CLASSROOM

experiences in movement:

GYMNASIUM

PLAYING FIELDS

W. B. SAUNDERS COMPANY
Philadelphia, London, Toronto

HOLLIS F. FAIT

Professor of Physical Education
University of Connecticut

physical education
for the elementary
school child

THIRD EDITION

with the collaboration of
GLADENE HANSEN FAIT

illustrated by
GREGORY FAIT *and* GERRY FAIT

W. B. Saunders Company: West Washington Square
Philadelphia, PA 19105

1 St. Anne's Road
Eastbourne, East Sussex BN21 3UN, England

1 Goldthorne Avenue
Toronto, Ontario M8Z 5T9, Canada

Library of Congress Cataloging in Publication Data

Fait, Hollis F

Experiences in movement.

First-2d ed. published under title: Physical education for the
elementary school child.

Includes bibliographies and indexes.

1. Physical education for children.   I. Fait, Gladene Hansen,
   joint author.   II. Title.

GV443.F34 1976   372.8'6   75–10384

ISBN 0–7216–3532–6

Experiences in Movement:
Physical Education for the Elementary School Child   ISBN 0-7216-3532-6

Last digit is the print number: 9   8   7   6   5   4   3   2

dedication

This book is dedicated with love and respect to my parents, *Harvey F. and Mussetta Heath Fait,* who together devoted over half a century of their lives to the teaching of elementary school children.

preface

This edition, like the previous two, has been designed for the use of those who are teaching or will be teaching physical education to elementary school youngsters, whether as teachers in the self-contained classroom or as teachers trained as physical education specialists. The new edition has been greatly expanded to present discussions of a number of exciting new developments and emerging trends in or directly related to physical education and to include descriptions of many more games, dances and rhythmic activities, stunts, and other motor activities. Among the new additions are a revised and expanded section on creative dance activity, a discussion of competition and its possible use and misuse in the learning process, and a comprehensive analysis of the current professional concern about the purpose of physical education.

As a result of the additions to this book, its usefulness as a source of reliable up-to-date information about teaching physical education to elementary school children is greatly enhanced. One of the most significant new trends is the use of the problem-solving method of teaching physical education; consequently, this edition includes a complete chapter devoted to a discussion of this method and its practical implementation. The traditional method, still the most widely practiced method of teaching physical education, receives the same comprehensive treatment it was given in the former editions. Recognizing that the exclusive use of one or the other of these methods is not always feasible or effective for an individual teacher, a synthesis of the two methods is suggested by the author, which, he believes, may well be the most successful method for many teachers. Another important trend is the emphasis being given to the development of creativity in children by educators who recognize the importance of creative thinking to an individual and to society. A section of this edition is devoted to a discussion of the nature of creativity and how it may be developed through physical education. Certain creative characteristics are identifiable in children at each grade level; these have been assembled by the author for inclusion with the expanded listings of physical, intellectual, and social characteristics. Other areas of concern in education relating directly to the teaching of physical education that are presented include the disadvantaged child, the nongraded or multi-age grouping, the community school, and the nursery school. Each of these is described extensively enough to give a general background and then is specifically considered in terms of the teaching of physical education.

The chapter "Techniques for Effective Planning and Organization" has been revised to include a comprehensive discussion of long-range objectives, curriculum objectives, and behavioral objectives. The way in which they are developed and written is explained, and the importance of viable objectives to presenting an educationally sound program is discussed. Material in the chapter discussing "low organized" games has been changed to reflect the new concept that physical education at the elementary school level should contribute to the development of basic motor skills specifically. Each game described in the chapter "Basic Skill Games" has been analyzed to determine the basic skills of movement utilized in its performance, and suggestions are made for using the games to promote the development of the specific basic skills.

This new edition, because it is more comprehensive than the preceding ones, has increased value as a handy reference for new games, stunts, dances, and fitness and skill developmental activities. These activities introduce variety into and stimulate enthusiasm for the physical education program. Throughout the book are countless practical suggestions and teaching hints, ranging from how to push the desk and lift the chair properly to improvising equipment for aquatic games. These suggestions are helpful to experienced teachers in making their teaching even more effective and to neophytes in their preparation for doing the best possible job of teaching physical education. Teachers without experience or training in sport skills will find the "correction charts" particularly useful in diagnosing and correcting the errors that children frequently make in the performance of motor skills such as running, throwing, catching, and batting. These have been supplemented with other original charts showing the development of problems when using the problem-solving method of teaching physical education. Of special interest and help to the classroom teacher are the practical discussions on conducting physical education in the classroom itself and on supervising and directing play during free play periods on the playground.

Particularly for the teacher in training, the first part of the book is devoted to a discussion of the foundations of physical education. The history of physical education is described so that the student may understand the forces which have shaped contemporary physical education. It is felt that such background information is essential in understanding the nature of physical education in today's schools and in appreciating the sport activities in present-day society. True understanding and sincere appreciation serve the best interest of education, because they ensure that physical education will concern itself with the development of each child according to his abilities.

Throughout the book the most recently available information concerning the physical, mental, social, and creative development of children has been correlated with the planning and teaching of the elementary physical education program. Special emphasis is given to the nature of motor learning, including perceptual-motor learning; the analysis of motor movement; and the development of attitudes and interests. This material, obtained largely from studies by psychologists and specialists in child development, has been included in response to a need expressed by numerous teachers of physical education at the elementary level for background information that will enable them to help children learn motor skills more effectively. Theories of learning and behavior have been interpreted into terms of practical application in teaching physical education to elementary and nursery school age children. Suggestions are made for activities suited to the needs, abilities, and interests of students at each grade level from kindergarten through eighth grade. Discussions of planning and organizing the program, motivating the learners, and evaluating the students and the program are realistic and purposeful. In each chapter presenting activities, a section is devoted to the use and care of equipment needed for the activities; and, wherever possible, ideas for improvising items of equipment have been included.

Because of the increasing enrollment in our schools of youngsters who have disabling conditions, an entire chapter is devoted to special physical education programs for these students. The comprehensive discussion presents all phases of the physical education program concerned with providing an experience in motor movement that will serve the special needs of youngsters who deviate from normal because of physical handicaps, mental retardation, emotional disturbance, extremely low levels of physical fitness, or inadequate motor ability. The material in this chapter is based upon the author's extensive work in special physical education.

This book is one of the few elementary physical education books to include a discussion of physical education for grades seven and eight. The reason for doing so is to provide specific background knowledge for those teachers who may teach at these levels; the training for secondary school teaching is generally not adequate preparation for coping effectively with the special needs, interests, and abilities of this age group.

The author, who has himself been an elementary school classroom teacher, recognizes the multiplicity of the problems which confront teachers who strive to present a good program of physical education. It is his sincere hope that the practical information and teaching suggestions presented in this text will help ease their task.

Hollis F. Fait

acknowledgments

To the numerous people who have shared with me their experiences, observations, and special knowledge of elementary school children, I wish to express my gratitude and acknowledge my indebtedness. I wish particularly to express my appreciation to Mrs. Mussetta Fait, who provided me with a large collection of games which she either had gathered for use in teaching young children or had originated in her classroom teaching over a long and successful career as an elementary school teacher.

Special recognition is given to **Ellen Moore**, Assistant Professor, University of Wisconsin, for writing the creative dance section and to **Dr. John Dunn**, Assistant Professor, Oregon State University, for revising the chapter "Foundations of Physical Education." The help of Angus Wooten in revising the chapter on aquatics is acknowledged with appreciation.

I wish to express my continuing gratitude for their able assistance to a number of people who helped in various ways during the preparation of the two earlier editions: Arden Curtis, Norwich Free Academy; Virginia Francois, Storrs Grammar School; Jean Calder, University of Queensland, Australia; Robert Harvat, Denver Public Schools; Dr. James Baley, Jersey City College; and Norris Fait, water safety instructor.

Sincere appreciation is extended to the following people of the Town of Vernon School System, Connecticut, who provided new pictures for this edition: Clare Albom, Supervisor of Health, Elementary and Girls' Physical Education; Principal Joseph Novac, James Herdic, and Terry Wolverton, all of Center Road School; Principal David Engleson and Joel Gitlin of Lake Street School; Principal Andrew Mannegia and Thomas Bowler of Maple Street School; and Principal Anthony Magliocco and Constance Kolesko of Talcottville School; and Charles Avedisian, Director of Physical Education, Darien Public Schools, Connecticut.

Other new pictures in this edition were furnished by several companies to whom I am most grateful:

Childcraft Education Corporation, 20 Kolmer Road, Edison, New Jersey 08817.

J. E. Gregory Company, Inc., 922 W. 1st, Suite 221, Spokane, Washington 99204.

World Wide Games, Inc., Delaware, Ohio 43015.

School—Tech, Inc., Wolverine Sports Division, 745 State Circle, Ann Arbor, Michigan 48104.

Lind Climber Co., 807 Reba Place, Evanston, Illinois 60202.

Hollis F. Fait

contents

foundations of physical education

HISTORICAL ASPECTS OF PHYSICAL
    EDUCATION
PURPOSE OF PHYSICAL EDUCATION

Modern day schools have accepted the challenge of contemporary society to develop the total capacities of each child so that in adulthood he will be equipped with the knowledge, sound thinking processes, physical stamina, and emotional maturity to live effectively in an ever-changing and highly complex society. Elementary school teachers bear a major portion of the responsibility in answering this challenge effectively, for the educational achievements of the elementary school years are, in effect, the girders on which all future learning will be built. That these "girders" may provide the best possible support requires an elementary school curriculum which ranges beyond the basic academic knowledges and skills to include experiences which will help the student to develop socially, emotionally, and physically as well as mentally.

Physical education is that area of the curriculum in which learning experiences are provided through the medium of motor movement. Like other subject areas, physical education provides opportunities for the development of desirable social behavior and satisfactory emotional adjustment. Physical education activities can be utilized to help motivate the learning of mathematics facts, spelling words, and the factual information of other subject matter areas. Used imaginatively, physical education is a worthy classroom tool in implementing all phases of the educative process. It is, however, unique in its contributions to the physical aspects of total learning. Of the subject areas which constitute the

1

Figure 1–1 Physical education is the only elementary school subject specifically concerned with the child's physical fitness and motor development. (Courtesy of Lind Climber Company.)

modern elementary school curriculum, physical education is the only one specifically concerned with the child's physical fitness and motor development. It is also the only subject area that promotes an understanding of the relationship of the body to the environment to give the child insight into the possibilities of how he can move his body in any environment.

The physical education of a child is achieved through his participation in physical activities. But it does not occur automatically as the result of his having engaged in play during the time allotted to the physical education period. Good physical education is the result of good program planning based on a thorough knowledge of how physical education contributes to the growth and development of children at each age level. All too often elementary school physical education is a haphazard affair in which the teacher supervises the choosing of sides or the assembling in formation for playing a game, which has been endorsed as a favorite by the youngsters, and then stands on the sidelines until the ringing of the bell signifies the end of the physical education period. Obviously, while such an activity may be "physical," it is not "education" to any significant degree. Playing a favorite game does offer some opportunities for desirable learning to occur, of course, but the contributions which physical education can make are seriously limited unless the time allotted for it is carefully planned and organized and the activities presented are selected with some knowledge and understanding of the contributions of various kinds of motor activity to human growth and development.

HISTORICAL ASPECTS OF PHYSICAL EDUCATION

The physical education program of today is the product of a long historical evolution. Some understanding of the historical and philosophical concepts which have shaped present-day physical education is useful to a teacher in dealing with the problems which arise in the teaching of physical education. It will be the purpose of this section of the chapter to present a brief discussion of physical education's history so that the teacher may more fully understand the basic nature of motor movement in man, appreciate the environmental forces and changes in cultural patterns which have given prominence to certain types of physical education activities, and analyze the causes for the continuous revision of the concept of physical education and its objectives through the ages.

The history of physical education is interwoven with the history of the economic, social, political, religious, and educational institutions of man. The objectives of physical education and the methods of teaching it have constantly changed just as the character of politics, religion, economics, and education has altered to reflect the needs and philosophical ideals of each age and civilization. The history of physical education is the record of man's use of motor activities to secure his livelihood, defend himself, improve his body, and entertain himself as his particular environment dictated.

In the dawn of man's existence, he developed certain patterns of movement which enabled him to survive the multiple hazards of his environment. He walked, ran, jumped, climbed, threw, and caught; all the activities of his daily existence were a repetition of these motor movements. Generally referred to as man's racial characteristics, these movements remain basic to human motor activity today.

Modern physical education has been influenced by the racial characteristics of man and the environment that has affected him throughout history. Knowing how primitive man reacted to certain stimuli and understanding the nature of his society enable the modern teacher to visualize more accurately the basic nature of motor activity. For a study of the physical education of prehistoric man, the Neolithic or New Stone Age is of greater importance than the other ages, for the man of this age, unlike the Eolithic or Paleolithic Age man, is the direct ancestor of modern man.

NEOLITHIC MAN. Neolithic man was the first to make nature work for him. As he began to fashion implements and weapons from the natural products of his environment, he developed previously unknown motor skills. The development of the bow and arrow, for example, necessitated the acquisition of special motor skills for drawing and releasing and insuring accuracy of aim. Later use of such improved weapons and implements as polished and chipped stone for arrows and axes is testimony to man's increased powers of perception and reasoning. As he refined his weapons, he undoubtedly began to realize the importance of practice to improve his skills in their use.

Anthropologists support the supposition that the basic aim of all educative processes of prehistoric man was self-preservation. Superior physical skills were important to self-preservation; survival was determined largely by physical competence in speed, strength, endurance, and coordination. Teaching the young to acquire these competencies was undoubtedly man's first physical education. The teaching likely consisted of demonstration of the skill for the young learners and practice of the correct techniques by them. To add interest to their practicing, the youngsters undoubtedly devised contests involving physical feats of strength, speed, and skill in the use of weapons and tools. Mimetic games of the hunt for food, the fight against the enemy, and the raising of children are known to have formed part of the education of the young of this prehistoric age much as they do in the lives of today's youngsters. It is known, too, that dancing had an important role in the lives of primitive people. It was usually identified with religion and as such gave the people a means of emotional expression. Because of its exalted position among primitives, many authorities have postulated that the dance satisfies certain basic needs of man; and, for this reason, it should be considered a basic motor activity.

BABYLONIANS AND EGYPTIANS. Some time between 5000 and 3000 B.C. the Neolithic Age came to an end with the rise of two cultures whose development of a form of writing has established them as the birthplace of modern Western civilization. One of these cultures was that of the Babylonians, located between the Tigris and Euphrates rivers; the other was the Egyptian civilization which flourished in the region of the lower Nile River. To the peoples of these early civilizations, intellectual activity was obviously very important, and they prized the type of training which enabled them to achieve economic, political, and social success. Physical education, which had held such a dominant position in the Neolithic culture, was less essential in the lives of these peoples and, consequently, came to be regarded as merely training in certain physical skills, such as swimming for recreational purposes or dancing for religious purposes among people of the higher social classes, and as training in the motor skills required by their jobs among people of the lower classes. Only among the warriors, who as a class shared some of the prestige of the upper classes, did physical education have status. For them physical education consisted of exercising to keep the body in top physical condition and practicing the skills of fighting. Its singular aim of producing soldiers capable of fighting for the homeland successfully has not been confined to this early period of history.

GREEKS. Among the societies of the ancient world, it was the early Greek civilization which most clearly exemplifies the contemporary spirit of physical education. The basic tenets of the humanistic philosophy that nourished this spirit were laid in the Aegean civilization between 1200 and 800 B.C. These early Greeks conceived the idea of man's total development of his mental and physical capacities which was to become their dominant philosophical precept. Sport activities were integral in the lives of these early Greeks as evidenced by the descriptions found in the *Iliad* and the *Odyssey* of the games played at the funerals of deceased leaders and important men.

It was in Athens during the fifth century B.C., prior to the Persian Wars, that physical education reached its zenith. Athenians regarded physical education as essential to the development of the complete man. They thought of it not only as the training of the body itself but also as the development of the total individual through the use of the body. The objectives of Athenian physical education were: 1. to develop a well-proportioned body; 2. to perform skills according to aesthetic standards with emphasis upon beauty of performance rather than outcome; 3. to maintain a moral standard in which loyalty to the elders, the state, and the gods was foremost; 4. to develop a citizen-soldier physically prepared to defend his country. While the statesmen were prone to stress the military objective of physical education, the philosophers emphasized a balanced physical education program through which all the objectives might be realized. The influence of the latter was such during this time that in the gymnasia of the land youngsters and adults alike were instructed in a variety of skills which made their physical education more nearly like modern day programs than that of any other time or place.

Following the Persian wars, however, an entirely different attitude about the purposes of physical education developed. It appears to have been the product of a philosophical concept that replaced the former practice of identification with civic goals with the gratification of individual desires. Luxuriating in the great power and wealth which were theirs as the result of the triumph over the Persians, the Greeks lost sight of the physical education objectives formerly so revered and relegated physical training to the professional athlete. The games that formerly had been participated in by nearly every citizen became dominated by the professionals while the majority became spectators. The great festivals lost their religious significance and became commercial enterprises. Costly prizes were awarded to winners and betting among spectators was common. Athletes no longer gloried in representing their city-states in contests but crassly sold their services to the highest bidder. The hero-worshipping public exalted skill in physical performance and those who excelled in these skills far out of proportion to their values. In the words of one physical education historian: "Physical education, which had once been a means of building a hardy, vigorous, morally sound nation, had by now twisted into an agency that was undermining and prostituting its power."[1]

The philosophers and critics raised their voices in protest against the professionalism in athletics. Xenophon admonished the citizens with the words of Socrates, "No citizen has a right to be an amateur in the matter of physical training." Plato decried the tendency toward professionalism and the use of competition for the purpose of amusing spectators, and Euripides deplored the hero-worship of athletes and the overemphasis on winning in athletic events. Their protests went unheeded.

ROMANS. By 300 B.C. the Grecian civilization had receded under the dominance of the conquering Romans. Although in the development of their culture the Romans assimilated much from the nations which they conquered, they were not influenced by the concept of physical education espoused by Plato, Socrates, Xenophon, and other notable Athenians. For them physical education had only a utilitarian purpose, that of creating military strength. In a manner similar to the later Greeks, but with added emphasis, the Romans developed professional sports and the general populace became mere spectators. But the athletic events which had been popular with the Greeks held no appeal for the Romans; they preferred the more brutal events of chariot racing and gladiatorial combat. Throughout the years in which the Romans were in power, they came to be characterized increasingly by luxurious and licentious living among the upper class and a corresponding decline in morality among the lower classes. This was the atmosphere which produced the downfall of Rome and in which the neglect of physical education activities probably played a considerable role.

MIDDLE AGES. In the period following, the overindulgence which had previously characterized Roman behavior was replaced by the asceticism of the early Christians who had grown in numbers during the last years of the declining Roman Empire. Asceticism reached its heights in the early medieval period (A.D. 400 to 800) during which the more extreme practitioners existed as hermits, grazed in the fields after the manner of animals, rolled naked in thorns, and lived in swamps infested with snakes. Such morbid practices were not typical of the majority of Christians, but it was typical of Christians to regard play and games as contemptible.

With the development of the monasteries (A.D. 500) the more morbid ascetic practices disappeared, and milder forms developed. The body was no longer subjected to torture for the benefit of the soul; however, bodily pleasures continued to be denied. The holy man of the time exemplified for those beyond the monastery walls the acceptance of poverty, obedience, devotion, and work as a way of life. Physical education could be said to receive attention only in the broader sense that physical skills were learned to increase efficiency in work. Physical education as play would never have been tolerated.

Physical education remained largely neglected until the period of chivalry in the Middle Ages (A.D. 800 to 1200). Its basic concept during this time may be illustrated by an examination of the training which knights received. Training began at the age of seven as a page. During this time the program of motor skill learning consisted of marbles, teeter-totter, tennis, and running. Later the page was introduced to swimming, jumping, fencing, boxing, and scaling walls. At the age of 14 he became a squire; and during this time he learned the skills of swordsmanship, horseback riding, and jousting. Knighthood was granted at the age of 21. The purpose of this systematic program of physical education was to develop skill in fighting and in contests for the admiration of the peers. In all of this there was no consideration of the Greek idea of total development.

RENAISSANCE TO THE 1900s.   With the Renaissance (A.D. 1300 to 1500) educational philosophy underwent a complete metamorphosis. As a result, physical education received renewed attention for its contributions to total development. From the end of the Renaissance to the 1900s the foundation was being laid for modern physical education. Philosophers such as John Locke, François Rabelais, Rousseau, Johann Basedow, and Johann Guts Muth preached that participation in physical education activities was "natural" to the child. While the physical education in the schools remained largely a program of formal gymnastic exercises, "play" began to be looked on more favorably as a positive contributor to the child's development.

UNITED STATES.   Physical education in the United States has been strongly influenced by two factors: the ascetic attitude of the early Puritan settlers and the individualism fostered by the rugged frontier life. The contempt which the Puritans felt for all bodily pleasures, including the playing of games, has had far-reaching consequences for physical education; the idea that play is the antithesis of education is still held by many people. The greater freedom of life on the frontier gradually broke down the Puritan concept of play. Men and women who worked hard and fought hard took particular pleasure in contests, games, and dancing during their few periods of leisure. Thus they helped to shape a national attitude of approval of play activities that encouraged educators to introduce physical education into the school curriculum in the closing years of the nineteenth century.

The physical education that was offered in the schools in these early years consisted largely of the formalized gymnastics which were being used in the schools of Europe; however, at the beginning of the new century, new influences were coming into focus that had a profound effect upon the country's physical education programs. Chief among these influences was John Dewey's philosophy of developmentalism. This philosophy as applied to physical education had as its objective the development of the mental, emotional, and social growth of the child through physical activity. Because sports seemed to the developmentalists to provide such an abundance of opportunities for achieving this objective, they were given top priority in the physical education curriculum. Among the advocates of the promotion of sports were such renowned physical educators as Thomas Wood and Clark Hetherington, and later, Jesse Feiring Williams, J. B. Nash, and Clifford Brownell.

At about the same time that this emphasis on sports began in the schools, sport pages began to appear in increasing numbers in American newspapers, reflecting a growth of interest in sports among the general public. This interest of laymen combined with the endorsement of sports as an educational tool by teachers and administrators resulted in the dominance of the developmentalists' philosophy of physical education from 1920 to 1950. In fact, the concept of the use of motor activity to promote social, emotional, and mental attributes was so dominant that its use for the purpose of developing physical attributes was frowned upon by many physical educators.

The great interest in and enthusiasm for sports led quite naturally to the development of more extensive varsity sports programs, first in college and then in the secondary schools. Before long, elementary schools also formed interscholastic teams for competition with other schools. For a time, this trend was supported vigorously by the physical education profession, as well as by the public at large. However, as the emphasis in the varsity athletic programs came to be placed more and more upon producing a winning team and entertaining the spectators, many physical educators began questioning the educational soundness of the program.

The initial area of concern was the interscholastic program at the elementary school level, in which the participants were particularly vulnerable to the dangers of overemphasis because of their physical and emotional immaturity. In 1947 the American Association for Health, Physical Education and Recreation[2] passed a resolution condemning interscholastic athletic competition in the elementary schools as being physiologically dangerous to participants and, in general, educationally unsound. However, a study by Fait[3] in 1951 influenced the reexamination by the profession of this resolution. The Fait study indicated that there was no scientific evidence that the physiological dangers of participation in competitive sports were greater for elementary school children than for older school children. Subsequent research by others confirmed Fait's findings. There was general agreement among the researchers, however, that a competitive program which placed greater emphasis on winning than upon the well-being and development of the participants was educationally unsound and could be physiologically and psychologically damaging to the children involved, regardless of their age. In 1952 a joint committee of the AAHPER and the Society of State Directors of Health, Physical Education, and Recreation[4] issued a report that was based on the research referred to above. The recommendations in this report regarding competitive sports for the elementary school age group now serve as the official policy of the physical education profession.

Although their argument that physiological harm might be done to the young participants has been invalidated, the critics have continued to protest varsity athletics in the elementary school on the basis that it is educationally unsound and wasteful of the educational dollar. Recently this attack has been carried into the higher educational levels as well. The arguments against interscholastic and intercollegiate athletics have considerable merit; however, judging by the number of programs currently in existence, the critics have had little influence in decreasing the emphasis upon such programs.

PERIOD FROM 1920 TO 1970.   During the period from 1920 to 1950 little emphasis was given to the development of the physical efficiency of the body through calisthenics and formal exercise except for a brief time during and immediately after World War II. Then in 1953 a comparison study[5] of back and abdominal strength and flexibility of European children and children in our own country was brought to the attention of the American public. The poor performance of our children in the tests of this study was generally attributed to the lack of the type of formal exercises which build up the body in specific respects. Concern and comment about the poor physical condition of the nation's youngsters was so widespread that President Eisenhower in 1956 called a White House Conference of national leaders to discuss the problems evidenced by the study. One direct result of the Conference was the appointment of a Citizens Advisory Committee on Youth Fitness to which was delegated the job of seeking ways of improving the physical fitness of the country's young people and implementing these in as many ways as possible. Subsequently, this committee was replaced by a permanent group, which is now known as the President's Council on Physical Fitness and Sports.

During the 1960s the major new influence on physical education came from a number of professionals who were experts in fields other than physical education. Kephart (a psychologist), Doman, Doman, and Delacato (a physical therapist, a medical doctor, and a physical therapist working as a team), and Getman (an optometrist) became interested in developing programs that would improve the cognitive domain of the children with learning disabilities with whom they were working. Hypothesizing that the basis of all intelligence is movement, these men developed programs of motor movement intended to improve perception of stimuli and so contribute to cognitive development. These perceptual-motor programs, as they are referred to, were intended primarily for use with mentally retarded, learning-disabled, and neurologically impaired youngsters; their use, however, quickly found its way into the elementary school physical education curriculum in anticipation of highly favorable results of their use with normal students. The perceptual-motor programs were implemented without adequate research, and the improvements expected with their use have not been realized. Research subsequent to the introduction of the programs does not support much of the original hypothesis on which they were founded or the concepts on which they focus.

Also during the sixties, there began a significant change in the way physical education was taught. Ever since the time of its introduction as a subject area in the schools, physical education had been taught with the same general method. Basically, this method consisted of showing the student how to perform a skill, providing for his practice of it, and helping him to overcome any errors. The formality of the procedure gradually diminished, but there had been no real change in the basic method of instruction. The change, when it came, was radical; it shifted the emphasis from teacher-directed instruction to pupil-directed learning. The new method was called by several different names during its infancy, but it is now commonly labeled the problem-solving method.

Initially, the problem-solving method was limited to use in teaching the basic skills through motor exploration. It is admirably suited to this area of physical education because it helps children to discover for themselves all the diverse movement possibilities of their bodies and to relate these to the learning of specific motor skills needed for the performance of everyday and play activities. Having observed the success of the problem-solving method in helping children to learn the basic skills, other teachers began experimenting with problem-solving in the teaching of game and sport skills. The good results encouraged others to try the method, and it gained—and continues to gain—wide support in the profession.

PRESENT DAY.   Introspection has been the most marked feature of the profession during the past few years. Among physical educators there is little argument as to the value of and necessity for providing movement experiences. There is considerable debate, however, as to the true rationale for providing such experiences. The extent of the disagreement is evidenced in the renaming of numerous college and university physical education departments with such titles as sport science, kinesiology, and human kinetics, to better reflect the true intent of physical education as conceived by the faculty involved. Contemporary literature reflects the conflicting opinions on the purpose of physical education; support for such differing concepts of physical education as play, movement, and sport has been documented. Controversy of this nature is healthy and indicative of a profession that is very much "alive." The result of such discussion can only serve to enhance the profession of physical education.

PURPOSE OF PHYSICAL EDUCATION

As suggested in the discussion of the historical aspects of physical education, the emphasis in the curriculum has shifted repeatedly in response to changes in the popular concept of the purpose of physical education. Because there is currently no general agreement about the purpose of physical education, the present-day curriculum may have one of several possible focuses, or it may amalgamate different views. The four major concepts of the central purpose of physical education advocated today can be identified as physical fitness, play, sport, and movement.

The purpose of physical education is in effect the foundation on which the framework of the curriculum is constructed. All elements of the planning process are directed by the purpose of the program. The objectives are formulated and the teaching procedures selected with consideration for the effective implementation of the purpose. It is, therefore, important to understand the nature of the four major purposes being advanced today and to assess the soundness of the scientific and philosophical bases by which they are supported.

PHYSICAL FITNESS.   There is ample research evidence that physical exercise is essential to the development and continued maintenance of a healthy and efficient body. Consequently, many physical educators contend that the most significant contribution the physical education program can make to the child is providing him with the proper exercise. The mechanical nature of our society, it is argued, deprives children and adults of the need to perform the kinds of physical activities which in a former age helped keep people in a desirable state of physical fitness. Since it is unrealistic to suppose that our school children will completely forsake buses and autos to walk to school, to the movies, and elsewhere, the only hope for improved physical fitness lies in a sound physical education program whose purpose is to develop a high level of physical fitness.

For the elementary school, this implies an emphasis on activities and instructional procedures that provide optimum exercise during the time allotted for physical education. Specific exercises that develop the several components of physical fitness are utilized to supplement games and activities. Running is stressed because of its importance to the development of cardiorespiratory endurance. Considerable time is devoted to testing for improvement in physical fitness in order to chart the progress of the students and to assess the success of the program in achieving its purpose. An important concern of the teacher is to provide knowledge of and appreciation for the value of engaging in conditioning activities so that they will be encouraged.

PLAY.   The importance of play activity in the life of children and adults is well documented. Play, as one authority has stated, "is a basic mode of behavior, an integrating thread in the design of life."[6] Conjecture as to why people play has intrigued scholars for many years. Some have suggested that play is an instinct or an attempt to re-enact the behavior patterns of one's ancestors. Others have viewed play as necessary for relaxation or as a safety valve for ridding the body of surplus energy. Although these and other theorists are not in concert with respect to a rationale for play, they are in agreement that play can contribute to one's mental, physical, and psychological needs.

In view of the benefits of play, one prominent psychiatrist has indicated it is unfortunate that ". . . too few people know how to play."[7] Successful participation in play activity is predicated upon the assumption that children will be taught the requisite motor and sport skills. The physical education class provides an environment which permits youngsters to practice these skills and progress from involvement in simple play activities to successful participation in a variety of sport forms. Those who support play as the focus of physical education regard integration of these skills into one's daily routine and utilization throughout life as the end to which all physical education experiences should be directed.

The emphasis in the play curriculum is upon individualized instruction and the creation of a learning atmosphere in which children are successful in play, thereby benefiting not only physically but psychologically from participation in physical activity. With successful mastery of the basic motor skills, students are encouraged to narrow their individual play interests and improve their competence in those activities which they find most rewarding. The choice of play activities is made with the assistance and guidance of the physical education teacher, but the final selection remains with the student. It is believed that, if students are permitted to improve their skills in those play activities which they find satisfying, their participation in motor activity throughout life is probable and they will continue to receive the physical and psychological benefits gained from such participation.

SPORT.   Support of sport as the focus of physical education is based on the popularity and prominence of sport activites in our society. It is argued that active and spectator participation in sports has reached such proportions that it constitutes a major social force with which youngsters should be educationally prepared to deal. Youngsters, therefore, need to be taught to understand and to engage with competence in sport. Physical education obviously provides the proper place for such educational preparation to occur.

The motor skills emphasized are those skills which are indigenous to performance in sport activities. Such skills are taught in conjunction with the games in which they are used, so that a student learns progressively the performance of the skills, their use in the game, and the playing rules and strategy. Proponents of sport believe, however, that opportunities to utilize the motor skills should not be limited to only a handful of sport activities. During the formative years of a child's life, exposure to a wide variety of sport activities would help to ensure that all children discover a sport activity which is suited to their needs. Development of general motor ability and physical fitness, which are essential to effective performance in sport, receive attention but are specifically directed toward achievement of the program's purpose.

The curriculum with a sport emphasis would also include the traditional discussion of sport rules and strategies as well as provide information to help students understand such concepts as why man engages in sport activity, the value of such experiences for the participant and spectator, and the total impact of sport on society. Sheehan and Alsop[8] have suggested that sport may be viewed as a "micro society" and within this structure social values such as cooperation may be learned. Sport sociologists caution, however, that changes in behavior will not occur unless such changes are planned and influenced through attitude modification techniques, which the program would attempt to do.

MOVEMENT.   In the consideration of the central intent of physical education, some see movement as the ultimate focus. Movement is regarded as being composed of three general kinds of human activity: motor skills of everyday living, sport skills, and muscular activity of a creative nature. Those who believe that movement should be the focus of physical education point out in support of their position that no other discipline is involved with the study of movement and all of its ramifications in the three areas of human activity. If movement is to receive the serious study that it must if mankind is to continue to improve, the proponents argue, physical education is the only discipline in which it can logically occur.

No clear delineation of the skills of everyday living has yet been made. However, there is general agreement that the skills with which the school physical education program should be concerned are those involving gross motor activity such as running, jumping, pushing, lifting, etc. Motor activities of the kind involved in grooming, eating, etc., are not included. Some authorities would classify activities such as throwing and catching as motor skills of every-day living since they are vital to the play of children; others prefer to classify these as basic sport skills. The creative movements are generally regarded as those exploratory activities in which children engage as they seek to discover new ways of moving or of expressing themselves as they do, for example, in certain kinds of dance activities.

A program that focuses on movement must obviously be a diversified one. Hence, such programs emphasize in the early years the learning of many basic motor skills that can effectively serve the child in his performance of common everyday tasks and play activities. There is great emphasis on creative and ex-ploratory activity, based on the reasoning that this helps children to develop confidence in their own ability to solve movement problems. Physical fitness and sport skill development are given consideration but only in terms of enhancing movement of the human body.

As is obvious from the foregoing discussion, even though physical educa-tion programs may have different focuses, they utilize many of the same kinds of physical activities to achieve their purposes. This is particularly true at the elementary school level where much basic motor skill learning must occur.

Figure 1–2 Developing an understanding of how the body moves is an important objective when movement is the focus of the physical education program. (Journal of Health · Physical Educa-tion · Recreation.)

Only an extensive and highly diversified activities program can provide the necessary learning environment for the comprehensive motor development of young children. Therefore, regardless of the focus, the program offerings are necessarily much alike. They are, however, given different priorities and different pedagogical emphasis in keeping with the specific purpose of the program. The decision about this purpose must remain an individual one, arrived at after weighing the supporting evidence and arguments. Regardless of one's decision, the common element which binds together all of the purposes is the concern with motor skill learning. This textbook provides information and ideas about motor movement and how it can be effectively taught in such a way that the prospective teacher of physical education will be able to apply the knowledge to the individual choice of purpose.

SUPPLEMENTARY READINGS

Brown, Roscoe C., and Cratty, Bryant J.: *New Prospectives of Man in Action.* Englewood Cliffs, New Jersey, Prentice-Hall, Inc., 1969.
Bucher, Charles A.: *Foundations of Physical Education.* Ed. 6. St. Louis, The C. V. Mosby Company, 1972.
Metzger, Paul, Jr.: *Elementary School Physical Education — Readings.* Dubuque, Iowa, Wm. C. Brown Company, Publishers, 1972.
Siedentop, Daryl: *Physical Education: Introductory Analysis.* Dubuque, Iowa, Wm. C. Brown Company, Publishers, 1972.
Slusher, Howard S., and Lockhart, Aileene: *Anthology of Contemporary Readings: An Introduction to Physical Education.* Ed. 2. Dubuque, Iowa, Wm. C. Brown Company, Publishers, 1970.
Van Dalen, Deobold B., et al.: *A World History of Physical Education.* Ed. 2. New York, Prentice-Hall, Inc., 1971.

BIBLIOGRAPHY

[1]Van Dalen, Deobold B., et al.: *A World History of Physical Education.* New York, Prentice-Hall, Inc., 1953, p. 69.
[2]American Association for Health, Physical Education and Recreation: "Policy." *Journal of Health • Physical Education • Recreation,* September, 1947, p. 432.
[3]Fait, Hollis F.: *An Analytical Study of the Effects of Competitive Athletics upon Junior High School Boys.* Doctor's Dissertation. Iowa City, University of Iowa, 1951.
[4]American Association for Health, Physical Education and Recreation: *Desirable Athletic Competition for Children of Elementary School Age.* Washington, D.C., American Association for Health, Physical Education and Recreation, 1968, p. 2.
[5]Kraus, Hans, and Hirschland, Ruth P.: "Muscular Fitness and Health." *Journal of Health • Physical Education • Recreation,* Dec., 1953, pp. 17–24.
[6]Ulrich, Celeste: *The Social Matrix of Physical Education.* New York, Prentice-Hall, Inc., 1969, p. 99.
[7]Menninger, William C.: "Recreation and Mental Health." *Recreation,* November, 1948, pp. 340–346.
[8]Sheehan, Thomas, and Alsop, William L.: "Educational Sport." *Journal of Health • Physical Education • Recreation,* May, 1972, pp. 41–45.

chapter 2

how and why children learn

NATURE OF MOTOR LEARNING
ANALYSIS OF MOTOR
   MOVEMENT
INTEREST AND ATTITUDE
CREATIVITY
CHARACTERISTICS OF CHILDREN AND
   THEIR IMPLICATIONS FOR THE
   PLANNING OF THE PHYSICAL
   EDUCATION PROGRAM

The successful physical education program is one which provides the kinds of activities children need to ensure their continued physical, mental, and emotional growth and development. In order to help each child to meet this challenge of developing to his optimum through physical education, the teacher must provide motor experiences that are appropriate to the child's abilities, that serve his needs, and that motivate him to extend his capabilities. Successful selection and presentation of such physical education experiences require the teacher to understand the nature of the learning process, particularly as it applies to motor movement. Knowledge is needed not only of the way children acquire motor learning but of the determinates that affect the degree and quality of learning. In addition, the general characteristics that children display at each age have important implications for the educative process that must be fully appreciated by the teacher.

NATURE OF MOTOR LEARNING

Motor learning—that is, the learning of any motor movement or combination of movements—is most successful in propitious circumstances. One of the conditions is the readiness of the student to learn. Others relate to the utilization of the mental processes, the rate of learning, the influence of emotions, and the amount of transfer of learning.

READINESS

The ability to learn a motor skill is influenced by growth and maturation. A child can learn a specific motor activity only when he has achieved the actual physical growth required to accomplish the movement. For example, a three year old child whose legs are so short in relation to his trunk and head that he cannot push his center of gravity over the midline of his body in a forward roll will probably not be able to learn how to perform a forward roll until his legs grow longer in relation to his body. In addition to having achieved the necessary physical growth, the child must be "ready" to learn a motor skill in other ways, i.e., he must have reached certain levels of motor, emotional, and social development.

MOTOR READINESS. Motor readiness is affected not only by physical size but also by the level of maturation of the neuromuscular system, i.e., the development of the systems of nerves and muscles to a degree that enables effective control and operation of the body. Maturation occurs as a result of experience and of the physiological changes which are produced naturally as age increases. In most children, one or the other of the two influences is more dominant at certain levels of their development. For example, in the very young the physiological changes caused by the passing of time affect the learning of a motor skill more than prior experience. The studies by Gesell and Thompson[1] offer evidence in support of this observation by demonstrating that a child who had received specific training in walking stairs at the age of 46 weeks did not learn to walk stairs any sooner than one who did not start until 53 weeks of age. Although experience has less influence at this age level, it is nevertheless extremely important. The child who has participated in a wide variety of activities and has engaged in much experimentation with random movement has a greater possibility of learning a specific activity at an earlier age than one who has not had such experiences.

There are limitations upon the learning of a motor skill determined by the physiological maturation of the neuromuscular function regardless of past experience. The limitations are greater for the baby at birth than for older children. They become less with each year of growth up to the age of 10. Although the evidence is not complete, it is generally accepted that most children above the age of 10 have the neuromuscular potential to perform many of the skills of coordination that an adult is able to do. This does not imply that the 10 year old has developed his capacity of strength and endurance to an adult level, but that he has developed the capacity to learn movements that a normal adult can learn.

EMOTIONAL AND SOCIAL READINESS.   Emotional readiness is a part of the total readiness for motor learning. A favorable attitude is essential to success in motor movement. Great anxiety, uncontrollable fear, or extreme dislike hinders the learning process. Evidence of the presence of such emotions is usually fairly obvious. Sometimes, however, subconscious restrictions are so infused with the inability to perform a movement that it is difficult to detect the true cause.

A phase of emotional readiness that is frequently disregarded in the presentation of physical education activities involving a number of participants is social maturation. A child who is not socially ready to adjust to situations in which others are involved will not learn as well or as easily as one who is socially mature.

APPLICATION OF THE PRINCIPLES OF READINESS.   In the application of the principles of readiness, the physical education teacher must be very sensitive to the reaction of the child to learning motor movement. Pressuring a child to learn an activity when it is beyond his ability may be detrimental to his learning. On the other hand, it is likely to be disadvantageous to the child if he is not exposed to experiences that promote his maturation so that he will be able to learn the skill in the future. Ways of determining when a child is "ready" to learn and the methods the teacher may use to prepare him to learn will be more evident after reading and discussing the section on characteristics of children.

BEST PERFORMANCE TECHNIQUE

The best way to perform any given skill is dictated by mechanical and physiological principles of movement; however, there is no one best way for every child because of anatomical and physiological differences. Over the years guidelines of good motor performance have been developed based upon principles of movement and empirical evidence. (Guidelines and suggestions on how best to perform a given skill are presented in each section of the book that discusses a specific skill.) These guidelines are applicable to most youngsters; but, in many cases, there will be a need to help the child explore how a particular movement should be performed to obtain the best results.

LEARNING A NEW MOVEMENT

In learning a new movement at any age level, mobilization of the higher mental processes is involved. The person learning the task is consciously trying to bring the correct muscles into play at the right time to make the desired movement. The performer calls upon an intellectualization process based upon insight derived from previous performances and similar movements as well as visual and proprioceptive feedback that provide him with information on the quality and quantity of a movement. Generally, first attempts of a specific movement are awkward and stiff, especially if there is considerable concern to do the movement correctly. Upon repetition of a skill, the awkwardness disappears.

There seems to be a reorganization of feedback control until the act becomes an organized and well-coordinated movement. As the act becomes well learned, i.e., a habit, there appears to be less need of the higher mental processes and the act becomes more or less unconscious. It has been suggested by some theorists[2] that a skilled act comes under the control of the lower portion of the brain. Hebb[2] contends that an acquired motor habit does not lose totally its dependency upon cortical organization, but, when the movement is thoroughly learned, the neural units themselves undergo more or less permanent alterations called "cell assembly." When cell assembly occurs, because of many different motor-perceptual experiences, one is able to perform the movement with less difficulty. Nevertheless, it is obvious that in the performance of a well-learned motor skill, the action does not depend upon conscious effort; rather, it is, more or less, automatic.

EXPLORING A NEW MOVEMENT

There is less conscious effort in learning a new movement through exploration than in learning it through motor response to description or demonstration. This does not imply that the higher level of the nervous system (cortex) is not involved in the former. Intellectualization does take place as the child conceives the nature of the movement that he wishes to make. Generally, the concept is not a clearly defined one, that is, the performer is not completely aware of the exact nature of the movement he is going to make until he makes it. It appears that a large portion of the movement is under the influence of that "center" which controls well-learned motor movement while a small part of the movement is under the control of the cortex. The opposite would appear to be true in following directions to learn a specific movement, at least until the movement is partially learned. It is postulated by the author that one of the values of movement exploration as a way of teaching motor movement is that the intellectualization is regulated in such a manner that the "center" or "function" in control of movements that have become habitual through "overlearning" takes over earlier in the learning process and, hence, motor learning is faster and more effective than in the traditional method of learning a specific skill.

REINFORCEMENT AND REPETITION

Repetition of motor movement tends to establish that movement as a part of an individual's repertoire of movement. However, to improve the quality of the movement and to establish it more firmly, the performer must be aware of the goal and the results of his movement, and, in general, be motivated to improve. Aimlessly practicing a movement or haphazardly repeating a movement has limited value in promoting learning of that movement.

Reinforcement must follow the motor response of the individual for optimum learning to occur. Reinforcement refers to any condition or event following a response that increases the probability that the response will be repeated. Reinforcement is often thought of as either a reward or a punishment.

However, knowledge that a certain effort produces a desired result is also a type of reinforcement and probably the most effectual in the teaching of motor skills.

PROGRESSION

A child will progress in the learning of movement at a specific rate that is uniquely his own pace. His interests and abilities, or lack of abilities, will determine what skills the child should have an opportunity to participate in and in what order these skills should be presented to him. Progression should be in terms of each individual child and at his own rate. Generally, the activities which the child is encouraged to learn should progress from simple to complex. Usually, a child needs to wait until the foundation skills have been mastered before he attempts to learn advanced skills.

For many types of physical education activities, a progression of successive skills, based on the degree of difficulty and successive relations, has been developed for use by teachers; however, caution should be exercised in adhering to "set" progression in any given activity. Progression should be based upon increasing the variety of activity which requires new or altered responses within the student's realm of capability.

EMOTION AND MOTOR LEARNING

It has long been noted that emotions have extensive influence on human action. Less evident is the effect of emotions on the learning process. Extreme emotional reactions can often be seen to be detrimental to learning, but suppressed feelings and emotions may have a profound effect and yet not be easily detected. Such feelings as anxiety, fear, and humiliation may not be evident to an observer but yet may be a strong deterrent to learning. Teachers who use techniques such as ridiculing a child's performance or pointing to the poorest performer in class as an example of how not to do a certain activity may be creating an emotional response in the child that may stifle learning for a considerable length of time.

The teacher is not alone in creating an emotional atmosphere that may hinder learning for some child; his peers play an important part also. Rejection or abuse by the peers can be a contributing factor in creating an emotional attitude that is devastating. Of course, each individual responds differently to ridicule, rejection, and failure; but, unfortunately, the individuals for whom they are most harmful are the most likely to be subjected to them by teachers and peers.

TRANSFER OF MOTOR LEARNING

There is much misunderstanding concerning the transfer of learning from one motor skill to another. It is commonly thought, for example, that employing the hands in a specific skill that requires vision develops eye-hand coordination or that developing agility in tumbling improves one's agility in other activities. These ideas are based upon the mistaken notion that there are general abilities of coordination and agility. The preponderance of evidence indicates, however, that there is no such thing as general coordination or agility that is basic to a number of motor activities; instead, motor skills are specific.[4] Consequently, learning to turn a rope for jumping in no way develops the general coordination of the arms so that learning to throw a ball, shoot a basket, or play jacks is easier. There are individuals who perform a number of motor skills well and seem to be generally well-coordinated, but there is no evidence to support the concept that the learning of one movement enhances the general ability so that the learning of another skill is easier; rather, the situation is that these individuals possess a number of specific abilities, or have great desire and interest, so that they are able to perform a variety of skills well.[5]

This explanation is not to be interpreted as denying that transfer of learning occurs. Transfer of learning does occur from one activity to another, but it is not necessarily automatic. It will occur only under certain circumstances. Transfer of learning can take place when two activities have identical elements,[6] and the performer is aware of the similarity of the two. Awareness is not a necessity when the activity involves an action that has become habitual. Furthermore, transfer of learning does occur when a principle learned in one situation can be generalized and applied in another situation.[7] Little or no transfer of learning takes place when an individual's past experience is complete; in a repetition of the experience, learning does not take place and no significant transfer of learning occurs.[8]

Because of the limitations and the circumstances in which transfer of learning occurs, the student must be exposed to many different physical education activities in order to provide him with such a wide variety of motor experiences that he will develop a large reservoir of skills. Then, when he is confronted with the execution of a new movement, he can utilize this background of acquired skills to produce the new movement successfully. Also, having experience with a great variety of skills helps the student to analyze more effectively and perceive more readily the elements in the new skill that are similar to those in skills already learned,[9] thereby enabling him to learn the new skill at a faster rate.

Analysis of research by the author indicates that meaningful generalizations and transfer of learning will be fostered by utilizing these procedures in the teaching process:

1. Provide a variety of different kinds of movement activities.
2. Include many different activities to develop body awareness (kinesthetic awareness).
3. Provide opportunities for the development of meaningful generalizations by using real situations, and provide practice in applying generalizations.
4. Point out the likenesses between activities in which transfer of learning can occur.
5. Allow the student to explore different kinds of activities and provide guidelines for determining good quality of movement and effective skills.

PERCEPTUAL-MOTOR LEARNING

How we perceive and react to stimuli has not been clearly established. Psychologists have advanced a number of theories, some of which are contradictory. There is general agreement, however, that perception is the act of receiving information from stimuli of the various senses, processing the information, and responding to its meaning through movement. The Gestalt psychologists of the early 1900s felt that perception was not a learned but a maturational aspect of development, i.e., that the perceptual processes mature relatively independently of experience. By the middle of the century, an opposing point of view was being expressed by Hebb,[10] who has had considerable influence upon present-day psychologists and physical educators. Hebb postulated that numerous repetitions of a sensation cause the cortical cells within the brain to organize into units that function together in what he has called "cell assembly." When certain combinations of cell assemblies are brought into action simultaneously over and over, they become integrated into increasingly complex functional units called "phase cycles," which affect how new sensations, derived from the senses, are perceived. Hebb also contended that lack of perceptional experiences causes deterioration of cell assemblies.

General acceptance by educators of Hebb's theory that ability to perceive can be increased through experiences gave a new dimension to education—that of providing the child with experiences specifically in perceiving and in interpreting the perception. In keeping with this objective some physical educators have developed specific perceptual-motor activities that are purported to exert a causative effect on a wide variety of perceptual and intellectual endeavors.[11] However, the evidence does not support the contention that only certain activities develop perception.

Some motor activities do involve different faculties of perception to different degrees in the act of learning. For example, a child attempting to stand on one leg with eyes closed depends chiefly upon the proprioceptors (involved with kinesthetic sense) and the semi-circular canals (organs of the inner ear involved with balance), while the child performing the same skill with his eyes open utilizes sight in addition to the proprioceptors and semicircular canals. The development of perception in motor performance is acquired through performing movements that place a demand on the various faculties of perception. Hence, physical education can best serve perceptual-motor learning by providing ample opportunities for the utilization of these faculties in a variety of motor activities.

FEEDBACK AND MOTOR SKILLS

Feedback has been referred to as knowledge of various kinds which the performer receives during and after his performance. The faculties of perception provide feedback to help in executing effective movement while the performer is in the process of moving. Additional feedback may be received following the performance; in this case it is the product of knowledge of the results and/or insight. Some authorities[12] believe that knowledge of results is the strongest and most important variable controlling performance and that improvement in performance does not occur without it. The implication of this for the teaching process is that students should be given immediate information by the teacher about their performance of a skill and aided in applying it in future attempts.

MOVEMENT AND THE COGNITIVE DOMAIN

Over the years there has been much speculation concerning the relationship between motor movement and the cognitive domain, that is, between doing and thinking. Thinking obviously occurs in the execution of a motor skill; to varying degrees, those who perform motor skills think about their performance. This is especially the case during the learning of a new skill when much thought must be given to which muscle movement must be made at what time. However, the extent to which the ability to think well influences motor skill performance has not been determined.

There is no evidence to indicate that there is a high correlation between intelligence and athletic success above the I.Q. of 70. (Studies have indicated that, below the I.Q. of 70, there is a low but positive relationship between intelligence and motor ability.) Researchers investigating the correlation between physical fitness scores and intelligence have produced equivocal results. Some studies showed a low but positive correlation while other studies, which appear to be in the majority, found none. With respect to the contention that participation in specific types of motor activities will enhance the intellectual potential, research does not strongly support such speculation.[13]

It has been observed that participation in motor activity does inter-react with academic achievement. It has been suggested that for some individuals mild or moderate exercise creates a relaxed state, in which they are likely to do better in academic tasks. On the other hand, vigorous exercise may fatigue an individual to the point where learning is impeded.[14]

Additionally, success in motor skills may motivate some individuals to make greater effort to be successful in other endeavors, including intellectual pursuits. For others success in athletics may provide an escape from the work of trying to succeed in academic subjects. Many individuals, especially elementary school children, are easlly motivated to participate in motor activities so that, when motor activities are used as a vehicle to teach academic subjects, interest in learning the subjects is, in most cases, greatly increased. For a complete discussion of the use of motor activities to enhance academic learning see "Classroom Games," Chapter 14.

EFFECTS OF COMPETITION ON LEARNING MOTOR SKILLS

Competition so often appears to have such successful results that teachers rely on it heavily to motivate students to learn. This has been particularly true of those physical educators who teach motor skills largely through the medium of sports and games. Because of the extent to which competition is utilized in mo-tivating the learning of motor skills, it is well to understand the nature of compe-tition and the educational effects of its use.

Competition takes two forms: direct and indirect. Direct competition may be defined as a contest between two or more individuals striving for an objec-tive which only one of them can accomplish. Indirect competition occurs when an individual is striving for a specific goal and the success or failure of his ob-taining that goal is not dependent upon other people. The competition of games and sports in physical education is predominately the direct variety. Most of the other kinds of activities that make up a physical education program are ones in which the individual competes against himself—the competition is indirect.

Direct competition is utilized in physical education classes to motivate children to improve their motor skills and their level of physical fitness. It is highly successful with those children who have the physical attributes neces-sary to win often enough to enjoy the thrill of success. They are usually mo-tivated to work harder and to learn more. Unfortunately, in direct competition there is at least one competitor who must fail for every one who is successful. One who fails to win in the competitive activities of the physical education class is usually one who has poor motor skills and/or is undeveloped physi-cally. He is therefore frequently, if not always, the loser. Such children generally avoid participation in all types of motor activity. They withdraw to sedentary ac-tivities in which they can compete successfully. In their case, competition can hardly be said to motivate them to improvement of their motor skills and physi-cal fitness.

In competition anxiety is often increased to a high level. It has been well established that strength and endurance increase while one is in an anxious state. However, performance level in tasks that require complex movements and intellectual endeavor is decreased by anxiety. Hence, learning is usually at a minimum in highly competitive situations. It would appear, then, that the more productive learning environment in physical education for the majority of students is the non-competitive play situation rather than the highly competitive one in which there is great anxiety about winning.

ANALYSIS OF MOTOR MOVEMENT

As has been pointed out previously, because there is no one best way for everyone to perform a specific activity, teachers of physical education must be able to help each child develop the most efficient movement. In order to do this effectively, it is necessary to have an understanding of the basic principles of movement. Such knowledge is the basis of movement analysis, i.e., determining why the child is failing to achieve effective performance and how he may improve the quality of movement.

TEACHING MOVEMENT PRINCIPLES TO PARTICIPANTS

There is some controversy among physical educators concerning how much time and effort should be given to the teaching of principles of movement in the physical education class. Research studies[15] are not in agreement concerning the effects of teaching mechanical principles to participants who are learning a motor skill—some students performed better and others worse when time was spent learning mechanical principles. Whether a student profited from the teaching of mechanical principles of learning motor skills appeared to be dependent in part on how the principles were presented. The author recommends that to utilize instruction in the principles of movement effectively as an aid to motor learning, these suggestions should be followed:

1. Select the principles to be taught in relation to the ability of the students to understand them.

2. Simplify the presentation, when necessary, to fit the situation and the ability of the students to comprehend.

3. Avoid belaboring the obvious—do not offer explanations when the concept is already well understood by the participants.

4. Avoid lengthy sessions of discussion.

5. Integrate the teaching of the principles with the teaching of a skill or movement.

MECHANICAL PRINCIPLES OF MOVEMENT

All movements, including human movements, are regulated by the laws of motion. In human movements, the chief elements are those related to maintaining equilibrium and stability.

PRINCIPLES OF STABILITY. The ability to achieve stability is important in all action as well as in all stationary positions. The successful performance of such activities as standing, sitting, running, jumping, and bouncing requires some degree of stability. In maintaining stability, the body is governed by certain principles:

1. When the center of gravity is lowered, greater stability is achieved.

2. The larger or wider the base of the support, the greater the stability.

3. When the center of gravity is over the base, stability is greater.

When the body is lowered, as in bending the knees, the center of gravity is lowered, thereby providing more stability to the body. In activities in which force must be received, as in catching a fast ball or being tackled by another player, greater stability can be created by lowering the body, making it more capable of receiving the force without losing balance. The principle applies also to such activities as pyramid building: a more stable pyramid can be built by participants on their hands and knees than on their feet because the center of gravity is lower. Stability is also increased because the "all fours" position makes the base larger.

A larger base allows a greater range of body movement before the center of gravity moves beyond the base to cause the loss of balance. This is particularly evident in walking a narrow beam or in moving on ice skates; maintaining balance in these activities is difficult because the base of support is relatively small. In movement that requires a stable base, the spreading of the feet creates a larger base. A case in point is the participant in hand wrestling or the bottom performer in a standing pyramid. Another example is offered by the head stand in which the triangle made by the head and the two hands must be relatively large in order to maintain balance in this position. In activities involving the receiving or giving of impetus to an object, such as catching or throwing a ball, stability is more readily maintained by widening the stance in the direction of the force.

It should be noted that a wide base does not always create the most efficient position. If the stance with the feet is so wide that the legs are at an extreme angle to the ground, muscular efficiency is decreased so that actually the advantage created for maintaining balance by a wide base is nullified by the decrease of the muscular efficiency of the legs used in maintaining balance.

When the center of gravity is near the center of the base, greater stability is created. Many directions for performing skills include a suggestion to distribute the weight evenly to give better balance to the body. Such distribution brings the center of gravity to the center of the base. If the participant must make a quick move or start in a specific direction, he leans the body in that direction so that the balance is easily disturbed by the shifting of weight. In starting a race, the body is leaned forward and the center of gravity falls near the front of the base. In running rapidly, the center of gravity falls in front of the base so that, in a sense, the body falls forward and the "legs run up under the body." When slowing from a fast pace, the body is straightened so that the center of gravity is brought back near the center of the base.

In balancing the body on a narrow base such as occurs when one is on a balance beam or standing on one leg, the center of gravity must be maintained over the base to keep the body in balance. This is achieved by aligning the parts of the body so that approximately the same amount of weight is distributed equally around the base. When movement of one part of the body upsets this even distribution of weight, another part must usually be moved to counterbalance the effect of the other and so maintain the desired equilibrium.

PRINCIPLES OF MOVING THE BODY.   The movement of the human body or of any part of it is governed by these laws of motion:

1. An object which is at rest will remain at rest, or if in motion will remain in motion at the same speed in a straight line unless acted upon by a force.
2. When a body is acted upon by a force, its resulting change of speed is proportional to the force and inversely proportional to the mass.
3. For every action, there is an equal and opposite reaction.

A tendency for the body to remain either in motion or stationary is known as inertia. The more the object weighs, the more force is required to overcome its inertia. Also, the faster the movement of the object, the greater the difficulty of overcoming its inertia. In initiating movement, the inertia is overcome by use of force. Once an object is moving, less force is required to keep it moving. In pushing a wagon, for example, less energy is required to push it after it is moving than to start it in motion. The same is true of the body. A performer attempting a pull-up will find it much easier to complete the pull-up entirely than to stop halfway and then continue after having lost the advantage of the momentum that had been created.

If each of two unequal forces is applied to objects of equal mass, the object to which the greater force is applied will move at a greater speed. If two equal forces are applied to two masses of different size, the larger mass will move at a slower rate. For example, if two boys are batting balls and one of the boys consistently hits the ball with more force, his ball will travel much farther; however, if the boys are hitting with equal force but one has a heavier ball, the heavier ball will travel less distance than the lighter ball.

The equal and opposite reaction is perhaps most easily illustrated by the swimmer pushing backward against the water—the water moves backward as the swimmer moves forward. This reaction is not so obvious when the performer pushes against a large solid object such as a wall or the ground because of the large size of the object in relation to the performer who is exerting force against it; the large object moves insignificantly in relation to the movement of the performer and, therefore, is not noticed. When the body is not supported by a surface but is in the air, the equal and opposite reaction occurs within the body itself; for example, when one has jumped off a diving board and swings one arm, which has been extended to the side, to the front of the body, the entire body will turn in the direction opposite to that in which the arm is moving. The speed of the turn is increased if the extended arm is bent as it is brought to the front. The rotary motion of turning is accelerated by shortening the radius of the body when the arm is brought close to the body. Conversely, the rotary motion is decreased when the radius of the moving body is increased. Application of this principle is, as should now be apparent, very important in diving and tumbling activities.

Even though the body while in the air can be turned on its own axis by an internal force generated by moving parts of the body, the speed of the body cannot be altered in this manner. Once the body is in the air, the center of gravity will follow a predetermined path set by the force executed when leaving its support. In a vertical jump, the height attained by the center of gravity is determined by the force executed in jumping; no movement in the air will alter this. However, the center of gravity can be lowered after the jump by changing the position of the body, e.g., lowering the arms from overhead. By thus lowering the center of gravity, the body will be projected higher into the air; this is an important principle in all jumping activities where height is the objective.

PRINCIPLES OF RECEIVING OR ABSORBING FORCE. In numerous activities the participant must repeatedly receive or absorb force. Examples of receiving force from objects are catching a ball, batting a ball, heading the ball in soccer, landing from a fall or a jump, and running into another object. A moving body possesses kinetic energy, that is, the energy of motion. Abrupt loss of kinetic energy can cause injury to the body. Injury in falling occurs when the body collides with the ground and the loss of kinetic energy occurs too quickly. To avoid injury from too abrupt a loss of kinetic energy, the loss must be made to occur more gradually. This can be done by increasing the distance over which the kinetic energy is lost. Landing with the knees bent and the hips flexed to enable them to bend farther to cushion the fall is one example. Another is landing, in falling at an angle, on a portion of the body and immediately rolling to another portion to prolong the time over which the loss of kinetic energy occurs.

Still another factor that must be considered in absorbing force is the relationship of the force to the size of the area which bears the brunt of the impact. Force concentrated on a small area of body surface is likely to cause more serious injury than the same amount of force spread over a larger area. For this reason, injury is more likely in a fall in which the weight is taken on one foot than equally on both feet.

In catching an object, both factors (absorbing the force over a longer time and spreading the force over a larger area while receiving it) are important for the safety and success of the performer in catching the object. Consequently, to catch a ball that has been thrown hard, the elbows are bent to help absorb the force; with large balls the body is leaned backward as the ball is caught. A glove helps to disperse the impact of the ball over a large area of the hand as well as lengthening the time it takes the ball to slow down. The padding acts as a cushion to reduce the force over a longer period of time.

PRINCIPLES OF IMPARTING FORCE TO AN OBJECT. Many of the activities in physical education require a projection of a ball or an object into the air. In throwing a ball there are three main concerns: (1) the speed of the throw, (2) the distance, and (3) the direction in which the ball will travel.

The speed and distance that the ball is thrown are dependent upon the speed at which the hand was traveling at the moment of release. The speed that the hand can acquire depends upon the distance it travels before the ball is released. Therefore, it is advantageous to make the backswing of the throwing movement as long as possible by rotating the body, shifting the weight, and taking a step. The use of these movements to create distance is effective only if they are synchronized so that each one is added to the preceding movement to take advantage of the momentum already created.

The distance that the ball will travel depends not only upon the force exerted in the throwing but also on the angle at which it is released. As soon as the ball leaves the hand, gravity has a tendency to pull it downward. The pull of gravity becomes more noticeable as the ball is slowed by the resistance of the air. A greater distance can be obtained if the ball is thrown upward as well as forward because the ball will stay in the air longer and, hence, travel farther. The best throwing angle to gain the most distance is approximately 45 degrees.

The follow-through is an important part of the throw. Stopping the movement immediately after the release of the ball tends to produce a short, jerky movement throughout the total throw and affects the direction and distance of the throw. Furthermore, stopping the throw abruptly may cause injury to the arm because the muscles that must contract for the throw may be damaged by the tremendous force exerted in the opposite direction.

The direction in which the ball travels depends upon the direction in which the force was applied at the moment of release. In most throwing, the hand describes an arc in the throwing process; when the ball is released, it goes off at a tangent to the arc described by the hand. The release of the ball must be timed so that the tangent is in the desired direction. It is easier to release the ball at the correct time when the hands are moved in a flatter arc at the time of release. A ball which is too large to hold in the fingers and must be held in the palm is more difficult to release at the right time than one held in the fingers.

Keeping the palm of the hand directly behind the ball as it moves in the desired direction will keep the ball moving in the direction intended.

Winds may influence the direction of flight as well as any spin that is placed on the ball when it is released. A spin to the right causes the ball to curve to the right; a spin to the left causes it to curve to the left.

When an implement such as a bat or a racket is used to apply force to an object, the implement becomes an extension of the arm. The arm in throwing or batting is a lever, and, with the addition of an implement, the resistance arm of the lever becomes longer and, hence, greater momentum can be created. When a bat is swung in an arc, the end of the bat is moving much faster than the hands that are holding it. Consequently, when the ball rebounds, it does so at a much faster rate than if the bat were only moving at the speed of the hands.

The direction the ball travels is even more difficult to control when using an implement than in throwing. The angle of the ball as it leaves the striking surface is determined by the angle at which it hit the surface. The ball will bounce from the object at an angle opposite to that at which it struck, so in batting a ball the bat must strike the ball at an angle opposite the direction of the intended flight of the ball. To cause the ball to rebound in the same direction that it came from, it must strike the implement at right angles.

INTEREST AND ATTITUDE

The urge to move is inherent within the human organism. Children's response to this urge is observable in the interest and enthusiasm with which they engage in motor activity. They love to run, jump, climb, and move in other forms of vigorous motor activity. Children lose this desire or urge to move only when play becomes an unsatisfactory or unpleasant experience.

Because of their high interest, a teacher of physical education does not have a difficult task motivating young children in motor movement. However, he must provide an environment in which children feel secure and at ease; he should control the learning situation so all the children have fun and success in motor tasks that are meaningful to them and so continue to be interesting to them.

Interests are reinforced by attitudes, and attitudes are a result of an individual's reaction to his experience. Sherif[16] defines attitudes as states of readiness which are formed in relation to definite stimuli and which are more or less lasting.

The stimuli that determine an attitude are either emotionally or intellectually based. An emotional attitude, according to Dewey and Humber,[17] is an "emotional relationship between the person and his environment, physical as well as social." They explain that "these attitudes are learned or acquired primarily by means of the autonomic nervous system and involve visceral-vascular reaction to stimuli." When a person responds toward another person, an object, or a situation with hate, affection, love, distrust, fear, repulsion, grief, or indifference, he indicates an emotional response. Essentially, such responses are the product of emotional attitudes.

Intellectual attitudes, on the other hand, may be described as the product of cortical involvement. They are formed as the result of valid reasoning and objective observation. An intellectual attitude is much more readily changed than an emotional one when new evidence is presented to support the need for change. One who has developed intellectual attitudes is less biased and prejudiced than one whose attitudes are emotional.

Because of the great benefits of physical activity to the body, it is desirable for teachers to promote in children an attitude favorable to lifelong participation in motor activity. The first step is ensuring that the children have a positive attitude toward their physical education experiences and this is, as implied above, closely related to their interest in and enjoyment of the activities presented. In addition, the teacher can discuss with the class the nature of physical education, and the values that accrue and the enjoyment to be derived from physical activity. The approach should be intellectual in nature on a level suited to the comprehension of the children. Emotional appeals may produce more immediate results in attitude formation, but such attitudes are less educationally sound because they tend to encourage prejudicial and biased points of view.

CREATIVITY

Creativity may be defined as a process of thinking that is characterized by imagination, originality, flexibility, and responsiveness to the new and unexpected. Creative thinkers are impelled to seek answers to the unexplained and to test the unknown and, in so doing, to take the inevitable risks. They are, of course, the discoverers, innovators, and inventors who make progress in all areas of human endeavor possible.

Creativity that results in new and important discoveries is of a high order possible for only a small number of people. Anyone can, however, develop the ability to think creatively, and it is to his benefit to do so. Studies have shown that creativity enables one to cope more effectively with life's frustrations and failures. Solutions to everyday problems are found more readily when approached with a degree of imagination. It is only when one is completely lacking in imagination and flexibility that he feels overwhelmed and unable to cope with the stresses of his life. It is not surprising that a lack of creativity has been shown to be a factor in poor mental health.

Schools are currently making a belated effort to develop creativity in children. Every area of the curriculum offers potential for the development of creativity. This is no less true of physical education than of other subject areas, although the possibilities in physical education may not be immediately apparent to those accustomed to the traditionally inflexible presentation of physical education. However, no less a person than Torrance,[18] whose research in creativity and promotion of programs to develop this quality in children are foremost in the field, has pointed out the important contributions that physical education can make to the development of creative thinking ability in school children.

How should the teacher of physical education proceed to stimulate the development of creativity?

The teacher must first of all show his students that he respects creativity. He can demonstrate his respect by the way he responds to their ideas and questions. Although he must give honest appraisals of the ideas and true responses to the questions, he must never be demeaning or sarcastic. He must never dismiss an idea or a solution because it is unorthodox or appears impractical. The contributions of his students must be valued for what they are. Some will be of little or no value, it is true, but the fact that the student has given thought to the matter must be honored. Students like to try their ideas out on someone, and the teacher is the logical person. If the teacher actually listens and then replies in a way that indicates he respects the creative thinking behind the idea, the student is encouraged to continue to explore new ideas and to work out original solutions to problems.

Not every teacher is able to inspire creativity, but certainly all can encourage it. Encouragement may take a number of forms: an expression of personal interest in the student's efforts; rewarding the achievement with praise or recognition; supplying the materials, resources, and environment for trying out ideas.

The teacher must deliberately plan situations that call forth creativity. It cannot be left to chance that opportunities will occur. The use of problem-solving is particularly effective in providing opportunities for older children to use creative thinking; for younger ones, movement exploration is better suited.

Pressure from peers to conform is responsible in a large part for the sharp drops found in the developmental curve of creativity at the ages of nine and 12. When the child reaches the age of nine, and again when he is about 12, he becomes very concerned about acceptance by his peers. He becomes wary of taking any kind of action or expressing an idea until he knows how his peers regard it. Unusual or original ideas or solutions to problems are often viewed with suspicion by peers and their reaction is consequently unfavorable. To avoid these negative responses from his peers, a child will often suppress his originality and try to conform to the thinking and behavior of those with whom he is associated.

Such children should be helped by the teacher to understand that it is not necessary to be like everyone else, to perform in the same way, to like the same things, or to dress in the same fashions as others. It is very important to impress upon the entire class that actions, beliefs, likes and dislikes should be based upon reason and facts, not upon majority opinions, attitudes, and mores.

The teacher must particularly beware of forcing children into set patterns. One of the greatest dangers in teaching is that the students might be propagandized rather than educated. When a teacher demands that children accept that which he accepts and believe that which he believes, little education occurs. Children should be taught at an early age to investigate ideas systematically. Simple concepts and techniques of research and investigation should be taught to enable children to find out the facts. The physical education teacher may introduce these through problem-solving in motor movement. However, he should not stop there but should encourage the use of the investigative techniques to test abstract ideas and concepts as well.

The ability to raise questions and identify problems is basic to creative thinking. Most children are helped in this respect by their immense curiosity. They have learned the importance of asking "why" to secure information long before they enter school. The teacher must continue to foster the children's curiosity and encourage them to continue asking why. Then he must help them learn how and where to find the answers. Not only should the child be encouraged to ask the teacher why, but he should be encouraged to ask himself why so that he will develop the ability to question his own concepts.

CHARACTERISTICS OF CHILDREN AND THEIR IMPLICATIONS FOR THE PLANNING OF THE PHYSICAL EDUCATION PROGRAM*

The successful physical education program is one which provides the kinds of activities which the children need to insure their continued physical, mental, and emotional growth and development. Physical education needs at any given grade level are determined largely by growth patterns, rate of maturation, social development, previous learning, and intellectual capacity. Consequently, it is useful for the teacher to be aware of the characteristics which children are likely to exhibit at a given chronological age. In the discussions which follow, an attempt has been made to present the patterns of physical, social, and intellectual developments which are most characteristic of each age and to show the implications that these have for the planning of a physical

---

*The physical, social, and intellectual characteristics and interests of children were compiled from information presented in the studies and books listed in the *Bibliography*.[19] The creative characteristics were compiled from the published sources and unpublished materials made available to the author by E. Paul Torrance, Calvin Taylor, and James A. Smith, eminent authorities on creativity.

Figure 2–1 Knowledge of the physical attributes which a child of a given age may be expected to exhibit is extremely useful in planning a physical education program to meet his needs. (Bureau of Publications, Baltimore Public Schools.)

education program which will meet the needs of the children in each grade of the elementary school from kindergarten through eighth grade.

In any given age group there will be some children who are tall and some who are short, some slender and some heavy, some who are alert and learn easily and some who are dull and learn slowly, some who are strong and agile and some who are weak and awkward. No one description of the characteristics of an age group will fit every child in a given room. It is unlikely that many children of a particular age will exhibit *all* of the characteristic traits ascribed to that age. It is possible that in some classes, very few will evidence a particular trait; for each child does, after all, grow and develop at his own individual rate. This rate may be influenced by socioeconomic background as well as inherited factors.

Children differ in their rate of development. They follow the same general pattern of development, but some progress at a faster or slower rate. Usually all aspects of physical development are accelerated or retarded at the same speed but not necessarily so. It is true that emotional and mental development usually parallel physical development but not in all cases; it may be found, for instance, that the motor skills of a child have developed, but emotional maturity has remained stationary. For example, certain children because of their physical and social maturity may be capable of playing complex games when they enter kindergarten at approximately five years of age while others who are the same age chronologically and possess the same motor skills development will not be ready to participate with success in these games because of emotional immaturity.

Changes in maturation, growth, and development are in continual progress; therefore, it should not be expected that the characteristics of one age will be immediately replaced by those of the next age as soon as the child is a year older. No such hard and fast lines can be drawn between the characteristic behavior and developmental progress of each age. However, scores made by children of a given age group in the testing of those traits which are measurable will generally fit the normal bell-shaped curve of probability. The majority will cluster around the mean for the trait, but others will vary between positive and negative extremes.

For the purpose of planning the physical education program, knowledge of the traits which will be exhibited by a majority of children in a given grade of the elementary school is extremely useful. From this information the teacher gains an understanding of the progress which a specific age group may have made in the past and may be expected to make in the year ahead. Then, too, the needs which many children experience at a given age can be assessed from a study of the traits they commonly exhibit. Armed with these facts and interpretations, the teacher is better able to select physical education activities which will produce optimum results. Toward this end, the characteristics common to children in each of the grades from kindergarten through eight are presented below together with the implications these have for the planning and teaching of physical education. In the presentation the physical characteristics are described in greater detail than the others because they are more basic to physical education. Additional information on the other characteristics is available in the references listed in the *Bibliography*.

FIVE YEAR OLDS
(Kindergarten)

Physical Characteristics

The overall growth of five year olds is relatively slow. Gain in height is greater than gain in weight. Children of both sexes lose subcutaneous fat from their first year until their fifth or sixth year. The arms and legs begin to slenderize, characteristic of the contour of the middle childhood figure.

There is a rapid increase in muscle tissue which increases the potential for the production of energy for movement, especially gross motor activities. Improved coordination is becoming evident with improved control and ease of body movement. However, large muscle control is still more advanced than that of small muscle control. Some improvement in the coordination of small muscles will be noticeable. Boys tend to be superior to girls in motor skills, and they generally perform with more vigor and forcefulness.

These children are extremely flexible, because there is more space between the joints and the relatively longer and less firmly attached ligaments than in older children. Their immature bones have proportionately more water and protein substances and less minerals and so have less resistance to pressure and muscle pull.

In five years, the skills of walking, running, and climbing have been learned, and, as opportunity is offered, they will be improved and extended. Children of this age show continued improvement in power and form while running and are therefore able to control to a considerable extent the start, stop, and turn.

Jumping and hopping can be performed successfully by most five year olds. Although most of them can do a gallop step and some can skip, few can give a skillful performance of these steps until later.

Climbing and descending stairs (the alternate foot descent may be a recent accomplishment) are established skills, as is the climb and descent of a ladder. However, the child will associate the height of the climb with the difficulty of the ascent; even children who climb well show cautious all-fours movement when the height is increased. At five years of age, boys and girls display equal ability in the skill. Children of this age enjoy climbing fences, and onto and under chairs and tables.

Some elements of mature throwing action are becoming evident, although most children at this stage still employ the off-balance step forward on the right foot as the ball is delivered with the right hand. The majority of the children will show improvement at an increasing rate both in throwing for accuracy and in throwing for distance.

Five year olds have short stubby fingers that make it difficult for them to catch objects in the hands. They are, therefore, not successful in attempts to catch small balls.

As with the other skills, there is a wide range of individual ability. This is shown in the bouncing of a ball. The size of the ball in relation to the size of the hand is important; although younger children may successfully bounce a large ball, the majority will be six years or older before they can bounce a small ball.

Ball bouncing is the only skill in which girls are likely to show superior performance to boys.

There is fairly marked improvement in dynamic balance. The children are able to stand on one foot and most can balance on the toes. Some improvement is shown in a kicking action, but the necessary controlled body balance and rhythmic leg swing have not yet been attained.

Although some five year olds can swim, most will not learn to swim at this age. They can handle a sled and a tricycle and may attempt to ride a bicycle.

Social Characteristics

Kindergarten age children play together for short periods in groups of three of four children with frequent shifting of the composition of the groups. Much of the time the children engage in parallel play alongside other children rather than actually participating in play together. The attention span of this age group is relatively short. These children both need and want supervision of their activities. They want approval but do not seek it as actively as those who are younger. They are less self-centered and less boastful than a year or two earlier.

Intellectual Characteristics and Interests

Five year olds are interested in learning to count and read. They are learning to print their names, and they know right from left. Imaginative play is intellectually stimulating for them. Imitating actions, acting out stories, and exploring movement are favorite activities.

Creative Characteristics

There is a decline in the creative abilities, especially imagination, at about the age of five when the children enter kindergarten. Torrance[20] feels that this decline is a direct result of the rigid educational programs and the strict discipline children encounter in kindergarten.

The ability in role playing has decreased since four years of age. Also, the attempt by the children to do what is expected of them tends to decrease their search for new and unique ways of doing things. Given proper direction and encouragement by the teacher, the children will overcome their inhibitions.

Implications

In planning physical education for kindergarten children it should be remembered that they are at a stage in which the opportunity to try out their skill with a variety of equipment is more important and enjoyable than success in use. The fun lies in the act of throwing the ball rather than in the distance or accuracy of the throw.

Because of their short stubby fingers, they often use their arms in catching rather than the hands. For this reason balls from 6 to 8 inches in diameter are recommended. Games with a ball which may be utilized to teach ball handling skills to five year olds are:

Teacher Ball using bean bags (page 201)

Rolling a Ball Through the Legs Relay (page 202)

Right Side Relay (page 202)

Left Side Relay (page 202)

For development of other fundamental skills at this age, activities such as those listed below may be used either singly or in various combinations.

Walking and standing while balancing a book or eraser on the head

Running slowly or fast as directed

Walking a straight line for balance

Rolling over

Forward roll

Climbing ladders

Climbing over Swedish boxes

Jumping over low objects

Balancing on a balance beam

Their short attention span makes it difficult for these children to listen to lengthy discussions of playing rules and safety regulations. Therefore, it is better for the teacher to say only so much as is necessary before starting play and to stop the class occasionally for rest during which time other essential information can be presented. Games should not be so long as to outlast the children's interest; those which may be terminated at any point, such as Brownies and Fairies (page 181) and Charlie over the Water (page 180), are especially suitable.

Games which keep most of the group moving most of the time are preferable to ones in which some children must stand idle for long periods awaiting their turns. However, for short periods, particularly following games which necessitate very vigorous play, games requiring each player to wait his turn are good because of the rest they afford the youngsters. Games which might be used in this way are:

Wild Horse Round-Up (page 179)

Rabbits and Foxes (page 179)

Animal Chase (page 180)

Chase the Rabbit Around (page 176)

Call Ball (page 202)

Because of their interest at this age in imaginative play, motor exploration activities can lead them in this direction. Rhythms have great appeal also; stepping, jumping, marching, and galloping to music are simple enough motor skills to be used effectively with kindergarten children. Improvised dances appeal to and satisfy certain needs of the child of five. Singing games such as those listed below provide additional opportunities for motor movement and rhythmic understanding.

The Farmer in the Dell (page 254)

Bluebird (pages 254–255)

The Muffin Man (page 255)

Danish Dance of Greeting (page 256)

Chimes of Dunkirk (page 256)

SIX YEAR OLDS
(First Grade)

Physical Characteristics

The sixth year of a child's life is an age of transition, with both physiological and psychological changes taking place. Growth continues to be slow and relatively uniform with the continued slenderizing of arms and legs and some elongation of the trunk. The large muscles are lengthening and 75 per cent of the weight gain is due to the increase of muscle tissue.

The six year olds are losing the knock-knees and protruding abdomen of early childhood. Their bones continue to have little resistance to pressure.

Increased flexibility continues on throughout childhood. Girls show their greatest flexibility of shoulder, knee, and thigh at six years of age.

Although generally healthy, the six year olds tend to be less robust than the five year olds and are subject to many of the childhood diseases. At this age, children, particularly boys, are prone to accidents.

The six year olds are very active. They are full of energy and seem to be in constant motion. They are boisterous and rough in play, but, at the same time, performance is more deliberate. Frequently, they appear to be clumsy as they overdo or overextend an action. Motor control is much improved, and they become frustrated with failures in tasks involving fine motor skills. However, the six year olds tend to show more interest in the actual performance of stunts and activities than in the level of their achievement.

The six year olds have acquired most of the basic motor skills and are now concerned with perfecting them and with combining skills.

Between the ages of five and six, children improve their running skill and are able to use this skill effectively in their play.

The steady increase in climbing ability is continued, with the majority of the six year olds being proficient in this skill. Boys may tend to be slightly superior to girls in climbing skills.

Skill in jumping is well established by the time children are six, but it is not until they reach this age that they are able to hop with skill. Even at this age, there is a wide range of ability in hopping. Girls from six to nine years old tend to be superior to boys in controlled hopping. Also, they show a more graceful action, hopping on the balls of their feet rather than using the flat-footed action generally employed by boys.

By the age of six, the majority of the children can skip (with variations in the level of performance). Although children can do a gallop step by the time they are four or five, most are six and a half years old before they accomplish this activity with skill.

Once the skills of jumping, hopping, skipping, and galloping are accomplished, children tend to experiment with variations, to improvise, and to incorporate the skills in other activities.

Six year olds have developed the level of balance, control, range of movement, and arm-foot opposition necessary in order to perform a skilled kicking action.

There is a continued increase in the proficiency of throwing a ball, but even at six years, there is a wide range of skill level from very awkward to highly proficient. By six and a half years, most boys are using a mature throwing action and are able to throw farther than girls.

There is a significant increase in the ability to catch a ball between the ages of five and six years. Many six year olds use a hand catch with the elbows at the side when catching a large ball but are not able to perform this skill when catching a small ball.

The ability to bounce a ball and to strike a ball is similar to that shown by the five year olds; the degree of progress is relative to the opportunity to practice these skills. The batting stance of the six year olds tends to be stiff, and the batting action is a type of swat.

There is an increase in dynamic balance ability between six and eight years. There is also a steady increase in static balance. An awareness of balancing his body in space is evident. Consequently, six year olds can handle a small bicycle, roller skates, bobsled, toboggan, and skis.

Many children at this age will learn to swim if exposed to swimming.

Social Characteristics

First graders enjoy group play although they shown preference for small groups. The composition of the groups is likely to change frequently as the group breaks up because of a quarrel, and members leave and others take their places. Boys and girls play together readily. Boys begin to fight and wrestle with others to demonstrate their masculinity or to express emotions which they cannot otherwise express. A sudden shift from good to bad behavior is to be expected. Taking turns, which was fairly well mastered during kindergarten, now appears to have been forgotten.

Children without pre-school experiences may need special help in adjusting to being away from home.

Intellectual Characteristics and Interests

Because they are being introduced to the mysteries of letters and numbers, these children delight in using their new reading and arithmetic skills. They are immensely curious and eager to handle different kinds of materials. They have vivid imaginations for the most part and enjoy using them in creative play activities. At this stage children are aware that simple rules must govern cooperative play, and they are willing to apply these and are able to do so with reminders from the teacher.

First graders like to use large blocks and furniture that they can push and pull around in order to build and climb on and in. They enjoy active games with singing and are able to join in the singing. Other favorite activities are skipping to music, crawling on all fours, playing tag, and swinging.

Creative Characteristics

Studies[21] indicate that after the decline of creative ability in children of five years of age, there is a rekindling of creative ability as they become six years old. A sharp increase is shown by the end of the year, unless creativity is severely restricted by teachers and other adults. Children at six are able to identify and produce many possible combinations or new relationships among objects, sounds, movements, and ideas; they respond well to encouragement to add, subtract, and mix these together to determine what will happen as a result.

Implications

Because of the child's physical development in his sixth year, he is sufficiently skilled to bounce, throw, and catch a ball. The ball should be of medium size because of the underdevelopment of the fingers. Skills of locomotion are such that the six year old can learn to kick a ball on the run, jump, skip, hop, chase, and dodge. First graders want to move about, to engage in vigorous play. Therefore, it is important to choose activities which provide full participation for everyone. The activities should not be too complex nor too long in duration as these youngsters have neither the interest span nor the skill for such activities yet. Safety should be emphasized because of the proneness to accidents in this age group.

At the beginning of the year the program should include many games that the youngsters are familiar with and have enjoyed. Generally these will be the more complex of their kindergarten games such as Call Ball (page 202) and the Farmer in the Dell (page 254). A review of the techniques of motor exploration is useful before introducing new experiences in motor performance. The fundamental skills of throwing and catching the bean bag; rolling, tossing, and catching a ball; and running at different speeds and in various directions need to be reviewed before exploring such new skills as dodging, ducking, twisting, and turning while running. Some games for this age group in which the new skills are emphasized are Skip Tag (page 183), Drop the Handkerchief (page 214), and Circle Stride Ball (pages 203–204).

Simple stunts and self-testing activities lend themselves to the first grade program because they are so easily adapted to the short interest span of the first grader. Some suggested activities are:

Forward Roll from a Squat (page 364)
Forward Roll from a Stand (page 364)
Shoulder Roll (page 365)
Foot and Toe Balance (page 358)
V-Sit (page 356)
Line and Beam Walking (pages 356–357)

Because their play patterns tend to be individual and small group, some physical education activities may be organized around these patterns. However, the children should be introduced gradually to play in larger groups so they can gain experience in participating with greater numbers of children. One easily accomplished way of doing this is to play games in which the number of players can be increased without affecting the essentials of the game. Examples of games that may be expanded from a small group to include any number of additional players are:

Partner Tag (pages 189–190)
Red Light (pages 215–216)

Tag the Line Race (page 193)
Club Relay (page 193)
Thread the Needle (page 194)
Pom-Pom Pull Away (pages 184–185)

Rhythmic activities arouse the eager and enthusiastic responses of children of this age. They also enjoy dramatizing in dance the information they have gained in their social studies. Folk dances learned in kindergarten will still be enjoyed, and to these may be added slightly more complex dances such as Loobly Loo (pages 256–257) and London Bridge Is Falling Down (page 258).

Games which employ their new reading and number skills should be included for the challenge and practice which they offer. Activities such as Letter Race (page 392) and Shuffle Letters (page 393) are appropriate.

To satisfy the prevalent curiosity about different materials, the teacher should attempt to introduce variety in the play equipment: different sizes and kinds of balls, bean bags, ropes, bars and ladders are suggested possibilities.

SEVEN YEAR OLDS
(Second Grade)

Physical Characteristics

The relatively slow and constant growth of middle childhood continues, with the limbs still growing proportionally more than the trunk. The hip-shoulder ratio of girls begins to change after six years of age with an increase in hip width. The general slimming of physique, characteristic of the beginning of middle childhood, is evident so that the figures of boys and girls are similar.

Some children may show a slight tendency to increase in subcutaneous fat. The bones of the body still have little resistance to pressure but are increasing in density. Growth in height over the year will be slow and regular; weight will increase less slowly than height.

Activity tends to be more variable with seven year old children; sometimes they are very active and at other times they are inactive. Movements and postures tend to be more tense than those of the six year olds. There is more use of both the large and small muscles of the body.

Throughout middle childhood there is a strong organic need for vigorous activity.

Second graders are significantly more accomplished in motor skills and eye-hand coordination than first graders. There is evidence of the beginning of patterns common to middle and later childhood in which there is a consolidation of growth, the perfection of known skills, and rapid learning taking place.

Social Characteristics

These children are less boisterous than they were as first graders, and they tend to be more cautious in their approach to activities. Their attention span has increased, but sitting still for long periods is still difficult. Their actions are more self-directed and less impulsive. Second graders begin for the first time to observe differences among their classmates. Some element of competition is usually observable in their social relationships.

Intellectual Characteristics and Interests

Most second graders are fairly facile with simple printed materials and enjoy using their reading skills. They have acquired basic addition and subtraction facts and like to make use of these, also. They are capable and willing to accept increased personal responsibilities. They welcome opportunities to act on their own. While they tend to engage in fewer new activities and ventures, they do show intense interest in certain activities for a period of time.

Seven year olds like to play running games and are beginning to show an interest in the skills of some of the major sports, particularly those involving the batting of a ball. Girls are interested in activities that require skipping or jumping with a rope. Both sexes enjoy running and galloping to music and may show an interest in dancing. Both boys and girls are likely to have a strong interest in swimming.

Creative Characteristics

There is a more dramatic increase in creative ability between the ages of six and seven than between the ages of five and six. The seven year olds develop an insatiable curiosity. They want to know the how and why of all that meets their eyes. The children of this age are able to produce increasingly more complex combinations of movement, using more abstract ideas in the combination of body movements and the manipulation of objects.

Implications

Motor skills have progressed to the point where these children are able to perform the basic skills of movement with a fair degree of accuracy and to use them with enjoyment in game situations. Second graders are able to jump, skip, and leap with more skill and coordination than during their previous year. It is desirable to begin to expand their basic skill learning. Motor exploration activities provide an excellent way of giving necessary insight into the movement possibilities of the human body. Second graders will not be ready to play games involving the more refined motor activities such as throwing and catching a ball, but they will be able to achieve considerable motor learning from such games as:

Circle Ball Passing (page 205)
Kneel Ball (page 204)
Bean Bag Circle Toss (page 387)
Bean Bag Passing (page 388)

Although second graders are less boisterous, they still enjoy moving about vigorously and making noise as they move. The physical education activities should not fail to provide sufficient big muscle movements to give them muscular (and vocal) release from the restraints of the classroom. Activities such as Pom-Pom Pull Away (page 184) and Chain Tag (page 185) are two good examples of the kind of game that might be included in the program to encourage the vigorous activity necessary to fill this particular need.

Because of the greater intellectual and social development of second graders, slightly more complex games than were played in first grade may be introduced. The games should still have few rules to follow but should give the youngsters more chances to use their initiative and to exercise individual judgment. Cat and Rat (page 183) and Red Light (page 215) are two such games.

Second graders react fairly well to competition; however, highly competitive game situations are contraindicated. They respond very well to self-testing activities in which each is competing against himself. Recommended self-testing activities are:

Bridge (page 355)
Forward Bend (page 355)
High Kick (page 358)
Cat Walk (page 356)
Foot and Toe Balance (page 358)
Walk on Heels and Toes (page 357)

A wonderful opportunity for expanding the child's knowledge of the people of different lands is provided by the budding interest evidenced at this age in the differences among classmates. A discussion of the likenesses and differences of other peoples might precede the teaching of folk dances from other lands such as:

Hopp Mor Annika (Sweden) (page 259)
Kinderpolka (German) (page 260)
Shoemaker's Dance (Denmark) (page 261)

EIGHT YEAR OLDS
(Third Grade)

Physical Characteristics

This is an age of diversity. Physically, the eight year olds begin to foreshadow the marked changes that will take place in later childhood, although such changes are yet barely discernible. During the eighth year children lose their baby body profile and reach a maturity level in which the two sexes are developing different characteristics. This will continue to be more apparent in physical development and in motor ability skills.

There are steady height and weight gains throughout the year. At eight years old, a child's arms and legs tend to be very thin with no marked development in musculature; the arms and legs are nearly 50 per cent longer than they were when the child was two years of age.

The eight year olds are generally healthier and less subject to fatigue than the seven year olds. As they grow older, there is an increase in strength, speed, and endurance.

They are aware of their own posture, and posture changes become more adaptive. Their movements show more control than previously, as their total pattern of body movement becomes rhythmical and graceful.

Middle childhod is a period when those who have made poor social adjustments tend to overeat to compensate for this failure. As a result, obesity may begin to become a problem with some children.

There is a marked improvement in throwing, catching, dodging, kicking, and striking a ball. A leveling off in ability in dynamic balance is evident, and there will be a slight decrease in flexibility, unless the proper physical activities are given to the child to prevent it.

Eight year olds may show a high level of skill in activities such as skating, swimming, and cycling. Coordination of small muscles begins to be evident, and there is a growing interest in games requiring this type of skill. Skills of major team games can be learned. However, small muscle work, such as writing, is still difficult and tiring for eight year olds.

Girls become increasingly skillful in their ability to skip with a rope. They learn to run in and out of a moving rope, although they still have difficulty in varying the step while working in the rope.

Social Characteristics

Group play in the third grade is maintained for a longer period without being dissolved as the result of disagreement. By the time children are eight years old, they are able to resolve their differences in play to a considerable degree. But, while they are able to work together for a common goal such as winning a relay game, they are not yet equal to the demands of more competitive play.

Both boys and girls are adventurous, but the play of the former tends to be considerably rougher and more challenging. Consequently, the sexes tend to separate into their respective groups during free play.

Intellectual Characteristics and Interests

Third graders usually become very much interested in the world beyond their local environment; they enjoy their introduction to history. The intellectual development is such that group discussions and projects can be conducted with considerable success.

Children at this age particularly enjoy rhythms of a spontaneous and dramatic nature. They demonstrate a fairly wide variety of play interests.

Creative Characteristics

At eight years of age children enter a more sophisticated quest for explanations. The questions of why expand into questions of how, who, when, and where. Eight year olds begin to develop a concept of the order of a sequence and willingly experiment and explore possible changes in the order by adding to or subtracting from the sequence to develop a completely new pattern.

Implications

Coordination is sufficiently developed in third graders for them to enjoy learning such advanced skills as hitting a moving target. They are also at an age to profit from practice to improve skills which they have previously learned; and many of them will express their interest in practicing to acquire proficiency in throwing, catching, kicking, batting, and rope climbing. The activities listed below are some which might be included in the program for the development and practice of these skills:

Circle Ball Passing (page 205)
Circle Dodge Ball (page 207)
Line Dodge Ball (page 207)
Line Soccer (page 209)
Call Ball (page 202)
Lower Away (page 362)
Chin Up (page 362)

Third graders have sufficient intellectual maturity to enjoy simple team strategy, but the time devoted to explaining and discussing strategy should not be so great as to reduce significantly the time devoted to actual play of the game, for vigorous movement is of primary importance at this stage of the child's development. Their social development is such that these children are able to engage in group play requiring limited cooperation with other team members and having restricted competitive elements. Recommended as activities which provide for competition and cooperation within the abilities of third graders are:

Partner Tag (page 189)
Prisoners' Base (page 187)
Chief Red Ball (page 188)
Bear in the Pit (page 188)
Bronco Tag (page 189)

Children of this age are capable of considerable resourcefulness in organizing and creating dance games and activities. Creative rhythms and motor exploration activities offer them opportunities for exercising this talent. Examples of suitable singing and folk dances for this age level are:

Hansel and Gretel (page 263)
Jolly Is the Miller (page 264)
Nixie Polka (page 265)

Because this is the beginning of the decline in flexibility, exercises and activities that provide opportunities to stretch the muscles and develop a wide range of movement should receive considerable attention in the program. Some activities of this type which might be included are:

Motor exploration
Touching the toes with the knees straight
Ostrich Walk (page 349)
Inchworm (page 350)
Chicken Walk (page 350)
V-Sit (page 356)

Since third grade is the time when the sexes first tend to separate for free

Figure 2-2 Because flexibility begins to decline at about age eight, many opportunities should be provided for stretching muscles and extending the joints. (Courtesy of Town of Vernon Schools, Rockville, Connecticut.)

play, it is important to encourage group play during physical education classes. This helps boys and girls to remain comfortable in each other's presence and to promote in them mutual respect and appreciation for the abilities and interests of the opposite sex. Dances and rhythms as well as games are good activities for joint participation.

NINE YEAR OLDS
(Fourth Grade)

Physical Characteristics

Prior to pre-adolescent changes, sex differences that exist are slight, and there is little difference in physique between boys and girls.

The nine year olds are at an intermediate age — between childhood and youth. Some of the girls will have commenced the accelerated growth spurt of the pre-adolescent period. They will also be at the start of a corresponding period of the greatest gain in strength.

A sequence of change in the rate of increase in height, body breadth, and body depth, and in heart size, lung capacity, and muscular strength, in addition to changes in other structures and functions, becomes evident in girls between the ages of eight and 12 years and in boys between the ages of nine and 13 years.

Self-motivation is a characteristic of the nine year olds who both work and play hard. They have a great deal of energy and tend to stay with an activity until exhausted. They may have difficulty in calming down after strenuous and exciting activities. They are often so active that it is necessary to provide extra rest periods for them.

The interest of the previous year in posture has been abandoned as the nine year olds show preference for careless or awkward postures.

An increase in ability in dynamic balance is evident.

Gross motor activity is still prominent as previously acquired skills are combined and integrated. The children are becoming aware of specific skills and are interested in practicing skills in order to improve performance. There is improved eye-hand coordination, and fine motor activities are becoming more skillful.

After the age of nine years, the earlier development of thigh and trunk flexion in boys becomes evident in the superiority of their jumping ability.

Between the ages of nine and 12 years, particularly on the part of boys, there is evidence of the sequence of development in the mechanics of the long jump. Boys progress toward a more mature and efficient manner of jumping. Improvement shown with age is greater for boys than girls, but there is a great deal of overlap.

Although the nine year olds have better control of their own speed, they may show some timidity of involvement in fast movement, such as sliding or skiing. They are interested in their own strength and ability to lift things. Boys still engage in rough-and-tumble play, such as informal wrestling and tumbling.

Skills acquired during middle childhood will depend on opportunities that are given the child to learn and practice skills and on what skills are popular with the peer group.

Social Characteristics

Antagonism toward the opposite sex may become evident, particularly if there is overt or subtle encouragement from the school or community. Fourth graders are less spontaneous in their relationships with adults and tend to move in exclusive groups. Gangs and clubs are formed to promote this exclusiveness.

Intellectual Characteristics and Interests

During the fourth grade students demonstrate a real interest in how things are made and in the cause and effect relationship. Reading skill is developed sufficiently to enable them to pursue special interests and hobbies on their own with little or no assistance from adults. The pursuit of these activities may become so dominant an interest among some children that they will not participate in vigorous play as much as they should. Others develop a keen interest in motor activity and show a great desire to perform finely coordinated activities with speed and skill. These youngsters will also begin to show an interest in team games and in learning the skills of these games.

Creative Characteristics

As they reach the fourth grade, children tend to be perfectionists and are therefore easily discouraged by undue adult pressure. There is a decline in creativity at this age caused chiefly by conformity to peer group standards. Only the unusual child of this age can withstand the pressure to conform. If given encouragement and a satisfying experience in creative endeavor, children are able to maintain their progress in creative growth. At this age, they do become more aware of a complex combination of objects and movements and are able to produce the new combinations and to make simple predictions from observations.

Implications

The improved strength, skill, coordination, and concentration of fourth graders increase the fun to be had in more complex games. Ball handling skills can be developed to a degree of considerable efficiency at this age level. New skills may be introduced, particularly in games which challenge their increased ability to perform; however, a review of skills previously learned should not be neglected. Games that they may have learned previously such as Line Dodge Ball (page 207) and Line Soccer (page 209) bear repeating because they are so generally enjoyed and because they encourage further skill development.

The prevalent gang spirit can be utilized by the teacher to promote team games. Some good lead-up games (Chapter 12) for the more advanced sports which these youngsters will learn later are:

Basketball Dribble Relay
Keep Away
Slow Pitch Softball
Three Grounders and a Fly
Circle Soccer
Alley Soccer
Newcomb

Skill drills or motor exploration problems for the more complex team games which should be emphasized are:

Dribbling a soccer ball
Kicking a soccer ball with inside of foot and with instep
Basketball passing; chest and bounce pass
Basketball dribbling
Foul shooting
One hand push shot
Batting
Volleying a volleyball against a wall

Because these children are so active as to require additional rest, the amount of time allotted to vigorous competitive play in class and in intramurals should be carefully planned.

Since the boys enjoy rougher play than the girls, some of the activities may be segregated; but it is important to promote good relatons with the opposite sex through numerous mixed activities. Vigorous games that appeal to boys of this age level are: Bronco Tag (page 189), Come Along (page 216), and Poison (page 216). Excellent mixed activities can be found among the rhythms and singing and folk dances. Especially good are:

Gustaf's Skoal (page 268)

Norwegian Mountain March (page 268)

Patty Cake Polka (page 269)

Seven Steps (page 269)

To add variety to the program and to encourage more complete physical development, self-testing and tumbling activities may be introduced. Some suggestions for these types of activity are:

Cartwheel (page 366)

Neckspring (page 366)

Assisted Straight Arm Handspring (page 369)

Handspring (page 370)

Balancing activities (pages 356–358)

Simple pyramids may be introduced in fourth grade. Care must be exercised that pyramid height be controlled to avoid placing undue stress and strain upon the child acting as the base of the pyramid.

Fundamental skills of body balance and good posture should be emphasized to increase the awareness of the advantages of maintaining good posture.

TEN YEAR OLDS
(Fifth Grade)

Physical Characteristics

Corresponding with the pre-pubescent growth spurt of the 10 year olds, there is a decrease in the percentage of weight gained, although there has been an increase in weight prior to this growth spurt. Girls, ahead of boys in sexual maturity, exceed boys in height during the ages 10 to 14 years.

Puberty begins for some 10 year olds. Secondary sex characteristics become evident in some girls, and there is a brief leg length growth spurt preceding the general growth spurt for girls.

A gain in bone and muscle tissue, contributing to the period of greatest gain in strength, occurs at this time.

A 10 year old boy is stronger than a 10 year old girl of the same age, height, and weight. Nearly half of the boys and almost all of the girls will not have sufficient strength to do pull-ups.

The chest will broaden and flatten, and the ribs will change from a horizontal position to an oblique one in both boys and girls, with the latter developing slightly ahead of the former. If the bones of the chest do not become firm enough to withstand pressures, chest deformities may result.

Although bones tend to become less flexible as the child approaches maturity, flexibility of the body continues throughout the middle childhood period.

Boys' hearts are a little larger than the hearts of girls throughout childhood, but from age nine or 10 to age 13 or 14, girls' hearts are the larger. Between four and 10 years the growth of the heart has been slow, and there is some evidence to indicate that during this period the heart is smaller in relation to the rest of the body than it will be at any other period. The heart beat slows down, and there is an increase in blood pressure as the child approaches maturity. Approximation to adult heart rate is reached somewhere between six and 12 years. From 10 to 13 years of age, girls evidence a higher blood pressure than do boys.

With the pubescent spurt, the chest cavity and lungs increase while the rate of breathing decreases.

After 10 years of age there tends to be a decrease in the occurrence of illnesses.

The overall pattern of organization displayed by the 10 year olds is more flexible than that shown when they were nine year olds. Although alert, 10 year olds tend to be more relaxed and casual than nine year olds. Their performance of activities is carried out with skill and speed.

There is a further increase in proficiency in motor performance. Boys, on an average, are superior to girls, but many girls are as physically skilled as some of the boys. Batting action has improved markedly since the initial attempts. There is now a good swing action and the footwork is more appropriate. Practice has made some contribution to this improvement, but the progressive growth changes of the total neuro-muscular system are also involved.

With the steady increments that have taken place in body size and strength, there is a corresponding consistent improvement in the basic skills such as running, jumping, and throwing.

There is an increase in skills relevant to team sports and other adult sports and games. Ten year olds are also beginning to concentrate on the development of selective motor skills.

By the time children reach 10 or 11 years of age, their games are frequently competitive. An interest is shown in hazardous activity, but boys are more active and more rough than girls.

Skill shown in fine motor activities is approaching an adult level. Sex differences are shown in the superiority of girls in manual dexterity and in the superiority of boys in gross muscle movements that involve strength, speed, and coordination.

Social Characteristics

The gang spirit continues into the fifth grade. Children of this age are organized and competitive. They are adventurous and enjoy an element of danger in their activities. They are likely, also, to show signs of a desire for greater independence. Their dependability is increasing when they are given responsibility. There is a broadening interest in team games, especially those that demand vigorous activity.

Intellectual Characteristics and Interests

Fifth graders are interested in the ideas and the achievements of others, particularly in motor skills. They are capable of evaluating and learning to express their own points of view adequately. At the age of 10, children are developing the ability to plan ahead and, consequently, are capable of handling fairly long-range assignments. They show an increased interest in motor activities and desire to improve their sport skills.

Creative Characteristics

The children entering their tenth year make some recovery from the decline of creativity in the previous year. They become more able to use a variety of skills for creative purposes and can discover ways of using their unique abilities. They can and do develop and utilize analogies in problem-solving. They are able to predict possible outcomes of specific situations and to discover incongruities in action. During this year children develop the ability to produce alternate possible solutions to a problem and to produce original movements in dramatizing abstract ideas.

Implications

The need to belong which manifests itself in gangs can be satisfied in the physical education program with group and team play. Contact sports suitable to the abilities and maturation of the students may be introduced to satisfy their desire for adventure and danger. Team games may be presented if there have been sufficient participation in lead-up games and appropriate development of skills. Lead-up games for basketball, softball, soccer, and volleyball may be introduced to both boys and girls; generally touch football is limited to boys. The following activities are good lead-up games for fifth graders.

For Basketball:
    Keep Away (page 301)
    Keyhole Basketball (page 301)
    Captain Basketball (page 301)
    Corner Goal Ball (page 300)
For Softball:
    Work-Up (page 312)
    Beatball (page 312)
    Three Grounders and a Fly (page 312)
    Bat Ball (page 312)
For Soccer:
    Soccer Keep Away (page 319)
    Line Soccer (page 320)
    Circle Soccer (page 320)
    Soccer Dribble Relay
    Soccer Goal Kick
For Volleyball:
    Circle Formation Volley (page 328)
    Line Formation (page 328)
    One Bounce Volleyball (page 328)
For Touch Football:
    Hot Potato (page 334)
    Five Step Football (page 334)

All these games provide opportunities for students to gain experience in accepting responsibilities. At this age students are capable of assisting as scorers, helpers, and demonstrators.

The strength and ability of both boys and girls are sufficient to permit the use of the more difficult self-testing activities. Those suitable for 10 year olds include:

Jump and Turn (page 358)
Russian Dance (page 359)
Stick Jump (page 359)
Wall Leap (page 359)
Chair Vault (page 360)

Stunts and tumbling activities possessing a degree of difficulty are also appropriate. Some of these are:

Monkey Walk (page 352)
Wheelbarrow (page 352)
Horse Walk (page 353)
Tandem Walk (page 354)
Headspring (page 367)
Knee-Shoulder Spring (page 368)
Handspring (page 370)

The popular chin up test for arm strength in boys is inadequate for testing boys of this age because the greater portion of them do not have sufficient arm strength to score on the test, negating the test's discriminatory power. For further information about testing see Chapter 4.

The interest which youngsters of this age begin to show in the ideas of others can be utilized to present the history of the development of various games and to introduce the dances of other lands and cultural groups. Dances from other lands appropriate for fifth graders are:

Crested Hen (Denmark) (page 272)
Ace of Diamonds (Denmark) (page 272)
Csebogar (Hungary) (page 273)
La Raspa (Mexico) (page 273)

ELEVEN YEAR OLDS
(Sixth Grade)

Physical Characteristics

There is a wide range of individual difference in the rate at which children mature, and at 11 years old this factor is becoming obvious. The rapid growth of the early maturer is contrasted with the slower, less intense growth of the later maturer, and, particularly with boys, there is a difference in body proportions between the two extremes. Girls between 11 and 14 years of age are generally taller than boys of the same age. After 11 years the ratio of sitting height to standing height tends to rise for girls.

At the age of 11, boys are entering the accelerated growth period of pre-adolescence, which is preceded by a brief leg length growth spurt. The earlier rapid growth rate of girls was accompanied by a widening of the hips, whereas the rapid growth rate of boys is marked by a broadening of shoulder width.

Between 11 and 12 years there is a beginning of marked gains in bone and muscle for boys which corresponds with a period when there are the greatest gains in strength.

Between the ages of 11 and 13 years there is an increase in the thickness of subcutaneous tissue. Girls make a rapid increase in weight and begin to show secondary sex characteristics; some girls may reach menarche.

At 11 years, boys are twice as strong as when they were six years old. Girls are not as strong as boys, but relative to the strength of boys, they are stronger in the legs than in the arms and hands. Jones[22] indicates that there is an apparent sequence of strength development—first leg power, then biceps and back, and later forearm.

The increase in muscle growth and the increasing sex differences in the relationship of muscles to body weight and in the development of skeletal structures has a marked effect on the skill performances of boys and girls after 11 or 12 years of age. Such sex differences are most apparent in skills involving jumping, running, and throwing. However, in addition to these biological factors, cultural expectations are involved in the increased sex differences in motor performance.

Boys are ahead of girls in physical endurance.

The relative increase in leg length will contribute to a higher percentage of failures in the reach-and-touch-the-toes test of flexibility.

The last wrist bone, which has appeared in girls at nine years, does not appear in boys before 11 years. The sesamoid bone in the hand, which indicates growth at pubescent level, appears in girls between 11 and 12 years of age.

Oxygen consumption is consistently higher for boys throughout childhood, but this difference becomes more pronounced after 11 years.

Girls tend to have greater control over hands and fingers and so display fine muscle movement superior to that of boys and particularly between the ages of 10 and 13 years. However, research[23] indicates that, even in cases in which there are significantly different levels of performance between the sexes in fine muscle movement and in eye-hand coordination, these differences are less than the range of variation that exists within either sex.

Some researchers find little improvement in balance after 11 years, which would indicate that a peak period has been reached. However, others claim that boys especially continue to improve through 14 years of age.[24]

At all age levels, boys are superior to girls in throwing for distance, and this difference in ability increases with age. As shown by boys, superiority in this skill is thought to be due partly to their more mature throwing pattern and partly to their mechanical advantage in propulsion of an object for distance. This last advantage is present because boys have greater forearm length, girth, and strength. There is not a marked sex difference in throwing for accuracy, although boys do tend to show superiority.

Social Characteristics

A desire for recognition is prevalent among 11 year olds. Being a member of a club or gang helps to fulfill this desire. Sixth graders experience increased independence of thought and action, and there is a genuine interest in being helpful to others. Interest in team play is high, and these children respond well to organized games. They are both willing and able to practice motor skills to improve their playing ability.

Intellectual Characteristics and Interests

By their eleventh year, youngsters are capable of dealing with fairly complex ideas. They have an understanding of the interrelationships of cause and effect. Assessment of their own capacities and abilities is greater than ever before. Ability to organize and to assume responsibility for doing a job is also greatly improved.

Eleven year olds show strong interest in their performance of the individual motor skills. Some will be self-conscious when learning new skills. Spectator interest in athletics begins to show definite development.

Creative Characteristics

During the eleventh year there is a continued recovery from the decrease in creativity experienced during the ninth year. Girls and boys show different preferences in exploration of activities. Girls like to explore and pretend in play, while boys prefer firsthand experience. At this age, there is less restlessness than was exhibited at an earlier age, and the children are able to give sustained attention to mental activity. Children at 11 years of age will try most anything for experience but tend to lack confidence if the results of their efforts are to be made public. The skills of creativity that begin to develop at 10 years of age continue to expand, and the child gains greater ability in them.

Implications

Self-testing and tumbling activities should receive considerable emphasis in the sixth grade program because of the increased interest in and ability to perform complex skills that youngsters at this age level demonstrate. Activities of this type which might be presented to this age group are:

Balance Beam Stunts (pages 356–358)

Double Kazotski (page 359)

Walk-Out Handspring (page 370)

For the development of strength and endurance in the boys, these activities may be offered:

Fireman's Carry (page 352)

Partner Handstand Walk (page 353)

Back Carry (page 354)

Some separation of the sexes for play is necessary because of the differences in strength and endurance. Generally team sports are segregated for instruction and for play. Good team games for sixth grade boys are touch football and football type games such as Five Step (page 334) and Hot Potato (page 333). Coeducation team play should not be neglected, however, because of the social benefits to be derived from playing together. Team games suitable for this purpose include volley-ball, basketball, softball, and soccer. The program should include dance and rhythmic activities in which boys and girls participate together. Dances such as Csebogar (page 273) and La Raspa (page 273) are very good for this age. Social dancing is sometimes introduced during the sixth grade. In classes in which the sex antagonism has been largely outgrown, social dancing is usually very successful. This factor as well as that of the attitude of the community toward social dancing should weigh heavily in the decision to include it in the sixth grade physical education program.

TWELVE YEAR OLDS
(Seventh Grade)

Physical Characteristics

Twelve years of age marks the period of the most rapid growth spurt for girls and is the time when an increasing number of boys will enter the growth spurt. More girls will reach menarche and some boys will show signs of the beginning of puberty.

The ages 12 and 13 indicate the period of most rapid growth in strength for girls. Boys have been gradually increasing in strength up to the age of 12 years, when the rate of increase will become rapid. At 12 years old, boys have reached about 50 per cent of the manual strength which they will have at 17.

Boys and girls who are more advanced toward sexual maturity tend to be taller and heavier than those who are maturing more slowly.

At 12 years, individual differences become even more marked, with a great amount of overlapping between age levels in characteristics and skills. Differences in body proportions between early and late maturing girls are not as pronounced as between early and late maturing boys.

Starting at 12 years of skeletal age, girls become relatively broad in the hips, whereas boys maintain the ratio between hip width and height. Girls of the same skeletal age show no difference in ratio, whether they be early or late in maturing, but there is a marked difference in boys according to the speed of maturity. Boys who mature early tend to have broad hips in relation to height, whereas boys who mature later tend to have slender hips in relation to height.

The arms and legs of a 12 year old girl are approximately the full length that they will be at maturity. This upset in proportion, resulting from relatively long limbs as compared to the trunk, may produce awkward and clumsy movements in many situations, even though her previous development has shown considerable ability and confidence in performance of skills.

Early maturing boys may show arrest in leg growth, but it will be three years later before the late maturing boys experience any arrest in the ratio of sitting height to standing height.

The pre-adolescent peak of fat increase is followed by a decrease as there begins a rapid increase in the development of bone and muscle tissue. This trend is less marked in girls who tend to maintain a higher level of subcutaneous fat.

A girl's twelfth year marks a peak in her flexibility. Generally, there is an increase in flexibility to 12 years, then there is a decline. The exceptions to this trend appear in the shoulder, knee, and thigh where girls show a gradual decline from six years to 18 years. Of all measures of flexibility, ankle flexibility is the most constant.

After 12 years, the basal heart rate, which has fallen gradually since birth, decreases more markedly in boys than in girls. Girls show a rise in pulse rate just prior to menarche; the progressive rise in systolic blood pressure ceases near menarche and then remains at a uniform level.

At 12 years, early maturing children are nearer adult levels in pulse rate, blood pressure, and metabolic rate than are late maturing children. Many 12 year old children reach adult maturity in some eye-and-hand coordination skills. Girls tend to show superiority in fine motor and manual dexterity skills, whereas boys are superior in activities that involve muscular strength, speed, and coordination of gross movements.

At pubescence there is a slackening in the rate of increase in motor ability. This slackening precedes the period of greatest growth.

Those 12 year olds who are physically more developed will demonstrate superior athletic skills, and the majority of those who excel in team sports will be those who are pubescent or post-pubescent.

With pubertal changes girls show a tendency to lose interest in strenuous activity and games, although between 12 and 13 years of age, they demonstrate a maximum increase in athletic skills. Physical ability becomes a very important factor for boys.

Social Characteristics

Seventh graders are unsure of their relationships with the group and with those in authority, and this gives rise to feelings of insecurity and frustration. The choice of activities in which these youngsters will participate is based more upon individual preference than any other consideration. Self-consciousness about learning new skills is evidenced.

Intellectual Characteristics and Interests

Increasing self-control is demonstrated by seventh graders. They are more and more capable of solving intellectual problems and can deal fairly capably with abstract ideas. There is likely to be considerable concern about the moral code of their society.

Although interest in team games in still high among both sexes, it may begin to diminish among girls unless there is much emphasis in their social group upon team play. Generally, they tend to find the partner and individual activities more interesting, with a definite preference for dancing, particularly social dancing. Boys maintain a high interest in the more vigorous games and activities.

Creative Characteristics

The third decline in creativity comes at the age of 12. This decline may be explained on the basis of conflicts arising with the onset of the physiological change of puberty. As the transition is made into early adolescence, social pressures to conform reassert themselves with greater strength than at any other time. These new demands and responsibilities often produce feelings of insecurity and inadequacy. The resultant anxiety makes creative thinking and action extremely difficult.

Implications

Seventh grade students should be given opportunities for successful participation in many sports. Basketball, softball, volleyball, soccer, track, tumbling, and swimming with the addition of touch football for boys might well comprise the core of their program. This does not mean that only team sports should be offered or even that they should constitute the dominant portion of the program. Since at this age self-consciousness about learning new skills will prevent these children from exploring new activities on their own, it is particularly important for the physical education program to introduce them to the largest possible variety of activities.

Sport skills for the above mentioned team sports (Chapter 12) which should be emphasized in the program are:

Basketball	Touch Football
Passing	Passing and receiving
Dribbling, feinting, and pivoting	Kicking
Shooting	Softball
Soccer	Catching
Kicking	Throwing
Trapping	Pitching
Tackling	Fielding
Volleyball	Base running
Volleying	Batting
Setting up	
Spiking	

Girls of this age need encouragement to continue strenuous activity in order to maintain their strength, speed, and endurance levels. Physical fitness activities suitable for this include sit-ups, endurance hang, squat thrust, and 50-yard dash. Boys of this age are highly motivated and respond well to the fitness activities without special encouragement.

If interscholastic sports are introduced at this grade level, the utmost care must be taken to insure that everyone, regardless of the level of skill ability, has a chance to learn the sport skills.

THIRTEEN YEAR OLDS
(Eighth Grade)

Physical Characteristics

The period from 13 to 16 years, which marks early adolescence, is a period of transition. Girls have reached a peak of acceleration in physical growth which will continue into their fourteenth year. Weight is increasing faster than height. By 13 years, most girls reach menarche or have passed it. Menarche marks the beginning of a stabilization of physiological functions in girls and a corresponding rapid approach toward the adult level of functioning.

Boys are near the period of most rapid growth. Some boys are pubescent at 13 years, but most will be in the middle stage of Stolz's three stage cycle of puberty.[25] At 13 years, the range of development shown by boys is from childhood to almost complete maturity.

Between 13 and 18 years, girls show an increase in the amount of subcutaneous tissue, while boys show a decrease in it.

Muscles of the body have grown to the extent that they now constitute nearly half of the body weight. The growth of the bones and muscles follows the pattern of total growth; however, if muscle growth has lagged behind skeletal growth, there is now a tendency for it to catch up.

During the periods of rapid growth, muscles and bones grow rapidly and establish a new ratio to one another. Important changes take place in body proportion with an increase in the rate of growth of the trunk, which has followed the earlier period of rapid growth of arms and legs. The 13 year old boy may not yet have reached this period, but, by the time he is between 13 and 14 years, his hands and feet will have reached a size that is very close to their total development at maturity.

The changes taking place in body proportions contribute to "adolescent awkwardness," but this will be less obvious in those who are becoming sexually mature at a slow rate and in those who had reached a high level of motor proficiency during childhood.

Anatomically, the girl has certain mechanical disadvantages in comparison to boys, and as she approaches maturity these become more obvious—the oblique angle of the attachment of the femur to the pelvis, the shorter arms and legs in proportion to the trunk, and the broader pelvis. Girls are larger than boys in girth of the thigh and boys are larger than girls in thoracic circumference and girth of forearm.

The rate of functional growth in strength is greater than the rate of anatomical growth in the cross section of muscle during adolescence.[26] Boys reach approximately 50 per cent of their 17 year old shoulder strength in both thrusting and pulling actions at 13½ years, which is about one year later than the equivalent development of manual strength. With girls, pulling strength is developed at the same rate as manual strength, whereas thrusting strength matures more rapidly, particularly in the year preceding menarche. The girl may reach approximately her adult level of strength as early as 13 years.

A distinct relationship between strength measures and motor performance is shown with boys, but no such relationship is apparent with girls. Hurlock[27] emphasizes that the development of muscle power following growth in muscle size will not alone guarantee muscular skill. Training, practice, environment, and motivation are all important contributory factors.

The motor performance of boys is positively and significantly related to all measures of maturity (chronological, anatomical, and physiological); there is no such correlation in the motor performance of girls. However, body build may show some significant relationship in the case of a girl with an exceptional performance level.

A typical characteristic of the pubescent child is muscular fatigue.

Endurance, as measured by the 600-yard run, shows continued improvement from six to 13 years. After this age, boys continue to improve, but girls show a loss in efficiency. Girls of 13 will score less in sit-ups than 10 to 12 year old girls.

Boys show increasing superiority in motor performance as they grow older, and this superiority is especially marked in skills of agility. As they grow older, girls tend to improve in balance, control, and strength, but they decline in agility.

Through 15 or 16 years girls show a steady increase in skill in throwing events, both those involving distance and those involving accuracy. Performance by boys in these events, although not as marked as in the target throw, is superior and will increase at a steady rate.

Social Characteristics

There are embarrassment and a lack of confidence in the performance of new skills at this age. As a consequence many of these students are likely to take spectator roles unless encouraged to do otherwise. Any antagonism toward the opposite sex that developed in earlier years has disappeared and has been replaced by a growing interest in boy-girl relationships. Individual friendships are important, but group membership is very desirable.

Intellectual Characteristics and Interest

These students have acquired a considerable body of knowledge which they are becoming increasingly capable of using in the process of logical reasoning. Ability to deal with abstract ideas is more in evidence, and a wide variety of interests is characteristic. An intelligent response to frustrating situations is more likely than an excessively emotional one. However, escape from undesirable experiences is often sought in identification with the real or imaginary idols of movies, television, and adventure fiction.

Interest in games and sports that require a great amount of physical energy reaches a peak in early adolescence. Hereafter, most girls show a definite preference for the less vigorous activities. There is a change in recreation interests, which is more pronounced in girls, who prefer being spectators to being performers. Exploring and outdoor activities are popular with both sexes.

Creative Characteristics

During the thirteenth year, there is a slight revival of creativity in some children; others never recover from their seventh grade decline. The majority of these children are capable of being creative, but they seldom attempt creative solutions or utilize creative approaches on their own.

Implications

Because of the difference in strength and endurance between most boys and girls at this age, they should not compete against each other in games that emphasize these factors. Although the sexes are often separated for all physical education, such separation is not necessary, or even desirable, for many activities. Among the possibilities for coeducational play are:

Bounce Basketball (page 298)
Basketball Wall Volley (page 300)
Bat Ball (page 312)
Beat Ball (page 312)
Soccer Home Ball (page 321)
Newcomb (page 326)
Wall Volley (page 328)
One Bounce Volleyball (page 328)

Team games and drills are of value and of interest to eighth graders of both sexes. Rhythms and exploration are enthusiastically received by girls; however, boys should be encouraged to participate in them, also, to develop skill and awareness of movement possibilities of the body. Girls need to be encouraged to work for increased strength and endurance in self-testing activities. Individual abilities should be given recognition in order to build interest in and desire for lifelong participation in vigorous play.

SUPPLEMENTARY READINGS

American Association for Health, Physical Education and Recreation: *Foundations and Practices in Perceptual Motor Learning—A Quest for Understanding.* Washington, D.C., American Association for Health, Physical Education and Recreation, 1971.

Breckenridge, Marian E., and Vincent, E. Lee: *Child Development.* Philadelphia, W. B. Saunders Co., 1965.

Broer, Marian: *Efficiency of Human Movement.* Ed. 3. Philadelphia, W. B. Saunders Co., 1973.

Cratty, Bryant J.: *Movement Behavior and Motor Learning.* Ed. 3. Philadelphia, Lea and Febiger, 1973.

Cratty, Bryant J.: *Physical Expression of Intelligence.* Englewood Cliffs, New Jersey, Prentice-Hall, Inc., 1972.

Cratty, Bryant J.: *Teaching Motor Skills.* Englewood Cliffs, New Jersey, Prentice-Hall, Inc., 1973.

Taylor, Calvin W. (ed.): *Creativity: Progress and Potential.* New York, McGraw-Hill Book Co., Inc., 1969.

Whiting, H. T. A.: *Acquiring Ball Skill.* Philadelphia, Lea and Febiger, 1969.

BIBLIOGRAPHY

[1]Gesell, Arnold, and Thompson, Helen: "Twins T and C from Infancy to Adolescence." *Genetic Psychology Monographs,* 1941, Vol. 24, pp. 3–121.

[2]Cratty, Bryant J.: *Movement Behavior and Motor Learning.* Philadelphia, Lea and Febiger, 1964, p. 62.

[3]Hebb, D. O.: *Organization of Behavior.* New York, Wiley, 1949, pp. 60, 107–34.

[4]Cratty, Bryant J.: *op. cit.,* pp. 267–72.

[5]Henry, Franklin, and Whitley, J. D.: "Relationship between Individual Differences in Strength, Speed and Mass in Arm Movement." *Research Quarterly,* 1960, Vol. 31, pp. 24–33.

[6]Thorndike, E. L.: "The Psychology of Learning." *Educational Psychology,* New York Teachers College, 1913, Vol. 2.

[7]Judd, C. H.: "The Relation of Special Training to Special Intelligence." *Educational Review,* 1908, Vol. 36, pp. 28–42.

[8]Hebb, D. O.: *op. cit., p. 109.*

[9]Cratty, Bryant J.: *Teaching Motor Skills.* Englewood Cliffs, New Jersey, Prentice-Hall, Inc., 1973. p. 50.

[10]Hebb, D. O.: *op. cit.,* pp. 79–106.

[11]Cratty, Bryant J.: *op. cit., p.* 5.

[12]Bilodeau, Edward A., and Bilodeau, Ina: "Motor Skill Learning." *Annual Review of Psychology,* Palo Alto, California, 1961, pp. 243–270.

[13]Cratty, Bryant J.: *op. cit., p.* 98.

[14]Gutin, Bernard, and DiGennaro, J.: "Effect of One-minute and Five-minute Step-ups on Performance of Simple Addition." *Research Quarterly,* March, 1968, Vol. 39, pp. 81–85.

[15]Singer, Robert N.: *Motor Learning and Human Performance.* New York, The Macmillan Co., 1968, pp. 230–1.

[16]Sherif, Muzafer: *An Outline of Social Psychology.* New York, Harper and Brothers, Publishers, 1948, p. 202.

[17]Dewey, Richard, and Humber, W. J.: *The Development of Human Behavior.* New York, The Macmillan Company, 1951, p. 209.

[18]Torrance, E. Paul: "Seven Guides to Creativity." *Journal of Health • Physical Education • Recreation,* April, 1965, Vol. 68, pp. 26–27.

[19]Bayer, L. M., and Bayley, N.: *Growth Diagnosis.* Chicago, The University of Chicago Press, 1959.

Bayley, Nancy, and Espenschade, Anna: "Motor Development and Decline." *Review of Educational Research,* 1950, Vol. 20. pp. 367–70.

Boynton, Bernice: *The Physical Growth of Girls.* Iowa City, University of Iowa Press, 1936, pp. 81–95.

Breckenridge, Marian E., and Vincent, E. Lee: *Child Development.* Ed. 5. Philadelphia, W. B. Saunders Co., 1960.

Clarke, H. Harrison, and Wickens, J. Stuart: "Maturity, Structural, Strength and Motor Ability Growth Curves of Boys 9 to 15 Years of Age." *Research Quarterly,* March 1962, Vol. 33, No. 1, pp. 26–39.

Espenschade, Anna: "Motor Performance in Adolescence," *Monographs of the Society for Research in Child Development.* Washington, D.C., Society for Research in Child Development, National Research Council, 1940, Vol. V, Serial No. 24, No. 1, pp. 48–60.

Espenschade, Anna, and Eckert, Helen M.: *Motor Development.* Columbus, Ohio, Charles E. Merrill Publishing Co., 1967.

Gesell, Arnold, and Ilg, Frances L.: *Child Development. An Introduction to the Study of Human Growth.* New York, Harper and Row, Publishers, 1949.

Gesell, Arnold, and Ilg, Frances L.: *Infant and Child in the Culture of Today.* New York, Harper and Brothers, Publishers, 1943.

Gutteridge, M. V.: "A Study of Motor Achievements of Young Children." *Archives of Psychology,* 1939, p. 244.

Hurlock, Elizabeth B.: *Developmental Psychology.* New York, McGraw Hill, Inc., 1953.

Meredith, Howard V.: *The Rhythms of Physical Growth.* Iowa City, University of Iowa Press, 1935, pp. 100–115.

Millard, C. V.: *Child Growth and Development.* Boston, D. C. Heath and Co., 1951.

Shirley, Mary M.: "The Motor Sequence." In Wayne, Dennis (ed.), *Readings in Child Psychology.* Englewood Cliffs, New Jersey, Prentice-Hall, Inc., 1963. pp. 72–82.

Sloan, William: "The Lincoln-Oseretsky Motor Development Scale." *Genetic Psychology Monographs,* 1955, No. 51, pp. 183–252.

Tuddenham, Read D., and Snyder, Margaret M.: *Physical Growth of California Boys and Girls from Birth to 18 Years.* Berkeley, University of California Press, 1954.

Wellman, Beth L.: "Motor Development from Two Years to Maturity." *Review of Educational Research,* Feb. 1936, Vol. 6, No. 1. p. 54.

[20]Torrance, E. Paul: *Guiding Creative Talent.* Englewood Cliffs, New Jersey, Prentice-Hall, Inc., 1962, pp. 62–64, 89–91.

[21]*Ibid.* p. 125.

[22]Jones, Harold E.: *Motor Performance and Growth.* Berkeley, University of California Press. 1949, pp. 160–76.

[23]Espenschade, Anna: "Motor Performance in Adolescence," *Monographs of the Society for Research in Child Development.* Washington, D.C., Society for Research in Child Development, National Research Council, 1940, Vol. V, Serial No. 24, No.1, pp. 48–60.

[24]*Ibid.* pp. 48–60.

[25]*Ibid.* pp. 71–73.

[26]Hurlock, Elizabeth B.: *op. cit.,* pp. 48–60.

[27]*Ibid.* pp. 48–60.

techniques for effective planning and organization

A good environment is essential for effective teaching. To ensure such an environment, a certain amount of planning and organization is required. Although physical education by its very nature engenders a more spontaneous and relaxed atmosphere than most other classes, the teaching of physical education must still be an orderly process. A number of factors are involved in the planning and conduct of a well organized physical education class, irrespective of the method of teaching that is used. The kind and extent of the facilities and equipment available and the time allotment must necessarily influence the content and organization of the program.

Even more important, however, is the use to which the equipment, facilities, and time are put; intelligent, imaginative, well organized use of these is extremely important to good teaching in physical education. This chapter presents specific techniques for planning the instruction and organizing the class which experienced teachers have found most helpful in creating a good environment for attaining the objectives of physical education. Both the classroom teacher who is in charge of the physical education instruction of his class and the physical education specialist in the elementary school will find the suggestions and information valuable.

FACILITIES

Physical education programs are dictated in part by the areas available for conducting the classes. Ideally, the elementary school would have a gymnasium for indoor use and a playing field for outdoor use. An increasing number of schools now approach the ideal, but many elementary school teachers must conduct physical education in corridors, in basement rooms, and on the stage of the auditorium. That the physical education is as successful as it is under these circumstances is a great credit to the teachers who have applied their imagination and ingenuity to planning a balanced program of activities which can be performed in the play space available to them.

The teacher entering a school system for the first time must be prepared to do the best possible job regardless of the physical limitations imposed by the facilities. It is well, however, for the teacher to be familiar with the kind of space requirements which are considered adequate for teaching physical education properly.

Gymnasium

A gymnasium solely for physical education is most desirable. However, many schools have an all-purpose room which is used as a gymnasium as well as for other school activities. With proper scheduling and effective use of the classroom and outside areas for certain aspects of physical education, it proves very satisfactory.

Recommended space for effective use of a gymnasium is a minimum of 40 feet by 60 feet. Large classes of over 50 pupils would necessitate larger spaces, approximately 40 square feet for each additional child over 50. Area in the gymnasium in which permanent seats are located cannot be construed as playing area for physical education. Beams of the ceiling should not be less than 18 to 20 feet from the floor. All supports should be at the sides of the floor and not in the playing area. Wall supports should not be closer than 3 feet to the boundary line of any game that requires strenuous activity.

The boundaries may be marked permanently on the floor for those games which will be played frequently. Differently colored lines may be used for different games. Suggested markings are:

1. Court lines for basketball and basketball type games.
2. Boundary lines for volleyball.
3. Several lines across and down the floor for games such as Crows and Cranes.
4. Circles and squares for games such as Dare Tag and Four Squares.

Ideally, there would be located adjacent to the playing area storage rooms, office space, lockers, and toilet, dressing, and showering facilities.

Playground

For the outside play area, it is recommended that there be a minimum of 5 acres with an additional acre for every 100 pupils over a 500 enrollment. For reasons of safety, there should be separate areas for primary grade children and for upper elementary grade students. On street sides the grounds should be enclosed with a chain link fence to prevent children from inadvertently running into the street to recover a ball. If it is necessary to have an entrance in the fence in an area where there will be considerable play activity, a double fence arrangement is highly recommended to eliminate the necessity for a gate. In this arrangement the opening is backed up by a short section of fence a few feet from the opening; it permits easy access to and from the playground without the opening and closing of a gate and also serves to prevent objects from rolling through the opening into the street. All fencing materials should be free of sharp points which may cause bodily injury and damage to play equipment.

It is desirable to have some portion of the play area near the school building hard-surfaced for use when the ground is wet. Court markings for such popular elementary school games as shuffleboard, hop scotch, and volleyball may be painted directly on the surface. Many professional physical educators strongly advocate that courts even for play by young children should be standard size; however, it is the author's conviction that learning the game for the pleasures and benefits to be derived from it should take precedence over other considerations and, if the space available is not adequate for a regulation court, a smaller court which is reduced proportionally in size is certainly permissible.

Every playground should have certain items of developmental equipment, which includes monkey and climbing bars and poles, high and low bars, and parallel ladders. When students are properly introduced to these, they enjoy them as much as the more traditional types of play equipment, such as swings and slides, and with far greater physical benefits, for these apparatuses provide exercise to certain sets of muscles which are not usually adequately exercised. Opportunities for creative muscular exploration, or kinesthetic expression, should also be provided. A number of companies now manufacture equipment designed for this purpose, but the same objective can be achieved with easily

Figure 3-1 A hard surface area enclosed with a chain link fence makes an ideal playground. Here court markings are painted on the surface and the posts are padded as an additional safety measure.

acquired materials such as packing boxes, barrels, and assorted pieces of lumber.

Classroom

The classroom offers a convenient place for a considerable variety of physical education activities in the lower grades, and it has a certain advantage in that the teacher need not move the students to another area. Moreover, the classroom is most appropriate for those games which can be well integrated with arithmetic, social studies, and other subject matter. Blackboard work in arithmetic or word recall exercises can be combined effectively with hopping, skipping, and similar kinds of muscular movements. In the modern classroom desks are readily moved to provide space for nearly all kinds of physical education activities. In some games the desks can be used as goals or obstacles for moving around. The classroom does have its limitations for games which require gross movements through space; vigorous activity can be engaged in, but it must be the kind that can be performed in a limited area to avoid accidental injuries resulting from bumping into fixtures and furniture.

EQUIPMENT AND SUPPLIES

The term *equipment* is defined as anything used for equipping a person for the act he is to perform, while the term *supplies* is used to describe items on hand or available for use. For budgetary purposes in schools, however, the terms are used to designate long-lasting materials and those which need to be replaced at regular intervals. Classified as equipment are such items as balance beams, trampoline frames, climbing equipment, and swings that have a relatively long life. In the category of supplies are expendable items with limited life, e.g., balls, trampoline beds, and jump ropes.

In selecting equipment or supplies, consideration must be given to several factors: design and safety features, quality of material and workmanship, cost of maintenance (both time and money), and the actual cost. In addition, and probably the most important factor, is the nature of the program and its objectives. If a new teacher is asked to recommend supplies and pieces of equipment for purchase before he has had an opportunity to analyze the program completely and develop specific objectives, he will need to think in terms of general objectives for a good physical education program at the grade level in question and make his recommendation accordingly.

Recommended equipment and supplies for the elementary school physical education program are listed below with the type of activity in which they are most frequently used.

Movement Exploration, Basic Skills, and Physical Fitness

Jouncing boards
Climbing equipment
Low and high chinning bars or door bars
Creative play apparatus
Parallel and vertical ladders
Portable stairway
Rocking boat
Climbing and building blocks
Crawl-through equipment
Carts, wagons, tricycles
Medicine balls or cage balls
Balls: playground and utility balls, sponge balls, tennis balls, yarn and fleece balls
Hoops
Jump ropes (long and short)

Stunts and Tumbling

Climbing ropes; knotted for the lower and middle grades
Balance beams
Trampoline
Climbing poles
Turning poles
Individual mats

Lead-up and Team Games

Balls: junior and regular size footballs, soccer balls, junior and regular basketballs, volleyballs, softballs
Volleyball net and standards
Softball bats
Softball catcher's mask and body protector

Basketball goals
Softball bases and backstop
Soccer goals
Jumping standards and cross bar

Rhythmic and Dance Activities

Record player and records
Piano
Percussion instruments: castanets, tambourines, bells, drums

Aquatics

Lightweight pole 8 feet long and other life-saving equipment
Arm- and leg-supporting devices
Several non-floating objects

Classroom

Bean bags
Rag ball
Wands for stunts
Indian clubs
Ring toss
Plastic bowling set

Adapted

Mirrors
Stall bars
Low and high chinning bars or door bars
Darts
Deck tennis
Table tennis
Plastic bowling set
Rubber horseshoes
Croquet
Shuffleboard
Table games

Miscellaneous

Whistles
Clip board
Ball inflator and gauge
Marking pen
Measuring tape
Scales
Plastic tape in assorted colors
First aid kit
Stop watch
Bags for carrying equipment
Portable chalkboard
Color arm bands for identifying teams
Swings
Slides
Sandboxes

Care and Repair

It is of utmost importance to establish a definite program for the care of equipment. Such a program will pay off in increased longevity of supplies and equipment and elimination of injuries due to failure to replace or repair worn and broken equipment. A well-organized program for the care of supplies and equipment requires: (1) an adequate room for storage, (2) a good marking system, (3) proper care, and (4) a positive effort to educate students to respect and care for the materials they use.

The storage room should be an easily accessible area which can be closed off from general use. The door to the area should be one that can be locked. If no suitable space is available, a section of the hallway or dressing room can be partitioned off with caging wire.

A marking system is valuable for ease in keeping track of supplies issued to different classrooms or teachers and also for determining the age and durability of the supplies. If each piece of a specific kind of supply is marked with a number, this number may be recorded when that piece is checked out. In this way it can be determined in whose possession any item is at any given time. Each item may also be stamped with the year of purchase to provide information about its age and hence, its durability. For example, a ball purchased in 1976 may be marked 1–76 and another 2–76, etc. All supplies purchased prior to the time of marking for which the purchase date is not known may be marked with some code number such as P–76 (prior 1976).

All equipment should be examined periodically for worn, broken, loose, and malfunctioning parts. Equipment that cannot be repaired immediately should be taken from service. Each school system should have a procedure for reporting losses and damages and securing repairs.

An area in the storage room should be made available for the items in need of repair. It is important that such items be removed from use and repaired immediately. Some of the simple repairs may be done by the teacher. Others will require the services of professional repair personnel. Local shoe repair firms or handicraft leather good stores can sew seam rips and make other repairs for leather goods. There are also firms that specialize in the repair of athletic goods of all kinds.

Proper care of equipment and supplies will reduce the frequency of repair and prolong their life. Recommendations for caring for items used in the various activities of the program are included in the chapters on the activities. In addition it is important that children understand that public property such as that used in physical education classes belongs to everyone; therefore each individual has an interest in its preservation. Knowing how to care properly for equipment is an essential first step in the development of an attitude that fosters respect for all public property.

Improvising Equipment

The teacher is likely to find that a piece of equipment needed to promote a certain activity is not available. Oftentimes the necessary equipment can be improvised from readily secured materials. Some improvised equipment serves just as well as the standard piece does; others serve only partially, but their use is justified because the main need is met. In improvising equipment special care must be taken to ensure that the equipment is safely constructed. Specific suggestions for improvising equipment are presented in the chapters discussing the various physical education activities. (Also see Appendix iii.)

TIME ALLOTMENTS

All students should participate in physical education activities daily. A minimum of 30 minutes of activity time exclusive of free play and extra-class activities is recommended, with at least half of this time devoted to vigorous activity. Table 3–1 indicates appropriate time allotments for the various categories of physical education activities which a good physical education program would include.

OBJECTIVES

Objectives are written statements describing the results that are sought in the instructional program. The statements may also be so written as to suggest an approach for teaching and a means of evaluation. Developing objectives for the program is essential because they serve as a guide to producing the best possible learning experience.

The writing of objectives has become a matter of concern in recent years. In the past it was generally agreed in educational circles that there were only two forms for written objectives, long-range and specific. The long-range objectives were those that described the broad general goals (aims) of the program, while the specific objectives were the more definite results being sought in a unit or daily lesson. Although the objectives were written to guide the choice of physical education experiences and their means of implementation, in actual practice there was often little relationship between the stated objectives and the actual instruction.

In response to the concern about the lack of relationship, new ways for expressing the objectives have been introduced to focus the teaching act on the desired outcome. Objectives can now be said to be of three types: long-range, specific or curriculum, and evaluation objectives. The long-range objectives continue to be written as they were formerly. The specific objectives, now also called curriculum objectives, translate the long-range objectives into statements describing specific behaviors (1) that can be readily identified, (2) for which specific teaching procedures can be selected to help the student progress toward the objective, and (3) for which evaluation tools are easily chosen to determine the degree to which the objective has been achieved. The evaluation objectives are those which indicate quality of performance and are so stated as to constitute the evaluation tool. Both the specific and the evaluation objectives are applicable in planning either the unit or daily lesson, al-

TABLE 3-1 Time Allotments

A. Activities	NURSERY SCHOOL, KINDERGARTEN, AND PRIMARY GRADES			
	N1 3 yrs.	**N2** 4 yrs.	**K-1** 5-6 yrs.	**2-3** 7-8 yrs.
Basic skill or low organized games		10-20%	20-30%	15-25%
Rhythms (70% movement exploration type)	40-60%	30-50%	25-45%	25-45%
Stunts and tumbling and self-testing activities	10-20%	10-30%	10-30%	10-30%
Basic skills of activity			5-10%	5-15%
Fundamental skills (50% movement exploration type)	10-30%	10-30%	10-30%	10-30%

	UPPER GRADES					
	4-5	**4-5***	**6**	**6***	**7-8**	**7-8***
Basic skill games or low organized games	5-10%	10-15%	5-10%	10-15%	2.5-5%	5-15%
Rhythms and dance	15-20%	20-25%	10-15%	15-20%	2.5-5%	5-15%
Stunts and tumbling and self-testing activities	15-20%	20-25%	15-20%	20-25%	20-25%	25-30%
Basic skills of sports	10-15%	10-15%	10-15%	10-15%	10-15%	10-15%
Fundamental skills	5-10%	5-10%	5-10%	5-10%	5-10%	5-15%
Aquatics	20-25%	—	20-25%	—	20-25%	—
Team activities	25-30%	30-35%	30-35%	35-40%	35-40%	40-45%
Physical fitness or developmental activities†	5-10%	5-15%	5-10%	5-10%	10-15%	10-15%

(Classroom games not included in total percentage)

B.	Percentages‡ (From A)	Total Time		Class Periods
		Hours	*Minutes*	
	1%‡	0	45	1½
	5%	4	15	8½
	10%	8	30	17
	15%	12	45	25½
	20%	17	0	34
	25%	21	15	42½
	30%	25	30	51
	35%	29	45	59½
	40%	34	0	68

*Time allotment when swimming is not available.

†Many activities overlap; nearly all make some contribution to physical fitness. The category here is restricted to those activities in which the chief contribution is to physical fitness such as pull-ups.

‡Based on a 30 minute class period, five days per week, 34 weeks per school year, the percentages are equal to the time allotments shown.

though the evaluation objectives are now used more frequently for daily lesson planning.

A type of evaluation objective called the behavioral objective is currently finding much favor among physical educators because it provides the teacher with an instant measuring device for determining if the objective has been met. Consequently, it is not necessary to prepare and administer tests and other evaluation tools. Another advantage is that both the teacher and the student know exactly what has to be accomplished before the objective is successfully met. These objectives are highly specific and indicate (1) the behavior to be exhibited, ie., the kind of activity to be performed, (2) the conditions that exist where the performance takes place, and (3) the criterion of desired performance. The way in which specific objectives may be converted to behavioral objectives can be seen in Table 3–3, page 73.

PLANNING

The success of the physical education program in accomplishing its objectives depends to a very considerable extent upon the deliberation and care which go into its planning. Planning may take two general forms: the *long-range* or *vertical* plan, which is in effect a blueprint of the program for an entire year or for several years, and the *short-range* plan, which involves a single unit of instruction, including the over-all plan for teaching the unit of work as well as the day-by-day lesson plans.

Long-range planning varies from school to school. Some situations call for complete planning by the individual teachers; others provide the teacher with a framework or previously prepared course of study on which unit planning shall be based. The most effective planning usually occurs when all the teachers and other personnel involved with physical education share in it. Long-range planning for several years has certain advantages over planning only one year's program in that it enables teachers to avoid duplication of activities and skills which the children have already been exposed to sufficiently, and it ensures a more comprehensive coverage of physical education. The long-range plan, for whatever length of time, should retain a degree of flexibility so that it can at any time be adapted to unanticipated shifts and changes in the physical education scene.

In creating a long-range plan, the planning group should consider first the broad general goals they hope to achieve during the period of time concerned. The program content should be based upon the chosen objectives. The next step is to determine the grade level at which the various objectives will be emphasized and which activities suitable to the grade in question will be most likely to result in accomplishment of the objectives. In determining the suitability of activities, consideration must be given to age, interests, needs, and abilities of each age group. Other factors which influence planning, such as class size, available facilities and equipment, and the time allotment must also be taken into account in the planning. Characteristics peculiar to the community should be given consideration also; dominant nationality groups, economic conditions, educational levels, cultural influences, and religious beliefs should be examined for possible implications in the selection and planning of physical education activities.

In choosing activities, the curriculum planners must consider the following questions:

1. Is the activity reasonably safe?
2. Are the students physically able to perform the activity?
3. Are the students sufficiently mature to understand how to perform the activity?

4. Are the students interested in learning this kind of activity; if not, can enthusiasm for learning it be engendered at this age level?

5. Does the activity have meaning so that students will be able to see the application of what is learned?

6. If an activity requires lead-up skill training, have these skills been mastered fully by the students?

7. Does the activity contribute to creativity?

8. Does the activity contribute to the objectives sought more effectively than another possible choice?

The crucial element in the success of long-range planning is the way in which the plan is utilized in the actual day-to-day teaching. No long-range plan has any great value unless each day's lesson is planned and taught in such a way as to accomplish the program's designated purposes. Many teachers have come to believe that the daily lesson should not be presented as an isolated segment of learning, unrelated to any learning which preceded or follows it, but that it should be correlated with other learning experiences into a unified whole. To create this desired unity in the daily lessons, a unit plan is frequently employed.

UNIT PLANNING

A unit refers to a sequence of learning experiences or a number of closely related experiences which encompasses a complete identity or meaningful whole. It serves as a method of organizing the teaching and learning procedures in a logical manner (Table 3–2).

Physical education lends itself well to unit organization; the information and skills which must be taught in such activities as tumbling, rhythms, movement exploration, basketball, volleyball, basic skills, and others are easily organized into a teachable unit, suited to the needs and abilities of an age group. However, physical education is not always presented in units. When it is not, the selection of activities must be made most carefully to achieve a well-balanced program. There are also times when the planned unit is temporarily abandoned to present an entirely unrelated activity for the purpose of generating greater interest and enthusiasm for the program or simply for the enjoyment that the particular activity gives to the group. Generally, however, the teaching of physical education activities as units is more desirable and produces a more satisfactory learning situation because of the planned sequence of learning experiences.

Resource Unit

In preparing to develop a unit for physical education, it is necessary to have certain materials available for reference. An accumulation of such materials is known as a resource unit and may include suggestions and recommendations for general objectives for the unit and the kinds of activities and subject matter that might be used; unusual and practical ideas for teaching the unit;

TABLE 3-2 Sample Volleyball Unit Plan for the Sixth Grade

SITUATION
1. Pupils—35 students, 16 boys and 19 girls. None have played volleyball previously. Majority of students have played Newcomb. No students are in need of adapted physical education.
2. Time allotted—3 weeks, 30 minutes daily for each class.
3. Equipment—Volleyball courts, standards and nets, volleyballs, and wall space for volleying ball against.

OBJECTIVES
1. To learn those basic volleyball skills of which sixth graders are capable.
2. To develop an appreciation of and interest in playing volleyball.
3. To learn the fundamental rules of volleyball.
4. To acquire knowledge of the care of volleyball equipment and to develop the proper attitude toward the care of school and other public property.
5. To engage in a competitive activity in a spirit of cooperation and fair play.
6. To develop and/or maintain some of the factors of physical fitness.

TECHNIQUES
1. Orientation—Discussion of history and values of volleyball; care of equipment and reason for necessity of caring for public property by users; the nature of fair play in volleyball and its relationship to fair play in other situations.
2. Skills—Serving and volleying: drills (T); exploration (PS); both (S).*
3. Exercises—General body conditioning and wrist and finger developmental exercises preceded by a short discussion of the value of such exercises: drills (T); exploration (PS); both (S).*
4. Competitive play—Team play and instruction on strategy and on cooperative effort in team play.

EVALUATION
1. Subjective ratings of skill performance and analysis of how well students demonstrated cooperation and fair play.

*T = traditional method; PS = problem-solving method; S = synthesis of both methods.

sources of suitable films, charts, and other teaching aids; directions for improvising equipment needed for teaching the unit; and a bibliography. The selection of materials for the resource unit should come about from consideration of the teaching situation and through investigation of the pertinent literature. It is recommended that the prospective teacher of physical education begin early to gather possible materials; the use of folders for clippings, notes, and lists of useful references and sources of teaching aids is very helpful.

Organizing the Unit

Organizing the unit from the resource materials which have been gathered is a matter of selecting the information and skills to be taught and planning the methods by which they can best be presented after having given thorough consideration to the needs, interests, and abilities of the students; the class size; the time allotment; and the equipment and facilities available. A good unit plan will include:

1. An evaluation of the class, including the general and specific experiences the students have had upon which the unit is being based.

2. The time allotment.
3. A list of equipment and materials required.
4. A list of the objectives sought in the teaching of the unit.
5. The types of activities to be used throughout the unit.
6. A description of the techniques to be used.
7. A description of the evaluation procedure if behavioral objectives are not utilized.

DAILY LESSON PLANNING

The daily lesson plan, as its name implies, is the plan for teaching each day's lesson (Tables 3–3 and 3–4). If a unit plan is being used, the specific items to be taught each day are selected from the unit content; when it is not, the choice of items to be included in the daily lesson plan is determined by the long-range objectives of the physical education program. In either case, the information and the skills to be taught and the methods and procedures of presenting them effectively as well as evaluating the success of the day's teaching should be specifically indicated in the daily lesson plan.

Daily lesson planning is a necessity for good teaching. The plan may or may not be in written form; but writing down the lesson plan tends to help the teacher, particularly the beginning teacher, to organize more effectively and provides him with the opportunity to give serious consideration to the teaching problem for the day. Moreover, it makes possible greater unity in teaching from day to day.

The total of the lesson plans for any one unit should accomplish the objectives set for the unit. One basic error that is made frequently by the ineffective teacher is the failure to provide for experiences in the daily lesson to meet the objectives of the unit. The objective most frequently neglected is emotional and social development. Often teachers list such objectives as developing leadership and self-confidence and then fail to plan specific ways of helping students to realize these objectives during the daily teaching of physical education.

A lesson plan must be flexible. Even the most carefully conceived plan may have to be altered to meet some unexpected demand or to capitalize on a teachable moment. This should not be interpreted to mean that little attention need be given to advanced daily planning, because the teacher who does not plan ahead cannot adjust to new circumstances as effectively as one who has planned the general content of the lesson. This is true largely because the non-planner will not have a sufficiently broad concept of the total situation to make impromptu teaching really effective.

ORGANIZATIONAL PROCEDURES

Dressing for Activity

Elementary schools throughout the country differ in their policies regarding the wearing of special dress for physical education. Some schools with locker

TABLE 3–3 Sample Volleyball Daily Lesson Plan for the Sixth Grade (Traditional or Direct Method)

SPECIFIC OBJECTIVES
1. To develop skill in serving and to continue practice in volleying.*
2. To provide an exercise to warm-up for volleyball activity and to give general exercise.
3. To provide an opportunity to participate in a team situation requiring cooperation.

BEHAVIORAL OBJECTIVES
1. Make an underhand serve so that the ball passes at least 3 feet above the net and lands in the back of the receiving court in three out of five tries.
2. Return a volley three times in succession using the fingers in overhead volleys and the closed fists in underhand volleys without carrying the ball.
3. Warm up before participating in the lesson by performing the jumping jack exercise for 45 seconds.

MATERIALS
Volleyballs, net, and standards.

FLOOR PREPARATIONS
Set up standards and net.

PROCEDURES
1. Warm-up exercise. Students in open file formation† for jumping jack exercise. Time—30 to 60 seconds.
2. With students still in formation, the underhand serve will be explained and demonstrated. Time—3 to 4 minutes.
3. Students to go through the motions of serving without a ball. The teacher will observe and correct errors. Time—4 to 5 minutes.
4. Students to be divided into groups of 6 or 8 and placed standing on the base line on each side of the net. Several balls to be used on each court. Students will take turns serving to players on the opposite side. The teacher will observe and correct faults; also point out nature of cooperation in this situation. Time—10 to 12 minutes.
5. Students form two teams for volleying. A server will serve and both sides working together will try to keep the ball going back and forth over the net as long as possible. The teacher will encourage students to handle the ball with their fingers for overhead volleys and closed fists for underhand volleys without carrying the ball. Time—10 to 12 minutes.
6. Class will close with entire group forming a large circle around the volleyball court. Students to stand equal distance apart. At the command of "Go" the students will run to the right and attempt to tag the person in front. Those tagged will drop out of the game and stand to the side. Time—1 minute.

EVALUATION
(This evaluation procedure will be used only if specific objectives are used. Behavioral objectives have their own evaluation tool.)
1. Ratings will be made based on observation of ability to serve and volley.
2. Notes are to be taken of the success of the techniques in accomplishing the objectives.
3. Suggestions for improvement will also be noted.

*This lesson plan is for a class that has already begun the volleyball unit. The time allotment for the instruction is 30 minutes.

†Formations for this lesson have been so planned as to avoid confusion and unnecessary consumption of time in moving the class into new formations.

TABLE 3–4   Sample Volleyball Daily Lesson Plan for the Sixth Grade*
(Problem-solving or Indirect Method)

OBJECTIVES
1. To develop skill in serving.
2. To provide an opportunity to warm up for volleyball activity.
3. To encourage independence in developing one's motor skills.
4. To develop an understanding of these concepts:
    (a) How a ball rebounds from the hand when hit at different angles.
    (b) The relationship between the force of the hit and how far the ball travels.
    (c) How the different parts of the body must work together to accomplish a desired movement.

MATERIALS
Volleyballs (one for each student)

FLOOR PREPARATION
None

PROCEDURES
1. Warm-up exercise. Random formation. Each student selects and performs an exercise that warms up his body for participation. Time—30 to 60 seconds.
2. Explanation of the objective of the serve. Time—2 to 3 minutes.
3. Questions to be posed to encourage students to think how the ball must be served.
    (a) Where must the ball be hit to make it rise high enough in the air to go over the net? *Variable—* space; *Variation—*bottom to top of the ball.
    (b) Where and how should the ball be held so as to allow it to be hit in the spot discovered in (a)? *Variable—*space; *Variation—*above the waist to below the waist.
    (c) What part of the hand should be used to hit the ball? *Variable—*space; *Variation—*finger tips to base of hand.
    (d) How should the arm be swung to allow the hand to come in proper contact with the ball? *Variable—*flow; *Variation—*shallow arc to full arc.
    (e) With how much force should the ball be hit? *Variable—*force; *Variation—*soft to hard.
    (f) How should the legs and body be moved while hitting the ball? *Variable—*space; *Variation—* stationary to forward movement of one leg with body weight coming over leg.

After each question is asked, the students will be encouraged to discuss their answers and their reasoning. Then students will take random positions on the floor for experimentation to determine if their assumptions are correct. The teacher will circulate to make suggestions and offer comments that will help the students reach a solution. Time—26 to 27 minutes.

EVALUATION
1. Self-evaluation.
2. Notes are to be taken of the success in accomplishing the objectives.
3. Oral test using the questions in Procedures, Item 3, above.

*The time allotment for the instruction is 30 minutes.

and shower facilities require children to wear either a prescribed uniform or a costume of their own choosing suitable for play. This is most commonly required of the seventh and eighth grades, although in some schools the practice begins with the fourth grade. Where children are dressing and showering, the teacher must plan the time allotment, supervision of the children, and proper storage of the gym clothing.

In many elementary schools, children change only from their street shoes to sneakers for physical education class. This can usually be handled most effectively by changing in the classroom before going to the area where the physical education class is being held. However, some schools do provide shoe lockers for the storage of the gym shoes. In this case the teacher must plan the assignment of lockers and designation of floor areas, usually at the sides and ends of the playing floor, where the children may sit to change.

Game Formations

Game formations are those patterns or positions which the children assume for the playing of various games. Nearly all group games which elementary school children play require one of the following basic game formations:

Circle Formations. The children stand an equal distance apart in a circle for a single circle formation; for a double formation, two concentric circles are formed. Children face in the direction required by the game. The shape and size of the circle are more easily controlled by having each child join hands with the child on either side. For a smaller circle the children step forward into closed ranks, and for a larger circle they step backward, dropping hands if necessary.

Semicircle Formation. The players form a half circle with the teacher or leader a few feet in front of the formation.

Line or File Formation. The children stand directly behind one another in a straight file.

Rank Formation. The children stand beside one another facing one direction.

Open Formation. The students take a rank formation and count off to 4. Those who are 2's step forward two steps, the 3's step forward four steps, and the 4's, six steps.

Zig-zag Formation. This formation is created from two line formations. Players move apart the required distance for the game, and then one line moves so that each of the players is directly across from a space between two players in the other line, rather than across from a player.

Shuttle Formation. Two teams in line formation face each other at a specified distance apart. The first person in line runs toward the first person in the opposite line, touches him, and takes a place at the end of the line. As soon

Figure 3-2 Children drill on the skills of scoop ball in rank formation. (Courtesy of Town of Vernon Schools, Rockville, Connecticut.)

as a player is touched, he may run to touch the first person in the other line. At the end of play, all will be on the opposite side from where they began.

Relay Formation.   Teams or squads for relay games are formed by counting off while standing in line formation. Children then form in lines at the points designated for each number.

Random Formation.   This is an informal arrangement of the class in which the students take positions of their own choice that are convenient and suitable to the activity. The teacher indicates the nature of the activity by such comments as: "You will need room to dribble in a stationary position without interfering with someone else," or "Gather around so that you can see the demonstration." Random formation is especially appropriate for problem-solving activities, but it may be used in any situation where a specific formation is not essential to playing the game or performing the activity.

Dividing the Class.   Counting off is one of the most efficent methods of dividing the class for team play. If the game to be played is one in which height is of distinct advantage, the class may be asked to take positions in a line formation according to height from the tallest to the shortest. When the line then counts off, for example in three's, each team will be assured of having a fairly equalized distribution of height. Choosing sides is a popular means of forming teams for a game; it is more time consuming than counting off and, since the selection is made for the most part on the basis of playing ability or popularity, it does call unnecessary attention to lack of ability or unpopularity of the youngsters who are always last to be chosen. When this method is used, it is a good idea for the teacher to appoint occasionally the children who are continually chosen last as the "captains" who choose the sides.

For many games, especially for primary children, it is necessary to select an "It." The teacher may simply ask for volunteers and make a selection from among them, being careful to distribute the choice as widely as possible. A favorite way of selecting "It," which from the standpoint of physical education is a particularly good one because of the vigorous activity involved, is that of having the class race to a designated goal with either the first or the last to arrive being "It" for the game. While this is very popular with older elementary school children, selection of "It" by means of a rhyme or jingle is enjoyed greatly by younger children. The children assemble in a circle formation for this, and the teacher walks around the circle repeating the jingle as she points to each child in succession. "It" is the one to whom the teacher is pointing on the last word of the jingle.

Use of Signals

For an orderly class presentation, which ensures that the class members are able to hear the teacher's explanation and to see the demonstration of the skills, it is necessary for the teacher to develop with the students a special signal for stopping play to listen. A drum beat, a chord on the piano, clapping hands, or blowing a whistle may be used satisfactorily as the signal. An elaborate system of signals for lining up, assuming game positions, and so on is unnecessary and may prove more confusing than effective. It is usually preferable to have a signal only for stopping play and focusing attention on the teacher. Many teachers like to use a visual signal, such as raising the arm over the head or extending two fingers, because this type of signal is appropriate for use in the classroom as well.

Attendance and Excuses

The physical education teacher, unless he is a classroom teacher instructing his own classroom of students, may be required to take class attendance. This job should be so organized that it subtracts as little time as possible from the total play period. Unless the class is small, calling the names on the roll will be too time consuming. It does, however, give the teacher an opportunity to learn the names of the children; and, because a better environment is created when the teacher knows the pupils by name, it is recommended as a procedure during the first few days of the new school year. Other methods for taking roll used successfully by teachers include:

Checking off the names as the students enter or leave the dressing room in those situations in which the students dress for the activity.

Checking off the names as the students enter the gymnasium or pool.

Assigning numbers to students which are checked off on the class roll as each pupil calls out his number in sequence.

Assigning floor spaces (which may have numbers painted on the floor) which are checked against a chart of the floor arrangement.

Assigning the class to certain lines or squads which are checked by student leaders who report to the teacher.

The policy on excusing students from participation in physical education will usually be established by the school. It is well to review these policies with the older students from time to time so that there will be no misunderstanding about them. As a guide for use in circumstances in which you, as the teacher, need to make a decision about excusing a child from physical education, it is well to remember that physical education has something to offer even to one who is severely restricted in physical activity. Suggestions for providing activities for such children are presented in Chapter 17.

Student Helpers

The use of student assistants can be of great help to the teacher as well as making a significant contribution to the development of the youngsters. Among the responsibilities which can be handled by student helpers in the upper grades are the securing and returning of equipment, helping to mark or lay out playing courts and fields, officiating, acting as time keepers, taking attendance if this is necessary, recording fitness tests scores, and assisting in the administration of these tests. Student helpers who do a particular skill well may also be used to demonstrate it for others who need to see it performed in order to do it themselves. They may also provide assistance on an individual basis to students who need special help either because of a disability or because of difficulties in learning the skill. Children in the primary grades will not be ready to handle the more complex of these duties, but they may be expected to get and replace the equipment or supplies for the games, help with score keeping, and assist in other ways.

The children who are to perform these duties should understand exactly what is expected of them and which class periods they will be "on duty." Teachers could well include the more specific of the physical education responsibilities on the chart of daily "housekeeping" duties such as erasing the boards and watering the plants in the classroom. The jobs should be distributed among the entire class so that all will have the chance to develop the initiative, responsibility, cooperation, and good judgment which the performance of these jobs entails.

SAFETY

Nearly 70 per cent of the accidents young children (nursery through eighth grade) incur happen while they are under the school's jurisdiction. It has been estimated that one out of every 33 children attending school is injured and that over half of these sustain their injuries in physical education or athletics. The grimness of these statistics suggests that teachers of physical education must do more to ensure the safety of participants. A serious injury to a child negates all the possible advantages that are gained from participation in the physical education or extra-class program. It is the responsibility of the teacher to conform to a standard of behavior that will not subject a pupil to an unreasonable risk of injury.

The safety of children in vigorous play is of such importance that it deserves careful attention to every detail which will help to ensure it. Equipment in good repair and a safe playing area free of obstructions and hazards are, of course, essential to safe play. Maintenance of equipment is usually the responsibility of the physical education supervisor or some other school official, but the teacher should assume a responsibility for observing the state of wear of the apparatus and other equipment and reporting the need for repair and attention to the proper person. Any equipment which appears dangerously worn should be removed from use by the teacher. The same holds true for hazards on the playground or indoor playing areas.

A more direct responsibility of the teacher is educating the youngsters in the proper use of equipment and the practice of certain safety procedures. Educating is as much a matter of developing the right attitudes about practicing the safety precautions as supplying the safety information. Attitudes are largely developed by the teacher's emphasis on the safety measures and his own observance of them. The stress placed on safety should be positive in nature rather than a series of "don'ts."

Suggestions for making pupils safety-minded are:

1. Plan with the children definite rules about the use of swings, jungle gyms, and other pieces of equipment. Children should understand the neces-

sity for standing outside the danger zones while waiting their turns to use equipment which is in motion.

2. Discuss with the class the need to practice common courtesies in taking turns, lining up, using equipment, and making remarks about the performances of others.

3. Work out a system for making equipment available without confusion or congestion; where necessary for safety assign participants activities according to size and maturity of physical development.

4. Prepare the students for the more difficult stunts and activities by a solid background of lead-up skills. The proper sequence of motor skills is very important in preventing accidents and injuries to muscles which haven't been sufficiently strengthened. Youngsters should be encouraged to try new skills but should not be pushed beyond their physical and mental "readiness." Reckless behavior and showing off should be emphatically discouraged.

5. When the classroom is being used for physical education, the hazards should be pointed out to the class since they may not be aware of these. Stress should be placed upon the need for safe conduct and courtesy in not disturbing those in other classrooms.

Safety-minded students have fewer accidents than students who are not safety conscious; nevertheless, accidents will occur and the teacher should be prepared to deal with them. If there is a school nurse on duty, she should be notified immediately so that she can give the injury proper care. The nurse will also take charge of making out the necessary reports. If there is no nurse, the teacher must give first aid to the injured child, notify the proper authorities about the accident, and make a written report of the accident for reference should it be needed. The teacher should never attempt more than first aid for such may be construed as "treatment" which is fraught with legal difficulties for one unqualified to administer it.

LIABILITY

The teacher should have knowledge not only of his educational responsibilities in preventing accidents in his program but also of the general area of legal liability. Such information will help the teacher to protect the students from accidental injury and so guard against the possibility of his being involved in litigation.

Legal liability for injury to a student occurs when a teacher is held to have been negligent in behavior involving the accident. Negligence is defined as the failure to act as a reasonably prudent person would act under the same or similar circumstances. A prudent person is considered to be one who is able to see the harmful consequences of a specific situation and acts to prevent the harmful consequences from occurring by adjusting the situation. Examples of the kind of situation referred to are:

(1) Defective equipment and unsafe facilities. Many injuries are the result of using equipment that is damaged, worn, or otherwise defective, and facilities that are hazardous. Examples of the former are broken or worn parts,

loose bolts, or ragged and sharp edges. Holes in the playing surfaces, protruding objects in the play area, and equipment left scattered around are examples of unsafe facilities.

(2) Allowing or encouraging students to take unreasonable risks. For many years injuries were accepted in physical education as a natural hazard of the program. It was felt that, particularly for boys, injuries were part of the toughening-up process that helps to make students courageous in physical acts and stoic about pain. Risks had to be taken as part of the process. Fortunately, few teachers hold such a view today, but many teachers do allow students to take unnecessary risks in performance or encourage them to excessive effort that can result in injury to them.

(3) Inadequate supervision and poor instruction. Accidents frequently occur when there is no or poor supervision of the playground or instructional area. A teacher is considered responsible for the conduct of students that may lead to an accident during physical education instruction and also for the injury of one member of the class by another. A teacher who is absent from his supervisory duties or engaged simultaneously in another activity would have difficulty showing that adequate supervision was being exercised. Inadequate preparation of the student for motor performance is another cause of accidents. Failure to prepare the student with appropriate lead-up skills prior to performing a complex skill is evidence of negligence. Students who have been extremely strongly motivated to succeed in an activity have a higher injury rate than those less motivated. This is one reason for the higher injury rate in varsity sports as compared to other physical education activities. Extreme fatigue and disregard of pain are the chief sources of serious injuries to the highly motivated player. Competitive sports and physical fitness testing are the situations in which such injuries are most likely to occur.

(4) Poor selection of activities. Certain activities are considered more dangerous than others because the incidence of injuries per exposure hour is higher. There are three commonly taught sports that are considered to be extremely dangerous: football, rebound tumbling, and boxing.

WORKING WITH THE PHYSICAL EDUCATION SUPERVISOR

It is an increasingly common practice for communities which have several elementary schools within their educational system to employ a physical education supervisor, a specialist trained in physical education and elementary education. Although the duties of the supervisor are varied by the circumstances and needs of the specific school system, the supervisor generally serves as a coordinator of physical education throughout the schools, working closely with the classroom teachers in planning the objectives of the program, constructing the curriculum, and otherwise implementing the best possible physical education for all the elementary school children of the community.

Although the supervisor is often responsible for certain administrative duties such as budgeting, purchasing supplies, maintenance of equipment, and directing the intramural and interscholastic activities, his chief concern is the physical education of each child. Toward this end the supervisor usually establishes a schedule of weekly visits to the classes of each school to observe the children firsthand and to consult with the teachers. The supervisor may teach the classes himself during the visit, but more frequently he will only observe. In either case recommendations may be made to the teacher for possible improvement and enrichment of the physical education experience.

The classroom teacher should regard the supervisor as a helper whose specialized knowledge about physical education will make the instruction of the teacher more effective. The supervisor is one to whom the teacher may turn for advice about methods of teaching, new games and skills to present, suggestions for helping children who lack certain skills, and means of dealing with behavior problems.

SUPPLEMENTARY READINGS

American Association for Health, Physical Education and Recreation: *Organizational Patterns for Instruction in Physical Education.* Washington, D.C., American Association for Health, Physical Education and Recreation, 1971.

American Association for Health, Physical Education and Recreation: *Planning Facilities for Athletics, Physical Education and Recreation.* Washington, D.C., American Association for Health, Physical Education and Recreation, 1974.

American Association for Health, Physical Education and Recreation: *Teaching Safety in the Elementary School.* Washington, D.C., American Association for Health, Physical Education and Recreation, 1972.

Appenzeller, Herb: *From the Gym to the Jury.* Charlottesville, Virginia, The Michie Company, 1970.

Bucher, Charles A.: *Administration of School and College Health and Physical Education Programs, Including Athletics.* Ed. 5. St. Louis, The C. V. Mosby Company, 1971.

Corbin, Charles B.: *Inexpensive Equipment for Games, Play, and Physical Activity.* Dubuque, Iowa, Wm. C. Brown Company, Publishers, 1972.

Mager, R. F.: *Preparing Instructional Objectives.* Palo Alto, California, Fearon Publishers, 1962.

Rubenstein, Irwin, and Hase, Gerald J.: *Student Teaching in Physical Education.* Englewood Cliffs, New Jersey, Prentice-Hall, Inc., 1971.

Willgoose, Carl E.: *The Curriculum in Physical Education.* Englewood Cliffs, New Jersey, Prentice-Hall, Inc., 1969.

chapter four

implementing the program

Implementing a good learning experience in physical education is a complex process. Children must be motivated to work toward the achievement of the objectives. They must receive instruction in the knowledge and skills which make the realization of the objectives possible; those who are unsuccessful must receive additional help, which requires knowledgeable diagnosis of the reasons for lack of success. Finally, the results of the instruction must be evaluated both in terms of the accomplishments of the students and the effectiveness of the teacher's instruction and selection of curriculum content.

MOTIVATION

Motivation may be said to be the nucleus of the learning experience. Success in learning is directly related to the motivation of the learner. When pupils are moved toward achievement by their own personal desires, urges, interests, and abilities, the need for external incentives is eliminated or, at least, greatly reduced. In every class, however, there will be a number of youngsters who need to be motivated to achieve the desired objectives.

Motivation of elementary school age youngsters in physical education is in most instances not a difficult task. Among preschool and primary school children the natural desire to play in itself provides sufficient motivation for successful learning in physical education. For these children, as yet unaccustomed to remaining seated and quiet for long intervals, play periods give welcome release from the discipline and tension of the classroom. The teacher has only to make the program appealing to the needs and interests of these youngsters to ensure the necessary motivation for achieving the desired objectives for a specific age group. Only children who have had unsatisfactory experiences in play will need special motivation. These youngsters will evidence their dislike for play by reluctance to participate, withdrawal from games, and preference for only those games and play activities in which they feel competent and successful. The best way to help such children is by a gradual introduction to other activities which have the same appeal as the ones they do enjoy and in which they feel competent. Movement exploration activities are an especially good choice for this purpose because of the great pleasure which most children take in discovering for themselves the great variety of movements of which their bodies are capable. By enlarging their experiences in play so that they can develop the skills and confidence necessary for enjoying physical education activities, their negative feelings about participation can be overcome gradually. Many such children need only the personal reassurance and individual attention of the teacher to overcome their fears of their own inadequacies.

Children in the intermediate grades are still largely motivated by their pleasure in participating in the variety of stunts, games, and dances which they are now skilled enough to perform well. Satisfaction and pride in their skill abilities now become the chief instrument of motivation; interest in improving their physical performance, particularly in sport skills, is a strong motivator. From the fifth or sixth grade on through the eighth grade, the prevailing interest in competition provides an additional motivational force. The appeal of competition will manifest itself not only in team sports but in self-testing activities in which the individual student competes against himself in an effort to better his previous score. The teacher should exercise caution, however, against relying too heavily on competition as a motivator because this may result in the development of a win-at-any-cost attitude.

By the time students reach seventh grade, and often earlier, they are also interested in the effects of exercise upon their bodies. Such interest is usually first indicated by enthusiasm for increasing muscle size and improving the body build. The teacher should capitalize on this strong interest to motivate learning in physical education. Some children of this age, however, form strong interests in hobbies of a sedentary nature which largely supplant their play interests so that motivating these pupils to participate in vigorous activity in their leisure hours, if not actually in the class, becomes a problem. An appeal to their intellectual interest in the effects of exercise upon the body made through discussions, supplemented by the many excellent visual aids available to the teacher, may provide an incentive to such students.

TEACHING METHODS AND TECHNIQUES

Teaching methods are general procedures for promoting learning. In physical education the most commonly used methods may be described by the terms: traditional or direct, problem-solving or indirect, and a synthesis of these. The synthesis is not generally recognized as a method, although it is widely practiced; for this reason, and for others which will be discussed later, the author includes it as one of the methods of teaching physical education. In any general procedure of teaching, certain techniques are utilized. Techniques of teaching may be said to be special ways of effectively handling classroom problems and dealing with the varied responses of different children. All techniques may be placed in one of three broad categories: verbalization, visualization, and kinesthesis.

TRADITIONAL OR DIRECT METHOD

Generally speaking, in the traditional method the teacher chooses the specific activity or skill that is to be learned. The teacher briefly describes the movements involved and demonstrates personally or through visual aid media how the movements are performed to achieve maximum effectiveness. The students then attempt the skill while the teacher corrects any errors that are being made by individual students. In making the corrections, the teacher may utilize such teaching techniques as verbalization, demonstration, or manual kinesthesis to help the student learn the correct movement. Usually an opportunity is provided to practice the skill before using it in a game situation. The students continue to receive instruction to improve performance during practice and also during actual participation when they have progressed to playing the game.

Practice of specific skills may be provided through drills in which the class participates as a whole, or the class may be divided into groups for practice of different skills. In the latter situation, practice proceeds more effectively if each group is provided with a worksheet or task card that lists several specific items the group is to attempt to accomplish. If there are sufficient portable blackboards, the tasks for each group may be written on them rather than reproduced on paper. Each task should have some inherent quality or quantity measure to enable the student to determine when he has reached the desired level and is ready to move on to the next task. An example of the task assignments that might be made for practicing the dribble in basketball is:

1. Dribble a basketball 20 continuous bounces, contacting the ball on the fingertips and using chiefly wrist and elbow action.
2. Dribble as above but use the opposite arm.
3. Dribble as in number 1 but on each bounce change hands.
4. Set up five chairs 10 feet apart; dribble between them making three consecutive trips at top speed without losing control of the ball.

Within a group, the students may be divided into pairs to work together, alternating as performers and observers. The observer's role is to provide information feedback to the performer about his level of performance and to help him determine when the task has been accomplished. As soon as a student has accomplished a task, he may ask the teacher to observe him performing it and check his card. He then proceeds to the next task. Students may progress as rapidly as their abilities allow.

PROBLEM-SOLVING OR INDIRECT METHOD

In the problem-solving method, the teacher presents a motor task to the students in the form of a problem. The nature of the problem is determined by the maturation level and past experience of the students and the objectives of the program. These factors influence the degree of complexity of the problem presented. For example, for young children who are just beginning to explore movement, the task may be as simple as determining how to move from one place to another without walking or running. In their attempts to solve this problem, the children experiment with various kinds of movements; some may hop, others may skip, and the more imaginative may leap frog or do a forward roll to propel their bodies to a new location. A more sophisticated problem for older children with more experience in motor movement might consist of discovering the angle at which the knee should be placed in preparation for making a vertical jump. In addition to experimenting with various knee positions, this task involves solving such other problems as how to estimate the degree of the angle, how to measure the height of the jump, and how to work with someone else in making these measurements. (A more detailed discussion of the use of the problem-solving method is presented in Chapter 5.)

Movement Exploration

Movement exploration is a form of problem-solving. It is chiefly concerned with discovering the movements of which the body is capable; encouraging the inherent love of movement; and developing an understanding of the relationship of emotion to movement as a basis for expressing emotions through movement.

In movement exploration, no rigid standard of correct movement is established as the criterion toward which the students should work. The correct movement is entirely dependent upon the individual and the particular situation. The problem is considered to have been satisfactorily resolved when the student, having made a number of attempts to solve it, has achieved a movement that satisfies him.

SYNTHESIS OF THE TRADITIONAL AND PROBLEM-SOLVING METHODS

It is usually assumed that the problem-solving method and the traditional method of teaching physical education are philosophically in total opposition and therefore incompatible. While it is true that there is a basic difference in the philosophies of teaching on which the two methods are based, a difference between telling or showing students how and guiding them to self-discovery of how to perform, the two methods are not so incompatible as to require the teacher to make an absolute choice of either one or the other. Effective teachers who would be classified as users of the traditional method have always utilized certain aspects of problem-solving. Recognizing that each child is an individual with certain abilities and certain limitations, these teachers have attempted to help him discover how to achieve optimum performance without rigid adherence to the "correct" way. Although they may rely to a large extent upon telling and showing their students how to perform skills in patterns that have been proven to be the most efficient for most people, they nevertheless recognize that not all children should be forced to adopt a particular pattern of performance or even that they should all be expected to attempt it. Within these classes, then, there has always been a certain amount of problem-solving, arising from an effort to serve individual needs. Moreover, effective teachers of the traditional method have always understood that children frequently learn best when they have an opportunity to question, to examine, and to experiment; and they have, consequently, operated from much the same premise as those utilizing the problem-solving method.

Further evidence that the two methods are not incompatible is found in the use of certain techniques of teaching, usually associated with the traditional method, to increase the effectiveness of the problem-solving. Demonstration by the teacher or by a skilled student or through the use of films and other visual aids is frequently employed by the teacher to give students a better understanding of the nature of the movements involved in a certain motor task or to present them with a standard of performance against which to evaluate the solution they have achieved. The visual media are likely to be as provocative as the teacher's verbalization, and they offer variety in presentation of problems to be solved.

On the basis of the evidence given above of the compatibility of the two methods, the author suggests that the most effective teaching of physical education to elementary school age youngsters can be achieved through a synthesis of the traditional and the problem-solving methods. The synthesis would unite the best of each method, leaving the teacher flexible in the choice of method best suited to any specific situation and to his own special talents and abilities. Such flexibility is greatly to be desired over the use of one particular method, regardless of its appropriateness to the situation, because of a conviction that it is the better method and must always be used in every teaching situation.

A synthesis of the two methods is likely to be far more effective in achieving the objectives of the program than exclusive use of either may be. It will produce a method of teaching that allows the child to be creative and experimental and impresses him with the possibilities of movement of which his body is capable. It will encourage him to think reflectively and to apply the process of logical reasoning to the solution of the problem. But at any time that the teacher senses a lack of security among the students with the problem-solving method, or confusion arising from failure to solve the motor task, he can shift to the more direct approach. When lack of time is a factor in developing a phase of the program, certain aspects of the motor problem being considered can be taught with the traditional techniques since they generally require less time. Review of formerly learned skills and evaluation of performance may also generally be more efficiently handled with traditional procedures.

The key to the teacher's successful synthesis of the two methods is the use of the method best suited to the teaching situation to ensure the optimum development of the individual child.

VERBALIZATION TECHNIQUE

Verbalization refers to use of the spoken word as a technique of teaching. Verbal explanations are necessary for describing how to do a skill, explaining rules and game strategy, answering questions from students, and giving directions during the conduct of the class. Verbalization is, in fact, so commonly used in teaching that little thought is usually given to making it more effective.

If the verbalization is to succeed, it must be clear and concise. The vocabulary must be within the comprehension of the students. A common failing in describing a skill performance is to give too many details and to use a technical vocabulary for which the children have no background. With very young children, particularly, the teacher is likely to introduce too much information about the game before play begins. These youngsters, as we have already noted, want to play as soon as the play period begins; they do not take well to standing around listening to details about the activity in which they are going to participate. With the younger age groups the teacher would do well to verbalize only so much as is necessary to get the activity underway and then to stop for periods of rest, needed at frequent intervals by primary age pupils, during which other information about the activity may be discussed.

VISUALIZATION TECHNIQUE

Visualization is a technique involving the visual attention of the students. Visual aids are motion pictures, film strips, charts, posters, pictures, and diagrams, which show how a particular skill is performed correctly, analyze good game strategy, and give instruction in the correction of errors.

Visualization is utilized less in problem-solving than in the traditional method, because it is felt that showing the student how to perform eliminates the need for experimentation and discourages free exploration. However, as pointed out above, there are times when the direct approach is useful in accomplishing the resolution of the problem, and such media as films, pictures, and demonstrations can be used most effectively.

Movies, slides, and film strips require considerable planning to ensure effective use. Unless they are school owned, which is rare, they must be ordered well in advance of the date of showing. Arrangements must also be made for holding the class in a room that can be made reasonably dark. An operator must be engaged if the teacher will not be operating the visual aid machine.

Because of the expenditure of time and effort involved, it is important that the visual aid to be shown will be sufficiently worthwhile. Judging its value is difficult without a preview showing, and this cannot usually be arranged before ordering. However, a preview before showing it to the class is possible and should be done as it helps the teacher to become familiar with the contents as well as providing an opportunity to reject it if it proves entirely unsatisfactory.

By becoming familiar with the information presented by the particular visual aid, the teacher is able to make better use of it in instructing the class. The students can be alerted before the showing about the significant things which they should watch for. Then, too, the teacher will be better prepared to make additional comments during the showing if this should seem desirable. A discussion of what has been seen and an opportunity for students to ask questions should always follow the showing of this type of visual aid, and a preview is usually helpful to the teacher in organizing the points of discussion.

Pictures, charts, and diagrams are useful in helping students understand the techniques of certain skill performances. Such visual aids may be placed in the area where the activity is being taught for students to study before and after class. The teacher may find that it is helpful to some students with special problems to look at them and discuss them together with the teacher during class. When not in use in classes, the pictures, charts, and so forth may be displayed on a bulletin board located in some strategic place. An attractively arranged and colorful physical education bulletin board can be a real asset, not only as a visual teaching aid, but as a stimulator of interest in the physical education program.

Printed material is another form of visualization which may be used with children who have acquired sufficient reading skill. Although books suitable for elementary age children are not numerous, it is likely that the school library will have books of games and how-to books on the more popular sport skills which may be used. While greater use of printed physical education materials should be encouraged at other educational levels, at the elementary school level it should not be expanded at the expense of time allotted to vigorous play, which is the most essential learning experience of the program for this age group. However, stimulating children to seek information from the printed page should be considered a function of physical education instruction.

Demonstration of skill performance is one of the most useful and important of the visualization techniques in the direct method of teaching. If the teacher is unable to perform the skill well, a student who has evidenced mastery of it may be asked to demonstrate. Many times, however, the teacher, although not capable of performing the skill in its entirety, is quite skilled in the execution of certain parts or components of the skill or in the performance of the entire skill in slow motion. A demonstration of parts or in slow motion is very acceptable and meaningful to the students. The various components of the skill are easily observed by them, and time is permitted for verbal explanation of the techniques as well.

Since the purpose of the demonstration is to show the students how a skill is performed, the teacher should arrange the class so that everyone is able to see the demonstrator. It is helpful to young students to have the demonstration performed in the same position that they will take when doing a skill that involves direction of movement, so, when demonstrating a skill like batting or dancing, the demonstrator should turn his back to the students rather than face them.

The demonstration should consume as little time as necessary to establish the techniques. Students are usually eager to try the demonstrated skill themselves, and it is difficult to hold their attention for long. In fact, the chief problem in using this method of teaching a skill is keeping the children from performing until they've watched the entire demonstration. A word of warning that they will not see everything and will keep others from seeing if they begin practicing before the demonstration is over is usually sufficient to restrain them.

There is some question as to whether it is better to demonstrate a skill at the beginning of the teaching unit or to wait until the children have had experience in trying to perform the skill. The time to use demonstrations cannot be arbitrarily established; it must be determined by the nature of activity and the objective sought. If the purpose of an activity is to encourage motor experimentation and exploration, demonstration may be a hindrance because it encourages performance in a specific way. The demonstration might, however, be used to advantage after the students have experimented for a time; they could then study and compare their own performances and their concepts of the movement with the demonstrated movement. If, on the other hand, the objective of the demonstration is to evoke a set response of performance by the students, it is best used before the skill is attempted by the class.

In the direct method, practice of the skill should follow the demonstration with the teacher watching for errors or difficulties in performing correctly. If it seems desirable, the practice may be interrupted for another demonstration during which special attention is directed to the most prevalent errors and problems in performance.

KINESTHESIS TECHNIQUE

Kinesthesis is a teaching technique that involves adjustment of the body segments to achieve successful performance of a skill through the realization of how it "feels." Kinesthesis may be manual or exploratory.

In the former, the teacher leads the segments of the student's body that are involved in the skill through the correct execution of it. For example, with a child who is having difficulty achieving a level swing of the bat (a common tendency among beginners is to strike down at the end of the swing), the teacher may stand behind the batter and, placing his hands over the child's, guide the bat through the swing at the proper level. After several repetitions, the child will get the "feel" of the correct movement and in future efforts at batting will be guided by this kinesthetic sense of correct form.

In contrast to manual kinesthesis, exploratory kinesthesis originates with the child. Given a certain objective in motor performance, he attempts various movements and then makes adjustments as seem necessary to him to accomplish his objective. Upon discovering a specific way of moving that is successful, he repeats it to establish a kinesthetic sense of the movement that will guide him in future performance of the movement. Children employ exploratory

Figure 4–1 The kinesthetic method is helpful in teaching a child who is having difficulty learning the overhand throw. (Courtesy of Town of Vernon Schools, Rockville, Connecticut.)

kinesthesis when they learn any kind of movement on their own through what is commonly called trial and error.

TEACHING NONGRADED CLASSES

An increasing number of elementary school systems are grouping students on bases other than chronological age. The principal ways of organizing the groups in these schools are: (1) homogeneous grouping based upon a level of academic performance, generally ability in language arts; (2) heterogeneous grouping combining several grades and utilizing multi-level instruction by a team of teachers; and (3) heterogeneous grouping combining several grades from which smaller groups are formed on a day-to-day or week-to-week basis according to ability in specific subject areas.

If either of the first two means of grouping is used in the school, the students in the physical education classes will exhibit a wide range of abilities and speed of learning in motor movements. To meet the varying needs and abilities of each individual within the group, the teacher will need to plan the physical education program so as to allow the children to progress at their own rate of speed and to work at their own level of ability. The problem-solving method can be used effectively to achieve this and is, therefore, highly recommended for nongraded classes in which motor ability has not been used as a criterion for grouping.

When the third means of grouping, described above, is employed, the physical education class can be organized and instructed to best advantage if the students are grouped according to motor ability. A common procedure for determining motor ability is testing by means of a physical fitness test battery that includes an agility test. Often only the agility test is used. Either procedure provides only a rough measurement of ability to perform in physical education and must be supplemented with subjective judgment. The traditional method of teaching may be used effectively with these homogeneous groups; however, the problem-solving approach is frequently used just as effectively. The choice is a matter of the method by which the individual teacher is best able to achieve the desired results.

EVALUATION

In physical education evaluation seeks to measure individual progress and the extent to which the objectives sought have been achieved. From evaluation the teacher may diagnose the specific difficulties being experienced by the students and determine possible weaknesses in techniques of teaching or lacks in the construction and organization of the program. Because of the importance of progression in skills in physical education, evaluation is also essential in determining whether pupils are adequately prepared for subsequent phases of the program.

EVALUATING THE ACHIEVEMENT OF OBJECTIVES

All too often the thoughtfully planned objectives for the physical education program are ignored in the actual teaching process. Few objectives can be realized without special effort being directed toward their accomplishment. To determine how practical the objectives of the program are and the extent to which they may be achieved, testing and evaluation are needed after the pupils have been exposed to the specific situation. In the process of this testing, the teaching techniques and program planning are also evaluated.

DETERMINING INDIVIDUAL PROGRESS

By determining the status of the student's abilities at specific intervals, the teacher can determine the progress the student is making. This is essential for determining whether or not the student is adequately prepared for subsequent phases of the program. These evaluations may be used also to determine the grades to be given for physical education.

Determining status and progress of students is useful in motivation. As students become aware of their progress and see the results of their efforts, they are more likely to try harder. This is not true with every child, of course, but many children are motivated to greater effort by the knowledge that improvement is possible.

For teachers using the traditional method, measurement of ability is helpful in classifying students for various activities. It is particularly desirable to equate groups for team play so that those with superior skills and strength will be distributed among the various teams. This is both more fun and a better learning situation for poorer players because they have more opportunities to contribute to the success of their team.

SELF-EVALUATION

The ability to judge his own progress is an important skill that every student should be taught to develop, for it is basic to the achievement of independence in the learning process. To evaluate himself, the student must first recognize the objectives that he is working toward and then determine how successfully he is accomplishing them.

Teachers using the problem-solving method must necessarily promote self-analysis and evaluation. Students are encouraged to examine their movements and, by means of careful analysis, to assess the effectiveness of their solutions to the motor tasks. In some instances, they may be able to use objective measuring devices such as a tape measure or stop watch. The evaluation is made by each student himself by comparing the results he has achieved with the objectives implied in the problem he is trying to solve.

Self-evaluation of the kind involved in problem-solving can, and should, be more widely utilized by teachers who use the traditional method exclusively or in combination with problem-solving. To institute self-evaluation in a more traditional program, the teacher must be certain that the objectives are clearly recognized by the students; involving them in setting up the specific objectives is an especially good way of accomplishing this. In addition, there must be less rigid adherence to preconceived standards of performance. Individual students must be allowed greater freedom to discover their own best way of accomplishing motor movements based upon their own analysis and evaluation of the progress they have made and may expect to make.

Evaluation—Behavioral Objectives

Behavioral objectives provide their own means of evaluation. If the objectives are successfully achieved, the quality and quantity of the performance are immediately apparent. Definitive information is available to the child for his self-evaluation and to the teacher for evaluation both of the students and of the teaching procedures used to accomplish the objectives.

DIAGNOSING DIFFICULTIES

In order that the teacher may help the student whose achievement is inadequate, he needs to know specifically what phases of performance the student is weak in. Testing may identify these. For example, a youngster who performs poorly in basketball may be given a series of diagnostic tests of his shooting, jumping, running, and other component skills in basketball. A poor score in one or more of these tests will reveal the weakness. The cause might also be attributable to a lack of physical fitness, which again could be discovered through diagnostic testing of the physical fitness factors.

As a teacher gains experience in observing the various types of skills used in play, he is able to identify many errors and weaknesses simply by watching the players carefully. The ability to recognize incorrect movements and poor skill techniques is of such importance to the successful teaching of physical education that every teacher in the physical education program should cultivate it. Discovering the weakness in a student's performance, whether by testing or by observation, is only the first step, however. The teacher must determine how to overcome the weakness or error and then must be able to analyze it clearly for the student so that he is able to understand where the fault lies and how to correct it. This should be followed by considerable drill on the correct technique or form under the supervision of the teacher. In this connection, the teacher will find the charts in Chapters 8, 12, and 15, which identify errors in skills performance and present means by which they may be corrected, exceedingly helpful.

EVALUATION FOR GRADING

The purpose of grading in physical education, as elsewhere, is to report progress toward accomplishing the objectives. Students need to be informed of their progress and helped in their appraisal of the quality of the work they have done; grading is a useful tool for this.

Grades in physical education are generally reported in one of two ways: (1) a written description of the pupil's progress, and (2) a single symbol indicating the level of achievement. In the written report, the objectives of the instruction are specifically stated and comments are made about the child's effort and ability in achieving these objectives. The most obvious advantage of this method of reporting is that the specific weaknesses and areas where improvement is possible are clearly identified for the child and for the parents.

Symbols used in the elementary schools to report physical education achievement are P and F for pass and fail; S and U for satisfactory and unsatisfactory; and the letter marks of A, B, C, D, and F. In the two symbol markings, the P and S are roughly equivalent to A, B, and C while F and U equate with D and F in the letter scale. The use of either of the two-symbol scales of marking tends to discourage close evaluation, and often students are awarded the higher mark if they make some effort to do the class work and have a good attitude. A similar lack of discrimination is sometimes evidenced by teachers using the A to F marking scale; however, when used with good judgment, it should be the better means of reporting achievement because it does permit the degree of progress and accomplishment to be indicated to the student.

Regardless of the symbols used, a teacher must relate the symbols to the objectives of the program. Since the course of study must encompass the objectives, the evaluation may be used to determine the extent to which each of the objectives is being accomplished. Each activity presented in the program is likely to have more than one objective. The percentage of class time spent in working toward the fulfillment of a given objective determines how much weight it should receive in the final evaluation. If, for example, 75 per cent of the time is spent on developing skills, the progress made in acquiring the skills should account for three-fourths of the grade.

Grades in physical education may be assigned on an absolute or a relative basis. An absolute grade is based entirely upon achievement while a relative grade is assigned on the basis of achievement in realizing potentiality. Those who favor relative grading point out that such a technique frequently fosters greater interest in improvement and will motivate the youngster who is poor in physical education because he knows that his native physical ability will not cause him to receive a poor grade if he shows improvement. Also, there are some who feel that skill in physical education cannot be likened to skill in a subject like English; and although good development of the body and in the skills of physical education are beneficial throughout life, these are not so fundamental to the educative process as the skills developed in English class. Consequently, a student who works to the limit of his physical capacity but does not achieve the desired level of performance for receiving a passing grade should not fail physical education, although one who achieves to the extent of his mental capacity without making a passing grade should fail English.

Those who oppose this line of reasoning point out that an educated person is a well-rounded person and as such should have developed some proficiency in physical education. Furthermore, assessing potentialities is very difficult and makes relative marking far from accurate.

Goal Record Card System

Schools that emphasize individualized instruction often utilize the goal record card system. A goal record card lists for the student all the important objectives to be achieved during a designated instructional unit. The objectives are specific in nature so that the requirements for meeting them can be readily determined. For example, the specific objectives for a sixth grade unit in volleyball might be listed as:

1. Demonstrate the correct form for serving underhand.
2. Serve three out of five attempts into the receiving court so the ball passes at least 3 feet above the net.
3. Demonstrate the correct way for volleying a ball that has fallen below the waist.
4. Demonstrate the correct form for volleying the ball above the head.
5. Set up a ball that has been tossed in the air so that it is volleyed close to and above the net three out of five attempts.
6. Spike a ball that has been set up by a toss into the forecourt three out of five times.

The goal card is developed by the teacher and is given to the children at the beginning of the unit so that they may take it home for the information of the parents. Children above the third grade can be given the responsibility of keeping their own cards and bringing them to class for checking by the teacher. When a child feels he has accomplished a specific goal, the teacher observes him as he performs the skill and marks the goal record card to indicate achievement, partial achievement, or failure to achieve the objective. The marks can be converted to letter grades, if that is desired.

Contract Grading

Another marking system that is being used with increasing frequency is the contract for a final grade. It is generally not an effective instrument for use below the sixth grade. To initiate the procedure the teacher establishes a list of requirements with respect to amount and quality of work that must be fulfilled for each grade. The student decides which final mark he wishes to receive and contracts with the teacher to do the required work. He then proceeds on his own to fulfill his contractual obligations, working at a pace determined by him as suitable to accomplish the work by the end of the time allotted to the unit. If the student fails to achieve a minimum standard in the requirements of his contract, he may elect to undertake additional work and attempt to achieve satisfactory performance, or he may choose a lower final mark.

Administering Tests

In using tests the teacher must observe the same rules that guide good teaching. Tests must be so administered that students will develop interest and concern for performing well. Every test which the students take should serve in some way just as every activity included in the program must serve the needs of the students.

Students should be informed of the results of the test as soon as possible after taking it. A long wait between the testing and the time when the students are informed about the results tends to subtract from the meaningfulness of the test for them. Not only the score of the test, but an interpretation of the score should be reported to the pupils. Information given about the meaning of a particular score should be on the level of their ability to comprehend and should be presented in such a way that each individual is able to understand his status and to recognize the evidence of accomplishment or lack of it, as the case may be.

Tests which point up individual success and improvement appeal to the upper elementary grades more than to the lower grades. For this age tests provide a means to prove ability in competition with peers; and for this reason, the types of tests being administered should vary to permit students with different abilities to excel. However, at this age level it is wise to help establish a good sense of values regarding motor excellence.

The teacher should be concerned especially that the importance of motor excellence not be overemphasized. The child who is naturally slow in movement and is basically poorly coordinated should not be placed in a situation where he is looked down upon by his peers because of his inability to come up to average performance. For students with low motor ability, success must come from improvement, however small, rather than outstanding performance; and the teacher must set the stage for the development of this attitude among the class members.

In planning how much of the time should be given to testing and evaluating, the teacher must consider the total amount of time available for physical education. To a certain extent evaluations may be made at the same time that teaching is occurring. Although there are limitations to a subjective measurement, this is an evaluation technique which a teacher can employ even as he teaches. Then, too, many tests are in essence exercises or activities which promote improved fitness or skills so that their use has teaching as well as testing value. The good teacher knows that testing is a device to improve teaching and, hence, learning. Testing is necessary to identify strengths and weaknesses and to measure progress; but the time devoted to testing must not be so extensive as to exclude ample opportunity for working toward the program's objectives.

Kinds of Tests

Tests for physical education can be divided into three categories—knowledge, social adjustment and attitudes, and motor tests.

KNOWLEDGE TESTS.   Since gaining knowledge is one of the objectives of physical education, it is worthwhile to use tests that indicate if this objective is being reached satisfactorily. Written tests serve this purpose best in the upper elementary level while verbal questions to children in kindergarten and the primary grades tend to be more successful because of the limitations in reading and writing. Objective and short answer tests are preferred generally when the teacher is testing a large number of students and has a limited time for evaluating papers. Of the different types of objective tests, the true-false, multiple choice, and matching tests are recognition tests; that is, a key for the right answer is supplied. In completion and simple answer tests, the answer is not suggested but must be recalled from memory. The definition of a term is an example of this type of test item.

Test Construction.   In constructing a test, the preliminary steps should include:

1. An outline of the scope of the proposed examination with the important topics identified.
2. Determination of the important items under each topic.
3. Listing of the items according to importance as far as possible.
4. Determination of the best type of test in accordance with the nature of the material.

Having taken these preliminary steps, a good selection of test items and an appropriate form for the test are more likely to result. Although it is not possible to ask questions covering all the facts that the class might be expected to know, there should be a question on every important topic.

In developing an objective test the instructor must determine its validity, that is, the degree to which it measures what it purports to measure. The reliability of the test, which refers to how constantly it gives the same results under like conditions, must also be ascertained. References at the end of the chapter may be consulted for a more comprehensive discussion of the means for determining the validity and reliability of tests.

Standardized Tests.   The teacher may wish to use some of the standardized tests which are available in physical education, particularly in physical fitness and motor skill testing. A standardized test is one for which norms and specific testing procedures have been established and the reliability and validity have been determined. Norms are the standard points of reference that provide a basis for judgment in evaluating any single score or group of scores.

Standardized tests have value beyond the teacher-made test in that they provide a means of comparing students with those in other schools or with students throughout the entire country. Additional advantages are that no time is required to prepare the test and the scoring is usually simple and quickly done.

Like other tests, standardized tests may be used to evaluate pupil achievement and to measure the effectiveness of the teaching procedures. For the evaluation of the latter to be meaningful, however, it is necessary to realize that community environment may be such as to offset the efforts of the physical education program. For example, in a community where the play and exercise opportunities outside of school are severely limited and the socioeconomic level is such that many children are malnourished or undernourished, the test scores in motor efficiency would be low regardless of the excellence of the school's physical education program and those who teach it. Consequently, an unfavorable comparison of one school with another does not necessarily mean that the quality of the physical education is less. Comparisons are significant only when the factors outside the school which influence the progress of the school population are equal or nearly so.

A drawback to the use of standardized tests, and it is an important one, is that of fitting the teaching to the tests. Extensive use of standardized tests necessitates that the physical education be planned to expose the youngsters to the activities they will be tested on. This puts too much responsibility for curriculum determination on the test maker. There is the further danger that the teacher will "teach the test" rather than concentrating on presenting a varied program of physical education which will promote its many objectives.

SOCIAL ADJUSTMENT AND ATTITUDES TESTS.   There have been no widely accepted devices developed for precise measurements of social adjustment and attitudes. However, there are several techniques to help clarify the teacher's subjective measurement of these qualities. Some of the techniques such as adjustment and personality tests, rating scales, and other psychological tests are best used and interpreted by the psychologist or psychiatrist. Procedures that are of practical use in physical education are the anecdotal record and the personal interview or conference.

Anecdotal Record.   An anecdotal record is a running account describing behavior in specific instances. File cards 3 by 5 inches in size are convenient for keeping the records. Cards should be dated and filed in chronological order so that, if the need to trace the history of a particular problem or to assess over-all progress should arise, it can be easily accomplished. Each card should contain a brief description of the circumstances in which the child was observed, any pertinent facts which the teacher knows about the child, and the teacher's interpretation of these.

The teacher should be warned that there is a tendency to record only unusual happenings and that to do so is likely to lead to an incorrect analysis of the student's general behavior patterns and to provide an incomplete picture of the child's true development and progress. It is equally important to know something about the child in a non-problem setting, that is, one in which he is not prompted to conduct himself in a way that calls attention to his actions. It is also important to know the extent to which the deviations in behavior occur, and for this reason the regular recording of observations over a period of time is greatly to be desired.

Interview. A personal interview or conference between the child and the teacher provides one of the best opportunities for the teacher to gain a better understanding of the reason behind a child's actions. Usually the area of concern is undesirable social behavior in the class or on the playground, but it might also be the child's inability to learn what is taught or lack of interest in participation.

Although its name suggests otherwise, the teacher's role in the personal interview is chiefly that of listener. Prodding the child to speak by asking too many questions tends to make most children resentful or apprehensive about the purpose of the interview. The child must be made to feel that the teacher is interested in him and his feelings rather than merely prying into his affairs. The child may need help in discussing his problem, and the teacher should be ready to make suitably encouraging comments, but he should refrain from arguing with or correcting the child's concepts and from giving comfort insincerely. The confidence of the child in the teacher is absolutely necessary to the success of the personal interview; only by building an atmosphere of trust and respect is the teacher likely to learn the facts he needs to improve the situation.

GENERAL MOTOR PERFORMANCE AND SKILL EVALUATION. Attempts to develop general motor performance and general coordination tests have not been successful. Most of the tests of this nature were developed in the 1930s and 1940s; at that time it was widely accepted that there was a general factor of motor ability and that it could be measured by a single test. However, as pointed out in the discussion of motor learning (pages 18–19), recent research indicates that motor ability is specific rather than general in nature. Consequently, tests of general motor ability cannot be devised, and existing tests are of no great use to the teacher. It is possible, however, to measure specific skills.

If behavioral objectives have been established for the course, these provide a ready means for evaluating achievements in specific skills. Evaluation under these circumstances is an assessment of the student's mastery of the stated objectives.

When only curriculum objectives have been established, an evaluation can be determined by tests measuring abilities in specific skills that comprise the objective. Such tests fall into two general categories—rating scales and objective motor skill tests.

Rating Scales. During the teaching of a skill, the teacher is making constant use of the rating scale techniques, that is; he is observing motor performance and making decisions as to how effective each student is. This technique can be made into a more precise testing tool by considering some of the factors that affect rating validity:

1. The skill or factor of motor performance that is being rated should be defined, insofar as possible, in terms of abilities which are observable to the rater. For example, in rating the performance in playing dodge ball one of the observable skills is the ability to retire the opponent by hitting him with the ball; another is the ability to keep from being hit by the opponents.

2. The rating of any skill becomes more accurate if the rater breaks the skill into its components. If performance in dodge ball is being rated, the game should be analyzed; the components which constitute the skills of the game should be identified, and their relative importance should be properly assessed. Some of the components which would be identified in this case are: the ability to throw a ball accurately, the speed with which the ball is thrown, the ability to dodge, feinting ability, and the ability to pass and receive the ball. The

Figure 4–2 To evaluate students' ability in soccer, the component skills must be rated through observation of the children in a play situation. (Journal of Health · Physical Education · Recreation.)

performer should be rated in each of the skills and these ratings should be taken into account in arriving at final evaluation of the total ability to play dodge ball.

Having arrived at an evaluation of each student's ability to perform a specific game or skill, the teacher may wish to use the scores to place the students into categories for purposes of grading them or for other reasons. The curve of probability is a simple and useful guide for developing such categories. The ranking of the students might be set up in this way: Category 1, representing very poor performance, with approximately 7 per cent of the student population in the age group being evaluated expected to score in this category; Category 2, poor, with 24 per cent; Category 3, fair, with 38 per cent; Category 4, good, with 24 per cent; and Category 5, excellent, with 7 per cent. The rater should understand, however, that no specific group will score in exactly the percentages indicated; such would be the case only with large numbers and if the group being tested represented a random sample.

Motor Skill Tests. Developing valid motor skill tests is a complicated procedure which is beyond the scope of this book. A limited number of skill tests for the intermediate and junior high school grades are available in published form. The teacher who wishes to make use of these is referred to the list of sources in Appendix I.

Physical Fitness Test. Tests for measuring the components of physical fitness are given in Chapter 7.

EVALUATING THE INSTRUCTION. The strength of any physical education program is measured by the progress of the students. Slow progress or lack of it as indicated by the evaluation procedures used in the class requires a thorough analysis to determine the causes. Low fitness scores, poor progress in the development of motor skills, and lack of information about the physical education activities should prompt the teacher to make an inventory of class organization, curriculum content, and teaching methods. Among the questions which might be asked are:

1. Was the allotted class time used effectively?
2. Did the activities which were taught develop total fitness, including all its components?
3. Does every child participate in accordance with his ability?
4. Were the skill problems diagnosed correctly and the children given proper understanding of their performance?
5. Were the children motivated to do their best?
6. Were the activities suited to the children's level of maturation and their needs and interests?
7. Was recognition given to individual differences and the program content planned and taught accordingly?
8. Did the program encourage creative responses by the children?
9. Were the problems or the discussions and demonstrations clearly and effectively presented to the children?
10. Did the teaching have continuity and were the lead-up skills thoroughly learned?

SUPPLEMENTARY READINGS

Gagné, Robert M.: *Learning and Individual Differences.* Columbus, Ohio, Charles E. Merrill Publishing Co., 1967.

Kuethe, James L.: *The Teaching-Learning Process.* Chicago, Scott, Foresman and Co., 1965.

Mathews, Donald K.: *Measurement in Physical Education.* Ed. 4. Philadelphia, W. B. Saunders Co., 1973.

Means, Richard K.: *Methodology in Education.* Columbus, Ohio, Charles E. Merrill Publishing Co., 1968.

Mosston, Muska: *Teaching Physical Education from Command to Discovery.* Columbus, Ohio, Charles E. Merrill Publishing Co., 1966.

Smith, James A.: *Setting Conditions for Creative Teaching in the Elementary School.* Boston, Allyn and Bacon, Inc., 1966.

Torrance, Paul E.: *Education and the Creative Potential.* Minneapolis, The University of Minnesota Press, 1963.

Vannier, Maryhelen, and Fait, Hollis F.: *Teaching Physical Education in Secondary Schools.* Ed 4. Philadelphia, W. B. Saunders Co., 1975.

chapter five

problem-solving

VOCABULARY OF PROBLEM-SOLVING
TYPES OF MOTOR MOVEMENT PROBLEMS
PRELIMINARY PLANNING OF THE PROBLEM
PRESENTING THE PROBLEM TO THE CLASS

Problem-solving is a time-honored method of teaching in academic subject areas, but it has become widely used in physical education only during the
last decade. The possibilities of teaching motor skills by this method came to
the attention of teachers in the United States as the result of its enormously successful application in England. During the early years of its use here, a variety
of terms were used to describe the method: problem-solving, movement education, motor exploration, and movement exploration. All were more or less
synonymous. In subsequent years, a distinction has developed among the
terms. In current popular usage, motor exploration and movement exploration
refer to discovery of the movements the body is capable of performing while
movement education is a term generally applied to physical education that is
predominantly taught through problem-solving.

As used by the physical education teacher, problem-solving involves setting
up a problem in motor movement to be solved by the individual student through
experimentation or exploration. It is an indirect method of teaching, for the child
learns through his own efforts to resolve the problem rather than by performing
in response to information supplied directly to him by the teacher. Because this
is so, it promotes independence in learning—the child must think through the
possible solutions, decide which ones to try, and then analyze and evaluate
them. The solution he finally selects as his best effort may be in the traditional
pattern of performance, but it may also be an entirely new way of performing the

skill. In this way creativity is encouraged. Another valuable asset of the method is that it allows each student to proceed at his own pace.

THE VOCABULARY OF PROBLEM-SOLVING

The body in motion is described in certain terms such as speed, power, and coordination. However, many teachers who use problem-solving and motor exploration extensively prefer to employ four general terms to identify the motions. These terms are:

Time—speed of movement.
Force—amount of strength and speed (power) exerted against resistance.
Flow—sequence of action in moving the body from one position to another (coordination).
Space—the area the body occupies at any given time (the position and level or plane of the body affects what space the body occupies).

Each of the elements described by these terms is a *variable,* that is, is subject to changes; for example, as time may be increased or decreased, force may be made greater or lesser. The performer, by controlling the variables, creates *variation* in movement. In problem-solving the student experiments with each variable to discover how best to perform the movement (his solution to the problem).

TYPES OF MOTOR MOVEMENT PROBLEMS

Problems in motor movement take three different forms:*
1. A SINGLE PROBLEM.   The single problem consists of a simple motor task to be solved by the entire class, such as, determine how far you can jump from a standing position. Several single problems that are interrelated, but vary in the degree of difficulty of their solution, may also be used. For example, the interrelated problems concerned with balancing might range from such simple problems as how to balance on both feet and on one foot to such complex activities as how to balance on one foot and one hand and on one knee. This kind of problem accommodates all degrees of ability from beginner to advanced. The student determines which of the problems he can already perform and which ones he wishes to experiment with and work on. It is, as can be readily seen, a highly individualized type of presentation.

The single problem places a minimum burden on students in solving the problem; therefore, it is most useful with young children or children with little or no experience in problem-solving.
2. SEQUENCE OF SUBPROBLEMS LEADING TO THE ANSWER OF THE MAIN PROBLEM.   This approach is also known as guided discovery, which is descriptive of the role of the teacher. The teacher presents the main problem to

*For a thorough discussion of these and other types and kinds of problems, refer to the reference in the *Supplementary Readings.*

the class and then guides it toward a desired solution by offering a series of clues, usually in the form of questions. Each student proceeds to find by experimentation the answer to each subproblem, finally combining all his answers to solve the major problem.

An example of a sequence of subproblems, together with the variables and some possible variations of the problem, is presented below.

Problem: How to dribble a basketball while standing stationary.

Subproblems:

1. In order to start the dribble, where is the ball dropped in relation to the body to maintain the best control? *Variable*—space; *Variation*—from the extreme left of the body to the extreme right and from close to the body to an arm's length from the body.

2. In what position is the body held? *Variable*—space; *Variation*—standing straight to a low crouch position.

3. What part of the open hand makes contact with the ball? *Variable*—space; *Variation*—from the palm of the hand to the finger tips.

4. How is the wrist used in coordination of the arms? *Variable*—flow; *Variation*—from a stiff wrist to extreme flexion of the wrist when the ball is stroked.

5. When is the ball stroked in relation to its bounce? *Variable*—time; *Variation*—from when the ball is bouncing upward to the top of the bounce to when the ball is falling back down.

6. How hard is the ball stroked? *Variable*—force; *Variation*—from very hard to very soft.

7. At what angle? *Variable*—space; *Variation*—from a 45° angle completely around the ball (left, right, front, and back) to a 90° angle.

3. INDEPENDENT DISCOVERY. As the name suggests, this form of problem-solving requires the student to work independently in the search for the solution to the motor problem. The problem in this instance is presented in terms of several broad subproblems for which the student must develop his own sequence of problems to be solved (similar to the ones given by the teacher in guided discovery). He then experiments with the variables of each problem in the

Figure 5–1 Children experiment to discover the part of the hand that should contact the ball in dribbling. (Courtesy of Town of Vernon Schools, Rockville, Connecticut.)

sequence of each of the subproblems until he has worked out a satisfactory solution to each subproblem. The solutions are then combined for his complete resolution of the main problem.

PRELIMINARY PLANNING OF THE PROBLEM

Effective use of the problem-solving method requires careful preparation. The teacher must first decide upon the general area of motor learning that will constitute the major problem and, if there is to be a sequence of subproblems, formulate the subproblems. The selection of the problem is made from among those appropriate for the age group. The bases for determining appropriateness are the physical, social, intellectual, and creative characteristics common to children at each grade level that were described in Chapter 2. Any type of physical education activity may be taught with the problem-solving method, including team sports.

If the subproblems are to take the form of a sequence leading to the solution of a main problem, they must be arranged logically. This requires careful analysis by the teacher of the activity to identify the steps involved. If he will think through the progression of movements required to accomplish the activity or movement stated in the main problem, the steps into which the problem should be divided will usually stand out fairly clearly. It may be helpful to the teacher to refresh his recollection of the steps in performing a skill by referring to a written description of how the skill is executed. To understand the usefulness of this procedure in formulating such problems, refer to the description of dribbling a basketball (page 296) and note how the author utilized the steps discussed here to aid him in developing the subproblems for the problem "How to dribble a basketball while standing stationary" on page 104.

In planning the sequence, it is necessary to decide if each step constitutes a relevant problem; for example, does it lead to the discovery of information that has a direct bearing on the final solution? If not, it should be eliminated from consideration for inclusion in the sequence.

As part of the planning process, the teacher must also give some thought to the possible solutions that the students may develop in response to any of the three types of problems. The possibilities of solution in most instances are numerous; therefore, it is necessary to anticipate what these may be and organize them according to their common variables. Then it is possible to redefine the problems in order to limit their scope and thereby reduce the number of possible solutions.

Final steps in planning are the class organization and the distribution of any items of equipment that will be used. Considerations of these matters are discussed in Chapter 3.

PRESENTING THE PROBLEM TO THE CLASS

When using the problem-solving method for the first time with children who have had no experience with it, the teacher should explain how the method works, stressing the responsibility of each individual in arriving at a satisfactory solution to the problems. For young children, the introduction may be kept very simple; but for older children, particularly those whose only experience has been with the traditional method, extensive guidance will probably be required initially and reinforced from time to time in the early weeks of the class.

The problem itself should be presented to the students in such a way that thought and experimentation are required before they respond. A direct question or an implied one, i.e., a statement that challenges the students to find an answer or solution, may be used for this purpose. As has already been stressed, the questions must be appropriate to the age and abilities of the children.

While the teacher is presenting the questions, he must be alert to the responses of the students. If they appear bored or restless, the questions are probably too simple and lack challenge for the abilities of the group; if, on the other hand, there is considerable confusion or complete lack of response, the questions may have been too complex or the concept too difficult. The set of questions that the teacher has developed to stimulate the group to experiment should be basic in nature so they can be easily reworded as necessitated by the response of the group. An example of such a basic set of questions is presented below. The questions have been developed from the major problem cited on page 104: How to dribble while standing stationary.

1. Take a ball and find a place on the floor where you have sufficient room to dribble while standing in one spot. (If there is an insufficient number of balls for each student to have a separate ball, the class may be divided into groups to take turns with the balls.)

2. Find a spot on the floor in front of you where it is easiest to bounce the ball with one hand.

3. With what part of the hand should you stroke the ball?

4. How hard should you stroke the ball? What happens when it is stroked easy? Hard?

5. How much should you bend your elbow and wrist when stroking the ball?

6. What happens if you stroke the ball when the ball is coming up from the bounce? At the top of the bounce? As the ball falls to the ground?

7. How do you make the ball bounce some other way than straight up? What makes the ball bounce to the left or to the right?

The carefully constructed problems are presented to the class either verbally or in written form depending upon the nature and the complexity of the problem. If complex problems are presented verbally, more time may need to be allotted for students to assimilate the presentation and to ask questions for clarification than if they have the written material in front of them. When students are old enough to be effective readers, the written form is usually preferable for complex problems because it generally requires less explanation and it places the information in the hands of each student so he may proceed at his own pace, according to his ability and interest. There is also desirable flexibility in that the student may choose his own order of problems to be solved. A sample written form is shown in Table 5–1. It could be prepared for reproduc-

TABLE 5–1 Sample Written Guide for Sequence Problem-Solving and Independent Discovery

SUBJECT: SPEEDBALL

Major Problem: How to pass the ball to a teammate by kicking it.

A. *How to kick a ball into the air so that it can be caught.*
1. At what place on the ball should it be kicked so it will rise into the air?
2. What part of the foot is used to kick the selected place on the ball?
3. How is that part held when it comes into contact with the ball?
4. What is the action of the kicking leg prior to kicking the ball?
5. How is the body balanced when the ball is kicked?
6. Where is the non-kicking leg placed in relation to the ball during the kick?
7. How hard should the ball be kicked in relation to how far away you are from the receiver?
8. What happens to the kicking foot after the ball has been kicked?

B. *How to make a long pass on the ground to a teammate.*
1. At what place on the ball should it be kicked so that it will travel on the ground?
2. What part of the foot is used?
3. How is that part held when it comes into contact with the ball?
4. What is the action of the kicking leg prior to kicking the ball?
5. Where is the non-kicking leg placed in relation to the ball during the kick?
6. How is the body balanced when the ball is kicked?
7. How fast should the body be moving when the ball is kicked?
8. How many steps should be taken before the ball is kicked?
9. How hard should the ball be kicked in relation to how far the ball is to travel?
10. What happens to the kicking foot after the ball is kicked?

C. *How to make a short pass on the ground to a teammate.*
1. What part of the foot should be used in kicking to send the ball in the direction of the intended flight?
2. Where should the ball be contacted when kicked?
3. What is the action of the leg prior to kicking the ball?
4. How is the body balanced when the ball is kicked?
5. How hard should the ball be kicked?

---

tion on a copier or duplicating machine, or it could be written on a permanent or portable chalkboard.

Each student is permitted to approach the resolution of the problem in his own way. Some students will go to their chosen spots on the floor or field and begin experimenting immediately. Others may spent time thinking through their responses before setting to work. The teacher should allow the student ample time to attack the problem; he must never allow himself to become so impatient for action that he interrupts the thought processes of a student. However, if the student very obviously needs help to get started, the teacher may provide assistance in the form of more highly refined subproblems.

It is likely that some students will be reticent about attempting solutions on their own. This attitude will be particularly prevalent if the class has had no previous experience with problem-solving. Such students should be encouraged by the teacher's positive comments on their initial attempts. The use of words of praise or, where praise is not justified, of acceptance is important not only with reluctant experimenters but also with the entire class. A feeling of success in finding good solutions is important as motivation for the student to attempt other solutions with greater freedom from his own inhibitions and those imposed by the presence of the teacher and peers.

Figure 5–2 The problem of going over a bar has a variety of individual solutions. (Journal of Health · Physical Education · Recreation.)

Teachers in their initial use of problem-solving are prone to expect conventional solutions to the problems. When students respond with a totally different solution that meets neither the established criterion of movement patterns nor the criterion of aesthetic performance, the solution is likely to be rejected by the teacher. The teacher must guard against rejecting unorthodox solutions, for in doing so he may destroy the student's confidence in himself as a problem-solver.

Throughout the class period, the students are involved in seeking and testing solutions. Their activity is self-directed. Self-evaluation is an important part of the entire process, as was pointed out in Chapter 4. The teacher's role is to move about the floor observing each student. He offers suggestions as needed to help an individual student, answers questions put to him by a student, and gives encouragement and praise to a student.

TEACHING HINTS

The use of the problem-solving method is not without certain difficulties for the teacher. One difficulty arises from the amount of time that may be consumed. Unless the presentation of the problem and the experimentation are carefully planned and guided, more time may be spent than the outcome warrants. There is always the possibility that the children will begin to lose interest in the problem when too much time is devoted to a certain phase of it.

Another common difficulty for the teacher is that, unless extreme care is exercised, the presentation of the problem may become so oversimplified that it loses its meaningfulness and usefulness for the children. Thought must be given also to the phrasing of the problems so that students will readily grasp the essence of the problem. It is very important that the problem be neither oversimplified nor overly complex.

SUPPLEMENTARY READINGS

American Association for Health, Physical Education and Recreation: *Physical Education '73*. Washington, D.C., American Association for Health, Physical Education and Recreation, 1973.

American Association for Health, Physical Education and Recreation: *Trends in Elementary School Physical Education*. Washington, D.C., American Association for Health, Physical Education and Recreation, 1970.

Bilbrough, A., and Jones, P.: *Physical Education in the Primary Schools*. Ed. 3. London, University of London Press, 1972.

Boyer, Madeline Haas: *The Teaching of Elementary School Physical Education*. New York, J. Lowell Pratt and Co., 1965.

Howard, Shirley: "The Movement Education Approach to Teaching in English Elementary Schools." *Elementary School Physical Education Readings*. Dubuque, Iowa, Wm. C. Brown Company, Publishers, 1972.

Mosston, Muska: *Teaching Physical Education from Command to Discovery*. Columbus, Ohio, Charles E. Merrill Publishing Co., 1966.

chapter six

movement or motor exploration

THE NATURE OF MOVEMENT EXPLORATION

The young infant moves his head from side to side, waves his arms, and kicks his legs. It is his basic nature to move. Movement helps him to discover what his body is capable of doing and how he can control it. These movements are, in effect, a kind of exploration for the infant and so have come to be called movement exploration.

The child will continue to explore movements as he progresses through infancy and early childhood. Some types of movement will be a combination of several simple ones acquired earlier. Thus, by the time he enters kindergarten, he will have several movement patterns in common with most other children his age; that is, he will walk, run, swing his arms, twist, and turn. The way he performs these movements as well as the extent and variety of any additional movements he uses will have been determined by the limitations or potentialities for movement exploration in his environment.

Restrictions within the environment naturally have a negative effect upon movement exploration. Lack of play equipment to push and pull, to climb over and crawl under, to hang from and jump over reduces the possibilities of discovering new ways to use the body. Space limitations place restrictions on the exploration of gross body movements. Then, too, the attitude of those in the child's environment may be such as to discourage the child from discovering new movement patterns. Lack of initiative in movement exploration can often be traced to an overprotective attitude in the child's parents. Parents may also have created a barrier to exploration by the very act of praising success in certain kinds of motor movements performed by their child. The child who experiences complete satisfaction in the successful performance of a limited number of movements may be deprived of the motivation to explore further his body's capacity to move in strange and interesting new patterns. In much the same way, the child's mimicking of the movements of others sets limits to his movement exploration. Mimicking is likely to provide such immediate satisfaction of the child's need to move as well as his need for approval that he never fully realizes the potentials in motor movement.

Enjoyment of movement is natural. By an early and continued satisfying experience with varied motor activities, a sound foundation for future enjoyment of motor skills is created. Those youngsters, and adults too, who have a great dislike or fear of motor movement have developed it; their dislike is the result of an environment, the nature of which produced this undesirable and harmful attitude.

Helping the child, when he reaches school, to continue the exploration of motor movements is obviously an important function of his physical education instruction. Movement exploration for the school child is directed toward:

1. Discovering the movements the body is capable of performing.
2. Encouraging the inherent love of movement, thereby establishing a positive attitude toward life-long participation in motor movement.

Figure 6-1 Exploration of movement encourages children to discover what the body is capable of. (Journal of Health · Physical Education · Recreation.)

3. Developing an understanding of the relationship of emotion to movement so that it will become possible to express emotions through movement.

Movement exploration as a unit of work in physical education can be included at every grade level; but because the experiences it affords are so basic to all the physical education that will follow, it should receive special emphasis from nursery school and kindergarten through the primary grades. Children in the intermediate and upper grades who have never had specific instruction in motor exploration should be given an introduction to it, using the methods which will be described below for younger children. Older children will, of course, progress more rapidly and at a more sophisticated level.

PROBLEMS IN MOVEMENT EXPLORATION

The problem-solving method lends itself admirably to teaching movement exploration because it promotes freedom to investigate various solutions, which is the very essence of movement exploration. In using this method, a problem concerned with movement possibilities is presented to the students, and they attempt to solve it by experimental motor movements. Students, however, are not trying to find the most effective way to make a movement, as is usually the case in problems directed toward determining the best way to perform a specific skill for maximum efficiency and effectiveness. Problems in movement exploration focus on the discovery of movement potential. Presented below are several significant problem areas in movement exploration around which the teacher may organize units of instruction appropriate for the age and experience of the pupils.

MOVEMENT IN A STATIONARY POSITION

The objective of this problem in movement exploration is to learn in what ways the body can move without locomotion, that is, without moving from place to place. By exploring the space around him through movements of his head, arms, legs, trunk, and other segments of his body, the child develops an understanding of his body's dimensions in space.

Because children generally think of movement as walking or running from one place to another, the idea of moving in a fixed position will be both startling and confusing to them. In setting up the problem, then, the teacher may want to begin by asking the children to move as many parts of their bodies as they can while standing in one spot. Nearly everyone will move his arms; some may lift one leg while standing on the other; a few may move their heads. As they explore the movement possibilities, they should be encouraged to tell what they have discovered. This will inspire new exploratory attempts, and soon the children will have discovered a great variety of ways to move their bodies without ever having taken a single step.

In this connection, it is fun for the children to discover that certain movements are not possible. The teacher could, for instance, present the suggestion to the children that they lift one foot and hold it in their hands and then lift up the other foot. There will be some earnest effort with this until they realize the limitations of their bodies in solving this particular problem.

Having introduced the class to these new possibilities in movement, the teacher may progress toward helping the children to determine their capacities in movement and encouraging them to try new ways to accomplish their motor tasks. The exploration of the reach is one possibility for working toward this objective. The initial attempts may be to discover how far they can reach and in what ways they reach. From the more familiar movements of reaching up and toward the front and side, the teacher should guide them toward exploration of the possibilities of reaching down, to the back, diagonally across the body. As a final step, children should attempt to reach without their hands, using instead their elbows, legs, trunk, and head.

Following the reaching activities, the ways in which the body can be stretched are logically introduced. Suggestions for helping the children progress beyond the initial exploratory movements in stretching the body are: showing the difference between big and tall, big and wide, and big and round; squeezing the body until it takes up the least possible room and then expanding it to take up as much room as possible; being a rubber band that is stretched and then released.

Children need also to discover differences in quality of movement. To begin with an activity that is familiar to them, the students may be asked to show with muscular movement how strong they are. This will bring forth a great show of flexing of the upper arm muscles and clenching of fists. This might be followed with a discussion of how a strong movement is achieved and with experimental attempts to achieve strong movements with other parts of the body. Contrast of strong with weak movements and rapid with slow movements offers other exploratory possibilities which help children to appreciate quality of movement.

Yet another facet of movement in a stationary position is movement at different levels. To give the class insight into the possibilities of this, the teacher may ask them how they would place themselves as close to the ground as possible. In response to this the children will lie down. The problem then becomes to find out how many different levels they can assume before they are standing upright. They will find they can squat, kneel, sit, and stoop. Other exploratory activities can be based upon the position of the body in these various levels.

Two possibilities using imagery are suggested because of the pleasure children find in performing them. The first is the spinning top. The class is asked: Can you spin like a top? Can you spin high? (standing) Spin low? (squatting) Can you spin from high to low and low to high? These activities might be followed by a discussion of how a top is constructed. It should be noted that a top's base is smaller than its upper part. The children may then try spinning with a wide base (feet spread) and with a narrow base (feet together). They will discover that it is more difficult to spin rapidly and smoothly with a wide base. The other possibility for an interesting exercise in movement at different levels is the corkscrew. Questions which might be asked to bring forth the motor response are: How does a corkscrew work? What happens when the cork is pulled out? Can you be the corkscrew being twisted into the cork? Can you be the cork when it comes out of the bottle?

EXPLORING LOCOMOTION

Locomotion is movement from place to place; the elementary skills of locomotion include rolling, crawling, walking, jumping, running, and variations of these. Children of school age, even those in kindergarten, have acquired these skills to some degree. Some children, particularly among the older age groups, will have done considerable experimentation with other means of locomotion and will thereby have acquired skills in hopping, skipping, leaping, and galloping, among others. The objective of the unit in exploration of locomotion is to encourage children to discover new ways of moving through space and to develop an understanding of the nature of locomotion—how the various forms are similar and different.

Attention can be focused on the variety of forms of locomotion by suggesting to the children that they move about the play area in the gait of several animals; the elephant, giraffe, rabbit, and turtle are only a few of the possibilities. The children will respond to this activity in different ways depending upon their past experiences with animals and with motor movement. However, the elements of slowness and deliberateness of movement will characterize the elephant's walk in most instances; and in portraying the giraffe, the children will walk on their tip toes and reach high into the air with their arms. For the rabbit

Figure 6–2 Children should be given opportunities to discover new ways of moving through space. (National Education Association.)

they will hop or jump about the room, and as turtles, they will move about very slowly.

In discussing this activity with the youngsters, the teacher should help them to understand that they have used variation in the size of steps and variations in the height of the steps. Size of the step and its relationship to speed of locomotion could well become the next problem to be explored by the class. Giant, medium, and tiny steps can be tried at slow and fast paces and the differences and likenesses compared. When the teacher is satisfied that the students have sufficient insight into this problem, variation in height of steps can be added to the exploratory exercise. Skipping, hopping, and galloping steps can be compared for the heights to which the feet are lifted. Further exploration may be encouraged by asking the youngsters if they can move by kicking their feet into the air above their waists, above their heads, and to the rear. Can they lift their knees high as they run? Can they lift both knees at once? The students may not realize until they try this that what they are really doing is hopping with both feet. Can they lift one knee while hopping on the opposite foot? This, of course, becomes skipping.

Locomotion need not always be forward, and children should be encouraged to explore the possible directions in which movement may be made: forward, backward, to either side, and diagonally at various degrees in between. Any of the various previously discovered speeds and heights of steps may be attempted in any of the directions. Another possibility is discovering the direction in which a specific kind of step, such as skipping, can be used most successfully.

Quality of movement in locomotion should also be explored. Such a lesson may begin by asking the children to make strong, slow movements. The imagery of a heavily loaded freight train or a big bulldozer might be used if needed to stimulate them. To point up the contrast in quality, the movement is changed to light and slow. Children may be snowflakes or gentle spring breezes. Both of these movements were slow; can the children now be swift and heavy and fast and light? For further contrast in movement quality, the children may run like rag dolls and like iron men. The difference in the quality of movement should be discussed, with the children being urged to describe how they felt and how they looked. If they are ever at a loss for words to explain themselves, they should be encouraged to demonstrate with movements as this will further promote movement exploration.

Direction in movement may be introduced by asking the children to move in a straight line to the wall and then come back in a line that is not straight. Some will return in a zig-zag pattern or a semicircle or half rectangle. The discussion might center around what objects and creatures move in a straight line and which do not. Among the things moving in a straight line the children will probably mention an arrow. The teacher may show that an arrow does travel in a straight line but gradually comes down to earth. The children can be "arrows" showing how the arrow loses altitude as it travels and at the end of its flight lands on the ground.

The class will know that an arrow will not stop until it hits something or comes down to the ground, but other things that are moving may stop. A mouse, for example, stops and starts again. Can the children show how the mouse starts quickly and stops suddenly as it runs across the floor? Can they start and then, quickly, change direction? In doing this, the children will discover that it is difficult to change direction rapidly while running fast. As they continue to experiment with changing direction at fast, slow, and moderate speeds, they will find that they must slow down from a very fast speed in order to change the direction of movement easily and gracefully.

COMMUNICATION THROUGH MOTOR MOVEMENT

In this phase of exploratory movement, youngsters learn the ways in which the body may be used to communicate emotions and ideas. The problems in exploration which are suggested below are designed to help children acquire a degree of skill in using their bodies as instruments of expression. They will serve also as a basis for creative dance and the dramatic arts.

To ensure that they have an understanding of the nature of emotional behavior and the ways in which it is expressed, the students may discuss the different kinds of feeling one may have: fear, hate, sadness, surprise, joy, and so on. They may then examine situations in which these emotions are expressed and analyze the facial expressions and body postures which are identified with each.

With these ideas in mind, the children may begin to explore the expression of emotions in body movement. Children who are less imaginative may tend to copy what they observe others doing and need to be encouraged to express their own concepts. One successful way of doing this is to divide the class into groups of two. One child is to express in motor movement some emotion that he feels. His partner is to express the emotion which is the opposite of it. For instance, if the first child demonstrated happiness, the other child is to show sadness in his movements. If necessary, until they develop some degree of skill in such communication, they may tell each other about the mood being portrayed. The children become enthusiastic about working with a partner, and this provides strong motivation for originality in creative movement.

A simple problem in communication of an idea may be developed around the locomotion skills. For example, the students may attempt to express the nature of something they are walking on or in. They might choose walking on a rail or on an icy sidewalk or in deep snow or sticky mud. Their problem is to communicate where they are walking by means of their steps and body postures.

A possibility for group activity is the description of the weather. Each group selects a weather condition such as gentle rain, snow storm, hurricane, or sunny and hot. The groups may be given a few moments to make their selection and to discuss how they will interpret it through movement. As each group moves through its description of the weather, those who are watching may discuss why the movements depict a certain kind of weather.

As the children gain experience with this type of group communication, they may be encouraged to work out more complex ideas. Depending upon the age and experiences of the children, these might include such things as a visit to the zoo, watching a baseball game, a ride in a Ferris wheel. The children should, of course, be guided toward thinking up their own ideas for these exercises in communication. Not all the work should be in groups; individual performances are desirable whenever the teacher feels that the students in the class have progressed to the point where they have lost their self-consciousness sufficiently to enjoy and profit fom performing alone.

EXPLORING RELAXATION

Muscular relaxation is another motor exploratory activity which should receive attention in the physical education program. There is a certain amount of automatic learning of muscular relaxation in the process of doing any of the other exploratory activities because the antagonistic muscles are in controlled relaxation while the opposing muscles are contracting. However, actual work on discovering how to relax the muscles is important because it promotes further control over the body, making it possible to contract and relax the muscles when one wishes.

To help the children discover the relationship of muscular contraction and muscular relaxation to movement, they may be asked to make the arm like an iron bar. They will, of course, contract the muscles. Then they are asked to change it to a limp piece of rope to which they will respond by relaxing the arm muscles completely. They should feel this arm in both instances with the hand of the opposite arm. The difference in what they feel should be discussed with them, for recognition of this difference is important for later work in relaxation. Establishing the meaning of the two terms, relaxation and contraction, is necessary also to ensure that they will be understood when used in future activities.

The next problem posed to the class might be why the arm does not always move when the muscles are contracting. If they cannot find out for themselves, the teacher may help them by showing them that, when both muscles on each side of the elbow are pulling the same amount at the same time, the arm does not move. The children will find that they are able to make the muscles fight each other and that, when one pulls less than the other, the arm will move toward the muscle that is pulling harder.

The teacher may have the children contract and loosen the muscles of the arm several times, each time making the muscle tighter and looser than the time before. The same process may be used for other parts of the body—the legs, the neck, the stomach muscles. When the "feel" of these various sets of muscles in contraction and relaxation has been established, the children will enjoy contracting one part of the body while relaxing another part. For example, they may walk about with the legs in rigid contraction and the arms hanging completely relaxed; or one arm may be contracted while the other is relaxed. They should be encouraged to try the other possibilities that will occur to them. However, children may find it difficult to do this until they have had a good deal of practice at it.

Other activities which use contraction and relaxation and are greatly enjoyed by the children can be based on the idea of the blown up balloon which is punctured and collapses or the breakdown of the mechanical man.

EXPLORING THE MANIPULATION OF OBJECTS

Having discovered movements that can be made with the body, children are ready to explore the possibilities for using the body to manipulate objects. The ball is perhaps the commonest play object in physical education experiences so it will be used to suggest ways in which movement exploration in the manipulation of objects may be approached by the teacher.

Exploration of movement possibilities with a ball may begin with the children in a fixed position. First, their problem is to discover how many things they can do with the ball while maintaining a grip on it with both hands. This may be followed by the use of only one hand. The children will find that they can hold the ball above the head, to either side, to the back, to the front, between the legs, etc., although success with two hands is greater than with one hand. Finally they may experiment with the ball leaving their hands, which will result in various kinds of throwing and catching, bouncing on the floor and against the wall, and with the more skilled, in forms of juggling.

Movement with the ball is the next problem. To initiate it, the possibilities of locomotion discovered earlier may be reviewed. Because the usual space limitations will make it impractical for the children to attempt many different means of locomotion at the same time, the children might be asked to select one or two of these to explore with the use of the ball. Among the movements the children will combine with ball handling are walking, jumping, skipping, and hopping. With older children the natural progression is to dribbling and kicking the ball.

Children who have considerable skill in handling the ball will enjoy experimenting with the creation of patterns of movements using the ball. They may begin with a simple pattern such as bouncing the ball a certain number of times with each hand and passing it under each leg without breaking the rhythm of the bounce. More complex patterns can be developed using other parts of the body, such as the elbow or chest, to bounce the ball. The possibilities are limited only by the skill and creativeness of the youngster.

Striking an object with a bat, cue, or stick is a manipulative skill that is a dominant feature of many games. Exploration of the striking movement is important to the young child because it enables him to discover the possibilities of hitting one object with another object.

The exploration may begin by striking a ball on the ground with a strong stick 3 or 4 feet in length to see how many different ways the ball can be hit with the stick. The problem should be worded in such a way that the children's first attempts will be gentle rather than vigorous to avoid the necessity of chasing the ball a long distance to retrieve it. Later, striking with increased force and speed as well as with a variety of striking implements may be explored. Various sizes of balls may be used as may other objects, e.g., a puck.

For older children, exploration in manipulation of an object can include striking a ball in the air. Initially, the ball may be attached to a cord suspended from the ceiling. Later, the ball is tossed to the child; balls of different sizes may be used.

PLAY EQUIPMENT EXPLORATION

Some pieces of playground equipment offer wonderful opportunities for movement exploration; and, because children seldom show reluctance to use these in their play, they have the advantage of needing no planned program of motivation. Equipment which encourages experimentation and exploration of the play possibilities includes ladders and other climbing apparatus, swinging and stationary bars, climbing ropes, balance beams, and obstacles to climb over, under, and through. Swings, teeter-totters, and slides, while greatly enjoyed by youngsters, offer little in the way of exploration because of the rigid nature of their design. Moreover, safe use of these pieces of equipment demands strict adherence to safety regulations which eliminates trying new ways to use the equipment. Free form types of equipment are particularly suited to imaginative and exploratory play. Their modernistic design combines in artistic form such familiar equipment as ladders, bars, tunnels, steps, and platforms, which encourages a variety of motor movements in new and unusual combinations.

Before children use any type of playground equipment, they should be taught how to use it safely. This instruction needs to be explicit without discouraging exploration. Daring children particularly will need to be shown the dangers inherent in their actions. On the other hand, timid and overly cautious

Figure 6–3 Free form playground equipment offers wonderful opportunities for movement exploration. (Recreation Magazine.)

children may need direct encouragement from the teacher to expand their use of the equipment. All children should understand the limitations of strength and skill in relation to their aspirations.

TEACHING HINTS

The approach to introducing movement exploratory activities must be determined by the maturity and background of the youngsters. The characteristic behavior of children discussed in Chapter 2 will give the teacher an indication of what kind of response the youngsters may make.

Resistance to participation at any age may have its roots in fears arising from inadequacies in skill performance; these pupils believe they do not have the ability to do the required movements. Other students will be fearful of the responses of others to their attempts in movement exploration. Still others will be disheartened by the strangeness of the activity when it is first presented.

In coping with these fears, the teacher must work to build confidence in the ability to do the movements successfully. Toward this end, trying to do the activity is emphasized over refining the quality of the movement. Students who are fearful for whatever reason must be brought along gradually so there will be no danger of undermining with failures any budding self-confidence. Praise should be given generously for honest effort. However, the attention of the class should not be focused on the performance of these children until they are doing well enough to enjoy being praised in front of the others. There are always a few students who will be obnoxiously boastful and overconfident about their performances. The teacher must recognize that in some cases this kind of behavior masks a feeling of inadequacy and that these students need the same kind of direction and encouragement as the shy, fearful ones.

Demonstration of the skill should be used sparingly. Showing children how to perform tends to destroy the spontaneity of the response. Movement exploration must be inner-directed if it is to succeed in its objectives. The student must explore rather than imitate. The teacher may chart the course, but the explorers must make their own trails, as it were.

In charting the course, the teacher supplies a problem to be explored, e.g., the ways in which the body can be moved without using the feet. The students are then encouraged to experiment with their bodies in order to solve the proposed problem. The encouragement may take the form of questions, the answers to which will suggest possibilities of movements. The less imaginative and more inhibited may need further encouragement and suggestions from the teacher. It is sometimes effective to hold a discussion with the children about the possible ways in which the body might be moved to solve the particular problem before any of them attempt the exploration. Such a discussion helps stimulate the imagination of the less fanciful students. It is good fun, too, for the students to try out all the suggested possibilities and to discover how impossibly ridiculous some of them are.

In instances in which the children have difficulty with a problem, the teacher may employ imagery, that is, it may be suggested to the pupils that they hop like a rabbit, spin like a top, use their arms like the wings of an airplane. (Other suggestions to encourage exploration of specific movements

TABLE 6–1   Mental Images to Encourage Motor Exploration

BODY MOVEMENT	IMAGERY
Balancing	Be a tightrope walker, a cat on a fence (use balance beams, old tires, boxes).
Bending	Be a rag doll, a loose rope.
Bouncing	Be a bouncing ball, Mexican jumping bean, corn in the popper.
Crawling	Be a snake, a worm, a caterpillar.
Galloping	Be a pony, a wild horse, a trained circus pony.
Hopping	Be a rabbit, a frog, a kangaroo.
Jumping	Be "Jack be nimble," "the cow that jumped over the moon."
Skipping	Be a pebble "skipping" across the water.
Stretching	Be a windmill, a giraffe, reach for a star.
Rocking	Be a rocking chair, a tree in a storm, a boat rocked by big waves.

common to young children are given in Table 6–1.) Imagery is very helpful in prompting certain movement responses in children because it gives them something familiar and concrete to work toward. The use of imagery should not be overworked, however, because it does have a certain inhibiting influence upon movement. This arises from the fact that when a child moves according to a preconceived pattern, as he will do when imagining that he is hopping like a rabbit, he is less free in his movements than if he were inspired to hop without the use of the image.

Movement exploration need not be confined to presentation as a unit in the physical education program. It can be incorporated into other units of instruction on the skills of specific games, sports, and dance activities, regardless of the teaching method employed. For example, in a unit on basketball taught by the indirect method, the problem of how to dribble while standing stationary, outlined on page 104, may be expanded to include questions that encourage exploration of ways of dribbling the ball other than using the hands. Questions for this purpose might be phrased in this way: Can you dribble the ball without the use of your hand? Can you dribble the ball without moving the arm? Such questions help students to discover the capacity of the body to move in the performance of specific skills, whereas the questions relating to dribbling while stationary are designed to lead the students to resolving the most effective ways to accomplish this particular skill. If the skills of dribbling are, instead, being taught by the direct method, a portion of the time allotted to drilling may be devoted to exploration of other possible ways of dribbling than the one being drilled. This not only offers variety in the class activities but gives students an opportunity to make comparisons and draw conclusions about the best method of dribbling for themselves.

SUPPLEMENTARY READINGS

Barlin, Ann, and Barlin, Paul: *The Art of Learning Through Movement.* Los Angles, Ward Ritche Press, 1971.

Deim, Liselott: *Who Can* (English text). Frankfort, Germany, Wilhelm Limpert Publishing House, 1967.

Gates, Alice A.: *A New Look at Movement—A Dancer's View*. Minneapolis, Burgess Publishing Co., 1968.

Hackett, Layne C., and Jenson, Robert G.: *A Guide to Movement Exploration*. Revised. Palo Alto, California, Peek Publications, 1967.

Halsey, Elizabeth, and Porter, Lorena: *Physical Education for Children*. New York, Holt, Rinehart and Winston, 1970.

Latchaw, M.: *A Pocket Guide of Movement Activities for the Elementary School*. Englewood Cliffs, New Jersey, Prentice-Hall, Inc., 1970.

Mosston, Muska: *Developmental Movement*. Columbus, Ohio, Charles E. Merrill Publishing Co., 1965.

Sweeney, R.: *Selected Readings in Movement Education*. Reading, Massachusetts, Addison-Wesley Publishing Co., 1970.

chapter seven

physical fitness

THE NATURE OF PHYSICAL FITNESS
IDENTIFYING THE UNDERDEVELOPED
PHYSICAL FITNESS TESTING
PROVIDING A PROGRAM OF FITNESS ACTIVITIES

Physical fitness refers to the ability of the body to do its work as efficiently as possible. To do this a state of general well-being and a capacity for vigorous work must be present. Any teacher, professionally trained in physical education or not, who is in any way involved with the physical education instruction needs to have a thorough understanding of the nature of fitness and how it may be achieved. Improved physical fitness will come about only as the result of careful planning and selection of activities based on the knowledge of how exercise affects the body.

THE NATURE OF PHYSICAL FITNESS

The level of physical fitness of the body is determined by the development of each of several different components. Until recently, the chief components were identified as coordination, balance, speed, muscular strength, flexibility, and cardiorespiratory and muscular endurance. Because some of these are more closely related to physiological capacity and others are more closely associated with neurological aspects or skill mastery, physical educators have found it desirable to classify them separately into physical fitness and motor fitness components. Hence, such qualities as muscular strength, flexibility, and cardiorespiratory and muscular endurance fall into the classification of physical fitness, and qualities such as coordination, balance, and speed are classified as motor fitness components.*

Let us examine each of the four physical components of fitness to better understand the nature of each and how it is influenced by exercise.

STRENGTH. Muscular strength is the amount of force which can be exerted by a particular muscle when it is contracted. The strength of a muscle is dependent upon its size and quality. Maturation, the number of muscle fibers present, nutrition, and exercise all affect the size of the muscle. As a youngster passes from childhood to adulthood, the muscle increases in size as a result of growth. The number of muscle fibers is inherited; only the size and quality change during the years. Optimum changes in the muscles take place during the maturation period if they receive the proper amount of exercise and nourishment.

Strength is specific to various muscles or sets of muscles. Nevertheless, a relationship among the strengths of sets of muscles exists. This does not, however, preclude the possibility of an individual having several strong muscle sets and also several that are relatively weak.

ENDURANCE. There are two types of endurance, cardiorespiratory and muscular. Muscular endurance refers to the ability of the muscle to continue contracting over a period of time or to sustain a contraction. It is, therefore, measured by the number of repetitions of the movement completed or by the amount of time the contraction is held. The number of contractions or the duration of the contraction is dependent upon cardiorespiratory endurance, or the ability of the cells of the muscle to get and use oxygen and to rid the muscle of waste products. Muscular strength and muscular endurance are not totally independent qualities; nevertheless, one can possess exceptional muscular endurance without exhibiting extraordinary strength. However, all things being equal, the stronger muscle has the greater amount of endurance.[1]

FLEXIBILITY. Flexibility is the range of movement possible in the joint. Range is determined first by bone structure; for example, the hyper-extension of the joint of the elbow is limited by the particular way the bones there are constructed. Other limiting factors are the ligaments and muscles which support the joints. Ligaments are stabilizers which are not affected by exercise. Muscles, however, can be stretched through exercise to increase flexibility. Inability to reach down and touch the toes without bending the knees is generally caused by the lack of stretching capacity in the hamstring muscles of the legs.

Development of Physical Fitness

The general concept on which scientific physical fitness conditioning programs are based is the principle of Specific Adaptation to Imposed Demands

---

*It is difficult to draw a distinct line between the two sets of components since the neurological and physiological aspects of the body are so closely interrelated as to be indistinguishable in many instances.

Figure 7-1 Dance activity helps to increase flexibility. (Courtesy of Ox Ridge Elementary School, Darien, Connecticut.)

(SAID).[2] The principle states that the body adapts rather specifically to the demands which are imposed upon it. For example, if the strength of a particular muscle group is to be increased, it must contract with a force greater than normal. The muscles adapt to the greater demand by becoming larger and stronger. The SAID principle also applies in a reverse situation as in the reduction of the normal load by decreasing the amount of the workload. The muscles adapt to the new level of demand by atrophying and becoming weaker.

All components of physical fitness respond in a like manner. In the above example, the body specifically adapted to the strength demand; it changed little in flexibility or cardiorespiratory endurance. To increase flexibility, stress must be specifically applied to cause the body to work through a greater range of motion; to increase cardiorespiratory endurance, the workload must be increased to place a greater than usual demand upon lungs, heart, and vascular system. The development of one component is rather specific and does not, in most cases, automatically or appreciably aid the development of others. (An exception is strength, which, as indicated previously, is related to muscular endurance to some degree.)

RECOMMENDATIONS

The President's Council on Youth Fitness and Sports[3] has recommended that: "All children in grades K–12 should be required to participate in daily programs of physical education emphasizing the development of physical fitness. . . ." To accomplish this, the Council recommends that the physical ed-

Figure 7–2 Muscles adapt to greater demand by increasing in size and strength. (Journal of Health · Physical Education · Recreation.)

ucation program "... should include a core of developmental and conditioning activities appropriate for each grade level." It is further recommended that the physically undeveloped pupils should be identified by using valid fitness tests.

IDENTIFYING THE UNDERDEVELOPED

There are several ways in which children who are physically underdeveloped may be identified. The periodic health examination, required of elementary school children by most states, will reveal conditions of physical underdevelopment caused by diseases and physical disabilities. Most of these children will require special physical education programs of exercise especially designed to meet their individual needs; such programs are fully discussed in Chapter 17. Lack of physical fitness development in children not identified by the health examination must be determined by observation of the children during participation in physical activity and by the use of valid fitness tests of the components described earlier in the chapter.

The teacher has an excellent opportunity to observe the quality of the physical performance while teaching the physical education class. He should watch for those who fatigue easily; telltale signs will be a flushed face and labored breathing. Of course, some knowledge of the capacity for work output is needed before deciding if such signs of fatigue are actually an indication of subnormal endurance or if they merely indicate a greater expenditure of effort and energy than usual. Other signs indicative of a lack of proper physical fitness development observable in physical performance are insufficient strength and limited flexibility. Because some students mask their physical inadequacies by withdrawal and reluctance to participate in the class activities, such behavior should also be regarded as a possible indicator of low fitness.

The instructor should be aware that there are other factors besides that of lack of proper exercise that contribute to subnormal fitness. In the analysis of the possible cause of low fitness, consideration must be given to physical defects or disorders, faulty nutrition, poor health practices such as insufficient rest and sleep, inherited factors which influence the development of physical efficiency, and psychological weaknesses such as the lack of ability or desire for optimum performance from the muscles. If low physical fitness is attributable to any of these, the cause must first be remedied before an activity program designed to raise the level of fitness can be successful.

Fitness tests for children in grades above the fourth grade can help to determine those who have low fitness as well as isolate the factors in which they are especially in need of improvement. Tests for this purpose are the same as those used for evaluating the progress of pupils in achieving physical fitness, which are described below.

With the possible exception of the Recovery Index Test, a low score in physical fitness tests does not mean that a child is unhealthy, nor does a high score indicate freedom from health problems. A low score does give an indication of lack of physical fitness; and in a large percentage of cases, this can be improved by proper exercise and activity.

PHYSICAL FITNESS TESTING

To determine if any objective is being achieved it is necessary to evaluate. To measure success in attaining the objective of improved physical fitness, certain tests of the various components of physical fitness are given. The results of testing these factors of fitness have demonstrated a high relationship to total body fitness. These tests, when given before work to improve physical fitness begins, also identify those students who have low fitness and furnish a statistical basis for determining the amount of improvement made by the students over a period of time.

PHYSICAL FITNESS TESTS

There are numerous physical fitness tests for elementary school children. Two most commonly used batteries are the Kraus-Weber Test and the Youth Fitness Test of the American Alliance for Health, Physical Education and Recreation. Others have been developed by certain states and by several organizations concerned with health and physical fitness; most have established norms.

The large majority of test batteries do not include tests for use with children below fifth grade because of the inability of younger children to maintain interest in the testing and to exert maximum effort. However, if an evaluation is greatly desired, a suitable battery could be composed from a combination of three items of the Youth Fitness Test, the sit-up, standing broad jump, a dash of 30 yards instead of 50 yards, and the Recovery Index Test. (Table 7–1 presents standards for judging the performance in these events of children in grades one through four.)

Recovery Index Test[4]

The recovery index test attempts to measure the cardiorespiratory resources of the individual. The final score obtained from the test is a rough indicator of the efficiency of these resources.

For giving the test, a sturdy platform or box 14 inches high is required. To start the test, the child steps with either foot onto the box at the command "one." At the command "two" he steps up with the other foot. He steps down with the first foot and then with the other foot at the commands of "three" and "four." The cadence of the count should be such that the steps up and the steps down are done in two seconds. The test continues for 4 minutes after which the student stops, sits down, and rests. One minute later, his pulse rate is taken for 30 seconds. Two minutes later it is taken again for 30 seconds. It is taken the third time 3 minutes after the second measurement, again for 30 seconds. The three pulse rates are added for a total score. The result can be compared to pulse count totals in Table 7–2 for interpretation. Anyone scoring "poor" should be referred to his physician.

Kraus-Weber Test

The Kraus-Weber battery tests the strength of the muscles of the hip flexors and back extensors, the elasticity of the muscles of the hamstrings of the legs, and/or the flexibility of the spinal column.

Strength of Abdominal Muscles and Hip Flexors. The subject is supine with the hands behind the neck and his feet held down by another person. He

TABLE 7–1   Evaluation of Fitness Test Scores (Ages 6 to 9)

AGE	POOR	AVERAGE	GOOD
Sit-up			
Girls 6	2	4	6
Boys 6	2	4	6
Girls 7	3	5	7
Boys 7	3	5	7
Girls 8	5	8	10
Boys 8	6	9	11
Girls 9	9	15	25
Boys 9	14	20	30
Standing Broad Jump (feet and inches)			
Girls 6	2'10"	3'5"	4'0"
Boys 6	2'10"	3'5"	4'0"
Girls 7	3'0"	3'7"	4'2"
Boys 7	3'4"	3'9"	4'4"
Girls 8	3'6"	4'0"	4'7"
Boys 8	3'7"	4'2"	4'10"
Girls 9	3'8"	4'3"	4'8"
Boys 9	4'0"	4'5"	5'0"
30-Yard Dash (seconds)			
Girls 6	10.0	9.5	9.3
Boys 6	10.0	9.5	9.3
Girls 7	8.8	8.6	8.4
Boys 7	8.7	8.5	8.3
Girls 8	7.7	7.4	7.1
Boys 8	7.2	6.8	6.5
Girls 9	7.0	6.7	6.4
Boys 9	6.8	6.4	6.1

attempts to roll into a sitting position, keeping his hands behind his neck. He must not perform a stiff back sit-up.

Strength of Abdominal Muscles with Minimum of Hip Flexors. The subject takes the same position as above but with the knees bent. He rolls to a sitting position as in the first test.

Strength of Hip Flexors with Minimum of Abdominals. The subject assumes a supine position with the hands behind the neck and the legs extended.

TABLE 7–2   Evaluation of Recovery Index Test Scores

TOTAL OF THE THREE 30-SECOND PULSE COUNTS	
199 or more	Poor
from 171 to 199	Fair
from 150 to 170	Good
from 133 to 149	Very Good
132 or less	Excellent

He lifts the legs 10 inches off the floor and holds for 10 seconds. The knees are straight.

Strength of Extensor Muscles of the Back. The subject is prone with a pillow placed under his hips so that it becomes a fulcrum for the body. With the hands behind the neck, the subject raises his chest, head, and shoulders and holds for 10 seconds. The feet are held down by another person.

Strength of Extensor Muscles of the Back. The subject takes the same position as for the above test except that his hands are placed so that the head can rest on them. In this test the subject's chest is held down and he raises his legs without bending them and holds the position for 10 seconds.

Elasticity of Hamstrings or Flexibility of Spinal Column. The subject removes his shoes and stands erect with his hands at the sides. With the feet together and the knees straight, he bends down slowly to touch the floor with his fingertips. The position is held for the count of three. Bending at the knees or crouching to reach the floor is not permitted.

There has been some misinterpretation of the Kraus-Weber Test as a physical fitness test. The total battery roughly evaluates the strength of certain muscles and the flexibility in one area by dividing the subjects into categories of pass or fail. The battery should not be interpreted as a measurement of total body fitness, because only the strength of the flexors and extensors of the back and the flexibility of the back and elasticity of the hamstrings are measured; furthermore, the test has limitations in discriminating levels of fitness since the score is either pass or fail.

Youth Fitness Test

The Youth Fitness Test consists of six items:

1. Pull-up for boys and flexed arm hang for girls to measure muscular endurance of the shoulder girdle.
2. Sit-ups to measure muscular endurance of the abdominal muscles and flexors of the trunk.
3. Shuttle run to measure agility.*
4. Standing broad jump to measure power of the legs, power being a combination of speed and strength.
5. 50-yard dash to measure the speed of running.**
6. 600-yard run-walk to measure cardiorespiratory endurance.

Pull-up (Boys). The subject takes an overhand grip on the bar, raises the body until the chin can be placed over the bar, and lowers the body to full arm extension.

Flexed-Arm Hang (Girls). The bar is placed at a position equal to the subject's standing height. An overhand grip is taken. The subject raises her body to a position of chin above the bar, elbows flexed, and chest close to the bar.

---

*Agility is closely related to coordination, and in this text it is considered as a motor fitness factor rather than one of physical fitness.
**Speed of running is related to the power of the legs.

Figure 7-3 An overhand grip is taken on the bar to execute the pull-up. (Courtesy of Ox Ridge Elementary School, Darien, Connecticut.)

Figure 7-4 Students may need to be instructed in the proper techniques of the standing broad jump. (Courtesy of Town of Vernon Schools, Rockville, Connecticut.)

Two spotters, one in front and one in back, may offer assistance. The subject holds the position as long as possible.

Sit-ups. The supine position is taken with the hands clasped behind the head, elbows on the floor. The knees are bent and the feet are placed 12 inches from the buttocks. The feet are held down. The subject rolls up to touch the elbows to the knees, and then returns to the original position.

Shuttle Run. At a signal the subject runs from the starting line to pick up one of two blocks which are behind another line 30 feet away. He carries the block back, sets it down behind the first line, and repeats with the second block.

Standing Broad Jump. With the feet together the subject jumps forward as far as possible. Three trials are allowed.

50-Yard Dash. The subject runs the dash as fast as possible.

600-Yard Run-Walk. The subject attempts to cover the distance in the fastest time possible; he is permitted to walk if necessary.

If the physical education program includes running as an integral activity, two optional tests are available: the 1-mile or 9-minute run for children 10 through 12 years of age and the 1½-mile or 12-minute run for those 13 years old.

The scores in Table 7–3 may be used as a rough measurement of poor, average, and good performances in the fitness tests by boys and girls of various ages. The scores are based on norms established by the American Alliance for Health, Physical Education and Recreation.*

ADMINISTRATION OF THE TESTS

Physical fitness tests should be given periodically during the year to establish a reliable indication of the progress being made and to point up where greater effort is needed to effect improvement. Those who have scored very low should be tested more frequently.

In administering the tests, procedures must be developed to ensure that the greatest number of students can be tested with the greatest accuracy. In small classes, the teacher is able to do the testing personally and so ensure the consistency in administering the tests and accuracy in recording the scores which are essential to good testing. But with large numbers of students in the classes, the difficulties of administering the tests as well as the amount of time required make other procedures necessary.

One such procedure is to set up several testing stations within the gymnasium or play area so that several tests may be given simultaneously with the students rotating from station to station until all tests in the battery have been completed. The use of student helpers is necessary to give the test and record the scores at each testing station. Consequently, this procedure is restricted to use with older children. The helpers should receive thorough instruction from

---

*Tables of percentile scores for each test in the battery are given in the *AAHPER Youth Fitness Test Manual,* available from the American Alliance for Health, Physical Education and Recreation, 1201 16th St. N.W., Washington, D.C. 20036.

TABLE 7-3 Evaluation of Fitness Test Scores (Ages 10 to 13)

	AGE	POOR		AVERAGE	GOOD		
Flexed-Arm Hang							
Girls	10–11	3		7	15		
Girls	12–13	2		6	13		
Pull-ups for Boys							
Boys	10–11	0		1	4		
Boys	12–13	0		1	5		
Sit-ups							
Girls	10–11	15		22	29		
Boys	10–11	25		43	68		
Girls	12–13	22		30	36		
Boys	12–13	34		55	96		
Shuttle Run (Seconds)							
Girls	10–11	12.5		11.8	11.0		
Boys	10–11	12.4		11.2	10.6		
Girls	12–13	12.2		11.5	10.9		
Boys	12–13	11.4		10.8	10.2		
Standing Broad Jump (Feet and Inches)							
Girls	10–11	4'3"		4'8"	5'2"		
Boys	10–11	4'7"		5'1"	5'6"		
Girls	12–13	4'5"		5'0"	5'6"		
Boys	12–13	5'2"		5'8"	6'2"		
50-Yard Dash (Seconds)							
Girls	10–11	9.0		8.5	7.9		
Boys	10–11	8.7		8.1	7.6		
Girls	12–13	8.9		8.2	7.8		
Boys	12–13	8.2		7.7	7.2		
600-Yard Run-Walk (Minutes and Seconds)							
Girls	10–11	3'11"		2'48"	2'31"		
Boys	10–11	2'46"		2'30"	2'16"		
Girls	12–13	3'13"		2'50"	2'32"		
Boys	12–13	2'33		2'17"	2'4"		

9-Minute/1-Mile Run

		Yards in 9 Minutes			Minutes for 1½ Miles		
Girls	10–11	1337	1525	1713	11:30	10:15	9:31
Boys	10–11	1516	1748	1983	10:14	9:01	7:38
Girls	12	1372	1560	1704	10:37	9:24	8:11
Boys	12	1606	1841	2078	9:39	8:21	7:03

12-Minute/1½-Mile Run

		Yards in 12 Minutes			Minutes for 1½ Miles		
Girls	13	1622	1861	2100	18:50	16:57	15:03
Boys	13	2305	2592	2879	12:39	11:29	10:19

the teacher in the techniques of the test with the importance of accuracy being stressed.

With classes of younger children, or in other situations where the use of student helpers is unsatisfactory, the teacher may use the procedure of giving the same test to several students at the same time. For the pull-up test, the number of students who can be accommodated on the bar at one time can be tested together. Other students may be assigned to stand behind those who are pulling up to remove the bench, if one is used, and also to assist the teacher in counting the number of pull-ups each student does. The sit-up test may be administered to the entire class at once by having the children form into pairs with one of each pair holding down the legs of the other and counting the number of successful sit-ups, which the teacher records.

To reduce the time consumed when recording scores in the longer running events, the teacher may call out the times as the runners cross the finish line to be recorded by an assistant. The runners are instructed to stay in a line in the order in which they finished after they cross the finish line. Their names can then be matched with their times. For the 9- and 12-minute runs the track can be marked at 50-yard intervals. Measurement of the distance run can then be easily and rapidly calculated by adding the number of markers the runner passed plus the distance from the last marker to the point he reached at the end of the allotted time.

PROVIDING A PROGRAM OF FITNESS ACTIVITIES

The activeness of children often creates a deceptive impression that they are receiving plenty of exercise to ensure the development of a high level of physical fitness. However, when one considers the different factors that make up physical fitness and the fact that different exercises contribute to the accomplishment of different phases of fitness to different degrees, it can be readily understood that the unplanned play program of children may not produce general physical fitness. This highly desired goal can be attained successfully only through a well planned program of physical education.

In the opinion of most physical educators, a daily period of 15 minutes of strenuous activity is the minimum that should be provided for effecting changes in physical fitness. It is generally agreed that a daily physical education period of 30 minutes exclusive of time spent dressing, etc., is highly desirable. This would permit at least 15 minutes of strenuous activity plus an additional 15 minutes for learning the skills of games and activities that will be played in after-school hours and in the years beyond school, thereby establishing a basis for continuing vigorous play throughout life.

SELECTING THE ACTIVITIES

The selection of activities to be taught in that portion of the program which is to be devoted to skill instruction should be determined largely by the needs and interests of the children of the particular grade. If the selection is sufficiently varied so that many different sets of muscles are used in the execution of the skills, a significant contribution to physical fitness may be expected from this part of the program even though its major objective is the learning of new skills and the improvement of formerly learned ones.

A wise selection of such activities must be based on a knowledge of the nature of the activities and the contributions of each to the physical development of children; these are discussed in other chapters. Our concern in this chapter is with the portion of the program which will present specific physical fitness developmental exercises and activities. The selection of these should be based upon the results of the physical fitness testing and identification of the deficiencies which exist in specific children and in the class as a whole. In anticipation of the test results in a given class, the teacher may think in terms of those physical fitness needs of elementary school children which have been demonstrated in the testing and observation of the general school population throughout the nation.

Strength

The strength of boys is comparable to that of girls until pubescence when boys begin to outdistance girls. Not only do the muscles of the male grow in size at a faster rate, but the quality of the muscles improves. The main factor in the difference in quality is believed to be caused by the increased activity of the gonads secreting the hormone testosterone. Among boys the increase in strength parallels an increase in height and weight during the pubescent growth spurt. Girls, after the pubescent period, tend to decrease in strength, attributed in part to a tendency to withdraw from strenuous activity.

Some children have developed muscular strength in some areas of the body while remaining relatively weak in other muscle areas. Noticeably weak areas in many boys and girls are the arms and shoulder girdle, the result of lack of participation in activities that would develop strength in these.

Suggested Activities for Developing Strength

PRIMARY GRADES
Race on Tip Toes
Jumping Jack (page 355)
Seal Race (page 349)
Crab Race (page 350)
Modified Push-up (from a kneeling position)
Hop Tag (page 182)
Bouncing Ball (page 351)
Chinese Back to Back (page 352)
Tug Pick-up (page 352)
Hanging and Climbing Activities
INTERMEDIATE AND UPPER GRADES (DUAL RESISTING EXERCISES AND COMBATIVES)

1. Two students face each other with arms at their sides and elbows bent. They place their palms against each other and push.

2. As above except the arms are fully extended.

3. Arms are completely extended in front; one student puts his palms against the back of the other and pushes forward while the other resists.

4. One student behind another interlocks his fingers around the forehead of the other and pulls slowly back while the other resists. This may be done to the front and to the sides, using the same techniques.

Figure 7–5 Dual resisting exercises develop muscular strength. (Courtesy of Ox Ridge Elementary School, Darien, Connecticut.)

   5. Partners face each other with their arms extended forward and upward. The fingers are interlocked and the hands are brought down, keeping the arms straight. The wrists are flexed in an attempt to force the opponent to superextend his wrist and come to his knees on the floor.

   6. Partners take a position on the knees so they can put right elbows on the mat with the forearms extended upward. Hands are grasped and an attempt is made to bring the other person's arm down in front of him until it touches the mat.

   7. Partners stand with the feet comfortably spread, each with the right foot forward in contact with the other's right foot. Right hands are grasped and an attempt is made to force the other person to move one foot or the other by pulling or pushing with the right arm while maintaining balance.

   8. Two students lie on their backs with the feet extended in opposite directions and the right arms linked at the elbows. At the count of three the inside leg is lifted and brought up until the heels are locked together. An attempt is made to bring the leg back down to force the opponent over in a forward roll.

   9. Partners stand one behind the other, facing the same direction. The one in front places his hands on the floor while the other lifts his legs at the knees. The first student walks forward on his hands with his partner holding his legs wheelbarrow fashion.

UPPER GRADES (WEIGHTLIFTING AND ISOMETRIC EXERCISES)

   Many junior high schools introduce weightlifting into the physical education program for boys and, in some instances, for girls as well. If weights are available for use, the activity can become a very satisfactory way of interesting students of this age in increasing strength. The two chief precautions which must be taken in presenting weightlifting are first, guarding against the participants' lifting too much weight before they have the necessary strength, and second, teaching the youngsters to lower the weights slowly, not drop them.

   Some use is also being made in the upper elementary grades of isometric exercises, which promote the development of strength through contraction of the muscles in pulling against an immobile object. Several kinds of isometric ropes and straps which attach permanently to the wall are currently available on the market at little cost. Many instructors look with favor on these devices because they make it virtually impossible to overload immature muscles.

Endurance

Elementary children because of their physical and emotional characteristics have a limited amount of endurance. In planning workloads, sufficient time must be allotted for recuperation. However, it should be the aim to provide a well balanced program of physical education that will increase muscular and cardiorespiratory endurance which promotes rapid recuperation from physcial fatigue and reduces the need for long and frequent intervals of rest.

Suggested Activities for Developing Endurance

PRIMARY GRADES
Midnight (page 177)
Bronco Relay (page 192)
Circle Relay (page 193)
Brownies and Fairies (page 181)
Cross Tag (page 189)
Line Relay (page 192)
Side Straddle Hop (page 356)
Running in Place
Tag
Rope Jumping

INTERMEDIATE AND UPPER GRADES
Circle Run (page 191)
Line Formation Volley (page 328)
Whirl-Away (page 215)
Baton Passing Relay (page 200)
Sprint and Long Distance Runs
Basketball (pages 302–304)
Soccer (pages 322–323)
Touch Football (page 334)

Flexibility

Children generally possess great flexibility. With each succeeding year of age, however, a certain amount of flexibility is lost unless they are subjected to specific activities that require a wide range of movement in many different parts of the body.

Suggested Activities for Developing Flexibility

PRIMARY GRADES
Eagle and Sparrows (page 181)
Wring the Dish Rag (page 352)
Inchworm (page 350)
Elephant Walk (page 352)
Ostrich Walk (page 349)
Bear Walk (page 349)
Chicken Walk (page 350)
Snake Crawl (page 349)
Forward Roll (page 364)
Touch Floor without Bending
  the Knees

INTERMEDIATE AND UPPER GRADES
Double Kazotski (page 359)
Stick Jump (page 359)
Heel Slap (page 360)
Single Leg Circle (page 360)
Front Swan (page 360)
Through the Stick (page 361)
Neckspring (page 366)
Headspring (page 367)
Forward Roll (page 364)
Backward Roll (page 365)
Sit-ups with Knees Straight

Power, Agility, and Speed

Although power, agility, and speed are not components of physical fitness as classified in this chapter, they are related to strength, which is a component of physical fitness, and are dependent in part upon the strength of the muscle involved. Activities that increase strength also increase power, agility, and speed (as it is measured in running).

Power has been called explosive strength[5] because it is the ability to achieve force at a specific moment. A release of force by the muscle involves both speed of contraction and strength of the muscle. Speed and strength must be combined to produce power. Fitness for such activities as throwing, jumping, and running requires power.

Agility has been defined as the ability to change the direction of the movement of the body, as a whole or in part. There is evidence to indicate that agility is a combination of other factors. Research[6] indicates that power (explosive strength) plays a significant role in the scores achieved in agility tests, especially those requiring rapid change of direction while running. It appears that the factor of agility can be increased not only by increasing the power of the muscle but also by developing the coordination of the muscle used in making a specific movement. Coordination of a muscle results from its use in activities in which the direction of movement is changed rapidly.

Speed of body movement depends upon speed of muscular contraction; the speed of contraction, in turn, depends upon the energy liberated during certain chemical reactions in the muscles. It is believed that the rate of the liberation of energy determines the speed of muscular contractions. The nature of the molecules of the muscle may also exert an influence; the ability of molecules to rearrange themselves when the muscle is shortened is postulated to be the factor involved. Not yet identified is the exact relationship of increase in the strength of the muscle to an increase in its speed of contraction. There is some evidence to indicate that as the strength of specific leg muscles is increased, speed of running is increased.

To increase power, agility, and speed children should be provided many opportunities to engage in a wide variety of activities that require speed, strength, and coordinated muscle movements. Children who are poorly coordinated have a tendency to withdraw from physical activity because they are so seldom successful. Consequently, many of them are underdeveloped in other aspects of fitness as well. So in addition to selecting activities that promote the development of coordination, the teacher can help the poorly coordinated child achieve a measure of success in physical activity by equalizing the competition so that he will not always fail. Young children have less speed than older children; overweight children have less than those of normal weight. A child who has stronger leg muscles can run faster than one whose muscles are weaker, all other things being equal. Therefore, in planning the fitness program for children who lack speed, consideration must be given to the age, weight, and muscular strength of the children.

Suggested Activities for Developing Power, Agility, and Speed

KINDERGARTEN AND PRIMARY GRADES

Spider and Flies (page 176)
Red Light (page 215)
Pussy Wants a Corner (page 213)
Cat and Mice (page 181)
Fire on the Mountain (page 216)
Squat Tag (page 175)
Circle Weave Relay (page 195)

INTERMEDIATE AND UPPER GRADES

Crows and Cranes (page 198)
Dodge Ball Games (pages 207–209)
Corner Goal Ball (page 300)
Captain Basketball (page 301)
Basketball (pages 302–304)
Touch Football (page 334)
Soccer (pages 322–323)
Sprints
Catch of Fish (page 218)
Object Race (page 214)

SUPPLEMENTARY READINGS

American Association for Health, Physical Education and Recreation: *Exercise and Fitness.* Washington, D.C., American Association for Health, Physical Education and Recreation, 1964.

American Alliance for Health, Physical Education and Recreation. *Youth Fitness Test Manual.* Revised. Washington, D.C., American Alliance for Health, Physical Education and Recreation, 1975.

American Association for Health, Physical Education and Recreation: *Your Child's Health and Fitness.* Washington, D.C., American Association for Health, Physical Education and Recreation. No date.

Fait, Hollis F.: *Special Physical Education: Adapted, Corrective, Developmental.* Ed. 2. Philadelphia, W. B. Saunders Co., 1972.

Fleishman, Edwin A.: *The Structure and Measurement of Physical Fitness.* Englewood Cliffs, New Jersey, Prentice-Hall, Inc., 1963.

Mathews, Donald K.: *Measurement in Physical Education.* Ed. 4. Philadelphia, W. B. Saunders Co., 1973.

President's Council on Physical Fitness and Sports: *Suggestions for School Programs, Youth Physical Fitness.* Washington, D.C., U.S. Government Printing Office, 1973.

BIBLIOGRAPHY

[1]McCloy, Charles, H.: Unpublished mimeographed notes. Iowa City, University of Iowa, 1950.

[2]Wallis, Earl L., and Logan, Gene: *Figure Improvement and Body Conditioning Through Exercise.* Englewood Cliffs, New Jersey, Prentice-Hall, Inc., 1964. p. 1.

[3]President's Council on Physical Fitness and Sports: *Suggestions for School Programs, Youth Physical Fitness.* Washington, D.C., U.S. Government Printing Office, 1973. p. 3.

[4]*Ibid.,* p. 9.

[5]McCloy, Charles H., and Young, Norma D.: *Tests and Measurements in Health and Physical Education.* Ed. 3. New York, Appleton-Century-Crofts, Inc., 1954. pp. 3–13.

[6]Fleishman, Edwin A.: *The Structure and Measurement of Physical Fitness.* Englewood Cliffs, New Jersey, Prentice-Hall, Inc., 1964, p. 99.

basic skills

Muscular movement is fundamental to life. The muscular movement of the heart and other vital organs is an automatic function, and the baby is born with these muscles functioning. He is also born with the potential for movement in the skeletal muscles, a potential which is gradually developed during the years of maturation.

Initially, the baby learns to move through observation and trial and error; he learns to lift his head, to grasp objects, to turn over. At first his movements are uncertain and ineffectual. Normal children soon learn to perform these activities fairly efficiently; those who don't generally need special attention and assistance to help them acquire these simple motor movements. However, as children mature and are confronted with the need to execute complex movements and motor patterns, they all benefit from instruction in performing movements and combining them to develop skills.

Before a child can effectively learn any motor skill, he must have acquired a repertoire of movements that he can draw upon. For example, he must have learned to grasp, raise the arm, and cock the wrist (to mention three of the many movements involved) before he can learn to perform the skill of throwing a ball. Other influences on the learning of motor skills were discussed in the chapter "How and Why Children Learn." Some skills are used more frequently and are more important in the daily life functions and play of children. They are generally termed *basic skills,* and it is the teaching of these with which this chapter is concerned.

The basic skills can be taught by the problem-solving method, the traditional method, or a synthesis of both. However, standing, walking, sitting, and, for older children, running, do not lend themselves to problem-solving as well as other basic skills do, because faulty mechanics may have already developed to the point where a child may be unable to identify his own problems and to establish procedures for alleviating them. For the other activities, with the possible exception of falling techniques, for which experimentation must be fairly restrictive to avoid possible injury, the problem-solving method can be utilized effectively. Subproblems are listed for the appropriate activities as samples of the problems and questions that may be developed for use in teaching basic skills by the problem-solving method. The Correction Chart at the end of the chapter, which has been designed to assist the teacher of the traditional method in identifying and correcting the errors made by students in performing the basic skills, will be helpful to the teacher using the problem-solving approach, in that the errors, results, and corrections can be used as the basis for formulating the problems that the students need to solve in order to discover the most efficient performance of the skills. The skills may be taught and practice afforded through the basic skill games (low organized games); refer to Chapter 9 for information about games that provide opportunities to learn specific basic skills.

BODY BALANCE IN GOOD POSTURE

Body balance must be developed in many different positions for posture is not static. An endless variation of positions or postures is assumed as one walks, stoops, sits, and performs the countless other movements necessitated by his work and play. Certain of these postures, however, such as standing, walking, and sitting, occur more frequently and are more fundamental to other positions than most of the body's postures. Moreover, good posture in these activities is more important to total body efficiency than, for example, some of the postures used only in performing special skills such as standing on one's head in tumbling, because the basic postures are in constant use day in and day out.

The body is not a single mass of materials but is made up of many different parts. How the individual parts are used in relation to other parts makes the difference between good and poor body posture. Because of the anatomical structure of the body, certain segments of the body best serve postural efficiency when aligned in a specific way; postural strain occurs when they are out of good alignment.

Proper alignment must be determined on an individual basis because people are not built alike. For example, some, because of the structure of their bones, will hold their shoulders forward more than usually occurs. Youngsters with this kind of structure will not be able to stand as erect as might appear to be desirable; but to force these children to conform to the erect posture of those children who have exceptionally good posture would actually be creating a less efficient rather than a more efficient posture for them. Each child should be helped to understand the nature of body balance and to discover the best alignment for the structure of his body.

STANDING

The teacher can determine to some extent which is the best standing posture for any specific body structure by directing the child to:

1. Balance the head on the shoulders; do not hold it forward or raise it backward. Keep the chin down.
2. Make the shoulders as wide as possible; do not throw them back.
3. Hold the breast bone up; do not throw the chest out. The stomach is held flat but relaxed.
4. Bend the knees very slightly; they should not be locked.
5. Place the hips under the trunk. Usually this position is assured if the knees are not locked.
6. Point the toes straight ahead with the weight of the body falling on the outside of the foot.

Physical education activities relating to posture should not be thought of as corrective or therapeutic exercises because such work belongs in the hands of the expert. The physical education program should, however, include activities that provide developmental exercises for the postural muscles that hold the body in an erect position. The following are suggested exercises for this purpose. The first 19 of these are designed chiefly for strengthening the muscles of the upper back that are largely responsible for holding the body in an upright position. Some of the exercises if not properly done can cause an increase in the angle of the lumbar curve (small of the back), which may lead to future posture problems; an appropriate cautionary note to that effect is given in the descriptions of these exercises. Exercises 20 to 24 inclusive are designed to prevent the development of excessive lumbar curve. All students can participate in these activities unless contraindicated.

Exercise 1. The student assumes a good standing position, and a book is placed on his head. He attempts to walk a specified distance without the book falling from his head. If it starts to fall, the book is replaced.

Exercise 2. The student reaches high into the air with both arms while standing on tip toes. The curve in the lumbar region (the small of the back) should not increase in size. (Not to be used by those who have arch difficulty.)

Exercise 3. A supine position (on the back) is taken on a mat, and the head is pushed forcefully down on the mat. The lumbar curve should not be increased.

Exercise 4. The student takes a sitting position and, placing his hands behind his head, interlocks the fingers. The head is then pushed back against the forward pull of the arms.

Exercise 5. Either a standing or sitting position is taken, and the head is thrown back as far as possible while the chin is held in contact with the neck.

Exercise 6. A helper stands in front of the student doing the exercise and locks his hands around the latter's head. With his arms braced against the student's shoulders, the helper pulls the student's head down while he attempts to push it back.

Exercise 7. The student stands with his feet placed slightly apart. The arms are crossed in front with the fists clenched and then flung upward and backward behind the head. As the arms are flung backward, the subject rises up on his toes to avoid increasing the size of the lumbar curve.

Exercise 8. The arms are raised at the sides until they are parallel to the floor. With the palms held up, the arms are moved so that they describe a circle backward, downward, forward, and upward.

Exercise 9. The elbows are raised to the height of the shoulders with the hands clasped approximately in front of the chin. A pull is made with each arm resisting the other.

Exercise 10. The student lies on his back in a hook position (knees raised to the chest). The hands are placed at the sides with the palms up. The arms are then moved horizontally to a position over the head and returned to the original position. The curve in the lumbar region should not change when the arms are moved.

Exercise 11. The student stands in a corner and places a hand at shoulder height with arms parallel to the floor on each wall forming the corner. The back is kept straight as the body is leaned toward the corner.

Exercise 12. The arms are raised over the head with the hands grasping a wand. The wand is moved over the head as far as possible while the arms are kept straight. The lumbar curve should not be increased.

Exercise 13. The student lies in a prone (on the front of the body) position with his hands clasped together behind the lower back. The head and shoulders are raised off the mat while the lower back is kept straight.

Exercise 14. As above, except that the arms are extended overhead.

Exercise 15. In a standing position, the student interlocks his fingers behind the back in the lumbar area. The elbows are pressed down and back in an attempt to bring the elbows together in the back. The head is held erect and the lower back is straight.

Exercise 16. The student stands or sits with the arms dropped to the sides. The shoulders are moved in a circle by first shrugging them, then forcing them backward, and finally dropping them to the original position. The forward movement should be passive and the backward movement, forceful.

Exercise 17. The student takes a supine position on a mat with his hands placed under his neck. As he inhales, he raises his shoulders and upper back off the mat. The head, elbows, hips, and legs remain in contact with the mat. The lower back should not be arched. As he exhales, he returns to the original position.

Exercise 18. In a sitting position on the floor, the student places his feet in front of him and his hands behind his body. The weight of the body is taken on the hands and feet and the body lifted off the floor as the student walks forward, backward, and/or sideways. This activity is called the crabwalk.

Exercise 19. The student hangs from a bar or rings with the arms straight. If his grip is not sufficient to hold him any length of time, a helper may stand on a bench beside him and aid him to hold on by grasping his hands.

Exercise 20. The feet are spread and the body is bent forward at the hips, keeping the knees straight with the arms hanging down between the legs. With the upper body relaxed, a bouncing movement is made so the trunk bobs up and down.

Exercise 21. As above, except the feet are together.

Exercise 22. Lying in a prone position, the student forces the small of the back toward the floor by rotating the lower part of the pelvis forward.

Exercise 23. The student lies on the floor in a hook position. The abdominal muscles are contracted and the small of the back is forced toward the floor.

Exercise 24. A hands and knees position is taken on the floor. The pelvic area is tucked in so as to flatten the back. This position is held for a count of five before returning to the original position. Extreme arching of the back should be avoided when returning to the original position.

Many of the above exercises can be utilized in game situations that add interest and variety to routine exercising. For example, the activity described in Exercise 1, walking with a book balanced on the head, can be used in a team relay activity. Exercise 8 is the basis for Eagle and Sparrows, a game that is described in detail on page 181. Both of these are suitable for young children. The activity in Exercise 12 is simulated in the game Sitting Relay of the Overhead Pass, which is presented on page 203; this is an appropriate activity for older children. The activity described in Exercise 18 can be developed into an individual race or a team relay. One kind of relay based on this activity is the Man, Monkey, and Crab Relay on page 195. The game of Follow the Leader can be played using the various postural exercises, varying them in difficulty according to the age group.

Poor posture can be caused by many different factors including physical abnormalities, such as poor vision; chronic fatigue; improper nutrition; insufficient strength and tonicity of the postural muscles; and psychological problems. Except for the factor of muscular development, these factors are generally beyond the scope of physical education and their solution will require outside help.

WALKING*

There is a basic pattern for walking efficiently and gracefully. The weight is shifted slightly to one leg while the opposite leg with the knee slightly bent is swung forward ahead of the body. The heel strikes the floor first as the back leg pushes off, transferring the weight to the leg in front. The body is not leaned forward until the leading foot strikes the ground. As the weight is transferred, the front foot rocks onto the whole foot while the rear foot comes onto the ball of

---

*Walking is a locomotion skill but is presented here in the discussion on "Body Balance in Good Posture" because it is one of the most common postures.

the foot. The transfer of weight is made without an exaggerated movement of the hips from side to side. The rear leg is brought forward for another step. The arms hang entirely relaxed from the shoulders. They swing back and forth from the shoulders in a small arc moving in the opposite direction of the foot on the same side of the body.

In taking the steps, it is generally best for the toes to point nearly straight ahead. Toeing out causes the weight of the body to fall on the inside of the foot which places undue stress upon the longitudinal arch. Toeing in, in addition to detracting from a graceful walking posture, contributes to a knock-kneed condition.

The following activities are suggested as good exercises for developing a pleasing and efficient method of walking. Exercises 1 to 14 inclusive strengthen the muscles of the foot. Exercises 15 to 18 inclusive are exercises that stretch the hamstrings (back muscles of the upper legs) that are important in maintaining proper curvature in the lumbar area. The other exercises are designed to help develop the proper techniques of arm and leg movements in walking.

Exercise 1. A standing position is taken with the feet slightly apart. The toes are pressed hard against the floor and an attempt is made to rotate the knees inward to lift the arches of the feet.

Exercise 2. A sitting position is assumed with one leg crossed over the other. Keeping the toes straight, the foot is circled, moving first in and then up, out, and down.

Exercise 3. Sitting on the floor with the knees bent and the balls of the feet touching while the heels are slightly apart, the student draws the feet toward the body, keeping the balls of the feet together and the heels apart.

Exercise 4. The student takes a supine position with the legs extended and the toes apart with the heels touching. The thighs are rotated inward until the toes touch and then are returned to the original position.

Exercise 5. Lying on the back with the knees bent, feet on the floor, and toes pointing straight ahead, the student spreads the knees as far as possible, allowing the feet to roll to their outer borders. A return to the original position is then made.

Exercise 6. The student lies on his back with the knees bent. The heels are raised and the balls of the feet are pressed to the floor. The outer edges of the feet and toes remain on the floor. The small of the back should not be arched.

Exercise 7. In a sitting position, the student places one foot on the knee of the other leg. The toe and heel are grasped by the hands and the leg is pulled upward.

Exercise 8. While standing the feet are tilted inward so that all of the weight of the body falls on the outer edge of the feet. The student walks backward and forward in this manner.

Exercise 9. In a sitting position, the feet are crossed with the outside borders resting on the floor. The body is leaned forward forcing the chest to the knees.

Exercise 10. A standing position is taken with the heels apart and the toes touching. Without raising the feet, the heels are slid together against the resistance of the floor.

Exercise 11. The student stands with his hands on the hips. One foot is raised and the sole of the foot is placed at right angles against the knee of the opposite leg. The weight is taken on the outside of the foot that is on the floor. The position is held for a count of six and repeated with the other foot.

Exercise 12. The student marches forward crossing, first, left foot over right and then right foot over left. The weight is borne on the outside of the foot.

Exercise 13. A series of ropes is laid down on the floor, a walking step apart. Beginning at the first rope, the student walks over the ropes by crossing the feet in each step over one of the ropes. The weight is taken on the outside of the foot.

Exercise 14. The student walks forward lifting the knees moderately high, keeping the weight of the body on the outer borders of the feet.

Exercise 15. The student takes a position on his right side with both legs extended. The left leg is moved forward as far as possible while the foot is flexed.

Exercise 16. Beginning in a sitting position with the legs extended, a sit-up is performed, both hands touching the feet without bending the knees.

Exercise 17. From a standing position with the feet 6 to 8 inches apart, a twist is made to the right and then, while twisted, the trunk is bent forward at the hip. The movement is then made in the opposite direction.

Exercise 18. With the legs apart and the knees straight, the student bends at the hips and tucks the head between the legs as far as possible.

Exercise 19. In a standing position, the student walks forward and backward on a straight line that has been drawn on the floor. He must not look down at the line.

Exercise 20. In a standing position the arms are swung gently back and forth from the shoulders, avoiding a wide arc and swing at the elbows.

Exercise 21. The student walks forward, first, with his body leaning forward in advance of the leading foot's contact with the ground; he then shifts the body to lean backward so the weight is on the back foot when the lead foot strikes the ground. After mentally taking note of the two positons, the student attempts to walk in a correct position with the body in proper balance.

Exercise 22. A tight line is stretched or a long stick is held at head height. The student walks beneath the line so that his head will not bob up and down and touch the line.

SITTING

School children spend a considerable amount of time at their desks. It requires more energy to sit in a desk chair and others like it which have a straight back than a lounge chair, but such chairs permit a greater freedom of body movement which is frequently necessary when working while seated. The most efficient position when resting the back against the back of the chair is to position the buttocks as far back in the seat of the chair as possible. The trunk is held erect and the shoulders are held up and wide. Prolonged hunching of the back creates fatigue faster and makes sitting for long periods more difficult. The young student must perform many different types of work at his desk. For much of the work it is necessary to bring the head and eyes over the work on the desk. In this position the back can no longer be supported by the back of the chair. The trunk leans forward slightly from the hips while the head, neck, and trunk are held in a relatively straight line.

It is desirable to develop the strength of those muscles which hold the body erect while seated. These exercises, suitable for use while sitting at a desk, might be included among the physical education activities conducted in the classroom.

Exercise 1. Sitting at the desk with the feet on the floor, the student pushes his head up, balancing it evenly, and attempts to stretch as tall as possible.

Exercise 2. As above but with the arms rested on the desk and the back held straight, the student leans forward at the hips until his chest touches the desk and returns to the original position.

Exercise 3. Sitting straight with his feet crossed, the student first bends to the right until his right hand touches the floor and then to the left. The head is kept in line with the trunk; it does not lead the trunk.

Exercise 4. Sitting with the arms crossed at the chest, the student turns the trunk as far as possible to each side in succession.

Exercise 5. The student extends his arms to the side palms up while seated. The arms are rotated describing a small arc. The arms move first back, then down, forward, and up.

TABLE 8–1 Basic Skills Correction Chart

Technique	Common Error	Probable Result	Correction
Standing	Improper balancing of head	Forward head	Balance head on neck with chin held down
	Failing to keep shoulders straight	Round shoulders	Make shoulders as wide as possible
	Locking the knees	Sway back	Flex knees very slightly
	Dropping the chest	Round shoulders	Raise breast bone up
Walking	Leaning forward before lead foot strikes the ground	Body balanced too far forward	Do not shift weight forward until lead foot strikes ground
	Carrying weight on the rear foot until after lead foot strikes ground	Body balanced too far to rear	Bring weight forward as lead foot strikes ground
	Exaggerated shifting of weight to supporting leg	Swaying of hips from side to side	Shift weight smoothly from rear leg to leading leg
	Swinging arms in too wide an arc	Slight swaying of body	Swing arms less vigorously
	Exerting force straight up from rear foot as step is made	Bobbing up and down	Push diagonally with rear foot rather than straight up
	Failing to swing arms at shoulders	Swinging of arms from elbows	Allow arms to hang loosely from shoulders
	Looking at feet	Slumped posture	Keep eyes focused straight ahead
	Rotating legs to side	Toeing out	Rotate legs inward to bring feet pointing straight ahead
Sitting at Desk	Sitting too far forward	Rounding shoulders and back	Move hips against back of seat and lean forward from hips
	Sitting on one foot	Shifting weight to one side	Place both feet flat upon the floor

TECHNIQUES OF MOVING HEAVY OBJECTS

Elementary school children should have a basic understanding of the most efficient procedures of lifting, carrying, pushing, and pulling. If the classroom is used for games, the children will need to help move the desks and chairs to prepare the room for activity. Young children, however, should not be allowed to lift extremely heavy objects because of the danger of strain and of injury to the fingers.

LIFTING

To lift light objects off the floor, the most efficient procedure is to bend at the hips and lean over. However, when the object to be lifted is heavy, the back should be kept relatively straight and the legs bent. The powerful muscles of the legs then supply the lifting force, rather than the weaker muscles of the back. The nearer to the center of the body the weight of the object can be placed, the greater will be the mechanical advantage and, hence, there will be less stress upon the body.

The grip taken for lifting a heavy object depends upon the shape and size of the object. If there are no protrusions on the object that enable a good grip to be taken, the object will have to be grasped either by placing the hands under the object or by placing them on each side of the object and pressing against it. Extreme care must be exercised in placing the hands underneath a heavy object to avoid crushing the fingers.

Figure 8–1   The technique of lifting heavy objects can be taught using folding chairs. (Courtesy of Town of Vernon Schools, Rockville, Connecticut.)

CARRYING

When a heavy object is to be carried, it should be placed as near to the vertical center of the body as possible. A new center of gravity is created when a load is carried, and in adjusting to this load the body should maintain a relatively straight posture. Any lean of the body away from the carried object to adjust to the new center of gravity should be made at the ankes while the rest of the body is held relatively straight.

PUSHING

To push heavy objects the hands are placed against the object with the elbows locked, or one shoulder is placed against the object. The body is leaned toward the object with one foot several inches in front of the other. The knees are bent and force is exerted by straightening the rear leg. The back must be held straight. As the object moves, the rear leg is brought forward. The length of the steps taken while pushing will depend on the speed with which the object is being pushed. As the leg is being brought forward, the other leg, which becomes the rear leg, continues to exert force.

When the object to be moved is relatively light, the crouch of the body need not be as great as with heavy objects. A light object may be moved with the use of the arms only while standing straight.

PULLING

In many situations a heavy object that cannot be pushed because of its location may be pulled. (Less force can be exerted by pulling than by pushing.) How the object can be pulled depends upon the grip that can be taken on the object. General techniques for efficient pulling which are applicable in most situations are:

1. The body is turned to the side.
2. The feet are placed parallel to one another and comfortably spread.
3. The body is lowered by bending at the knees and hips.
4. The pull is exerted by leaning the body away from the object and straightening the leg nearer the object.
5. Small side steps are taken as the force is being exerted.

Teaching the Skills of Moving Heavy Objects

In teaching the skills of moving heavy objects by the direct method, the teacher first explains the principles involved in the effective performance of the skills. Demonstration of the skills usually follows. The pupils simulate the skills and then practice with suitable objects. Lifting and carrying may be practiced

TABLE 8–2 Problem-Solving:
Sample Subproblems for Teaching Lifting, Carrying, Pushing, and Pulling

1. What is the most effective grip to take in lifting a specific object? *Variable*—flow; *Variation*—depends on shape of object.
2. Where is the weight held in relation to the body while lifting heavy weights? *Variable*—space; *Variation*—from close to the body to arm's distance away.
3. Where are the feet placed while lifting a heavy object? *Variable*—space; *Variation*—from feet together to legs apart, spread side to side or front to back.
4. How are the legs and back used in lifting a heavy object? *Variable*—flow; *Variation*—legs straight and back bent to legs bent and back straight.
5. How does the body lean while lifting heavy objects? *Variable*—flow; *Variation*—from toward the object to away from the object.
6. How close should a heavy object be held to the body when lifted? *Variable*—space; *Variation*—from arm's length from the body to as close to the center of gravity of the body as possible.
7. How high should a specific weight be lifted if it is to be carried a given distance? *Variable*—space; *Variation*—from just off the ground to arm's length above the head.
8. How fast should the body move when carrying a heavy object of a specific weight? *Variable*—speed; *Variation*—from very slow to very fast.
9. How long a stride should be taken when carrying a heavy object of a specific weight? *Variable*—space; *Variation*—from a very short to a very long stride.
10. How should the arms be held in pushing a heavy object? *Variable*—space; *Variation*—from arm against the body to arm straight out from the body.
11. How is the body leaned in pushing a heavy object? *Variable*—space; *Variation*—from leaning backward away from the object to leaning forward toward the object and letting the object balance the body.
12. How do the legs move when pushing a heavy object? *Variable*—flow; *Variation*—from short powerful strides to long strides.
13. In what position is the back held while pushing a heavy object? *Variable*—space; *Variation*—from a swayed back to a flexed back.

---

with bar bells or chairs and tables, depending upon their weight and the age of the children doing the lifting. Tables and desks may be used for practice of pushing techniques; immovable objects, such as a wall, offer another possibility. Pulling techniques may be practiced with tables and other heavy objects, or pupils may pull against a rope tied to an immovable object. A game of "tug-of-war" is a good activity for utilizing proper techniques of pulling in a competitive situation.

In using the problem-solving method to teach the skills of moving heavy objects, the teacher must develop problems with appropriate subproblems to help the students determine the most effective way to lift, to carry, to push, and to pull. Examples of suitable subproblems are given in Table 8–2. In both methods, it is advantageous to the teaching process for the students to have an understanding of the mechanical principles of movement, discussed in Chapter 2, so that, as they attempt to perform the skill, they will have an idea of what to expect from specific body movements.

FALLING WITHOUT INJURY

Falling occurs commonly in the play of children. Breaking a fall to avoid injury is an essential and basic skill that should be taught in any physical education program. Falling is the result of the loss of body balance.

TABLE 8–3   Basic Skills Correction Chart
Lifting, Carrying, Pushing, and Pulling

Skill	Common Error	Probable Results	Correction
Lifting Heavy Objects	Holding the object too far from the body	Lack of power	Hold weight against body
	Failing to bend at knees	Injury to back	Bend knees
	Failing to bend at hips	Injury to back	Bend at hips
	Lifting with back muscles	Injury to back	Keep back straight and extend knees
Carrying Heavy Objects	Holding the object too far from the body	Lack of power	Move weight against body
	Failing to lean from ankles	Loss of balance	Adjust lean by bending at ankles
	Failing to adjust the lean of the body to weight lifted	Loss of balance	Lean the body away from the weight
Pushing Heavy Objects	Failing to lock elbows	Loss of power	Straighten arms and lock elbows
	Standing straight	Loss of power	Lean body toward object
	Swaying the back	Injury to back	Keep back straight and body in a slight crouch
	Taking too-long steps	Loss of power	Take short steps
Pulling Heavy Objects	Leaning backwards	Loss of power and injury to back	Turn to the side
	Holding feet close together	Loss of balance and lack of power	Place feet parallel to one another and spread comfortably
	Holding body straight	Loss of power	Lower body by bending at knees and hips
	Taking too-long steps	Loss of power	Take small steps as force is exerted

Figure 8–2 Techniques for efficient pulling of objects may be practiced in a tug-of-war. (Courtesy of Town of Vernon Schools, Rockville, Connecticut.)

In many cases of lost balance, it is actually safer to "go with" the fall than to fight desperately to maintain a position on the feet. Going with a fall refers to an attempt to lower the body to the ground and reduce the shock of impact by decreasing the distance through which the body falls and increasing the length of time of the fall.

Most falls occur when forward movement is in progress, and consequently the person falls forward. When the fall is to the side or back, one should attempt to fall toward the front because this is the area of the body which is best able to withstand the impact of the fall without injury. A front fall is effected by turning the head and shoulders in the direction of the fall. Some of the force of the landing can be dissipated by rolling in the opposite direction from which contact was made with the ground. During the fall, the body is lowered by bending at the knees.

If the body falls forward onto the hands and arms, the arms must absorb some the the shock of the fall by giving with the force (controlled relaxation). This is accomplished by bending the elbows as the hands come in contact with the ground; the muscles are partially contracted and giving with the weight as they are forced to bear it. Every effort should be made to avoid landing on the elbow or knee since landing on these areas will not allow the lowering of the body to the ground in controlled relaxation.

In falling to the rear, if the hands are used by placing them in back of the body, they should "give" in controlled relaxation in much the same way as in the forward fall. The head should be protected from coming in contact with the ground or floor. It can be protected by tucking the chin on the chest, taking the force of the fall on the buttocks, and then rolling onto the upper back. In falling forward the head should be held high and protected by taking the fall on the hands and arms.

When the fall occurs from a height with no forward movement, the feet should be kept under the body. One should land with the feet slightly spread but no farther than the width of the hips. The weight of the body should be taken first on the balls of the feet and then transferred rapidly to the total foot, ankles, knees, and hips. As the knees and hips take the weight, the muscles in these areas are slightly relaxed to allow the downward motion of the body to be slowed gradually. Tucking the body and going into a roll will aid the body in absorbing the shock of the fall.

Teaching the Skills of Falling

Because of the hazards of experimental break-falling, the inexperienced teacher is advised not to use the indirect method to teach this skill. For instruction with the direct method, the principles of falling to avoid injury should be explained to the children in language they understand. A demonstration in which the principles are identified as they are applied is desirable. Practice of controlled falling should start from either a squatting or a standing position. Utmost care must be taken so that no child will attempt a controlled fall from a height at which injury is likely to occur.

Many of the activities learned in tumbling are applicable in breaking an accidental fall. The principles of performing the forward roll and backward roll are the same as those used in breaking an uncontrolled fall. The landing technique in broad jumping is also applicable to falling correctly, and practice in broad jumping and in tumbling activities will help students develop skill in falling without injury.

LOCOMOTION SKILLS

Locomotion is the act of moving from place to place. The human being achieves such movement in a variety of ways: walking, running, hopping, leaping, jumping, skipping, galloping, crawling, and climbing. These examples are only the most commonly employed skills of locomotion; the body is, of course, capable of other ways of moving from place to place. Children should be given opportunities to discover these other means of locomotion (or to rediscover the skills of locomotion of their infancy) through movement exploration or through problem-solving.

RUNNING

Running is an important activity in the everyday lives of children. It is also an integral part of many games played during the elementary school years and in the years beyond. In much of the running that occurs in game situations, the runner starts from an upright position rather than from a crouched one used by runners in a race. To start the run in an upright position, the feet should be spread comfortably with one foot in front of the other. Both feet should be pointed in the direction in which the runner intends to go. If the runner does not know in which direction he is to run, as happens in many game situations, his feet should be approximately parallel. In preparing to take the first step from an upright position, the body is leaned forward in the direction the runner intends to move. The first few steps are shorter than the normal stride of the runner. Each subsequent step is greater in length until the runner is taking full strides. Usually this will be after two to three steps.

In situations in which a starting position is not warranted as when starting to run to catch a player who is already running, the runner must adjust his body and his first running step to fit the position he is in at the moment. If, for example, he was in a walking position, his body weight shifts forward and the rear foot comes forward in the running step. A short stride will be taken in the first few steps as in running from a stationary position.

When running at full speed, the body is at a slight angle. The rear leg, which has completed its drive, is brought forward and extended in front. The knee of the leg that is now back exerts a force that drives the body up and forward off the ground. Contact with the ground is made on the ball of the foot with the toes straight ahead. At full speed the heel never comes in contact with the ground. As the front foot contacts the ground, the knee of this leg is in front of the foot and the body weight is well over the foot so that, when the leg starts its extension, the body will be pushed forward. The arms are swung from the shoulders with the elbows bent at right angles. When the leg is brought forward, the opposite arm is swung forward. The arms are swung forward and backward; they should not cross in front of the chest. The head should be held in a natural position and not thrown from side to side.

In running long distances, speed is reduced and a much shorter step is taken. The trunk is held more vertically and the arm action is less vigorous. Most long distance runners use the total sole of the foot rather than the ball of the foot as in speed running. In using the entire foot, the heel makes contact with the ground first.

In running a straight line the stride for each leg is of equal length, while in running a circle the inside leg must take shorter strides. The tighter the circle, the shorter the stride must be. In a tight circle the knee of the inside leg is never completely straightened. The body is leaned toward the center with the outside leg acting as a force to bring the body to the proper angle. The outside leg is not flexed to any great exent as it is brought forward, particularly if the circle is very tight.

Running in games and sport activities often requires a change of direction. To change direction while running requires a stable base at the moment the change is made (see Principles of Stability, page 23). To obtain the necessary stability, the speed is decreased, the stride is lengthened, and the body is lowered.

To decrease the speed, the body must be straightened and stride shortened for several steps. Each time a foot is brought forward the weight is increasingly taken on the rear of the foot to produce a braking effect. The power of the rear leg is decreased with each step.

The speed must be reduced sufficiently to enable the runner to place the leg on the side opposite the intended direction of movement as it is brought forward to increase the width of the stance. (The actual distance it is placed to the side is determined by the angle of the turn and speed of the movement.) As the leg is placed wide, the body is lowered and leaned in the direction of the turn. The body is lowered by bending at the knee (experimentation will inform the runner as to the desired width of placement of the forward leg and the body lean.) Then, as the body weight comes up over the forward leg, the rear foot pushes the body in the direction of the lean. In the next step, the rear foot moves in the direction of the turn.

To stop from a full run, if not required to stop quickly, the speed is gradually reduced by shortening the stride, by decreasing the force exerted by the rear leg. To stop rapidly, the speed of running is decreased rapidly by shortening the stride very quickly and using the legs to brake the body by coming to a more erect position and shifting the weight on the forward foot from the toe to the rear of the foot in each stride. To reverse direction while running, the forward speed must be reduced considerably. When the speed has slowed sufficiently, the weight is shifted so that it is balanced between the two feet. A pivot is made in the direction of the rear foot, and the weight is then taken on the leading foot. The rear foot pushes on to the next step.

DODGING

Dodging may require a change of direction (for description of the technique, see above.) In some activities after an initial change of direction, it is necessary to change the direction again immediately and continue in the original direction. In other instances the need to avoid a number of objects or individuals requires several changes of direction for successful dodging.

A dodge sometimes necessitates the movement of only a portion of the body away from the object or person to be avoided, such as a tagger with outstretched arms. If it is desirable to move the upper portion of the body without changing direction, the preparation for the move is similar to that in the change of direction. The speed is slowed, a wide step is taken with the inside leg in the direction of the object or person, and the body is leaned away from the object. The next step is then made straight ahead and the body is straightened.

A change of pace is an effective way to dodge a pursuer. The secret of an effective change of pace to elude a chaser is to run at nearly top speed but not at the fastest possible speed until the chaser is within reaching distance, and then burst into full speed as the chaser attempts to tag. Because he is taken by surprise and cannot accelerate his own speed rapidly enough, the chaser will be successfully eluded. The change of pace technique works most effectively when the chaser is coming from the side.

If the lower portion of the body is to be moved away from an object as in the case of a tagger attempting a tag on the leg, the speed is again reduced and a wide step is taken with the outside leg in a direction away from the tagger. As much weight as possible is placed on that foot. The upper portion of the trunk is swung toward the tagger while the leg near the tagger is swung away from him.

HOPPING, LEAPING, JUMPING, SKIPPING, GALLOPING

The activities of hopping, leaping, jumping, skipping, and galloping are similar to each other in that the force of gravity must be overcome in order to lift the body off the ground. Hopping occurs when the force that overcomes the gravity is exerted by one foot and a landing is made on this same foot. When the landing is made on the other foot, a leap has been executed. In skipping there is a hop on one foot, a step forward on the other, and a hop on that foot. Galloping is accomplished by taking rapid steps in which the lead foot and the rear foot retain their relative positions throughout. The weight of the lead foot is taken on the heel and then transferred to the total foot while the weight of the rear foot is chiefly at the front of the foot. In the gallop, as in the activities above, both feet are off the ground at the same time.

The force that projects the body into the air for the hop, leap, and jump is created by a rapid extension of the legs and ankles aided by an arm swing. In preparation for the execution of a hop, leap, or jump the hips, knees, and ankles are bent. The depth of the crouch is determined by the force desired. The arms are swung in the direction toward where the movement is being made. (The techniques of long jumping are discussed in Chapter 12.)

CRAWLING AND CLIMBING

Crawling and climbing are learned early in life, crawling preceding climbing. However, the skill developed at an early age is very limited. It is not until well after the child has learned to walk and run that he develops extensive skills in crawling and climbing over, under, and through objects. There are various ways of crawling and climbing and each situation in which the child finds he must crawl or climb requires somewhat different performance of the skills. Some of the common ways of crawling are on hands and knees, on the stomach, and on the knees only. Climbing may involve all of these positions as well as an upright position using only hands, only feet, or both.

Teaching the Skills of Locomotion

The procedure in teaching the locomotion skills will depend upon the method chosen for the teaching process. In most cases the teaching of running is best taught by the direct method, especially if the students have developed bad habits of running (a correction chart like that in Table 8–6 is helpful in determining which students have poor skills in running). The students should be informed of the corrections that need to be made and how to make them. Opportunities to practice the proper skill techniques are of the utmost importance in overcoming poor running habits.

Hopping, leaping, jumping, skipping, and galloping lend themselves readily to teaching by either the direct or problem-solving method. Running in a circle, changing directions, and dodging are especially well suited to the prob-

**TABLE 8–4   Basic Skills Correction Chart
Hopping, Skipping, Leaping, and Galloping**

Skill	Common Error	Probable Results	Correction
Hopping	No push-off from ball of foot	No hop off foot	With knee bent transfer weight rapidly from total foot to ball of foot and forcefully extend knee
Skipping	Lack of coordination between hop and step	No forward movement	Hop on one foot and step forward with opposite foot and then hop on that foot and step forward
	Failing to hop on non-dominant leg	Hopping on one foot and then other rather than skipping	Hop on one foot and step forward
Leaping	Failing to exert force on the rear foot and landing on the other	No upward propulsion of body	Push off hard on ball of foot of rear leg and reach forward with other leg
Galloping	Weight not taken on heel of lead foot	Loss of balance	Increase length of stride of leg in front
	Failing to stay on toes of foot in rear	Poorly coordinated gallop	Lean weight forward and take shorter steps on rear leg

TABLE 8-5 Problem-Solving:
Sample Sub-Problems for Teaching Locomotion Skills
(Running and Walking not included)

1. How can one move from one place to another using only one leg? *Variable—flow; Variation—*hopping.
2. How high should the hop be to move forward on one foot rapidly? *Variable—space; Variation—*from very high to very low.
3. How can one move by hopping first on one leg and then on the other? *Variable—flow; Variation—*skipping.
4. In skipping, where should the weight be taken on the foot? *Variable—space; Variation—*from toes to heel.
5. How fast should one run to leap a long distance? *Variable—speed; Variation—*very slowly to very fast.
6. How should the arms be moved when the leap is made? *Variable—flow; Variation—*arms held stationary, synchronized with a leap.
7. How high should the leap be made for a long distance? *Variable—space; Variation—*from very high to very low.
8. In changing directions abruptly how slowly must one be moving? *Variable—speed; Variation—*from very slow to very fast.
9. How is the body moved at the moment that a change of direction is made? *Variable—flow; Variation—*from body lean in the new direction to body lean in the opposite direction, and from body held erect to body lowered.
10. How far is the leg placed to the side in the last step before a change of direction is made? *Variable—space; Variation—*from a full step to a few inches.
11. In running in a circle, in what direction and how far is the body leaned? *Variable—space; Variation—*from toward the center of the circle to away from the circle and from a nearly erect position to an extreme lean.
12. How are the legs held in running in a tight circle? *Variable—flow; Variation—*inside leg from extreme angle to moderate angle; outside leg from straight knee to slightly bent.
13. In a dodge made by moving only the upper portion of the body, how are the legs moved? *Variable—flow; Variation—*from inside leg stepping toward object to be avoided to legs remaining stationary.
14. In dodging by moving only the lower portion of the body, how are the legs moved? *Variable—flow; Variation—*from a step to the side with the inside leg to a step to the side by the outside leg.
15. In galloping, how close is the closing foot brought to the forward foot? *Variable—space; Variation—*from very close to very far away.
16. In galloping, where is the weight taken on the forward foot? *Variable—space; Variation—*from the toe to the heel.
17. In galloping, where is the weight taken on the rear foot? *Variable—space; Variation—*from the toe to the heel.

lem-solving method since the way the skills of each of these activities are actually performed is dependent upon individual differences and specific situations. The skills can also be taught effectively by the direct method. Drills that may be used are described below.

Drill 1. Students are placed in line and from a standing position start a run of 10 yards, then stop, and line up for a return run.

Drill 2. An obstacle course is set up of chairs or other readily available large objects. The students run around these, avoiding touching them as they run.

Drill 3. Students run forward and change direction to either right or left upon command of the teacher or student leader.

Drill 4. Students "follow the leader," who leaps, jumps, skips, and gallops.

Drill 5. Students run forward four steps and execute a hop, a skip, and a jump, attempting to achieve maximum distance.

TABLE 8–6   Basic Skills Correction Chart
Locomotion

Skill	Common Error	Probable Results	Correction
Running	Allowing arms to flop at sides	Body movement from side to side	Bend elbows at right angles
	Crossing arms over chest	Body movement from side to side	Reach forward with each arm as if grasping for something in front
	Rearing head far back	Shortened stride	Look straight ahead in direction of run
	Throwing rear foot out to side after driving off it (especially common in girls)	Slow running speed	After leg drive, keep leg straight behind until recovery for next step
	Moving the body side to side	Decrease in speed	Synchronize arms with legs
	Holding arms and trunk muscles tight	Increase in use of energy	Relax and synchronize arms with legs
	Throwing head from side to side	Body weaves, decreasing forward speed	Hold head in natural position
	No push-off from the ball of foot	Shortened strides	Land on ball of foot and stay on the ball of foot
	Landing flat on foot	Loss of power in pushing off from the foot	Bend knee on forward leg and land on ball of foot
	Holding body erect	Shortened strides	Place body forward at a slight angle
	Failing to bring body weight over lead foot as it contacts ground	Loss of power in pushing off from the leg	Bend knee and bring weight over lead foot
Running in a Circle	Holding body erect	Slow running speed	Lean body toward center
	Failing to bend inside knee sufficiently	Slow running speed	Straighten outside knee and bend inside knee
	No increase in length of stride as speed increases	Slow running speed	Increase size of step until running is at full stride
	Taking normal steps for first two or three steps	Slow acceleration	Shorten length of first few steps
Change of Direction	Failing to decrease speed sufficiently	Shallow turn	Shorten stride and brake with lead foot
	Holding body straight	Shallow turn	Lean body in direction of turn
	Failing to lower body	Shallow turn	Lower body as it is leaned
	Bringing feet close together as turn is initiated	Shallow turn	Widen stance before turning
Change of Pace	Running at full speed to dodge a chaser	Failure to elude chaser	Run at less than top speed
Dodging by Moving Portion of the Body	Failing to move portion of body to avoid tagger	Failure to elude tagger	Slow speed slightly and change center of gravity of body by making necessary body moves in right direction

Games especially suitable for developing skills of locomotion are:

During drills and games, the teacher should make suggestions for the improvement of the skills.

The crawling and climbing skills are readily taught through motor exploration. Problems can be so constructed that the child will experience many different ways of crawling and climbing, or a specific problem may be posed so that the child will find the most efficient way to crawl or climb in a given situation. The special equipment (portable stairs, building blocks, inclined mats, climbing and crawl-through apparatus) discussed in Chapter 10 is useful for both exploration and reinforcement.

THROWING AND CATCHING

Throwing and catching are basic to many different kinds of games. There are several basic patterns of throwing: the side arm throw, the overhand throw, the underhand toss, and the push pass. Games in which elementary school children engage generally require only the last three of these. Catching techniques are very much the same for all patterns of throwing, although some adjustment in the position of the hands may be made in response to the speed, size, height, and other factors relating to the object being caught.

THROWING

The overhand throw is most frequently used when speed is desired and distance required. With the ball gripped in the hand, the elbow is bent and the ball is raised to the back of the head at about ear level. The elbow is away from the body and on the level of the shoulder. The wrist is superextended (cocked). The leg opposite the throwing arm is placed forward in the direction of the throw. As the ball is brought back behind the ear, the trunk is twisted toward the arm. The ball is thrown by bringing the elbow forward and the hand past the ear. The arm is then fully extended and the wrist is flexed releasing the ball about shoulder height. The trunk is rotated forward at the same time as the arm is brought forward. After the release of the ball, the arm follows through in a forward and downward direction, and the weight of the body is shifted forward.

Different sport activities frequently require that objects of different sizes and weights be thrown. Regardless of size, weight, or shape the techniques of throwing are similar; however, the grip that is taken for making the throw differs, depending upon the size and shape of the object. For a ball the size of a softball, the grip for elementary school children consists of holding the ball with the first three fingers on top of the ball and the thumb on the bottom. With a smaller ball only two fingers are placed on top. The grips and throwing techniques used with a football and basketball are described in Chapter 12.

The underhand toss is used when speed is not necessary or the distance is very short. The ball is gripped as in the overhand throw. The toss is made with a forward swing of the arm from its hanging position at the side of the body. A back swing, follow through, or the use of the body is not necessary since the force needed is minimal.

CATCHING

Catching a ball involves the same principles as breaking a fall. The arms of the body must absorb the impact of the moving ball by means of a short recoil of the arms. In getting ready to receive a ball, the feet should be spread to provide good balance with one foot slightly ahead of the other. In catching the ball, the body should be placed facing the line of flight of the ball. The palms of the hands and not the fingers are directed toward the ball. If the ball is coming toward the catcher below his waist, the palms are held so the little fingers are close together. If the ball is above the waist, the thumbs are held together as the ball is caught. For balls the size of a tennis ball or smaller, the fingers or thumbs should be touching. For larger balls, they will have to be spread farther apart. Larger balls such as basketballs are caught on the cushions of the finger tips while smaller balls are caught in the palms. To avoid injury to the fingers, they should be held straight out but always flexed slightly. One of the most important factors in catching the ball successfully is that of watching the ball throughout the catch.

Teaching the Skills of Throwing and Catching

Many games give practice in catching and throwing; however, young children should have ample opportunity to develop some skill in throwing and catching before being placed in game situations requiring skill beyond their abilities. A simple drill for the young ones, as well as for others who have difficulties and need additional practice, consists of forming two lines facing one another to throw the ball back and forth. The teacher watches for errors and makes corrections as needed. If the problem-solving method is being used, subproblems like those in Table 8–7 may be developed to guide the students in finding the most effective ways of throwing and catching.

TABLE 8–7 Problem-Solving:
Sample Subproblems for Teaching Fundamentals of Catching and Throwing

1. Which method of throwing, overhand, underhand, or push pass, is most effective when speed and distance are desired? *Variable*—flow; *Variation*—overhand, underhand, push pass.
2. Where should the elbow be held when the ball is raised to the back of the head position in the overhand throw? *Variable*—space; *Variation*—from elbow vertical to elbow horizontal.
3. How is the trunk moved in the overhand throw? *Variable*—flow; *Variation*—from stationary to rotation forward with the forward movement of the arm.
4. How does the wrist move in the overhand throw? *Variable*—flow; *Variation*—from flexed to superextended.
5. How are the legs moved in the overhand throw? *Variable*—flow; *Variation*—from a step forward by the leg opposite the throwing arm to a step forward by the leg on the same side.
6. How is the grip for throwing taken with one hand on a ball of a specific size? *Variable*—flow; *Variation*—from a grip with three fingers to the use of the entire hand.
7. How are the hands held to catch a ball at waist height? Head height? *Variable*—space; *Variation*—from hands apart to close together; from thumbs together to little fingers together.
8. How can the ball be cushioned so that it will not rebound from the hands when caught? *Variable*—flow; *Variation*—from arms held rigid to arms giving with the ball.
9. How are the feet placed when catching a ball? *Variable*—flow; *Variation*—from feet spread to feet close together.
10. How much follow-through must be made to throw a ball a long distance? *Variable*—flow; *Variation*—from none to complete follow-through.

STRIKING

Striking and batting are movements frequently employed in play and every-day activities. The kind of striking movement used is determined by the circumstances: a stationary object being struck by a moving instrument as in golf, or both object and instrument moving as in batting a thrown ball. Regardless of the circumstances, however, there are some basic principles that are applicable to all striking:

1. A stationary or moving object will move in a new direction only if the force applied is sufficient to overcome the inertia of the object.

2. When two opposing forces come together, there are two equal and opposite forces exerting influence. When a ball is hit with a bat, the reaction against the bat is just as great as the reaction against the ball. The direction of the thrown ball will be reversed only if the force of the bat is greater than that of the ball. The force of the ball in a new direction, after it is hit, is equal to the sum of the forces of the moving bat and ball. The force exerted upon both the bat and the ball depends upon their weight and the speed at which they are moving.

3. The speed of the striking instrument is determined by its length. A longer instrument will move faster at the extreme end than a shorter instrument if the speed at the near end is the same. The speed also depends upon the length of the back swing. The longer the distance through which a force can be applied, the greater the force will be.

4. The speed of the object rebounding from the instrument depends not only upon the force of the object and the instrument at the moment of contact,

but also upon the firmness of the two objects. If the surface of the striking instrument does not have sufficient resistance for the force of the object, the object will not rebound. For example, the golf ball struck against a practice net does not rebound but falls to the ground because of the lack of firmness of the net.

5. The direction of the rebound of an object from a striking instrument depends upon where it is hit in relation to its center of gravity. A foul ball in softball, for example, is the result of its having been hit off-center. Another factor involved in the direction of the rebound is a spin imparted to the object as it is thrown or struck.

Teaching the Skills of Striking

Students should be provided with many different kinds of objects to strike, some of them stationary and some moving at various speeds in the air and on the ground. The process of introduction should be gradual, however. Usually only one striking instrument and one object to be struck should be used in a single lesson. The speed and height of movement of the object to be struck can be varied to give experience in striking the same object in different situations.

A traditional striking act, such as batting a ball, hitting a croquet ball, or striking a hockey puck, can be taught equally well by the traditional method and the problem-solving method. However, if an assortment of striking acts using varied objects and instruments is to be taught, the differences in the

Figure 8-3 Field hockey provides experience in striking both a stationary ball and a moving one. (Courtesy of Ox Ridge Elementary School, Darien, Connecticut.)

techniques of striking will need to be understood. Problem-solving is generally more effective in such circumstances.

BALANCING

Balance is a state of equilibrium acquired through proper distribution of the body weight. Achieving balance in a stationary position on a hard surface is a different problem from that of maintaining balance throughout movement. In the first type of balancing, called *static balance*, weight must be distributed equally around the center of gravity which is relatively fixed. In the second type, known as *dynamic balance*, the center of gravity changes continually so that it is necessary to make constant, often complex, adjustments of the body to keep the weight equally distributed.

Balance is basic to nearly all movement. Few activities of daily existence and almost no play activities can be successfully performed without good balance. For this reason, it is important to provide balancing experiences in large measure in the elementary school physical education program.

Balancing stunts and activities for inclusion in the program are almost limitless in number and variety. They range from the simple activity of balancing on tiptoe to balancing on a narrow beam, a relatively complex stunt. Variations of the balancing activities may be achieved by varying the support—the body may be supported by the feet or a foot, by other portions of the body such as a knee, or by combinations of parts of the body such as the knee and hand. Ingenuity is the only limiting factor in devising balancing activities.

The balance beam and jouncing board, described in Chapter 10, provide excellent balancing experiences for very young children; an old bed spring and mattress can also be used. The trampoline, a very popular piece of gymnastic equipment, is an outstanding teaching instrument for all ages of children. Activities which may be performed on trampolines are described in Chapter 13. Useful in teaching the fine body control required in balancing on a tilting object is the balance platform, which is a 1-foot-square piece of wood bolted to a rounded piece of wood (Fig. 8–6). The child should learn to balance on it with two feet before attempting variations.

Teaching the Skills of Balancing

Balance can best be taught to young children through motor exploration and problem-solving because it is easier for them to develop an understanding of good balance if they experience both success and failure in their attempts to maintain balance in a variety of situations. Older children will profit from being given the basic information about the principles of stability, discussed on pages 23–24. The direct method is perhaps the more effective way to impart this knowledge. During practice of the designated balance activities, in checking for errors, the teacher can point out which principles of stability are being violated and identify the kinds of movement required to adhere to the principles.

TABLE 8–8   Basic Skills Correction Chart
Catching, Throwing, Fielding, Dribbling, Striking, and Kicking

Skill	Common Error	Probable Results	Correction
Catching	Failing to catch ball on cushions of finger tips	Fumbled ball	Spread fingers wide and curl fingers slightly
	Holding fingers straight	Injured fingers	Curl fingers slightly
	Failing to give with ball	Ball bounces from hand	Allow arms to give in controlled relaxation
	Failing to watch ball	Ball doesn't strike hand properly	Watch ball as it comes onto cushions of finger tips
Two-Hand Chest Pass	Catching ball on flat of hands	Fumbled ball	Catch ball on cushions of finger tips
	Failing to step in direction of pass	Ball lacks speed and is frequently intercepted	Take one step in direction of pass and shift weight forward
	Lack of wrist snap as ball is released	Throw lacks speed	Place thumbs behind ball; emphasize wrist snap by bringing thumbs forward so they will face in direction of pass after release of ball
Bounce Pass	Catching ball on flat of hands	Fumbled ball	Catch ball on cushions of finger tips
	Failing to step in direction of pass	Ball lacks speed and is frequently intercepted	Take one step in direction of pass and shift weight forward
	Lack of wrist snap as ball is released	Throw lacks speed	Place thumbs behind ball; emphasize wrist snap by bringing thumbs forward so they will face in direction of pass after release of ball
	Failing to bounce ball closer to receiver than thrower	Ball bounces too high and is frequently intercepted	Aim ball at a spot approximately two-thirds the distance between thrower and receiver
Dribbling	Using palms of hands	Ball is struck too hard; ball is uncontrolled	Stroke ball with cushions of finger tips; fingers should be used as if they were trying to grasp ball
Catching— One Hand	Failing to keep eyes focused on ball until caught	Ball does not make proper contact with glove	Watch ball throughout flight until caught
	Failing to give with ball	Ball bounces from hands and/or stings hand	Allow arm to give in controlled relaxation

**TABLE 8–8   Basic Skills Correction Chart
Catching, Throwing, Fielding, Dribbling, Striking, and Kicking (*Continued*)**

Skill	Common Error	Probable Results	Correction
Throwing—Overhand	Failing to use body properly	Ball may fall short of its goal	Turn body away from direction of throw as hand is brought back behind head and turn it forward as ball is thrown
	Lack of wrist snap	Ball falls short of its goal	Cock wrist as it is brought back behind head and snap it forward when ball is released
	Holding elbow close to body	Ball falls short of its goal	Bring upper arm parallel with ground and point elbow away from body as ball is brought back behind head
Fielding	Failing to watch ball as it is batted	Fielder not in proper position	Watch ball leave thrower's hand and follow it wherever it goes
	Failing to keep eyes on ball during catch	Ball does not contact mitt correctly	Watch ball throughout catch
	Running under a fly ball	Ball goes over head	Stay well back of where it appears ball will land and then move up rapidly as it comes down
	Failing to give with ball in catch	Ball bounces from hand and/or stings hand	Allow arms to give in controlled relaxation
Striking	Improper alignment of hands	Inability to control striking object	Depends on nature of striking object
	Failing to watch object to be struck	No contact with object	Keep eyes open and on object
	No back swing	Loss of power	Depends on location of object
	Lack of synchronization in use of arms and wrist	Loss of power, no contact with object	Move each part of body in proper order
	No follow-through	Loss of power	Continue movement in direction of stroke after object is hit
Kicking a Ball on the Ground	Failing to contact ball on center of toes or instep	Loss of control of ball	Contact ball in center of toes or instep
	Failing to watch ball	No contact with ball	Keep eye open and on the ball
	Lack of coordination of step and kick	No contact with ball	Take one step, swing opposite foot forward
	Back foot not aligned with ball	No contact with ball	Swing foot forward and then backward in straight line

Figure 8–4 *A, B,* and *C,* Ingenuity is the key to providing varied balancing activities that are also great fun. (Courtesy of Town of Vernon Schools, Rockville, Connecticut.)

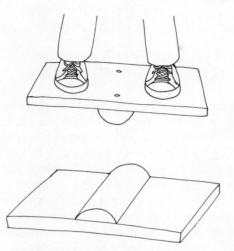

Figure 8-5 Balance platform.

Figure 8-6 Young children develop an understanding of balance through attempts to maintain balance in various situations. (Courtesy of Town of Vernon Schools, Rockville, Connecticut.)

OTHER BASIC SKILLS

In addition to the more commonly recognized basic skills discussed above, there are a number of others not so readily identified but so frequently used in the play of children as to qualify as basic skills. The skills discussed in succeeding paragraphs are considered to be in this category.

Chasing and Tagging

Chasing requires continuous attention to the maneuvers of the one being chased. The chaser must be alert to the possibility that the person being chased may at any moment employ a change of pace or dodging tactics. If a change of pace occurs, the chaser must be ready to increase or decrease his speed accordingly. If dodging tactics are used, the chaser must respond to the moves of the dodger. Dodging techniques are discussed on page 155.

Tagging is an important skill in many favorite children's games. It is a simple skill, readily learned. Most children learn the skill from observing others or through experimentation. For some, however, instruction in tagging may be necessary.

In tagging a moving target, the movement of the arm toward the target should not begin until the tagger is close enough to reach the target. Then, if the tagger is running, the arm is brought up from the running position quickly and forcibly directed toward the nearest part of the target. A follow-through is important so that, if the target with a burst of speed tries to elude the tagger after the arm movement is started, the arm may still make contact with the target. If a tag is made at the point anticipated by the tagger, the arm follows through in a downward direction to decrease the force of contact on the target and the tagger's arm.

Synchronized Movement and Side-stepping

Some children's games require synchronization of movement with that of a partner or a group. Synchronizing a movement requires prearrangement between partners of the movements that each will make at a given time. The two most frequently synchronized movements are running and side-stepping. A common activity using synchronized running is the Sack Relay (page 198).

In side-stepping, the legs are moved in unison, regardless of whether a couple or a long line is moving. All start the step with the leg closer to the direction of movement and step at the same time. The other leg is moved in a sliding or stepping motion to a position to the inside of the other leg.

Turning the Body from a Stationary Position

In turning the body in any direction, the body is led either by a foot and leg, arm, or head and shoulders. As the part of the body is moved in the desired di-

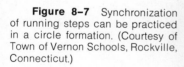

Figure 8–7 Synchronization of running steps can be practiced in a circle formation. (Courtesy of Town of Vernon Schools, Rockville, Connecticut.)

rection, the rest of the body follows. The smaller the radius of the body, the faster the turn can be made. Hence, by shortening the radius of the body by bringing the arms from outstretched position to the center of the body in a vertical turn, or by bending the head and flexing the knees and hips in a tuck, the speed of the turn is increased (see pages 24–25 for Principles of Moving the Body). In reversing the body while standing, the feet are moved so that one foot is in front of the other; the body is turned in the desired direction by pivoting on both feet.

Turning to the side and stepping out in a new direction requires a forceful drive from the leg on the side opposite to the direction to be turned; at the same time the body is turned and leaned in that direction. After the drive with the leg, it is brought across the front of the body to step in the new direction. The second step is also in the new direction.

Moving the Plane of the Body

Sitting, squatting, kneeling, and lying down or rising up from these positions require a change of plane of the body. Raising the plane of the body requires overcoming gravity. To exert sufficient force to move the body up from a lying or sitting position usually requires the use of the arms. When lying or sitting (including sitting crossed-legged) on the floor, the body is rolled or moved to a position on all fours (knees and hands are on the floor). From this position the body is raised to a kneeling position by pushing with the hands and straightening the body. Then a leg is lifted and the foot is placed on the floor and the weight is taken on the foot, bringing the body to an upright position. To increase the force generated, both hands can be placed upon the knee and pressure exerted downward to help in lifting the body upward.

When lowering the body from a higher plane to a lower plane, the force needed is supplied by gravity. The speed of lowering the body can be increased by extending the arms in the opposite direction of the intended movement (see discussion of Equal and Opposite Reaction, page 25). However, it is generally not feasible to do this. In most situations the body is allowed to move downward through controlled relaxation of the muscles involved. In cases where greater speed is desired, the body is allowed to drop as rapidly as possible. The fall will need to be cushioned by taking the weight partially on the hands and then lowering the body rapidly. The weight should *never* be taken on the arms with the elbows locked because of the possibility of injuring the elbow.

Clasping Hands

Clasping the hand of another player is common in the basic skill games. There are three distinct ways of clasping hands. One way is to grasp the hands so the palms touch; the thumb and fingers curl over the other's hand. This grip is the most commonly used and is effective in holding secure if both partners have equal strength in their grip. If one partner has a stronger grip than the other, a more effective hold can be taken by each grasping the other's wrist. A third way, which also produces a secure grip, consists of both partners flexing their fingers and partially closing their hands. The grip is then taken by hooking each other's closed fingers. Children should be encouraged to experiment with various grips during play to determine which is the most effective for a given situation.

Feinting

Feinting is a movement made in order to deceive an adversary by an attack aimed at one place or point merely as a distraction from the real place or point of attack. It is a very effective procedure in games where a good feint often forces the opponent to commit himself to a move in one direction while the person feinting moves in another.

A feint can be made by any part of the body; however, the most effective feints in most games are made with the upper portion of the body. In most movements of the body, the movement begins with the head and shoulders; hence, a feint with the head and shoulders is very effective because the opponent is usually watching for such a movement to give him an idea of which way the player is going to move.

The eyes are also used in feinting. Most individuals look first in the direction of their intended movement. Consequently, looking in the direction of the feint at the same time the feint is made with the head and shoulders increases the success of the feint.

Teaching Other Basic Skills

In most cases these skills are readily taught in the actual activity that requires their use. For example, the teacher may take a moment from an activity that requires the clasping of hands to explain the different techniques and then, during the activity, make suggestions to those who are having problems with their grip. Or when there are activities that require moving the plane of the body in a specific way, the teacher may demonstrate, or have demonstrated, the most effective way to make the movements as an aid to those who are having difficulty. Other skills that lend themselves well to instruction during actual play are chasing, tagging, side-stepping, and feinting.

At other times or for other situations, drills may be developed. In the case of tagging, the skill may be practiced by partners who take turns chasing and tagging each other. The drill should be limited to a small area to increase the tagging opportunities. Practice on the contact and follow-through can be provided by forming two lines of students facing each other with each holding his hand in front of his body with the palms facing the partner. He moves his hand when the other attempts to tag it. Neither player may move from his original position.

To learn synchronized movements, the class may be divided into groups of two. One of the partners may be assigned to perform a specific movement while the other moves at the same time with him. Singing games and folk dances offer other opportunities to learn synchronized movement. Feinting may be taught by forming the children in groups of three. One takes a place in the center; the other two try to keep a ball away from him. The two with the ball must remain stationary.

SUPPLEMENTARY READINGS

American Association for Health, Physical Education and Recreation: *Perceptual-Motor Foundations: A Multidisciplinary Concern.* Washington, D.C., American Association for Health, Physical Education and Recreation, 1969.

Broer, Marion R.: *Efficiency of Human Movement.* Ed. 2. Philadelphia, W. B. Saunders Co., 1973.

Davies, Evelyn A.: *The Elementary School Child and His Posture Patterns.* New York, Appleton-Century-Crofts, Inc., 1958.

Espenschade, Anna, and Eckert, Helen: *Motor Development.* Columbus, Ohio, Charles E. Merrill Books, Inc., 1967.

Fait, Hollis F.: *Special Physical Education: Adapted, Corrective, Developmental.* Ed. 3. Philadelphia, W. B. Saunders Co., 1972.

Fait, Hollis F.: *Health and Fitness for Modern Living.* Ed. 2. Boston, Allyn and Bacon, Inc., 1967.

Lowman, Charles Leroy, and Young, Carl Haven: *Postural Fitness Significance and Variances.* Philadelphia, Lea and Febiger, 1960.

Ubell, Earl, and Strong, Arline: *The World of Push and Pull.* New York, Atheneum Publishers, 1964.

Wickstrom, Ralph L.: *Fundamental Motor Patterns.* Philadelphia, Lea and Febiger, 1970.

chapter nine

basic skill games (low organized games)

TAG GAMES
RELAY GAMES
BALL CONTROL GAMES
MANEUVERING FOR POSITION GAMES
SCOOTER GAMES
SCOOP GAMES

Planned motor activity is the tool by which the teacher achieves the desired goal in physical education. Many of these activities are the familiar games of childhood which require little or no equipment and only the simplest organization. Because they are so easily played, they are often called low organized games; however, the title of basic skill games seems more fitting because these games provide vigorous activity for the development of physical fitness, for social interaction, and for the practice and development of the basic motor skills which are fundamental to everyday life and to the advanced team and individual sports in which the youngsters will participate as older children and as adults.

These games have an important place in the physical education for young children, regardless of the amount of emphasis placed on movement exploration and problem-solving in the program. Many of the games, such as Hide and Seek and Tag, are known to have existed in all historical periods and in every corner of the world. Commenting on their constant and continuous popularity among all children, Dr. Hevig Kéri, a Hungarian therapist, has stated this is "proof how high these games stand among human achievement and how permanent their value."[1]

In the descriptions of the games included in this chapter, the grades for which each game is most suited, as determined by the abilities, interests, and needs of the children, are indicated. The teacher will find, however, that the enthusiasm shown by the students for a game has a direct relationship to the way in which it is presented to them. Even very simple games will interest older children if the teacher makes them appropriately appealing. Consequently, while the grade level indicated may be used as a guide in selecting activities for the program, teachers need not be restricted to these if they wish to try to interest the children in other games. It is always necessary, however, that the children have the skill ability to play the chosen games.

Many of the games are similar in nature but utilize a different imagery; for example, in one tag game the chaser is a cowboy or cowgirl and those being chased are cows, and in another game which is played very much the same way the chaser is a fox who tries to catch chickens. Usually children think of such games as being very different because the imagery takes precedence in their minds over the way the games are played. Hence, the teacher need not be too concerned about the similarity of games when choosing games for the class to play. The teacher may wish to substitute a different imagery for that traditionally employed in a game in order to provide an additional experience. For example, Animal Tag, in which children take the names of various animals, might be changed so that the children choose the names of various inanimate objects such as a lamp, chair, and table. For additional motor experience and enjoyment, the children try to be as much like the chosen object as possible; thus, a "lamp" could run with his arm outstretched to suggest a lampshade, a

Figure 9–1 Imagery adds to the enjoyment as well as to the variety of motor experiences in basic skill games. (Courtesy of Ox Ridge Elementary School, Darien, Connecticut.)

"chair" in a modified squat position, and "table" on all fours. The teacher should not miss the opportunity to involve the children in changing the imagery, for this increases interest in the game.

In some of the games all the children are active all the time while in others only few are engaged at any one time. The teacher should take the amount of participation into consideration in choosing games. If all the children have been very active for an extended period, a game that has periods of inactivity during which players may rest is an appropriate selection.

The chief basic skills that are developed have been listed for each game. The basic skills are described in Chapter 8. Games should be chosen to give children experience in the various basic skills. Many children will not be able to perform all the basic skills adequately and will require practice on those which they perform inefficiently or inadequately.

When a new game is introduced requiring a basic skill that the children are not able to perform effectively, the game may be played for a short time after it has been introduced. Then play may be stopped for discussion and demonstration or exploration of the basic skill(s) that the children need help in learning to perform better. When the children resume playing the game, the teacher must continually observe the movements of the children in order to identify which children need further assistance in learning to perform the skill effectively.

The recommended number of players who can play a game is indicated for each game. However, this does not mean that more or fewer could not play the game but only that the recommended number is the most appropriate for maximum enjoyment and safety. Also indicated are the types of playing areas most suitable for the games. However, the games may usually be played in other types of playing space if modified to the size and nature of the space.

The procedures for organizing the class into the playing formations required by these games were presented in Chapter 3. With small classes, assembling the children into a formation can be relatively informal but with large groups, confusion and loss of time may result unless a routine is established for moving quickly into formation. In either case, it is important to create an atmosphere which fosters fun and freedom of movement rather than one of military precision and strict enforcement.

Playing equipment for these games is restricted to balls, tires, stools, boxes, tin plates, batons, and Indian clubs. These items are cared for simply by proper drying and cleaning when they become wet and dirty. Most of the equipment is readily available or easily improvised. Any smooth sticks of wood may be substituted for batons. If Indian clubs are not available, pieces of wood or large sticks approximately 3 or 4 inches in diameter and about 12 inches in length may be used instead.

TAG GAMES

Games in whch one or more players chase and try to catch one or more individuals under specified conditions have been played by children in all ages and in all parts of the world. The conditions governing the tagging have developed in an interesting variety with respect to areas where the tag may be made, safety areas where tagging may not be done, and where and how the player may be tagged. Imagery is often introduced to add still more variety to the tagging conditions. Playing tag games utilizes several basic skills: running, dodging, chasing, feinting, and tagging. Other basic skills may also be required in specific games. Because of the great appeal of the tag games for young children, they are excellent activities to provide practice of the basic skills.

Squat Tag

> Grades: K–1
> Number of Players: 5–30
> Playing Area: playground
> Equipment: none
> Basic Skills: dodging, chasing, tagging, running, moving from upright to squat position

DESCRIPTION OF GAME. One child is chosen to be "It." He attempts to tag one of the other players who evade him by running or dodging. They cannot be tagged if they are squatting. A child tagged in an upright position becomes the new "It."

Teaching Hints. The teacher should stress the chaser's avoiding running into the squatting child. The basic skill of dodging is used in avoiding the squatter.

Flowers Blowing in the Wind

> Grades: K–1
> Number of Players: 10–30
> Playing Areas: playroom, gymnasium, playground
> Equipment: none
> Basic Skills: chasing, tagging, walking, running, reversing direction

DESCRIPTION OF GAME. Two parallel lines are drawn 20 to 30 feet apart. The participants are divided into two equal groups, one "flowers" and the other, the "wind." The flowers take a position behind one of the lines while members on the wind side take their position behind the opposite line. The name of a common flower is selected in secret by the flowers, and then they walk slowly toward the wind. Each player who is a part of the wind has a turn to guess the name of the flower. If a correct guess is made, the wind chases the flowers back to their line. As long as the guesses are incorrect, the flowers continue to advance. However, if any flower reaches the wind's line before the name of the flower is guessed, the sides change roles.

Teaching Hints. If those who are the wind have difficulty in guessing the flower's name, they may be assisted by being given hints such as the first letter of the name of the flower and its color.

The Farmer Is Coming

> Grades: K–1
> Number of Players: 10–30

Playing Areas: gymnasium, playground
Equipment: none
Basic Skills: chasing, tagging, walking, running, reversing directions
DESCRIPTION OF GAME. All the players except one, the "farmer," stand behind the starting line. The farmer, who is seated 35 feet from the starting line, gives the signal for the children to walk forward. The children walk forward, coming as close to the farmer as they dare. The farmer, when he believes it will be to his greatest advantage, claps his hands and shouts: "The farmer is coming!" With this shout, he attempts to tag one of the players. The child tagged becomes the new farmer and the farmer becomes one of the players.

Teaching Hints. If the farmer is having difficulty catching a runner, he should be encouraged to wait until the runners are very close before clapping his hands.

Chase the Rabbit Around

Grades: K–1
Number of Players: 6–12
Playing Areas: classroom, hallway, playroom, gymnasium, playground
Equipment: 2 bean bags
Basic Skills: carrying an object, chasing, tagging, running in a circle
DESCRIPTION OF GAME. Players sit or stand in a single circle formation facing the center. One bean bag is identified as a "rabbit" and the other as a "fox." The game is started by a child who passes one bean bag, the rabbit, to the child on his right, who runs with it around the outside of the circle. The other bean bag, the fox, is given to another child, who chases the player with the rabbit. When he catches him, that game ends and a new one is begun. If the child with the rabbit returns to his position safely, he is entitled to run again, chased by a new player with the fox.

Teaching Hints. The game could be made progressively more difficult by increasing the number, size, and shape of the objects being carried around the circle. The direction of movement could also be changed from clockwise to counterclockwise.

Spider and Flies

Grades: K–2
Number of Players: 10–30
Playing Areas: gymnasium, playground
Equipment: none
Basic Skills: dodging, chasing, tagging, running, moving from a squat to
    a running position
DESCRIPTION OF GAME. To play this game it is necessary to mark two goal lines 40 feet apart and a circle between the goal lines large enough to hold all the players. One player is a "spider" and squats in the circle while the rest of the players are "flies" and stand behind the goal lines. All flies advance toward the circle and walk around to the right. When the spider jumps up, all flies run toward a goal while the spider tags as many flies as possible before

they get back behind either goal line. Those tagged join the spider in the circle and help catch the remaining flies. The last fly caught is the spider in the next game.

Teaching Hints. To make it easier for the spider to catch the flies, the circle may be made smaller.

Midnight

Grades: K-2
Number of Players: 10-30
Playing Areas: gymnasium, playground
Equipment: none
Basic Skills: chasing, tagging, running, walking, reversing direction
DESCRIPTION OF GAME. Two children are selected to be "Mr. Fox" and "Mother Hen." All the other players are "chickens." The hen and chickens have a goal line 30 yards away from the fox. Mother Hen leads the chickens to Mr. Fox and asks, "What time is it?" Mr. Fox replies with any time he chooses, but when he answers "midnight," the hen and chickens run toward their goal with the fox chasing them. Those tagged become "Mr. Fox's helpers." The last one caught is the winner.

Teaching Hints. If Mr. Fox is having difficulty catching the chickens, the latter may be encouraged to come closer to ask the time.

Frog in the Sea

Grades: K-2
Number of Players: 5-10
Playing Areas: classroom, hallway, playroom, gymnasium, playground
Equipment: none
Basic Skills: tagging, feinting
DESCRIPTION OF GAME. A circle, about 6 feet in diameter, is scratched or drawn on the playing surface. A child is selected to be the frog. He sits cross-legged in the center of the circle. The other children chant:

> "Frog in the sea
> Can't catch me!"

When the children step into his circle, the frog attempts to tag them without leaving his sitting position. Anyone tagged becomes the frog. If the frog leaves his sitting position to tag someone, the child tagged does not become the frog.

Teaching Hints. A large class can be divided into groups, each with its own frog; or the circle could be made large and three or four frogs could be used.

A Dillar a Dollar

Grades: K-2
Number of Players: 8-10

Playing Areas: gymnasium, playground
Equipment: none
Basic Skills: dodging, skipping, chasing, tagging, running

DESCRIPTION OF GAME.   The children form a circle. The child who is "It" stands 40 or 50 feet away from the circle. The children in the circle skip around the circle and then stop, put their hands to their eyes as if shading them from the sun, look at the child who is "It," and chant:

> "A Dillar, a Dollar—a ten o'clock scholar!
> What makes you come so soon?
> You used to come at ten o'clock
> And now you come at noon!"

One of the children asks: "Where have you been, scholar?" "It" replies:

> "I've been to sea to catch a fish
> And on my way I made a wish!"

The same child in the circle who spoke before asks: "What did you wish, scholar?"

"It" replies: "I wished there were no one who could run fast enough to catch me."

The child who asked the questions gives chase to "It." If "It" is caught, he joins the circle and the child who caught him becomes "It." If "It" is not caught in a reasonable amount of time (2 to 3 minutes), he returns to the circle and another child is chosen to ask the next question.

Teaching Hints.   For younger children, the teacher will need to supply the right words in the chant, questions, and replies when they forget what to say. Those who have not developed the skill of skipping may substitute galloping or running.

Old Mother Witch

Grades: K–2
Number of Players: 5–10
Playing Areas: playroom, gymnasium
Equipment: none
Basic Skills: dodging, chasing, tagging, running, moving from a sitting to a running position

DESCRIPTION OF GAME.   A goal line is marked across one end of the playing area. A circle with a diameter of approximately 9 feet is drawn at the other end of the playing area. A child is selected to play the "Old Mother Witch." Old Mother Witch settles herself in a sitting position within the circle. The children chant:

> "Old Mother Witch
> Fell in a ditch,
> Picked up a penny,
> And thought she was rich!"

While chanting, they run into and through her circle. The witch asks them repeatedly: "Whose children are you?"

They answer with any name or person that occurs to them. The witch does nothing. However, when any child says "yours!" that is the signal for the witch to give chase. The children run toward their goal line. A child tagged before reaching the goal line becomes the witch and the play continues.

Teaching Hints. If Old Mother Witch cannot move quickly enough to catch anyone, two or more witches could be used.

Wild Horse Round-Up

Grades: K–2
Number of Players: 8–30
Playing Area: playground
Equipment: none
Basic Skills: dodging, chasing, tagging, running, change of pace

DESCRIPTION OF GAME. The boundaries of the playground define the "range." A circular "corral" of 9 to 12 feet in diameter is marked with chalk or scratched out on the ground to one side of the range. Four to eight of the children are "cowboys" and "cowgirls" and all the others are "wild horses." One of the former is designated as the "foreman." When the foreman calls out "wild horses!" the horses must run from the "mountains" (the area immediately surrounding the range) into the range. The horses must stay within the confines of the range until they are caught by one of the cowhands. When the horses are caught, they go to the corral. The last child caught becomes the new foreman, who chooses three other players as cowhands who have not served in that capacity previously.

Teaching Hints. To avoid rough play, tagging should be employed rather than catching.

Rabbits and Foxes

Grades: K–2
Number of Players: no limit
Playing Area: gymnasium, playground
Equipment: none
Basic Skills: dodging, chasing, tagging, running, change of pace

DESCRIPTION OF GAME. The class is divided into two teams, one called the "rabbits" and the other the "foxes." Members of both teams stand behind their respective goal lines. The rabbits come out to play in front of their goal line. A fox calls out: "Run, rabbit, run!" The foxes try to catch the rabbits before they can return to their goal line. Rabbits caught become foxes and play continues until there are no rabbits. The game is then repeated with all the players changing sides.

Teaching Hints. The game may be played inside, but the number on each side would need to be limited.

Animal Tag

Grades: K–2
Number of Players: 10–30
Playing Areas: gymnasium, playground
Equipment: none
Basic Skills: dodging, chasing, tagging, running, change of pace

DESCRIPTION OF GAME.   A "den" is marked off in each of two corners of the playing field. Each den is large enough to accommodate all the players. Each child is named after a different animal. There may be several children representing one animal if the group is large. All the children begin in one den. One child, the "chaser," stands between the two dens. He calls out the name of an animal—"bears," for example. All the bears attempt to run across the playing area to the other den without being tagged by the chaser. Any players caught become chasers.

Teaching Hints.   The chaser may be positioned at different points to make the catching easier or more difficult, whichever seems necessary.

If the children are young, several may represent one animal to keep the number of different names of animals to a minimum.

Charlie Over the Water

Grades: K–2
Number of Players: 8–15
Playing Areas: classroom, playroom, gymnasium
Equipment: none
Basic Skills: skipping, tagging, galloping, running in a circle, moving
        from an upright position to a squat

DESCRIPTION OF GAME.   The children start in a single circle formation with hands clasped. One of the children stands in the center of the circle. He is "Charlie." The players walk, skip, gallop, or run to the left (or the right) around the circle chanting:

> "Charlie over the water,
> Charlie over the sea,
> Charlie caught a blackbird
> But he can't catch me!"

As the children say "me," they squat quickly. Charlie attempts to tag one of the children before he can squat. A child tagged becomes Charlie and the game continues.

Teaching Hints.   If Charlie experiences difficulty in tagging someone, the circle should be made smaller or two or more Charlies should be used. Changes may be made from time to time in the direction of movement, the action (skipping, running, galloping), and the safety position (squat, front lean rest, stand on one foot).

Cat and Mice

Grades: K–3
Number of Players: 8–15
Playing Areas: playroom, gymnasium
Equipment: none
Basic Skills: dodging, chasing, tagging

DESCRIPTION OF GAME. The children form a large circle with four "mice" in the center and a "cat" on the outside. On the signal, the cat runs into the circle and tries to tag all the mice. The mice may run anywhere within the circle to avoid being tagged. When tagged, a mouse takes a place in the circle. The last mouse caught is the cat for the next game. The leader then chooses four new mice.

Teaching Hints. In a large group, more "mice" may be used in the center, or for older children, several different circles may be used.

Brownies and Fairies

Grades: K–3
Number of Players: 20–30
Playing Areas: playroom, gymnasium
Equipment: none
Basic Skills: tagging, running, turning to run from a stationary position

DESCRIPTION OF GAME. The children are divided into two groups, one called the "brownies" and the other, the "fairies." Goal lines are marked across both ends of the play area about 40 feet apart. The members of each team line up along their own goal line. The members of one team have their backs turned toward their opponents. The members of the other team, on a silent signal from the teacher, advance quietly toward their opponents until they are 10 or 15 feet away from them (or within distance for a good chase) when the teacher shouts: "The brownies (or fairies) are coming!" The members of the team which have been standing suddenly whirl about and give chase to their opponents. Any child tagged must go back to the goal line of the child who tagged him. Those tagged become members of the opponent's team. The other team then receives its opportunity to do the tagging.

Teaching Hints. The children should be instructed to disperse themselves over the entire area so that they will not get into one another's way. By varying the distance the advancing team is permitted to approach toward the opponents before calling the signal, the game is made more interesting.

Eagle and Sparrows

Grades: K–3
Number of Players: 5–20
Playing Area: gymnasium
Equipment: none
Basic Skills: dodging, chasing, tagging, rotating arms, change of pace

DESCRIPTION OF GAME. One player is chosen as the "eagle." The other players are "sparrows" whom the eagle chases in an attempt to catch one. The sparrows must stretch their arms out to the sides, palms up, and rotate them up, back, down, and forward as they run. (see Exercise 8, page 143). A sparrow who is tagged becomes the eagle. Sparrows may not stop rotating their arms while being chased; anyone who does becomes the eagle.

Teaching Hints. Before the game is played, the children should learn to rotate their arms in a way that will help them gain maximum benefit from this postural activity.

Hop Tag

Grades: K–3
Number of Players: No limit
Playing Areas: classroom, hallway, playroom, gymnasium, playground
Equipment: none
Basic Skills: dodging, tagging, hopping

DESCRIPTION OF GAME. One player is "It." Hopping on one foot, he tries to tag one of the other players who are also hopping. When a player is tagged, he becomes the new "It." From time to time the teacher calls, "change feet," and then all those who are being chased must hop on the other foot. "It" may tag anyone while the change is being made.

Teaching Hints. With younger children, the teacher should watch for signs of fatigue in hopping on one foot and make the call for change of feet accordingly.

Japanese Tag

Grades: K–4
Number of Players: No limit
Playing Areas: classroom, hallway, playroom, gymnasium, playground
Equipment: none
Basic Skills: dodging, chasing, tagging, change of pace

DESCRIPTION OF GAME. Any player who is tagged must hold his hand on the spot where he was tagged while attempting to tag others.

Teaching Hints. Because running with the hand held on the leg is difficult and disadvantageous to the chaser, everyone may be required to hold his hand on his leg when the chaser must do so.

Shadow Tag

Grades: K–4
Number of Players: No limit
Playing Area: playground
Equipment: none
Basic Skill: dodging

DESCRIPTION OF GAME. The children are dispersed over the playing area. The teacher selects one child to be "It." "It" attempts to step on the shadow of another player's head. If he succeeds, the player whose "head" was stepped on becomes "It."

Teaching Hints. The game may be played inside if the lighting can be arranged to cast shadows.

Skip Tag

Grades: 1–2
Number of Players: 12–24
Playing Areas: classroom, hallway, playroom, gymnasium, playground
Equipment: none
Basic Skills: skipping, tagging

DESCRIPTION OF GAME. The players form a single circle facing center. The player who is "It" stands on the outside of the circle. "It" skips around the outside of the circle, tags a player who skips after him, attempting to tag him before he can skip back to the vacated position. If "It" is tagged, he continues as "It." If he reaches the empty place before he is tagged, the chaser becomes the new "It."

Teaching Hints. Skipping around the circle more than once before tagging someone and favoritism in tagging should be discouraged. Hopping and jumping may be substituted for skipping.

Run for Your Supper

Grades: 1–2
Number of Players: 10–15
Playing Areas: classroom, hallway, playroom, gymnasium, playground
Equipment: none
Basic Skills: tagging, running in a circle, turning to run from a stationary
   position

DESCRIPTION OF GAME. Players form a circle. A child selected to be "It" walks around the inside of the circle. He stops in front of two players and, thrusting his arms between them, says "Run for your supper." He remains in this position while the runners go in opposite directions around the outside of the circle. The one who returns and tags the outstretched arms of "It" first is the winner and becomes the next "It."

Teaching Hints. If the group is large, more than one circle may be formed.

Cat and Rat

Grades: 2–3
Number of Players: 8–30
Playing Areas: classroom, hallway, playroom, gymnasium, playground
Equipment: none
Basic Skills: dodging, chasing, tagging, running, clasping hands to hold
   securely

DESCRIPTION OF GAME. All the children except two stand in circle formation holding hands. One of the two children, the "rat," stands inside the circle; the other, the "cat," stands outside. The cat and the rat hold the following conversation:

> Cat: "I am the cat."
> Rat: "I am the rat."
> Cat: "I will catch you."
> Rat: "No! You can't."

With this last statement the cat attempts to tag the rat. The children in the circle allow the rat to enter and to leave the circle at will but do not accord the same courtesy to the cat. When the cat tags the rat, he becomes the rat and the teacher selects another cat.

Teaching Hints. The teacher should instruct the children about safety procedures to be used when a child runs into the locked hands. If, in doing so, the child is swung from his feet, he should be lowered slowly to the ground by the two children into whose hands he has run.

Chinese Wall

Grades: 2–3
Number of Players: 10–30
Playing Area: playground
Equipment: none
Basic Skills: dodging, chasing, tagging, running, change of pace

DESCRIPTION OF GAME.   All the players except one stand behind the goal line. The remaining player is the "guard." He positions himself in the "Chinese wall"—an area 10 feet deep running the width of the playing area and across its center. The playing area is roughly 70 feet in length. When the guard yells "Go!" all the players rush from their goal line through the Chinese wall and to the opposite goal line. Any player tagged by the guard within the Chinese wall area becomes a guard and must tag the others. Players passing through the Chinese wall area without being tagged are "free." The players not tagged line up on the goal line and on the signal "Go!" from the guard they again try to get through the Chinese wall without being tagged. The game continues until all players have been tagged except one. This one then becomes the guard for the next game.

Teaching Hints.   This game is similar to *Pom-Pom Pull Away* (see below), except that the area in which the tag can be made is smaller. This version should be used when the runner is to be favored over the chaser.

Pom-Pom Pull Away

Grades: 2–3
Number of Players: 10–30
Playing Area: playground
Equipment: none
Basic Skills: dodging, chasing, tagging, running, change of pace

DESCRIPTION OF GAME.   This game is played in an area a minimum of 20 by 60 feet. Lines are drawn near each end of the area. The players are behind one line. One player who is "It" stands between the two lines and faces the other players. He calls "pom-pom pull away" three times. This is the signal for all players to dash to the safety of the other line. Any player tagged by "It" during this dash joins him in tagging others. The last player tagged is the winner.

Teaching Hints. This game is used when it is desired that the tagger be favored (see Teaching Hints for *Chinese Wall,* above).

Hill Dill

Grades: 2–3
Number of Players: 10–30
Playing Area: playground
Equipment: none
Basic Skills: chasing, tagging, running, change of pace

DESCRIPTION OF GAME. *Hill Dill* is another tag game similar to *Chinese Wall* and *Pom-Pom Pull Away,* the only difference being that the call is "Hill Dill Come Over the Hill." For some unknown reason *Hill Dill* has been, in the past, more popular with younger children than *Pom-Pom Pull Away* and *Chinese Wall.* Elementary textbooks often recommend *Hill Dill* be played by younger children while the other two games are recommended for older children.

Teaching Hints. As indicated above, *Hill Dill* is frequently played by younger children only, but there is no valid reason that it could not be enjoyed by older children as well.

Red Rover

Grades: 2–3
Number of Players: 10–30
Playing Area: playground
Equipment: none
Basic Skills: dodging, chasing, tagging, running, change of pace

DESCRIPTION OF GAME. Two lines are drawn 70 feet apart. One player is "It" and stands between the lines. All others stand behind one of the lines. "It" calls, "Red Rover, Red Rover, let (a player's name) come over." The player whose name is called runs to the opposite line while "It" attempts to tag him. If the runner is caught, he helps "It" catch other players.

Teaching Hints. To speed up the game, the names of several players may be called at the same time.

Chain Tag

Grades: 2–4
Number of Players: 10–30
Playing Area: playground
Equipment: none
Basic Skills: dodging, chasing, tagging, synchronized running

DESCRIPTION OF GAME. Two players who are "It" join hands. Two others also join hands and are the other "It." Both pairs attempt to tag other players who are dispersed around the playground. Pairs must not release their hand grips. Any player tagged must join hands with the pair which tagged him. If at any time the hand grips are broken, the players must stop and rejoin hands. Anyone tagged when the links are broken is still free. The game ends when all have been caught. The winner is the team with the most players.

Teaching Hints. The number of "Its" may be increased for larger groups or if the game moves too slowly.

Count Three Tag

Grades: 2–4
Number of Players: 10–30
Playing Areas: playroom, gymnasium, playground
Equipment: any object that can be held in the hand
Basic Skills: dodging, carrying an object, chasing, tagging, running

DESCRIPTION OF GAME. One player is selected to be "It." Another player is given an object to carry (bean bag, towel, etc.). "It" attempts to tag the child with the object who may at any time give (but not throw) it to another player. That player *must* take the object. If "It" tags a player while he has the object in his possession, that player becomes the new chaser and the object is given another child. 'It" must count to three before he can begin the chase.

Teaching Hints. Larger objects may be used as students' abilities permit to give experience in maneuvering large objects.

Steal the Bacon

Grades: 3–4
Number of Players: 10–30
Playing Areas: hallway, playroom, gymnasium, playground
Equipment: bean bag or similar item
Basic Skills: tagging, running, feinting

DESCRIPTION OF GAME. Two lines are marked on the floor or ground parallel to one another and approximately 20 feet apart. Half the class members are lined up along one line and the other half along the other line. The two teams face one another and count off starting at their own right end from 1 through to the last member of each team. Like numbered players on opposing teams will be diagonally opposite one another. The "bacon" (cap, hat, bean bag, or other suitable item) is placed midway between the two teams. The teacher or leader calls out a number at which the players with this number run out and attempt to snatch the bacon and return to the safety of their own goal line before being tagged by the opponent. The runner may employ various feints to throw the tagger off guard. A player succeeding in reaching safety earns 1 point for his team. If he is tagged, his opponents receive 1 point. The team with the higher score is the winner.

Teaching Hints. Large groups can be divided into several small groups each with its own number caller and score keeper. The game can be made more complex by calling two or three numbers at one time.

Chase the Bulldog

Grades: 3–4
Number of Players: 5–10
Playing Areas: playroom, gymnasium, playground
Equipment: none
Basic Skills: dodging, chasing, tagging, running, moving from a squat to
  a running position

DESCRIPTION OF GAME. A 30 foot square area is marked on the floor or ground. One child is the "Bulldog," and another child is the "Master." The Bulldog squats on the ground beside his Master in the center of the square. The other players stand on a line facing the Master. The Bulldog chooses a color (substitute any type of item) and whispers it to the Master. Other players try to guess the color. When someone does, the Master says, "Chase the Bulldog." The child who tags the Bulldog becomes the next dog and chooses his own Master. If the Bulldog runs out of the playing area, he is considered caught.

Teaching Hints. If more than five or six players are playing, the square may be enlarged to increase the possibility of the bulldog's avoiding being tagged too easily.

Man from Mars

Grades: 3–4
Number of Players: 10–30
Playing Areas: playroom, gymnasium, playground
Equipment: none
Basic Skills: dodging, chasing, tagging, running, change of pace

DESCRIPTION OF GAME. All the players except "It" stand on a line and call to "It" who is in the center of the playing area, "Man from Mars, may we chase you to the stars?" "It" replies, "Yes, if you have on white" (or any other color he chooses). All children wearing that color attempt to tag "It." They may chase him anywhere on the entire playing area. The child who tags him becomes "It" for the next game.

Teaching Hints. Children should be encouraged to call different colors in order that all will receive a turn.

Prisoners' Base or Dare Base

Grades: 3–4
Number of Players: 10–20
Playing Area: playground
Equipment: none
Basic Skills: dodging, chasing, tagging, running, change of pace

DESCRIPTION OF GAME. Children form packs of four or five players. Each pack has an area marked out as its "den." The dens are distributed along the edges of the playing area. The members of each den try to capture members of other dens by tagging them when they are outside their dens. Those tagged must come with their captor to his den. While taking a captive to his den, the player is immune to capture. He takes his captive by the hand and brings him directly to his den. The captured child becomes a member of the pack which caught him. A player may capture only opponents who left their den before he left his. For example, if "A" left his den first, "B" left his second, and "C" left his third, "A" can capture neither "B" nor "C"; "B" can capture "A" but not "C"; and "C" can capture either "A" or "B". If "A" returns to his den and then comes out again, he may capture either "B" or "C". The pack which captures all the other players is the winner.

Teaching Hints. The children may be shown the strategy of putting a player out as a decoy to lure an opponent into position to be caught by pack members on the alert in the den.

Chief Red Ball

    Grades: 3–4
    Number of Players: 10–20
    Playing Areas: gymnasium, playground
    Equipment: none
    Basic Skills: dodging, chasing, tagging, running, change of pace
    DESCRIPTION OF GAME. A player chosen as "Chief Red Ball" stands between two goal lines which are 40 feet apart. All players wait behind a goal line until "Chief Red Ball" calls "Red Ball" three times. All the children run to the opposite goal as the chief chases them. Players caught become chasers, too. Any player who leaves the goal too soon is considered caught.

Teaching Hints. The chief may be encouraged to try to fool players by calling "Red Ball, Red Ball, Blue Ball" or whatever he chooses.

Bear in the Pit

    Grades: 3–4
    Number of Players: 10–15
    Playing Areas: gymnasium, playground
    Equipment: none
    Basic Skills: dodging, chasing, tagging, crawling, clasping hands to hold
      securely
    DESCRIPTION OF GAME. All the children except one form a circle holding hands. This one, the "bear," stands inside the "pit" (circle). He tries to break out of the circle by breaking through the children's clasped hands, crawling under their arms or in any other manner. When he breaks out, the others chase him around the area. The one who catches him is the new bear.

Teaching Hints. The teacher should instruct the children about safety procedures to be used when a child runs into locked hands. If, in doing so, the child is swung from his feet, he should be lowered slowly to the ground by the two children into whose hands he has run.

Skunk Tag

Grades: 3–4
Number of Players: 10–15
Playing Areas: classroom, playroom, gymnasium, playground
Equipment: none
Basic Skills: chasing, tagging, running, moving from a running position to a balance position

DESCRIPTION OF GAME. The game is played like simple tag except that a player can avoid being tagged by holding his nose with one hand and his foot with the other. The player tagged becomes "It."

Teaching Hints. The teacher should encourage players to scatter over the entire playing area. Bumping and pushing of players who are in the safety position should be forbidden. The safety position may be assumed either in a squatting position or while standing on one foot.

Bronco Tag or Loose Caboose

Grades: 3–4
Number of Players: 10–25
Playing Areas: gymnasium, playground
Equipment: none
Basic Skills: chasing, synchronized side stepping

DESCRIPTION OF GAME. The children form several files of three to six children in each file. The files are arranged like the spokes of a wheel with "It" in the center. Each file is a "bronco." All the children in a file hold on to the hips of the one in front of them. "It" attempts to latch-on to the "tail" of the bronco by grasping the hips of the last child in the file. If "It" latches on to a "tail," the "head" of that file becomes "It."

Teaching Hints. The teacher should encourage the first child in the file or the "head" to keep himself between "It" and his "tail." He must also know where his "tail" is at all times.

Cross Tag

Grades: 3–4
Number of Players: 10–15
Playing Areas: gymnasium, playground
Equipment: none
Basic Skills: dodging, chasing, tagging, running, changing direction

DESCRIPTION OF GAME. The players scatter around the playing area. One player who is "It" runs and tries to tag another player. If another player crosses between the chased player and "It," he must change and chase the crossing player.

Teaching Hints. To make a more active game, a larger number of "Its" may be used.

Partner Tag

Grades: 3–6
Number of Players: 10–25

Playing Areas: playroom, gymnasium, playground
Equipment: none
Basic Skills: dodging, chasing, tagging, running, synchronized running
DESCRIPTION OF GAME.   The children assume a double line formation. They pair up and each pair links arms. Every child must have both of his hands on his hips. One child who is "It" chases another who attempts to escape by hooking another child's arm. The partner of the child "hooked" becomes "It" and gives chase to the child who had been "It." If "It" succeeds in tagging the child he is chasing before he can hook on to another child, the child tagged becomes "It" and chases the former "It."

Teaching Hints.   The distance between pairs may be varied according to the age and skill of the players.

Goal Tag

Grades: 4–6
Number of Players: 10–30
Playing Areas: playroom, gymnasium, playground
Equipment: none
Basic Skills: dodging, tagging, running, stopping
DESCRIPTION OF GAME.   Each player chalks a square at random throughout the playing area which he occupies as his own base. One player is selected as the tagger. When the tagger leaves his base, all others must leave their bases and stop in a new square. The tagger attempts to tag any player seeking a new base. No player may return to the base which he has previously occupied until he has stopped at three different squares. Two players may not share the same base. The person who is tagged becomes the new "It" and the game continues.

Teaching Hints.   Encourage rapid play and restrict playing area to a feasible size.

Labyrinth Tag

Grades: 5–6
Number of Players: 10–30
Playing Areas: classroom, hallway, playroom, gymnasium, playground
Equipment: none
Basic Skills: dodging, running, clasping hands to hold securely
DESCRIPTION OF GAME.   A runner and tagger are selected; the remaining players stand in parallel lines. There should be the same number of players in each line as there are number of lines, so that when all players turn, the lines will be the same length. Players face forward and grasp the wrists of their neighbors on either side. The runner, in order to avoid the tagger, runs up and down the lanes formed by rows of players. A leader calls out, "Face Left," "Face Front," "Face Right," or "Face Rear." When the players hear each command, they drop wrists, face the prescribed direction, and grasp the wrists of their new neighbors. The runner may not break through the links, nor may the tagger reach across outstretched arms to tag the runner. Play continues until

the chaser tags the runner or until a designated time limit expires. A new runner and tagger are chosen and play resumes.

Teaching Hints. The leader should make frequent commands in order to prevent the runner's capture. The tagger and runner should be changed frequently.

Circle Run

Grades: 5–8
Number of Players: 10–15
Playing Areas: playroom, gymnasium, playground
Equipment: none
Basic Skills: tagging, running in a circle

DESCRIPTION OF GAME. The children stand in circle formation with a distance of 5 to 7 feet separating players. At the signal, all run clockwise around the circle, each player trying to tag the one in front of him while avoiding being tagged by the one behind him. When the signal is again given, the players turn and run in the opposite direction. A player who is tagged must step toward the center of the circle where he waits until the finish of the game with the others who have been tagged. The last player remaining is the winner.

Teaching Hints. This game makes an excellent warm-up activity but is very tiring. The last players should be watched for signs of fatigue. It may be advisable to stop the game momentarily to allow a rest before determining a winner. When there is a large number of players, they should be numbered from one to three, four, or five. When one of these numbers is called only those with that number run. The others step outside the circle until their number is called, then they may begin running.

Capture the Flag

Grades: 5–8
Number of Players: 10–30
Playing Area: playground
Equipment: 2 flags
Basic Skills: dodging, tagging, running

DESCRIPTION OF GAME. Two or more flags (pieces of cloth on a stick) are required. A rectangular or square area is marked out with a line running through the center. A "prison" area is marked out along opposite goal lines at opposing corners of the area. A flag is stuck into the ground at the center of each goal line. The players are divided into two teams of equal numbers. The members of each team try to capture and carry the opponents' flag into their own half of the field without being tagged. All defenders of the flag must stay at least 10 feet from the flag at all times. Players tagged while in enemy territory go to prison. Teammates may rescue a prisoner by going into the prison, taking his hand and running to their own court with him without being tagged. If rescuer or prisoner are tagged while in enemy territory, both become prisoners. Rescuers may recover only one prisoner at a time.

Teaching Hints. Each team may be given several flags. The team capturing all of the opponents' flags is the winner.

RELAY GAMES

Relay games are activities in which a number of players relieve one another or take turns performing a certain task, such as carrying an object. In all relay games the players form teams, and generally the objective of the game is for all members of one team to perform the required task before any other team. Under the teacher's guidance, children enjoy relay games very much, but do not engage in them spontaneously as they do tag games. These games require more organization and, as with all team games, more cooperation among the team members. Because of the cooperative effort required and because they provide experience in using the basic skills, the relay games are excellent choices for the physical education program. The skills utilized depend upon the particular relay, but they range from ball control to running and maneuvering the body into specific positions.

Line Relay

Grades: K–2
Number of Players: 10–30
Playing Areas: classroom, hallway, playroom, gymnasium, playground
Equipment: none
Basic Skills: running, starting

DESCRIPTION OF GAME. Players form teams in parallel lines and count off. A leader calls a number and this player on each team steps out to the right and runs counterclockwise completely around the team back to his original position. The player who returns first scores one point. The team that first scores 15 points wins.

Teaching Hints. To increase the length of the run, the distance between players in the line may be increased.

Bronco Relay

Grades: K–2
Number of Players: 10–30
Playing Areas: classroom, hallway, playroom, gymnasium, playground
Equipment: one broom stick for each line
Basic Skill: synchronized running

DESCRIPTION OF GAME. Players form lines of an even number of players. One stick, which may be a broom handle, is needed for each line. Each line divides into partners. The first couple, one behind the other, straddles the stick at the starting line. On the signal, they ride the stick to a specified turning line and back to the starting point where they give the stick to couple number two who repeats the same action. The line in which all the couples complete the relay first is the winner.

Teaching Hints. If there is an uneven number of players, one player may run twice.

Circle Relay

Grades: K–2
Number of Players: 6–8 for each circle
Playing Areas: classroom, hallway, playroom, gymnasium, playground
Equipment: handkerchief for each circle
Basic Skill: running in a circle

DESCRIPTION OF GAME. Players form circles. Number one in each circle is given a handkerchief. He runs to his right around the circle and gives the handkerchief to number two who repeats the same procedure. The relay continues until each person has had a turn. The first circle finished is the winner.

Teaching Hints. The size of the circles may be decreased or increased either by the number of players or by the amount of space between players.

Tag the Line Race

Grades: 1–2
Number of Players: 12–32
Playing Areas: classroom, hallway, playroom, gymnasium
Equipment: none
Basic Skills: running, reversing direction

DESCRIPTION OF GAME. A starting line and a finish line are marked on the playing surface 20 feet apart. The children form files of six to eight players behind the first child who stands on the starting line. On the signal the first child in each file runs to the finish line to touch the line or beyond it with his foot, turns around, and runs back to the starting line. The first player back makes 1 point for his team. Each child takes his turn in order until all have run. The team with the most points is the winner.

Teaching Hints. When children have begun to develop the team concept, the relay can be run by having them touch off the succeeding runner and then go to the end of the line.

Club Relay

Grades: 1–2
Number of Players: 12–32
Playing Areas: classroom, hallway, playroom, gymnasium
Equipment: one Indian club for each team
Basic Skill: running in a circle

DESCRIPTION OF GAME. The children line up behind the starting line in single files of six to eight children in each file. An Indian club is placed in front of each team 20–40 feet away. On the signal, the first child in each file runs to the Indian club, counterclockwise around it, and back to touch off the next child in line.

The action is repeated by each child in the line until all have run. The first line through is the winner.

Teaching Hints. The difficulty of the game may be increased by requiring the runners to go around the Indian club two or more times.

Thread the Needle Relay

Grades: 1–2
Number of Players: 10–30
Playing Areas: hallway, playroom, gymnasium
Equipment: two Indian clubs for each team
Basic Skills: running, reversing directions

DESCRIPTION OF GAME.   Teams of five to six children line up in single file behind the starting line. On the signal *all* the children on all teams race forward and run between the two Indian clubs which have been placed about 2 feet apart and 40 feet in front of each team. After running between the clubs without knocking them down, they race back to the starting line. If a club is knocked over, the runner must stop and set it up before continuing. The first team to have its last member over the starting line is declared the winner.

Teaching Hints.   The winning team can be more easily determined if the students are instructed to form a straight line and raise an arm after the last runner has crossed the starting line.

Tire Relay

Grades: 2–3
Number of Players: 12–30
Playing Areas: playroom, gymnasium, playground
Equipment: one tire for each team
Basic Skills: running, crawling

DESCRIPTION OF GAME.   A starting line and a touch line 50 feet away are needed. Teams of 6 to 10 players are lined up single file behind the starting line. The automobile tire is placed in front of each team midway between the starting and the touch line. On the signal, the first child in each line runs to the tire, crawls through it, runs to touch his foot on or beyond the touch line, runs back to the tire, crawls through it, runs to the starting line, and touches off the next player in line. When all members of a team have run, they sit down on the ground in single file. The first team with all its members sitting on the ground is declared the winner.

Teaching Hints.   To increase the complexity of the activity, another obstacle, such as a barrier or rope to climb or jump over, may be placed at the touch line.

Rescue Relay

Grades: 2–4
Number of Players: 10–30
Playing Areas: classroom, hallway, playroom, gymnasium, playground
Equipment: none
Basic Skill: synchronized running

DESCRIPTION OF GAME.   The class forms two or more teams. They stand in file formation with a leader from each team standing behind a goal line which is 25 feet from the starting line. The leader runs to the first player on his team, grasps the player's hand, and runs back with the player to the goal line. The rescued player runs back and gets the next player until all have been rescued.

Teaching Hints. To shorten the time required to complete the race or to involve more players at one time, the runner may be permitted to rescue two players at a time.

Circle Weave Relay

Grades: 2–4
Number of Players: 12–30
Playing Areas: classroom, hallway, playroom, gymnasium, playground
Equipment: none
Basic Skills: dodging, running

DESCRIPTION OF GAME. Players form circles—six to eight players to a circle. One player from each circle starts the relay by running to the outside of the player to his right, to the inside of the next, and continues weaving in this pattern around the circle to the starting position. He then tags the next player to his right who similarly runs to his right around the circle. The relay continues until everyone in the circle has had a turn. The first circle to complete the relay is the winner.

Teaching Hints. For older children, the game can be made more challenging by requiring every other player to run to his left.

Circle Jump Relay

Grades: 2–3
Number of Players: 10–30
Playing Areas: classroom, hallway, playroom, gymnasium, playground
Equipment: none
Basic Skills: jumping, running in a circle

DESCRIPTION OF GAME. The class is divided into teams. A circle is drawn 15 feet in front of each team and a square is drawn 15 feet beyond the circle. The teams stand in file formation facing the circles. The first one from each team runs up to his circle, runs around the circle three times, and continues running to the square. Here he jumps up and down three times and returns to his team. Each member of the team repeats the procedure until all have had a turn.

Teaching Hints. To aid young children in keeping track of the number of times they have run around the circle and jumped in the squares, the team can count aloud in unison.

Man, Monkey, and Crab Relay

Grades: 2–4
Number of Players: 6–30
Playing Areas: classroom, hallway, playroom, gymnasium, playground
Equipment: none
Basic Skills: crawling, crab walking

DESCRIPTION OF GAME.   There will need to be marked a starting line and a touch line 30 to 50 feet away. Participants line up behind the starting line in single files of 3 to 12 children. The number in each file must be a multiple of three. The children in each file count off by three's. Number 1's are men. On the signal they race to the touch line and back to touch off the number 2's. Number 2's are monkeys. They run on all fours to the touch line and back to touch off the number 3's. Number 3's are crabs. The crabs on all fours with their faces up race to the touch line and back to touch off the next number 1's. The first team finishing is the winner.

Teaching Hints.   Each time the relay is run, the children should be in different positions in order to experience all of the movements.

Tight Rope Relay

Grades: 2–6
Number of Players: 5–30
Playing Areas: classroom, hallway, playroom, gymnasium, playground
Equipment: none
Basic Skill: walking heel to toe

DESCRIPTION OF GAME.   Players form teams and stand in file formation at the end of a 25-foot line drawn in front of each team. Each player walks heel-to-toe the length of the line and back, tags the hand of the next player, and goes to the end of his team. If a player goes off the line with either foot, he must stop, put both feet back on the line, and resume the walk.

Teaching Hints.   To reduce the amount of time the players stand in line, the length of the line may be decreased.

Pin Relay

Grades: 2–6
Number of Players: 10–30
Playing Areas: classroom, hallway, playroom, gymnasium, playground
Equipment: one Indian club for each team
Basic Skills: running, stooping

DESCRIPTION OF GAME.   A bowling pin or Indian club for each team is set in a small circle drawn on the floor 25 feet in front of each team. The players stand in file formation facing their circle. On "Go," the first child on each team runs to the pin, knocks it down, runs back to his team, tags the next player, and goes to the end of the line. The second player runs up, sets up the pin, and returns to his line. Play continues in this way until each player has a turn.

Teaching Hints.   To facilitate selecting the winning team, the teacher may have the children form a straight line and raise their right arms upon completion of the run.

Walking Relay

Grades: 3–4
Number of Players: 10–30

Playing Areas: classroom, hallway, playroom, gymnasium, playground
Equipment: none
Basic Skill: walking rapidly

DESCRIPTION OF GAME. Players are lined up behind the starting line in single files of 5 to 15 players in each file. Each player, in his turn, walks to the touch line and returns to touch off the next player. A player who does not keep one foot in contact with the floor at all times disqualifies his team. The winning team is the one whose players have all had their turn and are back in their places first.

Teaching Hints. The complexity of the relay may be increased by having the players walk backward.

Back and Forth Relay

Grades: 3–6
Number of Players: 10–30
Playing Areas: hallway, playroom, gymnasium, playground
Equipment: none
Basic Skills: running, reversing direction

DESCRIPTION OF GAME. Teams are formed of five to 10 players each. A line is drawn 15 feet in front of each team and another line is drawn 10 feet beyond the first line. From a file formation, the first player from each team runs over the second line, turns and runs back over the first line, turns and runs back over the second line, turns and runs back over the first line, runs once more over the second line, and then returns to his team. Both feet must cross over the lines before moving to the next line. Each successive player repeats these movements. The winning team is the first one to complete the race.

Teaching Hints. If the game is played with young children, the teacher may have teammates count aloud for the runners so that he will know the number of times he has crossed the starting line.

Pilot Relay

Grades: 3–6
Number of Players: 6–33
Playing Areas: classroom, hallway, playroom, gymnasium
Equipment: none
Basic Skills: running, running backwards

DESCRIPTION OF GAME. The class is divided into teams of multiples of three. A turning line is marked 25 feet in front of each team. The first player faces the turning line and takes the hands of the second and third players who have their backs to the turning line. The first player runs forward to the line while the second and third players run backward. When returning to their team line, the first player runs backward as the second and third players run forward. The race continues in this way until all have had a turn. The team to complete the race first is the winner.

Teaching Hints. Before participating in this relay, the students should be given experience in running backward.

Jump Rope Relay

Grades: 3–7
Number of Players: 10–30
Playing Areas: classroom, hallway, playroom, gymnasium, playground
Equipment: 5-foot length of rope for each team
Basic Skills: running, jumping

DESCRIPTION OF GAME.   There should be a starting line and a touch line 30 to 40 feet away. The class should be lined up behind the starting line in several single file formations of 6 to 10 players in each file. The rope is placed on the touch line in front of each file. On the signal, the first child in each file runs to the touch line, picks up the rope, runs back to his file, gives one end of the rope to the second child and then both run back along their file holding the rope about 6 inches above the floor as their teammates jump over it. Upon reaching the end of the file, the first child falls in at the end of the file while the second runs with the rope to touch the touch line, runs back, hands one end of the rope to the second child and repeats the procedure followed by the first child. This procedure is repeated until all team members have taken their turn. The first team to finish is declared the winner.

Teaching Hints.   The children should receive instruction on how to hold the rope to avoid tripping anyone.

Sack Relay

Grades: 4–6
Number of Players: 12–32
Playing Areas: playroom, gymnasium, playground
Equipment: sack for each two runners
Basic Skills: synchronized running

DESCRIPTION OF GAME.   Two lines 50 to 100 feet apart are marked on the floor or ground. The players are divided into teams of four with two from each team stationed at each of the lines. The pairs at one line are given a sack in which they place their opposite legs and wrap an arm around each other's waist. At the command "Go" the pairs, synchronizing their steps, run from one line to the other, remove the sack, and hand it to the other pairs for the return trip. The line in which all couples complete the relay first is the winner.

Teaching Hints.   The pairs should be instructed to hold the sacks tightly around the legs to make synchronizing the movements easier.

Crows and Cranes

Grades: 4–6
Number of Players: 10–30
Playing Areas: hallway, playroom, gymnasium, playground
Equipment: none
Basic Skills: tagging, running

DESCRIPTION OF GAME.   The playing area is divided with a line in the center and a goal line at each end of the area. Players divide into two groups.

One group is called "crows" and the other, "cranes." They stand facing each other at the center. The leader calls "crows" or "cranes." The group called runs to the goal line behind it with the other group chasing. Players tagged go to the other group. Crows and cranes return to the center line. The leader gives the call again, and the action is repeated until the game is terminated.

The group with the largest number of players at the end of the playing time wins.

Teaching Hints. For added interest, the leader may be encouraged to prolong the "cr" sound of the word he plans to call, thereby keeping the players in suspense.

Indian Club Relay

Grades: 6–7
Number of Players: 12–30
Playing Areas: classroom, hallway, playroom, gymnasium, playground
Equipment: three Indian clubs for each team
Basic Skills: running, reversing directions, picking up objects
DESCRIPTION OF GAME. Players line up behind the starting line in files of 6 to 10. A circle is drawn in front of each file just beyond the starting line. Three X's are marked on the floor in line with each file and 6 feet apart, the first being 6 feet from the starting line. An Indian club is placed on each X. On the signal, the first player in each file runs to the first Indian club and returns to place it in the circle. He does the same with the second and third Indian clubs. He then touches off the next player in line who returns the clubs one by one to their original places. He touches off the third player who repeats the action of the first player, and so on down the line. The clubs must always remain standing. If a club falls, the player must return to stand it up before proceeding to the next step. The team finishing first with all of its players having run and back in their places is the winner.

Teaching Hints. To shorten the time the game requires and to speed up the action, two clubs may be used rather than three.

Push Ball Relay

Grades: 6–7
Number of Players: 12–30
Playing Areas: classroom, hallway, playroom, gymnasium, playground
Equipment: basketball and wand for each team
Basic Skill: ball control
DESCRIPTION OF GAME. The children line up in single file formation behind the starting line. There should be 6 to 10 players in each file. A basketball is placed on the starting line in front of each file. The first player in each file is given a wand. On the signal he pushes the ball with the wand to the touch line which is about 30 feet away, picks up the ball, runs back to hand the wand to the next child, and places the ball on the starting line. Each team member repeats this procedure until all have run. The team finishing first is the winner.

Teaching Hints. To make the game easier, the ball may be carried; to make it more difficult, the ball may be pushed in both directions.

Throw and Run Relay

Grades: 7–8
Number of Players: 10–30
Playing Areas: classroom, hallway, playroom, gymnasium, playground
Equipment: basketball for each team
Basic Skills: throwing, catching, running

DESCRIPTION OF GAME. Two lines are drawn on the ground or floor 20 to 30 feet apart. Half the members of each team line up single file behind one line while the other half of each team lines up single file behind the other line and directly opposite the other half. The first player in each team on one line has a basketball. On the signal, he throws it to his teammate in the opposite line and runs across to the end of the opposite file. Succeeding players repeat this procedure until all are back in their original positions. The team finishing first is the winner.

Teaching Hints. A player who fumbles the ball must retrieve it and return to his position before passing it. Players should be encouraged to pass accurately in order that the teammates can catch the ball more easily.

Baton Passing Relay

Grades: 7–8
Number of Players: 8–32
Playing Areas: playground
Equipment: baton for each team
Basic Skills: running, passing a baton

DESCRIPTION OF GAME. Four to 6 players make up a team. Lines are marked on the ground 40 to 60 feet apart, one line for each member of the team. The first player behind the starting line has a baton. On the signal, he runs with the baton to pass it to the player standing on the next line who carries it to the next, and so on until the last player receives it and runs across the finish line. The team whose last runner first crosses the finish line is declared the winner.

Teaching Hints. Players should be taught to carry the baton in their right hand and to place it in the next runner's left hand.

BALL CONTROL GAMES

The games described under this heading are those in which players attempt to control the ball. The control is exercised in a variety of ways: keeping the ball away from others, maneuvering with it around or over objects or other players, and kicking, batting, and rolling it at various speeds and heights. Skill in ball control is important to success and enjoyment in playing many games throughout the school years and beyond. The basic skill of ball control necessary for later acquisition of the more complex skills needed in these games can be developed through experience in the games in this section.

Line Ball

Grades: K–1
Number of Players: 10–30
Playing Areas: classroom, hallway, playroom, gymnasium, playground
Equipment: large ball
Basic Skills: throwing, catching, running

DESCRIPTION OF GAME. Three parallel lines are drawn on the ground 10 feet apart. The first line is the rolling line; the second line is the goal line; the third line is the starting line. A child is chosen as "It." He stands behind the rolling line while all other players stand behind the starting line. "It" rolls the ball toward the other players and calls the name of one player. The player named must run from the starting line and catch the ball before it rolls over the goal line. If he is successful, he changes places with "It." If the ball rolls past the player who was called, it may be caught by any player, who then rolls the ball back to "It."

Teaching Hints. To make it easier for the players to catch the ball before it crosses the goal line, the starting line may be moved closer to the goal line.

Teacher Ball

Grades: K–1
Number of Players: 6–10
Playing Areas: classroom, hallway, playroom, gymnasium, playground
Equipment: ball
Basic Skills: throwing, catching

DESCRIPTION OF GAME. Six to eight children are in rank formation with one child 8 to 10 feet in front of the group and facing them. He is the "teacher." The teacher throws the ball to each player in turn, and each child throws it back to the teacher. A player missing the ball goes to the foot of the line. If the teacher misses, he goes to the foot; the player at the head of the line becomes the teacher and play continues.

Teaching Hints. Bean bags, which are easier to catch, may be used by younger children. As skills improve, the distance may be increased.

Wonder Ball

Grades: K–2
Number of Players: 6–30
Playing Areas: classroom, hallway, playroom, gymnasium, playground
Equipment: ball or bean bag for each team
Basic Skill: ball handling

DESCRIPTION OF GAME. Six to 10 players form circles. One ball or bean bag is needed for each circle. The ball is passed around the circle from child to child while they repeat the following verse:

"The wonder ball goes round and round,
To pass it quickly you are bound,
If you're the one to hold it last,
You—are—OUT!"

The child holding the ball on the word "Out" is out of the circle. The player left alone in the circle is the winner.

Teaching Hints. Use a small ball. Instead of "Out" leaving the circle, the child has one point scored against him. The player having the lowest score is declared the winner.

Call Ball

Grades: K–3
Number of Players: 5–20
Playing Areas: classroom, hallway, playroom, gymnasium, playground
Equipment: large rubber ball
Basic Skills: throwing, catching
DESCRIPTION OF GAME. The players are in single circle formation with one child in the center. He throws the ball up and calls the name of one of the other players. The child whose name is called attempts to catch the ball either on the fly or on the first bounce. If he catches the ball, he becomes the thrower. If he fails to catch the ball, the child in the center continues to throw.

Teaching Hints. The position in the center can be made the penalty position rather than the reward position by having those who fail to make a successful catch go to the center.

Overhead Pass Relay

Grades: K–4
Number of Players: 12–50
Playing Areas: classroom, hallway, playroom, gymnasium, playground
Equipment: one large ball for each line
Basic Skills: ball handling, running
DESCRIPTION OF GAME. Players are arranged in two or more single file formations of 6 to 15 children in each file. The first player in each line holds a large ball such as a volleyball, basketball, or soccer ball in both hands. On the signal, the first player in each line passes the ball over his head to the next player. All succeeding team members pass the ball over their heads to the player behind. The last player in the line, on receiving the ball, runs along the right side of his file to the head of the file and passes the ball back overhead again. This procedure is repeated until all players have returned to their original places. The first team through is the winner.

VARIATIONS. *Through the Legs Relay.* Each team member passes the ball backward between his legs to the next player.

Roll Through the Legs Relay. The first team member rolls the ball backward between his legs through the straddled legs of his teammates. If he rolls it accurately, none need touch it.

Bounce Between the Legs Relay. Each player bounces the ball backward between his legs to the next player who catches it on the first bounce.

Over and Under Relay. The first player passes the ball backward over his head. The second player passes the ball backward between his legs.

Right Side Relay. Each team member passes the ball to his right side.

Left Side Relay. Each team member passes the ball to his left side.

All the above relays may be played without any running if players will face in the direction of travel of the ball after they have completed their pass.

Sitting Relay. Team members sit cross-legged and pass the ball overhead.

Teaching Hints. The overhead passing activity should be used frequently because it is an excellent posture exercise.

Hit the Basket

Grades: 1–2
Number of Players: 6–10
Playing Areas: classroom, hallway, playroom, gymnasium, playground
Equipment: ball
Basic Skills: throwing, catching
DESCRIPTION OF GAME. A circle approximately 12 feet in diameter is drawn, and a wastebasket is set in the center. One child stands in the center for retrieving purposes and six to eight players take positions outside the circle. Each player, in turn, tries to throw the ball into the basket from outside the circle. The center player gets the ball and passes it to the next player. A point is scored for each basket. After all players have had an equal number of turns, the player with the highest score wins.

Teaching Hints. To give everyone an opportunity to throw, the game should be kept short and a different retriever should be chosen for each new game.

Beat the Bunny

Grades: 1–2
Number of Players: 8–10
Playing Areas: classroom, hallway, playroom, gymnasium, playground
Equipment: large ball and small ball
Basic Skill: ball handling
DESCRIPTION OF GAME. A circle is formed, and a small ball and a large ball are given to players on opposite sides of the circle. The "bunny" (small ball) is started and is passed around the circle. Simultaneously, the "farmer" (large ball) is started and proceeds in the same direction. If the "farmer" catches the "bunny," one point is scored for the "farmer." If the "bunny" catches the "farmer," the "bunny" scores a point.

Teaching Hints. If the "farmer" is not scoring, the balls can be changed so the "farmer" is the smaller ball and the "bunny," the larger ball.

Circle Stride Ball

Grades: 1–2
Number of Players: 10–30
Playing Areas: playroom, gymnasium, playground
Equipment: large ball
Basic Skill: ball handling

DESCRIPTION OF GAME. The children are in a single circle formation facing the center with their legs straddled and the outside edges of their feet touching the outside edges of the feet of the player to either side of them. One child who is "It" stands in the center of each circle with a ball. He attempts to roll the ball between the players' legs. Players may not move their feet but they may stop or deflect the ball with their hands. A child allowing the ball to pass between his legs becomes "It," and the other child takes his place in the circle.

Teaching Hints. The children should be required to keep the ball low in order to avoid striking players by rolling it with an underhand throw. After the children have developed a measure of skill, two or three children with balls may be placed in the center.

Square Keep Away

Grades: 1–3
Number of Players: 4 for each square
Playing Areas: classroom, hallway, playroom, gymnasium, playground
Equipment: large ball for each square
Basic Skills: throwing, catching

DESCRIPTION OF GAME. For each group of four players, a court is drawn on the ground, composed of four squares each measuring eight feet square. One player occupies each square of the court. The players in the squares diagonally opposite each other are partners who try to keep the ball away from the other pair of players. The ball is played by rolling or bouncing. When a player steps on or over the boundary lines, the ball goes to the opposing team.

Teaching Hints. Playing the ball must be limited to rolling or bouncing to give opportunity for interception which would be less than if throwing over the heads were permitted.

Kneel Ball

Grades: 2–3
Number of Players: 8–30
Playing Areas: classroom, hallway, playroom, gymnasium, playground
Equipment: ball
Basic Skills: throwing, catching

DESCRIPTION OF GAME. The children are in two rank formations about 20 feet apart and facing one another. The player on the right of one rank throws the ball to the player on the right of the other rank. This player throws the ball to the player in the opposite rank who is second from the right end. Players continue throwing the ball diagonally across the two ranks. Any player failing to catch the ball must kneel and remain in that position until he successfully catches the ball in his turn after which he may again stand.

Teaching Hints. Unskilled players may have to remain on their knees for too long and should be allowed to return to the standing position when they successfully stop the ball.

Circle Ball Passing

Grades: 2–3
Number of Players: 10–30
Playing Areas: playroom, gymnasium, playground
Equipment: several large balls
Basic Skill: ball handling
DESCRIPTION OF GAME. The players are divided into two or more teams. All players form one single circle, facing the center with 5 to 8 feet distance between players. A ball is passed around the circle from player to player. Additional balls are introduced, all being passed around successively until five or six are going rapidly around the circle. When a player drops a ball, a point is scored against his team. At the end of a predetermined period of time, the team with the lowest score is declared the winner.

Teaching Hints. Balls of differing sizes and weights may be used to increase the difficulty of the game. A scorer should be appointed for each team.

One Step and Throw

Grades: 2–4
Number of Players: 10–30
Playing Areas: playroom, gymnasium, playground
Equipment: one ball for every two players
Basic Skills: throwing, catching
DESCRIPTION OF GAME. Pairs of players face each other 6 feet apart. The game starts by passing the ball from one to the other. Upon completion of each successful pass and catch, one step is taken backward. If a successful catch is not made, the players remain in place until a pass is caught. The size of the area will limit the number of steps that can be taken.

Teaching Hints. If only one or two balls are available, the players may be placed in a circle, arms' length apart, to throw the ball around the circle. After each successful catch, everyone in the circle takes one step back, making the circle wider. If a player fails to catch the ball, the throw is repeated until he is successful.

Overtake

Grades: 3–4
Number of Players: 10–30
Playing Areas: classroom, hallway, playroom, gymnasium, playground
Equipment: two balls
Basic Skills: throwing, catching
DESCRIPTION OF GAME. Half the class stands on an outer circle; the other half stands on an inner circle with all players facing each other. Each circle counts off by twos—all number one players are on one team, and all number two players are on the other team. On a signal, a player from one team in the outer circle and a player from the other team on the inside circle each start passing a ball diagonally to a teammate in the other circle—inner to outer,

outer to inner, and so forth. Both balls go in the same direction. A ball must make two complete trips around the circle. The team finishing first with the ball back in the starter's hands scores one point. If one team overtakes the other team's ball, they score an additional point.

Teaching Hints. To speed up play when the class is large, several smaller circles may be formed.

Toss

Grades: 3–4
Number of Players: 8–10
Playing Areas: classroom, hallway, playroom, gymnasium, playground
Equipment: large ball
Basic Skills: throwing, catching
DESCRIPTION OF GAME. All players stand inside a circle drawn large enough to accommodate about 10 players. One of the players has a ball and tosses it straight up into the air and calls another player's name. That player, "It," runs to catch the ball as other players scatter outside the circle. When "It" catches the ball, he calls "Stop." Everyone stops in place and may not move. "It" tries to hit one of the players below the waist with the ball. If the ball hits fairly, he takes the ball back to the circle. The players return to the circle, and play resumes. If he misses the player at whom he aimed, that person gets to toss the ball from the center and call a name.

Teaching Hints. Only a soft playground ball should be used to reduce the possibility of injury to a player.

Four Square

Grades: 3–6
Number of Players: 4 for each square
Playing Areas: classroom, playroom, gymnasium, playground
Equipment: volley ball or tennis ball for each square
Basic Skill: ball handling
DESCRIPTION OF GAME. The playing court is a square 12 by 12 feet which is divided into four smaller squares. One square is designated as the number 1 square and the others are numbered consecutively around the square. Four players may play at one time. Each player stands in or at the edge of a square. The game is started by the number 1 player who bounces the ball and then hits it underhanded into another square. The receiver lets the ball bounce once and then hits it underhanded, directing it into another square. Play continues in this way. If the ball is missed, is not hit on the first bounce, or goes out of bounds, the player at fault goes to the last square (number 4); the others move up accordingly. The player in the number 1 square when the game is concluded is the winner.

Teaching Hints. Young children and those who have difficulty hitting the ball may be provided with a large playground ball.

Square Ball

Grades: 3–6
Number of Players: 12 for each court
Playing Areas: classroom, playroom, gymnasium, playground
Equipment: playground ball
Basic Skills: dodging, throwing, catching

DESCRIPTION OF GAME. The four square court may be used for this game or a court of similar dimensions may be drawn on the ground. A ball approximately eight inches in diameter is needed. Two teams of not more than six players each play on one court. One team positions itself around the outside of the square and the other team stands in the center of the square. The players on the outside pass the ball to each other around the square, attempting to bounce or roll it across the square when they think the other team may be caught unaware. If the players in the center catch the ball, they try to hit one of the opponents with it. The opponent may dodge the ball but may not move away from the square. A point is awarded to the team in the center for each player hit, while the other team receives one point for each miss. When a team has ten points, the two teams change places.

Teaching Hints: If the players outside the square are unsuccessful in hitting any players inside the square, they should be encouraged to pass the ball more rapidly and to feint.

Line Dodge Ball

Grades: 3–6
Number of Players: 5–10
Playing Areas: hallway, playroom, gymnasium, playground
Equipment: ball
Basic Skills: dodging, throwing

DESCRIPTION OF GAME. Two lines are drawn about 20 feet apart. A box about 4 feet square is drawn halfway between these lines. A player stands in the box while half of the remaining players stand behind one of the lines and the other half behind the other line. Players along both lines throw the ball at the one player in the box attempting to hit him below the waist. The player in the box may dodge but must have at least one foot in the box at all times. A player successfully hitting the player in the box exchanges places with him.

Teaching Hints. For large groups, more than one square may be drawn between the lines.

Circle Dodge Ball

Grades: 3–6
Number of Players: 15–30
Playing Areas: playroom, gymnasium, playground
Equipment: large ball
Basic Skills: dodging, throwing, catching

DESCRIPTION OF GAME. A circle is formed by about two thirds of the players; the other one third of the players are inside the circle. Those in the circle attempt to strike the players inside the circle with the ball below the waist. When a player is hit, he joins the circle. The last player remaining is the winner.

Teaching Hints. Players should be encouraged to pass the ball to others occasionally to increase the chances of catching those in the center off guard.

Team Dodge Ball

Grades: 4–5
Number of Players: 10–30
Playing Areas: hallway, playroom, gymnasium, playground
Equipment: ball
Basic Skills: dodging, throwing, catching

DESCRIPTION OF GAME. The players are divided into two equal teams. A large circle is drawn on the playing surface. The members of one team are in single circle formation facing the center. The members of the other team are inside the circle. The members of the team forming the circle attempt to "put out" as many of their opponents as possible within a predetermined time limit of 1 to 3 minutes by hitting them below the waist with the ball. The team within the circle may not handle the ball. At the end of the period the teams change places. The team which has put out the greater number of players in the allotted time is the winner. Players put out remain out until the teams change places.

Teaching Hints. The game may be varied in the following manner. Players on both teams are scattered at random throughout an area with marked bound-

Figure 9–2 A player inside the ring in Circle Dodge Ball utilizes a jump to avoid the ball. (Courtesy of Town of Vernon Schools, Rockville, Connecticut.)

aries. Each team takes its turn on offensive for a predetermined period of time. The ball must be played from where it is caught within the marked boundaries. Each team takes its turn on offensive for a predetermined period of time. When a ball goes outside the boundaries, it must be brought within the boundaries by an offensive player before being played. If a defensive player steps outside the boundary, he is put out. The time limit should be kept short to avoid long waits before a child is back in play.

Two Division Dodge Ball

Grades: 4–5
Number of Players: 10–30
Playing Areas: hallway, playroom, gymnasium, playground
Equipment: two volleyballs
Basic Skills: dodging, throwing

DESCRIPTION OF GAME. This game is played in the same manner as is *Team Dodge Ball* except that two teams in adjacent courts play against each other by attempting to "put out" the greater number of players in the 2 or 3 minute period. The team which puts out more players during the period is the winner.

Teaching Hints. To avoid long periods of waiting to play by the children who are out, the game should be kept short.

Line Soccer

Grades: 4–5
Number of Players: 10–30
Playing Areas: playroom, gymnasium, playground
Equipment: soccer ball
Basic Skills: running, kicking

DESCRIPTION OF GAME. Players are organized as for the game *Steal the Bacon.* A soccer ball is placed in the center and each player attempts to kick the ball over his opponent's goal line when his number is called. A point is scored for the team each time one of its members kicks the ball over his opponent's line.

Teaching Hints. One member of each team should be designated as "retriever." His job will be to retrieve the ball which has gone over the goal line and to bring it back to the center. This responsibility should be rotated among all players. The game can be made more complex and challenging by calling out two or more numbers at one time. As the children grow in skill, the ball may be rolled in to require players to kick a rolling instead of a stationary ball.

Kick the Can

Grades: 5–6
Number of Players: 6–30
Playing Areas: hallway, playroom, gymnasium, playground

Equipment: 6 to 10 tin cans or Indian clubs and a soccer ball
Basic Skills: kicking, trapping

DESCRIPTION OF GAME.   A row of cans or similar objects is placed in the center between two lines which are 30 to 60 feet away on either side of the cans. Each team stands behind its own kicking line. One player kicks the ball at a can. Opponents stop the ball with their feet as it rolls to them and kick it back toward the cans. The game continues until all the cans are down. Each team is awarded one point for every can it knocks down, and the team with the higher score is the winner. The ball may be blocked by the body, but if the ball is touched with hands, it is a foul, and the opponents are given a point.

Teaching Hints.   To speed up the game, two balls may be used; however, this decreases the difficulty of scoring points as the cans are more easily knocked down.

Push Ball

Grades: 6–8
Number of Players: 10–12
Playing Areas: hallway, playroom, gymnasium, playground
Equipment: push ball
Basic Skill: ball handling

DESCRIPTION OF GAME.   A playing area of about 50 feet in length with goal lines marked on either end is necessary. There are two teams composed of five or six members. The teams face each other a short distance apart with the players on each team standing very close together. Two opposing players lift the ball into the air. On signal, both teams try to push the ball toward their goals. The team which first succeeds in doing so is declared the winner.

Teaching Hints.   To equalize the teams, tall players should be equally distributed between the teams.

Wall Ball

Grades: 6–8
Number of Players: 2–12
Playing Areas: playroom, gymnasium, playground if a free wall is available
Equipment: ball
Basic Skills: throwing, catching

DESCRIPTION OF GAME.   A restraining line is drawn the length of the wall at a distance of 6 to 10 feet from the wall. One player is given a ball. He starts the game by throwing the ball against the wall in such a way that it will bounce back to him. The other players attempt to catch the ball before he retrieves it. Anyone who catches the ball must throw it again immediately.

Players may not shove or push in attempting to get the ball. The ball may be caught in front of the restraining line but it must be thrown from behind it. The thrower may maneuver to get in the best position to catch the ball after it has bounced from the wall.

Teaching Hints.   The farther the restraining line is drawn from the wall, the more difficult it is for the thrower to catch the ball. If only a few children are playing, the line should be drawn closer to the wall than if a large number is playing.

Four Team Wall Ball

Grades: 6–8
Number of Players: 12–32
Playing Areas: playroom, hallway, gymnasium
Equipment: a ball for each team
Basic Skills: ball handling, running

DESCRIPTION OF GAME. A restraining line is drawn 20 to 40 feet from a wall. Four teams are formed with from three to eight players on each side. The teams form a line, facing the wall behind the restraining line. The player at the head of each line has a ball. Each ball should be a different color or marked distinctly. At command, each player with a ball rolls it forward to get it as close to the wall as he can. Then the player runs forward and retrieves any one of the other balls that have been rolled in by other players and returns to his original position. The first player back in place receives one point. The players then go to the ends of their respective lines, and the balls are returned to the original teams. The procedure is repeated until all of the members of the team have had a turn. The team with the highest score wins.

Teaching Hints. The players should be encouraged to roll the ball as close as possible to the wall to force the other players to run farther.

Medicine Ball Roll

Grades: 6–8
Number of Players: 10–30
Playing Areas: hallway, playroom, gymnasium
Equipment: several small balls (tennis balls) and one medicine ball or deflated basketball
Basic Skill: throwing

DESCRIPTION OF GAME. Two lines 20 feet apart are drawn parallel to each other. The players are divided into two teams. Each team takes a position behind its respective line. The medicine ball is placed in the center between the two lines. The object of the game is to throw the smaller balls against the medicine ball, forcing it across the opponents' line to score. The small balls may be retrieved within the 20 foot zone by players on either side, but they must return behind the line on their side before making the throw.

Teaching Hints. For younger children a slightly deflated basketball should be used instead of a medicine ball because it will move more easily when hit with another ball.

MANEUVERING FOR POSITION GAMES

This classification is one made by the author for those games whose main element is the maneuvering of the body into a given position. The games so classified require gross movements of the body to put it into a space that is sought by another player or to move it to a specific place at a given time. An example of the former is *Pussy Wants a Corner*; *Red Light* is an example of the latter. Games that utilize maneuvering the body as only one of several other elements that may include tagging, relay procedures, and ball control are not included here. Effective utilization of gross body movements in maneuvering is an important basic skill. Activities that provide for development of skill in maneuvering the body should be included frequently in the program.

One, Two, Button My Shoe

Grades: K–1
Number of Players: 5–30
Playing Areas: classroom, playroom, gymnasium, playground
Equipment: none
Basic Skill: running

DESCRIPTION OF GAME. Two parallel lines are drawn 30 to 50 feet apart. All the players are behind one of the lines except the leader who stands to one side. When the game begins, the following dialogue takes place:

Players: "One, two"
Leader: "Button my shoe"
Players: "Three, four"
Leader: "Close the door"
Players: "Five, six"
Leader: "Pick up sticks"
Players: "Seven eight"
Leader: "Run, don't be late."

The players pantomime the directions given by the leader in his responses. When the word "late" is spoken by the leader, the players run to the other line and back again. The first child who returns to the starting line becomes the new leader.

Teaching Hints. Excitement is added to the game if the leader is encouraged to vary the time he takes to say the last word. No child may begin to run before the word "late" is completely pronounced.

Squirrel in the Trees

Grades: K–1
Number of Players: 10–30
Playing Areas: classroom, playroom, gymnasium, playground
Equipment: none
Basic Skill: running

DESCRIPTION OF GAME. Partners form "trees" by placing both their hands on the other's shoulders. Another child becomes a "squirrel" in the tree by standing between the partners. One extra squirrel stands outside the trees. At a given signal all squirrels change trees, and the extra player tries to find a tree that has been vacated. Only one squirrel is allowed in a tree.

Teaching Hints. To provide everyone an opportunity to be a squirrel, squirrels may be required, as they enter a new tree, to change places with one of the partners who has not yet been a squirrel.

Pussy Wants a Corner

Grades: K–1
Number of Players: 4 for each square
Playing Areas: classroom, hallway, playroom, gymnasium
Equipment: none
Basic Skill: running

DESCRIPTION OF GAME. Squares are drawn on the floor for each player. One player, called "pussy," walks to different squares saying, "Pussy wants a corner." The player in the circle answers, "Go to my nextdoor neighbor." Meanwhile, as pussy is at other squares, the remaining players signal each other and attempt to exchange places. Pussy tries to occupy a square left by another player. The one left without a square becomes the new pussy.

Teaching Hints. If one player continues as pussy too long, he may call, "all change," and quickly find a vacant square as everyone changes squares.

Duck, Duck, Gray Duck

Grades: K–1
Number of Players: 8–30
Playing Areas: classroom, hallway, playroom, gymnasium, playground
Equipment: none
Basic Skills: tagging, running in a circle, walking

DESCRIPTION OF GAME. The children form a circle. One child is chosen to be "It." His place in the circle is left vacant to form an opening to the center of the circle. "It" walks around the outside of the circle touching certain children and saying, "Duck, duck." Whenever he touches a child and says, "Duck, duck, gray duck," that child must give chase, attempting to catch "It" before he can reach the opening and run safely into the center of the circle. If "It" is caught, he takes the place of the child who caught him, and this child becomes the new "It."

Teaching Hints. If "It" is not caught in a reasonable length of time, another child may be chosen to replace him.

Firemen

Grades: K–2
Number of Players: 10–30
Playing Areas: gymnasium, playground
Equipment: none
Basic Skill: running

DESCRIPTION OF GAME. The class is divided into lines of six or less, each group having a number. These groups stand on a goal line facing another goal line 40 feet away. One child is selected as the "fire chief" and stands at the side between the goal lines. The chief gives the alarm, "Fire, Fire, Station Number Three!" The group named runs to the opposite goal line and back. The first runner to return is the new chief, and the game continues. If the chief calls, "Fire, Fire, General Alarm," all groups run to the line and back.

Teaching Hints. The chief should be encouraged to call all the numbers so that everyone has a chance to run.

Drop the Handkerchief

    Grades: 1–2
    Number of Players: 8–20
    Playing Areas: classroom, hallway, playroom, gymnasium, playground
    Equipment: handkerchief
    Basic Skill: running in a circle

DESCRIPTION OF GAME. Players stand in single circle formation facing the center. One child who is "It" walks around the outside of the circle with the handkerchief. He drops it close behind another player and runs around the circle attempting to reach the vacated position before the other player. The player behind whom the handkerchief was dropped picks it up and runs around the circle in the opposite direction attempting to return to his position before "It" does. The player who reaches the position first is safe and the other player is "It" and repeats the procedure.

Teaching Hints. Large groups can be divided into several circles of 6 to 10 players. Children should be encouraged to drop the handkerchief behind a child who has not played.

Two Deep

    Grades: 1–3
    Number of Players: 15–20
    Playing Areas: classroom, playroom, gymnasium, playground
    Equipment: none
    Basic Skills: dodging, tagging, running in a circle

DESCRIPTION OF GAME. One player is chosen to be the chaser and one to be the runner. The rest of the players form a circle, facing its center and standing arms' length apart. The chaser tries to tag the runner who runs around the outside of the circle. To avoid being tagged, the runner may stop in front of anyone in the circle, who then becomes the runner. When the chaser tags the runner, the positions are reversed and the runner becomes the chaser.

Teaching Hints. To involve more participants, the runner may be limited to running only once around the circle before he must stand in front of a player. To accommodate more players, two concentric circles may be formed with players in both circles facing the center. When a runner steps in front of a player, the child in the outside circle becomes the runner.

Object Race

    Grades: 1–3
    Number of Players: 10–30

Playing Areas: playroom, gymnasium, playground
Equipment: miscellany of small objects
Basic Skills: carrying an object, running

DESCRIPTION OF GAME.   Two lines are drawn on the floor or ground parallel to one another and approximately 50 feet apart. The objects are placed along one line. The players are behind the other line. On the signal the players race to the far line and attempt to pick up one of the objects. Since there is always one less object than there are players, there will be one player without an object. Empty-handed players are eliminated. The race is run again and again, each time with one less participant and one less object. The winners are the players remaining when the game is concluded.

Teaching Hints.   The game should be kept short so that the children will not have to wait a long time before they play again.

Whirl Away

Grades: 1–3
Number of Players: 10–20
Playing Areas: hallway, playroom, gymnasium, playground
Equipment: none
Basic Skill: running

DESCRIPTION OF GAME.   Two parallel lines approximately 50 feet apart are marked on the floor or ground. Two teams are formed. The members of one team are in rank formation along one line and the members of the other team are in rank formation along the other line. The players are numbered consecutively from opposite ends. The teacher calls a number and the two players (one from each team) with this number run to the center, lock arms, whirl around, and run back to their positions. The one to reach his position first earns 1 point for his team. The team with the most points is the winner.

Teaching Hints.   To increase participation, more than one number may be called at a time.

Red Light

Grades: 1–3
Number of Players: 10–30
Playing Areas: gymnasium, playground
Equipment: none
Basic Skills: running, stopping

DESCRIPTION OF GAME.   There are two goal lines. All the players except "It" are lined up on one goal line. "It" is on the other goal line with his back to the other players. He counts aloud from 1 to 10, shouts "red light!" and turns about to face the other players. Players race toward the opposite goal line while "It" is counting from 1 to 10, but the moment he shouts "red light!" they must stop. If "It" sees anyone moving after he has said, "red light," he sends him back to the starting line and he starts from there at the next count. When a player reaches the finish line, the game is over and that player is "It" for the next game.

Teaching Hints. The instructor has an opportunity to teach sportsmanship and objectivity by encouraging "It" to call only those players whom he actually sees moving and by encouraging those children caught to go back cheerfully and without argument.

Fire on the Mountain

Grades: 2–4
Number of Players: 10–30
Playing Areas: playroom, gymnasium, playground
Equipment: none
Basic Skill: running in a circle
DESCRIPTION OF GAME. The children form two circles with one circle, called the "trees," standing inside the other circle, called "people." In the center is one player who is "It." He begins clapping his hands as he calls, "Fire on the mountain. Run, 'people,' run!" The "trees" remain standing while the "people" run to the right behind them. When "It" stops clapping, he and the "people" run to stand in front of a tree. The one who does not find a place to stand becomes the new "It."
Teaching Hints. If the game is played more than once, the players should change roles for each successive game.

Come Along

Grades: 3–4
Number of Players: 10–30
Playing Areas: classroom, hallway, playroom, gymnasium, playground
Equipment: none
Basic Skill: skipping
DESCRIPTION OF GAME. Players are in single circle formation, standing shoulder to shoulder and facing center. One player who is "It" skips around the outside of the circle. He pulls a player out of the circle saying, "Come along!" The two players join hands and continue to skip around the circle until the second player pulls out a third, the third a fourth, and so on. On a signal all the players skipping around dash for a vacant position in the circle. The player unable to secure a position is "It" for the next game.
Teaching Hints. Running, hopping, or galloping may be substituted for skipping.

Poison

Grades: 4–6
Number of Players: 8–15
Playing Areas: playroom, gymnasium, playground
Equipment: none
Basic Skills: pulling, pushing
DESCRIPTION OF GAME. The players are in a single circle formation facing the center with hands clasped. A circle is drawn on the floor 3 to 4 feet

inside the circle of players. On a signal, all the players attempt, while keeping their hands clasped, to pull or push other players into the inner circle. Anyone stepping on or inside the inner circle is out of the game. The last players remaining at the conclusion of the game are the winners.

Teaching Hints. The game should be kept short to avoid long waits before a child is back in play.

Snake Catcher

Grades: 4–8
Number of Players: 5–10
Playing Areas: playroom, hallway, gymnasium, playground
Equipment: one jumping rope
Basic Skills: chasing, running, stooping, catching a moving object

DESCRIPTION OF GAME. One player is the "snake," who is provided with a jumping rope which he drags after him. On the command all the other players try to catch the dragging end of the rope in their hands. As soon as a player catches the rope, he becomes the snake.

Teaching Hints. It should be impressed upon the players that they are not to step on the rope but must catch it in their hands.

Catch the Cane

Grades: 4–8
Number of Players: 5–15
Playing Areas: classroom, hallway, playroom
Equipment: cane
Basic Skill: running

DESCRIPTION OF GAME. The children form a circle approximately 50 feet in diameter and count off around the circle. One child is standing in the center holding a cane or stick balanced on end on the floor. He calls a number and at the same time releases the cane. The child whose number is called must catch the falling cane before it tumbles to the floor. If he doesn't do so, he takes the place in the center of the circle, and the other child takes his number and place in the circle.

Teaching Hints. To give more children a chance, the teacher may stipulate that a number cannot be called more than twice during the game.

Circle Guard

Grades: 5–8
Number of Players: 4–28
Playing Areas: classroom, playroom, gymnasium, playground
Equipment: none
Basic Skills: dodging, side-stepping, tagging

DESCRIPTION OF GAME. Three children clasp hands forming a circle. A fourth child who is "It" stands outside the circle. He attempts to tag a designated member of the circle. The other children in the circle attempt to help keep the third one from being tagged without releasing hands. "It" is not permitted to go under the clasped arms or through them.

Teaching Hints. Unnecessary roughness may be avoided by not allowing body contact to be made.

Jump the Shot

Grades:　5–8
Number of Players:　5–12
Playing Areas:　classroom, playroom, gymnasium, playground
Equipment:　rope attached to a ball or object of similar weight
Basic Skill:　jumping

DESCRIPTION OF GAME. Players form a circle. One child stands or sits in the center and swings the rope attached to the object so that it will pass under the feet of those standing in the circle when they jump in the air. A jumper who fails to clear the ball or rope changes places with the player in the center.

Teaching Hints. The player in the center is encouraged to keep the ball low at first and continue to raise it as he spins the rope until a jumper misses.

Catch of Fish

Grades:　6–8
Number of Players:　10–30
Playing Areas:　playroom, gymnasium, playground
Equipment:　none
Basic Skills:　dodging, synchronized running, clasping hands to hold
　　securely

DESCRIPTION OF GAME. Two parallel lines 20 feet long and 50 feet apart are marked on the floor or ground. The players are divided into two equal teams; each team stands behind its goal line. Members of the team called the "net" clasp hands. Members of the other team, called the "fish," attempt to reach their opponents' goal on the signal. The net tries to catch as many fish as possible by surrounding them. The fish may attempt to escape by circling around the open ends of the net, but they may not go under the arms of their opponents nor may they go outside the side boundaries of the area. All fish inside the net when the ends close together become members of the net team. The teams then return to their own goals. The fish next join hands to become the net. The teams alternate in being fish and net until all players on one side are caught or time has run out.

Teaching Hints. The net will be more successful if it closes rapidly and the fish more successful if they spread out.

SCOOTER GAMES

Scooter games are an interesting addition to the basic skill games of an elementary physical education program. The scooter is a flat board approximately 14 by 18 inches to which four rollers have been attached to permit the

Figure 9–3 As the rope is spun in Jump the Shot, it is slowly raised until a jumper misses. (Courtesy of Ox Ridge Elementary School, Darien, Connecticut.)

scooter to roll freely in any direction. The rollers are constructed of material that will not mar the floor.

Scooters may be made from three-fourths inch plywood. The corners should be rounded, and a rubber stripping should be glued firmly around the edges. The four casters are attached to the bottom of the board about two inches from each corner.

The children take a position on the scooter and propel themselves by the use of their hands or their feet or both. Among the more common positions that may be taken are: lying prone (face down), kneeling on both knees, kneeling on one knee and pushing with the other leg, sitting with the feet placed on the floor, and squatting with one foot and one hand on the scooter. Scooters may be used by partners. One child may ride while the other pushes. In another position two participants sit back to back and lock arms. A third possibility is the wheelbarrow. One child lies on the scooter on his stomach while a partner lifts up his legs and pushes as he would a wheelbarrow.

The instructor should stress the safety rules for the use of the scooter before any active games are taught. The children should not be permitted to

Figure 9–4 Scooter board. (Courtesy of SCHOOL-TECH, INC., Wolverine Sports Division.)

GYM DOLLY

stand on them as skate boards or to push them around recklessly. Students should be warned to take utmost care to prevent pinching or smashing fingers. Unless it has cushioned sides, the scooter should never be grasped along its edge while being propelled.

Many of the basic skill games and relays can be modified for play using the scooter. Suggested modifications of selected games and relays are described below. Other possibilities will suggest themselves after reading these.

Scooter Basketball

Grades: 5–8
Number of Players: 8–16
Playing Area: gymnasium
Equipment: basketball, two wastebaskets, scooter for each player
Basic Skills: hitting a target, scooter skills

DESCRIPTION OF GAME. All players take a kneeling position on a scooter; they must remain on the scooter throughout the game. They propel themselves with their hands. Each team tries to advance the ball toward its basket by passing to teammates or by dribbling. One point is scored when the ball goes into the basket.

Teaching Hints. To involve all the students in the class in the game, those not on scooters may be divided into two groups and placed on one or the other of the teams. They line up around the boundary lines alternately with players from the opposing team. They are permitted to retrieve the ball when it goes over the boundary line but may not move more than 3 feet from their original position. They must throw the ball to a player on a scooter. Players on scooters may pass to players on the side.

To avoid possible collision or the running over of fingers by the scooters, players should not be allowed to come closer than 3 feet to each other.

Figure 9–5 The lying and kneeling positions on the scooter. (Journal of Health · Physical Education · Recreation.)

Scooter Soccer

Grades: 5–8
Number of Players: 16–20
Playing Area: gymnasium
Equipment: soccer ball, two Indian clubs, scooter for each player
Basic Skills: kicking, scooter skills
DESCRIPTION OF GAME. There are two teams with eight to 10 players on a side. An Indian club is set up at each end of the court. Players take a sitting position on their scooters. They may propel themselves with their hands or feet or both. Each team tries to advance the ball toward the opponents' Indian club by kicking it. A point is scored when the Indian club is successfully knocked over by a kicked ball. One player from each team is designated as the goalkeeper to guard the club and prevent a score.

Teaching Hints. Members of the class not included on the teams may be lined up around the boundary lines as described in scooter basketball. However, in this instance, the players must be seated and may only play the ball with their feet.

Scooter Hockey

Grades: 5–8
Number of Players: 16–20
Playing Area: gymnasium
Equipment: soccer ball, two Indian clubs, scooter for each player
Basic Skills: kicking, scooter skills
DESCRIPTION OF GAME. Two teams are formed of eight to 10 players per team. An Indian club is set at either end of the court. The players kneel with one knee on the scooter and propel it with the opposite leg.

The players propel the ball forward by bumping it with the front end of the scooter. They attempt to knock down the opponents' Indian club and then score when they are successful in doing so. One player of each team is designated as the goalkeeper to guard the club.

Teaching Hints. Players should not be allowed to make contact with each other's scooter in order to avoid the possibility of injury to the fingers.

Scooter Relays

Grades: 5–8
Number of Players: 10–30
Playing Area: gymnasium
Equipment: minimum of two scooters
Basic Skills: running, scooter skills
In developing relay races, any one of several formations may be used. The two most commonly used are the rank file and shuttle formations. Using the rank file formation, two or more teams are formed. Each team lines up facing the same direction. At the command of "Go," the first player in line propels his scooter in any manner to the designated goal and returns to the starting line. He passes the scooter to the next child in line and takes a place at the end of the

line. The relay continues in this manner until the last child has returned to the starting line. The first line to complete the relay is the winner.

For a relay using the shuttle formation, two or more teams are formed. Each team divides into two lines of equal numbers. The first person in each line faces his teammate who is first in the other line. The other players are lined up behind them. At the command of "Go," one of the two players at the head of the lines moves forward on his scooter to the head player in the other line, who in turn mounts the scooter and propels himself to the second person in the other line. After his turn, each player goes to the end of the line. The race continues in this fashion until all members of the team finish. The team completing the relay first is the winner.

Teaching Hints. The contest can be varied by requiring the players to take a specific position on the scooter. To increase the difficulty of the race, an obstacle course of chairs can be set up a few feet in front of each line. Each participant must maneuver his scooter around the chairs before returning to the starting line.

SCOOP GAMES

The scoop games, which are played with a scoop-like device, are adaptations of commonly played games and activities. Scoops are available from commercial firms, but they are easily improvised. The construction of the scoop is simple enough that even young children can make their own. To make a scoop a large plastic bleach bottle is cut in the shape of a scoop (Figure 9–6). The plastic can be cut with a knife, heavy scissors, or tin snips.

SCOOP THROWING AND CATCHING

Scoop games provide interesting opportunities for learning the basic skills of catching and throwing. The basic skills of the overhand, the underhand, and the side-arm throw can be taught using the scoop. The other skills are more or less unique to play with the scoop, such as the snap throw and backhand throw. The snap throw is done completely with the wrist. In the backhand throw the ball is thrown backward in a sideward, backhand motion. The total arm is used but the snap of the wrist plays an important part in giving speed to the ball.

The fundamentals of catching with one hand may also be taught with the

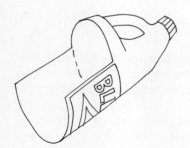

Figure 9–6 Improvised scoop made from a plastic bleach bottle.

use of the scoop. There are three basic techniques in catching: overhand, underhand, and to the side. In the overhand catch the scoop is held vertically and the ball is caught near the tip of the scoop and allowed to roll to the back end. In an underhand catch the scoop is held parallel with the ground and the ball is allowed to drop into the scoop. For the catch to the side, the scoop is held so that its opening faces the ball and it is caught as in the overhand catch. A "dead ball" is retrieved by placing the end of the scoop over the ball and pulling the ball toward the body; the scoop is then twisted with a flip of the wrist so that it comes up under the ball.

TARGET SCOOP ACTIVITIES

An activity that can be introduced to practice the game requires the formation of lines of players facing each other 20 to 60 feet apart. Each player throws the ball with the scoop to his opposite number of the other line, who catches it and throws it back. Throws may be overhand, underhand, or to the side (for the sidearm throws sufficient distances must be established between players in the lines). As skill in throwing increases, specific areas may be designated for throwers to aim at, e.g., a foot above the head or an arm's length to the side.

Activities that provide practice hitting targets are easily arranged. A bull's eye may be drawn on the wall with each ring being given a different value for scoring purposes. An Indian club or clubs may be placed at one end of the gymnasium for an activity in which the player attempts to knock down the clubs by throwing the ball at them with the scoop. A box or old tires may be used as the target for a similar game. An especially interesting target may be developed by rolling an old tire down the middle of two rows of students facing each other at a distance of 20 feet. As the tire passes in front of them, the students attempt to throw a ball through the rolling tire.

Scoop Goalball

The class is divided into two teams. On a large field there can be as many as ten players on a side; in a gymnasium or smaller playing area six to eight players to a side is a more appropriate number. A goal 5 to 20 feet wide is marked at each end of the playing area, depending on its size. A line is also marked at mid-field. On a soccer field the soccer goal and the center line may be used. At the beginning the teams face each other on either side of the center line. One side is given the ball to start the play, and, by passing the ball among its teammates, tries to move the ball downfield to score by throwing it across the opponents' goal. Players may not hold the ball in their scoops longer than 10 seconds. They may take three steps while carrying the ball. No body contact is allowed. Opponents may try to intercept but may not touch a player's scoop.

Scoop Wallball

A court 20 by 30 feet is marked on the floor with one line of the court being formed by the junction of the floor with the wall. The wall surface above the court must be unobstructed. The game is started by one player throwing the ball against the wall with a scoop. The other player must catch the ball after it hits the wall or after the first bounce on the floor. A player who allows the ball to bounce more than once before catching it forfeits the point to his opponent. Each player takes a turn at serving.

SUPPLEMENTARY READINGS

International Council on Health, Physical Education and Recreation: *ICHPER Book of Worldwide Games and Dances.* Washington, D.C., American Association for Health, Physical Education and Recreation, 1967.

Latchaw, Marjorie: *A Pocket Guide of Movement Activities for the Elementary School.* Ed. 2. Englewood Cliffs, New Jersey, Prentice-Hall, Inc., 1970.

Miller, Arthur G., and Whitcomb, Virginia: *Physical Education in the Elementary School Curriculum.* Englewood Cliffs, New Jersey, Prentice-Hall, Inc., 1969.

Mulac, M. E.: *Games and Stunts for Schools, Camps and Playgrounds.* New York, Harper and Row, Publishers, 1964.

Wickland, Ralph L.: *Fundamental Motor Patterns.* Philadelphia, Lea and Febiger, 1970.

BIBLIOGRAPHY

[1]Frosch, John, and Ross, Nathaniel: "Ancient Games and Popular Games, Hedvig Kéri." *Annual Survey of Psychoanalysis,* 1958, pp. 342–343.

chapter ten

movement and special equipment

Increased interest in the motor education of very young children and children with motor learning problems has prompted teachers to seek new ways of providing motor experiences. One result has been the utilization for instructional purposes of supplies and equipment that formerly were used only in casual play. Teachers have discovered that many of the items can be improvised from materials that are readily available. The commercially produced play items range from portable stairways to target games. While some of these are specially designed for motor skill development, others are not but can be used for that purpose by the imaginative teacher.

The teacher who is unaware of the contributions these more special pieces of equipment and supplies can make to motor skill learning must exercise good judgment in deciding to buy or improvise specific items. A poor decision is not, of course, as serious when the item has been improvised as when it has been purchased since the amount of money involved is insignificant by comparison. When considering an item for purchase, it is well to remember that appearance may be deceptive, as may be the claims made in its behalf. It is suggested that, before purchasing special equipment, the teacher resolve these questions to his satisfaction:

1. Does it provide movement experiences that are not easily provided elsewhere?

2. Does it motivate the child to participate in activities?

3. Does it provide a reasonable degree of safety to those using it?

4. Is the price reasonable in relation to its contribution to the education of the child and time saved for the teacher?

5. Does it provide for learning skills that add appreciably to the total development of the child?

On the pages that follow are described some of the less familiar commercial products that may be used to enhance the learning of motor skills. Also described are several items that can be readily improvised by the teacher. Suggestions are made for ways in which both the commercial and the improvised varieties can be used in teaching basic motor skills to very young children and in helping those with disabilities to improve their motor movement.

Three-Step Portable Stairway

Stairways are available in wood or in vinyl-covered urethane foam. They may be used singly or in pairs for such activities as stepping, crawling, and jumping; they also lend themselves to imaginative play. Some wooden stairs have an attachment for the support of a balance beam (Figure 10–1) for use in balancing activities.

The stairways are very helpful in teaching the skill of walking up and down stairs to those with physical or mental handicaps who have not developed such skill. The problem-solving method is very effective for instruction but may need to be supplemented by the kinesthesis technique with youngsters who have difficulty.

Rocking Boat

This piece of play equipment is a wooden rocker built so that, when inverted, it becomes a stairway (Figure 10–2). As a series of steps, it offers most

Figure 10–1 Wooden stairs with attached balance beam. (Courtesy of Childcraft Education Corp.)

Figure 10–2 Inverted rocking boat becomes a set of steps. (Courtesy of Childcraft Education Corp.)

of the possibilities for play on the three-step stairs. As a rocker, it provides experience in balancing similar to that of the swing.

When it is in use, children should be directed away from the floor space near the rocker to avoid the possibility of smashed fingers. Also, there may be a need to place a limit on the vigorousness of rocking the "boat" since it has a tendency to move along the floor when the rocking movement is strenuous.

A rocking "raft" is easily constructed by someone with simple carpentry skills using the runners of an old rocking chair and a flat piece of board large enough to accommodate a seated child. A diagram of its structure may be seen in Figure 10–3.

To teach the techniques of balancing with either the rocking boat or the rocking raft, a procedure like that suggested for teaching balance on the swing may be used (see page 444).

Jouncing or Bouncing Board

A jouncing board is a wide board elevated a short distance above the ground by suitable supports (Figure 10–4), or with one end resting on the ground. The board has a certain amount of flexibility so that it can be bounced upon to the delight of most children. A jouncing board is an effective tool for teaching kinetic balance, similar in nature to balance in bouncing on the trampoline. The board can also be used as a balance beam.

Figure 10–3 Improvised rocking "raft."

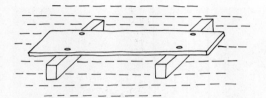

Figure 10–4   Jouncing board.

Climbing and Building Blocks

Blocks for climbing are popular with the young child. They are available in several sizes and shapes, constructed of wood, plastic, or covered urethane foam. They provide opportunities for balancing, jumping, climbing, and crawling as well as lifting and pushing when used in building designs and structures. Blocks have proven to be especially useful in teaching the skills of the everyday movements of stepping, pushing, pulling, and lifting to the mentally retarded.

Blocks of unusual shapes of foam-filled nylon-vinyl casings are excellent for building creative forms. These blocks vary in size from ones small enough to be manipulated by the hands to those large enough to require pushing, pulling, and lifting. Also available on the market is a type of blocks equipped with buttons, buckles, snaps, zippers, and lacings for practicing the skills needed for independence in dressing and undressing. Their use is recommended for preschool and exceptional children.

One of the most economical and versatile building and climbing blocks is the plain wooden box. A packing crate may be utilized as the frame for constructing the box, or the frame may be made from 2 × 2s as shown in Figure 10–5. Three-fourths inch marine plywood is used to cover the frame.

Covered foam log-shaped forms, triangles, and incline mats offer nearly unlimited opportunities for skill building activity. The logs lend themselves to "log-rolling," rolling the body over, and various balancing activities. The triangles may be used for balancing, crawling, and climbing. The incline mats become interesting "hills" for tumbling and rolling. All of the forms can be used

Figure 10–5 Construction of a building block.

as giant building blocks, and they may also be put together to create an obstacle course for the performance of a series of different motor activities.

Crawl-Through Equipment

Crawling through objects provides a child with the unique experience of manipulating his body in a small place. Equipment that can be utilized for this purpose is readily available. An old barrel open at each end, low parallel bars with mats thrown over the top, or chairs lined in a row all make excellent crawling equipment. In addition there is an extensive assortment of manufactured crawl-through equipment. Some pieces are built in circles, squares, or triangles; some take the shapes of letters; others are made like padded tubes. Attractive shapes and designs add to the interest of the children in using them. Different kinds of movements in crawling through them are required by the various shapes.

Some children, especially if they are handicapped, may need individual help in learning to crawl through the pieces of equipment. With the physically handicapped, the teacher will need to explore with the student various possibilities to determine the most effective way to move through the space. The severely mentally retarded may need to be taught crawling skills by kinesthesis.

Climbing Equipment

Climbing equipment is available in various shapes and sizes, ranging from a simple vertical ladder to a complex arrangement of vertical and parallel ladder rungs. A very simple but versatile piece of climbing equipment is the Lind Climber (shown in Figure 10–6). It consists of two saw horses with several cross bars, each of which can be placed at several levels to provide opportunities for different forms of activities.

Hoops

The hoop has been used in many different ways in childhood play throughout the years. The old rolling hoop of an earlier day was converted in more recent times to the hula hoop, which was placed around the waist and spun by moving the hips. Currently, the hoop is used for balancing and spinning on a stick, throwing and catching, and crawling through as well as rolling and "hula hipping."

Hoops may be purchased from a manufacturer but old tires provide a successful substitute for many hoop activities. They may be used for rolling and climbing in, out, and through, and they may be stacked like building blocks for yet another kind of activity.

A type of hoop called the play-all is a three-piece circle that can be disassembled and put together to make other shapes and forms. Among its possible

Figure 10–6 Lind Climber. (Courtesy of Lind Climber Co.)

uses are a hoop to roll, a tunnel to crawl through or roll in, a teeter-totter, and an object to be climbed on, over, or under (Figure 10–7).

Carts, Wagons, Wheelbarrows, and Tricycles

These mobile vehicles have special significance and importance in the nursery school program: not only are they very popular with children, but they provide experience in pushing, pulling, lifting, and balancing.

Figure 10–7 *A, B* Play-All. (Courtesy of Childcraft Education Corp.)

Figure 10–8 Wheelbarrow. (Courtesy of Child-craft Education Corp.)

It is well to teach children the most effective way to lift, push, or pull the wheelbarrows, wagons, or carts, as well as to move on and to control the tricycles. Demonstration and supervised practice are good ways of teaching these skills. However, the problem-solving method offers the child the opportunity to explore and determine for himself the most effective movements.

A specific play area should be established for using the vehicles; this area must be kept free of other children to avoid the possibility of injury. Playing on the floor in the area should be prohibited.

Stilts

Walking on stilts is an activity that children have enjoyed over the years. Generally, it has not been included in the school's physical education programs; rather, the children have on their own built the stilts and learned the skills. Walking on stilts can be an exciting experience for a child because of the interesting problems in balance it presents.

Stilts can be made of scrap lumber (Figure 10–9). For young children the foot rest should touch the ground; for older children it may be attached several inches or even a foot or more above ground level.

Stilts can also be made from two large cans. Holes are punched at opposite sides of the can near the closed end. A cord is run from each side through the holes and secured with a knot tied inside the can. The loop that is made should be long enough to enable a child to hold the loop at about waist height when standing on the cans (Figure 10–10).

In using the stilts, earth or grass provides the best traction. Cement, vinyl, and wooden floors often prove slippery and therefore dangerous. In learning to use the stilts children should initially receive assistance in getting on the stilts and balancing on them as they walk. Help can be withdrawn when they are able to maintain balance by themselves. Stilts of different heights should be

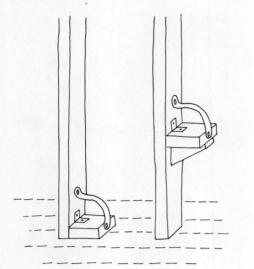

Figure 10–9 Stilts.

available, but a child should not progress to higher stilts until he has fully mastered walking on low stilts.

Active Table Games

Table games, although generally limited in the amount of motor activity they provide, do promote certain hand and arm skills. As such these games have a place in the child's physical education. They are especially useful in a physical education program for handicapped students who have limited movement in the trunk and lower limbs.

Some of the common table games are described below:

Skittles

Skittles is a game in which a top is spun in a box in which pins are set, each having a number value (Figure 10–11 *A* and *B*). The object of the game is

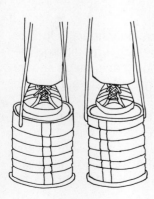

Figure 10–10 Stilts from coffee cans.

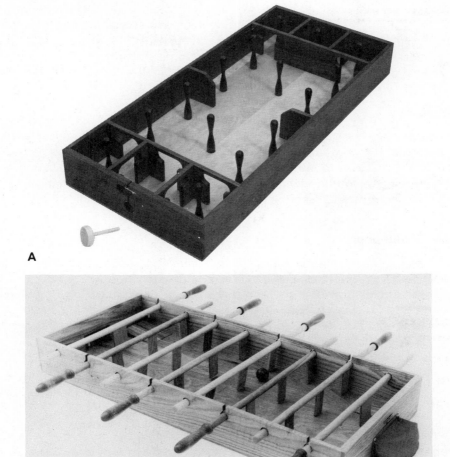

Figure 10–11   *A,* Skittles. *B,* Table cricket. (Courtesy of World Wide Games, Inc.)

to knock down as many of the pins as possible with the top to get the highest number of points.

Table Cricket

Table cricket is played using a box with eight handles, four on each side (Figure 10–11*B*). The handles control paddles inside the box. There are goals at each end. A player attempts to manipulate the paddles so as to propel the ball inside the box through the opponent's goal to score.

Labyrinth Games

A labyrinth game consists of a box with a control handle that will slant the top of the box in different directions. The object of the game is to pass a steel ball along the route marked on the top until it reaches the end without dropping into a hole. Each hole has an assigned number, and score may be kept for two or more players by adding up the numbers of the holes into which the steel ball falls. Each player takes the same number of turns. The winner is the one with the fewest points when the agreed-upon number of turns has been taken.

Box Hockey

Box hockey is a game played in a box that can be placed on a low table or on the floor. The box has a center piece with several holes through which a puck is to be passed to the goals at either end (Figure 10–12). Two to four people play the game at one time. Each player holds a stick in one hand and attempts to score by knocking the puck through the goal to his left.

Table Shuffleboard

There are many different types of table shuffleboard. Basically they consist of a board 15 to 20 feet long with sideboards on each side. Some boards have numbered circles drawn at one end of the board; others have divided spaces that are used for scoring. The players stand at one end and slide the puck with the hand to the other end to score, each taking one turn at a time. Four to six pucks are played for each game. Scoring consists of adding the numbers of the spaces where the pucks are standing after each game.

Target Games

There are various forms of target games, available commercially or from scrap materials. They range from darts, bean bags, and ball throws at a target to ring toss at hooks or stakes on a board.

Figure 10–12　Box hockey. (Courtesy of World Wide Games, Inc.)

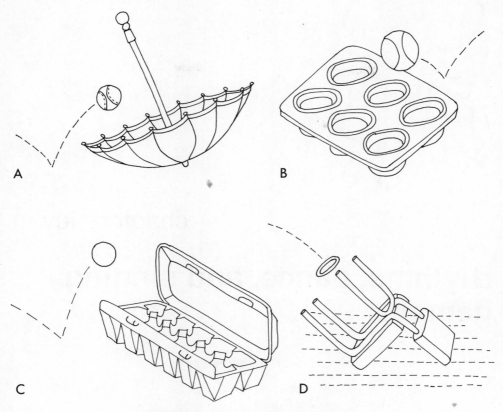

A   B

C   D

Figure 10–13 *A, B, C, and D* Improvised targets.

Many target games can be created using cast-off items. An old umbrella makes a good target for thrown balls; a muffin pan, several old cups, or an egg carton serves well as a target for bounced table tennis or small rubber balls; an old waste basket placed on a chair becomes a bean bag target; and the legs of an inverted chair make an excellent target for ring toss.

chapter eleven

rhythms, dance, and singing games

FUNDAMENTAL LOCOMOTOR RHYTHM
 PATTERNS
CREATIVE DANCE ACTIVITY
TRADITIONAL DANCE STEPS
SINGING GAMES AND FOLK DANCES
SQUARE DANCES
SOCIAL DANCE

Dance is as old as man. Since primitive times, man has found in rhythmic movement a medium for expressing his inner thoughts and deepest feelings. The dance and associated rhythmic activities have reflected and interpreted the culture of every society in every age. Today most dancing is thought of as a joyous activity, one of fun and sociability, but it is also recognized as an activity that involves considerable motor skill. Consequently, rhythms and dancing have become an integral part of the physical education program.

A program in rhythmic and dance activities is valuable not only in teaching basic movements, but in developing balance, coordination, poise, self-control, and self-confidence. The activities provide opportunities to develop a sense of belonging and adequacy; they contain the essential elements for satisfying the individual's needs for recognition, satisfaction, and creative self-expression. Moreover, they help to develop appreciation of dance as an art form.

ORGANIZATION

It is difficult to separate one rhythmic activity from another, but for purposes of efficiency of presentation, the following divisions have been made: (1) fundamental locomotor rhythm patterns, (2) creative dance activity, (3) traditional steps, (4) singing games and folk dancing, (5) square dancing, and (6) contemporary social dance steps. Included in the presentation of each of these are suggested methods of organizing the instructional unit, selecting activities appropriate to the grade, and teaching hints which will prove useful to the inexperienced teacher in presenting an effective learning experience in rhythms and dance.

SELECTION OF DANCE AND RHYTHMIC ACTIVITIES

The grade at which a given dance or rhythmic activity should be taught is difficult to ascribe, since the previous experience of the students is an important factor. In the descriptions of the dances and rhythmic activities that follow, the grade level at which they can generally be introduced successfully is given as a guide to the teacher; however, in making suitable selections, the following questions should be considered:

1. Have the children previously learned to perform the steps and movements required in the dance?
2. If not, can they be learned quickly and easily as the dance is being learned?
3. Do the children have sufficient background to understand and appreciate the activity?
4. Will the children be able to unite the various parts of the activity with a minimum of difficulty?

A variety of rhythmic and dance activities and singing games are suggested in the pages that follow; complete descriptions are given for some to indicate the pattern of movement. When these patterns are used, the record that is listed for accompaniment should also be used, because the music differs from record to record and the described pattern may not be suited to the music.

EQUIPMENT

The most commonly used pieces of equipment for the rhythmic and dance activities are phonograph and records, percussion instruments, and piano. The use of the piano and accompanist for these activities is highly desirable because it permits the teacher to stop and to repeat at will and to give full attention to the class. However, few schools are able to furnish a piano for use in the gymnasium or play area where dance is taught or, if the piano is available, to provide an accompanist to play it for class instruction. Consequently, most teachers rely on records for musical accompaniment. Although the need to stop the machine for instruction of the class or for repetition of the movements does restrict to some extent the attention the teacher can give to the class, the use of the phonograph is extremely satisfactory. Percussion instruments, both commercial and improvised, are useful in many phases of the dance activities.

CARE.   The phonograph and records represent a considerable investment and the teacher should learn the specific operation of any machine he may be using and teach this to any children who may assist in operating it. Proper care of the records is important to keep them from becoming scratched and warped. All who use the machine should understand the importance of grasping the plug near the socket to remove it rather than yanking it out. An adequate and convenient storage area should be arranged for storing the various pieces of equipment when not in use.

Improvised Equipment

Percussion instruments are readily improvised and children delight in making them. A very satisfactory drum may be made from any large cans from which both ends have been removed. The drum heads are made from old inner tubes cut in a circular shape about 3 inches larger than the diameter of the end of the can. These pieces are laid over the ends of the can and made secure by threading heavy cord through the overlapping edges, going back and forth from top to bottom around the can. Another kind of drum may be improvised from old metal trays. When struck with a padded stick, these produce a tone like a kettle drum.

Sand blocks are simply made. Coarse sandpaper is attached by thumbtacks to pieces of wood of any desired size. Suitable pieces may usually be secured from the scrap pile of the industrial arts room or from a carpenter in the community.

FUNDAMENTAL LOCOMOTOR RHYTHM PATTERNS

Fundamental locomotor patterns are natural movements which take the body through space and can be joyful, happy experiences when used as free informal activity. There are eight basic patterns: walk, run, hop, jump, leap, slide, skip and gallop.

Almost every element of rhythmic activity or movement has its basis in the locomotor patterns. For example, the run and hop combine to develop the schottische step; the gallop forms the basis for the polka step; and the skip, when slowed, becomes the step-hop. Although locomotor patterns occur repeatedly throughout the dance and elsewhere in life's activities, they should be stressed especially in the physical education of the kindergarten and the first three grades since this is the period when habits of well coordinated natural movements are being developed.

TEACHING HINTS

Praise should be used when deserved; it does much to improve effort and skill. After children are doing well at a normal tempo, the tempo may be changed. For example, when teaching the walk, the change of tempo may be from long slow steps to short fast steps; from heavy noisy steps to soft tiptoeing steps. In teaching the skip, both the speed of the skip or the height of the skip may be varied. Combinations of locomotor patterns may be emphasized beginning in the third grade. At this time it is advisable to use groups and partners. Fun and enjoyment should be stressed rather than perfection. In some cases, it may prove more effective to teach locomotor patterns for short intervals during the class than to devote the entire class period to them.

PRESENTATION

A generally effective organization for the presentation of fundamental locomotor patterns is:

Listen to the drum beat (or any good substitute for a drum).
Clap to the rhythm of the drum, or count out loud.
Let everyone try. (Sometimes when space is limited or numbers are large, let half perform, while others accompany by hand clapping.)
Use music.
All listen to the music.
Clap the rhythm of the music (count out loud).
Let everyone try.
Have volunteers demonstrate.

Walk (even rhythm)

The weight is transferred from one foot to the other as a step is taken.

count 1	count 2	count 3	count 4
walk right	walk left	walk right	walk left

Run (even rhythm)

The running step is similar to a fast walk except the weight is carried on the ball of the foot. Momentarily both feet are off the floor at the same time.

count 1	count 2	count 3	count 4
run right	run left	run right	run left

Hop (even rhythm)

The hop is a spring from the floor from one foot landing on the same foot. Either foot may be used. The push off and the landing are done from the ball of the foot.

count 1	count 2	count 3	count 4
hop	hop	hop	hop

Jump (even rhythm)

The jumping step is a spring from the floor from both feet landing on both feet. The push off is from heel to toe, the landing from toe to heel.

count 1	count 2	count 3	count 4
jump	jump	jump	jump

Leap (even rhythm)

The leaping step is similar to a slow run. The deeper knee bend at the beginning and the end distinguishes it from the simple walking step. The leap is a transfer of weight from one foot to the other with both feet off the floor at the same time. There is a push off with a spring, landing on the ball of the foot, letting the heel come down with slight bending of the knee.

count 1	count 2	count 3	count 4
leap right	leap left	leap right	leap left

Skip (uneven rhythm)

The skipping step is a step hop on the same foot. It divides a walking tempo beat into three counts, two for the step and one for the hop.

count 1	count 2	count 3	count 4
step-hop	step-hop	step-hop	step-hop
right right	left left	right right	left left

Gallop (uneven rhythm)

The gallop divides the walking tempo beat into a long-short rhythm. It is a step followed by a quick leap onto the other foot on the short portion of the beat. The closing foot never passes the leading foot.

count 1	count 2	count 3	count 4
step close	step close	step close	step close
right left	right left	right left	right left

Slide (uneven rhythm)

The sliding step is a sideward movement with the lead foot followed by a quick close with the following foot. The transfer of weight is made on the short beat. The following leg does not pass the leading leg. The slide may also be done with a leap.

count 1	count 2	count 3	count 4
step close	step close	step close	step close
right left	right left	right left	right left

CREATIVE DANCE ACTIVITY*

Small children particularly enjoy creative activity and spend a great deal of their out of school hours in imaginative play. These qualities of creativity and imagination are capitalized upon in presenting creative dance activity; they are, in effect, the ingredients which are added to the fundamental locomotor patterns previously presented and practiced. Instead of walking to music, the child becomes an Indian stepping quietly through the woods looking for a deer or a lion stalking through the heavy forest undergrowth.

As a result of a conscientiously conducted creative dance activity program, children not only gain an outlet for self-expression and creativity but develop motor skills, exercise large muscles, and gain social poise. This type of activity also helps to foster an awareness of rhythm in the total environment.

Motor exploration activities are readily utilized in the dance program. Exploring movement to music or rhythmic beat adds to the enjoyment of the activity and often helps in the release of inhibitions in those with limited experiences in motor exploration.

The emphasis in creative dance activity differs for the age groups because of their interests and needs. Children from kindergarten through the second grade enjoy the world of make-believe. They love to discover imagery in the ways their bodies can move, to notice that moving an arm in a quick small way makes them feel animal-like. They like to comment on their images. Third and fourth graders prefer more complicated combinations of movement with more continuity. These boys and girls are able to participate in groups and with partners while younger ones are more inclined to perform individually or alongside others rather than with them. Beyond the fourth grade (and earlier if the group is sufficiently mature and skilled) children should have an opportunity to create dances out of their past experience in locomotion, creative activity, and traditional dance steps.

TEACHING HINTS

Children will most enjoy classes if they feel successful at what they are doing. Being asked to think, to attempt, to explore, and to help shape the class

---

*This section was adapted from unpublished material by Ellen Moore and from Moore, "Dance Techniques Through Problem Solving." (See Supplementary Readings.)

keeps them lively, motivated, and learning to take responsibility for what happens to them. The following reminders relate to these observations:

The children will understand and be able to contribute if the teacher starts from the simplest beginning of a problem and builds it one step at a time so that they can participate at all times in its development.

The teacher can avoid frightening the children with the possibility of failure by keeping directions clear and simple. If the directions prove to be confusing or too difficult, the teacher may explain this to the children and then modify or abandon the directions.

The teacher needs to be ready to modify the plans for the class depending on what appears to be right at the moment for the energy level of the students.

The children will develop a taste for making choices if they are reminded to choose things they like, and to stop moving and rest when they've had enough. (Thus they are helping the teacher pace the class.)

The children will be more relaxed and happier in a class where a few activities are presented well with time to explore, rest, perform, and chat about what's happening than in one where they are hurried and intensely exposed to a greater number of events.

PRESENTATION

Because of the nature of creative dance activity, presentation must necessarily be flexible. However, there are some suggestions that can be made with respect to general organization of the instruction. Each class should provide for:

Tension release activity (with special attention to breathing freely).
Presentation of a movement problem for exploration.
Free exploration.
Periods of rest.
Suggestions of possible use of space and then time, or vice versa.
Clarification of locomotor patterns used.
Possible addition of drum beat or music or both (drum first, probably).
Possible performance.
Possible free improvisation of some aspect of the day's work.

Personal achievements toward which the creative dance activity program is directed are: (1) release of physical and emotional tension, (2) understanding of oneself, (3) improved motor skills, (4) appreciation of the creative process through interrelating with others, and (5) self-confidence in performance. These may, of course, be realized in a variety of ways. Some suggestions are offered below as representative of the larger possibilities. Directions for these sample activities are given in terms of suitability for typical third graders; they can be modified for younger or older children. It should be noted that any of the activities suggested as a means of effecting personal achievement in any one area may contribute to that in other areas as well, but each is presented under the achievement goal to which it makes the greatest contribution.

Release of Physical and Emotional Tension

The necessity for limitations on physical and vocal expression in the classroom often results in physical and emotional tension in the child. A release from such accumulated tension is extremely beneficial to the student. Creative dance is a particularly helpful activity for this purpose because its choices allow children greater opportunities to find personally satisfying ways of achieving a more relaxed state. Because of its importance to the child, release of tension should be the initial focus of every class in creative dance activity.

Suggested activities with which to begin the class are those that are innately relaxing such as manipulating the body in rolling and swinging movements or alternating maximum with minimum muscular contraction. Some specific possibilities for alternating actions are given below. The children should be allowed to time these activities themselves (within reasonable limits) to ensure that each has as much time as necessary to become relaxed and free of tension. Encouragement should be given the children to breathe freely as this helps greatly to reduce tension in the trunk muscles and allows much better quality of movement.

Alternating Actions

(1) Stretching—dissolving

(2) Reaching—dropping

(3) Stiffening into rigid body shapes of the child's choice—dissolving

(4) Exhaling of breath with controlled collapse of body—free breathing in and out with gradual restoration of erect body shape.

(5) Closing tightly —opening suddenly or gradually

(6) Shaking fast in a nearly vibratory action—shaking gradually more slowly allowing each shake to become larger.

Children will receive the most value from these activities if they do them close to floor level first and then expand the movements in directions they themselves discover and find interesting. It is desirable that they be given short moments of rest throughout the class period for complete or partial recovery from demanding activity when the activity itself doesn't provide respite.

Understanding of Oneself

In dance activities the child uses his mind and feelings as well as his body in making choices. The integration of intellect and emotion with physical performance stimulates an awareness of personal responses and capabilities and thus enhances self-understanding.

Through solving movement problems the child comes to accept and appreciate the physical characteristics of his body and its movement potential; his pacing of himself for comfort and efficiency; his reaction to the fast, moderate, and slow pacing of others; and his own physical effort compared to others. He begins to appreciate his own personal rhythms, the fascination of the effect of changing energy on speed and distance.

The ability to "internalize" intellectual understanding of basic space, time, and energy concepts is developed by experiencing them emotionally as well as physically. The teacher can assist this development by directing the child's attention to the feelings that accompany his movement choices. Simple reminders such as, "Did you notice how that felt?" or "Let's see how it feels to do that in slow motion," will help to do this.

Movement problems that help to achieve an understanding of the self can be either predominantly inner- or outer-directed. Predominantly inner-directed problems, for which the child closes his eyes and concentrates intently on his own kinesthetic and emotional feedback, have to take place near the floor where balance is less of a problem. In presenting an inner-directed movement problem to the class, the teacher might say: "Get into a position near the floor which you want to be in right now. Stay in it as long as you enjoy it. Notice how it feels. Move just your head and see how that changes it. When you have had enough, find another position that you like and that feels different from the first." This can go on until the children have had time to satisfy their need for exploring freely, and the teacher senses they are ready for a change.

The teacher can begin to prepare them for outer-directed activity through space by giving them vigorous work to do in problem-solving near the floor. This will enable them to warm up their muscles, and at the same time develop movement understanding and body awareness. Let them start gently. The problem might be presented to the class in this way:

Think about the heaviness of the various parts of your body. Choose a part which is medium heavy. (Children often like to exchange opinions about their choices. Letting them do this briefly is a way of letting them approve of themselves.) See if you can find a way to use one of your hands to throw it (the part of medium weight) somewhere in such a way that it doesn't get hurt.

Then let the children try throwing a heavier part—with or without help from a hand. For the heavier part of the body, students will likely choose the head or hip in contrast to their earlier selection of an arm or leg as a part of medium heaviness. In this problem the students are dealing with weight, anatomical accommodation, and protection from injury. They have to judge effort and direction and find out what is possible.

Throwing parts of the body can evolve into more familiar ways of warming up limbs for vigorous moving on the feet, such as free arm and leg swings or kicks and kneading the feet against the floor.

With guidance children can discover their own ways to warm up through understanding and experiencing how they can stretch themselves, or resist or throw part of their own weight. Their experimentation will involve them in choices of timing and spatial organization. They can also learn to work with and against each other's weight. The more they utilize the weight of their trunks in such efforts, the more dynamic the activity will be to the children; therefore, directions should be given which promote the involvement of the trunk as much as possible. Two examples of ways in which this might be done are the problems presented below:

See if you can make a shape with your partner. Without talking about it, find out what new shape it can be turned into. Let the new shape you make turn into another new shape. Let your bodies stop for a moment each time you think you've found a new shape you like.

Sit back to back with a partner. Let your backs "talk" to each other when they're ready. Go slowly and easily. Learn what you can do together. (When students are ready, the teacher encourages them to explore more expansively.)

Improved Motor Skill

As discussed elsewhere in this text, children should be provided with opportunities to develop a wide variety of specific motor skills. Because creative dance activity encourages exploring space at various speeds, with different movement qualities, and with varying forces, it contributes significantly to skill development in a variety of motor movements. To plan appropriate activities, the teacher needs to be familiar with the concepts of space, time, flow, and force outlined below.

Spatial Concepts

Direction
Forward
Backward
Sideward
Diagonal
Around

Distance
Large
Medium
Small

Floor Pattern
Straight
Circular
Zig-Zag
Scalloped
Serpentine

Level in Space
High
Low
In-between

Size (Range) of Body Action
Large
Medium
Small

Body Facing
Front of body addressing different direction than that of its locomotion

Spatial Concepts (continued)

Front of body addressing same direction as its locomotion

Eye Focus
Head facing in different direction from body
Head facing same direction as body

Time Concepts

Fast
Medium
Slow
Rhythmic pattern

Flow Concepts or Movement Qualities

Smooth-flowing
Interrupted
Hitting
Throwing
Swinging
Collapsing
Resisted

Force Concepts

Strong
Weak

Parts of classes can be devoted to exploring the locomotor patterns, working from a simple walk to the more complex slide and gallop, with some of the above variations in direction, speed, level, etc., and a drum or musical accompaniment to add interest. Children can also explore possible swinging, hitting, or throwing action, for instance, of arms or head with some of the leg patterns; or they can try to determine how they can use rotation of legs, arms, or spine in conjunction with the locomotor activities. In these actions students are trying to synchronize one action with another—a very challenging part of the process of developing more complex motor skills.

Children like the fundamental locomotor patterns, with their intrinsic repeating rhythms, and they enjoy being challenged to coordinate them in various simple combinations and performing them in strong group unison. They like to let their trunks, arms, and heads respond freely, and to consume as much space and energy with their movement as they can. They also like the contrast of making some movements very small. The locomotor pattern activities are an excellent complement to the unmetered movement explorations described above.

To initiate this type of activity, the children may be asked to do four slides facing the (clock) wall and four slides facing the opposite wall. When they have solved this, the teacher can decide if they can reduce the pattern to three or two slides or possibly one slide, altering the last slide to a fairly tricky skip (step hop) turn. Children appreciate the teacher's continuing help until they have successfully solved the problem. If any activity proves too difficult for them, the teacher should tell them so to alleviate unnecessary feelings of frustration or failure. They also like the attention of being watched in separate rows to see if they are doing the right number of slides. They enjoy counting out loud for each other. The teacher must watch them closely and provide them with a good strong beat, knowing in which patterns the beat is even and in which uneven, at a tempo suitable to their length of leg and rate of movement.

After mastery of the four-slide pattern above, four skips may be added. Patterns are more challenging and fun when they have more than one thing happening, so that the child experiences motor relief and contrast.

Any of the basic steps from the folk dances in this chapter can be used in the same way. The teacher can help the children understand the folk dance steps by presenting them all as time-effort variations of the weight transference of the walk, or combinations of the eight basic locomotor patterns. For instance, the Norwegian Mountain March on page 268 can be prepared for in the warm-up by giving attention to the pushing foot action in running. The teacher can then suggest that the children add movement accents, such as stamps or claps, on every third beat. A waltz could be played, and the children could begin to coordinate their accent with the accent in the music, which is count 1. They could then replace or reinforce the clap or stamp with emphasis by the leg on the accented beat, and they would have accomplished the first figure of the Norwegian Mountain March.

On the same or another day the children could work in groups of three to invent a pattern of their own, using the idea of joining hands to run in circles and under each other's arms while crossing the room to the music of the Norwegian Mountain March. It is likely that children will have more appreciation for learning a set pattern if they have dealt with the problem of making one of their own first. Letting the children find dynamics and pleasure in the separate movement ideas of the folk dances before attempting the additional task of putting the movements together helps them to perform better and with more pleasure and appreciation of dance quality when they come to assembling the steps of the dance.

Appreciation of the Creative Process Through Interrelating with Others

Children can learn to appreciate their own uniquenesses and to respect the personal quality of others through mutual effort in a creative activity. Working with another child on a problem necessitating close timing to create a movement structure which propels them both is an experience in which they both internalize the importance of mutual support and the equal importance of each child. Children gravitate to other children with whom they've had intimate experience of support through direct physical contact. Having exchanged trust physically, they tend to share respect and sympathy. The development of such feelings is essential to successful participation in the creative process and to the broader appreciation of the art act.

To achieve such development, the teacher may, for example, have children select partners and take turns leading and following each other through movements of their choice. This is often called "mirroring." At first children may follow simultaneously for mutual support; later they may be encouraged to try the activity with the follower taking his time to respond and omitting what he does not want to do. Most children love to "mirror" both with and without music, but they usually become more deeply involved with exploration of mutual dynamics without music.

Involvement in the dance activity is easily generated by the use of outside objects, which dancers often call "props" (short for stage properties). Children are delighted to have a prop as a partner. Anything that stimulates movement or imagination usually works—e.g., crepe paper streamers, ropes, a badminton net on the floor or hanging limply from its supports, floaty fabric, balloons, a flat piece of cardboard, newspapers, and cardboard cartons. The first very appropriate and dance-like response of the children is to see how they can move with the object. (If their movements indicate destructive feelings toward the props, the teacher can appropriately encourage a dance of destruction and praise them for putting their anger into a dance.) Once they've found some movements that are fun to use with their props, the children can often "rhythmetize" these movements easily by repeating a favorite part of the total pattern and sensing the rhythm in it. The teacher can help a child feel the rhythm by providing a suitable drum accompaniment.

Children are unpredictable as to whether they can relate their movements with props to music. Their ability to do so really depends on the prop and the response it evokes. When done in silence with a sense of conscious performance, these improvisations often acquire dramatic overtones.

As the children experience appreciation and pleasure in their own dance fragments, formed out of their own selection of movements, and receive admiration for their discoveries from their classmates, they begin to experience the essence of the art act: the making of choices, the manipulation of tools of the art toward greater pleasure, and interest in the end product.

Self-Confidence in Performance

A very important ingredient in all dance activity experiences is the need for the child to appreciate his ideas, his feelings, his ability to understand and to solve problems alone and with others, the rightness of his solutions for himself, and his final motor and artistic achievement—that is, the child needs to develop confidence in his abilities as a performer.

There are essentially two ways in which a teacher can help a child achieve self-confidence. One is to give him verbal encouragement and approval as he works with movement exploration, labeling his discoveries when possible, e.g., "You're doing a good gallop, Timmy." The other is to give children chances, to the extent time permits, to show their discoveries. Children quickly learn to relish performance alone and in small groups and often extend their skills and awareness markedly during their more intense concentration in performance. Caution should be taken, however, to avoid so much emphasis on performance that the child loses sight of moving for his own pleasure and discovery.

CHOICE OF RECORDS

Records for creative dance activity can be chosen from several sources. For locomotor activities with strong rhythmic patterns, imported authentic folk dance records are delightful and can be used for many kinds of dance ideas. Two very useful ones are: "Theme from Zorba the Greek" and the "Israeli Folk Dance Festival."

Songs by American folk singers such as Pete Seeger and Joan Baez are good possibilities so long as the selections don't slow down or speed up. There are always current pop tunes, too, which have playfulness or simplicity which makes them appropriate for use with children. Examples of these are songs by John Denver, Cat Stevens, Burt Jansch, and John Renbourn. Two songs that are actually very good waltzes of usable tempo are John Denver's "Take Me Home" and Cat Stevens' "Morning Has Broken."

Classical music to symphonic orchestra is often overwhelming in creative dance activity. Instrumental groups with fewer instruments are usually a less frightening accompaniment for children's bodies. There are exceptions, however. The teacher might consider Khachaturian's "Masquerade Suite" or Kabalevsky's "Comedians," or Debussy's "Children's Corner Suite."

TRADITIONAL DANCE STEPS

Almost all of the traditional dance steps have their foundation in the fundamental locomotor patterns. Before attempting these steps a strong basic understanding of the locomotor patterns should be established. Most folk dances involve one or more of the traditional dance steps, and much of the social dancing has its basis in traditional dance steps.

TEACHING HINTS

Sometimes it may be valuable to use these dance steps as a warm-up at the beginning of a period or even as stunts during a tumbling period.

The teacher should learn and use the cue words that will keep the children with the music. For example, when teaching the schottische the cue words are: run-run-run-hop.

PRESENTATION

A generally good procedure for teaching a traditional dance step follows:

If possible give the background of the step.
Listen to the music.
Learn the step without music and without a partner.
If possible do the step in a stationary position, then add movement.
Add the music, do the dance individually.
Do the dance step with a partner and music.

A suggested grade placement for introducing each traditional dance step will be indicated. It must be remembered that this is only a suggestion, and the needs and abilities of the class will determine the speed at which the steps will be introduced.

Step-Point (Grade 2)

The step point is a step on the left foot, pointing the right foot in front. This action is repeated stepping on the right foot.

count 1	count 2	count 3	count 4
step left	point right	step right	point left

Step-Hop (Grade 3)

The step-hop is a step on the left foot and a hop on the right foot. This action is repeated using the right foot.

count 1	count 2	count 3	count 4
step left	hop left	step right	hop right

Step-Swing (Grade 3)

The step-swing is a step on the left foot followed by a swing of the right foot across in front of the left. This action is repeated stepping on the right foot.

count 1	count 2	count 3	count 4
step left	swing right	step right	swing left

Bleking (Grade 3)

The bleking step is a jump landing with the left heel forward. This is held momentarily before the left foot is brought back as the dancer jumps with the right heel forward and holds, then jumps left, right, left in quick time and holds. This action is repeated starting with the opposite foot.

count 1	and	2	and
jump right		jump left	

count 1	and	2	and
jump right	jump left	jump right	hold

Balance Step (Grade 4)

The balance step can be done in any direction. The dancer steps left and closes right to left rising on the balls of both feet.

count 1	count 2	count 3
step left	close right	rise on toes, lower

count 1	count 2	count 3
step right	close left	rise on toes, lower

Schottische (Grade 4)

The schottische step is a step on the left, step right, step left, hop left. The action is repeated using the right foot. The steps are taken so quickly as to become a run.

count 1	count 2	count 3	count 4
run left	run right	run left	hop left

count 1	count 2	count 3	count 4
run right	run left	run right	hop right

Minuet (Grade 4)

The minuet step is a step left, step right, step left, point right, step right, point left, step left, point right.

count 1	count 2	count 3	count 1	count 2	count 3
step	step	step	point	—	step

count 1	count 2	count 3	count 1	count 2	count 3
	point	step		point	

Polka (simple) (Grade 4)

The simple polka is a step on the right, close left to right, step on right, hold. The action is repeated using the opposite foot.

count 1	and	count 2	and
step right	close left	step right	hold
count 1	and	count 2	and
step left	close right	step left	hold

Polka (heel-toe) (Grade 4)

The heel-toe polka is a step on the left placing the right heel forward; the right toe is placed to the rear; the dancer then steps right, closes left to right, steps right, and holds. The action is repeated using the opposite foot.

count 1	and	count 2	and
	heel		toe
count 1	and	count 2	and
step	close	step	hold

Polka (hop) (Grade 5)

The polka step is a hop on the right, step left, close right to left, step left. The action is repeated beginning with a hop on the left.

and	count 1	and	count 2	and
hop	step	close	step	hop

count 1	and	count 2	and
step	close	step	hop

Two-Step (Grade 5)

The two-step is a step on the left, close right to left, step left. The action is repeated beginning right.

count 1	count 2	count 3
step left	close right	step left
count 1	count 2	count 3
step right	close left	step right

Waltz (box) (Grade 6)

The waltz step is a step forward left, step sideward right, close left to right, then a step backward right, step sideward left, close right to left.

count 1	count 2	count 3
step left (forward)	side right	close left
count 1	count 2	count 3
step right (backward)	side left	close right

Mazurka (Grade 6)

The mazurka step is a step on the left bringing right up to left with a cut step displacing left, and a hop right while bending left knee so that left approaches the right.

count 1	*count 2*	*count 3*
step left	cut right	hop right
count 1	*count 2*	*count 3*
step right	cut right	hop right

SINGING GAMES AND FOLK DANCES*

Singing games and folk dances not only serve as popular recreational activities providing enjoyment, relaxation, and physical activity, but promote real understanding and appreciation of peoples and cultures of many countries. With careful planning, singing games and folk dances may be successfully integrated into many other subject areas including social studies, music, and art.

Because the singing games and folk dances involve dancing with a partner or in a group, they afford excellent opportunities for children to learn desirable social skills and attitudes. Like most other rhythmic activities, many of the singing games and especially the folk dances provide vigorous activity which contributes significantly to the physical development of the participants as well as providing experiences for their social development.

The attitude of the teacher toward an activity is extremely important, and this is especially true in presenting these games and dances. Not only must the specific activity be well in mind, but the presentation must generate enthusiasm and sincere interest.

The grade level at which the singing games and folk dances may be introduced is indicated with the descriptions below. This should serve only as a guide. After discovering the abilities and needs of the class, the teacher will determine when an activity should be introduced. After an activity has been introduced and learned, it should be reviewed at subsequent grade levels to reenforce the skill learning and for sheer enjoyment.

TEACHING HINTS

Almost every singing game or folk dance involves one or more of the fundamental locomotor patterns. Depending upon the skill abilities of the class, some review of these may be necessary. The ones most closely related to the activities of the present unit should receive the most emphasis.

---

*Records are available for all singing games and folk dances. See the list at the end of the chapter on pages 289–290.

Dances and singing games may be repeated often, since children enjoy repetition. Enjoyment and participation are more important than perfection, and too much drill is to be avoided.

Securing Partners

Getting a partner is not a significant problem in kindergarten, first, second, and third grade; in fact, it is permissible for boys to dance with boys or girls with girls. From fourth grade to eighth grade, certain problems arise. Discussions should be held with the class on selection of partners. It is best to avoid allowing children to choose partners. Many times certain children are chosen last or not at all, so that an arbitrary method of obtaining partners is preferable. A grand march is one excellent way (see p. 267). Any method of selecting partners should be as impersonal as possible. It is especially important with older children to change partners often.

It is an unusual class, indeed, that has the same number of boys and girls. Provision should be made, especially in the older grades, for an uneven number of boys and girls. An arm band, or similar device, can be used to designate a girl taking a boy's part or vice versa. Children should never sit out of the activity for extended periods of time.

PRESENTATION

The following presentation may be used with success:

Singing Game

Give the background of the dance, if possible.
Listen to the music.
Teach the words without music, then with the music.
Teach the action of the dance without music, then with music.
Combine words, music, and action.
If space is limited or numbers large, half of the class may sing while the other half dances.

Folk Dance

Give the background of the dance, if possible.
Listen to the music to get an idea of character, quality, and speed.
Describe and demonstrate the dance.
Teach the difficult steps or figures separately.
Do the steps individually first without music, then add music.
Use partners without the music; then add music.

KINDERGARTEN AND FIRST GRADE*

The Farmer in the Dell, English Singing Game

FORMATION. The children form a single circle and join hands facing the center. One child in the center is the "farmer."

MEASURES	VERSE 1
1–2	The farmer in the dell,
3–4	The farmer in the dell
5–6	Heigh-ho! the dairy-o!
7–8	The farmer in the dell.

	VERSE 2
1–2	The farmer takes a wife,
3–4	The farmer takes a wife,
5–6	Heigh-ho! the dairy-o!
7–8	The farmer takes a wife.

VERSES 3–9

The wife takes the child, etc.
The child takes the nurse, etc.
The nurse takes the dog, etc.
The dog takes the cat, etc.
The cat takes the rat, etc.
The rat takes the cheese, etc.
The cheese stands alone, etc.

EXPLANATION. *Verse 1.* The children circle clockwise singing.

Verses 2–8. The children continue to sing and circle. The farmer chooses a wife who joins him in the center of the circle. The wife then selects a child, etc.

Verse 9. At this time the children forming the circle stop, face center and continue to sing. Those in the center crowd around the cheese and clap over his head. At the end of this verse, those within circle, except the cheese, join the circle. The child chosen to be the cheese remains in the center and becomes the farmer for the new game.

Bluebirds, U.S. Singing Game

Formation. The children form a single circle facing center with hands joined high to form arches. One or more children selected as "bluebirds" are on the outside of the circle.

---

*See record list on pages 289–290 and references.

MEASURES	VERSE 1
1–4	Bluebird, bluebird, through my window,
5–8	Bluebird, bluebird, through my window,
9–12	Bluebird, bluebird, through my window,
13–16	Oh Johnny, I am tired.

	VERSE 2
1–4	Take a little boy (girl), tap him on his shoulder,
5–8	Take a little boy (girl), tap him on his shoulder,
9–12	Take a little boy (girl), tap him on his shoulder,
13–16	Oh Johnny, I am tired.

EXPLANATION. *Verse 1.* The bluebird goes in and out through the arches, using his arms as wings and moving them in rhythm, while the other children sing.

Verse 2. The bluebird stops behind a child in the circle and, in rhythm, taps him (her) on the shoulder while singing. On the word "tired," the bluebird gently pushes the one being tapped into the circle. The one pushed is now the bluebird. The game is repeated. The old bluebird occupies the vacant spot.

The Muffin Man, English Singing Game

FORMATION. A single circle is formed with the children facing center. One child in the center is the "muffin man."

MEASURES	VERSE 1
1–2	Oh, have you seen the muffin man,
3–4	The muffin man, the muffin man;
5–6	Oh, have you seen the muffin man
7–8	Who lives in Drury Lane?

	VERSE 2
1–2	Oh, yes, we've seen the muffin man,
3–4	The muffin man, the muffin man;
5–6	Oh, yes, we've seen the muffin man
8–8	Who lives in Drury Lane.

VERSES 3–6

Two have seen the muffin man, etc.
Four have seen the muffin man, etc.
Eight have seen the muffin man, etc.
All have seen the muffin man, etc.

EXPLANATION. *Verse 1.* Everyone, except the one in the center, walks or skips clockwise around the circle singing.

Verse 2. Those forming the circle stop and face center while singing. The one in the center skips around within the circle and stops in front of another child.

Verse 3. The one chosen moves into the circle and joins hands with the one who chose him. Both skip counterclockwise around the circle, while all sing.

Verses 4–5. Partners release hands and each chooses another partner. Four then skip counterclockwise around the circle while all sing. This is repeated until all have been chosen. Each time the number in the song is doubled.

Verse 6. All skip counterclockwise around the circle singing.

Danish Dance of Greeting, Danish Folk Dance

FORMATION. The children form a single circle, facing center with partner on the right.

MEASURES	PART 1
1	Clap hands twice and bow to partner.
2	Clap hands twice and bow to neighbor (one on left).
3	Stamp twice in place, still facing center.
4	Turn once around in place using four running steps.
5–8	Repeat measures 1–4.

	PART 2
1–4	All join hands and circle clockwise with 16 running steps.
5–8	Repeat counterclockwise.

Chimes of Dunkirk, Belgian Folk Dance

FORMATION. The children form a circle, with partner on the right. Partners then face each other for Part 1.

MEASURES	PART 1
1–2	Stamp in place three times.
3–4	Clap own hands three times.
5–8	Join hands with partner, and turn once around opposite line of direction (clockwise) with 8 skipping steps.

	PART 2
1–8	All join hands and circle clockwise with 16 skipping steps.

Looby Loo

FORMATION. Children form a single circle facing the center.

MEASURES	CHORUS
1–2	Here we go Looby Loo,
3–4	Here we go Looby light.
5–6	Here we go Looby Loo,
7–8	All on a Saturday night.

VERSE 1

1–2	I put my right hand in,
3–4	I put my right hand out;
5–6	I give my right hand a shake, shake, shake
7–8	And turn myself about.

CHORUS

VERSE 2

1–2	I put my left hand in,
3–4	I put my left hand out;
5–6	I give my left hand a shake, shake, shake
7–8	And turn myself about.

ADDITIONAL VERSES

3. I put my two hands in, etc.
4. I put my right foot in, etc.
5. I put my left foot in, etc.
6. I put my head 'way in, etc.
7. I put my whole self in, etc.

EXPLANATION. *Chorus.* Children join hands and slide, skip, run or walk to left or right.

Verses. While singing a verse, they stand in place and act out lyrics. Repeat the chorus after each verse.

Did You Ever See a Lassie?

FORMATION. Children form a single circle facing the center. One child is selected to be in the middle.

MEASURES

VERSE

1–8	Did you ever see a lassie (or laddie),
	A lassie, a lassie,
	Did you ever see a lassie
	Go this way and that?

CHORUS

9–16	Go this way and that way,
	Go this way and that way,
	Did you ever see a lassie
	Go this way and that?

EXPLANATION. *Measures 1–8.* All join hands and skip left or right. Center player decides what action to display.

Measures 9–16. Children in circle stop and mimic the center player's movements.

Repeat song with a new leader in center.

London Bridge

FORMATION.   Two players join hands and form an arch over their heads. Other players form a single line facing the arch.

MEASURES	VERSE 1
1–2	London Bridge is falling down,
3–4	Falling down, falling down,
5–6	London Bridge is falling down,
7–8	My fair lady.

	VERSE 2
1–2	Build it up with iron bars,
3–4	Iron bars, iron bars,
5–6	Build it up with iron bars,
7–8	My fair lady.

	VERSE 3
1–2	Off to prison you must go,
3–4	You must go, you must go,
5–6	Off to prison you must go,
7–8	My fair lady.

ADDITIONAL VERSES

Build it up with gold and silver, etc.
Gold and silver I have not, etc.
Build it up with pins and needles, etc.
Pins and needles rust and bend, etc.
Build it up with penny loaves, etc.
Penny loaves will tumble down, etc.
Here's a prisoner I have got, etc.
What's the prisoner done to you, etc.
Stole my watch and bracelet too, etc.
What'll you take to set him free, etc.
One hundred pounds will set him free, etc.
One hundred pounds we don't have, etc.
Then off to prison he must go, etc.

EXPLANATION.   *Verse 1.*   Children in line walk through arch. On the words "My fair lady," children forming arch drop their hands to capture prisoner.

Verse 2.   Children forming arch sway from side to side while prisoner moves forward and backward.

Verse 3.   Arch players and prisoner move away from rest of group. The prisoner is asked to choose one of two items such as gold or silver. The two arch players each select one prior to the game. The prisoner then stands behind the arch player who represents the item he selected. Repeat until all players have been caught. The side with the most players wins.

Go Round and Round the Village

FORMATION. Half the children join hands in a single circle. The remaining children stand around the outside of the circle.

MEASURES	VERSE 1
1–2	Go round and round the village,
3–4	Go round and round the village,
5–6	Go round and round the village,
7–8	As we have done before.

	VERSE 2
1–8	Go in and out the windows, etc.

	VERSE 3
1–8	Now stand and face your partners, etc.

	VERSE 4
1–8	Now follow me to London, etc.

EXPLANATION. *Verse 1.* Children in circle stand still. Those outside the circle skip around circle to left or right.

Verse 2. Children in circle raise their arms. Those on outside skip in and out of circle under raised arms.

Verse 3. Each outside player faces a circle player.

Verse 4. Partners hold hands, and all skip around to left or right.

SECOND GRADE

Hopp Mor Annika, Swedish Folk Dance

FORMATION. The children form a double circle, boys on inside, all facing counterclockwise, with partners' hands joined.

MEASURES	INTRODUCTION
1–2	Face partner and bow or curtsey.

	PART 1
1–8	Take 16 walking steps forward (counterclockwise), swinging arms alternately forward and back.

	PART 2
9–16	Continue moving counterclockwise with 16 skipping steps, swinging arms. End facing partner.

	PART 3
17	Clap own hands, clap right hands with partner.
18	Clap own hands, clap left hands with partner.
19	Clap own hands, clap both hands with partner.

20	Clap own hands three times. Hold last count.
21–24	Repeat 17–20.
25–32	Couples face counterclockwise and skip 16 steps, swinging joined hands.

Carousel, Swedish Singing Game

FORMATION. The children form a double circle, facing center; dancers in the inside circle join hands, while those in the outside circle place both hands on shoulders of partners.

MEASURES	PART 1
1–2	Little children young and gay, carousel is running,
3–4	It will run 'til evening, little ones a nickel,
5–7	Big ones a dime, hurry up, get a mate, or you'll surely be too late.

	PART 2
1–2	Ha, ha, ha! happy are we,
3–4	Anderson and Henderson and Peterson and me.
1–2	Ha, ha, ha! happy are we,
3–4	Anderson and Henderson and Peterson and me.

EXPLANATION. *Part 1.* Dancers, while singing, move sidewards clockwise using a step together—step left (count 1), close right to left (count 2). This is repeated 13 times.

Part 2. Dancers continue singing and moving clockwise sliding to the faster tempo and using short quick steps.

Kinderpolka, German Folk Dance

FORMATION. The children form a single circle, partners facing. Arms are extended, hands joined, shoulder high.

MEASURES	PART 1
1–2	Move toward center of circle taking two slide close steps, ending with three steps in place.
3–4	Repeat, moving away from center of circle.
5–8	Repeat measures 1–4.

	PART 2
9	Slap own thighs with both hands, clap own hands.
10	Clap both hands with partner three times.
11–12	Repeat measures 9–10.

	PART 3
13	Point one foot forward and shake forefinger at partner three times.

14	Repeat using other foot and hand.
15–16	Turn once around with four running steps and stamp three times.

Shoemaker's Dance, Danish Singing Game

FORMATION. The dancers form a double circle, partners facing.

MEASURES	PART 1
1	Wind, wind, wind the bobbin,
2	Wind, wind, wind the bobbin,
3	Pull, pull,
4	Clap, clap, clap.

	PART 2
5	Wind, wind, wind the bobbin,
6	Wind, wind, wind the bobbin,
7	Pull, pull,
8	Tap, tap, tap.

	PART 3
1–8	Tra la la la la, etc.

EXPLANATION

MEASURES	PARTS 1 AND 2
1	Arms bent at shoulder level and hands closed to form a fist. Move one fist over the other in a circling movement while singing.
2	Reverse circling.
3	Pull elbows back vigorously, twice.
4	Clap own hands three times.
5–7	Repeat measures 1–3.
8	Hammer own fists together three times.

	PART 3
1–8	Partners join inside hands and take 16 skipping steps moving counterclockwise.

A-Hunting We Will Go

FORMATION. Two parallel lines face each other. Partners face each other, six girls in one line and six boys in the other.

MEASURES	VERSE
1–4	Oh, a-hunting we will go, A-hunting we will go,

| 5–8 | We'll catch a fox and put him in a box,
And then we'll let him go. |

CHORUS

| 1–4 | Tra la la la la la,
Tra la la la la la, |
| 5–8 | Tra la la la la la la la la la,
Tra la la la la la. |

EXPLANATION. *Verse. Measures 1–4.* The first set of partners (head couple) join inside hands and skip between lines to end of set. Other players clap to music.

Measures 5–8. Head couple turns, changes hands, and skips back to head of set.

Chorus. All partners join hands and skip to left in a circle. When the head couple reaches the end of the set, they form an arch under which all other partners pass. The head couple remains at the foot of the set while the second couple becomes the new head couple.

Repeat dance until all partners have returned to their original position.

Pop Goes the Weasel

FORMATION. Double circle in sets of four children. Girls are on partners' right. Couples facing clockwise are couples one; couples facing counterclockwise are couples two.

MEASURES	VERSE 1
1–4	'Round and 'round the cobbler's shop Monkey chased the weasel,
5–6	In and out and 'round about,
7–8	Pop, goes the weasel.

	VERSE 2
1–4	I've no time to wait or sigh, To wait for bye and bye;
5–6	Kiss me quick, I'm off — good-bye,
7–8	Pop, goes the weasel.

EXPLANATION. *Verse. Measures 1–4.* Join hands in circle of four and circle left with skipping or sliding steps.

Measures 5–6. Walk forward two steps raising joined hands, then back two steps lowering hands.

Measures 7–8. Number one couples raise joined hands to form an arch as number two couples pass under and continue forward to meet new couples.

Oats, Peas, Beans, and Barley

FORMATION. Children form single circle facing center with hands joined. Select one child for the center who is the "Farmer."

MEASURES	VERSE 1
1–2	Oats, peas, beans, and barley grow,
3–4	Oats, peas, beans, and barley grow,
5–6	Do you or I or anyone know
7–8	How oats, peas, beans, and barley grow?

	VERSE 2
1–2	First the farmer sows his seed,
3–4	Then he stands and takes his ease,
5–6	Stamps his foot and claps his hand,
7–8	And turns around to view the land.

	VERSE 3
1–2	Waiting for a partner,
3–4	Waiting for a partner,
5–6	Open the ring and choose one in
7–8	While we all gaily dance and sing.

	VERSE 4
1–2	Now you're married, you must obey,
3–4	You must be true to all you say,
5–6	You must be kind, you must be good,
7–8	And keep your wife in kindling wood.

EXPLANATION. *Verse 1.* "Farmer" stands in center of circle while others circle left.

Verse 2. Children in circle stop, face center, and pantomime the words.

Verse 3. Children in circle skip left as "farmer" skips around inside of the circle and picks a partner. "Farmer" and partner skip around inside.

Verse 4. Two "farmers" continue to skip while others join hands and circle left. Old "farmer" joins ring and new "farmer" repeats four verses.

THIRD GRADE

Hansel and Gretel, German Singing Game

FORMATION. The children form a double circle, partners facing.

MEASURES	VERSE 1
1–2	Partner come and dance with me,
3–4	Both your hands now give to me,
5–6	Right foot first, left foot then,
7–8	Round and round and back again.

VERSE 2

1–8	Tra la la la la la la, etc.

VERSE 3

1–2	With your feet go tap, tap, tap,
3–4	With your hands go clap, clap, clap,
5–6	Right foot first, left foot then,
7–8	Round and round and back again.

VERSE 4

1–2	With your head go nip, nip, nip,
3–4	With your fingers snip, snip, snip,
5–6	Right foot first, left foot then,
7–8	Round and round and back again.

EXPLANATION

MEASURES   VERSE 1

1–2	Boys bow and girls curtsey.
3–4	Join both hands.
5–6	Jump placing right heel forward; repeat placing left heel forward.
7–8	With four skipping steps turn partner around moving clockwise.

VERSE 2

1–8	Join inside hands and take 16 skipping steps around the circle moving counterclockwise.

VERSE 3

1–2	Partners stop and face each other, dropping hands. Stamp feet three times. Clap own hands three times.
5–6	Join hands and jump placing right heel forward; repeat placing left heel forward.
7–8	With four skipping steps turn partner once around moving clockwise.

VERSE 4

1–2	Drop hands and nod three times.
3–4	Snap fingers three times.
5–8	Repeat measures 5–8 as in Verse 3.

Jolly Is the Miller, U.S. Singing Game

FORMATION.   The children form a double circle facing counterclockwise, partners inside, hands joined. One or more extra dancers are in the center of the circle.

MEASURES   VERSE

1–2   Jolly is the miller who lives by the mill,
3–4   The wheel turns around of its own free will,
5–6   One hand in the hopper and the other in the sack,
7–8   The hub goes forward and the rim turns back.

EXPLANATION.   Partners walk or skip counterclockwise around the circle. On the word "back" in the last line of the song, partners release hands; those in the inner circle step forward; those in the outer circle step backward to get a new partner. The extra dancer attempts to get a partner at this change. The one without a partner moves to the center of the circle.

Nixie Polka, Danish Folk Dance

FORMATION.   The dancers form a single circle facing center. One or more children in the center act as the "Nixies."

MEASURES

1   Jump placing right heel forward, hold.
2   Jump placing left heel forward, hold.
3–4   Repeat action of measures 1–2.
5–16   Take 24 running steps in place. The Nixie takes 24 running steps moving counterclockwise around the inside of the circle. On the last step the Nixie stops in front of a partner.
1–4   Repeat measures 1–4 above. The Nixie dances in front of partner. On count one of measure four the Nixie jumps turning back to partner. The partner places hands on the Nixie's shoulders.
5–16   Repeat running steps in place. Nixie and partner run counterclockwise on inside of circle. On last step Nixie stops in front of another partner.
                Repeat dance until all are in line behind the Nixie. The Nixie then leads the group counterclockwise into a circle.

Bleking, Swedish Folk Dance

FORMATION.   Partners face each other with both hands joined.

MEASURES

1   Jump lightly to left foot placing right heel to floor (Bleking). Seesaw arms by extending right arm forward with elbow straight and left arm back with elbow bent. Reverse arms and jump onto right foot, placing left heel on floor.
2   Repeat step.
3–8   Repeat measures 1–2 three times.

9–16	Extend arms sideward and turn clockwise with 16 step-hops, alternately raising and lowering arms and kicking free leg to side.
	Repeat entire dance.

Pawpaw Patch, U.S. Singing Game

FORMATION.   Four to six couples form a double line with partners facing each other. The first name of the girl is used as each new couple take their place at the head of the lines.

MEASURES	VERSE 1
1–2	Where, oh where is sweet little (Bonnie)?
3–4	Where, oh where is sweet little (Bonnie)?
5–6	Where, oh where is sweet little (Bonnie)?
7–8	Way down yonder in the pawpaw patch.

	VERSE 2
1–2	Come on boys, let's go find her,
3–4	Come on boys, let's go find her,
5–6	Come on boys, let's go find her,
7–8	Way down yonder in the pawpaw patch.

	VERSE 3
1–2	Pickin' up pawpaws, puttin' them in a basket,
3–4	Pickin' up pawpaws, puttin' them in a basket,
5–6	Pickin' up pawpaws, puttin' them in a basket,
7–8	Way down yonder in the pawpaw patch.

EXPLANATION.   *Verse 1.*   First girl turns to right and skips around the entire group.

Verse 2.   Girl encircles group again, and the line of boys follows her and returns to original position.

Verse 3.   Partners join hands and follow first couple around to right. When head couple reach foot of line, they form an arch and other couples skip under it.

Repeat entire dance with each new first girl leading.

Come, Let Us Be Joyful, German Singing Game

FORMATION.   Each person selects two partners and joins hands. Form a circle, every other trio facing the opposite direction, thus making sets of six. Allow six short steps between facing trios.

MEASURES	VERSE
1–4	Come, let us be joyful,
	While life is bright and gay;
5–8	Gather its roses
	Ere they fade away.

9–10	We're always making our lives so blue,
11–12	We look for thorns and find them, too,
13–16	And leave the violets quite unseen,
	That on our way do grow.

EXPLANATION

MEASURES

1–4	Facing trios take three short steps toward each other; boys bow, girls curtsey, and trios step back to place.
5–8	Repeat measures 1–4.
9–10	Center person faces right hand partner, links elbows, and turns once. Left hand partner turns in place alone.
11–12	Center person faces left hand partner, links elbows, and turns once. Right hand partner turns in place.
13–16	Repeat measures 9–12.
	Repeat measures 1–4.
	Repeat measures 5–8. Trios advance three steps, drop hands, and pass through opposite trio, each passing right shoulder to right shoulder.

FOURTH GRADE

Grand March

CALL.   (1) Come down the center in twos.
(2) Twos right and twos left.
(3) Come down the center in fours.
(4) Fours right and fours left.
(5) Come down the center in eights.

EXPLANATION.   The musical accompaniment may be any march. The boys and girls line up on opposite sides of the room, facing the rear of the room. The teacher, who makes the calls, stands in the center at the front of the room. As each call is given, the leaders of the two lines respond accordingly and the others in the lines follow them.

(1) The boys and girls march to meet one another at the rear of the room. They turn, join hands, and march toward the teacher. (2) The first couple turns to the right, the second to the left, and so on. (3) As the two head couples meet at the rear of the room, they join hands and march toward the teacher. (4) The first group of four turns to the right, the next group turns to the left, and so on. (5) As the two groups of four meet at the rear of the room, they join hands and march toward the teacher, where they stop.

If the Grand March is being used to pair the couples for a dance that is to follow, the above pattern is reversed.

CALL.   (1) Fours right and fours left.
(2) Come down the center in fours.
(3) Twos right and twos left.
(4) Come down the center in twos.

EXPLANATION. The group of eight divides in half, each group of four going in the opposite direction. (2) As they reach the rear of the room, the groups of four take the position of one behind the other. (3) They march toward the teacher and divide into groups of twos, each group of two going in the opposite direction. (4) When they meet at the rear of the room, they line up behind each other and march down the center toward the teacher and stop.

Gustaf's Skoal, Swedish Folk Dance

FORMATION. The dancers form a square, girls on partners' right. Couples are numbered counterclockwise 1, 2, 3, 4. Head couples are 1 and 3; side couples are 2 and 4.

MEASURES	PART 1
1–4	Head couples take three steps forward, bow and curtsey on count four. Return to place using four steps.
5–8	Side couples repeat measures 1–4.
1–8	Repeat measures 1–8.

	PART 2
	Side couples join inside hands high to form arches.
1–6	Head couples take four skipping steps forward, drop partner's hand, turn a quarter turn away from partner and join hands with the opposite. With opposite go under nearest arch with four skipping steps. After going through the arch release opposite's hand and, with four skip steps, return to original places.
7–8	Head couples join both hands, skip once around in place with four skipping steps.
1–8	Side couples repeat measures 1–8.

Norwegian Mountain March, Norwegian Folk Dance

FORMATION. The dancers form triangle sets of threes facing counter-clockwise. The leader, number 1, extends both arms backward joining outside hands with numbers 2 and 3. Number 2 is to the left of the leader, number 3 is to the right of the leader. Numbers 2 and 3 stand behind number 1 and join inside hands.

MEASURES	PART 1
1–8	All run forward with 24 light running steps. Take three steps to a measure, accenting the first step in each measure.

	PART 2
1–2	Number 1 dances backward under the raised arm of numbers 2 and 3 with six running steps, accenting the first step. Numbers 2 and 3 dance in place.

3–4	Number 2 dances across, with six running steps, under the right arm of number 1. Numbers 1 and 3 dance in place.
5–6	Number 3 turns under own right arm with six running steps. Numbers 1 and 2 dance in place.
7–8	Number 1 turns under own right arm with six running steps. Numbers 2 and 3 dance in place. All finish in starting position.

Patty Cake Polka, U.S. Folk Dance

FORMATION.   The dancers form a double circle, partners facing with both hands joined. Boys form the inner circle, girls the outer circle.

MEASURES   PART 1

1–2	Boys place left heel diagonally to the side and return left toe beside instep of right foot. Girls do same action starting on right foot. Repeat.
3–4	Partners take four slides to the boys' left, moving counterclockwise.
5–8	Repeat action of measures 1–4, with boys starting right, girls starting left.

PART 2

	Release hands.
9	Clap right hand with partner three times.
10	Clap left hand with partner three times.
11	Clap both hands with partner three times.
12	Slap own thighs three times.
13–14	Hook right elbow with partner, turn once around in four walking steps.
15–16	With four walking steps move left to new partner.

Seven Steps, North European Folk Dance

FORMATION.   The children form a double circle, inside hands joined, facing counterclockwise. Boys are on inner circle.

MEASURES   PART 1

| 1–2 | Take seven steps forward, starting with the outside foot. Stamp on count seven and pause. |
| 3–4 | Take seven steps backward, starting on the inside foot. Stamp on count seven and pause. |

PART 2

| 1 | Take three steps moving diagonally away from partner, starting with outside foot. On count four stamp inside foot and clap. |

2	Repeat first measure of Part 2 returning to partner, starting on inside foot.
3–4	Partners hook right elbows and take seven running steps around in place.

PART 3

1–4	Repeat measures 1–4 above.

Troika, Russian Folk Dance

FORMATION. Form groups of three facing counterclockwise. Boy in center holds inside hands of girls. Girls' outside hands are on hips.

MEASURES

1	Four running steps diagonally forward to right.
2	Four running steps diagonally forward to left.
3–4	Eight running steps directly forward in circle.
5–6	Girl on right of boy runs eight steps under arch made by boy and girl on left. Boy turns under own arm, and girl on left runs in place.
7–8	Girl on left runs under arch; repeat as in measures 5–6.
9–11	Trio joins hands in circle and runs 12 steps around to right.
12	Stamp left, right, left.
13–16	Repeat measures 9–11 running around to left and stamp right, left, right.
	Boys move on to new set each time dance is repeated by going under arch made by two girls.

Virginia Reel

FORMATION. Four to six couples in parallel lines with partners facing each other. Boys are on caller's right.

MEASURES	CALLS
1–8	Bow to your partner.
	Go forward and back.
	Go forward and back again.
9–12	Forward again with right elbow swing
	And back again.
13–16	Forward again with left elbow swing
	And back again.
1–4	Forward again with a two hand swing
	And all the way back.
5–8	Forward again with a do si do.
9–16	The head two sashay down the middle,
	All the way back to the head of the set.

1–8	Cast off, boys going left And girls going right.
9–16	Form an arch and all pass through.

EXPLANATION

MEASURES

1–8	Dancers take three skips forward, curtsey or bow, and skip back. Repeat.
9–12	Partners hook right elbows, swing once around, then step back.
13–16	Partners link left elbows, swing, and step back.
1–4	Partners join both hands, swing clockwise, and step back.
5–8	Partners walk forward, pass right shoulders, move to right passing back to back, and step into own position.
9–16	Head couple slides down center of set and back.
1–8	Boys' line goes left and girls' line goes right, ending at foot of set.
9–16	Head couple joins hands and forms an arch at foot of the set. The second couple leads other couples through arch and moves to head of line. Repeat dance with each new head couple.

Bingo

FORMATION.   Partners form double circle facing counterclockwise. Girls are on their partners' right in promenade position.

MEASURES	VERSE
1–2	There was an old farmer Who had an old dog,
3–4	And Bingo was his name.
5–10	BINGO, BINGO, BINGO,
11–12	Bingo was his name.
13–14	B–I–N–G–O,
15–16	Bingo was his name.

EXPLANATION

MEASURES

1–12	All promenade as they sing song.
13–14	Take partner by right hand as all say "B". A grand right and left follows as each person takes the next person by the left hand and says "I," the next by the right and "N," the next by the left and says "G," and the next by the right and says "O".
15–16	Persons meeting on "O" swing once around and prepare to promenade again with new partner.

FIFTH AND SIXTH GRADES

Crested Hen, Danish Folk Dance

FORMATION.   Children join hands in sets of threes.

MEASURES	PART 1
1–8	Take seven step-hops moving clockwise, ending with a stamp.
9–16	Repeat measures 1–8 moving counterclockwise.

	PART 2
	Open to form lines of three.
1–4	Center dancer and left hand partner raise joined hands to form an arch. The partner on the right with four step-hops passes under the arch and returns to starting position. The center dancer unwinds by passing under own raised arm.
5–8	Repeat action of measures 1–4 with the left hand partners passing through the arch.
9–16	Repeat measures 1–8.

Ace of Diamonds, Danish Folk Dance

FORMATION.   The dancers form a double circle, partners facing. Boys' backs are to the center.

MEASURES	PART 1
1	Clap own hands and stamp with left foot.
2–4	Partners hook right elbows and take three polka steps once around, starting with hop on left foot.
5	Repeat measure one doing the stamp with the right foot.
6–8	Repeat measures 2–4 hooking left elbows and starting with a hop on the right foot. End with partners facing, hands on hips.

	PART 2
9–12	Boys take four step-hops backward while girls take four hops forward, starting on right foot.
13–16	Return to starting position, the boys taking four step-hops forward while the girls take four step-hops backward, starting on right foot.

	PART 3
	All turn to face counterclockwise, inside hands joined.
17–24	Take eight polka steps forward, starting with hop on the inside foot. Finish facing partner.

Csebogar, Hungarian Folk Dance

FORMATION. The dancers form a single circle facing center, all hands joined. Girls are to the right of partners.

MEASURES	PART 1
1–4	Take seven slide steps sideward clockwise using the eighth step as preparation to reverse direction.
5–8	Take seven slide steps counterclockwise.

	PART 2
1–4	Take four walking steps forward raising the arms; return to starting position taking four steps backward and lowering the arms.
5–8	Hook right elbows with partners and turn clockwise using eight skip steps.
	End in a single circle facing partner. Boys facing counterclockwise.

	PART 3
1–4	Partners join both hands and moving sideward take four draw steps to the center as follows: count one step sideward left, close right to left, the right taking the weight. Boys start left; girls start right.
5–8	Repeat measures 1–4 moving away from the center. Boys start right; girls start left.

	PART 4
1–2	Take two draw steps sideward toward the center.
3–4	Take two draw steps away from the center.
5–8	Hook right elbows with partner and turn clockwise using eight skip steps. End in a single circle facing center, girl to the right of partner.

La Raspa, Mexican Folk Dance

FORMATION. The children form a double circle, partners facing with hands joined and arms extended and held shoulder high.

MEASURES	PART 1
1	Hop on the left foot, placing the right foot forward; at the same time push the right arm forward and pull the left elbow back. Jump to the right foot, placing the left foot forward, reversing the elbow action.
2	Jump to the left foot, placing the right foot forward, reversing the elbow action and hold.
3–4	Repeat measures 1–2, starting with left foot forward.
5–8	Repeat measures 1–4.
1–8	Repeat measures 1–8 so action is done a total of eight times.

PART 2

1–4	Partners hook right elbows, holding left hands high, and turn opposite direction, using eight skipping steps. Release elbows and clap on count eight.
5–8	Repeat measures 1–4, hooking left elbows.
1–8	Repeat measures 1–8.

Kalvelis, Lithuanian Folk Dance

FORMATION. Approximately eight couples form a single circle facing counterclockwise.

MEASURES

1–8	All polka eight steps right without hop.
1–8	All polka eight steps left without hop.

CHORUS

9–16	Clap own hands, partner's right hand, own hands, and partner's left hand. Grasp partner's hands and skip to left four times, then skip to right four times.
9–16	Repeat chorus.
1–8	Girls do four polka steps into circle, turn, and repeat back.
9–16	Repeat chorus.
1–16	Girls weave around circle, going behind the first dancer and in front of the next and so on for sixteen polka steps. Boys do the same.
1–16	Repeat chorus twice.
1–16	All grand right and left.
1–16	Repeat chorus twice.
1–8	All join hands and polka eight times to the right.
1–8	All join hands and polka eight times to the left.

Sicilian Circle, Sicilian Folk Dance

FORMATION. From circle with sets of four, each couple facing another couple. Girl is on partner's right.

MEASURES	CALLS
1–4	All step forward and back.
5–8	Circle four hands around.
1–4	Ladies chain.
5–8	Ladies chain back again.
1–4	Right and left through.
5–8	Right and left through back.
1–4	Forward and back.
5–8	Forward again, pass through.

EXPLANATION

MEASURES

1–4	Join hands with partner. Step forward four steps to opposite couple and back four steps.
5–8	Four people in set join hands, circle left with eight walking steps, and stop in original position.
1–4	Girls extend right hands to each other, pass by and extend left hand to opposite boy who takes her left hand in his left hand, places his right arm around her waist, and turns backward to face opposite couple.
5–8	Girls repeat with own partner.
1–4	Couples walk toward each other and each person passes through the opposite couple, boys on outside passing right shoulders with opposite girl. After passing through, boys turn partners as in girls' chain, and couples face each other again.
5–8	Repeat same movement, returning to original position.
1–4	Partners walk forward and back.
5–8	Partners walk forward eight steps, passing opposite's right shoulder, to meet new couple.

Tantoli, Swedish Folk Dance

FORMATION.   Form double circle with couples facing counterclockwise. Boy is on left with right arm around girl's waist. Girl places left hand on boy's right shoulder. Outer hands are on hips.

MEASURES

1–8	Beginning with outer foot, take eight heel-and-toe polka steps forward.
9–15	Partners face each other. Boy places hands on partner's waist; girl's hands on partner's shoulders. Circle while taking 14 step-hops in place. Boy ends with back to center of circle.
16	Boy lifts partner in air and sets her down to his diagonal right in front of another boy. Repeat with new partners.

SEVENTH AND EIGHTH GRADES

Varsouvienne, U.S. Folk Dance (Put Your Little Foot)

FORMATION.   Couples are scattered informally on the floor. The girl stands in front and slightly to the right of the boy. They join left hands, shoulder high; the boy extends his right arm behind the girl's shoulder and grasps the girl's raised right hand.

MEASURES	PART 1
1	On the pick up beat (count three), swing the left foot across in front of the right foot, step left, close right to left, the weight ending on the right foot.
2	Repeat measure one.
3	With three walking steps the girl crosses in front and to the left side of the boy without releasing hands. The boy takes three steps in place.
4	Point right toe diagonally forward.
5–8	Repeat measures 1–4, starting with the right foot.

	PART 2
1–2	Starting left, the boy leads partner across to left hand side with three steps. Point right toe diagonally forward.
3–4	Starting right, the girl returns to right of boy. Point left toe.
5–8	Repeat measures 1–4.

The Roberts, Scottish Folk Dance

FORMATION. The dancers form a double circle, partners facing, and boys' backs to the center; they join both hands.

MEASURES	PART 1
1–2	Starting with boy's left foot, girl's right foot, take two side steps, moving counterclockwise.
3–4	With four walking steps, partners drop hands and, turning away from each other, the girl circles right and the boy circles left. End facing partner, both hands joined.
5–8	Repeat measures 1–4. End facing counterclockwise, inside hands joined.

	PART 2
9–10	Starting with outside foot do one heel toe step and take one two-step forward.
11–12	Repeat measures 9–10, starting with inside foot.
13–16	Take four two-steps forward, moving counterclockwise.

Little Man in a Fix, Danish Folk Dance

FORMATION. Two couples form a set. Partners on boys' right. Boys hook left elbows, placing right arm around partners' waists. Girls place left hand on partners' left shoulders.

MEASURES	PART 1
1–8	All run forward with 24 small running steps, revolving the set counterclockwise.
1–2	Boys release elbows to join left hands, forming an arch. Girl moves out to join inside hands with partner. This action is done with six running steps.
3–4	With six running steps girls pass under the arch, turn toward partners, and join right hands with opposite girl above the joined hands of the boys.
5–8	Continue moving counterclockwise with 12 small running steps.

PART 2

1–8	Move into social dance position with partner and take eight waltz steps.

Schottische, U.S. Version Involving Two Couples

FORMATION. The dancers form sets of two couples, one couple standing in front of the other. Partners join inside hands, the outside hands joined linking the two couples together. Front couple is couple number 1, back couple is number 2. All face counterclockwise.

MEASURES	
1–2	Do two basic schottische steps (left, right, left, hop left; right, left, right, hop right).
3–4	Taking four step-hops, couple one releases hands and, turning away from each other, moves to the outside and end behind couple two, again joining hands. Couple two is now the front couple.
(Variation)	
3–4	Taking four step-hops, couple one backs through the raised arms of couple two. Couple two does "wring the dish rag" movement in order to straighten out. Couple two is now the front couple.
1–4	Repeat measures 1–4 with couple two turning out or backing through the arch.

Jesse Polka, U.S. Folk Dance

FORMATION. Couples spread informally on floor in Varsouvienne position; they move counterclockwise.

MEASURES	PART 1
1	Place left heel in front, step left in place.
2	Place right toe behind, touch right toe in place.
3	Place right heel in front, step right in place.

4	Place left heel diagonally forward, bring left foot across in front of right.

PART 2

5–8	Take four two-steps forward counterclockwise.

Road to the Isles, Scottish Folk Dance

FORMATION. Couples form double circle facing counterclockwise in Varsouvienne position. Boy stands back and to left of girl, both facing in the same direction. Boy holds girl's left hand in his left hand at shoulder level. Boy's right arm extends behind girl's shoulders and holds girl's raised right hand in his right hand.

MEASURES

1	Point left toe forward to left.
2–3	Place left foot behind right, step right to right side, place left foot in front of right and hold.
4	Point right toe forward to right.
5–6	Place right foot behind left, step left to left side, place right foot in front of left and hold.
7	Point left toe forward.
8	Point left toe backward.
9–12	Beginning on left, take two schottische steps forward. Turn to right and face in opposite direction on hop.
13–14	Beginning on left, take one schottische step. Turn to left on hop and finish in original position.
15–16	Stamp in place—right, left, right.

Cotton-Eyed Joe, U.S. Folk Dance

FORMATION. Closed dance position with partner.

MEASURES

1	Boy starts with left foot and girl starts with right foot; each takes one heel-toe, and then step, step, step.
2–4	Repeat three times.
5–8	Eight polka steps.
9–10	Hook left ankles with partner, grasp partner's left hand, lean back, and hop eight times on right foot, turning clockwise.
11–12	Repeat measures 9–10, using opposite ankle and hand and turning counterclockwise.
13	Couples face each other and take four push steps. Place toe of left foot sideways, pushing slightly, and step sideways to the right on right foot. Right foot remains close to the floor and carries most of the weight except for the slight transfer of weight to the left on push.

14   Repeat measure 13 in opposite direction.
15–16   Repeat measures 13–14.

Gay Gordons, Scottish Folk Dance

FORMATION.   Couples in Varsouvienne position.

STEPS

1   Both start on left foot and take four walking steps for-
                ward. Reverse and take four walking steps backward
                but continue in same direction.
                Repeat.
2   Boy holds girl's right hand high with his right hand and
                polkas forward as girl does four polkas clockwise,
                turning under boy's arm.
3   Taking social dance position with partner, take four
                polka steps, turning clockwise.
                Repeat entire dance.

Black Hawk Waltz

FORMATION.   Closed dance position with partner.

MEASURES

1–4   Balance forward on left foot, backward on right.
                Repeat.
5–8   Beginning on left foot, take four waltz steps.
9–12   Repeat measures 1–4.
13–16   Beginning on left foot, take two waltz steps, followed by
                six walking steps forward beginning on left foot.
17   Boy places left foot (girl opposite) across in front of right
                foot and places weight on it.
18   Place right foot across left foot in same manner.
19–20   Cross with left foot again, followed by a step sidewards
                to right with right foot, step left behind right foot and
                point right foot sidewards to right.
21–24   Repeat measures 17–20.
25–32   Repeat measures 17–24.

SQUARE DANCES*

Square dancing, as we know it, has developed from two sources, the New
England Quadrille and the Kentucky Running Set. European folk dances

---

*Records are available for all square dances. See the list, p. 290.

influenced square dances with many figures coming directly from them. There are a variety of ways to square dance, depending on geographical location in the United States.

Square dancing can be a very valuable experience for participants of all ages. Through square dance they continue to expand their experience in moving to music. Because partners change frequently, each individual participates with many different people and is thereby afforded unique opportunities for social interaction. Square dancing is a vigorous activity which promotes the objectives of physical education; moreover, it is an activity which students can participate in throughout their adult years.

TEACHING HINTS

Square dancing is not difficult to teach. The teacher need not be an expert caller to have successful square dancing. Keeping the calls brief and clear is important. Records with calls may be used, but are not as desirable as the teacher's or an aide's doing the calling. A caller is able to set the speed to the group's ability and can stop when the class is having difficulty.

Generally, square dancing is started in the fourth or fifth grade. The teacher may have a class with varying backgrounds of square dancing, from skilled to beginners. The advanced children will enjoy the repetition and can help others who have difficulty. Therefore, varying levels of skill should present no problem to the instructor.

The teacher should start with simple movements and changes: Old Arkansaw, Irish Washerwoman, Cut Away Six, Four, and Two.

Dancers should be instructed to refrain from stamping or clapping when the dance is being taught. After the dance has been learned, controlled clap-

Figure 11-1 Folk dances provide vigorous activity which contributes significantly to the physical development of the participants as well as providing experiences for their social development. (Courtesy of Town of Vernon Schools, Rockville, Connecticut.)

ping and stamping may be helpful, giving some individuals something to do with their hands and feet to relieve embarrassment and awkwardness.

As the class progresses, a different call for each active couple may be used for greater variety and enjoyment. The teacher should work for enjoyment, not perfection. Dances may be reviewed often, not only so they will be remembered, but because the children have fun doing dances they know.

PRESENTATION

A suitable sequence for teaching a square dance is:

Give the background of the dance, if possible.
Listen to the music (discover speed, tempo, and beat).
If the pattern is difficult, diagram it on chalkboard.
Demonstrate, using one square or couple.
Everyone walks through the pattern, no music.
Try the dance with music.
Stop and explain if some dancers are having difficulty.

TERMINOLOGY

Formation of the Square. A square is made up of four couples, each couple standing on the side of an imaginary square facing one of the four walls of the room. Allow approximately 10 feet across for each square. Girls are always to right side of partners.

Number of Couples. The side of the square each couple occupies determines the number of the couple. Generally, the couple standing nearest to, and with backs to music is designated as couple one. The couple to their right is couple two; the couple opposite couple one is couple three, and the couple to the left of couple one is couple four. Couples always return to this position (home position).

Center. The area in the middle of the square.

Corner. The boy's corner is the girl on his left; the girl's corner is the boy on her right.

Heads. Couples one and three.

Head Couple. Couple one.

Head Couples. Couples one and three.

Sides. Couples two and four.

Side Couples. Couples two and four.

Opposite. The one standing in the opposite position across the set.

SKILLS AND CALLS

Basic Step. An easy light step from one foot to the other moving forward. It can be distinguished from a walk in that the weight is transferred from the ball of the foot to the heel or kept on the balls of the feet. The feet remain lightly in contact with the floor.

Balance. Partners face each other, take two steps back and bow and step together two steps (this is done quickly).

Swing. Partners place right sides together, either in regular dance position or joining both hands together, and turn once in place.

Grand Right and Left. Partners face and join right hands; each advances forward passing right shoulders, giving left hand to the next person and passing left shoulders. All continue around, alternating hands until partner is met.

Promenade. Partners progress counterclockwise around the square, the girl on the boy's right. Hands are held in skating position, boy's right arm on top.

Alemande Left. Boy faces the girl on his left (corner girl). They join left hands and move around each other, returning to home position.

Do-Sa-Do. Partners move forward, passing right shoulders, and step sideward, back to back. Without turning around, they move backward to place. (Arms are usually folded across the chest.)

Do-Si-Do. The dancers form a circle of four and release hands. Girls pass left shoulders and join left hands with partners, pass behind partners, release hands and join right hands with opposite. They then pass behind opposites and return to partners with left hands. Boys place right arms around partners' waists and they turn once around in place.

Elbow Swing. Dancers hook right or left elbow with person indicated and swing once around.

Introductory Calls

Call 1. All jump up and never come down,
         Swing your partner 'round and 'round,
         And promenade, boys, promenade.

Call 2. Honor your partner and the lady by your side,
         All join hands and circle out wide,
         Break and swing and promenade home.

Call 3. All eight balance and all eight swing,
         Now promenade around that ring.

Grand Right and Left Patter

Call 1. Alemande left with your left hand,
         Partner by the right and right and left grand.

Call 2. Swing on the corner like swinging on the gate,
         Now swing your own if it's not too late,
         Alemande left with your left hand,
         Right to your partner, right and left grand.

Call 3. Alemande left as pretty as you can,
Right to your honey,
And right and left grand.

Promenade Patter

Call 1. Promenade, promenade 'round and make those big
feet jar the ground.
Call 2. Promenade eight, promenade all,
Promenade to a hole in the wall.
Call 3. Meet your Sally, meet your Sue,
Promenade just two by two.

Endings

Call 1. Promenade—you know where and I don't care,
Take her out and give her some air.
Call 2. Honor your partner, corners all,
Wave to the gal across the hall,
Thank you, folks, I guess that's all.

Do-Si-Do Patter

Call 1. Four hands up and around you go,
Break it up with a do-si-do,
One more change and on you go.
Call 2. Do si do and a little more dough,
Like a chicken in a bread pan pecking out dough,
Grab your partner and on you go.

SQUARE DANCE FIGURES

No grade placement is suggested for square dance figures. A beginning group, no matter what age, can use the square dance figures suggested.

Old Arkansaw

CALL. (1) First couple balance and first couple swing,
(2) The lady (gent) lead out to the right of the ring,
(3) Swing your paw, swing your maw,
(4) And don't forget Old Arkansaw.

EXPLANATION. (1) The first couple balance and swing; (2) first girl (or boy) moves to the second couple (3) and swings the boy of couple two, then swings the girl of couple two, (4) and then returns home and swings partner. The girl (or boy) of couple one repeats the figure with couples three and four. The figure is repeated with the girl (or boy) from couples two, three, and four.

Irish Washerwoman (sung in time with music)

CALL.   (1) Oh! it's all of the gents to the right of the ring,
           (2) When you get there you give her a swing,
           (3) When you get through remember my call,
           (4) Alemande left and promenade all.

EXPLANATION.   (1) All of the gents move to the girl on the right; (2) and (3) boys swing the right-hand girl; (4) boys alemande left with girl on the left. Boys return to right-hand girl and promenade to home positions. (Boys are all in original places, girls have moved one place to the left.) Repeat three more times to return to original partners.

Cut Away Six, Four, and Two

CALL.   (1) First couple balance and swing,
           (2) Go down the center and split the ring,
           (3) Cut away six,
           (4) Swing when you meet at the head and the feet; side couples the same.
           (5) Go down the center and cut away four,
           (6) Swing when you meet at the head and the feet,
           (7) The side couples the same.
           (8) Go down the center and cut away two,
           (9) Swing when you meet at the head and the feet.
        (10) The side couples the same.

EXPLANATION.   (1) The first couple balance and swing. (2) First couple goes down the center between boy and girl of couple number three. (3) The first couple separates, the girl going right, behind couple number two, the boy going left behind couple number four. (4) The first couple meets at home position and swings; couple three also swings; then couples two and four swing.

(5) The first couple goes down the center, the girl going between couple three and couple two and behind couple two; the boy going between couple three and couple four, and behind couple four. (6) Again they meet at home position and swing; couple three also swings, (7) Then couples two and four swing. (8) The first couple goes down the center once more, the girl going between the girl and boy of couple number two and behind the boy of couple number two; the boy goes between couple four and behind the girl of couple four. (9) Once again they meet at home position and swing; couple three also swings; (10) Then couples two and four swing.

The formation is repeated, using second, third, and fourth couples.

Birdie In the Cage

CALL.   (1) First couple balance and swing,
           (2) Lead right out to the right of the ring, circle four.
           (3) Birdie in the cage with four hands 'round,
           (4) Birdie hops out and the crow hops in,
           (5) Crow hops out and circle four,
           (6) On to the next.

EXPLANATION. (1) First couple balance and swing. (2) Couple number one leads to couple number two and they circle four. (3) The girl of couple one steps into the circle and the others circle three. (4) The girl of couple number one steps out; the boy of couple number one steps in; the others circle three. (5) The boy of couple number one steps out between the two girls, and all circle four. (6) Couple number one moves to couple three. Then the call is repeated. The couple then moves to couple four.

They repeat with couples two, three, and four doing the action.

Forward Six and Fall Back Six

CALL.   (1) First couple balance and swing,
          (2) Lead right out to the right of the ring, circle four,
          (3) Leave that lady and on to the next, circle three,
          (4) Take that lady and on to the next, circle four,
          (5) Leave that lady and go home alone,
          (6) Forward up six and fall back six,
          (7) Forward up two and fall back two,
          (8) Forward up six and pass right through,
          (9) Forward up two and pass right through,
             (Repeat last four lines.)
        (10) Swing your own.

EXPLANATION. (1) First couple balance and swing. (2) First couple advances to the second couple and they circle four. (3) Boy of first couple leaves his partner, goes to couple number three, and they circle three. (4) Boy of couple number one takes the girl of couple three (places her on his right) and moves to couple number four. Boy of couple three remains alone. Boy of couple one and girl of couple three circle with fourth couple. (5) Boy of couple one returns to home position. Girl of couple three remains with couple four.

(6) Two lines of three advance four steps and back. (7) Boys of couples one and three go forward four steps and back. (8) Two lines of three move forward, passing right shoulders, and face about on the opposite side of the set. (9) Boys of couples one and three pass through, passing right shoulders, and face about on the opposite side of the set. Repeat back to place. (10) Boys swing partners.

Repeat using couples two, three, and four.

Oh Johnny (sung in time with the music)

CALL.   (1) Oh! you all join hands and circle the ring,
          (2) Stop where you are and give her a swing,
          (3) Swing that girl in back of you,
          (4) Swing your own when you get through,
          (5) Alemande left your corners all and do-sa-do your own,
          (6) Now you all run away with your sweet corner maid, Singing
              Oh! Johnny, Oh! Johnny Oh!

EXPLANATION. (1) All join hands and circle clockwise. (2) Boys swing partners, (3) swing corners, (4) return to partners, and swing. (5) Then they alemande left their corners; do-sa-do their partners; (6) and promenade counterclockwise with the corner girl as a new partner. The action is repeated three more times to return to original partners in the square.

Texas Star

CALL. (1) Ladies to the center and back to the bar,
        (2) Gents to the center and form a star,
        (3) With right hands crossed,
        (4) Back to the left and don't get lost,
        (5) Meet your pretty girl, pass her by,
        (6) Hook the next gal on the fly,
        (7) The gents swing out, the ladies swing in,
        (8) Form that Texas Star again,
        (9) Now the gents swing in and the ladies swing out,
      (10) Turn that Texas Star about,
      (11) Now break and swing,
      (12) Alemande left just once,
      (13) And promenade the one you swung.

EXPLANATION. (1) Girls walk to center and back to place. (2) and (3) The boys form a right hand star in the center of the set. (4) The boys reverse direction, forming a left hand star. (5) and (6) The boys pass own partners and take the next girl by placing right arm around her waist. The star continues counterclockwise. (7) The boys break the star. The couples turn counterclockwise once and a half, (8) the girls now forming a right hand star in the center, moving clockwise. (9) The girls break the star. (10) The couples turn clockwise once and a half, and the boys again form a left hand star, now moving counterclockwise. (11) The boys break the star and swing, (12) alemande left the corner, (13) return to the girl on the right, and promenade to the boy's home position.

Repeat three more times to return to original partner.

SOCIAL DANCE

Social dancing is an activity that can be engaged in with pleasure throughout adulthood. It is a popular recreational activity among teenagers. Consequently, many schools offer youngsters an opportunity to learn social dancing in the physical education classes from grade six upward.

Usually the social dance instructions consist of such traditional dance steps as the fox trot and the waltz, but these steps are seldom danced by today's young social dancers. Nevertheless, the steps may be taught to beginning social dancers as a transition from folk dancing to the contemporary dance steps currently in vogue.

LEADING AND FOLLOWING

The boy leads his partner by indicating his intended movements with pressure from his right hand and the upper part of his body. The pressure should be firm and decisive and the subsequent movement should be likewise. The girl takes her cue from the pressure of the boy's hand and trunk. Generally the boy begins by stepping with his left foot and the girl with her right foot.

TEACHING HINTS

Social dancing need not be taught as such if there are reasons why it should not be. Many basic social dance steps are taught in folk dances; the waltz and two step, for example, are included in many folk dances. The social dance positions may be incorporated with appropriate folk dances to provide experience in this aspect of social dancing. The boys and girls should have opportunities to practice the traditional steps moving in various directions and making turns. Stress should be placed on smoothness and continuity of movement.

The teaching of a social dance step may be accomplished by the following method:

Listen to the music to get the idea of character, quality, and speed.
Describe and demonstrate the step.
Do the step individually first (without music, then with the music).
Use partners (without music, then with the music).

POSITIONS USED FOR SOCIAL DANCING (FOX TROT AND WALTZ)

Closed Position. Partners stand facing each other, toes straight ahead. The boy's right arm is around the girl, the hand slightly under the left shoulder blade. The girl's left arm and hand are placed on the boy's upper arm and shoulder. The boy's left arm is raised to the left, the girl's right hand is held gently in the palm.

Open Position. The girl stands to the right side of partner; both are facing the same direction. The boy places the right arm around the girl's waist. The girl places the left hand on her partner's right shoulder. The boy holds the girl's right hand in his left hand.

Conversation Position. This position is the same as the open position except the boy's left and the girl's right hand are not joined.

Fox Trot (Grades 6–8)

There are several varieties of Fox Trots; probably the easiest and most relaxing is the medium slow (Arthur Murray's "Magic Step"). The basic rhythm is 4/4 time with the accent on the first and third beats.

BOY'S PART. Step forward left, *slow (2 counts).*
Step forward right, draw left to right *slow (2 counts).*
Step to left with left foot *quick (1 count).*
Close right foot to left, transferring the weight, *quick (1 count).*

GIRL'S PART. Step backward, right *slow (2 counts)*.

Step backward left, draw right back to left *slow (2 counts)*.

Step to right with right foot *quick (1 count)*.

Close left to right, transferring the weight, *quick (1 count)*.

After the basic step has been established, the youngsters should practice in other positions, moving in various directions, making turns, and using music of various tempos.

Waltz (Box) (Grades 6–8)

The waltz is a slow graceful dance done to three-four time. The pattern of the steps outlines a box on the floor.

BOY'S PART. Step forward left *(1 count)*.

Step sideward right, transferring the weight *(1 count)*.

Close left foot to right *(1 count)*.

Step backward right *(1 count)*.

Step sideward left, transferring the weight *(1 count)*.

Close right foot to left *(1 count)*.

GIRL'S PART. Step backward right *(1 count)*.

Step sideward left, transferring the weight *(1 count)*.

Close right foot to left *(1 count)*.

Step forward left *(1 count)*.

Step sideward right, transferring the weight *(1 count)*.

Close left foot to right *(1 count)*.

When the basic step has been learned, practice should be devoted to moving in various directions and making turns.

RECORDS

Creative Dance Activity

Bert Jansck, Birthday Blues
W Reprise 6343
Cat Stevens, Teaser and the Firecat
A.M. SP 4313
Freda Miller, Music For Rhythms and
Dance
Album Number 4
John Denver's Greatest Hits
RCA CPL-0374 Stereo

John Renbourn, The Lady and the
Unicorn
Reprise 6407
Israeli Folk Dance Festival
Tikva Records, T 88
Theme from Zorba the Greek
Four Corners FCS-4222

Kindergarten — First Grade

Farmer in the Dell
    Folkraft 1182
    RCA Victor WE 87 (album)
Bluebird
    Folkraft 1180
Muffin Man
    Folkraft 1188
    RCA Victor WE 87 (album)
Danish Dance of Greeting
    Folkraft 1187
    RCA EPA 4132
Chimes of Dunkirk
    Folkraft 1188
World of Fun M-105

Looby Loo
    Folkraft 1184
    RCA Victor WE 87 (album)
Did You Ever See a Lassie?
    Folkraft 1183
    RCA Victor WE 87 (album)
London Bridge
    RCA Victor WE 87 (album)
Round and Round the Village
    Folkraft 1191
    RCA Victor EPA 4144
Sing a Song of Sixpence
    Folkraft 1180

Second Grade

Hopp Mor Annika
    RCA Victor EPA 4142
Kinderpolka
    Folkraft 1187
Shoemaker's Dance
    Folkraft 1187
Carrousel
    Folkraft 1183
A-hunting We Will Go
    Folkraft 1191
    RCA Victor WE 87 (album)

Pop Goes the Weasel
    Folkraft 1329
    World of Fun M 104
Oats, Peas, Beans and Barley
    Folkraft 1182
    World of Fun M 111
    RCA Victor WE 87 (album)

Third Grade

Hansel and Gretel
    Folkraft 1193
Jolly is the Miller
    Folkraft 1192
    RCA Victor WE 87 (album)
Nixie Polka
    RCA Victor EPA 4145

Bleking
    Folkraft 1188
Paw Paw Patch
    Folkraft 1181
    RCA Victor WE 87 (album)
Come Let Us Be Joyful
    Folkraft 1195
    World of Fun M 102

Fourth Grade

Gustaf's Skoal
    Folkraft 1175
    World of Fun M 108

Norwegian Mt. March
    Folkraft 1177

Patty Cake Polka
    Folkraft 1260
    World of Fun M 107
Seven Steps
    Folkraft 1163
    World of Fun M 101
Virginia Reel
    Folkraft 1249

Troika
    Folkraft 1170
    World of Fun M 105
Bingo
    Folkraft 1189
    RCA EPA 4138

Fifth and Sixth Grades

Crested Hen
    Folkraft 1159
    World of Fun M 108
Ace of Diamonds
    Folkraft 1176
    World of Fun M 102
Csebogar
    Folkraft 1196
    World of Fun M 101
La Raspa
    Folkraft 1119
    RCA Victor EPA 4139
    World of Fun M 106

Kalvelis
    Folkraft 1051
    World of Fun M 101
Sicilian Circle
    Folkraft 1115
    World of Fun M 104
Tantoli
    RCA EPA 4133

Seventh and Eighth Grades

Varsouvienne
    Folkraft 1165
    World of Fun M 107
The Roberts
    Folkraft 1161
    World of Fun M 121
Little Man in a Fix
    World of Fun M 121
Schottische
    Folkraft 1172
    Shaw 7-153-4

Jesse Polka
    Folkraft 1071
Black Hawk Waltz
    Folkraft 1046
Road to the Isle
    World of Fun M 110
Cotton Eyed Joe
    Folkraft 1035
Gay Gordons

Square Dance Records

Oh Johnny
    Folkraft 1037
Texas Star
    Educational Activities
    Album HYP3

Irish Washerwoman
Forward Six and Fall Back
    Six
    Educational Activities
    Album HYP4

Record Sources

A & M Records, Inc., P.O. Box 782, Beverly Hills, California, 90213.
Educational Activities, Inc., P.O. Box 392, Freeport, Long Island, New York, 11520.
Four Corners Records, N.Y., N.Y. 10022.
Freda Miller Records for Dance, 131 Bayview Avenue, Northport, New York, 11768.
Folkraft Record Company, 1159 Broad Street, Newark, New Jersey, 07114.
The Lloyd Shaw Foundation, Inc., Box 203, Colorado Springs, Colorado, 80901.
RCA Victor Record Division, 1133 Avenue of the Americas, New York, New York, 10036.
Reprise Records, Warner Bros. Records, Inc., 4000 Warner Blvd., Burbank, California.
Tikva Records, 1650 Broadway, N.Y. 19, N.Y.

SUPPLEMENTARY READINGS

Andrews, Gladys: *Creative Rhythmic Movement for Children.* Englewood Cliffs, New Jersey, Prentice-Hall, Inc., 1954.

Barlin, Anne, and Barlin, Paul: *The Art of Learning Through Movement.* Los Angeles, Ward Ritchie Press, 1971.

Boorman, Joyce: *Creative Dance in Grades 4–6.* Ontario, Longmans Canada Ltd., 1971.

Boorman, Joyce: *Creative Dance in the First Three Grades.* Ontario, Longmans Canada Ltd., 1969.

Dimondstein, Geraldine: *Children Dance in the Classroom.* New York, The Macmillan Company, 1971.

Gilbert, Acile: *International Folk Dance at a Glance.* Minneapolis, Burgess Pub. Co., 1974.

Joyce, Mary: *First Steps in Teaching Creative Dance.* Palo Alto, California, National Press Books, 1973.

Kraus, Richard, and Sadlo, Lola: *Beginning Social Dance.* Belmont, California, Wadsworth Publishing Co., 1964.

Latchaw, Marjorie, and Pyatt, Jean: *Folk and Square Dances and Singing Games for Elementary Schools.* Englewood Cliffs, New Jersey, Prentice-Hall, Inc., 1960.

Moore, Ellen: "Dance Techniques Through Problem-Solving." *Journal of Health · Physical Education · Recreation,* June, 1974.

Speisman, Mildred C: *Folk Dancing.* Philadelphia, W. B. Saunders Co., 1970.

Vick, Marie: *A Collection of Dances for Children.* Minneapolis, Burgress Publishing Co., 1970.

chapter twelve

lead-up and team games

BASKETBALL AND LEAD-UP GAMES
SOFTBALL AND LEAD-UP GAMES
SOCCER AND LEAD-UP GAMES
VOLLEYBALL AND LEAD-UP GAMES
TOUCH FOOTBALL AND LEAD-UP GAMES
TRACK AND FIELD
     Conducting Track and Field Meets

Team games provide important experiences for elementary school children. They help fulfill the need for vigorous big muscle activity and for further development of the basic skills. Participation in team sports appeals to the strong interest of children at the intermediate and upper elementary levels in group membership. Through team play children have an opportunity to learn to recognize and respect the abilities of individuals and to work with them in a cooperative effort for the good of the team. In addition to developing an appreciation for motor activity as an avenue to healthful living and worthwhile leisure, playing team sports helps to give the participants an understanding of sports as a part of modern American culture.

Team games are, in general, more complex than the previous play experiences of young children. They involve a greater number and variety of skills as well as more rules and playing strategy. The latter will, in fact, be largely a new experience for most youngsters. Among the team games which can be played with considerable success by children from the fifth grade upward are basketball, softball, soccer, and touch football as well as the track and field events. All of these may be played in class, intramurals, or interscholastic program.

Highly organized team play between schools is best suited to seventh and eighth grades; however, some schools sponsor interscholastic competition in some of the team sports, particularly basketball, in the intermediate grades. Other schools do not sponsor interscholastic sports because of the problems involved in making them a truly educational experience or because the cost to serve a relatively small portion of the student body is prohibitive.

ORGANIZING THE INSTRUCTION

The importance of progression in learning skills has been established in connection with other motor activities; it bears repetition here. A solidly built foundation of skills is necessary for success in any team sport. To ensure proper progression of skills in the team sports, class instruction is usually organized, when the direct method of teaching is used, in this sequence:

Instruction and practice in the less difficult skills
Playing of lead-up games which provide practice of the skills in game situations
Repetition of skill practice
Instruction and practice of the more difficult skills
Playing lead-up games which provide practice of the skills in game situations
Repetition of skill practice
Playing the team game
Drill on skills

The introduction to team game skills will begin usually at the fourth grade, but the actual playing of the game will not usually be feasible before fifth grade, although the interest, needs, and abilities of the particular group will determine the grade at which these are presented. The progress of the group in acquiring the skills is a determinant in the amount of time devoted to the teaching of this phase of the sequence, and consequently the grade level at which any phase is taught varies from school to school.

For the skill drills as well as for some of the lead-up games, the formations described in Chapter 3 will be used. The more highly organized team games have specific formations and patterns of play, which are described below.

Team games require different players to do different jobs. Consequently, when learning the game, players should rotate positions as much as possible in order to give everyone a chance to play and acquire the skills of the various positions. Generally, it is the practice for boys and girls to be separated for playing the team games. However, where conditions are favorable, mixed teams may be used with benefit to both sexes. Softball is perhaps the best suited to coeducational play because it is less vigorous and the skills of the two sexes are more nearly equal. The rules for the games presented in this chapter are the same for both sexes.

When actual playing of the game begins, the class may be divided into teams with the team membership remaining the same throughout the entire unit.

This saves time in organizing the teams at each class meeting and allows teammates to become more familiar with each other's special abilities and style of playing. However, dividing the teams frequently also has an advantage in that the participants are exposed continually to new playing situations from which much can be learned. The teacher should experiment with both procedures and use the one which is preferable in the particular circumstances. To distinguish the teams during play, different colored jerseys or pinnies may be worn.

The size of the teams is determined by the number in the class and whether the facilities will accommodate more than two teams. If it is possible to have only two teams and these would be excessively large if the class were to be divided equally between them, the size of each should be reduced to an appropriate number and other groups formed to work on skills in lead-up games or on drills as may best suit the circumstances. Having youngsters standing around waiting to be sent into the game or waiting their turn to practice is to be avoided.

Procedures that may be used in teaching the skills of team sports by the problem-solving method are described in Chapter 5. Suggested problems for each sport are presented in Tables 12-2, 12-4, 12-6, 12-8, 12-10, and 12-12 in this chapter.

SELECTING THE ACTIVITIES

The selection of the particular skills, lead-up games, and team games to be taught to a class is dependent, first of all, upon the skill development of the youngsters. Consideration must be given to the sport experiences outside the school as well as to school experiences. If, for example, a large number of students in a class have had experience in community sponsored competitive baseball programs, account must be taken of this in selecting the softball skills to be presented.

Team games are of a seasonal nature and so the time of year enters into the selection of activities: touch football and soccer are fall sports; basketball, a winter game; and softball and track and field, spring activities. The availability of courts and fields must necessarily also influence selection.

EQUIPMENT

Equipment for any of the lead-up or team games should be sufficiently adequate to prevent children from having to stand around waiting their turn. The available stock of balls, bats, etc., can be increased by proper care which prolongs the life of old equipment so that money budgeted for replacements can be spent instead on additional pieces.

CARE OF EQUIPMENT. The balls used for playing the team and lead-up games of basketball, football, volleyball, and soccer will be made either of leather or some synthetic material. Leather balls must be cleaned with saddle soap or a leather preservative while the others may be cleaned simply with a damp cloth. Balls should not be overinflated as this causes them to lose resiliency. The correct number of pounds of air pressure required by each ball is stamped on it.

The leather gloves used in softball should be given the same care as leather balls. A glove that has become wet should be shaped and allowed to dry slowly away from direct heat. Wet softballs should also be dried out slowly. Broken bats are caused by improper use. One of the first rules of batting which children should learn is to hold the bat so the trademark is up or down; a bat is much more likely to break if it is held with the trademark turned toward or away from the pitcher.

These items of equipment as well as others such as volleyball nets, softball bases, and track and field equipment should be cleaned of dirt and stored where it is dry, but not excessively hot.

BASKETBALL AND LEAD-UP GAMES

Basketball is perhaps the most popular game among boys in the country today. Interest among girls is growing rapidly owing both to changes in playing rules and regulations and to growth in opportunities for play. Rule changes have made the girls' games much more exciting for players and spectators alike. A need to provide equal sport opportunities for girls has encouraged the formation of girls' basketball teams and greatly increased the interest of girls in the game.

FUNDAMENTAL TECHNIQUES AND SKILLS

Many of the ball-handling skills learned early in childhood provide a good basis for teaching basketball skills. Techniques of catching, throwing, and dodging, all prerequisites to good basketball playing, should be well-developed when the actual teaching of the game of basketball commences.

Catching a Basketball (Grades 4–8)

In catching a ball the elbows are bent and are close to the sides of the body. The hands are extended toward the oncoming ball. The fingers are spread and slightly flexed. When catching a ball waist high or higher, the thumbs are together. For a lower ball the little fingers are together. The ball is received on the finger tips. As the ball is caught, the arms give with the ball.

The ball is watched throughout the catch. If the catcher is stationary, he should take a step toward the oncoming ball; in most cases, however, the catcher will be moving rather than standing still.

There are situations where the above techniques are not appropriate. One example is that of a wild throw nearly out of reach of the catcher who must move the body so that the ball can be reached and controlled by at least one hand. As the ball is brought under control, both hands grasp the ball.

Passing (Grades 4–8)

The speed of the teammate receiving the pass as well as the distance between the receiver and passer will determine how hard the ball should be thrown and the type of pass used. The ball must be thrown so that it reaches the teammate in the shortest possible time and yet can be caught by the receiver without fumbling.

The passes most commonly used in basketball are the two-hand chest pass, the bounce pass, and the overhand pass.

The two-hand chest pass is used for short distances. In making the pass the ball is brought to the chest with both hands. The ball is held on the cushions of the finger tips. Both elbows are flexed. A step must be taken toward the direction of the intended pass. As the arms are forcefully extended, the ball is released from both hands with an outward snap of the wrists, bringing the palms of the hands facing toward the released ball. As the pass is completed, the weight is well forward on the front foot and the arms are completely extended.

The bounce pass is most frequently made with two hands. The two-handed bounce pass is accomplished in a manner similar to the chest pass. In making the pass the arms are extended outward and downward to drive the ball to the floor. The ball is released at about waist height. The bounce should be made so that when the ball reaches the teammate, it has bounced waist high. For this to happen, it is necessary for the ball to make contact with the floor closer to the receiver than to the passer. The bounce pass is very effective when passing to a player near the basket who is being closely guarded.

The overhand pass is most effective for long distances. It is used chiefly to pass the ball above the reach of the opponent, Also, the position for making the pass is one that lends itself readily to feinting a pass that will throw the opponent off guard.

The ball is brought back behind the shoulder about head high. Then the ball is released by bringing the arm forward with a quick extension of the elbow and wrist. The arm follows through in the direction of the pass. The feet are comfortably spread. The ball is brought overhead with both hands, the wrists are cocked, and the elbows are slightly bent. Then the arms and wrists are straightened, and at the same time the arms are brought forward to propel the ball upward and forward.

Where the ball is thrown in any pass is dependent upon whether the receiver is stationary or moving. If the receiver is stationary, the ball should be thrown to him about waist high. If he is moving, the ball should be thrown sufficiently in advance of him so that it will still be in front of him when he reaches it. The thrower should not telegraph the intended direction of his throw.

Dribbling (Grades 5–8)

In dribbling, a low crouched position is taken. The ball is dropped in front of the body. The head is held up and the ball is watched with peripheral vision; however, the beginner will need to look directly at the ball. The ball is stroked with the fingers, not slapped or hit with the hand. It is bounced at an angle so that when the player steps forward, it will be in the proper position to be stroked again. When opponents are close, the ball is bounced low to protect it from interception. If speed is desired, a higher bounce is necessary.

Pivot (Grades 5–8)

The pivot is a turn of the body in which one foot is in constant contact with the floor. The player may move the non-stationary foot in any direction he wishes. The pivot is used to evade a closely guarding opponent and, hence, the turn is made away from the opponent.

One-Hand Push Shot (Grades 5–8)

The most frequently used shot in basketball is the one-hand push shot. In most cases it is easier for the very young to learn the one-hand push shot than the set shot (described below).

The ball is carried on the cushions of the finger tips. In the case of small hands, the ball will have to rest on the palm as well. Both hands bring the ball into position in front of the body. If the player is right-handed, the ball is shifted to the right side of the body and balanced on the right hand with the left hand steadying it. The left hand is removed as the right arm is extended full length and the wrist is flexed. The ball should make a high enough arc so that it will drop straight into the basket. The player keeps his eyes on the basket throughout the shot. When the player uses this shot under or very near the basket, it is called a lay-up shot.

Two-Hand Set Shot (Grades 6–8)

This shot is usually attempted when the opponent is not guarding closely. However, many players prefer to use the one-hand set shot in such situations, as well as when closely guarded, to eliminate the need to perfect two types of shooting styles.

For the shot, the feet are spread comfortably. The ball is held chest high with both hands and with the finger tips on the top part of the ball. The body is slightly crouched.

The weight is on the balls of the feet and the elbows are held close to the body. Preparatory to the release of the ball, the knees are bent slightly more and the wrists are dropped (Fig. 12–1). The wrists are then raised and the arms are extended upward and outward. At the same time the knees and body are straightened. The ball is released toward the basket with a snap of the wrists. An equal amount of force must be exerted on the ball by both hands. The eyes are focused on the basket during the shot.

Defensive Stance (Grades 5–8)

The player on defense stays between his opponent and the goal. He faces his opponent and the goal with his feet spread comfortably apart with one slightly behind the other. Usually he watches the ball. The arms are extended to the sides. In moving to the side, the feet are shuffled rather than crossed over.

Figure 12-1 The ball is held by the finger tips and the wrists are dropped preparatory to releasing the ball in the two-hand set shot.

LEAD-UP GAMES FOR BASKETBALL

Bounce Basketball (Grades 3-4)

DESCRIPTION OF GAME. There are 5 to 10 players on each of two teams. A basketball is used. There are two goals laid out on the floor at each end of the court. These goals are circles 3 feet in diameter. The center of each circle is 4 feet from the end line of the court. To score 1 point the ball must be bounced into the circle. Players may pass to teammates by bouncing the ball to them. Only one step is allowed while in possession of the ball and no dribbling is permitted.

TABLE 12-1   Basketball Correction Chart

Technique	Common Error	Probable Result	Correction
Catching	Failing to catch ball on cushions of finger tips	Fumbled ball	Spread fingers wide and curl fingers slightly
	Holding fingers straight	Injured fingers	Cup fingers slightly
	Failing to give with ball	Ball bounces from hand	Allow arms to give in controlled relaxation
	Failing to watch ball	Ball doesn't strike hand properly	Watch ball as it comes onto cushions of finger tips
Two-Hand Chest Pass	Catching ball on flat of hands	Fumbled ball	Catch ball on cushions of finger tips
	Failing to step in direction of pass	Ball lacks speed and is frequently intercepted	Take one step in direction of pass and shift weight forward
	Failing to snap wrist as ball is released	Throw lacks speed	Place thumbs behind ball; emphasize wrist snap by bringing thumbs forward so they will face in direction of pass after release of ball

TABLE 12–1   Basketball Correction Chart (*Continued*)

Technique	Common Error	Probable Result	Correction
Bounce Pass	Catching ball on flat of hands	Fumbled ball	Catch ball on cushions of finger tips
	Failing to step in direction of pass	Ball lacks speed and is frequently intercepted	Take one step in direction of pass and shift weight forward
	Failing to snap wrist as ball is released	Throw lacks speed	Place thumbs behind ball; emphasize wrist snap by bringing thumbs forward so they will face in direction of pass after release of ball
	Failing to bounce ball closer to receiver than thrower	Ball bounces too high and is frequently intercepted	Aim ball at a spot approximately two-thirds the distance between thrower and receiver
Dribbling	Using palms of hands	Ball is struck too hard; ball is uncontrolled	Stroke ball with cushions of finger tips; fingers should be used as if they were trying to grasp ball
	Watching ball	Ball is stolen	Watch ball with peripheral vision
Pivoting	Failing to pivot when closely pressed	Ball is tied up by opponent	At end of dribble, when a pass is not possible, pivot away from opponent to clear for a pass
One-Hand Push Shot	Failing to carry ball on finger tips	Ball often falls short of goal	Catch ball on cushions of finger tips and keep it on tips as ball is rolled onto right hand
	Failing to flex wrist	Ball falls short of goal	Super extend wrist when ball comes on fingers and flex it as shot is made
Two-Hand Set Shot	Handling ball with flat of hands	Ball falls short of goal	Use only finger tips
	Exerting more force with right arm than left arm	Ball goes to right of basket or its arc is too flat	Prevent rotation of right hand under ball
	Failing to snap wrist	Ball falls short of goal	Place thumbs behind ball; emphasize wrist snap by bringing thumbs forward so they will face in direction of pass after release of ball
	Flat arc of ball	Ball bounces too hard off backboard	Throw ball higher so it will have to drop down into basket

TABLE 12–2 Problem-Solving: Sample Subproblems for Teaching Catching, Passing, and Shooting a Basketball

1. What part of the hand comes in contact with the ball when catching, passing, or shooting? *Variable*—space; *Variation*—palms, whole hand, or fingertips.
2. What movement do the arms make when the ball is caught? *Variable*—flow; *Variation*—push arms toward the ball, hold arms stationary, or give with the ball.
3. What movement do the legs make when catching or passing the ball from a stationary position? *Variable*—flow; *Variation*—stand still, step forward, or step away from the ball.
4. What movements do the wrists make when the ball is thrown with two hands? *Variable*—flow; *Variation*—stationary to a sharp snap.
5. Where is the ball thrown in relation to a moving receiver? *Variable*—space; *Variation*—at the receiver or in front of him.
6. Where is the ball thrown in a bounce pass? *Variable*—space; *Variation*—close to the receiver, in-between the passer and receiver, or near the passer.
7. How hard is the ball passed to a receiver who is close? Far away? *Variable*—force; *Variation*—easy to very hard.
8. How is the ball brought into position when shooting a one hand push shot? *Variable*—flow; *Variation*—with one hand or two hands.
9. How high should the ball go into the air when shooting into a basket? *Variable*—space; *Variation*—slightly above the basket to several feet above the basket.
10. How hard is the ball thrown on a bank shot? *Variable*—force; *Variation*—soft to very hard.

Basketball Wall Volley (Grades 3–4)

DESCRIPTION OF GAME. A basketball is needed and sufficient wall space to bounce a ball. As many may participate as the wall space can accommodate. A horizontal line is marked on the wall 6 feet above the floor. Beginners may stand 4 feet from the wall, but those who are more skilled should stand farther back from the wall. The point from which they are to shoot is marked on the floor. Each player in turn throws the ball against the wall above the line and catches it without crossing the throwing line. The player's score is the number of catches in 30 seconds.

Corner Goal Ball (Grades 4–6)

DESCRIPTION OF GAME.   Two teams of 10 players each are needed for this game. A basketball is the only equipment required. A 4 foot square is drawn on each corner of the basketball court. The two squares at one end of the court belong to one team while the other two belong to the opponents. Each team has a player stationed within each of its squares. The players must keep at least one foot inside the square at all times. The other eight members of the team may play anywhere on the court as in basketball. The game is started with a jump ball between two opponents at the center of the court. In order to score a team must pass the ball successfully to one of its corner players. One point is scored each time a pass is caught by one of the corner players. After a score is made, play is resumed with a throw-in by the opponents from the end line nearest the corner.

Regulation basketball rules are followed in passing the ball. No player may get into the opponent's corner. If a foul is committed, a free throw for the corner is awarded. This throw is taken from the spot where the foul occurred. If the throw reaches the teammate without touching the floor, a score is made. Opponents are not allowed to guard during a free throw.

Captain Basketball (Grades 4–6)

DESCRIPTION OF GAME. Two teams are made up of from 7 to 21 players each. One basketball is used for the game. Each team chooses a captain who stands under his basket in a circle 3 feet in diameter which has been drawn on the floor. The team is divided into two groups, guards and basemen. The basemen are placed in 3 foot circles that have been drawn at intervals around the keyhole. The guards are stationed at the other end of the court to guard the opposing basemen. The basemen may not leave their circles, and guards are not permitted to leave their half of the court or enter the circles.

Each team tries to get the ball to its captain. Guards may not make a direct pass to their captain. A successful try scores 2 points. The game is started with a toss up between two guards at the center of the court.

Keep Away (Grades 4–8)

DESCRIPTION OF GAME. Twelve to 20 children can play this game in an area 50 by 50 feet or larger. A basketball is required. Two teams of 6 to 10 players are scattered throughout the playing area. The game begins when a ball is thrown into the area. Players attempt to recover the ball and to pass it back and forth among their teammates while their opponents attempt to intercept the passes. In the event opponents catch the ball simultaneously, the teacher tosses the ball up between the two players, who try to bat it to one of their team members. The game may be highly informal and provide much enjoyment for the participants. On the other hand, the game can be made more complex by adding such rules as a time limitation on how long the ball may be held.

Keyhole Basketball (Grades 5–8)

DESCRIPTION OF GAME. Five to 10 players using one basketball play at each end of the court. Eight marks are made equal distances apart around the keyhole on the basketball court. Each player, in turn, attempts to shoot a basket successfully from each of the eight marks. Those who make the eight baskets are declared the winners. When a basket is missed, the player must drop out until the next round of shooting. He begins at the point where he previously dropped out.

Twenty-One (Grades 5–8)

DESCRIPTION OF GAME. Five to 10 players can play this game at one basket. Each player, in turn, takes a long shot from 15 to 20 feet from the basket. If he is successful, he scores 2 points. If he does not make the basket, he must pick up the ball from wherever it landed and, with no more than one dribble, shoot again. A successful short shot scores 1 point. The first player to score 21 points wins.

Freeze Out (Grades 5–8)

DESCRIPTION OF GAME. Three to 10 children can play this game using one basket of a basketball court. Larger groups can participate if several games go on simultaneously at different baskets. One basketball is required for each game. Players stand in line formation behind the free throw line facing the basket. Each player takes his turn shooting at the basket. When a player is successful in making a basket, the player following him must also make a basket or be eliminated from the game. The last player remaining is the winner.

Teaching Hints. Since the poorest players are eliminated first, this game should not be continued for long periods. The shot may be made from various points other than from the free throw line.

Five-Three-One (Grades 5–8)

DESCRIPTION OF GAME. Three to 10 players participate in this game as a group; however, several games could go on simultaneously at the different baskets in the gymnasium or playground. A basketball is required for each group. The players are in line formation behind the free throw line. Each player in his turn, shoots from behind the free throw line, recovers the ball to shoot again from the spot where the ball was recovered, and recovers the ball once again to shoot a third time. Five points are awarded for a basket made on the first shot, 3 points for one made on the second shot and 1 point for one made on the third shot. Out of bounds balls are brought inside the court at the point where the ball went out and the shot is taken from that point. After the third shot, the player passes the ball to the following player waiting at the free throw line. The player with the highest score at the end of the period is the winner.

Teaching Hints. Players may call out their own scores after each shot or a scorer may be appointed. Players should be encouraged to make quick recoveries after each shot.

BASKETBALL
(Grades 5–8)

Historically, basketball for girls and boys has been two separate and distinct games. Today, however, the rules and regulations for play by both sexes vary little from each other.

An official basketball court is marked with a mid-court line, a center circle, and two free throw circles and lanes. On each end of the court, 10 feet* above the floor, are the baskets (Fig. 12–2). The team for an official game is composed of two guards, two forwards, and one center.

Two points are made by throwing the ball through the basketball hoop. One point is scored for a successful free throw which is awarded to the offended player as a result of infraction of the rules. At the beginning of each half, the ball is put into play with a jump by the two opposing centers in the center

---

*A height of 8 feet is recommended below seventh grade.

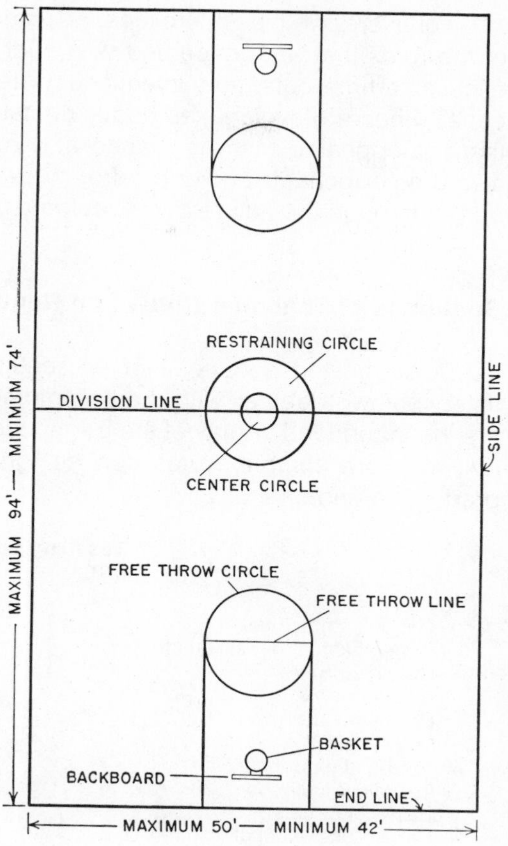

Figure 12–2 Basketball playing court. (Fait, H., et al.: *Manual of Physical Education Activities.* Ed. 3. W. B. Saunders Company.)

RESTRAINING CIRCLE

DIVISION LINE

SIDE LINE

CENTER CIRCLE

FREE THROW CIRCLE

FREE THROW LINE

BASKET

BACKBOARD

END LINE

MINIMUM 74'

MAXIMUM 94'

MAXIMUM 50'— MINIMUM 42'

circle. During the game, the jump is used when there is a held ball, such as when two opposing players have possession of the ball at the same time or when it is uncertain which side knocked the ball out of bounds.

A player is permitted to take only one step while holding the ball. Taking more than one step constitutes traveling with the ball. Dribbling is an action in which the hand pushes the ball repeatedly as it is bounced on the floor. The player is not permitted to continue dribbling once he has ended his dribbling. A player may advance the ball by dribbling if he does not violate the traveling rule. A ball is out of bounds when it touches a player, the floor, or any object which is on or outside the boundary line.

A violation is a certain kind of infraction of the rules. The penalty for a violation is loss of the ball to the opposing team, which throws it in from the boundary line. Violations which elementary school players might be expected to know about and to be held responsible for include:

1. Causing the ball to go out of bounds.
2. Running with the ball, striking it with the fist, or kicking it intentionally.
3. Dribbling a second time.
4. Touching the ball first when the player or his team has caused it to go from their front court to their back court.

Fouls are two types, technical and personal. Technical fouls are infractions of the rules that are concerned with such things as unsportsmanlike conduct, excessive time outs, and intentionally delaying the game. A personal foul is called when a player makes bodily contact with an opponent in such a manner that the opposing team is placed at a disadvantage. Fouls are penalized by awarding opponents one or two free throws. The number of free throws awarded depends upon the nature of the foul and when it occurs.

Sequence of Teaching Rules and Regulations

A suggested sequence of presenting the rules to beginning players is listed below, together with the recommended grades in which the rules may first be introduced. If play of the game begins at the fifth grade, as recommended, the more complex rules can be ignored until students reach the higher grade level indicated.

Teaching Sequence

Rule or Regulation	Grade
Out-of-bounds rules	3
General nature of basketball court	4
Double dribble	4
Scoring	4
Personal fouls	4
Traveling	5
Hold and jump ball	5
Technical fouls	6
Back court rules	7
Dimensions of court	7

Teaching Procedures

Teaching procedures will vary in accordance with the method used and the ability of students. If the direct method is employed, the instruction could be organized as follows.

Catching and throwing are presented first. The two skills may be taught together since throwing is an integral part of any drill that may be used to teach catching. Before setting up catching and throwing drills, the techniques are discussed and demonstrated. It is helpful to the children to go through the movements initially in slow motion without the ball. The teacher observes and makes suggestions and corrections as necessary.

The first throwing skill to be introduced is usually the two-hand chest pass. For the demonstration the class may be formed into two lines facing each other; they will then be ready for practice without loss of time in getting into formation.

The drill itself consists of passing the ball successively between players in the two lines. If the supply of balls permits, one ball should serve no more than eight to ten students. As skills improve, the distance between the lines should be increased. The same procedure may be used to teach the other passes.

Dribbling is the next skill to be presented. It is first thoroughly explained and demonstrated. Special attention is directed to the use of the fingers. For a simple preliminary drill in dribbling the class forms several lines of equal length at one end of the gymnasium. The first person in each line dribbles the length of the gymnasium and back to the starting position where the ball is handed to the next in line. The dribbler then takes a place at the end of the line. After several trial runs, competition among lines may be introduced to determine which line can complete the drill in the shortest time.

When introducing shooting skills to a beginning group, it is best to concentrate on the one-hand shot. The set shot should be taught first. A demonstration of the shot is followed by students' executing the movement in slow motion. The teacher observes and makes corrections and suggestions. The class may then try shots at the basket using a line formation at each basket. The teacher moves about to provide individual help to those who need it. Drills for practice in shooting can be expanded to include practice in dribbling, passing, and recovery from the backboard. One drill of combined skills will serve as an example: Students line up on the right side of the basket facing it. One player is stationed near the basket to pass the ball to the first player in line as he runs towards the basket. He receives the pass, shoots, and then recovers the ball and takes the position near the basket to pass the ball to the next player. The player who made the pass goes to the end of the line (Figure 12–3).

While drills are valuable teaching aids, it is in actual play that the greatest learning occurs, for it is in team participation that the skills are brought together into a functioning unit and the necessity for team strategy makes itself felt. Because interest is high and the desire to succeed as a team member is great, this part of the instructional unit requires less motivation than practice on drills and discussion of rules and related information.

The beginning teacher often makes the grave error of thinking that, *having brought his students to the point of actual game participation, he can relax his vigil for errors and retire to the sideline to enjoy the game.* Not so! He must con-

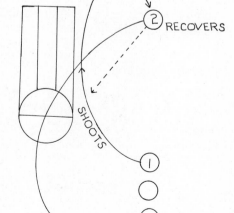

Figure 12–3 Basketball drill formation.

tinue to be alert to form, tactics, and attitudes demonstrated by the class in play. Sometimes he may wish to stop the game and make an explanation to the entire group; at other times he may give instructions to a single player who needs individual advice or correction.

Evaluation

There are several tests used to evaluate specific abilities in playing basketball. They are easily administered and provide definitive results that can be compared with the test results of others who take the test.

Test 1 — *Dribbling Against Time* (straight dribbling)

Two lines are drawn 60 feet apart. The dribbler starts at one line and dribbles to the other. A stop watch is used to time the completion of the dribble. Three trials are allowed. The score may be the average or the best time of the three attempts.

Test 2 — *Dribbling Against Time* (zig-zag dribbling)

Four chairs are set up in a line 10 feet apart. A line is drawn 10 feet in front of the first chair. The dribbler starts behind the line and dribbles the length of the chairs, passing on one side of the first chair and on the opposite side of the next chair and so on down the line. Then the dribbler turns and dribbles back in the same zig-zag pattern. The score is the time, recorded by a stop watch, required to complete the entire procedure.

Test 3 — *Ball Handling*

The player stands 5 to 10 feet from an unobstructed wall and passes the ball from behind the line to rebound from the wall as many times as he can in 30 seconds. He may retrieve the ball from in front of the line, but he must return behind the line before he throws it. The score is the number of rebounds made during the allotted time.

Test 4 — *Shooting*

The student stands at a designated distance from the basket to shoot as many times as possible during a period of 30 seconds. The number of baskets made is the score. Another shooting test may be devised by substituting the one-hand set shot from various distances.

SOFTBALL AND LEAD-UP GAMES

Softball attracts the interest of older children in the elementary school who enjoy playing the game in their leisure time. Hence, teaching softball in the physical education program provides children with recreational skills as well as contributing to general development of motor ability. The major emphasis in teaching the game on the elementary level should be on the fundamental techniques and skills, utilizing the lead-up games. Usually the game is not taught as a team sport until the fifth grade.

FUNDAMENTAL TECHNIQUES AND SKILLS

Although the foundation for many of the softball skills is established as early as the second and third grades, it is not until the fourth grade that specific softball skills are introduced.

Throwing and Catching (Grades 3–8)

The skills of throwing and catching a softball are identical to those described on pages 159–160. Older children may grip the ball with two fingers (Fig. 12–4). It is recommended that a softball glove be worn for catching in a softball game.

Fielding (Grades 4–8)

Fielding refers to catching the ball after it has been batted. Fielding a ball that is rolling or bouncing on the ground requires the fielder to maneuver himself into a position directly in front of the ball if at all possible. He keeps his eyes focused on the ball from the time it is hit with the bat until he catches it. The feet during the catch are spread comfortably with the right foot slightly behind the left. The arms are extended forward with the hands parallel and close to the ground and the fingers extended toward the ground.

As the ball comes into the glove hand, the arm is relaxed to give with the ball. At the same time the other hand is brought over the ball to secure it in the pocket of the glove.

In fielding a fly ball, the fielder watches the ball but notes the surrounding terrain with his peripheral vision. When the ball is high in the air, the fielder

Figure 12–4 Grip on a softball as made by an older child.

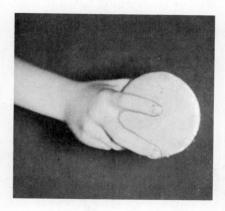

should stay well back from where it appears the ball will land; there is a tendency to misjudge and run under the ball. It is easier to run forward than to run backward while making a catch. The palms of the hands are parallel and, if possible, face in the direction of the oncoming ball. The arms give as the ball makes contact with the glove and the opposite hand is brought over the ball.

In fielding a ground ball or a fly ball, a right-handed player should catch the ball with his left foot forward to be in a position to throw the ball immediately.

Batting (Grades 4–8)

If the batter is right-handed, the bat is grasped with the left hand near the end of the bat with the right hand just above the left. For younger children or in cases where the bat is too heavy for the child, the hands may be moved slightly up from the end of the bat. This is called *choking.*

The top hand should be so aligned with the bottom hand that the third joint of the little finger rests between the second and third joints of the index finger of the lower hand. The trademark on the bat should face upward when the bat is swung over the plate.

The right-handed batter stands facing the plate with the left shoulder toward the pitcher. The corner of the plate should split the center of the batter's body. He stands just close enough to the plate to allow the heavy part of the bat to swing comfortably over the center of the plate.

The bat is held out from the right shoulder, not resting on it. Both elbows are bent and the right wrist is flexed with the left wrist straight as the bat is brought back at the beginning of the swing. The elbows are held away from the body. The batter keeps his eyes focused on the ball as it leaves the pitcher's hand. As the ball travels toward the strike zone, the bat is swung forward in a horizontal plane to meet the ball squarely. As the bat is swung forward, the body weight is transferred from the right to the left foot. After hitting the ball, the bat continues swinging around in a follow-through. *The bat is dropped, not thrown,* as the first step is taken toward first base. Young children should be instructed to carry the bat two or three steps before dropping it until the habit of dropping the bat becomes firmly established.

Player Positioning (Grades 5–8)

PITCHER
Backs up third base on throws from the outfield.
Covers first base on balls the first baseman fields.
Backs up the catcher on throws to the plate.
CATCHER
Covers area around home plate.
Backs up first base when no one is on base.
FIRST BASEMAN
Stands about 8 feet toward second base and a few feet behind the base line.
Fields bunts on his side.
Backs up second on throws from outfielders.

SECOND BASEMAN

Stands about 15 feet toward first and 10 feet behind the base line.

Backs up the first baseman on balls hit toward first and on double play throws.

Covers second on throws from the catcher.

Goes out to relay throws from the outfield.

THIRD BASEMAN

Stands about 8 feet toward second and a few feet behind the baseline.

Runs in on bunt on the third base side.

SHORTSTOP

Stands about one-half to two-thirds of the distance between second and third, and 8 to 10 feet behind the base line.

Takes flys and relays throws from the outfield.

Covers and backs up the second baseman.

Backs up the third baseman.*

FIELDERS

Left—backs up the center fielder on fly balls.

Center—backs up the left and right fielders on fly balls.

Right—backs up the center fielder on fly balls.

Short fielder (optional)—may play anywhere in the field.

All fielders back up the infield.

Pitching (Grades 5–8)

The pitcher faces home plate with the feet 6 to 8 inches apart and both feet touching the pitching plate. The ball is held with both hands in front of the body at the beginning of the pitch. For a right-handed pitcher the right arm is brought back as far as possible past the right hip. Beginners may hold the ball with the palms facing downward. As a player develops skill in pitching, the arm, when it is brought back, is slightly bent at the elbow and the wrist is twisted so the palm is up and the elbow is pointed toward the ground. Delivery is made in both cases by swinging the arm forward in an arc. The ball is released with the palm facing forward and with a snap of the wrist. The ball leaves the hand about shoulder height. As the arm is brought forward, a step is taken forward with the left foot. The arm follows through and the right foot is brought up parallel with the left foot in a position to field the ball if necessary.

LEAD-UP GAMES FOR SOFTBALL

Throw Ball (Grades 3–4)

DESCRIPTION OF GAME. This game is played on a diamond shaped field with two teams. There may be 10 to 12 players on each team. A volleyball

---

*Playing a base is of secondary importance because players are so situated that at least two players are available to cover every base. Thus, fielding the ball is of primary importance.

TABLE 12–3   Softball Correction Chart

Technique	Common Error	Probable Result	Correction
Catching	Failing to keep eyes focused on ball until caught	Ball does not make proper contact with glove	Watch ball throughout flight until caught
	Failing to give with ball	Ball bounces from glove and/or stings hand	Allow arm to give in controlled relaxation
Throwing Over-hand	Failing to use body properly	Ball may fall short of goal	Turn body away from direction of throw as hand is brought back behind head and turn it forward as ball is thrown
	Failing to snap wrist	Ball falls short of its goal	Cock wrist as it is brought back behind head and snap it forward when ball is released
	Failing to keep elbow away from body	Ball falls short of its goal	Bring upper arm parallel with ground and point elbow away from body as ball is brought back behind head
Fielding	Failing to watch ball as it is batted	Fielder not in proper position	Watch ball leave pitcher's hand and follow it wherever it goes
	Failing to keep eyes on ball during catch	Ball does not contact mitt correctly	Watch ball throughout catch
	Running under a fly ball	Ball goes over head	Stay well back of where it appears ball will land and then move up rapidly as it comes down
	Failure to give with ball in catch	Ball bounces from hand and/or stings hand	Allow arms to give in controlled relaxation
Batting	Failing to align hands properly	Swing is not free and easy	(Right-handed batter) Place left hand near end of bat with right hand just above it; third joint of little finger of top hand is aligned so it rests between 2nd and 3rd joints of index finger of lower hand
	Standing too close or too far from plate	Ball cannot be hit with proper swing	Adjust distance so that heavy part of bat swings over center of plate
	Resting bat on shoulder	Ball is missed due to slow swing	Move elbows away from body
	Swinging bat vertically	Ball is missed	Move elbows away from the body and swing bat on a horizontal plane

TABLE 12-3   Softball Correction Chart (*Continued*)

Technique	Common Error	Probable Result	Correction
	Failing to focus eyes on the ball	Ball is missed	Watch ball until it strikes bat
	Throwing bat	Possible injury to other players	Carry bat two or three steps before dropping it
Pitching	Failing to snap wrist	Ball lacks speed	Cock wrist as ball is brought back in wind-up and flex it as ball is released
	Failing to take proper wind-up	Ball lacks speed	• Bring ball back as far as possible past right hip
	Failure to follow through	Ball lacks speed	Bring right foot up parallel with left foot
	Failing to release ball at proper height	Ball goes too high or too low	Release ball shoulder height

is used. One team is stationed on the field in regular softball positions. The pitcher throws the ball to the "batter" who catches and immediately throws it out into the field. After the throw the game is played just like softball, using softball rules with the exception that there is no stealing of bases and a batter is considered out if he "hits" a foul ball.

VARIATIONS.   The batter may be required to throw the ball under his leg, with his left hand, or turn around and throw it over his head into the field.

TABLE 12-4   Problem-Solving: Sample Subproblems for Teaching Fielding,
Batting, and Pitching of Softball

1. Where is the body positioned in fielding a ball? *Variable*—space; *Variation*—to the side or front.
2. How are the feet placed while fielding a ball? *Variable*—space; *Variation*—close together, spread apart, the left foot in front, or the right foot in front.
3. Where is the body positioned when fielding a fly ball? *Variable*—space; *Variation*—under the ball or back away from the ball.
4. Where is the bat gripped in batting? *Variable*—space; *Variation*—end of the bat or further up on the bat.
5. Which hand is placed above the other in batting? *Variable*—space; *Variation*—left or right hand.
6. How does the batter stand at the plate? *Variable*—space; *Variation*—sideways to straight on, far away or close to the plate.
7. How is the bat held? *Variable*—space; *Variation*—resting on the shoulder, in back of the shoulder, or in front of the shoulder.
8. How is the bat swung? *Variable*—flow; *Variation*—swung down on the ball, swung level, or swung up.
9. How does the pitcher stand at the pitcher's mound? *Variable*—space; *Variation*—facing home plate or the side to home plate, feet spread or together, or one foot ahead of the other.
10. Where is the arm brought before the forward pitching movement begins? *Variable*—space; *Variation*—beside the hip or back beyond the hip.
11. When is the ball released? *Variable*—time; *Variation*—at shoulder height or above shoulder height.
12. What is the position of the hand when the ball is released? *Variable*—space; *Variation*—from palm up to palm down.
13. What movement is taken with the legs when the ball is thrown? *Variable*—flow; *Variation*—standing stationary or taking a step forward.

Bat Ball (Grades 4–5)

DESCRIPTION OF GAME. Two teams play this game using a home plate and first base and a volleyball as the ball. There are 10 to 12 players on a team. The batter strikes the ball with the hand or fist into the field. He then runs to the base and back to home plate. The fielders who are positioned on the field to cover it adequately field the ball and attempt to hit the runner; no fielder may take more than two steps with the ball in his possession, but he is permitted to pass to other teammates.

Beatball (Grades 4–5)

DESCRIPTION OF GAME. Beatball is played with a volleyball on a softball diamond with two teams. There are 10 players on each team. The batter throws the volleyball into the field and runs the bases consecutively from first to home. The fielder, after recovering the ball, must throw it to the first baseman, who must throw it to the second baseman, and so on around the bases. If the runner reaches home before the ball does, he scores one point; otherwise, he is out.

Three Grounders and a Fly (Grades 5–6)

DESCRIPTION OF GAME. A ball and a bat are needed to play the game. One player is the batter and the remaining players scatter across the playing area. The batter tosses the softball up and bats it into the field where the other players attempt to catch it. When a player in the field has caught one fly ball or three grounders, he may exchange places with the batter.

Work-Up or One Old Cat (Grades 5–8)

DESCRIPTION OF GAME. Four to seven children can play this game on a softball diamond. A softball bat and softball are required. A home plate and first base bag would be helpful. There are a pitcher, catcher, batter, and one or more fielders. The pitcher pitches the ball, underhand, to the batter who attempts to knock the ball by striking it with the bat so that he can run to first base and back to home plate without being put out. The batter continues to bat until he is put out. He may be put out by another player catching a fly or foul ball, by swinging at a pitched ball and missing three times before hitting fairly, by being tagged with the ball by one of the other players before returning to home plate after a fair hit, or by the catcher or pitcher tagging home plate before he can touch it after returning from first base. When the batter is put out, he moves to play the last fielding position. As successive batters are put out, he will move through the fielding positions, to pitcher, to catcher, and finally back to batter.

SOFTBALL
Grades 5–8

The size of the diamond should be adapted to the age of the children playing. For older children, the suggested distance between bases is 50 to 60 feet with the pitcher's box 38 feet from home plate. For younger children, it is suggested that the distance between bases be reduced to between 35 and 40 feet and the pitching distance to between 24 and 28 feet.

Inning. An inning is the period during which both teams have been up to bat and have been retired after three outs. An official game has seven innings, but the number that children play may be reduced to fit the abilities of the players and the time available.

Strike. A strike is a ball that is legally thrown above home plate in the strike zone which the batter either fails to strike at or strikes at and misses. The strike zone is the area over the plate between the batter's knees and shoulders. For beginning players, it is recommended that strikes be called only when the batter strikes at the ball and misses.

A batter is out after three strikes. A foul ball, one that is hit outside the baseline between home and first or home and third, which is not caught is a strike if the batter has less than three strikes.

Ball. A ball is a pitched ball that does not enter the strike zone.

Walk. After four balls, the batter is permitted to walk to first base. It is recommended that for beginners balls not be called.

Outs. The batter is out when:

1. A foul ball is hit and is caught.
2. There are three strikes except on the third strike when the catcher fails to catch the ball, and there is no one on first base.
3. An infield fly is hit and there are runners on first and second bases with less than two outs.

The runner is out when:

1. An opposing player reaches first base with the ball before the runner touches the base.
2. The runner is touched with the ball while going to any base.
3. The runner leaves the base before the ball leaves the pitcher's hand in a pitch to the batter.
4. The runner runs to the next base on a fly ball that is caught if he leaves the base before the ball was caught.

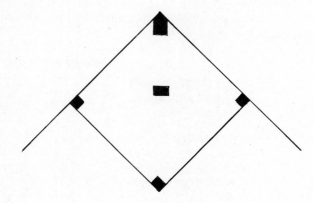

Figure 12–5 Softball diamond.

MODIFIED SLOW PITCH SOFTBALL*
Grades 5–8

This version of softball is excellent in that it permits greater participation by students in the various facets of the game, thereby affording more opportunities to practice all of the skills of softball. It is played like softball with the following exceptions:

1. The hitting team provides its own pitcher. He must remain on the mound during any play, and may in no way interfere with any fielders. The hitter is retired as penalty for interference. (Note: The pitcher takes his regular turn at bat, and is relieved by another member of the hitting team.)
2. The batter receives a maximum of two pitches. If he accepts the first pitch, and swings, he must hit a fair ball or he is out. The hitter may elect to let the first pitch pass, but he must then hit a fair ball on the second pitch or he is out. (Foul balls are out, a swing and miss is out.)
3. No bunting is allowed. The hitter must take a full swing at the ball or else he is called out.
4. Stealing bases is not allowed.
5. Sliding is not allowed. (Because of the lack of proper equipment). The base runner is out as penalty for sliding. (Regardless of whether or not slide was accidental.)
6. All members of the hitting team, with the exception of the batter, pitcher, base runners, and the "on deck" batter, must be on the "bench." If benches are not available on the field, an area is marked off with chalk lines, and the hitting team is confined to that area.
7. The batter must drop his bat entirely within the area chalked off along the first base line. The batter is out as penalty for infraction. Note: In case of infraction of 6 or 7 after, or concurrent with, the third out, the penalty is carried over to the next inning.

Sequence of Teaching Rules and Regulations

A suggested sequence of presenting the rules to beginning players is listed below, together with the recommended grades in which the rules may first be introduced. If play of the game begins at the fifth grade, as recommended, the more complex rules can be ignored until students reach the higher grade level indicated.

Teaching Sequence

Rule or Regulation	Grade
General nature of diamond	4
Strikes and strike zone	5
Foul ball	5
Fielding positions	5

*Adapted from "Ideas that Score (Softball Modified)," by George Wigton, *Journal of Health · Physical Education · Recreation,* Vol. 33, No. 8, Nov. 1962, p. 61.

Teaching Procedures

If problem-solving or synthesis of methods is used, subproblems like those in Table 12–4 must be developed. After the experimentation has given students sufficient insight into the skill performance, the teacher may wish to use the drills of direct method to establish the pattern.

Before the drills of throwing and catching begin, the techniques are demonstrated. Even though the skills have already been learned, a review of the skills is desirable. Footwork and body control and the proper grip in throwing the ball should be emphasized. The teacher should be particularly alert to the position of the elbow during the throw since beginners tend to bring it in close to the body rather than keeping it well out at shoulder level. Speed and accuracy in throwing the ball receive increased attention in each practice session. Moving into position to make the catch and the placement of the hands in receiving the ball are the most important elements to be stressed in teaching how to catch. Beginning fielders should be instructed to catch a bouncing ball at the height of its first bounce; as they become more skilled, they can learn to field the ball by smothering the bounce. The importance of moving to meet a ground ball must also be stressed.

Practice of the overhand throw employing the base touch is provided by a drill that simulates a game situation. Two files of players face each other. One file stands near a base. The first player in the other file throws the ball to the first player in the file near the base, who catches it and touches the base before throwing the ball to the first player in the opposite file. As each person makes his throw, he goes immediately to the rear of the opposite line. The drill may be used for competition among several groups of players. Judges may be assigned to watch the bases to make sure the players have not failed to touch them during or after the catch.

For practice of throwing and catching on a diamond, students form lines five and six deep at each base including home plate. The first one in line may throw around the bases or may follow any one of a number of assigned patterns devised by the instructor. Upon completion of the pattern, the players involved go to the rear of their respective lines.

Pitching skills may be practiced initially by two players. After the students demonstrate a degree of proficiency, the class can be divided into groups of three to work with the plate—one student pitches, another catches, and the third calls the balls and strikes. After several pitches positions are rotated. For younger children less emphasis should be placed on the skill. If modified slow pitch softball is to be used, the toss pitch is taught. This is a pitch that is thrown over the plate so that it is easily hit.

The demonstration of batting should emphasize several points: the position in the batter's box, the position at the point of contact with the ball, the follow-through, and the dropping of the bat. One good drill for practice of batting utilizes a squad consisting of a pitcher, a catcher, three or four fielders, and several batters. A pitching mound and a home plate or facsimiles are provided for each squad. The pitcher throws five easy strikes across the plate, and the ball is played accordingly before positions are rotated. As the batting skill increases, the speed of the pitch can be increased.

Evaluation

To evaluate softball skills, tests of throwing, fielding, and base running may be used. The test scores can be used to compare the achievement in skill development of students.

Test 1 — Throwing for Distance

From behind a designated line, each student throws a softball as far as possible. Only one step is allowed before throwing. The score is the distance thrown.

Test 2 — Throwing for Accuracy

A circle is drawn on the wall or a tire may be hung from the ceiling. The thrower stands 40 to 50 feet away and attempts to throw the ball within the circle or through the tire. The score is the number of successful throws out of 10 tries.

Test 3 — Fielding

Students take a position behind a line marked on the field. The teacher or aide throws three grounders and three flies to each one. The score is the number of balls caught. All throws must be consistently difficult to catch.

Test 4 — Running Bases

Students run the bases. Each runner is timed with a stop watch. The score is the time required to complete the run around the bases.

SOCCER AND LEAD-UP GAMES

Soccer is a very popular sport in many parts of the world. Although it does not enjoy comparable popularity in the United States, it is making rapid gains in some sections of the country. Soccer and soccer lead-up games offer students unique opportunities to learn kicking skills, which so many other games do not emphasize.

FUNDAMENTAL TECHNIQUES AND SKILLS

The fundamental skills of soccer include kicking, trapping, tackling, heading, and charging. Of these, kicking is suitable for introduction at the fourth grade level. The other skills can be taught beginning in the fifth grade.

Kicking (Grades 4–8)

The ball is propelled by three different types of kicks: a kick made with the instep of the foot, a kick made with the outside of the foot, and a kick made with the inside of the foot.

In the instep kick the contact of the ball with the foot is at the laces of the shoe. To make the kick, a step forward on the opposite foot is taken as the kicking leg swings back. The forward step is made on the ground beside the ball as the kicking leg swings forward to kick the ball. The toe comes close to the ground so that the ball is contacted on the instep of the foot. For the inside kick, the leg swings outward from the hip, then across the body. The ball is contacted on the inside of the foot. The ball may be kicked from a stationary or running position. The outside kick is accomplished by swinging the leg out to the side contacting the ball with the outside of the foot. The leg is held straight and swings from the hip.

In kicking a ball that is in the air (volley kick), the kicking foot is placed behind the other in a kicking position with the weight on the forward foot. As the ball descends, the weight is shifted to the other foot. The kicking foot is brought through with the knee slightly bent and toe pointing down. Contact with the ball is made on the instep. The punt, a kick which only the goalkeeper may use, is

Figure 12–6 The long kick may be practiced in line formation. (Courtesy of Town of Vernon Schools, Rockville, Connecticut.)

made in a similar manner except that the ball is held in front of the body and dropped. It is held in both hands and extended at arms' distance in front of the body before it is dropped. The kick is preceded by two steps. The body is bent slightly at the waist. As the ball is dropped, the kicking leg swings forward, contacting the ball on the top of the instep.

Trapping (Grades 5–8)

The skill of trapping should be taught before soccer is played at all. Unless children are taught trapping before they begin play, they may instinctively bend over to use their hands to stop the ball, exposing themselves to possible injury from those who are kicking at the ball. Also, without the skill of trapping, the ball cannot be controlled effectively.

In *body trapping* the ball is stopped by a part of the body, the portion being determined by the height of the ball; for high balls the upper trunk is used while for low balls the hip, thigh, or shin is used. Junior high school girls should be permitted to cover the chest with the arms for protection when blocking with the chest. To check the bounce of the ball in trapping with any portion of the body, the body should give with the ball so that it will drop close to the feet ready for play.

There are two other basic traps for elementary school students. One is a *foot trap*, in which the ball is trapped, as it rolls forward, with the sole of the foot by placing the sole on top of the ball as if pressing down to the ground (Fig. 12–7). The other trap is a *leg trap*, made with both legs. The feet must be close together. The ball is trapped between the front of the lower legs and the ground by bending at the knees and lowering the shins to the ground.

Tackling (Grades 6–8)

Tackling refers to the taking of the ball away from the opponent. A tackle may be made directly from the side of an opponent or in front of him. The hook tackle is the most effective for use by elementary school children. To execute it, the tackler reaches in from the side with the foot nearer to the opponent and hooks or pulls the ball away.

Figure 12–7 Trapping with the foot.

Heading (Grades 7–8)

Heading is a technique employed when the ball is dropping from overhead. The player jumps to meet the ball, making contact with the forehead at about the hair line. The direction of the rebound may be controlled by the angle of the jump or by the side of the head which is used.

Charging

Charging involves body contact and is a legal tactic in boys' rules. However, it is not usually recommended for elementary school children.

LEAD-UP GAMES FOR SOCCER

Soccer Keep-Away (Grades 4–5)

DESCRIPTION OF GAME. There are two teams with 10 to 15 players on each side. The game is begun by throwing the ball out into the playing area.

TABLE 12–5   Soccer Correction Chart

Technique	Common Error	Probable Result	Correction
Dribbling	Failing to use inside of foot while dribbling	Loss of control of ball	Turn foot to outside and make contact with ball with inside of the foot
	Kicking ball too hard while dribbling	Loss of control of ball	Kick less vigorously and aim for shorter distances
Body Trapping	Using arms to propel ball	Foul is committed	Hold arms to sides
Foot Trapping	Failing to wedge ball securely between foot and ground	Ball bounces away	Hold heel about five inches from ground with toes raised slightly; press foot down firmly as ball rolls under foot
Trapping with Both Legs	Failing to time bending of knee properly	Ball bounces away	Flex knees in anticipation of bending more deeply to trap ball
Punting	Rushing kick	Kick goes off side of the foot	Take more time and concentrate on kicking
Tackling from the Side	Failing to time correctly forward thrust of leg toward ball	Ball is missed	Keep eyes focused on ball and, in anticipation of where ball will be when foot reaches it, thrust leg forward
Heading	Failing to jump to meet ball	Opponent heads ball	Time jump so as to contact ball at top of jump
	Failing to use head to direct ball	Ball bounces out of control	Control direction by angle of jump and by contacting ball with side of head

TABLE 12–6   Problem-Solving: Sample Subproblems for Teaching Kicking or Trapping with the Feet and Legs, Punting, Tackling, and Heading in Soccer

1. What part of the foot is used in kicking the ball (kick to the right and left, long kicks and short kicks, dribbling)? *Variable*—space; *Variation*—outside and inside of foot, toe, and instep.
2. How is the bounce of the ball checked when a body trap is made? *Variable*—flow; *Variation*—body stationary or giving with the ball.
3. How is the foot held when trapping a ball with the sole of the foot? *Variable*—space; *Variation*—from a vertical position to a 90 degree position.
4. How is the trapping leg held when trapping with the inside of the thigh? *Variable*—space; *Variation*—leg vertically straight to nearly horizontally straight.
5. When are the legs bent in trapping with both legs? *Variable*—time; *Variation*—just before the ball hits the legs, as the ball hits the legs, or after it bounces from the legs.
6. What portion of the foot contacts the ball in a punt? *Variable*—space; *Variation*—toe or instep.
7. Where is the tackler when a tackle is made? *Variable*—space; *Variation*—behind, side, or in the front.
8. How is the foot used in tackling? *Variable*—flow; *Variation*—hooking or placing the foot on the ball.
9. What part of the head is used in heading? *Variable*—space; *Variation*—top of head, forehead, side of head.
10. When is the jump made to head the ball? *Variable*—time; *Variation*—when the ball hits the head, or as the ball is descending.

One team attempts to keep the ball away from the opponents by trapping, dribbling, or passing the ball while the other team attempts to gain possession.

Line Soccer (Grades 4–5)

DESCRIPTION OF GAME.   Goal lines are marked at the ends of a playing area that is approximately 30 by 30 feet. Two teams of 10 to 15 players each stand on their goal lines facing each other. A soccer ball is required. On signal the player on the far right of each line comes forward to play the ball that has been placed in the center of the playing area. Each attempts to knock it over the opponents' goal. Players must touch the ball with a foot (dribble) before kicking the ball hard. The opposing players defend their goal by kicking the ball away when it comes near them. They must keep one foot on the goal line at all times. When a goal is made or the ball goes out of bounds, players return to the goal line, and the next player who is now at the beginning of the line becomes the next one to try to play the ball.

Circle Soccer (Grades 4–5)

DESCRIPTION OF GAME.   The class is divided into two teams, each team making up half of a circle. Six or eight players are on a team. Each team tries to kick the soccer ball out of the circle through the half of the circle composed of opposing players. The ball must be kicked with the inside of the foot and must be kicked below the shoulders of the opponents. A moving ball must be trapped and stopped before it may again be kicked. Team members must kick the ball from their place in the circle. If the ball becomes stationary, a player may go after it and dribble it back to his position in the circle. A score is made when the ball goes through the opponents' half of the circle. A ball kicked above the shoulders gives a point to the opponents. The first team to score 10 points is declared the winner.

Soccer Home Ball (Grades 5–8)

DESCRIPTION OF GAME. This game may be played by 10 to 24 children using a softball diamond and soccer ball. Two teams of equal numbers are formed. The players of each team are numbered from 1 through to the total number of players on the team. The ball is placed on home plate. Number 1 of the team at bat kicks the ball and then attempts to circle and to touch as many of the bases as he can before being put out. The number 1 player of the team in the field controls the kicked ball and attempts to dribble and kick the ball so that it will pass over home plate to put out the "batter" before he can circle the bases and return to touch home plate. He is the only member of the fielding team permitted to touch the ball. The "batter" earns 1 point for his team for each base he touches before being put out. The batter may not run on "foul" balls, i.e., kicked balls which go behind the lines running from home to first and to third base. On all foul balls the "batter" kicks again. Players on the team "bat" in numerical order and the players on the opposing team with the same number as the "batter" field the ball. Three "outs" will "retire" a team, at which time, the teams exchange places. The game may be played for a designated period of time or for an agreed upon number of "innings." In an inning each team is up to bat once and out to field once. The team with the most points at the end of the agreed upon time period or number of innings is the winner.

Teaching Hints. Enlarging home plate to a size of 3 by 6 feet decreases the probability of collisions at home plate in the event batter and field reach there at the same moment.

Figure 12–8 A game of Soccer Home Ball. (Los Angeles City Board of Education.)

SOCCER
Grades 5–8

Different rules govern soccer play by boys and girls; however, no great need exists for separate rules until the seventh or eighth grade or such time as charging is introduced into boys' play. Girls on the junior high level should not be penalized for crossing their arms over their chests for protection in blocking, provided that the ball is given no impetus by the arms.

The rules* below will help lay a sound foundation in soccer when taught to boys and girls together. When the sexes receive separate instruction, the rules for boys and the rules for girls may be used with the respective groups; however, the rules which follow could be utilized for class instruction of either group.

Positions. There are 11 players on a team. All players have a definite position. The forwards (left wing or outside, left inner or inside, center, right inner or inside, and right wing or outside) play offense and attempt to advance the ball into the opponents' territory and score a goal. The halfbacks (left, center and right) play offense in that they follow the forward line to the opponents' goal and feed the ball to the forwards. They play defense when the opponents have possession of the ball, and are responsible for guarding a specific opponent, i.e., right halfback guards, or covers, the left wing; the fullbacks (left and right) play defense and guard (or cover) the opposite inners (left fullback versus right inner). The goalie defends the goal.

Kickoff. The game is started with a kickoff in the center of the field by the center forward of one team. The ball may not be played again by this player until it has been kicked by another player of either team. No player may cross his restraining line until the kickoff is made by a center forward. A goal may not be scored on a direct kick at the kickoff.

Offensive Play. The forwards try to advance the ball down the field to the opponents' goal by means of dribbling and passing. They should try to kick the ball through the 6 foot goal. If they do so, they score two points. The game consists of four 5 minute quarters with 2 minute rest periods between each quarter.

Out-of-bounds over the Side Line. The ball is kicked in from the ground by the nearest halfback of the opposing team at the point where it went out. If it is sent out-of-bounds by two opponents, the ball is rolled in at the spot where it went out, between the two opponents.

Out-of-bounds over the End Line, not Through the Goal, by a Member of the Attacking Team. The ball is kicked in from the ground by a member of the defending team at the point where it went out. If it is kicked out by a member of the defending team, it is kicked in at the nearest corner of the end line by a wing of the attacking team.

On any out-of-bounds ball, all other players must stay 10 yards away until the ball has been kicked.

Goalie's Privileges. The goalie may catch the ball coming into the goal area and throw it out, may catch and punt the ball out, and may guard the goal in

*Adapted from *Physical Education for the Elementary Schools of Colorado.* Preliminary Ed. Colorado State Department of Education, pp. 101–102.

the usual manner by blocking and trapping the ball and clearing the ball with a kick.

Fouls. Holding, pushing, kicking, or tripping an opponent, using the hands or arms on the ball (except the goalkeeper), and unnecessary roughness are fouls.

Penalty. A free kick on the spot where the foul occurred is awarded to the opposing team. The free kick is usually taken by the nearest halfback. All other players must remain 10 yards away until the free kick has been taken. A penalty kick is awarded for holding, pushing, etc., if the act is committed by the defense within its own penalty area. The ball is kicked 12 yards from the goal, and only the goalkeeper may be in the penalty area.

Sequence of Teaching Rules and Regulations

A suggested sequence of presenting the rules to beginning players is listed below, together with the recommended grades in which the rules may first be introduced. If play of the game begins at the fifth grade, as recommended, the more complex rules can be ignored until students reach the higher grade level indicated.

Teaching Sequence

Rule or Regulation	Grade
Out-of-bounds rules	4
General nature of soccer field	4
General rules of advancing the ball	4
Scoring	4
Kick-off	5
Fouls	5
Specific rules of advancing the ball	6
Rules of goalie's privileges	6
Dimensions of field	7

Teaching Procedures

Soccer lends itself well to the problem-solving method. Many youngsters will not have had extensive experience with kicking or the other soccer skills so that experimentation can be very fruitful. The skills should be introduced in the same order described in the discussion of the direct teaching method which follows. Suggested subproblems for use in stimulating experimentation are given in Table 12–6.

When teaching the skills by the direct method, the procedure is a demonstration of the techniques of the skill, followed by group practice. The teacher watches for faults during the practice and makes corrections and suggestions for improvement as needed.

The teaching of kicking should progress from the inside of foot through the outside of foot to the instep. The class may be lined up with from five to six players to a line facing each other for practicing the various kicks from a stationary position. A circle formation may also be employed for practice kicking. Players are spaced around in a circle at 10 foot intervals, and the ball is passed around the circle. The passes are made clockwise around the circle when kicking with the inside of the right foot or the outside of the left foot and counterclockwise when using the inside of the left foot or the outside of the right foot.

In teaching the trapping skills, trapping with the sole of the foot should precede trapping with both feet. After watching the demonstration of each trap, students attempt the traps on a slowly moving ball. As skill increases, the trap should be practiced in conjunction with a kick and a dribble. Practice should also include trapping a fast moving ball.

For preliminary drills in trapping, the class may be divided into groups which form two lines facing each other about 10 feet apart at staggered intervals. The first player in line 1 passes to the first person in line 2, who traps the ball and then passes to the next person in line 1.

The presentation of blocking or body trapping should include chest blocking and blocking with the thighs or abdomen. A drill in blocking may be devised from the same shuttle formation suggested for practicing trapping. The toss of the ball to the blockers may be made for the special type of block which is being practiced; for variety, the students may be allowed to toss the ball for any type of block so that the blockers will not have a chance to anticipate the block.

Heading the ball is introduced with a demonstration, followed by practice heading a tossed ball. For this the class may be placed in short lines or in circles with a leader tossing the ball to each person in turn. The first practice of heading should be of short duration. It is recommended that volleyballs be used in place of the harder soccer balls for heading until the techniques are well mastered.

Tackling should be practiced first on a rolling' ball, then on a player dribbling slowly down the field, and, finally, on a player dribbling at full speed.

To practice on a rolling ball, the class may be divided into groups of 12 to 14 players. The players face each other in lines 15 feet apart. The first player in line 1 kicks the ball slowly toward the first player in the opposite line, who advances to tackle the imaginary opponent in possession of the ball. He then kicks the ball toward the second person in line 1, and in this manner the ball is played back and forth down the lines.

The formation for a drill which offers excellent practice in timing the tackling and in passing to avoid the tackle consists of two lines facing each other 10 feet apart. The first two players advance, dribbling and passing the ball toward the player who is stationed about 15 feet out. This player attempts to tackle while the other two try to avoid being tackled. If the number of players in the formation is small, the rotation of players can wait until the end of the line; otherwise, they may be shifted after several attempted tackles.

Timing is the most important factor in successful punting; therefore, the teacher should stress the rhythmic pattern of the punt when demonstrating it for the first time. Simple line formations with the two lines facing each other 25 yards apart may be used to practice punting back and forth from stationary positions.

Evaluation

The tests for soccer include ability tests in the fundamental skills. Scores can be compared with others taking the test.

Test 1—Kicking and Trapping

A line is drawn 5 to 10 feet from an unobstructed wall. Standing behind the line, the player kicks the ball against the wall as many times as he can in 60 seconds. The player may kick the ball in front of the line but he cannot score with that kick.

Test 2—Dribbling

Four chairs are arranged in a line 4 yards apart. A line is drawn five yards from the first chair. Starting from behind the line, the player dribbles the length of the chairs, passing between the chairs. At the end of the line of chairs, the player turns and dribbles back, again going between the chairs. The score is the time required to complete the dribble.

Test 3—Punting for Distance

Each player punts from behind a restraining line. The score is the longest kick out of three attempts.

Test 4—Kick for Accuracy

Three circles 2 feet in diameter, labeled 1 to 3, are drawn on an unobstructed wall. They are placed so that the circles are on different vertical and horizontal planes. The kicker has six trials to hit the targets (two per target) from a distance of 25 feet. A point is given for each successful hit on a target. The maximum number of points that may be earned from hitting any one target is two.

VOLLEYBALL AND LEAD-UP GAMES

Volleyball, like most team games, is a more effective teaching tool at the higher grades than at the lower ones. However, the skills of striking a ball with the hands can be taught to the younger children, using soft rubber balls as substitutes for volleyballs. Other skills related to volleyball may be taught through the lead-up or basic games of Newcomb, Wall Volley, Volleyball Fungo, and Four Squares as early as the third and fourth grades.

FUNDAMENTAL TECHNIQUES AND SKILLS

A volleyball game is not very successful unless players have a good foundation of skills. The skills must be taught with attention to proper techniques of ball control.

Serving (Grades 5–8)

The underhand method of serving is the most easily mastered and is a very effective serve. In this serve, the right-handed server places the left foot ahead of the other. The ball is held in the palm and fingers of the left hand slightly below the waist. The right hand is held with the fingers closed so that the tips come near the base of the fingers. The right arm is swung backward, the knees are bent forward, and the entire body pivots to the left. As the arm is brought down, the body twists back around to the left. The ball is hit below its center with the heel of the hand. The knees are straightened as the ball is hit, and the arm follows through forward and upward.

Volleying (Grades 5–8)

The manner in which a player handles a ball will depend on how the ball is coming to the player. Usually the balls will be dropping from overhead. If the ball is above the head, the thumbs are placed close together and the ball is played with the hands over and slightly in front of the head. Only the fingers and thumb come in contact with the ball as it is deflected into the air. The ball must bounce from the hands. It cannot be carried momentarily. If the ball has fallen below the waist before it is struck, the arms must come under the ball below the waist. The hands, clenched into fists, are brought together; contact with the ball is made with the thumbs and wrists to propel the ball upward and forward.

Spiking and Setting-Up (Grades 7–8)

A spike can be made only when the ball is close to and higher than the net. The spiker must jump up to make the hit. He should hit the ball near its top, sending it downward into the court of the opposing team.

In setting-up a player bats the ball high into the air near the net in his own court to enable the spiker to spike it. By the time older children have developed the skill of spiking, they may be expected not to play the ball into the opponents' court until it has been set up.

LEAD-UP GAMES FOR VOLLEYBALL

Newcomb (Grades 4–5)

DESCRIPTION OF GAME. Two teams are on opposite sides of a volleyball net with six to eight players on a side. The game consists of throwing a volleyball back and forth over the net. The ball is thrown over the net from the spot where it was caught. To start the game the ball is thrown from the end line. A score is made when a team fails to catch a thrown ball that lands in its playing area. If the ball is thrown out of bounds, the other team scores a point. The winner is the team which first scores 15 points.

TABLE 12-7 Volleyball Correction Chart

Technique	Common Error	Probable Result	Correction
Serving	Failing to hit ball in proper place	Ball hits net	Make contact with ball below its center near completion of arm swing
Volleying	Failing to handle ball on cushions of finger tips	Loss of control of ball	Contact ball on cushions of finger tips and with fingers slightly flexed
	Carrying ball momentarily	Loss of serve or point	Make sharp contact with ball; avoid giving with ball as it contacts fingers
	Knocking ball back to opponents on first volley	Loss of opportunity to spike ball	Volley ball high into air close to net
Spiking	Failing to hit ball on its top to drive it downward into opponents' court	Ball goes into net or high into opponents' court	Jump sufficiently high into air for hand to make contact near top of ball
	Failing to time jump to be at height of jump when striking ball	Ball goes into net or high into opponents' court	Time jump to be at its height when ball is slightly higher than net

Volleyball Fungo (Grades 3–4)

DESCRIPTION OF GAME. Ten to 15 players take a random formation facing a player who is to be the batter. The batter, with a clenched fist, strikes the ball, knocking it toward the players. The player who catches the ball exchanges places with the batter.

TABLE 12-8 Problem-Solving: Sample Subproblems for Teaching Serving, Setting Up, and Spiking a Volleyball

1. Where are the feet placed while serving underhand? *Variable*—space; *Variation*—together, spread apart, or one in front of the other.
2. How is the ball held in the non-serving hand? *Variable*—space; *Variation*—on palm, fingertips, or palm and fingertips.
3. How is the serving hand held? *Variable*—space; *Variation*—fingers closed, open hand, or tightly closed fist.
4. Where is the ball hit so that it will go high over the net? *Variable*—space; *Variation*—near the top of the ball or under the ball.
5. How hard is the arm swung in hitting the ball in an underhand serve? *Variable*—force; *Variation*—soft to extremely hard.
6. What part of the hand makes contact with the ball in volleying? *Variable*—space; *Variation*—palm, fingertips, or palm and fingertips.
7. How high above the net should the ball be set for a spike? *Variable*—space; *Variation*—several feet above the net to just above the net.
8. What part of the ball is hit on a spike? *Variable*—space; *Variation*—near the top to near the bottom.
9. When should the jump be made in relation to the ball in making a spike? *Variable*—time; *Variation*—as the ball is going up to as the ball is coming down.
10. How hard should the ball be spiked? *Variable*—force; *Variation*—soft to very hard.

Wall Volley (Grades 4–5)

DESCRIPTION OF GAME. The available wall space limits the number who can participate. Players volley the ball against the wall above a line 6 feet high which is marked on the wall. The number of times a player volleys the ball successfully constitutes his score. With older students, the score may be determined by the number of volleys in a 30 second time limit.

One Bounce Volleyball (Grades 4–5)

DESCRIPTION OF GAME. Two teams composed of any number of players are stationed one on each side of the net. The volleyball is put into play with a serve. The receiving team may let the ball bounce once before batting it back. The ball may bounce only once before being returned over the net. Any number of players may play the ball one time before it is hit over the net. A score is made when the receiving team fails to return the ball over the net within bounds. The receiving team gets the ball for service when the serving team misses. Team members rotate before each serve as in volleyball.

Circle Formation Volley (Grades 5–6)

DESCRIPTION OF GAME. There are six to eight players in a circle with any number of circles. The ball is volleyed from player to player around the circle to the right and then to the left.

Line Formation Volley (Grades 5–6)

DESCRIPTION OF GAME. Two lines are formed of six to eight players in each line. A volleyball is used. The leaders of the lines face each other about 10 to 15 feet apart. Other members line up behind the leaders, one behind the other. One leader throws the volleyball to the first player in the opposite line and then runs to the end of his line. The receiver volleys the ball back to the other line and then retires to the end of his line. Volleying continues back and forth.

Keep It Up (Grades 5–6)

DESCRIPTION OF GAME. Ten to 40 children can play this game in an area a minimum of 30 by 30 feet. A volleyball will be required for each team. Players are formed into two or more teams with five or six players on each team. Each team is in single circle formation facing center with a distance of 2 to 3 feet between team members. Each team has a volleyball which it endeavors to keep in the air by batting. The team keeping its ball up the longest wins 1 point. The team earning the most points within the playing period is the winner.

Teaching Hints. Players should be taught to hit the ball with the tips of all the fingers, with the elbows turned outward, and to lift the ball with both arm and leg extension much as the set-up in volleyball is executed. The ball must be clearly hit and not caught and then pushed.

VOLLEYBALL
(Grades 5–8)

The net for volleyball is 6 feet in height for players in the fifth and sixth grades and 6 1/2 feet for seventh and eighth graders. Teams may be composed of from 6 to 12 players. If 6 players compose a team, they form two rows; if 8 or more players, they form three rows.

The game begins by serving the ball anywhere behind the back boundary line. The ball is served by striking the ball with the hand. Each team member serves in turn and may have one trial to serve the ball over the net. The server continues to serve until his team fails to return the ball; then the serve passes to the opposing team.

The ball must be batted. It cannot be momentarily caught. Each team has three hits to return the ball over the net. The net may not be touched by any player while the ball is in play. No player may hit the ball twice in succession. All offensive players rotate clockwise one position when a new player begins to serve. One point is scored if the receiving team fails to return the ball. The receiving team gets the ball to serve but does not score if the serving team fails to return the ball.

MODIFICATIONS. The serve goes automatically to the opponents if 5 consecutive points are scored by one server. If a server does not have the power to get the ball over the net, he may be permitted to move up to a mark which is 25 feet from the net.

Sequence of Teaching Rules and Regulations

A suggested sequence of presenting the rules to beginning players is listed below, together with the recommended grades in which the rules may first be introduced. If play of the game begins at the fifth grade, as recommended, the more complex rules can be ignored until students reach the higher grade level indicated.

Teaching Sequence

Rule or Regulation	*Grade*
Nature of the court	4
Out-of-bounds rules	4
Position of players	5
Rotation of players	5
Serving rules	5
Ball-handling rules	5
Net rules	6
Court dimensions	7

Teaching Procedures

The teacher may use the problem-solving method to assist the students in determining the most effective way to control the ball; or he may use the direct method, beginning with demonstrations of the skill, followed by diagnosis of movement in performance and direction to overcome movement errors.

Ball-handling is the basis of good volleyball, and it can best be developed by repeatedly handling the ball. Many types of activities can be devised to provide such opportunities. The most effective are those that give everyone a chance to handle the ball many times rather than waiting around for a turn to play, which is so often the case in game situations.

A good ball-handling activity for beginners consists of students' lining up 8 to 10 feet from the wall to volley the ball against the wall as rapidly as possible. This activity is most effective if there are plenty of balls and large areas of unobstructed wall surface.

Another good activity is the circle volley drill. For this six to eight players form a circle. One of the players begins by tossing the ball into the air to the player beside him who volleys it to the next person. This is repeated around the circle as many times as desired.

The straight underhand serve should be taught first to beginners as it is the easiest to master and is, at the same time, extremely effective. Following the explanation and demonstration on serving techniques, the class may be divided into two lines facing each other about 30 feet apart to explore or practice the serve. The ball is served back and forth from one side to another with each player having an opportunity to serve. After the skills are developed sufficiently, the distance between the lines can be increased to 55 or 60 feet, which approximates the serving requirements in game situations.

For the upper grades setting up a spike may be included in the unit. Practice in setting up may be accomplished in circle formations of six to eight players. The ball is played high into the air from one player to the next around the circle, simulating the set-up.

Evaluation

Since volleying and serving are two of the most important skills in volleyball, evaluation of ability in these skills is helpful in assessing a player's total performance. Two tests are recommended as good indicators of ability in these skills.

Test 1—Accuracy Serve Test

The receiving court is divided in half by a line drawn parallel to the net. The back half is divided into three equal parts. The server stands behind the serving line and attempts to serve into one of the three sections. A ball that lands in one of the two outside sections scores two points; one that lands in the center section scores one point. Ten serves are allowed. The score is the total number of points.

Test 2—Wall Volleying

A line is drawn 4 feet from an unobstructed wall. Another line is drawn on the wall parallel to the floor 6 or 6 1/2 feet above the floor. The student stands behind the line and attempts to make as many volleys against the wall as possible in 30 seconds. He may volley the ball when in front of the line, but the volley does not count in the scoring. The total score is the number of volleys made in 30 seconds from behind the line that strikes the wall above the mark.

TOUCH FOOTBALL AND LEAD-UP GAMES

Touch football is very popular among students at the elementary level. Instruction usually commences at the fifth or sixth grade. Care should be taken that the student be familiar with the correct form of falling before attempting to play touch football. The emphasis should be upon learning the touch football skills and appropriate rules and not upon developing successful team play.

FUNDAMENTAL TECHNIQUES AND SKILLS

The fundamental skills of touch football that are usually taught in the elementary school are passing, pass catching, centering and kicking. In addition the running and dodging techniques are emphasized as are the tagging skills. Blocking is usually not taught to elementary school students.

Passing (Grades 5–8)

Because of their smaller hand size, children below the seventh grade should use a junior football; seventh and eighth graders have sufficient grip to use a regulation football.

In making a forward pass, the ball is grasped at the end of the football. The fingers are well spread. The throwing arm is brought back behind the ear and slightly above it. The weight is on the rear foot. The arm is then brought forward close to the head, and finally fully extended as the ball is released with a wrist snap and the weight shifted to the forward foot.

In throwing to a receiver who is running, the ball is thrown in front of the receiver so that it will be an arm's length in front of him when he reaches that spot.

Figure 12–9 The proper grip using a junior football.

Pass Receiving (Grades 5–8)

A pass should be caught in the fingers, never with the body. Whenever possible, both hands are used to catch the ball. The arms should give as the ball comes in contact with the hands. After the ball is securely caught with the fingers, it is brought to the body.

In a game situation there is a greater possibility of the pass not being knocked down by a pass defensive player if the receiver can get into the open. A *change of pace* is a good technique to use for eluding a defensive man. The receiver runs at moderate speed; as he comes near the defensive man, he puts on a burst of speed, passing the defensive man before he can adjust his speed.

Centering (Grades 5–8)

The center pass is an underhand pass which is thrown between the spread legs. The same grip is taken on the ball with the throwing hand as in passing. The opposite hand rests lightly along the opposite side and to the rear of the ball to act as guide. The pass is made with the arm and wrist.

A modification that may be used in touch football is the side center. The player stands to the side of the ball and bends over and grasps the ball by the point as it rests on the ground. The ball is snapped in a sweeping motion of the arm so that it is thrown back and up to a backfield player.

Kicking (Grades 5–8)

The punt is the most frequently used kick. The ball should be held about waist high. For kicking with the right foot, the right hand is held under the ball at

Figure 12–10 A teacher shows a player the correct placement for the ball prior to centering. (Courtesy of Ox Ridge Elementary School, Darien, Connecticut.)

TABLE 12–9 Touch Football Correction Chart

Technique	Common Error	Probable Result	Correction
Passing	Balancing ball on hand	Ball is pushed rather than thrown, falls short of its goal and/or goes wide of its mark	Grasp ball at one end; if ball is too large to do this easily select a smaller ball
	Failing to snap the wrist	Ball lacks speed and "floats" through air	Snap wrist forward as ball is released to impart a spin to it
Pass Receiving	Standing still while receiving ball	Pass is intercepted	Keep moving so that passer has to lead receiver
	Catching ball in arms and against body	Ball bounces off body and is not caught	Catch ball on cushions of finger tips
Punting	Tossing ball into air	Foot does not make contact with ball correctly	Drop ball from a few inches above point where foot will contact it
	Flexing toe	Ball goes straight into air	Point toe
Place Kicking	Taking eyes off ball before kick is completed	Ball goes wide of its mark or is too low	Keep eyes on ball throughout kick and continue to watch spot where ball was for a fraction of a second after kick

about the center of the ball. The left hand is on the front end and to the side of the ball. In kicking the ball, one step is taken forward with the left foot. The right leg should start the swing forward with the knee slightly bent. The toe is pointed inward slightly. The ball should be dropped a very short distance before the foot comes in contact with it. The ball falls upon the instep. Contact is made about knee high and the foot continues to follow through to finish above the head.

In a place kick the ball is held for the kicker by a teammate. The holder places the point of the ball on the ground with the fingers of one hand on the top of the ball. The ball is tilted slightly toward the kicker. The kicker runs forward two or three steps and stops so that his left foot is approximately 6 inches behind and to the left of the ball. His right foot comes forward in a swinging arc and makes contact slightly below the center of the ball with his toe.

LEAD-UP GAMES FOR TOUCH FOOTBALL

Hot Potato (Grades 5–6)

DESCRIPTION OF GAME. Any number of participants form a circle and a ball is handed around counterclockwise. When the teacher calls "Hot," the player who has the ball is given 1 point. The player who has accumulated the least number of points after a designated period of play wins the game. To speed up the game several balls can be passed at one time.

TABLE 12–10 Problem-Solving: Sample Subproblems for Teaching Passing, Receiving, Centering, and Kicking a Football

1. Where is the ball gripped in passing? *Variable*—space; *Variation*—from in the middle to near the end.
2. How is the wrist used in passing? *Variable*—flow; *Variation*—held stiff to a sharp snap.
3. With what part of the body is the ball caught? *Variable*—space; *Variation*—arms and body, fingers and palm, or tips of the fingers.
4. What movement do the arms make when the ball is caught? *Variable*—flow; *Variation*—stationary to giving with the ball.
5. Where is the ball thrown in making a pass in relation to the runner that is to receive it? *Variable*—space; *Variation*—at the runner or in front of him—above his waist or below his waist.
6. How is the wrist of the dominant arm used in centering? *Variable*—flow; *Variation*—held stiff to a sharp snap.
7. Where should the ball be held in preparation for a punt? *Variable*—space; *Variation*—from above to below the waist.
8. How is the kicking leg moved? *Variable*—flow; *Variation*—swing through straight or with bent knee.
9. What position should the toe be in when the ball is kicked? *Variable*—space; *Variation*—90 degrees to as straight as possible.
10. In a place kick where should the ball be contacted by the foot? *Variable*—space; *Variation*—from near the top to near the bottom.

Five Step Football (Grades 5–6)

DESCRIPTION OF GAME. Two end lines are established 200 feet apart. Two teams with any number of players are at opposite ends of the playing area defending their end line. One team puts the football into play 70 feet from its end line by passing or kicking it toward the opponents. The opposing team attempts to catch the ball. At the point where the ball is first touched by the opponents, it is thrown or kicked back.

If a player catches the ball, he may take five steps forward before throwing or punting it back. Opponents cannot come closer than 10 yards to a kicker or passer. The game is won when a pass or kick that is not caught is made over the opponent's end line. The player touching the ball must make the kick or pass.

TOUCH FOOTBALL
(Grades 5–8)

The number of team members may vary from six to nine. The boys who play on the line of scrimmage are known as linemen. On a nine man team there must be at least five linemen (two ends, two guards and a center); for a six man team there must be three linemen. The remaining members make up the backfield.

The ball is first put into play by a team kicking the ball from the 10 yard line on their side of midfield. The opponents cannot cross over the center line. At all other times the ball is put into play from the line of scrimmage by a center pass to a backfield man. As a substitute for the center pass, the player may squat beside the ball and toss it back to a backfield player.

The line of scrimmage is an imaginary line which extends from the spot where the ball rests to both side lines. A team must advance the ball 10 yards in four downs or lose the ball to the other team; or the game may be played that the ball must be advanced the length of the field in six downs.

After the ball has been centered, it may be advanced forward by running with it or passing it to a teammate. Only one forward pass may be made in each play, and it must be thrown from behind the line of scrimmage. An incompleted pass is counted as a down and the ball is put into play from its original position. A backward or lateral pass may be made anywhere on the field.

The ball is dead when the ball carrier is touched by an opponent. Handkerchiefs or flags may be carried under the belt in the back of each player, and pulling the flag from the belt may be substituted for touching.

The player who is blocking must stay on his feet throughout the block. In touch football the only blocking permitted should be that of getting in front of the opposing player to prevent his getting the ball. Pushing and use of the shoulders should not be permitted. The blocker may not use his hands in any way.

Six points are scored when the ball is advanced over the goal line. The team with the highest number of points at the end of the playing period wins.

Flag Football (Grades 5–8)

Flag football is played in the same way as touch football except for the manner in which a player is tagged. In flag football, players wear a special belt to which a flag (strip of heavy cloth) is snapped, or they tuck the end of the flag in a pocket. Instead of tagging a player, the flag is pulled from the pocket or belt. The ball is down at the point where the removal occurs.

Figure 12-11 In the game of Flag Football, flags are worn on the belt or tucked into a back pocket. (Courtesy of Ox Ridge Elementary School, Darien, Connecticut.)

Sequence of Teaching Rules and Regulations

A suggested sequence of presenting the rules to beginning players is listed below, together with the recommended grades in which the rules may first be introduced. If play of the game begins at the fifth grade, as recommended, the more complex rules can be ignored until students reach the higher grade level indicated.

Teaching Sequence

Rule or Regulation	Grade
General nature of differences between touch football and football	5
Putting the ball into play	5
Out-of-bounds rules	5
Receiving and advancing ball	5
Incomplete pass rule	5
Scoring	5
Positions	5
Off-side	5
Line of scrimmage	5
Field marking	6
Kick-off	6
Penalty plays	7
Formations	7

Teaching Procedures

The instruction in the skills can begin with passing and receiving, since these phases of the game have strong appeal to most students. The explanation and demonstration of the grip for passing should be presented first if the direct method is used; otherwise, exploration of how to achieve the most effective grip is encouraged by posing appropriate subproblems (see Table 12–10). Because there will probably not be enough balls for everyone to have one, several students may be assigned to use one ball.

For experience in passing, the class may form two lines facing each other 20 to 30 feet apart. The first person in line 1 begins by passing to the first person in line 2, who catches it and passes it back to the second person in line 1. The ball is passed back and forth down the line until all have had a turn.

An activity for practice in centering may be provided by dividing the class into groups of four or less. Each student takes a turn centering the ball to another person in his group. The skill should be practiced at 10 feet from the receiver, at 5 feet, and, if the standard style of centering is taught, from the T formation.

For practice in punting and punt receiving, the class may be organized into two lines facing each other at a distance of 25 to 30 yards. The first person in line 1 punts to the first person in line 2, who catches it and punts it to the second person in the line opposite. Punting continues back and forth down the lines.

In organizing teams for class competition it is well to put players of equal ability on a team and to have teams of equal ability play each other. If the small size of the class limits the division into teams, the distribution of skilled and less skilled should be made as evenly as possible.

Plays for the game should be introduced in the general discussion of team strategy. The teacher should plan two or three simple plays with which everyone in the class can easily become familiar. The explanation of the plays should be clarified by diagraming them on the blackboard. When possible, it is highly desirable to have the plays mimeographed for class distribution so that the students will have them for reference later as they plot their own team plays.

Evaluation

General ability in touch football may be evaluated subjectively in game situations. However, specific skill tests may be used to provide more objective evidence of ability in certain skills. Some of the tests used in skill evaluation are described below:

Test 1 — Pass Receiving

The player runs down the field a designated distance (15 to 25 yards) and cuts to either right or left to receive a pass from a thrower who stands at the point where the runner started. Each receiver has five tries and scores one point for each successful catch. Failure to catch a pass that was not within reasonable catching distance does not count as a try.

Test 2 — Passing

A tire is suspended by two ropes from the goal posts. The passer stands 10 to 30 yards away. The tire is swung back and forth. The passer must throw the ball through the tire while it is swinging. The score is the number of successful passes in 10 attempts.

Test 3 — Punting for Distance

The kicker stands behind a line and punts the ball as far as possible. The score is the distance the ball is punted. The distance is measured to the spot where the ball lands, not to which it rolls.

TRACK AND FIELD

Track and field events have not been popular physical education activities at the elementary level. However, interest in track and field is readily generated, especially if the school sponsors an interscholastic sports program that includes track and field. A unit of track and field provides additional opportunities to teach the basic skills of running, jumping, and throwing.

FUNDAMENTAL TECHNIQUES AND SKILLS

There are three distinct types of events in track and field: running various distances, jumping, and throwing. Teaching of track and field generally starts in the fifth or sixth grade; however, the basic skills of running, jumping, and throwing should be established before students reach the fifth grade.

All of the events should be taught to every child. If this is not possible, at least one event of each type should be presented. Once a child has been exposed to and learned the fundamentals of each type of event, he may be encouraged to select one or more of the events for concentrated work. Such concentration occurs more frequently in the upper grades than in the middle grades.

Sprints (Grades 4–8)

The most common events in a track and field meet on the upper elementary school level are the 50-, 60- or 100-yard sprints, distance runs of 440 or 500 yards, the running long jump, the high jump, and the shot put or softball throw.

To start the running of short distances, a sprint style starting stance is used. If there are no starting blocks available for use, two holes are dug in which the runner may place the toes of each foot. To determine where the holes should be dug (or where the starting blocks should be placed), the runner faces away from the direction in which he is to run and places the heel of the right foot at the starting line and the left foot directly ahead with the heel touching the right toe. The first hole is dug under the middle of the left foot. The right foot is placed even with the center of the hole on the left side and the heel of the left foot is placed against the toe of the right. The second hole is made under the center of the left foot.

At the command by the starter of "Go to your marks," the runner places his toes into the holes with the left foot in the front hole. The knee of the rear leg is placed on the ground. The thumbs and fingers are placed adjacent to the starting line. The arms are held parallel with the elbows locked. On the command of

Figure 12–12 The sprinting start may be practiced inside when the weather is inclement. (Courtesy of Town of Vernon Schools, Rockville, Connecticut.)

"Get set," the knee is lifted off the ground and the hips are raised so they are slightly higher than the shoulders. A portion of the weight of the body is balanced on the hands and the eyes are focused down the track to the finish line. At the command of "Go," both legs drive with the back leg coming forward immediately after the drive.

As the front leg continues to drive while in the hole, the rear foot lands a few inches in front of the starting line. The actions of the arms are opposite to the legs; the left arm comes forward as the right leg is brought forward. The body is kept low in the first few steps; with each successive step the body will be straightened to the proper sprinting angle. The body should not be straightened before six or seven steps have been taken.

The sprinting stride is described in Chapter 8. When coming to the end of the run, the speed should not be slowed nor the stride shortened until after the runner "breaks the tape." The runner should practice running through the tape.

Distance Running (Grades 5–8)

For running longer distances it is not as important to get as fast a start as in sprinting so that a standing start is frequently used to conserve energy. This start is described in Chapter 8. The stride that is used is also described in that chapter.

Distance running requires extensive conditioning. Interval training is a popular type of conditioning among distance runners. Basically it consists of running at a set speed for a stipulated distance and then walking about four times the distance of the run. The sequence is repeated several times. It is desirable that the walking distance should be such that, at the end of the walking period, breathing has nearly returned to normal.

Long Jump (Grades 5–8)

In the long jump the jumper must run toward the take-off board before jumping. The length of the run is determined by the distance the jumper needs to gain top speed. For older children it will be 90 to 100 feet. For younger children the distance will be less. In order to assure stepping off the take-off board with the correct foot, the jumper should adjust his run to the right distance. He may mark one to three check points along the run to help him to step on the board correctly. As he approaches the take-off board, he must slow down slightly before jumping. This allows him to prepare to raise the body off the ground. On the step before the take-off the weight of the body is lowered by going down to the heel of the foot. On the take-off the jumper lands heel first and then rocks up on the toe as the leg straightens to force him up into the air. Once in the air the jumper maintains balance and extends the feet forward as far as possible. The landing is made on the heels and the body is brought forward, bringing the weight on the hands and knees.

High Jump (Grades 6–8)

In the high jump the barrel roll style is very effective and is one of the most common and easiest styles to develop. The approach to the bar should not be over seven steps. The jumper approaches the bar from the left at about a 30 to 45 degree angle to the cross bar. The take-off should be made at about arm's length from the bar. In approaching the bar the steps are short and are made on the balls of the feet. At the next to the last step before jumping, a flat footed step is taken with the right foot where the heel comes in contact with the ground. The left foot lands heel first with the knee bent. As the body moves forward over the take-off leg (left), the leg is straightened and the body is driven into the air. The right leg aids the upward motion by swinging up toward the bar. The arms are swung up in front of the body. At the peak of the jump, the jumper faces the bar and goes over on his stomach. As he goes over the bar, he straddles it. Then as the left leg is lifted over the bar, the clearance is completed. The right leg is dropped so that the landing will be made on the right foot and both hands.

Shot Put (Grades 6–8)

A 12 or 8 pound shot is used for upper elementary school participants. The beginner throws from a stationary position. The shot is held in the right hand at the base of the three middle fingers, balanced on the sides by the thumb and little finger. It is raised to rest against the neck on the collarbone and along the jawbone. The elbow is bent and the shot is held with the fingers pointing up. The beginner should put the shot from a standing position. A stance is taken with the left side facing the direction of the intended put or throw. The feet are spread with the left foot forward; the weight is shifted to the back leg which should be bent at the knee. The front or left leg is kept fairly straight and it slides forward as the body goes back to maintain balance. The trunk is bent over the right knee. The right knee is then forcefully extended bringing the body forward. As the body swings forward, the right leg will be pulled forward up to the leg. The shot moves with the body until the body weight is over the left leg. The elbow is straightened and the wrist and fingers are extended to propel the shot upward and forward. The shot should be pushed rather than thrown.

Softball Throw (Grades 4–8)

The softball throw is sometimes substituted for the shot put event. Techniques for throwing the softball are described in Chapter 8.

Passing the Baton (Grades 6–8)

Passing the baton is an important skill in relay racing. The open or sight pass is the one most frequently recommended for use by elementary school children. In this pass the outgoing runner must time his departure to permit the incoming runner to overtake him quickly. The incoming runner holds the baton in his left hand well ahead of his body where his teammate can grasp it easily. The outgoing runner reaches back with the right hand palm up and turns his head to watch the baton exchange. As he receives the baton, he turns his head to look down the track. He switches the baton from his right to his left hand in preparation for passing it to the next runner.

TABLE 12–11   Track and Field Correction Chart

Technique	Common Error	Probable Result	Correction
Starting	Taking a long strike in first step	Slow acceleration	Make first step land just a few inches in front of starting line
	Toeing out in first step	Balance is lost	Place foot with toes pointing straight ahead
Running	Allowing arms to flop at sides	Body moves from side to side	Bend elbows at right angles
	Crossing arms over chest	Body moves from side to side	Reach forward with each arm as if grasping for something in front
	Rearing head far back	Shortened stride	Look down track to finish line
	Throwing rear foot to outside as it drives off ground	Slower running speed	Hold leg straight out behind and then bring it forward in recovery for another step
Long Jumping	Failing to bring take-off foot down on take-off board	Feet go over board and jump doesn't count; or distance of jump is reduced	Use check points along run to insure proper position for take-off
	Trying to exert force forward rather than up on take-off	Distance of jump is reduced because height was not gained	Jump up on take-off foot and allow speed of run to carry body forward
High Jumping	Running with too much speed toward bar	Bar is knocked off due to lack of height	Slow speed while running forward
	Failing to come down on heel of foot on next to last step and on take-off	Insufficient spring to gain necessary height	Drop down on heel on last step and on take-off
	Failing to lift trailing leg	Bar is knocked off by trailing leg	Lift trailing leg as opposite leg is brought down
Putting Shot	Failing to hold shot on base of fingers	Lack of wrist snap	Place shot at base of three middle fingers, balanced on side of thumb and little finger
	Attempting to throw shot instead of putting it	Injury to arm	Keep elbow behind shot as it is brought forward for release

Teaching Procedures

The class should be organized so that all members have an opportunity to participate and develop skill in all the events presented. One effective way of doing this is to divide the class into the same number of groups as the number of events being taught. In this way after the skills are demonstrated and discussed with the entire class, each group can form to work on the skills of the specific event assigned to it. After several class periods, the students rotate to

TABLE 12–12   Problem Solving: Sample Subproblems for Teaching the Long Jump, High Jump, and Shot Put

1. What distance should the jumper run before the take-off? *Variable*—space; *Variation*—from short to long distance.
2. How are the leg and foot moved on the step before the take-off? *Variable*—flow; *Variation*—on the toe, flatfooted, or on the heel.
3. At what angle does the high jumper approach the bar in the barrel roll style? *Variable*—space; *Variation*—from straight on to near a 10 degree angle.
4. How are the leg and foot moved on the next to the last step in the high jump? *Variable*—flow; *Variation*—before the weight moves over the planted foot, when the weight is over the planted foot, or after the weight has moved over the planted foot.
5. How is the body held as the jumper goes over the bar? *Variable*—space; *Variation*—the trunk is straight or in a tuck; straddle the bar or legs together.
6. How is the landing made in the high jump? *Variable*—flow; *Variation*—on hands, hands and one leg, both legs, or all fours.
7. How is the shot held in the hand? *Variable*—space; *Variation*—from on the palm to balancing on the fingers.
8. Where is the shot put rested in preparation for the put? *Variable*—space; *Variation*—held out from the body or resting against the neck.
9. How are the arms and fingers used in propelling the shot? *Variable*—flow; *Variation*—elbow straightened and the wrist and fingers extended, elbow used without wrist and fingers, or elbow used without one or the other (wrist or fingers).

work at a different skill. The teacher moves from group to group to observe and assist those in need of help.

The running events can be taught to the entire class at one time. If it is a large class and the number of running lanes is limited, the class may be lined up several deep in each line to run in waves for the sprints and middle distances.

If the track and field skills are to be taught with the problem-solving method, a set of subproblems will need to be developed for each skill (see Table 12–12). Students may work alone or with a partner to solve the problems. The teacher moves among the students to watch them resolve the problems. If necessary, new subproblems are offered to help a child in re-evaluation of answers to previous problems to determine if the most effective solution to the major problem has been reached.

CONDUCTING TRACK AND FIELD MEETS

The learning of the skills of a game is culminated in the playing of the game itself, but track and field skills are not so directly applicable in a game situation. Consequently, a track and field meet is frequently planned to offer youngsters the fun and opportunity of trying their newly acquired skills in a series of competitive track and field events. The meets may be intra-class, intramural, or interscholastic.

The organization of a meet requires that certain details must be cared for in advance of the day of the meet. For intra-class competition such planning may be included in the lesson planning; however, the plans for intramural and interscholastic meets may need to be more elaborate and to be made far enough in advance of the chosen day to allow the teams involved sufficient time to prepare for participation.

A general announcement about the meet should be sent to the participating schools no later than a month before date of the meet. The announcement may include these items of information:

1. The date, place, and time of the meet.
2. The events and the approximate time that each will begin.
3. The eligibility requirements; the number of entrants permitted, and the number of events each person may enter.
4. The method of scoring which will be used.
5. The awards to be given (if any).
6. A request to return the enclosed entry blank by a specified date indicating on it the number of participants in each event.

For the safety of the participants and for efficiency in conducting the meet, certain rules for the conduct of the meet should be subscribed to. The rules which follow are recommended:

1. When a large number of teams is participating, the number of entries from each school may need to be limited to two for each event. However, unless the number of lanes and the amount of time are limiting factors, the number of participants should not be restricted; this is particularly true in intramural and intra-class meets.
2. No participant may be entered in more than two events in order to give greater opportunities to more students to participate and to protect participants from overexertion.
3. Each participant who enters the meet must have been in training for a minimum of three weeks previous to the meet and have had a medical examination.
4. No spike shoes are permitted to be worn unless all participants have them.
5. Participants are classified according to age or the McCoy Classification Index (see page 492). In some instances, classification according to sex will be necessary.
6. Three or five places may be awarded with the scoring as shown below:

5 points for first place	5 points for first place
4 points for second place	3 points for second place
3 points for third place	1 point for third place
2 points for fourth place	
1 point for fifth place	

7. If awards are given, they should be inexpensive tokens made in recognition of achievement. Ribbons or certificates are preferable.
8. The events are limited to sprints, distance runs, high and broad jumps, and shot put or softball throw.

Organization

The track and field must be prepared in advance of the meet. The lanes must be marked, the pits prepared, and the shot put or throwing area marked. The equipment which will need to be assembled and made ready includes high jump standards and bar, rakes, shovels, three stop watches, gun and blanks or whistle, cotton yarn for the finish tape, officials' badges, scoreboard, megaphone or loud speaker, tables and chairs, and pencils and paper for the scorers.

The shot put or throwing area should be roped off so spectators will not wander into the area and be exposed to possible injury from the thrown shot. Dressing rooms for each team should be labeled, and a place for the storage of valuables made available.

The number of running lanes available determines the number of participants who can run in a specified heat (a preliminary race). If there are six lanes and 34 runners, six heats will need to be run with six runners in four of the heats and five runners in the other two. Only the winner of each heat is chosen to participate in the final race.

Officials

The referee is the official in charge of the meet. He decides all questions in regard to the meet which are not definitely assigned to other officials.

In the running events, there should be a judge for each place that is to be picked. Each judge is then assigned to determine the winner of one particular place.

It is the job of the clerk of the course to notify the participants to appear at the starting line. He is in charge of establishing the heats and the drawing for lanes. The head scorer records the names of those who place and the order in which they finish.

Three timers are needed for each running event. The time as indicated by at least two of the watches is accepted as the correct time. If all three watches disagree, the watch having the middle time of the three times is accepted.

The starter is in charge of starting all running events. His commands will be, "Go to your marks," "Get set," followed by the firing of the gun or blowing of the whistle. A minimum of two seconds must elapse between the last command and the starting signal.

Field judges are in charge of the field events. There may be one judge for each event. The shot put or softball throw judge calls each participant when it is his time to put or throw. The judge must also be responsible for checking that the participant is behind the line or within the circle, that the distance of the effort is measured, and that the winner's name is reported to the scorer.

The high jump and long jump officials call the participants in turn; they must also check to see that the pit is properly prepared for each jump. In the long jump the judge must check on overstepping the take-off board. Both officials report the winners in their events to the scorer.

SUPPLEMENTARY READINGS

Bailey, Ian C., and Teller, Francis: *Soccer.* Philadelphia, W. B. Saunders Co., 1970.

Blake, Volp: *Lead-up Games to Team Sports.* Englewood Cliffs, New Jersey, Prentice-Hall, Inc., 1964.

Division of Girls' and Women's Sport: *Guides* (Various Sports) Washington, D.C., American Alliance for Health, Physical Education and Recreation. Published biennially.

Fait, Hollis F., et al.: *A Manual of Physical Education Activities.* Ed. 3. Philadelphia, W. B. Saunders Co., 1967.

Meyer, Margaret, and Schwarz, Marguerite M.: *Team Sports for Girls and Women.* Ed. 4. Philadelphia, W. B. Saunders Co., 1965.

Slaymaker, Thomas, and Brown, Virginia H.: *Power Volleyball.* Philadelphia, W. B. Saunders Co., 1970.

Vannier, Maryhelen, and Fait, Hollis F., editors: *Saunders Physical Activities Series* (Series of booklets on sports). Philadelphia, W. B. Saunders Co., 1969–1976.

Vannier, Maryhelen, and Poindexter, Hally Beth: *Individual and Team Sports for Girls and Women.* Ed. 3. Philadelphia, W. B. Saunders Co., 1974.

chapter thirteen

stunts and tumbling

ANIMAL STUNTS AND RELAYS
SELF-TESTING ACTIVITIES
STUNTS ON CLIMBING ROPES
TUMBLING AND BALANCING
PARACHUTE PLAY
PYRAMID BUILDING

Stunts and tumbling activities make a unique contribution to the physical fitness and motor skill development of elementary school children. General body conditioning and total physical fitness are promoted in the well organized unit of stunt and tumbling activities. The nature of these activities is such that they provide exercise for parts of the body which most other physical education activities leave undeveloped; a case in point is the shoulder girdle, the muscles of which are rarely sufficiently exercised except in stunts and tumbling activities. Moreover, these activities provide opportunities for developing flexibility and specific types of balancing abilities which most other activities fail to contribute to significantly.

Many stunts, from the simple animal relays to the most complex tumbling routines, encourage exploration of movement. For the very young, many of the stunts supply needed opportunities for imaginative play which relates the world of make-believe to their own.

The basic skills of falling correctly and controlling the body in positions other than on the feet are readily learned and developed in stunts and tumbling.

ORGANIZING FOR INSTRUCTION

Organization for instruction in these activities depends upon the method of instruction used by the teacher. Traditionally, stunts and tumbling have been taught by the direct method. The indirect method can be effectively employed, however; and many teachers use it with success particularly in teaching the basic skills of tumbling.

When the direct method is used, many of the activities can be introduced to the entire class at once; and then, as actual practice begins, the teacher may give individual instruction as needed. The introduction may be a demonstration of the stunt by the teacher or by a skilled student. The teacher should point out the essential elements of a successful performance in good form. Such verbal explanation should always be clear and concise. Wall charts and other visual aid materials illustrating the techniques of the stunt are also good for mass instruction.

For certain types of activities, such as the forward roll or cartwheel, the class can be lined up in rank file and moved forward to the mats to perform one at a time while the instructor observes and offers instruction as each individual takes his turn.

Activities such as the foot and toe balance which do not require forward movement can be taught in a circle formation. This enables the teacher to observe everyone easily and to move about the circle giving help to any who need further instruction. For advanced activities and more skilled students, the circuit technique of teaching may be utilized. The students are divided into groups according to the activity they are working on; for example, one group may be working on the hand stand, another on forward rolls, yet another on backward rolls. The teacher moves from group to group to instruct. In order for this to be successful, the students must have developed sufficient insight into the skill so that they are able to help each other and understand any hazards involved.

When the indirect method is utilized, the emphasis shifts from requiring the children to perform a skill in a specific way to encouraging them to discover ways of performing the skill effectively. This necessitates some changes in the organization of the instruction from that described above. The class organization is less formal, and questions and problems replace directions on how to accomplish the skills. The problems for stunts and tumbling should be designed so that they lead the child to explore movement that is consistent with his ability.

SELECTING ACTIVITIES

Activities are chosen to ensure progressive development of the students from kindergarten through eighth grade. Some activities build on others; that is, they utilize skills learned in activities presented earlier. It is, of course, essential to their safety that students be able to perform these lead-up skills before attempting the more complex skills. The activities described below have been arranged in order of their complexity so that those which are lead-up skills are presented before those activities which are comprised of one or more of the basic stunt skills.

Past experience and skill development need to be taken into consideration when selecting activities for any grade. As a general guide, the grade level at which each of the described activities may be presented is indicated. However, if the pupils in a given grade lack experience in these kinds of activities or are below average in physical development, they may not be ready for the indicated activities. On the other hand, their experience and development may be such that they are ready for much more advanced stunts and exercises. It should be pointed out, however, that almost any activity can be presented so that any age group will enjoy and profit from it; it is entirely possible, for example, for seventh and eighth graders to enjoy the animal relay games as much as kindergarten children if they are presented in a way that is appropriate to their years.

SAFETY

Before this unit of work begins, students should have an understanding of the general safety precautions: no horse play while performing; no shoving and pushing; no congregating around the performer. In addition many of the advanced activities require spotting by the teacher. Specific spotting techniques are given after the description of each activity for which spotting is necessary. Generally speaking, the spotter should place himself on the side to which the performer is likely to fall but out of the way of the performer, although, in trampolining a spotter is needed on each side of the trampoline. The support given to the performer by the spotter should be as light as possible and at the same time be effective in maintaining the position and safety of the performer. The procedure used for spotting is determined by the nature of the stunt; the four general procedures are holding, pushing, lifting, and catching the performer.

The teacher should be alert to signs of fatigue in performers. Periods of rest may be necessary to prevent overfatigue that often induces accidents.

Children should avoid lifting and supporting heavy loads, particularly in stunts requiring deep knee bends. It should not be assumed, as it frequently is, that heavy youngsters are capable of carrying heavy loads. Extremely overweight youngsters may suffer from weak epiphyseal lines (growth areas in the bone) and are, consequently, less capable of supporting heavy loads without injury than are children of less weight. Children working together on the couple stunts should be paired as nearly as possible according to size and weight.

EQUIPMENT

Many of the stunts require no equipment of any kind and can be done inside the gymnasium or in the classroom. Others need mats for safe and satisfying performance. Mats 5 by 7 feet in size are the most convenient. They are small enough to be easily moved from place to place but are large enough for most activities. They can be used singly for one man stunts and placed side by side for greater mat area when needed for dual or multiple stunts.

Trampolines smaller than regulation size are available for use with elementary school children. However, the regulation trampoline is much more effective for performing, and there is much less possibility of falling off the larger bed.

CARE OF EQUIPMENT.   Mats will last longer if they are properly handled. They should never be dragged across the floor as this causes undue wear. To move them properly, several students may carry them into place or a mat cart designed specifically to transport mats from place to place may be used.

Plastic mats and those treated with a rubberized paint are readily cleaned with soap and water. Trampolines require no special care except replacement of broken springs and worn canvas. These should be replaced immediately to avoid possible injuries to performers.

IMPROVISED EQUIPMENT.   Instructors in a school which does not have mats can improvise by using old mattresses, which can usually be acquired through donations. For sanitary purposes, these should be covered with plastic or cloth which can be washed as needed. Carts for transporting mats are easily constructed by nailing together boards to form a platform to which rollers are attached.

ANIMAL STUNTS AND RELAYS

Animal Stunts

DESCRIPTION OF ACTIVITY.   The animal stunts are imitative activities. No equipment is needed, and they may be performed almost anywhere, in the classroom, in the gymnasium, on the playing field. They may be performed as mass exercises or incorporated into relays as described below. The children should have developed some skill in the stunts before attempting relays.

VARIATIONS.   *Bunny Hop (K–2).*   A squatting position is taken with the hands on the floor between the feet. A hop is made forward, maintaining the position.

Elephant (K–2).   The child bends forward at the waist until the trunk is parallel to the floor. The hands are clasped in front and the arms swung from side to side as long lumbering steps are taken.

Lame Puppy Run (K–3).   The child bends forward to place both hands on the floor. The legs are bent slightly. Then one leg is lifted and the child moves about on his two hands and one foot.

Kangaroo Hop (K–3).   From a squatting position with the arms folded over the chest, the child leaps forward and returns to the squatting position.

Snake Crawl (K–3).   The child takes a prone position and moves forward in any manner, pulling and pushing with the arms and toes, wiggling, or a combination of these.

Seal (1–3).   The child assumes a "front leaning rest" position and walks on his hands, dragging his legs. The back is extended and the head is up.

Ostrich Walk (2–4).   The child bends at the hips to grasp his ankles. He then walks forward keeping the legs fully extended.

Bear Walk (2–4).   Bending over to place his hands on the floor, the child walks on all fours with the legs and arms fully extended and the head up. The arm and leg on the same side of the body move together.

Inchworm (2–4). A "front leaning rest" position is taken. Keeping the hands in place and the arms extended, the child walks forward until his feet are behind his hands. The knees should not bend. Then, with the feet remaining in position, the child walks forward with his hands.

Ape Walk (2–4). The child walks keeping the legs straight and the trunk parallel to the floor and swinging his arms freely with the finger tips just grazing the floor.

Chicken Walk (3–4). In a squatting position, the child reaches around behind and between the ankles to grasp the front of each ankle. He moves forward and backward maintaining this position.

Crab (3–8). A squatting position is taken with the hands placed on the floor behind the hips. With his back toward the floor and his abdomen up, the child walks on his hands and feet. The body should be held straight from the knees to the head.

Donkey Kick (4–8). The kick is achieved by diving forward and upward from a squatting position into a semi-handstand and then snapping down to the feet. At the start of the stunt from the squatting position, the child drives the elbows up and backward, at the same time springing from both feet to upend near the handstand position. The knees are bent; as the body falls off balance, the knees are extended forcefully and the hips flexed to land on the feet. The knees are bent upon landing. The shoulders are kept low and the head pulled backward throughout the stunt. Considerable practice is necessary before incorporating the stunt into a relay.

Animal Relays

DESCRIPTION OF ACTIVITY. Space requirements may range from a hallway or classroom to a large playing field. No equipment is needed. The children form as many single file lines of 5 to 10 children as are necessary to give all an opportunity to participate. On the starting signal, the first child in each line progresses toward a line at an appropriate distance away while imitating a selected animal. Upon reaching this line, he will turn about and race back to touch off the next child in line who then repeats the procedure. When all the children of a team have taken their turns, they line up single file with their right arms raised. The first team so lined up is declared the winner.

Teaching Hints. The children may be lined up abreast to count off by the number of relay teams to be organized. For example, if there are 30 children, they may count off by sixes and form six teams of five members each. In establishing the distance between lines, account should be taken of the strenuousness of the particular skill required by the relay and the abilities of the youngsters.

VARIATIONS. The first child on each team imitates one animal (the bear, for example), the second child, another animal (the bunny), the third, still another animal, etc.

A series of lines are drawn and each child must imitate a certain animal (the seal, for example) until he comes to the first line; then he must imitate another animal (the ape) to the second line, and so on. The total number of skills to be done, the total distance, and the distances between lines are dependent upon the age, level of physical fitness, sex, and the degree of strenuousness of the skills selected.

The contestants run to the line and perform the assigned skill on the return trip.

Stunt Relays

DESCRIPTION OF ACTIVITY. There are no special space requirements or equipment for these relays. Procedures for teaching the stunts and conducting the relays are the same as those described for the animal relays above. Among the stunts which may be presented as relays are:

Backward Walk or Run (K–3).

Hopping Forward or Backward on Two Feet (K–3).

Hopping Forward or Backward on Right or Left Foot (K–3).

Walking on Toes or Heels Only (K–3).

Goose Step (1–3). With each step, the forward leg is extended to waist height without bending the knee. The opposite arm is swung in a fully extended position to shoulder height with each step.

Skipping (1–4).

Toe-hold (2–3). The right knee is raised to the chest and the right toes are grasped in the right hand. Forward movement is accomplished by hopping on the left foot.

Hop, Step, and Jump (3–4). The contestant progresses forward by first hopping on both feet, then stepping forward immediately, followed by a jump.

Knee Walk (4–6). In the kneeling position with the hands grasping the ankles, the child walks forward on his knees. A slight forward lean will help to maintain balance. A mat should be used.

Partner Stunts and Relays

DESCRIPTION OF ACTIVITY. An entire class may participate in these activities in any area which will accommodate them. They require no special equipment. For the partner relays, the teams should form two adjacent parallel files. When all contestants of a team have taken their turns, they should signify that they are finished by standing in their files with partners holding inside hands raised over their heads. This procedure is most helpful in identifying the winning team.

Teaching Hints. The teaching hints presented for the animal stunts and relays apply also to these stunts and relays. All of them may be used for class work in stunts, and all except the first four may be utilized in partner relay contests.

VARIATIONS. *Bouncing Ball (1–3).* The first child is the "ball" and takes a semisquatting position in front of the second child who pushes down on his head as if bouncing a ball. As the push is made on his head, the first child does a deep knee bend and returns to the original position ready to be bounced again.

Wring the Dish Rag (1–3). The partners stand facing each other and join hands. They raise the arms on one side and lower them on the other and then turn under the raised arms, ending in a back-to-back position. They then raise the opposite pair of arms, turning under them to face each other again.

Chinese Back to Back (3–6). Partners stand back to back with elbows locked. They push against each other's back while taking several short steps forward and then sit down on the floor simultaneously. They should not let go of each other's arms.

Teaching hints. To increase the difficulty of this stunt for older children, the partners are instructed to rise from the sitting position without releasing their arms. To do this, the knees are bent and the feet placed close together. Then, as force is being exerted against the back of the partner, the legs are extended.

Tug Pick-Up (4–6). A short rope with loops tied at both ends is needed for this stunt. If several ropes are available, more children will be able to participate at one time. Two blocks, books, or similar objects are also needed for each set of partners. The objects are placed about a foot behind each partner who is holding on to one end of the rope. On a signal each partner tries to pick up the object behind him by pulling the other child toward him.

Teaching hints. The participants are not permitted to jerk the rope but must apply a steady pull. In this way better exercise is provided as well as precaution against the possibility of rope burns on the hands.

Wheelbarrow (4–6). The first child assumes a "front leaning rest" position. The second child grasps first child's ankles and holds them as though they were handles of a wheelbarrow. The "wheelbarrow" walks on his hands.

Teaching hints. The activity can be made easier for younger children by having the second child grasp and lift one leg only (Fig. 13–1).

Elephant Walk (5–8). The first child stands with feet apart. The second child starts by standing facing first child with his hands on his shoulders. The second child next jumps to straddle his legs around first child's waist. He then bends backward to place his hands on the floor between his partner's feet. The first child then bends forward to place his hands on the floor. The second child places his hands on his partner's ankles, and extends his arms.

Monkey Walk (5–8). The first child stands with his feet apart. The second child lies on his back between first child's legs with his legs in front of his partner's feet and his head behind them. The first child bends forward to place his hands on the floor to either side of his partner's legs. The second child wraps his legs around his partner's chest, reaches upward to place his hands on his partner's back with his arms outside his hips and pulls himself off the floor. The first child walks forward on all fours. By rolling halfway over to right or left, the partners can reverse positions.

Fireman's Carry (5–8). The first child stands with feet apart. The second child stands facing his partner, and squats to place his right arm between his partner's legs. The first child lies across the back of the second child's shoulders. The second child's arm passes around his partner's right leg to enable him to grasp his partner's right wrist with his own right hand. He then extends his legs to come to the erect position meanwhile keeping his back perpendicular to the floor. Partners should be paired so that their weight and height are reasonably equal.

Figure 13-1 Lifting only one leg makes the wheelbarrow easier for young children. (Austin Public Schools, Austin, Minn.)

Saddle Back Carry (5–8). The first child is standing. The second child stands facing sideward with his right shoulder against his partner's chest. He then squats and stoops placing his right arm around and behind his partner's knees. The first child lies across his partner's back. The second child places his left arm around his partner's shoulders and then comes to the erect position.

Piggy-back Carry. The first child is standing. The second child, from a standing position directly behind his partner and facing the same direction, jumps onto his partner's back with his arms on his shoulders and his legs around his waist. The first child grasps his partner's legs.

Horse Walk (5–8). The first child stoops forward to place his hands on the floor well in front of him. Both his arms and legs should be fully extended. The second child lies prone on his partner's back, facing the opposite direction. He wraps his legs around his partner's chest, places his hands on his partner's heels, and extends his arms. The first child walks forward on all fours.

Partner Handstand Walk (6–8). The first child stands with feet apart. The second child, facing his partner, stoops to place his hands on his partner's feet and upends into a handstand. The first child wraps his arms around his partner's legs and walks forward.

Tandem Walk (6–8). The first child stoops to place his hands on the floor about 2 feet in front of his feet. The second child stands in front of his partner facing the same direction. He bends forward to place his hands on the floor and then places his lower legs on his partner's back. Partners walk forward.

Back Carry (6–8). Partners stand back to back with arms locked. First child bends forward to lift the second child up onto his back. The second child lifts his legs until they are perpendicular to the floor.

Double Walk (6–8). The first child stands on his partner's feet facing him. Partners grasp one another's upper arms. As second child walks forward, first child shifts his weight from side to side in synchrony with his partner's movements. Partners may also stand back to back, elbows locked. On the signal, one will walk forward while the other walks backward. It will be necessary for one child to move his left leg forward, while the other moves his right leg backward.

Group Relays

DESCRIPTION OF ACTIVITY. Space requirements may range from a hallway to a playing field. No equipment is needed. An indefinite number of children may compete simultaneously.

Teaching Hints. Many of the teaching hints presented for animal relays are applicable to group relays. Teams may be selected in the same manner. The distance from start to finish line will be dependent upon the degree of vigor of the stunts, the age of the children, their sex, and their present physical fitness status. The teacher should provide explanation, demonstration, and practice in each of the stunts (briefly) before the relay races are begun.

VARIATIONS. Following are descriptions of several group relays of a stunt nature:

Chariot Race (K–3). Three children toe the starting line abreast of one another. The child in the center hooks the left elbow of the child to his right with his right elbow and the right elbow of the child to his left with his left elbow. A larger group than three may be used.

Centipede (1–4). Children stand directly behind one another and facing in the same direction. Each child wraps his arms around the chest of the one directly in front of him and clasps his own hands. Any number of children may run as a unit.

Forearm Carry (5–8). Three children line up abreast facing in the same direction. The two on the outside bend their inside arms so that the forearms are horizontal. They may reach across their own bodies with their outside arms to grasp their inside wrists to lend greater support. The child in the center grasps the wrists of the outside youngsters and extends his arms to lift himself several inches off the floor. The two children on the outside walk forward carrying their partner.

Walking Chair (6–8). Children line up behind one another and facing in the same direction. Each holds the hips of the child in front. All sit back on the thighs of the one behind but continue to support their own weight. All move forward in step.

Double Wheelbarrow (6–8). Child "A" stands facing the finish line. Child "B" stands facing the same direction directly in front of "A." He then stoops down to place his hands on the floor and lifts his legs so that child "A" can grasp his lower legs directly behind the knees. Child "C" stands directly behind child "A" and facing the opposite direction. He stoops down to place his hands on the floor and lifts his legs to place them between child "A's" arms and body. Child "A" walks forward holding the legs of "B" and "C" firmly while "B" walks forward on his hands and "C" walks backwards on his hands.

Tandem Wheelbarrow (6–8). Children "A," "B," and "C" stand directly behind one another facing the same direction. Child "B" assumes the front leaning rest position while "C" holds his ankles. Child "A" then assumes the front leaning rest position and places his lower legs along "B's" back. "C" walks his "tandem wheelbarrow" forward as "A" and "B" walk forward on their hands.

SELF-TESTING ACTIVITIES

DESCRIPTION OF ACTIVITY. Self-testing stunts are those activities in which the individual child competes against his own previous performance. Through these stunts and other self-testing activities, the child learns about himself—the capacity of his body, his physical courage, and his ability to control his environment. The following are among the best of the self-testing stunts which may be used in the elementary physical education program.

Agility and Flexibility Stunts

VARIATIONS. *Jumping Jack (K–3).* The child squats with his hands on his hips. He jumps to a standing position and throws his arms out to the sides. The difficulty of the activity may be increased by spreading the legs in the jump and bringing the arms up over the head.

Forward Bend (K–3). The child stands with feet apart and bends forward to touch his fingers to the floor.

Teaching hints. The teaching principles of progression and of providing an attainable but challenging goal apply even to simple stunts such as this one. Moving the feet closer and closer together makes the stunt increasingly difficult. When the child can touch his fingers to the floor with his feet together, he is ready to place his palms on the floor, then to bring his head to or between his knees and finally to bring his elbows close to or down to the floor.

Trunk Extension Flexibility (1–4). The child is in a prone position with his hands clasped behind his neck. Another child is needed to hold the one being tested. He should stand between the feet of the first child, kneel down with his knees outside those of his partner and place his hands on his partner's buttocks. The child being tested attempts to lift his head and chest as high off the floor as he is able. The vertical distance from his chin to the floor may be measured. (Children with exaggerated lumbar curve should not perform this exercise.)

Bridge (2–4). The child lies on his back with both feet flat on the floor near his buttocks, knees bent, hands flat on the floor under his shoulders with his fingers pointing toward his feet. He then extends his knees, hips, and arms to finish in an arched position. (Children with exaggerated lumbar curve should not perform this exercise.)

Arching (2–4). The child is in a prone position with his hands clasped behind his neck. He pulls his head, shoulders, chest, legs and feet as high off the floor as he is able by contracting all the posterior muscles. Only his hips and lower abdomen maintain contact with the floor. The number of repetitions, length of time held, and distance of feet and head from the floor may be varied. (Children with exaggerated lumbar curve should not perform this exercise.)

V-Sit (3–6). The child assumes a supine position with his arms extended beyond his head. He simultaneously lifts his legs and his trunk as he swings his arms upward and forward to grasp his ankles. He may also try to maintain balance while in the V-sit.

Backward Leg Raise (3–6). The first child is in a prone position with his hands clasped behind his neck. The second child places himself in a kneeling position facing his partner's feet with one knee at each side of his head. His hands are placed on his partner's shoulder blades. While his partner helps him to hold his chest in contact with the floor, the first child lifts his extended legs as high as he is able. He should hold his feet together. The perpendicular distance from his ankle bone (external malleolus) to the floor may be measured with a yardstick. (Children with exaggerated lumbar curve should not perform this exercise.)

Turk Stand (3–6). In a standing position, the child crosses one foot over the other and folds his arms over his chest. He then sits keeping the feet and arms in their original positions. In returning to the standing position, he must move his body forward to bring the weight over his feet and then lift upward.

Side Straddle Hop (3–6). The child jumps to a straddle position from a standing position with the arms at the sides. At the same time the hands are brought over the head. With the next hop, he returns to the original position.

Push-up and Chest Slap (5–8). Child assumes a front leaning rest position. He then does a push-up vigorously enough so that he can slap his chest with both hands before catching himself again in push-up position.

One-Arm Push-up (7–8). The child supports himself on three points—one hand and the two feet. His feet should be 3 to 6 inches apart. His body should be turned sideward. If he bends slightly at the hips as he lowers himself and extends the hips again as he pushes up, the stunt will be made slightly easier.

Line or Beam Walking (Grades K–8)

DESCRIPTION OF ACTIVITY. Excellent activities for developing balance are the line and beam walking stunts. Lines may be drawn or painted on the playing surface for the performance of most of these stunts. If beams are available, they may be placed from 18 inches to 3 feet above the floor in a horizontal position. For some stunts an inclined beam or a graduated beam (one that gradually becomes more narrow) may be used to increase the difficulty of the feat for more advanced students.

VARIATIONS. *Cat Walk Forward or Backward (K–2).* Both hands and feet are used; short steps are taken.

Figure 13-2 Performing a stunt on the graduated balance beam adds to its difficulty. (Courtesy of J. E. Gregory Co., Inc.)

Hop Forward or Backward (K-3). Arms may be held forward, sideward, overhead or behind back. Eyes are open or closed.

Walk on Heels or Toes (K-3). The child walks forward or backward with arms forward, sideward, overhead, or behind back. Eyes are open or closed.

Sidestep (K-3). The left foot is moved left, and the right foot brought next to the left foot.

Side Cross Step (K-3). The right foot crosses to the left of the left foot and then the left foot slides left.

Turn (K-3). A 180 degree turn is executed on the balls of the feet.

Jump Turn (5-6). Standing sideward across the line or the beam, the performer leaps into the air, does a 180 degree turn and lands in balance, facing the opposite direction. He takes a low jump, looks over the left shoulder, brings the left arm slightly behind the body, and finally brings the right arm across the front of the body.

Full Turn on One Leg (5-6). The turn is made on the ball of the foot. The arms are extended sideward for better balance.

Squat on One Leg (6-8). The shoulders are forward and the arms are extended sideward. The non-supporting leg is forward.

Sit on Beam (6-8). The performer leans well forward during the squat on one leg. He squats as deeply as possible before dropping the buttocks to the beam. The arms are extended sideward. To return to the standing position, one foot is placed on the beam as close to the buttocks as possible, and the body is rocked forward over the supporting foot and the supporting leg is extended.

ADVANCED VARIATIONS (6–8). Many other stunts at a more advanced level can be done on the balance beam. These include such stunts as forward and backward rolls, cartwheels, splits, front vaults, rear vaults, flank vaults, handstands, headstands, etc.

Jump Stunts

VARIATIONS. *Jump and Tuck (3–6).* The child leaps into the air drawing his knees to his chest with legs bent, grasps his shins, releases, extends his body and lands in a standing position.

Teaching hints. The performer's back should remain vertical. He must not lean forward to bring the chest to the knees; rather he must bring the knees to the chest. The head is erect.

Jump and Straddle Toe Touch (3–6). The child leaps into the air lifting his extended legs forward-upward with feet apart so that he can touch his toes.

Teaching hints. Same as for Jump and Tuck. The legs are fully extended.

Jump and Jackknife (4–6). The child leaps into the air lifting his extended legs forward-upward with feet together to touch his toes.

Teaching hints. Same as for Jump and Straddle Toe Touch.

Jump and Half Turn (4–6). The child leaps into the air throwing his left arm behind his hips and his right arm across the front of his hips as he looks over his left shoulder to execute a half turn before landing on his feet.

Teaching hints. The body should be fully extended and the arms in close to the body to rotate around the vertical axis of the body.

Jump and Full Turn (5–6). The child leaps into the air and executes a full turn before landing on his feet.

Jump and Full and a Half Turn (6–8). A full and a half turn is executed before the landing.

Jump and Swan (6–8). The child leaps into the air driving his arms high over his head as he pulls his body into an arched position. The landing is made on the feet with the body erect. (Children with exaggerated lumbar curve should not perform this exercise.)

Teaching hints. The hips are forward, head and feet pulled backward hard, and legs extended in the arched or swan position.

NOTE. All of the jump stunts described above can be done from a run, from a stand facing forward off a springboard, from a run and hurdle off a springboard, or from a stand facing rearward off a springboard. They could also be done from a platform of varying heights, a diving board, or a mini-tramp.

Balance and Coordination Stunts

VARIATIONS. *Foot and Toe Balance (K–3).* The child lifts one foot off the floor or balances on toe of one foot and maintains balance. Arms may be extended forward-sideward.

High Kick (1–3). The child holds his right or left arm extended forward at shoulder height and attempts to kick his hand.

Indian Squat (3–6). The child stands with his ankles crossed and his arms folded across his chest. He then squats fully until he is almost seated.

Russian Dance (5–8). The child begins in a full squatting position with one leg extended in front. He hops into the air, reverses the positions of the two legs, and continues in rhythm.

Teaching hints. The child must keep the back vertical. The weight is shifted to the side of the supporting leg.

Double Kazotski (5–8). The child starts in a full squat position. He then leaps upward extending both legs forward at right angles to the body simultaneously and bends them again to drop into the full squat position. The stunt may be done repeatedly and in rhythm.

Teaching hints. The back must be vertical. The performer must kick the legs out and bend them again quickly.

Thread the Needle (5–8). The child starts standing with his hands clasped in front. He then bends over and steps over his clasped hands with his right foot and then with his left foot to finish with his still clasped hands behind his back. The child may also start with the hands clasped behind the back and finish with them in front.

Heel Click (5–8). The child stands with his feet about 12 inches apart and then leaps into the air and clicks his heels together before landing. The child may click the heels together two or three times before landing, or click the heels together to either side of the body as his skill increases.

Ankle Grasp Jump (5–8). The child bends forward with his knees bent to grasp his ankles. He then jumps forward several times without releasing his grip.

Stick Jump (5–8). The child holds a wand in both hands in front or behind his body. He then attempts to jump over the stick without releasing his grip.

Teaching hints. The wand should be held lightly in the fingertips so that it will be knocked out of the hands in the event of a failure on the early attempts. The wand is swung under the legs as they are drawn upward. The child should not attempt to jump with forward or backward motion; the trajectory of the jump should be straight up and down.

Pick-up (5–8). The child stands with his back to a wall and attempts to pick up a clean handkerchief or a piece of paper placed on the floor in front of him.

Foot Throw (5–8). The child stands with the toe of one foot against the heel of the other. A small light object is placed on the toe of the rear foot. The child jumps into the air and attempts to "throw" this object as far as he can by quickly removing the forward foot and kicking the rear foot forward.

Ankle Throw (5–8). The child places a ball between the feet. By means of a quick thrust of the feet backward and upward, the object is flung over the child's head and he then attempts to catch it.

Pat and Plaster (5–8). The child attempts to rub his head in a circular motion with one hand while he pats his chest with the other. The procedure is then reversed.

Stoop Throw (5–8). The child places a ball on a line and stands straddling the ball. He then reaches around behind his legs to grasp the ball and to throw it as far as he is able through the legs. The ball must be thrown with both hands without losing balance.

Wall Leap (5–8). The child stands facing a wall with one foot against the wall about 12 inches above the floor. Then keeping the foot on the wall, he jumps his other foot over the one against the wall executing a half turn as he does so.

Blind Balance (5–8). The child stands with his right foot placed against his left knee, hands on his hips, and eyes closed. He attempts to maintain his balance for as long as he is able.

Heel Slap (5–8). The child leaps up as high as he is able bringing his heels up behind him and slaps both heels one or more times with his hands before he lands.

Dip-Snap (5–8). The child kneels on both knees with his hands clasped behind his back, bends over, and attempts to pick up a crumpled piece of paper with his teeth. The paper should be placed about 12 inches in front of his body.

Rocker (5–8). The child starts in a prone position. He then grasps his ankles and rocks forward and backward. (Children with exaggerated lumbar curve should not perform this exercise.)

Wand Balance (5–8). The child balances a wand on his chin or forehead without using his hands, squats, lies down, and then returns to the standing position while balancing the wand.

Heel-Toe Spring (5–8). The child places his heels on a line, bends down to grip his toes with his hands, and jumps backward over the line.

Teaching hints. By leaning slightly forward the child will gain impetus for the backward jump. He can also try to jump forward while in this position.

Chair Vault (5–8). The child places one hand on the seat and the other hand on the back of a sturdy chair. He then vaults through the space between his arms without touching the chair with his feet. The performer may also vault backward between the arms and over the chair to finish with the chair in front.

Single Leg Circle (5–8). The child assumes a squatting position with both hands on the floor. His left knee is between his arms. His right leg is extended sideward. He swings his right leg forward, and when it meets his right arm, he lifts his right hand and places it to the right of the right leg. He shifts his weight to his right arm as his right leg continues to circle under his left leg and hand.

Teaching hints. The child should not lean forward but should keep his back nearly vertical. He shifts the weight to the right arm and keeps the left leg bent.

Front Swan (5–8). The child starts in a standing position. He bends forward at the hips lifting his extended right leg up behind him until his right leg and trunk are parallel to the floor. The leg and back form an arch. (Children with exaggerated lumbar curve should not perform this exercise.)

Teaching hints. The arms should extend diagonally forward-sideward with palms down to help maintain balance. The head is held up to look at a point on the wall directly in front at head height. For good form both legs and both arms should be fully extended.

Coffee Grinder (5–8). The child assumes a side leaning rest position; that is, with the body extended and his weight supported on one hand and his feet. His other hand is raised over his head. He then walks around his supporting hand with his body extended, pivoting around the hand.

Corkscrew (5–8). The child stands with his feet about 15 inches apart and places a piece of paper at the toe of his right foot. He then brings his left arm across the front of his body and behind and between his legs to pick up the paper.

Cut the Wand (5–8). The child holds the end of a wand in the right hand with the other end resting on the floor in front of his feet. He releases the wand and quickly lifts his right leg over the wand, catching the wand before it falls.

Head and Toe. The child stands on one foot, grasps the other foot with both hands, and by bending forward and pulling brings the foot to his head.

Through the Stick (5–8). The child stands holding a wand grasped in both hands behind his back with his palms forward. He then brings the wand up over his head and in front of his body without releasing the stick. Next, he brings his right leg around his right arm, between his hands, and over the stick. Finally, he crawls through head first and back over with his left foot.

Games Using Self-Testing Activities (Grades K–8)

Several games follow in which many of the self-testing activities described above may be used:

FOLLOW THE LEADER. The class follows the movements made by the teacher or a selected leader.

INDIVIDUAL COMPETITION. The instructor constructs a chart with children's names running down the left hand vertical column and the stunts listed across the top horizontal column. Children may be given a mark for each stunt mastered. If a point is awarded for each stunt, selection of a class winner may be made.

TEAM COMPETITION. The class is divided into two or more teams. A point is awarded to a team each time one of its members masters one of the stunts. The winning team is announced at the end of the unit.

SIMON SAYS. The children are arranged in a circle formation with a distance of approximately 2 yards between each child and his nearest neighbor. One of the children who has been selected as the leader moves to the center of the circle. The leader gives commands and executes the particular skill called for. Some of his commands are prefaced by the words "Simon says" and some are not. The children respond only to those commands prefaced by the words "Simon says." Any player who responds to a command not preceded by the words "Simon says" is eliminated.

Teaching Hints. To avoid long periods of inactivity for those who have been eliminated, the game should be ended and started over at frequent intervals.

I SAY STOOP. The children are in the same formation as they are for Simon Says. The leader, who is in the center of the circle, gives the command, "I say stoop" or "I say do the front swan." He may do the action he has called for, or he may do another action. Students follow the leader's commands and not his actions. Those not executing the action called for sit down. Those failing to perform properly a skill called for sit down. If the leader attempts a skill and is unsuccessful, he sits down and the teacher selects a new leader. The activity should begin with simple actions and gradually increase in complexity and difficulty.

Teachings Hints. To avoid long periods of inactivity for those who have been eliminated, the game should be ended and started over at frequent intervals.

STUNTS ON CLIMBING ROPES

Lower Away (Grades K–4)

The child stands in front of the rope with his feet about 15 inches apart and holds the rope with both hands at shoulder height. Keeping his body straight, he lowers himself hand under hand until his back touches the mat. He then pulls himself back to the standing position.

Chin Up (Grades 4–8)

The child grasps the rope as high above his head as he is able to reach. He then pulls himself up to touch his chin to his hands and lowers himself again.

Ascending Techniques (Grades 5–8)

CLIMB WITH FOOT AND LEG LOCK. The child grasps the rope at chest height. The rope passes in front of his body, between his legs, behind his right leg, and then across the instep of his right foot. The left foot steps on the rope across the instep. The child climbs by pinching the rope between his feet as he extends his legs to reach for a higher hand grip. He then pulls himself up and repeats the procedure.

Teaching Hints. During the upward pull the slack is taken up with the left foot by moving it sideward with the rope over it.

CLIMB WITH STIRRUP. The child grasps the rope with both hands. The rope hangs to his right side and passes under his right foot and over his left foot. To climb, the child will flex his knees to bring them up as high as possible allowing the rope to slide between his feet as he hangs on. He will then clamp the rope between his feet as he extends his legs to reach for a higher hand grip. The procedure is repeated.

SHINNY-UP. The child grasps the rope over his head. The rope passes down between his legs and over the instep of one foot. It is clamped to the foot by the back of the ankle of the other foot.

Teaching Hints. The legs aid the arms in climbing by clamping the rope and extending the knees in synchrony with the arm pull.

CLIMB WITH HANDS ONLY. The child climbs using his hands only. The rope passes in front of his body and between his legs. His legs are almost fully extended and are at right angles to his trunk.

Teaching Hints. The weight should be shifted from side to side. The legs kick in a walking motion, and the shoulders rotate with each pull of the arms.

Descending Techniques (Grades 5–8)

DESCENDING WITH THE ROPE BETWEEN THE ARCHES OF THE FEET. The rope is pinched between the arches of the feet while the child lowers himself hand under hand.

Teaching Hints. The performer should keep the legs straight and the hips slightly bent.

SHINNY-DOWN. The body and rope positions are identical to those in the shinny-up. The child descends either by relaxing the foot pressure or by flexing the knees as he lowers himself.

DESCENDING WITH A STIRRUP. The body and rope positions are the same as in the climb with a stirrup. The speed of the descent is controlled by the distance between the feet.

Advanced Techniques (Grades 6–8)

MAKE FAST. The rope passes across the front of the body, between the legs, around the right leg, and over the instep of the right foot. The bottom of the left foot presses the rope against the right instep. The right leg is extended fully. The left hand grips the rope at shoulder height and is pressed into the right armpit. The right arm is moved in a horizontal plane forward to outward and backward. This will cause a backward traction on the rope. The left hand can then be released and both arms brought behind the body to grasp the right wrist with the left hand.

Teaching Hints. The climber should keep his legs fully extended. When the final position is achieved, the head is held erect and the chest out.

INVERTED HANG AND MAKE FAST. The child grasps the rope above his head and inverts himself by swinging his legs upward. He pinches the rope between his feet with one foot behind and the other in front of the rope. He next releases the rope with his right hand and grasps it below his head to wrap it behind his back and across his chest under his armpits. He can now hang inverted without using his hands.

Cargo Net Climbing (Grades 4–8)

A cargo net securely attached to the ceiling offers a number of opportunities for unique climbing experiences. The net may be used for climbing normally on a regular rope ladder, for climbing sideways while remaining parallel to the floor, or for climbing diagonally up and down. More skilled children can do hanging stunts or climb in and out of the rope squares. Climbing while others are also on the net increases the complexity and challenge of the activity, because their weight as they move about continually changes the shape and stability of each rope square.

Figure 13–3 Children experiment with various ways of climbing a cargo net. (John Read Middle School, Redding, Conn.)

TUMBLING AND BALANCING

Forward Roll

FROM A SQUAT (GRADES K–3). The child squats with his arms between his legs and his hands on the floor shoulder width apart, fingers pointing forward. He then elevates his hips, tucks his chin into his chest, lands on his neck and shoulders (the head should not touch the mat), tucks into a tight ball, and rolls over grasping his shins to pull on them to pull his feet under his buttocks. The forward roll may be done from a squat with the arms outside the legs also.

FROM A STAND (GRADES K–3). The child starts from a standing position, squats to place his hands on the mat with his arms outside his legs and moves directly into the forward roll.

FROM A WALK (GRADES K–5). When one leg is forward during the walk, the child stoops to place his hands on the mat well in front of his body, puts his chin on his chest, permits momentum to carry his hips over his head, tucks into a tight ball, grasps his shins, and completes the roll.

WITH A HALF TWIST (GRADES 1–5). The child begins as for a regular forward roll, but when he is in an inverted position, he crosses his legs. Then as he comes to his feet, he spins on his toes to finish facing the opposite direction.

Teaching Hints. Children imagine the spin occurs during the roll. This is not true. The roll is completed before the spin is executed.

SHOULDER ROLL (GRADES 1–5). The child stands facing the direction of his roll. He throws his right arm across his waist, turns his head to the left, drops to his right knee breaking the fall with his left hand, and rolls around the vertical (long) axis of his body. As he completes the roll, he comes to his left knee and right foot, and then stands up facing sideward.

Backward Roll

FROM A SQUAT (GRADES 2–5). The child squats with his back toward the mat. He then drops back to his buttocks and rolls around on his back until his shoulder blades contact the mat. At this time, he places his hands on the mat, palms down with fingers pointing toward his body. As he pushes against the mat with his hands to give his head room to come through, he pulls his knees towards his chest and comes around to his feet.

Teaching Hints. The head is held forward throughout the roll. During the push with the hands, the knees are pulled into the chest to shorten the radius and thereby accelerate the speed of rotation. Children can assist one another by placing one hand under their partner's shoulder to lift him and one on his back to help him to rotate.

FROM A STAND (GRADES 2–5). The child starts from a standing position with his back toward the mat. He squats and goes immediately into the backward roll as described above.

IN A STRADDLE POSITION (GRADES 2–5). The child starts in a standing position with his back toward the mat and his feet wide apart. He stoops to bring his hands to the floor. He then falls backward keeping his legs fully extended and keeping his hands in touch with the mat. He then rolls around his rounded back with his head well forward. When his shoulder blades come in contact with the mat, he places his hands on the mat, pushes, tightens his pike (pulls the extended legs closer to his body), and comes around to his feet.

Teaching Hints. The child should lean well forward during the backward drop to the buttocks. He must tighten the pike during the final stages.

IN A JACKKNIFE POSITION (GRADES 2–5). The child starts in a standing position with his back toward the mat and his feet together. He stoops to touch his toes and falls backward to his buttocks keeping his legs fully extended during the fall and continuing to touch his toes. When his shoulder blades contact the mat, he places his hands on the mat under his shoulders, pushes, and comes around to his feet.

Teaching Hints. The performer should lean as far forward during the drop as flexibility will allow. He should tighten the pike after the hands come in contact with the mat.

WITH AN EXTENSION (GRADES 3–6). The child begins the backward roll with an extension in the same manner as he does the backward roll in jackknife position; however, after he places his hands on the mat under his shoulders, he extends vigorously at the hips to "shoot" his feet vertically upward, pushes hard with his arms, pulls his head backward, "shoots" into the handstand position, then flexes at the hips to snap his feet to the mat.

Teaching Hints. The teacher can grasp the ankles of the child as he "shoots" into the handstand and pull him upward toward the handstand. This will help the child to orient himself. Obviously, obese or frail children would find this stunt not only frustratingly difficult but hazardous.

Cartwheel (Grades 4–8)

DESCRIPTION OF ACTIVITY. The child starts by standing oblique to his proposed direction of travel. He bends forward-sideward to place his left hand on the mat, meanwhile swinging his right arm across his body and to the mat. He then swings his extended right leg directly upward over his head at the same time springing off his left foot. These actions will cause him to upend into a handstand position. He will then flex forward-sideward at the hips and push off his hands to bring first the right foot and then the left foot to the mat to finish in a standing position facing the side of the mat.

Teaching Hints. While upended the child's head should be pulled backward, and he should look at a point on the mat between and slightly in front of his hands. The rhythm is hand, hand, foot, foot or 1, 2, 3, 4 in contacting the mat. Both hands and both feet do *not* contact the mat at the same moment. All four points of support—the two hands and the two feet—should contact the mat along a straight line.

Headstand (Grades 4–8)

DESCRIPTION OF ACTIVITY. A squat is assumed with the knees wide apart. The hands are placed on the mat at the same width as the spread of the knees. The elbows are tucked on the inside of the knees. By rocking up onto the hands, the balance of the body can be secured over the hands. (This position is called the tip-up.) The head is lowered to the mat to make an equilateral triangle with the hands. The hips are brought over the head to an inverted stand with the neck and upper body arched. The weight will be distributed between the hands and the head. As the balance is gained, the legs are brought up overhead.

Neckspring (Grades 5–8)

DESCRIPTION OF ACTIVITY. The child starts in a supine position with his hands under his shoulders, palms on the mat, fingers pointing toward his feet. He lifts his extended legs up over his head until his toes touch the mat beyond his head. He then rolls forward on his shoulder blades until his back is at a 45 degree angle to the floor. At this point he whips his legs around by extending at the hips, pushes with his arms, and brings his head forward to land on his feet.

Teaching Hints. The vigorous extension at the hips must be made at precisely the correct moment during the forward roll of the body in order (1) to utilize the momentum of the body, (2) to get the feet under the hips (if the extension occurs too late the performer will be unable to get his feet under his hips), and (3) to avoid shooting straight up. The legs must remain extended until the feet contact the mat in order to have a longer lever arm which is necessary to

Figure 13-4 The first step in a successful headstand is a tip up. (Journal of Health · Physical Education · Recreation.)

generate the needed momentum. The instructor must insist upon good assistance or spotting procedures. The spotter kneels on both knees to the left side of the student and facing him. He places his left hand on the child's lower back and his right hand under the child's left shoulder. The spotter's right forearm should rest on his thigh for better leverage. The spotter's left hand will prevent the child from striking his back and his right hand will ease him down if he should shoot straight up.

NECKSPRING TO A STRAIGHT LEG LANDING. The legs are "whipped" slightly earlier during the forward roll; "whipping" the legs more vigorously and pushing harder with the arms will enable the child to land with legs fully extended.

NECKSPRING WITH HANDS ON KNEES. The child places his hands on his knees and pushes against his knees instead of against the floor. This is slightly more difficult.

Headspring (Grades 5–8)

DESCRIPTION OF ACTIVITY. The child squats to place his hands on the mat shoulder width apart. He then places his head on the mat in front of his hands at such a position that, if a line were drawn connecting the three points of support, an equilateral triangle would be formed. Next, he brings his hips up over his head keeping his toes on the mat with his legs extended. He then tilts forward until his back is at a 45 degree angle to the floor with his toes still near the floor. When he is about to lose balance, he vigorously extends his hips and pushes with his arms to come about to his feet.

Teaching Hints. Each child must be spotted while learning this stunt. It is spotted in the same manner as is the neckspring. Following are common errors in execution of the headspring which prevent success: 1. Extending the hips as they are brought over the head, thereby shortening the radius of rotation during the "whip" of the legs. 2. Bending the knees during the "whip" of the legs. This also shortens the radius of rotation limiting the amount of momentum which can be generated. 3. "Whipping" the legs around too soon. The child must wait until his back is at a 45 degree angle to the floor.

HEADSPRING FROM A STAND, WALK, OR RUN. The child bends forward to place hands and then head on the mat. He takes off from both feet simultaneously keeping his feet low as his hips move above and beyond his head. When his hips are beyond his head, he vigorously extends his hips to whip his legs around and under himself. Due to the momentum resulting from the run, this whip is made slightly earlier than the headspring is done from a standing position.

HEADSPRING IN SERIES. After completing the first headspring, the child immediately places his hands and then his head down on the mat and executes another headspring. These can be continued for the full length of the mats.

HEADSPRING TO A STRAIGHT LEG LANDING. The child should execute the "whip" slightly sooner and more forcefully and should push harder with his arms to land with his legs fully extended.

HEADSPRING TO A SEAT. Instead of landing on his feet, the child lands in a sitting position. To do this, he does not hyperextend his hips, his push is more horizontal, and his feet do not come under his body. The landing is made with the entire underside of both legs contacting the mat at almost the same instant. The heels, however, contact the mat slightly before the other parts of the leg.

Handstand (Grades 5–8)

DESCRIPTION OF ACTIVITY. The stunt is begun with the hands on the mat in front of the body about shoulders' width apart. The right knee is drawn up close to the chest. The body weight is brought forward on the arms, and the right leg is kicked upward followed by the leg. The legs end in a nearly straight line with the body and arms. The head is held well forward to aid in maintaining balance.

Lead-Up Stunts to Handspring (Grades 5–8)

KNEE-SHOULDER SPRING. This is a partner stunt which leads to the front handspring. One child, called the understander, lies on the mat supine with feet on the floor and knees drawn up. His arms are extended vertically. The other child, called the topmounter, runs toward the understander, places his hands on his knees and his shoulders on the topmounter's hands and kicks his legs over his head to come around and land on his feet.

Teaching Hints. The topmounter must extend his arms horizontally in order that the understander receive his full weight on his hands. The under-

Figure 13–5 Student assistants are helpful in learning to do the handstand on the balance beam. (Courtesy of Ox Ridge Elementary School, Darien, Connecticut.)

stander must lift his head to watch the approach of his topmounter. The topmounter must keep his head pulled backward during the stunt. He should not tuck or pike. His body should be extended and pulled backward during the stunt.

ASSISTED STRAIGHT ARM HANDSPRING. The understander lies supine on the mat with his arms extended vertically and his legs apart. The topmounter runs toward his partner taking his last step between his partner's legs. He bends quickly at the hips to place one hand on either side of the understander's chest and "whips" his legs over and around his head to land on his feet. The understander assists the topmounter by placing his hands on his partner's shoulders and pushing as he comes around.

Lead-Up Stunts to Handspring (Grades 6–8)

HANDSPRING OVER A ROLLED-UP MAT. A mat is rolled up tightly and placed in the center of two mats placed end to end. Children should first learn the handspring by placing their hands in front of the rolled mat. To do this, the child takes a short run toward the mat, skips on the final step to enable placing of his hands closer to his feet to establish greater rotary momentum, "whips" his legs over and around his head to land on his feet.

Teaching Hints. The arms are fully extended throughout the stunt. The head is pulled backward throughout. As the body passes through the handstand position, a push is made upward from the shoulders (not the elbows). The hips are pushed upward by hyperextending the back after the handstand position has been passed. The arms are perpendicular to the floor throughout the stunt. A spotter should be seated astraddle the mats and place one hand under the performer's shoulder and the other on his upper back to assist him around.

HANDSPRING ON A ROLLED-UP MAT. The child executes a handspring placing his hands on top of the mat. The techniques of execution are identical to those described above for the handspring over the rolled-up mat.

Teaching Hints. The two spotters position themselves next to the mat on the side opposite the approach side. As before, they place one hand on the tumbler's upper back. The other hand, however, is used to grasp the tumbler's wrist or arm.

Handspring (Grades 6–8)

DESCRIPTION OF ACTIVITY. Having mastered the preceding stunts, the child is ready to attempt a front handspring. The techniques of execution are as previously described as are the spotting procedures.

WALK-OUT HANDSPRING. In the walk-out handspring, the legs are kept apart and the tumbler lands first on one foot and then the other. In other respects, the techniques of execution are identical to those previously described except that a more vigorous "whip" and shoulder push must be utilized.

Figure 13–6 Spotting the handspring. (Courtesy of Town of Vernon Schools, Rockville, Connecticut.)

Handspring (Grades 7–8)

ONE-ARM HANDSPRING. The techniques of execution are identical to those previously described for the handspring with the exception that only one arm is used.

ROUND-OFF. The child takes a short run to the mat, skips on his right foot, whips his arms downward and quickly flexes his hips to place his hands on the mat directly in front of his feet, fingers pointing sideward. His legs whip up over his head; his body turns 180 degrees; he flexes at the hips and knees to snap his feet down to the mat. Both feet contact the mat simultaneously.

Teaching Hints. The turn cannot be easily made unless the hands are placed on the mat in the proper position. They should be close together with fingers pointing to the side of the mat and the forward hand further toward the side than the other hand. The hand should be pulled backward and the arms extended throughout the stunt.

ONE-ARM ROUND-OFF. The techniques of execution for the one-arm round-off are identical to those described for the round-off, the obvious difference being that only one hand touches the mat.

TRAMPOLINING (REBOUND TUMBLING)

Basic Techniques (Grades 1–8)

GENERAL SKILLS. At the start of the jump the feet are about shoulders' width apart on the bed. They are brought together as they leave the bed. The arms are bent with the hands moving directly upward close to the body. The hands continue their upward movement to reach their highest point just as the body reaches its highest point. The shoulders are also lifted.

As the body drops down toward the bed, the arms are brought downward directly to the side of the body in an extended position. This downward movement should be timed so that the arms are at shoulder height at the moment of contact with the bed. The downward swing of the arms continues as the bed is depressed. When the body stops its descent, the jump is completed. To kill the spring, the knees and hips are bent as the feet make contact with the bed.

Teaching Hints. It is important that the child hold his head erect throughout the jump, as looking at the landing spot will bring the head forward, producing a rotary motion to the body. The child should be encouraged to establish the habit of looking at the end of the frame.

Children should not be permitted to bounce as high as they are able when learning the general skills and basic stunts; these should be mastered with a low bounce before attempting heights.

LEAD-UP JUMPS. The lead-up jumps help the beginner to learn body control and to maintain balance while unsupported in the air. In the first three jumps described below, it is important that the performer not bring his trunk forward.

The jump-and-tuck consists of drawing the knees to the chest and grasping the shins and then immediately extending the legs again to land on the feet.

In the jump-and-straddle toe touch the extended legs are lifted to a straddle position in order to touch the toes. Then the legs are dropped to land on the feet.

The jump-and-jackknife is performed the same as the jump-and-straddle toe touch, except that the feet and legs are held together.

To do the jump and half turn the performer throws his right arm across the front of his hips and pulls his other arm above his head. Both actions occur as he is leaving the bed. By springing higher and throwing harder with his arms, he may do a full turn and a full and a half turn.

KNEE DROP. The performer lands simultaneously on the knees, shins, and insteps of both legs and feet and rebounds back to his feet. As his lower legs contact the bed, his hips should be straight (but his back should not be arched and he should not "cave in" at the hips). An arched position of the back may produce a strained back; caving in absorbs the impact and prevents lift.

KNEE DROP WITH A HALF TWIST. The performer executes a knee drop and as he lifts off the bed, he adds a half twist to land on his feet facing in the opposite direction.

KNEE DROP WITH A FULL TWIST. This stunt is done in the same manner as the preceding stunt, except that the twist is executed with great vigor.

SEAT DROP. As he drops toward the bed, the performer flexes his hips to lift his extended legs so that he lands simultaneously on his buttocks and the entire undersurface of his legs. As he lifts off the bed from his buttocks, he leans slightly forward and comes up to his feet. He may place his hands alongside his hips with his fingers pointing forward upon landing on his seat.

SEAT DROP WITH A HALF TWIST. As he rebounds from his seat, the performer lifts his arms over his head pulling his left arm backward and his right arm across his face. At the same time, he turns his head to the left and extends his hips (the body will rotate more effectively on its long axis when it is extended). Having completed the half twist, he lands on his feet.

SEAT DROP WITH A HALF TWIST TO THE SEAT. This stunt is executed in the same manner as the previous stunt, except that as he completes the half twist, the performer flexes his hips to land on his seat instead of his feet.

HANDS AND KNEE DROP. As the performer leaps upward, he lifts his hips to bring them to the same elevation as his head. He then lands simultaneously on his hands, knees, and shins and rebounds to his feet by lifting his head, pushing with his hands, and bringing his hips forward.

FRONT DROP PROGRESSIONS. The performer leaps upward into a loosely tucked position with his hips as high as his head. As he drops downward, he extends his hips and knees to land on the bed in a slightly arched position, with his upper arms at a 45 degree angle to the long axis of the body and the forearms at a 135 degree angle to the upper arms.

His abdomen should contact the bed first and at the point where his feet left it. His trajectory should be straight up and down. After rebounding from his abdomen, he flexes his hips to bring his feet under his hips in order to land on his feet.

The front drop may be done from a jackknifed position by lifting the hips above the head, then extending the hips to make the front drop landing.

The front drop may also be done from a swan or arched position by pulling the trunk and legs directly into the arched position and then dropping to the front drop. At the height of the leap, the body should be at a 45 degree angle to the bed with the head at the highest point. The body will then pivot about its horizontal axis so that the student will land on his abdomen.

TURNTABLE.   As he rebounds from a front drop, the performer pushes sidewards against the bed with his hands, tucks, and pulls his head and trunk sidewards. He pivots about his hips 180 degrees with his front facing downward and then extends to land on his front. His feet should move around to the side of his hips and not under them.

A full turn can also be done with a higher spring and more forceful push off and a consequently faster spin.

BACK DROP PROGRESSIONS.   Leaping into the air, the performer lifts his legs to pivot about his hips, drops to his upper back with his hips flexed and his feet above his head, kips (extends his hips), and comes back to his feet. As his trunk moves backward during the drop to his back, the head should move forward. The first efforts should be made with a low bounce.

Back drops may also be done in *swing time,* going immediately from one back drop to the succeeding one. To do this, the performer, in coming to his feet, should not come fully to the erect position but should keep his back slightly behind a perpendicular line drawn from his feet. The slight body lean facilitates moving into the succeeding back drop.

The performer may do a backdrop from a *layout position* by pushing his chest and hips upward while letting his legs drag. He pivots about his hips in an arched position, and, just before striking the bed, he flexes his hips to lift his legs and land on his upper back.

The student may go from back drop to back drop by "kicking" his legs directly upward and keeping his head and shoulders low on rebounding from his back. To aid in preventing his trunk from pivoting upward, his feet and legs should be kept over his head at all times.

The back drop with a *half twist* may be done by pulling the right arm across the chest and turning the head to the left on leaving the bed from the back. The landing is made on the feet, facing in the opposite direction.

PYRAMID BUILDING

There are many different types of pyramids. In the true pyramid, the highest point is the center; in a modified pyramid, there may be a series of high points or the high points may be on each side. Pyramids may be designed so that all units are joined, or there may be a series of unjoined patterns, each more or less complete in itself. The pyramid may be made in a straight line, in a circle or semi-circle, in the pattern of wheel spokes, in a triangle, or in an open or closed square or rectangle.

Basic Pyramid Stunts (Grades 5–8)

For safe and enjoyable participation in performing the basic pyramid stunts and building pyramids, the teacher should: 1. place the participants properly with the heaviest forming the base; 2. make certain each participant knows exactly what he is to do; 3. keep the designs for beginners simple, and 4. have the children master the smaller units of a pyramid before constructing the entire pyramid.

FRONT LEAN BALANCE. Partners take a front leaning position (the position for the push-up), facing each other. A third child stands on the two partners by placing one foot on the shoulders of each.

THE WHEELBARROW. One performer stands behind another who is bent over at the hips with his hands resting on the floor. The one in back grasps the other performer by the ankles to lift his legs to simulate a wheelbarrow, or he may place his partner's ankles on his own shoulders.

HORIZONTAL STAND. One partner lies on the mat with his knees bent and his feet on the floor. His partner places his hands on the knees of the one who is down and supports himself while the down partner lifts the feet of the top partner.

THIGH MOUNT. Partners stand one behind the other grasping each other's hands. The one behind bends his knees slightly. The front partner steps up on the knees of the other. The partner who is holding may balance his partner by holding him at the knees rather than by the hands.

Figure 13–7 Thigh mount. (Courtesy of Town of Vernon Schools, Rockville, Connecticut.)

Figure 13–8   Double thigh mount. (Courtesy of Town of Vernon Schools, Rockville, Connecticut.)

DOUBLE THIGH MOUNT.   Two performers stand side by side with their feet spread and knees slightly flexed. The third performer, who stands behind the other two, steps from behind to mount the thighs of the two in front. He is balanced in this position by the grasp of the other two·on his thighs.

ANGEL BALANCE.   One performer lies on his back on the floor and lifts his legs into the air with the knees flexed. His partner places his lower abdomen against the upraised feet and grasps the bottom performer's hands. He then lifts his feet and balances his body. The partner on the bottom drops his arms, while the one on top arches his back and raises his arms as in the swan dive position.

THREE MAN MOUNT.   Two performers take a position side by side on their hands and knees. The third performer gets on top of the other two, placing one hand and one knee on the back of each, or he may stand upright, placing one foot over the hips of each.

THE FAN.   Three performers stand side by side with their feet as close together as possible. The center one grasps the shoulders of the two outside performers. They in turn grasp his shoulders with their inside hands and lower their bodies an arm's length to the side of the center performer. Five performers may be used if they possess sufficient strength to hold each other in position.

STAND ON PARTNER.   One performer takes a hands-and-knees position. The other performer stands on his back by placing both feet over the hip area of his partner or by placing one foot on the hip and the other on the shoulder. Weight should never be placed on the small of the back because of possible injury to this relatively weak area of the back.

STAND ON PARTNERS' KNEES.   Two performers kneel on one leg facing each other. The third performer stands on the thighs of the two who are kneeling. He may be supported by a hand extended by each of the two kneeling partners or he may be unsupported.

SITTING MOUNT. The partners stand one behind the other. The one in back kneels on one leg and bends over to place his head between the legs of the one in front. At the same time, he grasps the thighs of his partner. He then straightens his legs and back to bring the partner to a sitting position on his shoulders. The one on top tucks his legs under the partner's arms and behind his back.

STANDING MOUNT. One performer stands behind another. The one in front takes a deep stride position with his hands raised up and over his shoulders. The one in back grasps the hands of his partner and places his right foot on the partner's right thigh. He steps with his left foot onto the left shoulder of his partner and then follows with his right foot to the right shoulder. The bottom performer gradually rises to an erect position, releasing the hands of his partner to grasp him behind the knees for support.

DOUBLE HEAD STAND. Two performers face each other 8 to 10 feet apart. A third performer stands in the center facing forward. On command the two on the sides go into a head stand. The center person grasps their ankles.

Pyramids (Grades 5–8)

The basic pyramid stunts are combined in various ways to form pyramids. For example, the most basic and simplest of the true pyramids may be built with six performers employing the techniques of the Three Man Mount. Two of the performers mount three others who are in a hands and knees position. The last one mounts the two after stepping up on the back of the center man of the three who form the base.

Figure 13–9 Double head-stand. (Courtesy of Town of Vernon Schools, Rockville, Connecticut.)

Figure 13-10 Pyramids.

Figure 13–11 Basic true pyramid. (Courtesy of Town of Vernon Schools, Rockville, Connecticut.)

At the conclusion of pyramid building, the performers dismount in reverse order; however, in the basic pyramid described above, the performers "squash" by extending their legs backward and lowering their bodies to their hands.

The use of other basic stunts as units in pyramid building are shown in the illustration in Figure 13–10, page 377.

PARACHUTE PLAY
(Grades 4–8)

Parachute play provides vigorous activity that adds an exciting dimension to physical education. Regulation 24 foot parachutes for use in class may be purchased from Army-Navy surplus stores.

To start parachute play, the chute is spread out on the floor with the class taking positions around it, equidistant apart. Twenty to 40 students can participate when a regulation size parachute is used. The students kneel on one knee and grasp the chute by its edge with both hands in any one of three ways: palms up, palms down, or one palm up and one palm down. The palms-down grasp is generally the most effective. Some parachutes have handles which make holding it easier for the children.

In lifting the chute into the air, height is achieved by everyone simultaneously raising the chute to the maximum of his reach. As the parachute fills with air, it rises to form a canopy above the children. A small aperture in the center of the chute permits enough air to escape in order to stabilize the parachute as it slowly descends.

Figure 13–12 *A*, Students take the palms-down grip on the parachute. *B*, They lift the parachute into the air to toss the ball. (Robert Demetry.)

Various actions are possible during the rise and descent of the parachute. Students may move to the right or to the left or in alternate directions. Their movement may be at various tempos: walking, running, galloping, skipping. Musical accompaniment may be used, if desired.

A mushroom can be created by bringing the rim of the parachute down to the floor quickly as it attains maximum height. The mushroom can also be made by taking two or three steps toward the center while the parachute is rising into the air. As the chute reaches its peak, the children return to their original positions. Variations in the shape of the mushroom can be achieved by varying the number of steps taken toward the center.

When the children have learned to raise the parachute and to make the mushroom, the elements of various games can be introduced. The objective of the games adapted to parachute play is to accomplish the goal of the game before the parachute collapses; for example, any one of the games in which participants try to change positions without being tagged by the one who is "It" may be adapted by having the students try to change places before the parachute descends. Another possibility greatly enjoyed by youngsters involves the use of a light ball. The chute is raised with the ball resting on top. The class attempts to bounce the ball or otherwise maneuver it about on the parachute. As they become skilled in playing the ball, the students may be divided into teams, one on each half of the chute, to attempt to roll the ball off the opponents' side of the chute.

There are also interesting possibilities for creative play. With the parachute held at waist height, different patterns of waves and billows can be created by each child shaking the chute in independent action. Unusual patterns can be created also by small groups working together to achieve a specific motion. To facilitate this activity, the children can be separated into groups of three or four to plan the movement they will contribute to the total pattern.

SUPPLEMENTARY READINGS

Baley, James A.: *Gymnastics in the Schools.* Boston, Allyn and Bacon, Inc., 1964.
Cooper, Phyllis: *Feminine Gymnastics.* Minneapolis, Burgess Pub. Co., 1973.
Edwards, Vannie M.: *Tumbling.* Philadelphia, W. B. Saunders Co., 1969.
Fait, Hollis F., et al.: *A Manual of Physical Education Activities.* Ed. 3. Philadelphia, W. B. Saunders Co., 1967.
Roys, Betty Maycock: *Gymnastics for Girls and Women.* Philadelphia, W. B. Saunders Co., 1969.
Vincent, William J.: *Gymnastic Routines for Men.* Philadelphia, W. B. Saunders Co., 1972.

chapter fourteen

classroom games

ACTIVE CLASSROOM GAMES
INTEGRATED GAMES
GAMES FOR SPECIAL DAYS AND
   PLACES

Often the classroom must double as a gymnasium. Some schools do not have a gymnasium or playground; many others do not have sufficient floor space to accommodate all the children who must participate at any one time, particularly in bad weather when the outdoor playing fields cannot be used. Even in schools with entirely adequate facilities for physical education, the classroom is the scene for much interesting physical education activity used by the teacher to relieve tension or fatigue, to promote learning in other areas of the curriculum, and to observe holidays and other special occasions. The use of active games for these purposes in the classroom helps to promote physical fitness and motor skill development, supplementary to the regular physical education program; whereas in the situations in which the classroom must substitute for a regular physical education playing area, the classroom games become the physical education program and must be organized and selected to meet its objectives.

Organization of the classroom activities requires a certain amount of preliminary planning much like the organization of physical education on the playground or in the gymnasium or playing room. Consideration must be given to such matters as the formations which can be used in the area available, equipment required for playing the games, the total time allotment as well as the time to be given to each kind of physical education activity, and the safety factors peculiar to the classroom. Planning the orderly movement of the class to the playing area is eliminated, but in its stead is the problem of keeping the noise of the activity at a minimum so that children studying in adjacent classrooms will not be disturbed. Excessive noise can be controlled in part by careful selection of the activities and in part by teaching the youngsters to accept their responsibility in avoiding unnecessary movements and loud shouting during play.

The classroom must be made ready for safe participation. The desks and aisles should be cleared and hazardous objects elsewhere in the room removed. When a large playing area is needed, desks and chairs will need to be moved. Children should be taught the skills of correct pushing and pulling before they are ever permitted to move the heavy classroom furniture. A plan of which furniture should be moved where, which can be followed routinely, is useful in avoiding confusion and conserving time. Children should be cautioned repeatedly about any safety hazards in the room which cannot be eliminated.

To simplify for the teacher the selection of games for specific teaching purposes, the games in this chapter have been divided into three major sections: Active Classroom Games, Integrated Games, and Games for Special Days and Places. All the games are *active* in the sense that they require a significant degree of muscular movement. There are numerous passive games, such as guessing games, games with cards, and board games, which are played frequently in the classroom; but, while contributing to learning and recreation, they do not require sufficient muscular movement to fulfill the needs of the child for gross motor movement.

Figure 14–1 The classroom space, although limited in size, can be used for many kinds of activities. (Robert Jensen.)

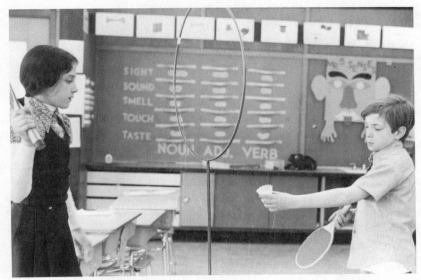

Figure 14–2 These students have devised a game for play in the classroom using a hoop, a stand, a badminton bird, and table tennis paddles. (Courtesy of Town of Vernon Schools, Rockville, Connecticut.)

In addition to the active games, many of the games and activities discussed in earlier chapters may be adapted to classroom use. Movement exploratory activities are especially adaptable; exploration may be from a stationary standing position or from a sitting position on the floor or at the desk. Specific exercises for improving body mechanics while seated at desks were described on page 147. Many of the stunts can be performed in the classroom; however, some require mats for the safety of the participants. By substituting walking for running, many of the tag, relay, and maneuvering for position games can be conducted as successfully in the classroom as on the playground; the substitution of bean bags, erasers, or balloons for the ball makes possible the use of many of the ball-handling games. Dances and rhythmic activities do not require modification if they are chosen with consideration of the space limitations.

ACTIVE CLASSROOM GAMES

Grouped under this heading are games suitable for play in the restricted space of the classroom. They are simply organized and require little in the way of equipment. But more significantly, they contribute to the physical education of the children and offer an alternative to the sedentary activities of the classroom.

On My Way To School (Grades K–1)

DESCRIPTION OF GAME. No equipment is necessary. One child stands in the front of the room and says, "On my way to school today I saw. . ."

and then he pantomimes what he saw. The others guess what he saw. The one guessing correctly goes to the front of the room and the game is played again. If no one guesses correctly, a child is chosen from the group by the one in front of the room.

Teaching Hints. The children hold up their hands and the teacher calls on someone to respond to ensure that everyone has an opportunity to participate.

Clapping Game (Grades K–1)

DESCRIPTION OF GAME. The game may be played by any number. No equipment is required. The children stand facing the teacher or a child who has been chosen to lead the game. The leader claps out a simple pattern with the hands. He calls upon someone to try to clap the same pattern. If that child is able to do so, he remains standing. If he is unsuccessful, he must sit down.

Teaching Hints. The younger the children, the simpler the pattern of clapping must be. For variety, a drum may be used instead of the hands.

Birds Fly (Grades K–1)

DESCRIPTION OF GAME. Any number of players may participate. Nothing is needed in the way of equipment. All the players stand by their seats except the leader who faces the group. The leader calls out, "Birds fly, butterflies fly, cars fly," etc. When he names something which flies, the group goes through the motion of flying by waving their arms up and down at their sides. When something that does not fly is named, they must not imitate flying. Anyone who does so when a nonflying object is named, or does not fly when a flying object is named, becomes the leader.

Teaching Hints. To give more exercise to the postural muscles, the teacher may have the children "fly" with the arms outstretched, palms up, rotating first down, then back, up, and forward. When they are not "flying," the fingers are interlaced behind the head.

Color on Color (Grades K–1)

DESCRIPTION OF GAME. Any number may play. A box of large colored crayons is needed. Several children close their eyes, while the teacher or a child chooses a crayon and places it next to some larger conspicuous object somewhere in the room. The children who have been hiding their eyes may open them and begin the search for the crayon as soon as the one who has placed the crayon returns to the group. Anyone who sees the crayon comes back to the group and says, "Red matches green," if, for example, red is the color of the crayon and green the color of the object near which it is located. The last one to discover the crayon returns it to the box, and the procedure is repeated.

Teaching Hints. If the child gives the wrong color cue, as is sometimes the case, the teacher should make the correction.

Poor Pussy (Grades K–1)

DESCRIPTION OF GAME.   No equipment is needed. A maximum of 25 children sit in circle formation. One child is chosen to be "poor pussy." Poor pussy kneels before a child and meows three times. The child whom he is facing must pat the pussy on the head after each meow and say "poor pussy" without laughing. If he laughs, he becomes poor pussy. If not, the pussy must try someone else.

Teaching Hints.   The teacher may encourage poor pussy to make faces or make a squeaky or peculiar meow to help evoke laughter.

Ringmaster (Grades K–1)

DESCRIPTION OF GAME.   The entire group participates. No equipment is needed. The children form a circle around one child who has been selected as the "Ringmaster." The "Ringmaster" points to a child and names an animal. The child gives his interpretation of the movements of this animal. When everyone has had a chance to imitate an animal, all the children form into a line for a parade led by the "Ringmaster." They move about the room, each imitating the animal he represents.

Teaching Hints.   The children should be encouraged to make different interpretations of the animal's movements if an animal is named more than once, as is often the case with young children with limited knowledge of the kinds of animals.

Statue (Grades K–1)

DESCRIPTION OF GAME.   Some type of music is required for this game. There is no limit to the number that may participate. The children are to mimic something, an elephant, a merry-go-round, etc. When the music stops, each participant stops instantly and holds the position as a statue. The teacher brings the attention of the rest of the class to the "funniest" statue.

Teaching Hints.   The children should be reminded that they are not to move after the music stops. Their statue position must be a spontaneous one.

Under the Bridge (Grades K–1)

DESCRIPTION OF GAME.   The whole class may participate. A record player or piano is required. All the children remain seated in rows except two. These two stand on each side of a desk and clasp hands over the desk. As the music is played, the two with hands clasped move down the row until the music stops. Then their arms are lowered around the child sitting at his desk. The one captured chooses a partner and the two join the couple already up. The game continues until no one is left in his seat.

Teaching Hints.   If the music stops when the couple is between two seats, they are to move forward to the next seat.

Hot Eraser (Grades K–2)

DESCRIPTION OF GAME.   There are 10 to 15 players to each circle. The number of circles will be limited by the space available. One eraser will be needed for each circle. When the teacher calls, "Pass the eraser," the eraser is passed either to right or left and continues being passed around the circle. When the teacher calls, "Hot," whoever has the eraser gets a point. The one with the least number of points over a period of time wins.

Teaching Hints.   The eraser must be passed, not thrown. Students should be encouraged against hesitation when it is their turn to take the eraser.

Climbing the Ladder (Grades K–3)

DESCRIPTION OF GAME.   A ladder is drawn on the floor with 10 rungs, each 1 foot apart. A ladder is drawn for each group consisting of not more than 10 players. The leader of each group climbs the ladder by stepping in between each rung. The other members of the group must do likewise. A player stepping on a rung goes to the head of the line and becomes the leader. When all have had a turn, the leader hops between the rungs and all must do likewise. The leader may skip, hop, walk backward, or move in any other way he chooses. All must follow him. The winners for each group are the last three in line after a designated period of time.

Teaching Hints.   The children should stay in line and turn to their right when returning from the top of their ladder to the bottom to facilitate their movement without collision.

Wastebasket Ball (Grades K–6)

DESCRIPTION OF GAME.   A basketball or volleyball and a wastebasket are needed. There can be 4 or 5 players for each wastebasket and ball. The players stand behind a designated line and throw the ball into the wastebasket. A score is recorded each time a basket is made.

Teaching Hints.   Teams may be formed to enhance competition. An underhand throw is the most effective in scoring, and there is less possibility of a "wild" toss with that type of shot than with a one-hand push shot or a two-hand set shot.

Chair Ring Toss (Grades K–6)

DESCRIPTION OF GAME.   A chair and three rings are needed for every four children. Any number of groups may play. The player stands behind a designated line and throws a ring in an attempt to ring one of the legs of the chair. If he does so successfully, he scores 1 point.

Teaching Hints.   The most effective throw is an underhand toss. The hand is brought waist high to the center of the body. The wrist is cocked. The arm is swung forward, keeping it parallel to the floor. As the ring is released, the wrist is straightened. The eyes are kept focused on the chair leg.

Do This, Do That (Grades 1–3)

DESCRIPTION OF GAME. No equipment is necessary. All players stand facing a child selected as a leader. The leader assumes any position or imitation of action he chooses and says "Do This." All players immediately imitate the action. If the leader says "Do That" instead of "Do This," all players must remain motionless. Any player who performs the movement must change places with the leader.

Teaching Hints. Gymnastic and stunt positions may be used to provide more vigorous exercise.

Squirrel with a Nut (Grades 1–3)

DESCRIPTION OF GAME. A piece of chalk or any object that is small enough to grasp in the hand is necessary. The entire class may play. All the children except one sit at their desks with their heads resting on their left arm. The right arm is stretched forward with the open palm up. One child is the "squirrel" with the "nut." With the object in his hand, he runs quietly down the rows and drops the nut in the open hand of some child. That child jumps up and chases the squirrel who races for his seat. If he is caught, he must be the squirrel again. If he reaches his seat before being tagged, the other child becomes the squirrel.

Teaching Hints. The child who is the squirrel should be encouraged to give the nut to one of the children who has not had a chance to run. To encourage more activity, a squirrel may be chosen for each row.

Spin the Platter (Grades 2–5)

DESCRIPTION OF GAME. Ten to 15 children may play this game in an area 30 by 30 feet. A metal pie plate is required. The children stand or sit in a single circle formation, and each child is given a number. The child who is "It" is in the center of the circle. He spins the pie plate as he calls a number. The child whose number was called attempts to catch the plate before it stops spinning. If he is successful, he becomes "It" and the game is continued.

Teaching Hints. The child may become "It" even if he does not catch the plate. The size of the circle may be increased as the children's skill is increased.

Bean Bag Circle Toss (Grades 2–3)

DESCRIPTION OF GAME. Any number may play; half as many bean bags as there are players will be needed. One bean bag should be of a different color or marked in some way so it will be readily identified. Players are in a single circle formation, facing the center and standing 3 to 6 feet apart. Every second player has a bean bag. The leader has the bag which is different. Players toss the bag to the player on their right and turn to the left to receive the next bag. The game ends when the special bag has traveled completely around the circle.

Teaching Hints. As the children's skill increases, the speed of passing may be increased, the distance between players may be increased, and/or the direction of passing may be reversed from time to time on command of the teacher.

Jump the Brook (Grades 2–3)

DESCRIPTION OF GAME. Chalk is used to draw two lines representing a brook. The lines should be approximately 3 feet apart and gradually increase in distance to 4½ feet, depending upon the age and skill of the children. It is suggested that there be no more than 10 players for each "brook." Players form a line and walk or run to the brook and jump over it at its narrowest point. If a child succeeds in jumping at the narrowest place, he moves to the next widest point. Those who fail should keep trying at the same spot. Each child moves along the brook as he succeeds at each spot. The student jumping the greatest distance is the winner.

Bean Bag Passing (Grades 2–4)

DESCRIPTION OF GAME. The entire class is divided into relay teams of six to eight members each. A bean bag is needed for each team. The team member at the head of each line holds a bean bag. On signal, he passes the bean bag to the teammate directly behind him. Each member, in turn, repeats this procedure. When the bag reaches the end of the line, it is passed back up to the front. The team whose bag is returned to the head of the line first wins. The bag may be passed with either or both hands. A team dropping a bag must begin again at the head of the line.

Last Seat (Grades 2–4)

DESCRIPTION OF GAME. The players sit in their chairs in rows. Nothing is needed in the way of equipment. A player stands behind each row. At the command, "Go," he runs forward to the head of the row and touches the first child in the row who stands. He takes this youngster's seat. The student who has just arisen touches the person behind who rises. He then takes that seat. This continues on down the row until the player in the last seat rises. He must run to the front of the row. The game continues until everyone returns to his original position.

Teaching Hints. The children should move to their right to return to the head of the row to avoid collision with other runners.

Catch the Cane (Grades 3–4)

DESCRIPTION OF GAME. Eight to 15 children may play this game in an area 30 by 30 feet. A cane or wand is required. The children stand in a single circle formation. All players are given a number. "It" is in the center of the circle, holding the cane upright on the floor with one end on the floor and the other end under the tip of his index finger. As he releases the cane, he calls a number. The player whose number is called attempts to catch the cane before it strikes the floor. If he catches it, he returns to his place in the circle. If he fails, he becomes the new "It."

Teaching Hints. Sawed-off broom handles may be used. The difficulty of the game may be increased by making the circle larger. Children catching the wand may become "It" instead of those failing to catch it.

Eraser Relay (Grades 3–4)

DESCRIPTION OF GAME. The entire class may participate. A clean eraser is needed for each row of seats. This eraser is placed on the floor next to the right of the seat of each child in the right-hand row of seats. The children are seated. On the signal, each child in the right-hand row picks up the eraser in his right hand, passes it to his left hand, and places it on the floor next to the seat of the child to his left. The child to his left repeats this procedure. The eraser is passed in this manner across the width of the room. The team which places the eraser on the floor in the left-hand outside aisle first is declared the winner.

Teaching Hints. To increase the activity of the game two erasers may be used. The second eraser cannot be passed until the first eraser has been placed on the floor on the left side of the room.

Clodhopper Relay (Grades 4–5)

DESCRIPTION OF GAME. Ten to 25 children can participate in this relay simultaneously in an area at least 15 by 30 feet. Two large shoe boxes will be needed for each relay team. The children are lined up behind the starting line in files of four to eight players. Two shoe boxes are placed on the floor in front of the first child in each file. On the starting signal, the first child steps into one of his boxes, balances himself on one foot, reaches back to grasp the other box in his hand, places it one step ahead of himself, steps into it with the foot which he has been holding in the air, balances on the forward foot, and repeats the previous procedures, progressing in this manner until he reaches the touch line. He then turns around and returns in the same manner. When he reaches the line, he hands the boxes to the second child and goes to the rear of the line. All members of the team take their turn. The team which finishes first is the winner.

Teaching Hints. Several extra shoe boxes should be on hand to replace the ones that come apart during the race. The shoe boxes may be re-enforced with tape.

Throw and Duck (Grades 4–6)

DESCRIPTION OF GAME. The entire class is divided into equally numbered rows. A bean bag, a slightly deflated ball, or other soft object is needed for each row. The first child in each row faces his line and on the signal "Go" throws a bean bag to the second player who catches it and returns it to the first player. The second player then squats. The bag is passed to the third player who catches it, returns it to the first player, and then squats. Passing continues until all players have caught and passed the bag. The first player then goes to the end of the line, and the second person passes the bag to others. Play proceeds until all players have had the chance to be the number one passer. The row completing the relay first is the winner.

Balloon Ball (Grades 4–6)

DESCRIPTION OF GAME. A durable balloon of any size is required. The entire class is divided into two teams. Every other row is a member of the same team. On one side of the room is the goal for one team; on the other side is the other team's goal. All players must remain seated. A balloon is tossed into the air in the center of the room. The players strike it and try to get it over their goal. Each goal counts one point. The winner is the team scoring the most points over a designated period of time.

Teaching Hints. If making a goal becomes too easy, a goalkeeper from each team may be chosen. He stands in the row in front of the opponents' goal. He must stay in the row, but he may move up and down the row to defend the goal.

Eraser Shuffleboard (Grades 4–6)

DESCRIPTION OF GAME. A hard-backed eraser and a pointer or some other stick are necessary. Four circles are drawn on the floor in any pattern. The children stand behind a designated line and shove the eraser on its back forward with the pointer. A score is made if the eraser lands in one of the four circles. An eraser stopping on the line is considered out.

Teaching Hints. For the younger children a shorter distance should be used and an eraser stopping on a line may be counted as a score. If a pointer is not available, the children may propel the eraser forward by shoving it with their hands.

Seat Tag (Grades K–6)

DESCRIPTION OF GAME. No equipment is necessary and the entire class may participate. One child is chosen to be "It" and stands in front of the room. The teacher calls the names of any two children who must arise and exchange seats. "It" tries to tag one of them before he reaches the other's seat. The one who is tagged becomes "It." If no one is tagged, the same child continues as "It."

Teaching Hints. The teacher may call the two names in such a manner that at first it is very difficult for "It" to catch a player. After a period of time, the teacher may make the call so it will be more difficult for the runners.

Classroom Tag (Grades K–6)

DESCRIPTION OF GAME. No equipment is necessary. The entire class may participate. A circle 5 to 10 feet in diameter is drawn on the floor. One person is chosen to be "It." The teacher calls any three names of children who then must attempt to get into the circle without being tagged by "It." If a player is tagged, he becomes "It." Those who are not tagged return to their seats.

Teaching Hints. The circle may be made larger or smaller to make it more difficult or less difficult to tag someone, depending upon the skill of the players.

Bowling (Grades 4–8)

DESCRIPTION OF GAME. A chair and a volleyball or softball are used for each four children. The class is divided into groups of four and chairs are set up one for each group about 10 feet apart. The children stand 20 to 30 feet away from the chairs, and each in turn attempts to roll the ball in between the legs of the chair. If he is successful, he scores one point. The highest score in 10 tries is the winner.

INTEGRATED GAMES

In this section are included games which have been successfully used by classroom teachers to help pupils increase their skills in reading, spelling, mathematics, etc., by incorporating them with motor movement activities. The integration of physical education with other subject matter has been shown to have motivational value. When some aspect of academic learning is attached to successful achievement of motor movement, children often become as enthused with the learning as with the movement. This is particularly true if the cognitive learning is fairly simple; observation indicates that the high level of enthusiasm for the activity is reduced when the learning incorporated into the game is complex.

In addition to the motivational value of integrated games, there is some evidence to indicate that academic performance may be improved by moderate exercise. In a research study[1] subjects who had been exercised moderately on a treadmill performed better in certain academic areas of study than did those who had not received the exercise. Although the reason for the better performance is not clearly established, the result seems to indicate that motor activity of a moderate nature is beneficial to the learning process for some students.

Integration of cognitive learning with motor activity seems to have still other advantages, particularly for young children and slow learners. The association of specific information with a certain movement provides a point of reference that makes the information more easily recalled. A longer period for assimilation of the information is provided by the game situation. Also, the opportunity to repeat a response may be greater in a game. Not all children need the slowed and repetitive learning process afforded by integrated games, but they generally enjoy the game for its own sake so that, while some profit more than others, all have fun and all experience the benefits of motor activity.

SPELLING AND LETTER RECOGNITION

Games are an excellent aid in the teaching of letter recognition and spelling. Some of the games described in this section give pupils experience in identifying letters in various type and case forms. Other games provide practice in recognizing the correct sequence of the letters in the alphabet and in spelling simple words.

Picking up the Alphabet (Grades K–1)

DESCRIPTION OF ACTIVITY.   The letters of the alphabet are drawn on small pieces of cardboard and scattered in a circle. Each child in turn goes forward and picks up the letter with which his name begins.

Teaching Hints.   As his ability progresses, the child may be asked to pick up the letters representing his initials or to pick the first letter of a certain word. Children who have learned to spell simple words may be asked to pick up all the letters that spell a specific word. This may be done by one child, or several children may each pick up one letter until the word is spelled.

Identifying Letters (Grades K–1)

DESCRIPTION OF ACTIVITY.   Letters of the alphabet are printed on pieces of cardboard and placed in a box. Each child draws a letter from the box, identifies the letter, and runs to the front of the room to place it against the wall.

Teaching Hints.   Children who have learned the alphabet can place the letters in their proper sequence.

Arranging Letters (Grades K–1)

DESCRIPTION OF ACTIVITY.   Letters are cut from cardboard and scattered on a large table. Children in turn select a letter, identify it, and place it so that it is in its proper position in the alphabet.

Letter Step or Letter Hopscotch (Grades K–5)

DESCRIPTION OF ACTIVITY.   Letters are drawn in chalk or painted on the floor. A letter is written on the board or spoken by the teacher, and the children, in turn, step on the letter indicated.

Teaching Hints.   For older children hopping may be substituted for stepping, and several letters may be given to each child. Also, instead of giving the child a letter, he may be given a word to spell by hopping on the correct letters.

Letter Race (Grades K–2)

DESCRIPTION OF GAME.   Fifty-two cards, blocks, or other suitable pieces with letters of the alphabet on them are needed. There should be two sets of cards lettered from A to Z, i.e., two A's, two B's, etc. through Z. The players are divided into two teams which are facing each other on opposite sides of the room. The members of each team are in rank formation a minimum of 4 feet from the side wall. One alphabet is scattered on the floor, face up, between the two teams. The other alphabet is placed on a table face down, at the rear of the room. On the starting signal, the first player in each line runs to the table, picks up a letter, runs back to the head of the line and passes the letter to the next player. The letter is passed quickly down the line until it reaches the last player who then runs to the letters on the floor, finds the matching letter, runs around the head of his line and behind it to the table, places both letters in a pile to his team's side of the table, takes another letter, runs to the head of his line, and passes the letter to the next player. This procedure is continued until all the letters have been picked up. The team with the most letters is declared the winner.

Teaching Hints. To increase familiarity with different kinds of lettering, the sets may be of different styles, e.g., one printed and one script or one capital letters and the other small letters.

Shuffle Letters (Grades 1–3)

DESCRIPTION OF GAME. Two complete sets of carboard letters of the alphabet are required. The two sets should be in contrasting colors. A list of words must be prepared in advance by the teacher. No letter of the alphabet may appear more than once in each word. A table will also be needed. The children are divided into two teams and each team is in rank formation on opposite sides of the room. The table is placed midway between the teams and the two sets of cardboard alphabets are thoroughly shuffled and placed face down on the table. The players on each team are numbered consecutively beginning at the right of each line. The teacher announces a word to be spelled and the number 1 player of each team runs to the table, searches for the first letter of the word, and after finding it runs back in front of his line holding the letter for all his teammates to see. When player number 1 reaches his position in line, player number 2 runs to the table, finds the second letter and runs to his place beside number 1. Succeeding players secure letters in this manner until the team has all the letters in the word. The team spelling the word correctly first is declared the winner. After having completed the spelling of one word, the letters are thoroughly reshuffled and returned to the table. The game is begun again with a new word with the player next in line to the one who secured the last letter of the previous word.

Radio Station (Grades 2–4)

DESCRIPTION OF GAME. No equipment is required. One of the children is chosen to serve as "It." "It" is in front of the class. The remaining children are standing next to their desks. "It" spells out action words as though they were letters of a radio or TV station and everyone does what the word spells. "It" may say: "This is station H-O-P," or "This is station R-U-N."

Team Spelling (Grades 2–5)

DESCRIPTION OF GAME. Two complete sets of cards 3 by 3 inches with one letter of the alphabet on each card running from A through Z are needed. The children are divided into two teams. The members of each team are in rank formation along the sides of the room. One alphabet is distributed among the members of each team. Some children might have two or more cards. The teacher calls a word which the children may be expected to spell. The children holding the letters in this word quickly step forward, arrange themselves in the proper order and, when the teacher indicates, step back into line. A point is scored for their team each time they spell out the word correctly before their opponents. The game continues in this fashion.

Live Letters (Grades 4–6)

DESCRIPTION OF GAME. Two alphabet card sets are needed. The cards should be between 6 by 6 inches and 12 by 12 inches in size. The cards can be strung so that the children may hang them around their necks or hold them in front of their chests. No cards are needed for the letters Q, X, Y, and Z. Two teams are selected and each team is arranged in a line formation. Each team has an alphabet card set. A captain is chosen for each team and a child is selected to play "It." "It" calls out a word. The captain of each team quickly gathers together the players holding the letters of this word, hurries them over to "It" and arranges them in the proper order. The captain getting his team in proper order first earns 5 points for his team. This procedure is repeated, until the time is up. If a letter is used twice in a word as "a" in salad, the holder runs back and forth pausing alternately between "s" and "l" and between "l" and "d." In a word with a double letter, as the letter "t" in butter, the holder waves his letter back and forth.

Spell and Wave (Grades 4–6)

DESCRIPTION OF .GAME.   The class is divided into two or more teams for a spelling bee. The teacher presents a word to each child which he spells except that instead of saying "a" he waves his right hand and instead of saying "r" he waves his left hand. For example, if the teacher pronounces the word "star," the player will say "st____" and then wave his right hand followed by a wave of his left hand. Five points are awarded to each team when a member spells a word correctly, and 5 points are deducted each time a member commits an error. The team with the greatest number of points is declared the winner.

Teaching Hints.   The list should be made up of words containing the letter "a" or the letter "r" or both, which the children may be expected to know how to spell. To increase the challenge of the game for proficient spellers, other letters may be placed on the "motion" list. It might be required that the letter "i" be indicated by winking the eye, the letter "s" by stamping the right foot, and the letter "t" by clapping the hands together.

OTHER LANGUAGE ARTS

Games may be useful in the development of language arts in children. They offer experiences in play situations that help to expand reading vocabulary, perfect pronunciation of words, and increase ability to interpret the meaning of words or describe a thought or observation.

Creative Movement Story (Grades K–3)

DESCRIPTION OF ACTIVITY. A story is read to the children, and at a certain point in the story the children are asked to express in movement the feelings generated in them by that part of the story. For example, Jack and the Beanstalk may be read to the children. The points in the story at which the teacher may ask for reactions are:

1. The mother's decision that the cow must be sold.
2. Jack taking the cow to town.
3. Jack meeting the merchant and trading the cow for the beans.
4. Mother's reaction to the trade when Jack returns home.
5. Jack's reaction next morning when he sees the vines.
6. Jack climbing the beanstalk.
7. Jack coming to the giant's castle.
8. Jack hiding from the giant.
9. Jack stealing the Golden Harp.
10. Jack running from the giant.
11. Jack cutting down the beanstalk.

Teaching Hints. Children should be encouraged to express their reactions in any way they desire. They need not necessarily pantomime the action of the story.

This Word Is Mine (Grades 1–2)

DESCRIPTION OF GAME. A number of words, the definition of which the children should know, are printed on cardboard or heavy paper. Each child is given a word. If the child can explain the meaning of the word, he is permitted to keep the word. If not, he must give the word back to the teacher. The children march around the room holding the words which they have successfully defined, stopping in front of the teacher to return the cards for another round of play.

Teaching Hints. To ensure everyone's having some success, the teacher should select words appropriate to each child's reading ability.

Phonic Train (Grades 1–2)

DESCRIPTION OF GAME. As many 3 by 2 inch oak-tag cards as there are children in the class will be needed. On each card are printed combinations of letters for sounds such as the following: "ing," "ack," "ay," "pl," "tr," "st," "ch," etc. A card is given to each child. The children are in line formation along the side of the room. Each child has his left hand on the shoulder of the child in front of him and holds the card in his right hand. The children march around the room making the sound "ch." When they reach their "depot" (the desk in front of the room), they stop and face the teacher who is sitting in the front row. Then each child, in his turn, utters the sound which he holds. The children then march around again with their left hand on the shoulder of the child ahead and repeat the "ch" sound. When they again reach their depot, they face the teacher and each, in his turn, presents a word which includes the sound that he holds. The child with "ing" could say "sing," one with "ack" could say "back," one with "pl" could say "place," etc.

Action Reading (Grades 1–3)

DESCRIPTION OF GAME.   A list of action words such as fly, hop, skip, whistle, clap, run, jump, sing, etc., is made from the children's reading vocabulary. The teacher writes the word "hop" on the board, asks a child or several children to perform the action, and then asks him to tell what he did as, "I hopped." The teacher presents several words in this manner. The children are then asked to remember all the words on the board as the teacher erases them. A child is then called upon to perform the several actions and to tell what he did. Example: "I flew, hopped, and skipped." Each day more action words may be added to the list.

Read and Act (Grades 2–3)

DESCRIPTION OF GAME.   No equipment is required. The children may remain in their seats except when they are called upon to perform. The teacher writes an action sentence on the board such as: "Hold up your hand," or "Stand up and sit down," using words which are known or can be sounded out. The teacher then points to or calls the name of a child. The child performs the action called for and tells what he did. The game can be made a little more complex by writing two or more sentences on the board, then erasing them and asking children to perform these actions and to state what they did.

Tell a Story (Grades 2–8)

DESCRIPTION OF ACTIVITY.   Each child selects a story to tell in movement. The other children interpret the movements and express their concept of the story verbally.

Teaching Hints.   The teacher should point out that interpretation is an individual response, and it is not necessary that all children agree in their interpretation or even agree with the performer. Nevertheless, the performer should strive to communicate to all; and to help him do so, he may be permitted to say a few key words as he performs.

Boiler Burst (Grades 3–4)

DESCRIPTION OF GAME.   Five to 15 children gather around a player who is telling a story. In his story he suddenly says, "boiler burst!" On this signal the children dash for the goal line or other safety zone and the story teller attempts to tag one. The child tagged starts a new game with a new story.

Have You Seen My Pal? (Grades 3–4)

DESCRIPTION OF GAME. Ten to 30 players form a circle facing the center. One child stands outside the circle. He is the "tagger." The tagger runs around the circle, stops behind a player, tags him, and asks: "Have you seen my pal?" The tagged player asks: "How is he dressed?" The tagger describes the clothing and appearance of a player in the circle. If the player tagged recognizes the player described, he runs around the circle attempting to reach the place he has vacated before the person described who, on recognizing his own description, runs around the circle attempting to reach the vacated place first. If the pal is tagged before he can reach the vacated poistion or, if the child chasing him reaches the position first, he becomes the tagger and the former tagger takes the pal's place in the circle. If the pal is not caught, the tagger and the person he tagged repeat their earlier conversation describing another player as the pal.

Teaching Hints. When the game is introduced to the students, explanation should be made of the techniques of describing objects and people.

Story Telling Game (Grades 4–6)

DESCRIPTION OF GAME. No equipment is necessary, but there is one less chair than the number of students. Players are each given the name of a stage coach part. One child tells a story about the stage coach mentioning all the parts assigned earlier. As the child's part is named, he gets up and runs around his chair. When the storyteller calls "Stage Coach," all players must change chairs with anyone except the player on his left or right. The leader tries to get a chair, and the player left seatless becomes the new leader.

Teaching Hints. Objects related to the children's studies may be substituted for the stage coach.

Block Writing (Grades 4–6)

DESCRIPTION OF GAME. Several blocks of wood, paper, and pencils are needed. A list of verbs to be conjugated is written on the board. The children are divided into as many teams as there are blocks. The members of each team line up behind their block of wood. On signal, the first child in each line steps up on the block, balances himself on one foot, and writes the conjugation of the first verb in the list on the paper. When he finishes, he steps down and hands the paper and pencil to the next child who repeats the procedure with the second verb of the list. This continues until all have had a turn. The team making the least number of errors in the shortest time is the winner.

Observation (Grades 5–6)

DESCRIPTION OF GAME. Eight to 10 players line up in front of the room holding some object. Other players observe items for one minute. The players holding the objects leave the room in order, and the observers write down the order in which the players were standing and what they were holding.

1	2	3	4	5	6
7	8	9	0	1	2
3	4	5	6	7	8
9	0	1	2	3	4
5	6	7	8	9	0
1	2	3	4	5	6

Figure 14–3 Hopscotch Numbers court.

Observers exchange papers, the players return to the room in order, and the papers are checked. The winner is the observer with the most correct answers.

MATHEMATICS

Numbers become more meaningful to young children when used in activities in which they are interested. For this reason, games designed to teach number recognition or number facts are popular choices in the classroom. Math experience can be extended beyond these specific games by involving the children in such activities as measuring playing courts, keeping scores and records, graphing and charting skills, and computing averages.

Hopscotch Numbers (Grades K–1)

DESCRIPTION OF ACTIVITY.   Letters are printed on the floor with chalk or paint as shown in Figure 14–3. The teacher calls out a number and a child hops or steps on the number.
Teaching Hints.   If the number that is called is more than one digit, the child can be instructed to hop on the numbers in the proper sequence.

Number Race (Grades K–2)

DESCRIPTION OF GAME.   Two sets of large plastic or cardboard numbers from one to 10 are needed. The players are divided into two teams who take rank formation a few feet from one another. The sets of numbers are scattered on the floor, face up, in front of each team. On the starting signal, the first player in each line runs foward, picks up number 1, returns to the head of his line, touches the child at the head of the line, and takes a place at the end of the line. As soon as he has been touched, the child who was at the head of the line runs forward to pick up number 2. This procedure is duplicated by each child in line until all the numbers have been picked up. The winner is the team who first picked up the numbers in the proper sequence.

Step Fast (Grades 1–2)

DESCRIPTION OF GAME.   A bottle or similar object that can be spun on the floor is needed. A circle with a diameter of 12 inches is drawn for each child at one end of the classroom. Each child is assigned a number and a circle. He writes his number in his circle. Another circle is drawn for each child on the floor at the opposite end of the play area. The circles may be drawn on the blackboard. Each child next writes his number in the new circle. All the children then return to their first circle. One child is appointed to serve as "bottle spinner." The bottle spinner stands to one side and in front of the group. He spins the bottle and when it stops, he claps his hands. The moment the bottle begins spinning the players walk as fast as they can toward their second circle counting their steps. When the bottle spinner claps his hands, the players stop walking and each writes in the second circle the number of steps he has taken.

Geometric Figures (Grades 1–3)

DESCRIPTION OF GAME. The entire class plays this game on the playground or in a classroom with movable chairs. The teacher must first acquaint the children with the various geometric figures by drawing them on the board with their names above them. The players are divided into two teams. A captain is appointed for each team. When the teacher calls the name of a figure, the captain of each team arranges his team members into the formation called for, i.e., circle, oblong, square, or triangle. The team which first correctly assumes the form called for earns 1 point. The team with the most points at the end of the playing period is declared the winner. Plus and minus signs, question and exclamation marks, stars, and ovals may also be called for.

Egg Market (Grades 1–3)

DESCRIPTION OF GAME. One child is appointed as "buyer" and another as "seller." The remaining children squat with their hands clasped behind their knees. The following conversation ensues:

> Buyer: "Have you any eggs to sell?"
> Seller: "I have."

The buyer and seller then go from child to child with the buyer on one side and the seller on the other. They grasp each child (egg) under the arms with both hands and swing him vigorously back and forth. If the egg does not release its hold, it is a "good" egg. If the egg does release its grasp, it is a "bad" egg and is "thrown out" of the market. The buyer asks the seller the cost of each egg. He names any amount within a limit set by the teacher according to the arithmetic level of the class. The buyer and seller add the total cost of the good eggs.

The Wheel (Grades 2–4)

DESCRIPTION OF GAME. Two concentric circles are drawn on the floor. The smaller circle has a diameter of 2 feet and the larger a diameter of 8 feet. Eleven "spokes" or lines are drawn equally spaced, from the small circle to the large circle. Each area defined by these lines is numbered from 1 to 11. A drawing similar in all respects is made a few feet away. The teacher appoints two players to serve as "It." Each "It" stands inside one of the inner circles. The remaining children are divided into two teams. Each member of the team stands in a numbered area in his team's circle. The teacher calls: "Circle number 1 — 5 and 4." "It" in circle number 1 steps or jumps into area number 5 and then into area number 4. "It" in circle number 2 steps or jumps into area number 9. The "It" who accomplishes his respective chore correctly first earns 1 point for his team. A new "It" is appointed for each new problem in addition, subtraction, or multiplication. The team with the most points at the end of the playing period agreed upon is declared the winner.

Teaching Hints. For problems in multiplication and for problems in addition with answers above 11, areas should contain two or more numbers. That is, numbers would run 1 through 11 once around the circle and then continue around again to 22 and around again to 33.

Fizz-Buzz (Grades 3–6)

DESCRIPTION OF GAME. The players are in a single circle formation. On the signal, they begin counting. The first child says "1," the second "2," and so on around the circle. Whenever a player receives a number containing a 7 or which is a multiple of 7, he says "buzz" instead of the number. Whenever a player receives a number containing a 5 or one which is a multiple of 5, he says "fizz" instead of the number. Each time a player makes a mistake, he must skip around the circle. For his second mistake, he must hop around the circle on both feet. For his third mistake he must hop around the circle on one foot.

Teaching Hints. When there are more than 10 players, two or more circles may be formed.

SOCIAL STUDIES

Games may be used to enhance certain concepts in social science or to help in the learning of certain specific information such as the names of state capitals. In addition to the games described here, the teacher can easily adapt any of the basic skill games that include identification of players by name or number by substituting names of products, locations, historical persons, etc., so that the game relates to the subject matter being studied.

Fruit Basket (Grades 1–3)

DESCRIPTION OF GAME. No equipment is needed. All players in a circle are named for different fruits, vegetables or other products. A leader in the center calls two fruits, and the two children bearing these names run and change places in the circle. The leader tries to reach one of the places first, and the player left without a place is the new leader.

Teaching Hints. Players may be sitting in chairs, and then the leader tries to capture an empty seat. If the leader calls "fruit basket," all must change seats. The choice of product may be related to the social studies unit.

Trades (Grades 2–3)

DESCRIPTION OF GAME. The game may be played either in the classroom or on the playground. The entire class is divided into two teams. One team is located at either end of the play area. Team 1 decides on some action (hammering, raking leaves, mopping) and walks up to Team 2. As they walk they say:

> Team 1: Here we come!
> Team 2: Where from?
> Team 1: (Name of town.)
> Team 2: What's your trade?
> Team 1: Lemonade!
> Team 2: Show us!

Team 1 stops close to Team 2 and performs the action. When Team 2 guesses correctly, they chase Team 1 back to its goal and those tagged must join Team 2. The game continues with each team visiting the other. The group having the most children at the end of the play period is the winner.

Postman (Grades 4–7)

DESCRIPTION OF GAME. A large map is required. A "postman" and a "pointer" are appointed. The postman goes to the blackboard and writes the names of various cities on the board. Each of the rest of the players, who remain in their seats, selects the name of one of the cities. The postman announces that a letter has been sent from one city to another. The children representing the two cities named attempt to exchange seats before the postman can take one of their seats. If the postman fails in his efforts, he continues as postman. If he succeeds, the child left out becomes the new postman. After the completion of this action, the pointer points to the two cities on the map.

Teaching Hints. A map of the county, state, nation, or world may be used, and the play restricted or expanded accordingly.

Keeper of the States (Grades 5–7)

DESCRIPTION OF GAME. The names of the 50 states are written on cards; there are two cards for each state. One set of cards is placed on one side of the room and the other set on the opposite side. The class is divided into two teams. A "keeper of the states" is chosen for each team. He takes his place by one set of cards, arranging them on the floor so that he can see them easily. The remaining players are lined up in two rank files at the rear of the room. The teacher, who is seated at a desk in the middle of the front of the room, calls out the name of a capital. The first player in each line runs forward to his keeper and with his help selects the correct state. He then runs to the desk at which the teacher is seated and places the card there. The first player there with the correct card receives a point for his team. The runner takes the place of the keeper who goes to the end of his line. Play continues in this way with the team scoring the highest number of points declared the winner.

Products (Grades 5–8)

DESCRIPTION OF ACTIVITY. Half of the players in a circle are given names of different fruits, vegetables, or other products. The others are each given the name of a country that exports one of the products. One student stands in the center of the circle and calls the name of a product. The child who has that name changes places with the child who has the name of the appropriate country. During the exchange, the child in the center tries to reach one of the vacated places. The player left without a place goes to the center.

Teaching Hints. Players may be seated in chairs in a circle rather than standing.

State Capital Ball (Grades 5–8)

DESCRIPTION OF GAME. This game might be played on an outdoor playing field or in the gymnasium as well as in the classroom. A bean bag or playground ball is needed for classroom play, but for play elsewhere a softball might be used. The class is divided into two equal groups. Each group takes a rank formation facing the other group several feet away (the exact distance depends upon the amount of space available). Each player in one rank is assigned the name of a state. Each player in the other line is given the name of a state capital. A child with the name of a state throws the bean bag up as high as he can and at the same time calls out the name assigned to him. This is the signal for the player in the opposite line who has been assigned the name of the capital of that state to run forward to catch the bean bag. If he succeeds, the bag is passed to a player in the line which has the names of states and the procedure is repeated. If the catch is missed, both the "state" and "capital" are eliminated.

SCIENCE

Motor activity is well suited to the teaching of specific scientific concepts. Understanding of such concepts as balance, force, inertia, and friction can be promoted through identification of their application to motor movements. For example, as children attempt the stork stand (balance on one leg) the principles of balance may be explained and demonstrated. Force may be more easily comprehended by young children when illustrated by such activities as hitting a ball with a bat or kicking it into the air. Inertia is easily demonstrated with a rolling ball, and the concept thus established can be applied to understanding why it is more difficult to stop or turn while running at full speed than at a slower speed. A comparison of the differences in ability to stop while running in rubber soled shoes or in stocking feet on the floor of the gymnasium promotes understanding of the concept of friction.

Many other examples might be cited, but the purpose here is only to suggest the possibilities for integrating science and physical education. The increased understanding that results from illustrating scientific concepts and principles in motor movement is beneficial to the child both in the enhancement of scientific learning and in the application of the scientific principles to motor movement in everyday activities and in game situations.

GAMES FOR SPECIAL DAYS AND PLACES

In this section are games for use in connection with class observances of special occasions and with the study of different lands and peoples. Children, particularly those in the primary grades, anticipate with pleasure all special days and holidays. Many teachers like to capitalize on this interest to promote certain other kinds of learning; it is with this in mind, that this group of special day games has been collected for use in physical education. The games for special places consist of games played by children of other lands and races. Appreciation of other races and nationalities is fostered by the enjoyment children experience in playing games that have their origin with these peoples. The development of understanding and recognition of the achievements and contributions of other peoples is important in the educational process and should be actively promoted by teachers. Games of other lands are often taught in conjunction with a social studies unit on the foreign country, but they should not be limited to this use. They may be presented at any time, introduced with appropriate commentary. Children in the class who are of the race or country of the game's origin should be encouraged to add to the discussion any information they know about the game and to teach the class other games from the same source.

HALLOWEEN

Halloween Stunts (Grades K–1)

DESCRIPTION OF GAME. No equipment is required. The teacher calls out "cats," "ghosts," "goblins," "witches," or "spooks" which the children imitate. Witches distort their faces, cackle, flex their wrists, fingers, and arms, and tip-toe around. Cats walk on hands and feet with backs arched, hiss, and leap. Ghosts stomp around with arms extended sideward and say "who-o-o-o." Goblins walk stooped over with knees bent, arms swinging between legs, and make horrible noises. Spooks tip-toe behind others, leap into the air and say "Boo!"

Ghosts and Hobgoblins (Grades K–2)

DESCRIPTION OF GAME. No equipment is required. Two lines are drawn on the floor at opposite ends of the room. The children are divided into two teams. The members of one team are "ghosts" and the members of the other are "hobgoblins." The ghosts are lined up along one line with their backs to the hobgoblins who are lined up along the other line. On a signal from the "head hobgoblin," the hobgoblins tiptoe as close as they dare to the ghosts. Then on a signal from the head hobgoblin, the hobgoblins shout "boo!" which is the signal for the ghosts to give chase. Any hobgoblins tagged before they reach the safety of their own goal line become ghosts. Then the ghosts take their turn in sneaking up on the hobgoblins. The team with the most players at the end of the playing period wins the game.

Witches' Race (Grades K–2)

DESCRIPTION OF GAME. An old broom will be needed for each contestant if the event is run as a race, or for each team if it is run as a relay. A starting and a finish line are drawn on the floor or ground. Contestants are lined up in rank formation straddling their brooms behind the starting line. On the starting signal, they race to the touch line and back to the starting line. The first one back is the winner. The event may also be run as a relay.

Ghost Treasure (Grades K–3)

DESCRIPTION OF GAME. Wrapped candy or nuts and numbered cards are needed. A small circle is drawn in the center of the room into which the candy or nuts are placed. Four circles about 6 to 8 feet in diameter are drawn, one along each wall of the room. The players are divided into four teams, and each team stands in one of the circles. The members of team 1 have cards with the number 1 taped to their backs. The same is true for the members of teams 2, 3, and 4. On the starting signal, all of the players run out of their circle to get the treasure. Each player may carry back to his circle only one piece at a time. Players guilty of taking two pieces at one time are disqualified. If a player's number is snatched off his back by an opponent, he is "dead" and out of the game. The winning team is the one collecting the greatest amount of treasure. All teams may eat their treasure.

Bluebeard's Key (Grades 3–6)

DESCRIPTION OF GAME. A string and a key are required. The players are seated in a circle holding the string which passes through the key. They keep their hands moving along the string constantly passing the key one direction or the other—or retaining it. "It," who is in the center of the circle, attempts to discover who has the key. Whenever he touches a player's hand, that player must open the hand touched to show whether he has the key. If he has, he becomes "It" and the game continues.

Apple Push (Grades 4–6)

DESCRIPTION OF GAME. A box of toothpicks and several apples are required. Two lines parallel to one another and 10 feet apart are drawn on the floor. The players are divided into two or more teams. Half the members of each are lined up behind one line while the other half are lined up facing them behind the other line. Each player is given one toothpick. An apple is placed on the ground before the first player of each team. On the starting signal, the first player rolls the apple with the toothpick which he holds in his mouth to his teammate behind the other line. This player then rolls the apple back in the same manner to the next player in the opposite line. The team whose players have all exchanged sides first is declared the winner. If a player breaks his toothpick, he must take the apple back to the line and start over. The members of the winning team receive a box of "goblin teeth" (marshmallows).

Broomstick Pull (Grades 4–8)

DESCRIPTION OF GAME. A pumpkin and a broomstick are needed. These are placed in the center of the playing area. Players are divided into two teams and are numbered. When the teacher calls a number, the two players with that number, one from each team, come forward, grasp the broom handle, and attempt to pull their opponent past the pumpkin. The player who succeeds earns 1 point for his team. The team with the greatest number of points is declared the winner.

Teaching Hints. More children can play by having several games go on simultaneously.

THANKSGIVING

Farmer and Turkeys (Grades K–2)

DESCRIPTION OF GAME. A pen is drawn at one end of the playing area. One child is appointed to serve as the "farmer." The remainder of the children are "turkeys" and are in the "pen." The farmer pretends to throw out seed to the turkeys who follow to eat the seed. When the farmer has led them a good distance from the pen he shouts, "Today is Thanksgiving Day!" which is the signal for the turkeys to run to the safety of their pen with the farmer in pursuit. Turkeys tagged become farmers. The game continues until all the turkeys have become farmers.

Thanks (Grades 2–4)

DESCRIPTION OF GAME. It is necessary that the word "Thanks" be printed in large letters on a piece of paper for each group of six players. This paper is then cut so that there is a single letter on each piece. Each player is given a letter. Players are distributed at random in the room. They are instructed to find others with the next letter necessary to spell the word "Thanks." As they discover players with the letters they want, they link arms and continue their search until they have all the letters necessary. No player may link arms with anyone other than those who have the letter immediately following or preceding his own letter. Members of the group which completes its task first may be awarded a suitable Thanksgiving prize.

Turkey Corn Shuttle (Grades 2–5)

DESCRIPTION OF GAME. Four corncobs, wooden blocks, or bean bags are needed for each relay team. A starting line is drawn on the floor or ground. The corncobs are placed on the ground in front of each relay team in a line at a right angle to the starting line and spaced 5 feet apart with the first being 5 feet from the starting line. On the starting signal, the first child on each team runs to the first corncob, picks it up, runs back to place it behind the starting line, and repeats this procedure with the second, third, and fourth corncobs. The second child in each team, after being touched off by the first, returns the corncobs one at a time to their original position. This continues until all team members have run. The team which finishes first is declared the winner.

CHRISTMAS

Christmas Toys (Grades K–2)

DESCRIPTION OF GAME.   The children are seated on the floor around the teacher. The teacher says: "On Christmas Eve, when everyone is asleep, some people say that the toys all come to life and play until the rooster crows to warn them that morning is near and that people will soon be about. Let's pretend that we are toys under a Christmas tree!" The following are suggestions (children should be invited to think of others):

Jumping Jack.   Children leap upward with arms and legs apart and bring them together as they drop quietly into a squatting position.

Walking Toys.   Children are supine and "awaken" by slowly stretching and coming to the erect position.

Rocking Horse.   Children stand with one leg forward and rock back and forth with legs stiff, alternately lifting the forward and the backward leg.

Top.   Children whirl around, wobble, and fall gently to the floor.

Dancing Doll.   Children dance stiffly on their toes with tiny steps, move their arms and bow stiffly.

Toy Soldier.   Children march around the Christmas tree with arms and legs fully extended while pretending to beat a drum or to carry a gun.

Train.   Children shuffle slowly forward increasing the tempo.

Crowing Rooster.   One child stretches upward on his toes flapping his wings and the other children run to their original places to assume their original positions and lie, sit, or stand without moving.

Christmas Relay (Grades 2–4)

DESCRIPTION OF GAME.   A chair and an empty box wrapped and tied appropriately for Christmas are required for each relay team to be organized. A starting line is drawn on the floor at one end of the classroom. The chairs with the boxes on them are placed at the opposite end of the room. The players are in line formation behind the starting line. On the starting signal, the first player on each team runs forward to his chair, unties, unwraps, rewraps, and reties his package and runs back to touch off his next teammate. This continues until all members of the team have run. The team finishing first is declared the winner.

The Night Before Christmas (Grades 4–6)

DESCRIPTION OF GAME.   No equipment is required. One child is appointed to serve as Santa Claus. All the other children are seated on the floor in a circle around Santa Claus. Each child is a character in the story "The Night Before Christmas." Santa Claus tells this story. Each time his character is mentioned, the child stands up, turns around, and sits down again. If Santa Claus tags him before he is seated, he becomes Santa Claus and he continues the story. Whenever Santa Claus says "Santa Claus," all the players stand up, turn around, and sit down again while Santa Claus attempts to tag one of them before he can sit down.

Wreath Ball (Grades 4–6)

DESCRIPTION OF GAME.   A wreath with a bell attached and a light ball will be necessary. The wreath is suspended from the ceiling. The children take turns throwing the ball through the wreath. One point is scored for each successful shot, and two points are scored if the shot is successful and the bell rings. The game may be scored individually or by teams.

VALENTINE'S DAY

Valentine Mail (Grades 1–3)

DESCRIPTION OF GAME.   One child is appointed to serve as the "postman." The remaining children stand in a single circle formation around him. The postman calls: "I have a valentine for (name of child) from (name of child)." The named players immediately change places while the postman tries to get into one of the vacated positions. The player left without a position becomes the new postman.

The Valentine Maker (Grades 3–6)

DESCRIPTION OF GAME.   One child is appointed to serve as the "valentine maker." A chair will be needed for each of the remaining players. These chairs are arranged in a row with alternate chairs facing in opposite directions. Each player is given the name of a material or tool used in making a valentine (hearts, arrows, papers of various colors, cupids, scissors, paste, rhymes, crayons, etc.). There may be several with the same name. The valentine maker marches around the chairs calling for the materials he needs in making a valentine. The players representing these materials rise and follow him as their material is called. Suddenly the valentine maker calls "posted," at which everyone, including the valentine maker, jumps for a chair. The player left without a chair becomes the valentine maker for the next game.

Tossing My Heart (Grades 6–8)

DESCRIPTION OF GAME.   Five to 10 children can play this game in an areas as small as 10 by 10 feet. A larger number of children can play if several games go on simultaneously. A wastebasket for each game and 5 to 10 cardboard hearts for each player will be needed. Players arrange themselves in a circle, a distance of approximately 6 feet from the wastebasket and attempt to toss the hearts into the wastebasket. A point is awarded for each heart tossed into the wastebasket. The player with the most points is the winner.

GEORGE WASHINGTON'S BIRTHDAY GAME

Shaking Cherries (Grades 1–3)

DESCRIPTION OF GAME. One of the players is blindfolded and is standing in the center of a circle of players who are marching around him singing:

"Oh, here's a tree with cherries ripe, cherries ripe, cherries ripe,
Oh, here's a tree with cherries ripe,
A tree both green and tall
We'll shake it now with all our might, all our might, all our might,
We'll shake it now with all our might,
And watch the cherries fall."

While the players are singing, one of them gently shakes the blindfolded child. He must try to guess who shook him. If he guesses correctly, the person who shook him must take his place. If he does not, the blindfolded player remains in the center until he makes a correct guess.

EASTER

Bunny Hop (Grades K–1)

DESCRIPTION OF GAME. One child is appointed to serve as the "bunny." All the other children hop along behind the bunny as he takes a walk and chant, "hippity, hippity, hop." The bunny answers, "You're not allowed to stop" and continues walking as the players hop after him and chant. Suddenly, the bunny claps his hands, turns, and chases the players. Any players tagged by the bunny must help him to tag others until all are tagged. The child tagged last is the bunny for the next game.

Bunny Race (Grades K–2)

DESCRIPTION OF GAME. No equipment is required. Players form several lines of equal length. They stoop, with hands to either side of the head like rabbit ears. On a signal, the first child in each line jumps in short hops on both feet to a goal line and back. The procedure continues until all children have had a turn. The line with the fastest bunnies wins.

Easter Egg Race (Grades 1–3)

DESCRIPTION OF GAME. The equipment consists of a bag of jelly beans (Easter eggs). The class is divided into teams of four players. Each team has four jelly beans placed about 5 feet in front of its respective line. On "Go" the first runner from each team runs to the beans, picks up one bean, brings it back to the line and places it in a square drawn on the floor or in a basket. The second runner goes after another bean, and so forth. The team getting all the jelly beans in their square or basket first is the winner.

APRIL FOOL'S DAY

Pop Sack Relay (Grades 5–6)

DESCRIPTION OF GAME.   Ten to 30 children can play this game in an area as small as 15 by 20 feet. A paper bag is needed for each player. Players are divided into two or more teams. Members of each team are in line formation. Each player is given a bag. On the signal, the last man in line on each team blows up his bag and pops it on the back of the player in front of him. This is the signal for this player to blow up his bag and to pop it on the back of the next player. This continues until the player at the head of the line is reached. He pops his bag on his own knee. The team all of whose members pop their bags first is declared the winner. Players may also run up to a chair where the bags are stacked and there blow up the bag and pop it before running back to touch off the next player.

GAMES FROM OTHER PLACES

The Winds, American Indian (Grades K–1)

DESCRIPTION OF GAME.   An Indian head band with feathers may be worn by each child for this game. The players stand in single circle formation far enough apart that they can extend their arms sideward without touching their neighbors' hands. The teacher stands in the center of the circle and calls out the names of various winds. The Indians imitate these winds. For south wind, they face south and wave their outstretched arms gently. For east wind, they face east and wave their arms from front to back with somewhat greater vigor. For west wind, they face west and swing their arms vigorously across their bodies. For north wind, they wrap their arms around their bodies and turn around and around shivering. For cyclone, they whirl rapidly around and around with their arms extended sideward. For tornado, they hop around in a small circle and howl.

African Dance Game (Grades K–2)

DESCRIPTION OF GAME.   As a substitute for a tree, which is used for this game by African children, a large circle is drawn on the floor. Everyone dances around the circle coming as close as possible to the line without stepping on or over it. Those who step on the line or into the circle are eliminated.

La Candelite (The Little Candle), Puerto Rican (Grades K–2)

DESCRIPTION OF GAME. The class forms a circle. One child, chosen to be "It," stands inside the circle. He approaches a child with his hand extended and says, "Give me a little candle." In reply, the child points to another child elsewhere in the circle and says, "There is a candle smoking over there." As "It" moves toward this child to repeat his request, the first child to whom he spoke attempts to change places with another child of his choice. "It" tries to reach one of the vacant places. If he is successful, the child who is left without a place becomes "It."

Bead Guessing, American Indian (Grades 1–3)

DESCRIPTION OF GAME. Players form a circle in front of the room. One player is selected to be in the center, and he holds a bead in one hand behind his back. He walks up to one player who tries to guess in which hand the bead is held. After each guess, the center player must disclose which hand holds the bead. If the guesser is correct three times, the one holding the bead runs to his seat; if the guesser catches him, he becomes the player in the center. Each player may guess three times, but unless he chooses the correct hand all three times, the leader moves on to another player.

Polish Game (Grades 2–3)

DESCRIPTION OF GAME. Players are in a single circle formation. One player who has been appointed as "It" walks around the outside of the circle. He taps another player on the shoulder and greets him with "dzein (jane) dobry (dough-bri)" which means "good morning." He then runs around the circle. The tapped player meanwhile runs around the circle in the opposite direction. When they meet one another, they shake hands, stoop three times, and say, "jak (yaak) sie (sheh) masz (ma-sh)" which means "How are you?" They then continue running to the vacant spot. The last one there becomes "It" for the next round and the game continues.

Verbos, Dutch; Tap-the-Line, Belgian (Grades 2–4)

DESCRIPTION OF GAME. This game is a favorite of both Dutch and Belgian children. The former call it "Verbos" and the latter, "Tap-the-Line." A goal is marked (or an object placed) 15 to 20 feet from where the players are standing in a circle. The child who is selected as "It" runs around the circle and taps someone in the circle on the shoulder. Both race to the goal. The one who arrives at the goal first is "It" for the next turn. The other player remains at the goal.

Calabash, African (Grades 3–6)

DESCRIPTION OF GAME. The class is divided into groups of three. Two children in each group form a "wall" by locking hands around the third child who stands between them. The latter is the calabash plant trying to grow beyond the wall; therefore, he attempts to escape from the locked hands. The other players try to prevent this by moving their arms up and down without unlocking their hands.

Chinese Game (Grades 3–6)

DESCRIPTION OF GAME.   Ten sticks about a foot long will be needed for each player. A starting line is drawn on the floor or ground. The players stand behind this starting line. Ten sticks are laid on the ground in a line in front of each player. The sticks are about 12 inches apart. On the starting signal, all the contestants begin hopping on one foot over the sticks. When they reach the last stick, they kick it away with their hopping foot and then turn around and hop back on the opposite foot. When they reach the first stick, they kick it away with their hopping foot. They continue in this manner until all except the last stick has been kicked away. The player who finishes first is the winner.

Exchange, French (Grades 4–6)

DESCRIPTION OF GAME.   The only equipment needed for this game is a piece of cloth to be used to blindfold the one who is "It." The players are seated in chairs or on the floor in a circle. They number off from 1. "It" stands in the center of the circle and calls two numbers. Those whose numbers are called exchange places while "It" attempts to catch one of them or to occupy one of the vacant places. The player who is caught or left without a place becomes "It." Players may not go outside the circle.

Eskimo Race (Grades 4–6)

DESCRIPTION OF GAME.   A starting and a finish line are drawn 10 or more feet apart. The children are lined up toeing the starting line with their feet together and their knees rigid. On the starting signal they travel forward by springing on their toes with the legs held straight. The child who reaches the finish line first is declared the winner.

VARIATION.   This game may also be organized as a relay. The players are divided into two or more teams. The players begin in line formation and each player in his turn hops to the finish or touch line, runs back, and touches off the next member of his team.

Hopi Indian Game (Grades 4–6)

DESCRIPTION OF GAME.   Two hoops, about the size of hula hoops, and six darts are required. The children can make the darts of corncobs with a small piece of wood inserted into one end and two feathers inserted into the other end. Two lines are drawn on the floor 15 feet apart. The children are divided into two teams and two captains are appointed. Each captain stands behind one of the lines with a hoop which the two roll back and forth to one another. The players stand midway between the two lines and several feet (depending upon ability of the players) from the path of the rolling hoops. Three players from each team, each with a dart, line up and attempt to throw the dart through the rolling hoop. If a player throws a dart through one hoop, he earns his team 1 point. If he throws it through both hoops at the same time, he earns 4 points for his team.

Teaching Hints. It is helpful to have two "Indians" serve as runners to return the darts. Runners, captains, and throwers should be cautioned about going into the throwing area while throwers are on the firing line. Throwers should line up and throw simultaneously as the hoops roll through the center area.

Stone, Paper, Scissors, Japanese (Grades 4–6)

DESCRIPTION OF GAME. The class is divided into two equal lines facing each other. Each player faces his partner with hands held behind his back. A player selected as the leader counts "1,2,3," and on "3" each player brings his hands forward in one of three positions: clenched fists represent the stone; open hands represent the paper; and an extension of the first two fingers represents the scissors. The winner is the one who "beats" his opponent. Because the stone dulls the scissors, it beats them. Scissors beat the paper, because they can cut it, and paper beats the stone, because it can enwrap it. A running score is kept, and the line acquiring the highest number of points is the winner.

African Game (Grades 5–7)

DESCRIPTION OF GAME. A particular kind of shuttlecock and a stick are needed for each player. The children make their own shuttlecock from a small stone, a piece of leather thong 12 inches in length, a twig 6 inches long, and a feather with a stiff rib. The thong is wrapped around the stone several times with about 6 inches left hanging. The end of the hanging piece is tied to the twig in such a fashion that there are about four inches of thong between the twig and the stone. The feather is firmly attached to the end of the twig. Players hold a stick three or four feet long in their hand. The shuttlecock is draped over the far end of the stick. Players fling the shuttlecock into the air with the stick and catch it again on the end of the stick. A point is awarded a player each time he catches the shuttlecock on the end of his stick.

Teaching Hints. There should be sufficient distance between individual players so that there is no danger of a shuttlecock landing on a player.

Piñata, Mexican (Grades 5–8)

DESCRIPTION OF GAME. A large paper sack, a piece of rope about 10 to 15 feet in length, a stick 3 to 5 feet in length, one roll each of red, white, and green crepe paper and enough candy, fruit, and nuts to fill the paper sack are needed. The filled sack is decorated with the red, white, and green crepe paper. (These are the colors of the Mexican flag.) One end of the rope is tied to the bag while the other end is thrown over an elevated support. A child is assigned to hold the free end of the rope. Another child is blindfolded and given the stick. The remaining children stand in a circle around the sack and the blindfolded player. The blindfolded player is allowed to feel the sack dangling before him. He is then told to strike at it hard enough with his stick to break the sack. However, each time he tries to hit it, the child holding the rope pulls the sack up out of his reach. When he has tried three times unsuccessfully, another child is chosen to make his three efforts. If, after several children have taken their turn, none has been successful, one is permitted to break the sack. When the contents fall out, all the children scramble to get as many pieces as possible.

Siamese Soccer (Grades 6–8)

DESCRIPTION OF GAME. A large size playground ball is needed. Players stand in a single circle formation. The ball is thrown up into the air, and the players attempt to keep it in the air by striking it with any portion of the body (hips, head, knees, shoulders, etc.) except hands and feet.

Teaching Hints. To provide more activity for more players, two or more games could be conducted simultaneously.

SUPPLEMENTARY READINGS

Cratty, Bryant J.: *Active Learning Games to Enhance Academic Abilities.* Englewood Cliffs, New Jersey, Prentice-Hall, Inc., 1971.

Halsey, Elizabeth, and Porter, Lorena: *Physical Education for Children.* New York, Holt, Rinehart and Winston, 1963.

Humphrey, James H.: *Child Learning Through Elementary School Physical Education.* Dubuque, Iowa, Wm. C. Brown Co., Publishers, 1974.

International Council on Health, Physical Education, and Recreation: *ICHPER Book of Worldwide Games and Dances.* American Association for Health, Physical Education and Recreation, 1967.

Miller, Arthur G., and Whitcomb, Virginia: *Physical Education in the Elementary School Curriculum.* Ed. 3. Englewood Cliffs, New Jersey, Prentice-Hall, Inc., 1969.

Sherman, Ripley G.: *The Book of Games.* New York, Association Press, 1961.

BIBLIOGRAPHY

[1]Cratty, Bryant J.: *Teaching Motor Skills.* Englewood Cliffs, New Jersey, Prentice-Hall, Inc. 1973. pp. 98–99.

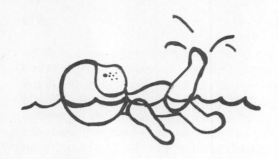

chapter fifteen

aquatics

OVERCOMING FEAR OF THE WATER
BEGINNING SWIMMING AND SURVIVAL
   SKILLS
INTERMEDIATE SWIMMING AND DIVING
   SKILLS
WATER GAMES

    The trend toward providing for swimming instruction in the elementary schools is a welcome one. Swimming provides a vigorous and beneficial exercise with lasting carry-over values; it is one of relatively few skills enjoyed as much by the sixty year old as by the six year old. In addition to its excellence as an exercise, swimming is a survival skill. With even rudimentary knowlege of how to keep the body afloat in the water, many accidental drownings could be avoided. Familiarity with water safety observances could avert many other disasters.

    The elementary school is in many ways the ideal place for swimming instruction. Non-swimmers of younger years have less fear of the water, as a rule, than older children, which makes it unnecessary to spend as much time with the preliminaries of overcoming fear of the water which must precede the actual teaching of swimming skills. Many older children who swim are likely to have been self-taught or to have been inadequately instructed and so have acquired poor swimming techniques which must be relearned. Such "un-learning" is frustrating and time-consuming; it is much easier for teacher and learner to begin the instruction before any ineffective skills have been acquired. Then, too, elementary school age children are more impressionable, and water safety observances inculcated during these years are more likely to remain with them always.

    Many as are the advantages of teaching aquatics in the elementary school physical education program, relatively few schools have been able to offer such instruction because pools are not generally included in the elementary school facilities. However, increasing numbers of schools have been able to work out arrangements with commercial pools and private clubs having pools to use these at hours when they would not otherwise be in use. Successful use has also been made by some schools of portable pools. Mounted so that they can be moved from school to school, these pools meet all the requirements for public health and sanitation and for good instructional techniques. Their big advantage lies in the nominal cost, particularly when shared with several other schools within a convenient distance of one another.

ORGANIZING FOR INSTRUCTION

Swimming instruction should be scheduled regularly for students beginning with the fourth grade, for by this time the skill development of most children is sufficiently advanced for them to profit readily from aquatic instruction. However, children younger than this are able to accomplish considerable swimming safety skill; and, if the time and facilities permit, first, second, and third graders should be included in the program.

Before any instruction begins, the teacher must establish firmly the safety and health regulations which are to be followed by the pupils from the time they enter the dressing room until they leave it at the end of the period. These might include:

No running in the dressing rooms or on the pool deck because of the danger of slipping on these surfaces when they are wet.

Take a cool shower before putting on a swim suit to ensure cleanliness and to help adjust the body to the temperature of the pool.

Use the bathroom before coming into the pool as water tends to stimulate the kidneys.

No pushing, shoving, shuffling, or ducking and splashing others at any time.

Use the footbath upon entering the pool area.

A maximum of 20 pupils per instructor is strongly urged in the interest of safety and good teaching. A preferred ratio is 10 pupils per instructor. Even with a small number the teacher will want to provide additional security checks. Perhaps the best of these is to develop the habit of an eye check of the water every 30 seconds; a sweeping glance over the pool at half minute intervals when there are students in the water will assure that anyone in distress is spotted in time to effect a rescue. The teacher may also want to employ a roll call check; for this each student is assigned a number which he calls out in succession during the check. Another highly recommended technique is the buddy system in which pupils are paired, with each responsible for knowing where the other is at all times. The buddies can also help each other when they are practicing skills. The teacher may simply number the children off by 2's for this; however, there may be an advantage in permitting them to select a buddy from among their special friends in the class as this will add to the pleasure and security they feel when working together.

Instruction for beginners should be in waist-deep water. The boundaries of the area which the beginners may use without danger should be clearly marked with buoys, and the class should be instructed in the importance of observing these boundaries. Areas to be used by intermediate and advanced swimmers should also be clearly identified.

The water temperature should be at least 80 degrees to ensure an environment conducive to pleasant relaxed activity in the water. Youngsters who are chilled and uncomfortable do not profit as much from the instruction.

The daily lesson plan should provide time for warm-up activities, review as needed of previously learned skills, demonstrations and instruction of new skills, and practice in the water. If the teacher is using the indirect method of instruction, the daily lesson plan should include the problems that will be directed to the students to guide them into warm-up activities and review of previously learned skills and to encourage them to explore and discover effective ways of performing new skills. Time should be allotted near the end of the class for a period of free swimming. During the free swim the youngsters may practice or play as their interests dictate. It is a time for them to enjoy the water which is important for the psychological impetus it gives to learning. Equipment for playing water games such as those described at the end of the chapter should be made available. The teacher will need to continue to supervise but should not offer instruction unless specifically requested by a pupil.

SELECTING ACTIVITIES

Experienced teachers of aquatics have found that swimming is learned most easily if each of the basic skills is taught separately and then combined later as required by a particular stroke. Effective presentation of the separate skills toward this end requires a carefully planned progression of skill learning. The content suggested below for aquatics in the elementary school physical education program is based on the progression of fundamental steps recommended by the American Red Cross.

No attempt has been made to suggest the grade level at which the various skills should be taught, for this will be determined by the grade at which instruction first begins in each particular school and by the individual progress of the students. Experience has shown that some boys and girls take as many as three years to learn what others are able to acquire in a year.

OVERCOMING FEAR OF THE WATER

Most non-swimmers have conscious or unconscious fears of drowning; consequently, the introduction to the water must be skillfully handled. The teacher should strive to make the introductory activities so much fun that the youngsters begin to feel secure in the water before they have time to be frightened. Standing in waist-deep water, the children should be encouraged to splash water over themselves; *no one should splash on another child.* They may experiment with bobbing up and down to their shoulders and eventually to their chins. In a circle formation with hands joined, the children may duck, sit on the bottom, and kneel. Simple water games which have been used with success in promoting a feeling of security in the water are described on pages 431–432.

Figure 15-1 Activities to introduce children to the water should be such fun that all fears of the water are forgotten. (Johns-Manville Celite Swimming Pool Filter Powder.)

Placing the Face in the Water

The children stand in the water, bend over, and holding their breath, briefly put their face in the water. They should be encouraged to repeat this until they are able to hold the face under for 15 to 20 seconds. The deep breath taken before putting the face in the water must be taken through the mouth.

Exhaling Under Water

When the children have accomplished the above, the next step is exhaling through the mouth while the face is in the water. It is sometimes helpful in establishing this technique to compare the exhaling to the blowing of bubbles with the mouth.

BEGINNING SWIMMING SKILLS AND SURVIVAL

Establishing Breathing Rhythm

The first step in establishing a definite rhythm pattern of inhalation and exhalation is to have the children bob the head up and down in the water, taking air into the mouth while the head is up and exhaling it through the mouth while it is down. When they have the idea, the teacher may ask them to do it to a count of one, two for inhalation and one, two, three for exhalation. A good game for practicing rhythmical breathing may be found on page 432.

Opening the Eyes

The teacher may begin to encourage the children to open their eyes as soon as they begin putting their faces in the water. Not all beginners are ready to do this, however, and specific games may need to be introduced to give them the incentive to open their eyes under water. Suggestions for such games are found on page 432. Picking up objects from the bottom of the pool also encourages opening the eyes to locate the objects. Objects which may be used are rubber hockey pucks, shiny metal disks, and non-buoyant colored waterproof toys.

Prone Float

The prone or "dead man's" float has important implications for the beginning swimmer; through it comes a realization of the body's buoyancy as well as the knowledge of how to regain the standing position in the water. The buddy system can be used for teaching the prone float. The buddies stand facing each other in water that is about waist deep and hold hands at arm's length. The child who is going to do the float places his face in the water and lifts his legs until he is fully stretched out. Support in maintaining this prone position is given by the buddy's hold on his hands. To regain the standing position, the hands are released so that they push downward, the knees are lifted up under the body, and the head is lifted. As the body becomes nearly vertical, the feet are placed on the bottom. The prone float should be practiced until it can be performed without the assistance of the buddy.

Children who tend to sink will find it helpful to: (1) extend the arms above the head and lift the hands out of the water; (2) bend the knees without lifting the thighs out of the water; and/or (3) take a bigger breath of air.

Prone Glide

When the above has been achieved, the child may be taught how to glide in the prone position. This is executed exactly like the float except that instead

Figure 15–2 Support in maintaining her position in the prone float is given this beginner by holding her hands. (James Baley.)

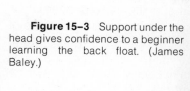
Figure 15–3 Support under the head gives confidence to a beginner learning the back float. (James Baley.)

of merely raising the feet, a push is given off the bottom to move the body forward in its prone float position. The recovery to the standing position is made in exactly the same way. The prone glide should be practiced until a glide of 5 feet or more is achieved.

Children may find it easier to push off from the side of the pool than from the bottom. To do this one leg is bent at the knee with the foot placed against the wall while the other foot remains on the bottom. The arms are extended, the face submerged, the foot on the bottom is lifted up to the other one, and a hard push is given with both feet to send the body forward in the glide. Practice in gliding can be movitated by competition to determine who can glide the greatest distance.

Back Float

To help the children visualize how to do a back float, the first step may be compared to sitting in a chair with the arms stretched out to the sides with the palms of the hands facing up and the head tilted back. The arms and ears must remain under water. In the next step the hips are lifted toward the surface of the water. Those who lack confidence may be given an assist by the teacher or buddy who stands to the rear and gives support at the shoulders or head. The recovery to standing is made by pulling the knees up, bringing the hands forward, and tilting the head forward.

Back Glide

For the back glide the position of the back float is taken and a hard push is made by the feet against the bottom before the legs are raised. Recovery is the same as for the back float. Children have a tendency to tip the head either too far back, causing water to run over the face, or too far forward so that the position of the body is not as completely supine as it should be.

Prone Glide with Kick

Learning the prone glide with kick is a matter of adding the swimming kick (flutter kick) to the prone glide learned earlier. The kick can be introduced with a land drill. The students assume a prone position and lift the legs alternately. The legs should be held straight without bending at the knees but relaxed, not rigidly stiff. The teacher may need to help the students by holding the legs to keep them from bending at the knees.

When the class is ready to practice the kick in the water, the buddy system may again be used. One child assumes the prone float position while the other takes him by the hands to tow him around the water. As he is being towed, the first child practices the kick with correct form. This is followed by practice without the assistance of the buddy.

Back Glide with Kick

When the students are able to propel themselves forward two body lengths, they are ready for the back glide with kick, which adds the flutter kick to the back glide. The kick is essentially the same as above, except the knees are bent more in the action. Land drill is advisable before attempting the kick in the water. In the water the student assumes the back glide position and kicks his feet. Support may be given at the shoulders or hips or at both if needed.

Human Stroke with Arms Only

The human stroke is executed much like the "dog paddle" except that the arms are fully extended and then pulled directly down and back to just beneath the shoulder; this is followed by lifting them to just beneath the surface and repeating the forward movement. The stroke is advantageous because it is closely related to the crawl which will be introduced later.

Practice of the stroke should be done on dry land first, followed by practice while walking in chest deep water, and finally accompanied by floating in the water. The arms must not be raised above the water during the stroke, and the face must remain in the water. In the final step, a prone glide with kick is made and the strokes added. It is recommended that this stroke be practiced until the child can move through the water at least 10 feet.

Complete Stroke in the Prone Position

This skill will combine several skills which have been learned earlier: breathing, kicking, and stroking with the arms. Standing in water up to the shoulders, the youngsters should move their arms through the human stroke. After an interval of practice, breathing is added; it is timed so that the face is turned with the strokes. Most children will turn their faces to the right to breathe. The face is turned to the right; then, as the left arm moves forward, the face is turned back to the water as the right arm comes forward. The student should strive for a smooth rhythmical execution of the head and arm movements. In additional practices, walking in the water can be added to the above.

Finally, the kick is added. To ensure successful performance of the combined skills, the child should do the prone glide with kick, add the arm strokes, and then the breathing. Complete mastery of this need not be expected before moving on to the next skill, but practice of it should be included frequently in subsequent class meetings. Kickboards and other flotation devices can be helpful at this stage to enable the learner to maintain a good working position and to increase the amount of sustained practice.

Complete Stroke in the Supine Position

With the mastery of this stroke, the students will acquire an important survival skill; for it is one that can be used to stay afloat for long periods of time without tiring greatly. The stroke is a combination of the back glide, kick, and finning movement of the hands. To teach the hand movement, a land drill may be used. The children lie on their backs with the arms to their sides. The elbows are bent slightly so that the hands will be about at the middle of the hips. In a continuous movement, the hands are moved so the palms are facing the feet and then returned to the original position. Repetition of the movement creates a finning motion.

The skill may be practiced in combination with a back glide in waist deep water. If support is needed, the buddy may give it by holding his hands under the shoulders. When the student is ready, the kick is added to the above movement. In the beginning the student need not coordinate the kicking and finning movements; breathing does not have to be timed with the strokes because the head is out of the water. Emphasis should be on making all movements as easy and relaxed as possible so that the learner maintains a comfortable position but still makes some progress in moving through the water.

Changing Position

With the skills of swimming forward and backward learned, students should learn how to move from one position to the other.

To turn from the crawl stroke to the back position, the learner turns on the arm extended in front, drops the shoulder, and turns the head away from the shoulder while the other arm is drawn across the body and extended to the opposite side. To turn from the back to the front position, the learner takes a breath, holds it, turns the head to the left, and draws the right arm across the chest; the body will rotate in the desired direction.

This is an important skill because it enables the swimmer to rest on his back when he becomes fatigued from swimming in a prone positon. Survival in the water may at some time depend upon such skill.

Changing Directions

Changing directions is easily learned by the young swimmer. To turn, the arm is extended in the direction the swimmer wishes to turn and the head is moved to look toward this arm. When swimming on the back, the swimmer moves his head toward the direction he wishes to take and a strong effort is made with the opposite arm.

Treading

Treading water is a skill that enables the beginner to keep his face above the surface with the body in a vertical position. The ability to tread water is important to the development of survival safety skill. With the arms outstretched just below the shoulder level, palms down and somewhat in front of the body, the hands move easily in wide circles, pressing slightly downward with the palms. The flutter kick already learned can be used, but the movement should be slower and wider. The kick is made simultaneously with the arm action.

The body may be bent slightly forward at the trunk. The arm and leg action should be sufficient to keep the head just high enough so that the mouth and nose are out of water for ease of continued breathing.

Jumping into the Water

Before the students practice jumping into the water, they should be instructed how to push off from the bottom and begin swimming as this is a necessary preliminary for the teaching of diving. The first jumps should be made in water which is chest deep with successive practice in shoulder deep water and finally in water just over the head. Some children may experience a degree of panic the first time they find themselves in water over their heads. Consequently, it is well for the teacher to describe what the experience will be like, using, of course, a calm voice and reassuring vocabulary. During the first practice session, it is a good idea for the teacher to be in the water just in front of where the children will jump to give assistance and reassurance.

Diving

The progression in teaching diving is the sitting dive, the kneeling dive, and the standing dive.

SITTING DIVE.   This should be taught in a water depth of at least 6 feet. Seated on the deck with the feet resting on the trough, the pupil must lean forward with the arms extended and the hands together. The knees are wide apart to allow the body to be bent close to the water before balance is lost. As the balance is lost, the child should push off with the feet. To return to the surface, the hands which are still together should be directed upward.

KNEELING DIVE.   As soon as the children acquire the "feel" of gliding

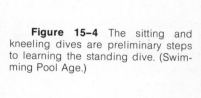

Figure 15–4 The sitting and kneeling dives are preliminary steps to learning the standing dive. (Swimming Pool Age.)

into the water and have sufficient self-confidence, the kneeling dive may be taught to them. Kneeling with either leg on the deck and the foot of the opposite leg resting on the gutter, the child leans forward until balance is lost. The arms are extended with the hands together. The chin should rest on the chest as he enters the water.

STANDING DIVE.   The water depth should be at least 8 feet for this dive. Standing with the feet close together, the toes are hooked over the edge and the arms are extended with the hands together. The child bends forward from the waist and, as balance is lost, gives a hard push-off from the deck. The chin is held down. Children who fail to hold the head down will "belly flop." Because of the depth of the water, the teacher should be ready to give assistance.

PERSONAL SAFETY SKILLS

Many unnecessary drownings occur within a few feet of safety and might have been prevented had anyone with some knowledge of rescue skills been present. The techniques of rescuing someone in danger of drowning are simple to apply and can be safely attempted even by a non-swimmer. People who know how to swim also number among the drowning victims. Often they could have saved themselves had they known the techniques of survival floating. Because of the universal value of developing rescue and survival skills, it is highly recommended that these elementary skills be included in the beginning swimming instruction.

Non-Swimming Rescue

In attempting a non-swimming rescue, i.e., without entering the water, the rescuer should avoid personal contact with the victim whenever possible and should always be certain to maintain firm contact with the shore, shallow water, or side of the pool. The rescuer's weight on the shore or the deck should be kept low or slanting backward, and if possible the rescuer should use some piece of equipment. The techniques to be applied in various circumstances are:

If the victim is within arm's reach, and no equipment is available, the rescuer lies flat on deck of pool and extends one arm toward the victim. Taking a firm grasp of deck with the other arm, he grabs the victim's wrist or arm and draws him slowly to safety. When using rescue equipment, he must be careful not to poke victim with the extended article, if it is a hard object, and must guard against being pulled into the water by the victim.

If the victim is beyond the reach of an extended article, the rescuer throws out any available line to pull the victim ashore or any available buoyant object to enable the victim to stay afloat until help can be summoned.

Survival Floating

The facedown floating technique combines a series of basic swimming skills and is designed to keep a person afloat for a long period with a minimum of effort and energy.

Resting Position: The swimmer starts with air in the lungs and holds his breath, letting his arms and legs dangle. The face is kept down. The swimmer rests and floats in this vertical position for a few seconds.

Preparing to Exhale: While maintaining this body and head position, the swimmer slowly and leisurely recovers or lifts the arms to about shoulder height. If leg action is also to be used, the swimmer slowly separates the legs into a modified scissors kick.

Exhalation: From a position with the back of the head at the surface, the swimmer raises the head no higher than necessary for the mouth to clear the surface. At the same time he exhales through the mouth and nose.

Inhalation: As soon as the head is vertical, the swimmer presses the arms downward and brings the legs together. This easy downward pressure should allow time for air to be breathed in through the mouth. The action of the arms and legs should not be vigorous enough to lift the chin out of the water.

Return to the Resting Position: The swimmer slowly allows the arms and legs to return to their original free dangling position, with face down in water, and relaxes. The cycle is repeated.

INTERMEDIATE SWIMMING AND DIVING SKILLS

As in the teaching of the beginning skills, the learning of separate skills to be combined later in specific strokes is recommended for intermediate skills. Consequently, the arm and leg strokes will be described separately for the intermediate skills given below before the way in which they are combined is discussed.

Elementary Backstroke

The kick for the elementary backstroke is executed by bending the knees and moving the *lower* legs so that the feet are as far apart as possible. The thighs remain stationary and close together. The toes are turned out as far as possible. Then, with a quick thrust, the lower legs are straightened and brought together. The toes are pointed for the glide. The land drill of the leg movement is best accomplished in a supine position, with the legs extended over the edge of the pool. In the water it may be practiced while holding on to the gutter or while in a back float position with the arms straight out or placed on the hips.

In the arm movement, the stroke begins with the arms fully extended at a 45 degree angle between the head and shoulders. The arms are then brought down to the sides of the body, in a sweeping arc. In the recovery the hands are brought up along the sides of the body until they reach the shoulders and are again extended. Students may practice this movement while standing or lying on the deck. For water drill, the feet should be supported either by a buddy or by resting them on a leg supporting device.

When both movements have been learned adequately, they may be combined. The legs are brought up and together at the same time as the arms are swept down to the sides. The arms recover along the body to the armpits before the legs start their recovery. As the legs start the recovery, the arms are moving outward for the pull. The swimmer should breathe normally throughout the stroke and relax momentarily for a glide between strokes.

Some land drill on coordinating the strokes is desirable. In the water students should be encouraged to work toward a smooth rhythmical stroke, with the glide phase 2 to 4 seconds in duration. A long glide is important because it is this period of inactivity which makes the backstroke a restful stroke, useful in long distance swimming and for staying afloat for long periods of time.

Figure 15–5 The kick of the elementary backstroke may be practiced while holding onto the pool gutter. (George Taterosian.)

Side Stroke

This is an important stroke because it is the basis for most life saving carries. The body is on its side so that the stronger arm is on top because it is this arm that must supply the power for the stroke; however, it is a good idea for students to practice on both sides so they will be able to swim either way if it should ever become necessary.

The leg movement is called the scissors. To execute it, the legs are drawn up slightly and the top leg is extended forward and the other backward. Then the knees are straightened and the legs are brought together like the closing of the scissors.

The leg movement may be practiced on deck with the legs extended over the edge of the pool or while lying on a bench or stool. While holding on to the gutter for support, the students may turn on their sides to practice the kick in the water; they should drill on both sides. Failure to straighten the leg in the backward motion is the most common error of beginning students.

The arm under the water is fully extended while the other one rests fully extended on the side of the body; this is the position for the glide with which the stroke begins and ends. The under arm is brought downward to a nearly vertical position and then the elbow is bent. As this is being done, the upper arm is pulled up to enter the water near the head. Reaching downward, it pulls back to the starting position at the side of the body. Meanwhile the other arm is executing a pulling movement toward the body before being extended for the next stroke.

Drills on the arm movement may be performed while standing on the pool's deck and while in neck-deep water. Practice in the water should also consist of propelling the body through the water using only the arm stroke.

The arm and leg movements are coordinated so that the legs reach out as the arms begin their movement, and both return to the starting position simultaneously for the glide. Holding the glide should be stressed by the teacher. One technique for doing this is to have the students hold the glide to a count of three by the teacher. Those students who have trouble maintaining their balance during the glide should practice pushing off into a glide from the side of the pool.

Crawl

To master the crawl the beginner has only to learn the arm stroke and synchronize it with the kick and breathing of the human stroke. To do the arm stroke, one arm is extended at arm's length into the water in front of the face and pressed downward against the water with the hand leading the rest of the arm. As the arm passes under the shoulder, the movement becomes a push rather than a pressing or pulling one which is continued until the release in which the shoulder is lifted and the elbow is raised to clear the arm from the water as it passes the hip. The recovery is accomplished by bending the elbow and continuing to lift the shoulder. The hand is brought forward with the fingers near the water ready for entrance and repetition of the stroke.

Figure 15–6 The feet may be hooked on the pool gutter to support the body while practicing a rhythmical crawl stroke with the arms. (George Taterosian.)

The movement of the arms is synchronized with the breathing so that inhalation occurs as the arm on the side to which the head turns is in the recovery position. The kicking of the legs is timed so that six kicks will be executed during the movements of both arms. To help achieve a rhythmical stroke, the swimmer may count to three each time a hand enters the water. If a record player and amplifier can be brought into the pool area, waltz music may be played to help the swimmers achieve the desired rhythm in their strokes.

The arm movements may be drilled on land standing or lying on a stool or bench and in the water by supporting the feet on the gutter or on a leg supporting device. Buddies may also be used to hold and maintain support of the feet during the arm drills in the water.

Treading

Treading at the intermediate level is used to maintain the body in a vertical position in deep water. The scissors movement with the legs learned in the side stroke may be applied to the vertical position. However, many students find it easier to use a pumping action like that used in bicycling. The leg movement should be practiced in deep water with the hands holding on to the gutter. An arm movement may or may not be used; when it is used, it is a sculling motion.

Sculling

Sculling is a rotating movement of the hands which is most often performed while in the back float position to provide a restful method of moving the body through the water. With the arms at the sides of the body, the hands are moved at the wrists in a rhythmical pattern of pushing and pulling against the water. A slow flutter kick may be used if necessary. The sculling movement of the hands

Figure 15-7 Sculling may be practiced in deep water as soon as the swimmers have learned to move the hands rhythmically. (George Taterosian.)

may be practiced first while standing in the water and then added to the back float.

Surface Dive

The surface dive is a means of getting under the water from a stationary or swimming position in the water. The body must be in a horizontal position to make the dive properly. Prior to initiating the dive, the swimmer should come to a position of full extension on the surface. Then, while still possessing momentum, he takes a breath of air. For a head-first surface dive, the arms are pulled back and the head is ducked into the water as the body bends sharply at the waist and the legs are lifted straight into the air. The body should enter the water in a vertical position as if standing on one's head. The eyes should be open and the hands remain in front of the head. Keeping the legs straight and the toes pointed are the chief difficulties for the learner.

To submerge feet first in the surface dive, the arms are pulled upward toward the surface from the horizontal position.

TEACHING PROCEDURES

Numerous specific techniques for teaching the swimming and diving skills have already been indicated in the discussion of the steps to be included in the aquatic unit. There are, however, other techniques, more generally applicable, which the teacher will find useful.

Demonstration of swimming skills is very important in helping youngsters understand the execution of the movements involved. In demonstrating, the teacher should place himself where he can be easily seen by the entire class. If elevation above the sightline of the children is desired, the teacher may give

TABLE 15-1   Aquatics Correction Chart

Technique	Common Error	Probable Result	Correction
Human Stroke	Lifting head above water	Legs sink and neck muscles fatigue quickly	Gain confidence by practicing prone glide
	Kicking from knees	Loss of power to propel body forward	Make kick from the hips
	Short arm strokes	Loss of power	Reach forward as far as possible in the recovery
Standing Dive	Failure to hold head down	Landing flat on stomach	Tuck chin on chest and bend over at hips
Elementary Back Stroke	Failure to keep thighs together	Loss of power	Keep knees together
	Failure to turn toes out	Loss of power	Rotate toes beyond the ankles
	Pause in action during recovery of arms	Develops greater water resistance against arms and power is lost	Pause only in glide position
Side Stroke	Kick straight back	Very little power developed	After legs are drawn up extend top leg forward and extend bottom leg back; knees are straightened and legs are brought together
	Pulling immediately with arms without going into glide	Eliminates glide	Pause after arm recovery until forward speed is slowed
Crawl	Lifting head above water	Legs sink and neck muscles fatigue	Gain confidence by practicing prone float and inhaling, and then exhaling under water
	Kicking from knees	Loss of power to propel body forward	Kick from hips
	Shortening arm by bending at elbow when pulling it through water	Loss of power	Keep elbow extended throughout pull
	Failure to lift elbow to clear surface of water	Increases resistance of water and slows forward speed	Rotate arm to turn thumb up as elbow is lifted
	Failure to lead with elbow in recovery of the arms	Makes getting arm above water more difficult	As arm is lifted elbow precedes lower arm
Treading	Failure to spread legs sufficiently	Will not stay afloat	Legs are spread wide in a scissor movement
Sculling	Jack-knifing at hips	Legs and hips sink	Straighten body and push hips up
Surface Dive	Attemping to lift legs up before hips are over body	Legs cannot be lifted over body	As head is ducked, bend sharply at waist

the demonstration from the diving board or from the deck with the children in the water. On occasion the teacher may wish to show the skill in the water with the class on the deck.

Verbalization which accompanies the demonstration must be clear and concise. Special attention should be directed toward those movements which may produce errors as, for example, the level of the head as it is raised for breathing or the straightness of the leg in the kick. Children who still have difficulty doing the skill after having seen it demonstrated and heard it described should be led through the movement to develop kinesthetic perception of it.

Reference has already been made to the use of land and water drills. Land drills may be given in any position, lying, standing, or sitting. The important consideration is space; students should be able to perform freely without getting in each other's way. Mass land drills on strokes may be given to start the class each meeting. This serves as a review of what has been learned and as a warm-up activity. The American Red Cross endorses a period of warm-up drills and calisthenics because it produces slight muscular fatigue which helps achieve relaxation in the water. Relaxation is, of course, highly desirable because it fosters learning.

The two formations most commonly used for mass water drills are the wave and stagger formations. For non-swimmers these are always held in shallow water. The wave formation consists of two or more lines of students which follow each other at intervals of about 10 feet doing the designated drill. The stagger formation permits greater attention to individual performance because the individuals start one after another. The first one in line begins and, when the teacher has watched the performance as long as he needs to evaluate it, he nods at the next in line to begin. The drill continues in this manner until all have had a turn. Drills for kicking and treading may be held with the students in lines along the pool's gutter to which they can hold for support while doing the designated leg movements.

It should be remembered that practice is needed for perfection! Consequently, the teacher should direct all of his imagination toward organizing the class drills so that maximum practice can be extracted from the instructional period. Keeping the children standing in long lines awaiting their turn is to be avoided as much as possible. A routine procedure for lining up quickly and without confusion in the drill formations for land and water practice should be established beginning with the first day the class meets; in the course of several weeks a considerable amount of time can be salvaged for practice in this way.

EQUIPMENT

There are several pieces of equipment that may be used in teaching swimming. The most necessary are those used for rescue and safety. A lightweight pole about 8 feet in length for reaching over the water is essential for giving assistance to children particularly when they first swim and dive in water over their heads. The children should be informed about the pole and shown how to grasp the end of it when it is extended before the need for its use arises, for then they may be too frightened to follow directions being given to them. The pole is also a useful teaching device for signaling corrections to swimmers without their having to stop for verbal directions. As an error is seen in the stroke, the teacher uses the pole to tap the arm, leg, or portion of the body which is being used incorrectly. Such use of the pole presupposes that the students already have considerable understanding of correct form and can therefore interpret the signals.

Non-floating objects to be placed on the bottom of the pool for training in opening the eyes and in diving may be considered part of the instructional equipment. These should always be removed from the water after each class and dried before storing.

Arm and leg supporting devices are other pieces of training equipment often used. It is recommended that these pieces not be used with nonswimmers as they may cause too much reliance on the artificial support and hinder the development of confidence and progress in staying afloat and moving through the water. After the beginning skills have been acquired, however, these devices are useful in helping the swimmer maintain a position while concentrating on the practice of leg or arm strokes. A kickboard is commonly used for kicking practice. It is a short board of buoyant material which is used to support the arms while the leg strokes are practiced. Small inflated tubes or waterwings perform a similar function by supporting the feet while the arm strokes are practiced. Care of these pieces is largely a matter of proper drying before storing.

Supporting devices may be improvised from easily accessible materials. Short thick pieces of wooden planks make suitable kickboards for supporting the arms. Used automobile inner tubes may be used as leg supporting devices.

WATER GAMES

OVERCOMING FEAR OF THE WATER

WALKING RACE.   The class lines up on one side of the pool where the water is shallow. At the command to begin, each walks as fast as he can through the water to the opposite side. The first to arrive wins the race.

CIRCLE TOUCH.   The class joins hands in a circle formation around an object such as a buoy or an inner tube, which is fairly large in size and which floats. The object of the game is to cause others in the circle to touch the object with some part of their bodies. Those who touch it are eliminated until one child remains who is declared the winner.

BALL TAG.   The child who is chosen to be "It" attempts to tag someone by touching him with the ball. The one tagged then becomes "It." A large rubber or plastic beach ball is suitable for this game. With nonswimmers it is important that the tagging be restricted to touching the individual with the ball rather than hitting him with a thrown ball.

FISH AND NET.   Half the class joins hands in circle formation to make a "net" in which they try to catch the other members of the class who are the "fish." The hands must remain joined during the catching of the fish. Those who are caught become part of the net. The last to be caught is the winner of that game. The teams are reversed for the next game.

FOLLOW THE LEADER. For the first time or two, the teacher may wish to be the leader with all of the class following. As the students begin to feel more at home in the water, leaders may be chosen from the class. The leader may do such things as splashing water on himself, ducking, bobbing up and down, sitting, kneeling, and walking about in the water.

CORK RETRIEVE. The class is divided into two teams. The teacher throws several handfuls of corks into the water and gives the signal for the teams to begin recovering as many corks as possible. The team with the greater number at the end of a designated time period is the winner.

ESTABLISHING BREATHING RHYTHM

SEE-SAW. Two children join hands facing each other. One of the pair takes a deep breath and ducks in a sitting position beneath the water while his partner remains standing. The first child holds the position for 2 or 3 seconds, exhaling through the mouth, and pops back into an upright position. Then it becomes the other child's turn to duck under the water while the first child remains upright. The action "see-saws" back and forth between the two as long as they are able to keep it up.

OPENING THE EYES

COUNTING FINGERS. The children are divided into pairs. One child ducks under the water while the other child remains in a standing position and extends any number of fingers under the water so the submerged child can see them. As soon as the latter has counted the fingers, he stands up and checks with his partner to see if he is correct. It then becomes the other child's turn to count the fingers.

FOOT TAG. The class is formed into groups of three. One in each group is "It" and must duck under the water and touch a foot of one of the other two in the group who remain in an upright position in one spot. They may lift one foot at a time in order to avoid being tagged but may not step away from their positions. The one who is tagged becomes the next "It."

RETRIEVE. The class is divided into two teams which line up along the sides of the pool in chest-deep water. Non-floating objects to be retrieved by the teams are placed in a line on the bottom of the pool midway between the two teams. On the signal to start, the first child in each line walks through the water to the objects, ducks under to pick one up, and returns to his team. The action is repeated in turn by everyone on the team. The first team on which everyone retrieves an object becomes the winner.

GAMES FOR PRACTICING INTERMEDIATE SKILLS

FOOT TAG. The one who is "It" must touch another swimmer on the foot to tag him. The one who is tagged becomes "It."

HEAD TAG. "It" attempts to tag another player by touching him on the head. To avoid being tagged, the player must submerge his head completely.

KEEP AWAY. The class is divided into two teams. The team in possession of the ball tries to keep it from falling into the hands of the opponents.

WATER DODGE BALL. The class is divided into two teams with one forming a circle around the others. The ball is thrown by those in the outside circle in an attempt to hit someone in the center. Those who are in the center may duck under the water to avoid being hit. Anyone who is hit must join the outside circle and help to eliminate those who remain in the center.

FOLLOW THE LEADER. The leader may lead the followers in a series of movements that combines all the strokes they have learned.

RETRIEVE. The class is divided into two teams which line up on opposite sides of the pool where the water is of sufficient depth for diving. A number of corks are placed in the water midway between the teams. At the command to start, the teams dive into the water and swim out to the corks to bring them back to the deck. The team gathering the most corks wins.

RACES AND RELAYS. The class may be divided into two or more teams to compete against each other in swimming any of the learned strokes. They swim certain designated distances determined by the teacher's knowledge of their endurance and skill. They may also compete in relay swimming races with each swimmer performing a certain stroke for a specified distance before touching a teammate who completes another "leg" of the relay in much the same manner as relays are run on land.

SUPPLEMENTARY READINGS

American Association for Health, Physical Education and Recreation: *Professional Standards for Aquatic Instruction.* Washington, D.C., American Association for Health, Physical Education and Recreation, 1971.

American Red Cross: *Water Safety Instructor's Manual.* Revised. Washington, D.C., American Red Cross, 1971.

American Red Cross: *Swimming and Diving.* Ed. revised. Washington, D.C., American Red Cross, 1970.

Counsilman, James E.: *The Science of Swimming.* Englewood Cliffs, New Jersey, Prentice-Hall, Inc., 1967.

Fait, Hollis F., et al.: *A Manual of Physical Education Activities.* Ed. 3. Philadelphia, W. B. Saunders Co., 1967.

Gabrielson, M. A., et al.: *Aquatics Handbook.* Ed. 2. Englewood Cliffs, New Jersey, Prentice-Hall, Inc., 1968.

chapter sixteen

physical education for the nursery school child

CHARACTERISTICS OF THE NURSERY
   SCHOOL CHILD
TEACHING IN THE NURSERY SCHOOL
THE PHYSICAL EDUCATION PROGRAM
      Equipment
      Selection and Presentation of Activities
      Music and Rhythmic Activities
      Story and Poetry Play
      Basic Skill Games
      Other Games of Low Organization
      Activities for Fitness

    It has long been recognized that children need experiences outside the home before they begin formal schooling to ensure their optimum development and preparation for the tasks of the classroom. The establishment of kindergarten, which serves five year olds, was a response to the awareness of the benefits to young children of carefully planned and directed preschool experi-

434

ences. Kindergarten has been an integral part of many school programs throughout the country for decades. A much more recent development is the nursery school for children younger than five years of age. Although nursery schools are just beginning to be included in the public school program, private nursery schools have been in operation in considerable numbers for many years.

The program of the nursery school is centered around play, for it is through play experiences that the young child learns about himself: who he is, what he can do, and how he relates to the world around him. It is through play also that he develops his body and motor skills and increases his physical well-being. Consequently, play is the focal point of the nursery school curriculum.

Because of the importance of play in the social, mental, and physical development of young children, teachers working in nursery school programs who have studied physical education have a great advantage. They will have a better understanding of the motor characteristics and growth patterns of the children and the ways in which this knowledge can be used to select play activities that make maximum contributions to children's total development, particularly physical development. They will have a wider repertoire of games, stunts, and exercises to choose from in order to ensure a well-balanced program of play activities. They will have a far better idea of how to plan the program and guide the youngsters toward fulfillment of the objectives.

It is difficult to state an exact age at which a child is ready for preschool experience, because children mature at different rates and the chronological age is not always the best indicator of maturity. Reliable evidence indicates that the large majority of children cannot benefit from an extensive school experience before the age of three. Pushing the child into a preschool experience before this age may be harmful if the child is ill-prepared for the social problems that he will meet.

It is granted that two year old children should have the experience of social contacts and play with children outside the home. However, this need can usually be more satisfactorily met by an informal experience, as when mothers bring their children together for an hour or so and stay with them the entire time, rather than by a formal preschool experience. The desirability of this kind of informal experience is confirmed by preschools that have experimented with the attendance of two year old children.

Whether three and four year olds should be in the same class together will depend on the individual child and how he relates to the group. In some groups providing opportunities for young children and older children to play together expands their opportunities to understand and learn how to play with both older and younger children. On the other hand, when the age range is wide, the younger children may disrupt the play of the older children, or they may completely withdraw from play because of severe competition from the older children. Generally, however, an age range of two years is not so great at the nursery school level as to cause unusual problems.

At or near the age of five, a nursery school child has usually matured sufficiently to be ready for kindergarten. At the age of six, the child is, as a rule, sufficiently mature to participate in the regular school program of the first grade.

CHARACTERISTICS OF THREE YEAR OLDS

Physical Characteristics

Gesell[1] points out that the third year is the transitional period between infancy and childhood. The three year old child is growing at a relatively slow rate compared to his rate of infancy. The average gain in weight during this period is about 4 or 5 pounds. Changes in height also tend to decelerate; the annual growth is from 2 to 3 inches. There will have been dramatic changes in body proportions since the period of infancy—the torso as well as the arms and legs will have lengthened. The bones have a high proportion of water and protein-like substance and less minerals and, therefore, are more liable to deformity under pressure. These growing bones have a rich supply of blood, and it is believed that they are more susceptible than mature bones to any infectious organism which may be carried by the blood.

Most three year old children have mastered the upright position, and there is very little sway and weave in walking. They are likely to be somewhat knock-kneed, but this tendency will disappear before the age of four. The protruding stomach, evidenced by the two year old, diminishes during the third year, as the musculature of the stomach develops.

Three year olds can balance on one foot for a brief moment, and some are able to walk upstairs, alternating the feet. They can jump off objects 12 to 14 inches high, landing on both feet, and jump down from a higher distance, landing on one foot. They can also jump upward using both feet. Most have developed enough muscular strength and coordination to be able to ride a tricycle. Also, they have begun to develop control over the use of a crayon and are able to make controlled marks for the first time.

They can catch a large ball with the arms fully extended but their arms do not recoil in catching. In throwing they use chiefly the arm and shoulder; they generally do not put one foot in front of the other while throwing but do turn the body by stepping forward on one foot.

There will be a tendency in some children toward handedness. The visual acuity is about 40/100 to 20/40.

Children of this age can feed themselves and pour liquids fairly well from one container to the next. They can unbutton buttons and use zippers; untie shoes and take them off; go to the toilet alone and usually do so. A nap of an hour during the day is common at this age.

Social Characteristics

At the age of three social activity has expanded considerably over the previous year. Gesell[2] states: "On a primitive and miniature level, the third year marks a kind of adolescence, a coming of age." Three year olds are eager to try new experiences on their own but slip back under the protection of parents or teachers when they encounter any difficulty. They have begun to cooperate with others to some degree and to understand the nature of taking turns. They are able to put off immediate gratification for later success if the period between the two is relatively short.

Children of this age are developing a desire to please others and are very concerned with gaining approval for their action. Although they are beginning to take an interest in playing with others, they spend a large share of the time playing alone or engaging in parallel play alongside other children. The three year olds have a keen interest in imitating and so will often do little tasks that they have seen others do when asked to do them. However, they frequently rebel at such requests, and sometimes this rebellion takes the form of violent reaction. They usually get over these rebellious moments very quickly.

Intellectual Characteristics and Interests

At the age of three, youngsters can talk in sentences. They have developed an understanding of shape and form, and so they are able to match simple shapes but cannot yet distinguish colors. They are able to translate simple directions into actions and are most willing to do so. Eagerness to learn and continual questioning are characteristic.

Three year olds love to imitate movements of other persons, animals, and moving objects. They enjoy simple songs and will attempt to join in singing them although without much success.

Creative Characteristics

At the age of three, imagination is developing at a very rapid rate. Hence, the children are very curious and greatly attracted to objects that are new and strange. There is considerable experimentation with toys and other objects in the environment to determine what they are like, how they feel to the touch, whether they come apart.

Three year olds are constantly attempting new movements—walking up and down stairs, climbing over and under objects, crawling through holes, and maneuvering into empty spaces.

Implications

Three year old children learn through the imaginative process. Through imagination they solve many problems that they cannot handle by cognition. In developing a physical education program for this group, many opportunities should be provided to allow children to explore movement and to participate in activities in which they may imagine themselves in a multitude of roles. The chapter on movement exploration suggests ways of developing these opportunities. Activities may be planned to allow the children to imitate movements of another person, animal, or some moving object (motor cars, planes, and the like). Stories in which the children can act out the movement of the characters give additional opportunities for freedom of expression in movement as well as experience in muscular movement.

Singing games provide another opportunity for creativity. The words of some songs suggest actions which can be performed by the children. At this age, most of the singing must be done by the teacher.

For early experiences in throwing and catching, bean bags are utilized; as the children gain skill in catching, large balls may be substituted. Bouncing activities should be included in the program for the development of balance. Opportunities must be provided for climbing, pulling, and pushing objects to aid in the development of the basic skills that are prerequisite to more advanced motor skills.

CHARACTERISTICS OF FOUR YEAR OLDS

Physical Characteristics

The four year olds' rate of growth is similar to that of the three year olds'—steady but slow. By the time the children are four, they have doubled their length at birth and have obtained almost one third of the weight that they will be at the age of 18. The bones of four year old children have made slight changes but are still relatively pliable and are subject to deformity from undue stress and strain. Vision has improved since the age of three and is generally somewhere between 20/40 and 20/20.

Leg musculature and coordination have strengthened and improved so that these children are much better runners at age four than at age three. They can change stride patterns and are beginning to learn to skip but as yet cannot hop. Balance has improved considerably, and they are now able to balance on one foot for several seconds and can walk on a wide balance beam easily. They can run smoothly at different speeds, turning sharply, and stopping and starting quickly.

They now attempt to catch a ball by giving with their arms and by using their hands more frequently than their arms in catching the ball. Although they will attempt to catch a ball with one hand, they have difficulty in doing so. When they grasp a small ball to throw, they now use thumb and fingers but favor the use of the medium finger rather than the index finger. Body and arm movements are combined in throwing. Boys throw the ball with a horizontal motion from above their shoulder, while girls throw the ball from above the shoulder with a downward sweep.

Four year olds are able to lace their shoes but still cannot tie them. They can dress and undress themselves with reasonable ease and have no difficulty in self-care at the toilet.

Many four year olds no longer nap during the day. If they do, they have a tendency to sleep longer during their nap than when they were three.

Social Characteristics

The four year olds prefer to play in small groups of two or three. While they do share with others, they do not do so consistently. Many times they become just as possessive about playthings as they were when they were three. In fact, it often appears that they purposely evoke social reaction by being overly possessive with playthings or bossy with playmates.

By the age of four, children have become aware of the opinions and attitudes of other people; their criticism of others and their opinions of themselves also have social implications. Four year olds have difficulty making clear distinctions between truth and fiction, which is a natural process of development in youngsters of this age. Unreasonable fears, such as fear of the dark, are slowly being overcome as they progress toward the fifth year.

Intellectual Characteristics and Interests

The four years olds are continually practicing their language skills. They chatter on and on. They ask questions incessantly, doing so more as a means of testing their own concepts than to learn new facts. There is a beginning of abstract reasoning in their thought process; they can place certain things in categories, e.g., this is big or this is little; they can also distinguish between one and many.

The children of this age continue to show interest in imitating movements. They enjoy singing games that require action.

Creative Characteristics

Children continue to develop their creative abilities during their fourth year, reaching a peak of creativity at about four and a half years of age. Imagination at this age is keenly developed. These children have insatiable curiosity and enthusiasm for learning and are constantly in search of the right answer. They learn about adult activity through role playing, experimenting with different roles in the imaginative play.

Implications

Many of the physical education activities offered to the three year old should be used in the program for four year olds. Movement exploration activities that are familiar from the previous year may also be repeated but encouragement should be given the children to expand their exploration beyond that which they have attempted at an earlier age. Role playing activities and stories to act out are sources of new movement experiences, as are singing games and rhythmic activities. The four year olds are able to participate in some of the simple low organized games, and the program should include games like those described on pages 451–455.

Large building equipment such as big blocks and wooden boxes that require muscular effort to move them will provide good exercise for building muscular strength as well as promoting opportunities for creativity. Experiences in pulling and pushing, crawling over and under objects, balancing, and climbing should be included in the program to provide for the widest possible experience in motor movement. Throwing activities should be provided to encourage the development of throwing and catching skills.

TEACHING IN THE NURSERY SCHOOL

Size of Class

The space that is available will dictate to some extent how large a preschool class should be; however, it is generally recommended that in a nursery school there not be over seven students to each teacher and not over a total of 21 in one group with three teachers.

Length of School Day

The school day at most nursery schools is approximately 3 hours in length. However, some preschools are in session as few as 2 hours and some, particularly those serving children of working mothers, have school days longer than 3 or 4 hours. A 2 hour session is too short to conduct a comprehensive program. On the other hand, longer sessions of 4 or 5 hours necessitate the teacher's being prepared to provide experiences that the child would otherwise have at home.

Arranging the Program

In arranging a program for any given group, these guidelines are important:

1. Vigorous activity should be alternated with more passive activity to avoid excessive fatigue.
2. Periods during which children are expected to sit in one place and listen should be relatively short.
3. If a rest period is scheduled, vigorous activity should not precede it.
4. Activity should be so arranged that there is an easy transition from one kind of activity to the next to prepare children for what is to follow and to avoid frequent rearrangement of the room for different activities.

Special Problems

There are some special problems that preschool teachers will have that other teachers will generally not have to cope with. They range from providing a rest and relaxation period to meeting the emergencies of the child not making it to the toilet in time. Some of the more common problems are discussed below.

Rest and Relaxation

Whether or not a rest period is scheduled for nursery school children depends on the length of the session. For sessions of less than 3 hours, there is generally no need for a rest period for most children. However, for a longer school day, a rest period ranging from 5 to 20 minutes is scheduled. If the rest period is short, the children can relax and remain quiet with heads on their arms while sitting at the table or desk chair. For longer periods, provisions should be made for the children to recline. Some preschools provide individual cots for the children. If these are not available, individual mats or rugs spread out on the floor make satisfactory resting places.

Preceding the actual rest period, the teacher may utilize a lesson in motor exploration of relaxation to set the mood for rest and to achieve complete relaxation. Playing of soft, soothing music also encourages relaxation and adds to the enjoyment of the period, as well as providing an opportunity for music appreciation.

Lunch and Snack Periods

Eating during the nursery and kindergarten session provides an interesting experience for children. It offers a pleasant break from play, and creates another kind of social experience. It is usually best to schedule a quiet activity prior to the time of eating to calm the children. Usually teachers schedule a quiet activity after lunch as an aid to digestion; however, there is no evidence that this is necessary from the physiological point of view. Normal youngsters can perform relatively strenuous activity after lunch without danger of upsetting their

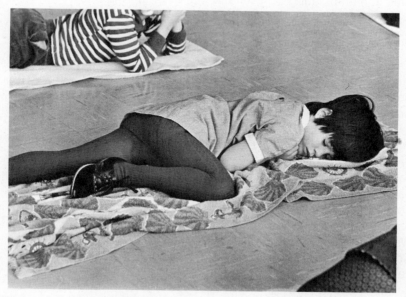

Figure 16–1 A nap is necessary for nursery school children if the length of the school day is long. (Journal of Health · Physical Education · Recreation.)

digestive systems. Extremely emotional situations do, however, interfere with proper digestion and should be avoided.

Use of Toilet and Lavatory Facilities

Children should be informed as to the location of the toilet facilities and how to use them on the first day of attendance. They should learn about washing their hands and using paper towels to dry them (which may be a new experience for most) and where to put the soiled towels. The boys should be instructed on how to use the urinal or how to lift the seats of the toilets.

Although children going to nursery school or kindergarten should be able to use the toilet facilities effectively, there will be accidents. When children are involved in interesting activity, they may forget to go to the toilet in time. Therefore, play activities that hold their interest intensely should not be conducted for long periods of time so youngsters will not delay going to the toilet because they don't want to leave the activity.

When an accident does occur, the teacher must take it in stride and treat the incident calmly and without causing embarrassment to the child. It is wise to request parents to provide a second set of underwear for each child with his name on it so dry underwear will be available in case of emergency.

THE PHYSICAL EDUCATION PROGRAM

Motor activity is an important phase of the nursery school program, both as a vehicle of play and as a tool for learning. The young child should be provided opportunities to learn what his body is capable of performing as well as learning skills in manipulating objects and maneuvering the body through space.

EQUIPMENT

Pieces of equipment that are valuable in developing motor skills in the nursery school child are listed below; the list is not complete but rather is offered as a suggestion for the beginning teacher who may be unfamiliar with the variety of items that may be utilized.

Mats	Kangaroo ball
Balance beam	Rhythm instruments
Jouncing or bouncing board	Dance props
Sand box	Playground balls of various sizes
Tricycles	Bean bags
Small wheelbarrows	Hoops
Wagons	Wading pool
Rocking boat	Gardening tools (junior size)
Large toy trucks	Shop tools (junior size)
Large wooden blocks and boxes	Swings
Climbing apparatus	Slides
Crawl-through apparatus	Teeter-totter

Figure 16-2 This rocking boat can be turned over and used as stairs for climbing. (Courtesy of Childcraft Education Corp.)

Instruction on the Use of Play Equipment

Instruction in the skills of using the various pieces of play equipment may utilize either the problem-solving or traditional method of teaching. For example, using the latter, the child is shown how the parts of his body must be moved to accomplish the skill; then he practices under the supervision of the teacher. In the problem-solving method questions are asked of the child to stimulate self-discovery of the most effective movements for his performance of the skill. For most pieces of equipment, little or no instruction will be needed because their use is simple enough for the children to learn by experimentation or imitation. Equipment that is potentially hazardous, such as swings and slides, requires special instruction to ensure safe and enjoyable use.

Swings. In teaching the young beginner to swing, his confidence must first be developed. He must be made to feel secure in getting in and out of the

Figure 16-3 Bouncing on a kangaroo ball.

seat and in moving gently back and forth in it. The seat should be lowered if necessary to permit his feet to rest flat on the ground. A seat with sidearms and back provides easier balance and a greater sense of security.

The child should be allowed simply to sit in the seat until all fears have been allayed. Then the swing can be pushed very gently and the motion gradually increased. In a short time the child will be ready for the regular swing seat and may be taught the techniques of balancing so that he can swing by himself. To teach the proper balance, the child is initially propelled manually by the teacher. The swing is brought back a short distance by the teacher who holds the child from the rear with one arm and with the other hand gently pushes his head and shoulders forward. As the swing moves forward, the teacher helps the child lean backward by pulling gently back with a hand against his chest. As the child gets the kinesthetic feel of these two movements, he is encouraged to try it without help. He should start with very shallow movements and increase the height of the swing gradually.

Safety precautions should be taught simultaneously with the skills of swinging. The child should never be allowed to stand behind or in front of a swing that is occupied. Swing sets with more than two swings should not be used by very young children. When used by older children techniques of approaching a center swing safely when the others are occupied should be stressed. The approach should be made from the front or behind the swing, never from the sides.

Slides.   In introducing the use of the slide, the teacher should have the child merely sit on the bottom end. As his confidence grows, he can be lifted and placed a short distance up the slide and allowed to slide down. The distance is gradually increased until the child is ready to try sliding from the top. With a steep slide, when the child tries it by himself, the teacher should wait at the bottom to help him in his landing until he has complete control.

Along with teaching the skills of using a slide, safety in its use should be stressed. Children should be taught not to stand in front of the slide when it is being used. Only one child should be on the slide at a time. Climbing up the slide or its supports should not be allowed.

Teeter-totter.   The teeter-totter or see-saw is the most popular of the various types of riding equipment. For nursery school children it must be lower than usual height and preferably be equipped with handles on each end to increase the feeling of security for the young rider. Instruction in the skills of riding may begin by supporting the child on the seat in the rest position to gain his balance. Then the teacher may slowly move the board up and down. As the child develops skill in balancing on the board, he is encouraged to use his feet as he comes to the ground to brake the downward movement and to exert force to move up again. When he can control his balance and exercise the necessary skill, he is permitted to ride by himself. The teacher should continue to watch for a time.

Children should not be allowed to stand beside the center of the board where they may get their fingers crushed. Nor should they ever jump off the board when the other child is up in the air on the other end. They must be instructed in the technique of getting off and raising the board for the safe descent of the other rider.

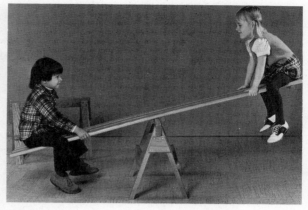

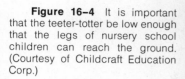
Figure 16–4 It is important that the teeter-totter be low enough that the legs of nursery school children can reach the ground. (Courtesy of Childcraft Education Corp.)

If there are other rides on the playground for nursery school children, the teacher should analyze the skills required in order to determine which techniques, including safety techniques, must necessarily be taught to prepare the children to use them safely. The teaching procedure may follow the ones suggested above for other equipment.

SELECTION AND PRESENTATION OF ACTIVITIES

Physical education activities are selected for children for the contribution they make to their development. The selection must, therefore, be analyzed in light of the desired objectives. Having determined the specific objectives to be accomplished, the physical education activities should be presented so as to provide abundantly for opportunities to develop the abilities, skills, and attitudes sought in the objectives.

One important consideration cannot be ignored and that is the interest of the child in the activity. Without interest the objectives sought are not likely to be accomplished; therefore, the interests of the children must be considered in choosing an activity. Of course, interest can be developed by the proper exposure to the activity so that new activities may become as interesting as the old favorites. Games and activities that are old favorites need not be discarded because it appears that all possible educational value has been extracted from them. Their great appeal to the children should be capitalized on by devising new ways to utilize these favorite activities to accomplish new objectives as well as to strengthen abilities already developed.

The games and activities selected need to be examined for safety hazards inherent within the game or activity. It must be determined if the participants have sufficient skill and insight to avoid such hazards if the activity is used. In some cases the activity may be modified to reduce the possibility of an accident, or a safety device may be utilized to eliminate the danger. Children should be taught the safe way to perform the activity. The instruction should be explicit without discouraging exploration and experimentation on the part of the student. If the students are encouraged to help establish the safety rules and regulations, they become more meaningful to the children and, hence, are more

Figure 16–5 Free-form play equipment encourages exploration of various types of movements. (Courtesy of Town of Vernon Schools, Rockville, Connecticut.)

likely to be observed. For example, in establishing the safe use of the swings, the children can help the teacher mark the danger areas around the swings to warn all against entering while the swings are being used.

In the nursery school children should have considerable opportunities to explore movement both on their own and with guidance. Play equipment and facilities should be of a design that encourage free play. A complete discussion of the utilization of movement exploration in physical education programs is found in Chapter 6.

Games and activities presented should be geared to the abilities of the children. The best activities are those that provide for a wide range of ability. The problem-solving techniques provide unique opportunities to provide challenging and satisfying experiences to all regardless of ability.

MUSIC AND RHYTHMIC ACTIVITIES

Because children love to move to music, singing games and rhythmic activities are important tools for teaching movement to children. Rhythmic patterns and the words of songs offer rich opportunities for creative activities as well as stimulating movement of learned patterns. Repetition of songs and movements are greatly enjoyed by children, and they should be encouraged to repeat old favorites as they have learned them but also with their own fresh interpretations.

The teacher may sing the song used for an activity or use any of the excellent records available. Children may join in as they are able. Some of the records supply the words, while others provide only the accompaniment for the teacher and children to sing the words.

Percussion instruments may be used to beat out rhythms for the various steps—walking, skipping, marching, running—or for various exploratory movements. On occasion, the children should be supplied with instruments of their own on which to beat the rhythms for their activities. Effective instruments may be made from boxes with their lids tapped on to resemble a drum. Other suggestions for improvised equipment are found in Chapter 11.

In planning the music and rhythmic activities for very young children, it is helpful to the teacher to understand the stages of development of abilities in these activities. The sequence of this development from approximately three to six years is outlined below. It should be understood that each child will pass through the stages in the sequence at an individual rate so that not all children of the same age can be expected to be at the same level of development.

SINGING DEVELOPMENTAL SEQUENCE

Listens to songs sung by others; may sing by himself as he plays.

Responds with actions to words of a song sung by others.

Joins in occasionally with words during group singing.

Sings with the group but does not always follow either the words or the time of the music.

Sings alone.

RHYTHMIC DEVELOPMENTAL SEQUENCE

Makes random movements to music or beat.

Moves rhythmically for short time spans.

Keeps time to familiar music with a strong beat.

Moves rhythmically when beat is emphasized.

Adjusts the body movements to slow or fast music.

Makes own beat on percussion instrument and moves other parts of the body to keep time to the beat.

STORY AND POETRY PLAY

Stories and poems or nursery rhymes may be used to suggest movements to be performed by the children. A suitable story or poem is one that has references to various kinds of movements throughout the entire composition, that is within the children's experiences, and that is fun for children to "act out." In presenting unfamiliar material, the teacher should have the children listen to the words first. Difficult words should be explained and questions from the children answered. Then before they attempt any movement, the children should be given a few moments to plan the kinds of movements they will make in response to the words of the story or poem.

An example of a short simple story that is very good for use with nursery school children is "Mother Cat and Baby Kitten." The story is acted out by two children as it is being told by the teacher or the rest of the class. Story: Mother cat and baby kitten are fast asleep. Baby kitten wakes up and runs away to hide. Mother cat wakes up and finds baby kitten gone. She calls, "Meow, Meow." Baby kitten answers, "Mew." The two children who are chosen for the mother and kitten perform the actions and make the call and answer. Several kittens may be used in increasing the number participating at one time. Boys may be daddy cat rather than mother cat if they prefer.

Many familiar children's stories can be used as story plays. In reading the story, the teacher should emphasize the main points to direct the children's attention to the parts that can be acted out. Examples are given for two stories:

Goldilocks and the Three Bears

Points to emphasize
(1) Tasting the three bowls of porridge
(2) Sitting in the three chairs
(3) Lying in the three beds

The Three Little Pigs

Points to emphasize
(1) Building the house of straw
(2) Building the house of sticks
(3) Building the house of bricks
(4) Blowing down the house of straw
(5) Blowing down the house of sticks
(6) Blowing at the house of bricks

The old favorite nursery rhyme "Jack Be Nimble" is a good illustration of the use of verse for "acting" by the children. A candlestick or some object about 6 to 8 inches high is needed. The children line up one behind the other to take turns jumping over the candlestick. They repeat the familiar lines as they jump:

Jack be nimble,
Jack be quick,
Jack jump over the candlestick.

With a large group, two or more lines may be formed to avoid long waits.

Other nursery rhymes in which the words are easily matched with actions are:

Jack and Jill

Jack and Jill went up the hill   (boy and girl walk up inclined mat)
To fetch a pail of water.
Jack fell down   (boy falls down)

And broke his crown   (holds his head)
And Jill came tumbling after.   (girl rolls down inclined mat)

Little Miss Muffet

Little Miss Muffet sat on a tuffet,   (children sit down)
Eating some curds and whey;   (imitate eating)
Along came a great spider and sat down beside her,
And frightened Miss Muffet away.   (children get up and run)

Humpty Dumpty

Humpty Dumpty sat on a wall,   (some of the children sit on a bench sur-
                                                      rounded by mats)
Humpty Dumpty had a great fall,   (children fall from the bench)
All the king's horses
And all the king's men   (the other children run over and pretend to patch
                                             up the others)
Couldn't put Humpty Dumpty together again.

Ring Around the Rosie

Ring around the rosie
A pocket full of posies   (children clasp hands and make a circle and
                                           move to the right)
Hush! hush! hush! hush!   (fingers are placed to the lips)
We all tumble down.   (children tumble to the floor)

One, Two, Buckle My Shoe

One, two, buckle my shoe   (children simulate each of the activities)
Three, four, open the door
Five, six, pick up sticks
Seven, eight, lay them straight
Nine, ten, do it again.

Finger Plays

Finger plays are very popular with young children. In presenting them for the first time the teacher should say the rhyme and explain the words after which the finger action should be demonstrated. The children then repeat the action while the teacher says the verse. Difficult parts may be repeated, and children having an especially hard time may be led through the motions by the teacher. As the children learn the finger play, they are encouraged to learn the verse.

For younger nursery school children, the very simple finger games, such as

Ten Little Indians and Here Is a Box, are more appropriate. Older children will be able to perform more complex finger plays. Examples are given below:

Ten Little Indians

Ten little Indians standing in a row,   (fingers are held straight up)
They bow to the chief, very very low.   (fingers are bent)
They move to the left and they move to the right,   (hands are moved first to the left and then to the right)
Then they all stand up ready to fight.   (all fingers are held very straight pointing upwards)

Here Is a Box

Here is a box with a lid.   (fist is clenched and other hand is placed over the top of fist)
I wonder what it hid?   (hand is removed from top of fist and a finger inserted in clenched fist)
Here it is without a doubt.
Open the box and let it out.   (fist is unclenched)

Five Little Crows

Five little crows sitting in a row.   (fingers of one hand are held up)
One fell down and then there were four.   (thumb is moved to palm)
Four little crows sitting in a tree.
One flew away and then there were three.   (bend one finger down)
Three little crows sitting in a shoe.
One hopped out and then there were two.   (bend second finger down)
Two little crows out for fun.
One got tired and then there was one.   (bend three fingers down)
One little crow sitting alone
He left and then there was none.   (close fist)

Two Little Blackbirds

(Peanut shells are placed on one finger on each hand)
Two little blackbirds sitting on a hill,   (hold up the fingers with shells)
One named Jack and one named Jill.
Fly away, Jack,   (one finger is bent and shell is taken in palm of that hand; finger is returned to original position)
Fly away, Jill,   (other finger is bent and shell is taken in palm; finger is returned to original position)
Come back, Jack,   (finger is bent and the end is stuck back in the shell and finger is straightened up again)
Come back, Jill.   (second finger does the same as the first)

Church and Steeple

Here is a church.   (fingers are interlaced, knuckles up, thumbs held side by side)

Here is the steeple.   (index fingers are lifted to touch at their tips)

Open the doors,   (thumbs are moved to side)

And see the people.   (fingers are wiggled)

BASIC SKILL GAMES

Games and activities should be selected on the basis of how well they serve each individual child. Games that force those who lose or are caught out of the game to sit on the side lines to watch the others are not serving the educational objectives for those children. In fact, games of this kind often deny the child who is in greatest need of the opportunity to participate. As a general rule, the games used should provide all children an opportunity to be involved throughout the game. At times, such as when space is limited or students need rest periods during the game, games which involve a few children while other children wait have a place in the curriculum.

Nursery school children generally are not ready to participate in games that require partners or cooperative team effort. However, some very simple games that require a minimum of interaction with a partner or teammates may be used with four and a half year olds who have had adequate play experiences during the early part of the nursery school year. A selection of such games is presented below. Additional information about the use of basic skill games is presented in Chapter 8. Many of the games described there for kindergarten can also be presented to older nursery school children.

How Do You Do

Number of Players: 7–21

Playing Areas: classroom, hallway, playroom

Equipment: none

Basic skills: lowering body to sitting position

DESCRIPTION OF GAME. One child is chosen to stand in the center. He beckons to a child in the circle, who comes forward to shake hands with the first child and then returns to his place in the circle. He takes a sitting position. The game continues until all are seated.

Teaching Hints. The children may be instructed to say nothing while playing the game as they enjoy going through the actions in absolute silence.

Catch the Balloon

Number of Players: 5–30

Playing Areas: classroom, hallway, playroom

Equipment: balloon

Basic Skills: throwing, catching

DESCRIPTION OF GAME. A circle is formed with one child in the center. He throws the balloon high into the air and calls a child's name. The child whose name is called attempts to catch the balloon before it falls to the ground. Regardless of whether he catches it or not, he becomes the next to throw the balloon.

Teaching Hints. For older nursery school children with more developed skills, a handkerchief may be used rather than a balloon.

Postman

Number of Players: 7–21
Playing Areas: classroom, hallway, playroom
Equipment: large ball
Basic Skills: ball handling

DESCRIPTION OF GAME. The ball serves as the postman. The children sit in a circle. One child starts the game by rolling the ball (the postman) to another child. If the ball touches him (delivers mail to him), he picks it up and rolls it to another child. If the ball touches no one, it is given to a child who has not yet had a turn.

I Sent A Letter

Number of Players: 7–21
Playing Areas: classroom, hallway, playroom
Equipment: none
Basic Skills: dodging, tagging, running

DESCRIPTION OF GAME. The children form a circle. One child is selected to be "It." He takes his place in the center of the circle. Another child is chosen as the "Postmaster." He says, "I sent a letter from (the name of one child in the circle) to (the name of another child in the circle)." As their names are called, the two children exchange places while the one who is "It" attempts to catch one of them. If he succeeds, the one who was caught becomes "It."

Going to Jerusalem

Number of Players: 7–21
Playing Areas: classroom, hallway, playroom
Equipment: chairs, piano or phonograph
Basic Movements: dodging, lowering the body to a sitting position

DESCRIPTION OF GAME. The entire group may play. Chairs are placed in a circle with their backs toward the center of the circle. There must be one less chair than the number of players. As music is played on the piano or phonograph, the children march around the circle of chairs. Whenever the music stops, the children sit in a chair. The one who fails to find a chair sits on the floor. Before the music begins again, one more chair is removed from the circle. The game continues in this way until all are sitting on the floor.

The Bear Pit

Number of Players: 7–21
Playing Areas: classroom, hallway, playroom
Equipment: none
Basic Skills: dodging, chasing, tagging, clasping hands
DESCRIPTION OF GAME. The children form a circle and clasp hands; this is the bear pit. One child is chosen to be the "Bear." He is in the center of the circle from which he tries to escape by going under the clasped hands or breaking through them. If he succeeds, the others try to recapture him. The child who catches him is the "Bear" the next time.

Leap the Puddle

Number of Players: 5–15
Playing Areas: classroom, hallway, playroom, playground
Equipment: none
Basic Skills: running, leaping
DESCRIPTION OF GAME. A large round "pie" is drawn on the floor with one triangular piece of the pie indicated. The piece, which is to be the puddle, should be large enough so that at the far end it is wider than anyone can leap. The children run around within the circle, leaping over the puddle as they approach it. Those with greater ability run closer to the outside of the circle and those with lesser ability, nearer the center.
Teaching Hints. Music may be played to start and stop the running.

Bean Bag Throw

Number of Players: 3–15
Playing Areas: classroom, hallway, playroom
Equipment: one bean bag for each player
Basic Skills: throwing
DESCRIPTION OF GAME. A circle 2 feet in diameter is drawn on the floor. The children stand 6 to 10 feet from the circle. Each player has a bean bag and takes a turn tossing it into the circle.
Teaching Hints. Children can be placed at distances commensurate with their abilities to increase the chance for success.

Classroom Obstacle Race

Number of Players: 1–21
Playing Areas: classroom, hallway, playroom
Equipment: see description of game
Basic Skill: varies according to nature of obstacles
Barrels, blocks, and similar large playthings, as well as classroom furniture, are set up to form an obstacle course. The children crawl through, run around, step over, and so forth as the nature of the obstacle suggests.

All Fours Race

Number of Players: 3–21
Playing Areas: classroom, hallway, playroom
Equipment: none
Basic Skill: crawling

The children form a line, facing a designated goal. They race on hands and knees to the goal. A variation of the race is achieved by racing backwards to the goal.

Rabbit Race

Number of Players: 3–21
Playing Areas: classroom, hallway, playroom
Equipment: none
Basic Skill: hopping

The children form a line. They hop on one foot to a designated goal and return to the starting line.

OTHER GAMES OF LOW ORGANIZATION

There are many games suitable for play on the nursery school level that do not contribute primarily to basic motor skill development but are valuable in promoting skills of visual, auditory, and tactile acuity. Examples of this type of games are given below:

Ring, Bell, Ring

Number of Players: 7–21
Playing Areas: classroom, hallway, playroom
Equipment: bell

DESCRIPTION OF GAME. The children are seated in their chairs. One child is selected to be the bell ringer. While the other children close their eyes, he goes as quietly as possible to some part of the room. Another child is selected to listen carefully for the ringing of the bell. When the bell ringer rings the bell, the listener must point in the direction from which he thinks the sound is coming. If he is correct, he becomes the next bell ringer. If he is wrong, the game continues with the same bell ringer.

Find the Thimble

Number of Players: 7–21
Playing Areas: classroom, hallway, playroom
Equipment: thimble

DESCRIPTION OF GAME. The entire group participates. A thimble or object of similar size is required. The thimble is hidden by the teacher or one of the children while the others close their eyes. One child is chosen to hunt for the thimble. When he finds it, he may be permitted to do the hiding for the next time.

Teaching Hints. An object larger than a thimble is desirable for very young nursery school children.

Guess What

Number of Players: 1–21
Playing Areas: classroom, hallway, playroom
Equipment: see description of game

DESCRIPTION OF GAME. A collection of objects such as a toy boat, airplane, car, and animals of various kinds, a block, a ball, and a pencil are needed. The teacher places three or more of the objects in a bag. The children attempt to identify the objects by feeling the bag.

The Blind Cat

Number of Players: 6–15
Playing Areas: classroom, hallway, playroom
Equipment: none

DESCRIPTION OF GAME. The children form a circle approximately 15 feet in diameter. One child, who is the "cat," is in the center of the circle. He must close his eyes and keep them closed. The children in the circle move to the right and stop on command. The cat then points to a part of the circle. The child pointed at must meow like a cat. If the child in the center guesses correctly the name of the one who made the sound, the two change places.

Teaching Hints. Another animal such as a dog, cow, mouse, etc., could be substituted for the cat.

ACTIVITIES FOR FITNESS

Some of the activities that are included in a program daily should stress the development of physical fitness. Children of this age are generally not in need of specific exercises designed to develop some factor of physical fitness. If the child is exposed to a variety of activities and motor experiences that give him an opportunity to run, jump, tumble, hang, and climb, there is a very good possibility that he will not need specific exercises. The more vigorous of the games that are described for basic skills development also contribute to the development of physical fitness.

SUPPLEMENTARY READINGS

Matterson, E. M.: *Plays and Playthings for the Preschool Child.* Ed. revised. Baltimore, Penguin Books, 1967.

Read, Katherine H.: *The Nursery School.* Ed. 4. Philadelphia, W. B. Saunders Co., 1966.

Vannier, Maryhelen, et al.: *Teaching Physical Education in Elementary Schools.* Ed. 5. Philadelphia, W. B. Saunders Co., 1973.

Willis, C., and Lindberg, L.: *Kindergarten for Today's Children.* Chicago, Follett Educational Corporation, 1967.

BIBLIOGRAPHY

[1]Gesell, Arnold, et al.: *The First Five Years of Life.* New York, Harper and Brothers, Publishers, 1940.
[2]*Ibid.*

chapter seventeen

special physical education

ADAPTED PHYSICAL EDUCATION
DEVELOPMENTAL PHYSICAL EDUCATION
CORRECTIVE PHYSICAL EDUCATION
SERVING SPECIAL NEEDS IN PHYSICAL
  EDUCATION

Modern educational philosophy is based on the premise that any child who is able to profit from the instruction should be able to enroll in our public educational system; consequently, an increasing number of children with physical, mental, and emotional conditions that were once considered too severely restricting to permit participation in the classroom with normal peers are now attending public schools. Today, in a typical elementary school, children will be found who have such physical disabilities as partial vision, impaired hearing, orthopedic handicaps, diabetes, epilepsy, allergies, and rheumatic heart conditions; who are mentally retarded; and who are emotionally disturbed. In addition, there will be children with such low physical fitness, inadequate motor skills, and/or poor body mechanics as to be handicapped to some degree in achieving normally successful educational development.

Nearly all of these children, regardless of their limitations, can benefit from some type of physical education. The physical education for a child with a handicapping condition must, however, be planned and conducted to serve his special needs. To accomplish this is the purpose of special physical education.

The term *special physical education* is an umbrella title, first utilized by the author, for the various kinds of physical education programs that have been developed over the years to serve those in the population who have special needs. Currently such programs have two major emphases: (1) modification of motor activities to permit the handicapped to participate in them and (2) the selection and presentation of physical education activities that develop the capabilities or movement possibilities of the participants. Programs of modified or adapted activities have been known historically as adapted physical education and have chiefly served the physically handicapped. Programs with the objective of the development of capabilities became prominent with the expansion of efforts to serve more effectively the mentally retarded and others with learning disabilities. Such programs were frequently described as developmental, and that term is now generally applied to programs that consist largely of motor skill developmental activities and, to a lesser extent, physical fitness activities.

It is difficult to draw a distinct line between the two types of programs because frequently the same elements are present in both. However, the emphasis varies considerably in the two programs. In the discussion which follows, a program that emphasizes adaptation of physical education activities will be referred to as adapted physical education, and one that emphasizes development of capabilities through improvement of motor skills and physical fitness will be termed developmental physical education; the term special physical education will be applied when speaking of these and similar programs as a whole.

ADAPTED PHYSICAL EDUCATION

Adapted physical education is a program of motor activities modified to fit the needs of the handicapped. Adapting the physical education activities to the abilities and limitations of the child ensures optimum benefits from participation and offers maximum protection against any possible aggravation of the handicapping condition. Among the benefits that the child may realize are:

IMPROVED MOTOR ABILITY IN BASIC SKILLS.   The basic skills of movement are important skills of everyday living. Improving ambulatory skills, balance, and control of the body in different positions is an important contribution to the total well-being of the physically restricted child. Moreover, the development of basic skills encourages participation in sport activities which adds to the enjoyment of life and fosters the maintenance of physical fitness.

HIGHER LEVEL OF PHYSICAL FITNESS.   It is as important for the physically handicapped child to develop physical fitness as for the normal child. The physical fitness level of the handicapped child is likely to be low because of the tendency to withdraw from activities and because of the limited opportunities to perform physically. In certain situations a high development of a specific factor of fitness, such as strength, may be essential to enable the child to make the necessary compensations for the motor limitations imposed by the handicap.

INCREASED FEELING OF INDIVIDUAL WORTH.   Handicapped children are quick to note the differences between themselves and the normal children, but they need help to see the ways in which people are all very much alike. The handicapped child is also likely to be greatly aware of his limitations but unaware of his potentialities. The physical education program can help him to gain greater respect for himself by showing him the many motor skills he can perform even with his limitations.

Organizing the Program

All those who need adapted activities for their physical education should be identified at the earliest possible time. All children should receive periodical physical examinations, and the physician should make the recommendations for the kinds of adapted activities when necessary. The examining physician should be made aware of the type of program the school is able to offer for various kinds of restricting conditions. This is most easily done by supplying the doctor with a form sheet such as the one shown in Figure 17-1.

In some cases parents are overly protective of their handicapped children and set restrictions upon their physical education participation which are actually not in the best interest of the children. Any restrictions should be determined by the family or school physician rather than by the parents. Some education of protective parents may be needed to ensure that they will support the program rather than fight it. A form letter like the one in Figure 17-2, which was designed for children in the upper elementary grades, may help parents to understand the nature of the adapted program and the benefits which accrue to their children from participation in it.

In most cases in the lower elementary grades children with physical limitations should participate within the limits of their physical restrictions in the regular program with the rest of their classmates. There may be times when it is desirable for a special activity to be organized for a handicapped child or group of children, but whenever possible they should play with children of normal physical abilities. They vitally need to be included in groups of normal peers so that they may realize that, although differences do exist, there are many ways in which all are alike. They need, too, to be brought to the realization that one's attitude toward the handicapping condition is more important than the condition itself.

The guiding principle for determining whether the child should be included in the regular program or be given special activities is the benefit he will receive. If he cannot participate to his advantage in the regular program, special activities from which he will derive benefit should be provided. The teacher should be aware not only of the physical aspects but the emotional and mental ones as well. If there is a danger of aggravating the condition or if the possibility of contributing positively to the child's well being is in any way in question, the child should not participate. On the other hand, even when there is no question on either score, the teacher may still wish to exclude the handicapped child from the regular class for a time due to an unfavorable emotional reaction to the situation which may prove detrimental to the accomplishment of the desired objectives.

SPECIAL PHYSICAL EDUCATION PROGRAM

_____School

Date_____

To Dr._____Family Physician for_____

Our program of physical education includes a wide variety of activities for all students in the school. The activities are adapted to fit the needs of each individual student regardless of his physical attributes, and any pupil who is unable to participate in the regular program is provided with special activities modified to meet his needs and to contribute to his welfare.

Please indicate the type(s) of activities that your patient cannot participate in and state the reason._____

_____

_____

Please state the length of time for which the patient is restricted from participation in the above activities:_____to_____; all year_____.

A list of the activities to be presented in the adapted physical education program this year is given below. Please check those in which your patient may participate.

Upper Elementary Grades		Lower Elementary Grades
bowling	shuffleboard	running games
badminton	weightlifting	skipping, hopping
table tennis	calisthenics	walking
golf	bag punching	bowling type games
tennis	dancing, social,	tossing and throwing activities
running	folk and square	climbing (ladder, jungle gym)
walking	squash	swimming
deck tennis	archery	dancing
volleyball	swimming (no diving)	rope jumping
softball	swimming (regular)	tumbling

Some of the above are generalized descriptions of the nature of the activity. If you wish a fuller explanation of the activity, please phone the physical education teacher at_____. Or you may wish to note briefly the types of movement that are contraindicated._____

_____

_____

Figure 17–1 Form sheet for the family physician.

Ways of Adapting Activities

The activity for the handicapped child in the regular class can be adapted so that his limitations are a minimum disadvantage in playing with others. For example, a boy on crutches cannot run bases in a game of softball; but he can be shown how to support himself with the crutches in order to free his hands for batting. This modification plus the substitution of someone to run the bases for him permits him to participate in the game to a degree that is personally satisfying and physically beneficial.

Many ways of modifying play activities are possible for nearly all types of restricting conditions. In general these modifications involve:

1. Substitution of a sitting or lying position for a standing position in activities such as shuffleboard and throwing bean bags at a target.

2. Substitution of walking for skipping or running.
3. Replacing throwing with underhand tossing.
4. Changing from two-handed skills, such as throwing or catching, to one-handed skills.
5. Decreasing distances.
6. Slowing tempo.
7. Providing more rest periods.
8. Supplying oral, visual, and kinesthetic cues to the player.

Which one of these suggested adaptations is used depends, of course, upon the conditions of the children involved. In cases of limited use of the arms and legs, the adaptation may have to be made in the type or amount of movement required by the game. For children who lack endurance or must not exert themselves, modification may be made to provide more frequent periods of rest and to decrease the strenuousness of the game by slowing the tempo or reducing the distance. For youngsters with impaired sight, it is desirable to supply oral cues, that is, to give them verbal directions and descriptions not required by those with full sight. Children with hearing problems can be given visual cues to compensate for the lack of verbal comprehension. Kinesthetic cues, which

_____ School

Date _____

Dear Parents:

The program of health and physical education at our school has a wide variety of activities to offer to all students. The activities are adapted to fit the special needs of each pupil regardless of his physical attributes. After receiving the recommendations of your family physician, it was found that your child could participate in the following activities which are being offered in physical education this year:

_____

_____

By giving your child an opportunity to participate in these physical activities, we hope to achieve these objectives:
develop his physical fitness and health to optimum potential;
develop skills in the basic motor movements of sports and everyday living;
develop a variety of sport skills for use in worthy leisure time activity;
promote a desire for continuous physical improvement;
promote an understanding of his physical limitations and potentialities;
provide opportunities to play and participate socially with others.

We hope that our plans meet with your approval. If you wish to discuss the program further, please call me at _____ .

Yours truly,

Figure 17-2 Form letter to parents. (From Fait: *Special Physical Education: Adapted, Corrective, Developmental.* W. B. Saunders Company.)

may range from a signal, such as a tap on the shoulder, to leading the child through the movement, are very helpful in nearly all situations.

Programs designed for those who are suffering from cardiopathic conditions, cerebral palsy, orthopedic handicaps, anemia, allergies, hernias, and other conditions that might be aggravated by improper activity should be checked with the family or school physician before participation by the children.

Teaching Hints

The problem-solving method is especially well suited to teaching the physically handicapped. A considerable amount of experimentation is generally necessary to determine the most effective way to perform a motor skill, and problem-solving enables the child to experiment in a productive way. The use of movement exploration is especially effective because it allows the handicapped child to explore movement in his own unique manner. Since no one way of movement is the correct way, physically disabled children have no difficulty fitting into a class of normal peers in movement exploration activities.

In teaching normal students by the direct method, the teacher relies heavily on verbalization and visualizations; however, when a student fails to grasp the techniques of the skill from watching a demonstration and listening to a description, the teacher often uses manual kinesthesis. The importance of kinesthesis in teaching handicapped children, particularly those with visual and auditory impairments, is obvious and serves as a perfect illustration of the fact that the teaching of exceptional children is essentially the same as teaching normal children.

Progress may come more slowly for the exceptional students, and the teacher must be extremely patient in teaching them. Each accomplishment, regardless of how small it may be, should be recognized and used to help the student gain group status and respect; however, the complimentary remarks should be sincere and be offered only for actual accomplishment.

In many cases children with handicaps who have not had the opportunity to participate in a wide variety of motor activities need to exercise certain safety precautions because they may lack sufficient strength and endurance. Until the level of fitness is near its optimum, care should be taken to avoid injury or harm from overexertion and fatigue. Students should be thoroughly instructed about the things they may and may not do. However, they should be encouraged to work to capacity within their tolerance level.

When the child cannot be worked into the regular physical education program, activities in which he may engage (depending upon his limitation and age) are:

jacks	table tennis
rope jumping	ball throwing and catching
hopscotch	basketball free throw
pitching and tossing games	badminton
self-testing activities	fitness exercises
darts	bowling and bowling type games
croquet	swimming
shuffleboard	bicycling
walking	archery

DEVELOPMENTAL PHYSICAL EDUCATION

Developmental physical education is concerned with the improvement of the physical fitness and motor ability of those children whose level of fitness or motor skills is below that which is considered desirable for effective functioning.

Low Physical Fitness

Generally, the level of physical fitness is raised through improvement of the separate components of physical fitness, such as strength, endurance, and flexibility. Some students will evidence low levels in all of the components, but a far greater number will be low only in certain physical fitness factors.

To determine the factors of physical fitness requiring special attention, children in grade four or above can be given a diagnostic physical fitness test. After identifying the specific weaknesses, appropriate physical fitness activities can be selected to effect improvement. Below the fourth grade, it is difficult to administer physical fitness tests as the children do not always exert maximum effort. Also, they are easily distracted, and it is difficult to keep their attention focused on the testing sufficiently to secure accurate measurements. Therefore, it is recommended that for children below fourth grade, a wide variety of activities from running and dodging to balancing and climbing be included in the program to ensure the inclusion of activities that will develop all factors of physical fitness. A comprehensive discussion on selecting activities that promote physical fitness in elementary school children and the administering of physical fitness tests to older elementary children is found in Chapter 7.

Poor Motor Ability

The evidence available indicates that there is no one set of activities that best promotes the general development of motor ability. As indicated in Chapter 2, general motor ability consists of specific skills, and the development of overall motor ability requires that specific skills be learned. Hence, raising the level of motor skill performance requires the identification of specific skill weaknesses.

To determine the skills that require special attention, an evaluation of the child's motor ability must be undertaken. Three diagnostic tests that have been used for this purpose are the Oseretsky Test, Denver Developmental Scale, and the University of Connecticut and Mansfield Training School Motor Skill Test.[1] An effective test for determining specific areas of motor inadequacy can also be developed by the teacher using the correction charts presented in Chapters 8 and 12. From the skills listed on each chart, a specific skill is chosen for evaluation, e.g., running. Then the chart in Table 8–6 is consulted for a description of the common errors that children make in running. These may be copied on a large sheet for record-keeping purposes. As many children as can be observed at one time are asked to line up facing the teacher at a distance of several yards. The children then run forward while the teacher observes and records movement errors. The errors noted become the basis for evaluating skill ability in running and for determining those who need specific assistance in developing greater proficiency in the skill.

For those skills for which correction charts have not been developed, the teacher may use a textbook description of the correct form to establish standards by which to evaluate the children as they perform the skill. The manner of performance of many skills such as maneuvering the body through a small space or climbing over or under various objects will differ greatly from one situation to the next because of the characteristics of the space involved. In these cases, the teacher will need to make a subjective judgment of the performance based upon the effectiveness of the child's use of his body in the given situation.

Kinds of activities that should be provided for promoting motor skill development are:

1. Running—straight, in a circle, zig-zag.
2. Dodging—changing directions, pivoting, chasing, tagging in tag games.
3. Balancing in various positions and in various situations.
4. Jumping, leaping, hopping, skipping, galloping.
5. Changing body positions to different levels, including falling correctly.
6. Pushing, pulling, lifting, and carrying.
7. Crawling and climbing in various ways and over various objects.
8. Maneuvering the body through small spaces.
9. Throwing and catching various objects and striking with various instruments.
10. Moving the body in various ways with and without locomotion.

The foregoing skills and their variations can be taught by the problem-solving or the direct method or by a synthesis of the two. Many of the skills are used in the basic skill games and can be taught through these games. Other skills lend themselves to learning through playing the lead-up and team games and performing stunts and tumbling. However, in most cases the child with low

Figure 17–3 Moving the body on hands and knees through a small space promotes the development of motor skills. (Courtesy of Childcraft Education Corp.)

motor ability will not be able to improve his skills markedly in game situations. Special activities will need to be developed for him, and stunt activities must be modified to fit his needs.

CORRECTIVE PHYSICAL EDUCATION

Corrective physical education generally refers to a program of exercises and activities to improve poor body mechanics of standing, walking, and sitting postures. These exercises and activities are generally designed to strengthen those muscles that are responsible for maintaining efficient posture.

The best way to strengthen the postural muscles of elementary school children is through basic skill or low organized games and activities. In general, any activities that involve strengthening the muscles of the back are activities that contribute to strengthening important postural muscles. Examples of these may be found in Chapter 8.

SERVING SPECIAL NEEDS IN PHYSICAL EDUCATION

Within the school population there are three groups of students who have unique needs that must be given special consideration in program planning beyond those already presented. These are the mentally retarded, the emotionally disturbed, and the disadvantaged. Each of the groups will be discussed in some detail as a separate entity although it is recognized that some children fall into more than one of the groups.

MENTALLY RETARDED CHILDREN

Many communities throughout the country are providing educational opportunities for the mentally retarded in the local schools. Schools providing instruction to mentally retarded students have approached the organization of physical education for them in different ways. Some schools provide separate classes segregated from normal students for all of the mentally retarded students together regardless of their chronological ages. Other schools integrate the more advanced students with their peer groups in regular physical education classes with special consideration given to planning for their special needs. The most successful organization is one in which the school schedules its physical education so that segregated and integrated classes are being taught simultaneously, thereby permitting the retarded students who can profit from the instruction being given at any one time in the regular class to participate in it but enabling them to move to the segregated class when they cannot participate to their benefit. This dual scheduling, because of its greater flexibility in programing, offers the best possibility of providing a good program suited to the individual needs of each mental retardate. Where this kind of organization is possible, it should be employed.

Levels of Retardation

Educators refer to the mentally retarded as totally dependent, trainable, and educable. Educable and trainable retardates are receiving their education in public schools in many parts of the country.

Totally dependent children are those, who because of the severity of their retardation, are incapable of being trained for economic usefulness, social participation, or total self-care. These children develop at only one-fourth the rate of average children. They will require nearly complete supervision and care throughout their lives, because they cannot care adequately for their personal needs, protect themselves, or communicate effectively with others.

Those mentally retarded children who have some potential for learning to care for their personal needs, for social adjustment in a group, and for economic usefulness are referred to as trainable. These children can be taught enough of the skills of personal care to make them generally independent of care by others. They are capable of learning to get along in the family and in a limited environment. Their mental development is approximately one-fourth to one-half that of the average child, and they are not generally capable of acquiring academic skills beyond the learning of simple words and numbers. Nevertheless, they are capable of learning to do simple tasks at home or for remuneration in a supervised situation outside the home. Some care, supervision, and economic support will be required throughout their lives.

Children who because of slow mental development cannot profit from the work offered in the regular elementary school but who are capable of learning some academic skills are identified as educable. They are generally capable of acquiring from second to fourth grade achievement in reading, writing, and arithmetic by the age of 16. Their development is approximately one half to three fourths as fast as the average child; consequently, their academic progress is also one half to three fourths the rate of the average child. Although their communication skills are definitely limited, they can be adequately developed for most situations. Most of the educable can learn to get along with others and can acquire enough skills to support themselves economically in adulthood. Emotional and behavior problems may limit their adaptability.

Curriculum Objectives

Some of the objectives that should be emphasized in the physical education program for the mentally retarded are:

TO DEVELOP THE BASIC SKILLS OF MOVEMENT THAT WILL ENABLE THE STUDENT TO PERFORM MORE EFFECTIVELY THE EVERYDAY SKILLS OF LIFE

The kinds of basic skills emphasized will vary in accordance with the mental level of the child. For the profoundly and severely retarded, such skills as lifting the feet over obstacles, climbing and descending stairs, and stepping across objects will become important specific objectives, while for the trainable and educable retardates, the basic skills that will be emphasized are the same as those taught to normal youngsters.

TO INCREASE THE LEVEL OF FITNESS

The majority of mental retardates who have not been exposed to good physical education programs will have low levels of physical fitness because of their tendency to be inactive and withdrawn from activities. Increasing the level of physical fitness will enhance the possibility of their successful performance of other motor skills.

TO DEVELOP THE FEELING THAT A SERIOUS EFFORT TO ACCOMPLISH IS WORTHWHILE AND TO INCREASE THE FEELING OF INDIVIDUAL WORTH

The mentally retarded child needs to know that trying is important—that nothing can be accomplished without making an effort. Since the mentally retarded will usually be more successful in physical activities than in academic endeavors, the physical education program can help the child to be successful and thereby foster a feeling of worth that may encourage him to try tasks in areas other than physical education.

TO ENCOURAGE INTERACTION WITH OTHER PEOPLE IN A PLAY SITUATION

Play and motor movement provide a wonderful opportunity for the mentally retarded to learn how to get along with other people. All types of physical activities provide opportunities to encourage the child to communicate and respond to directions in a play situation and to develop the ability to be a part of an orderly group.

Teaching Hints

One of the most crucial factors in teaching the mentally retarded is motivation, i.e., getting them to want to accomplish. Motivation is difficult for two basic reasons: they do not expect to succeed in any attempt because of repeated past failures, and they are unable to comprehend and appreciate the value of a certain type of behavior or action.

Because of the history of failures throughout their lives, mental retardates learn to expect to fail in everything they try; therefore, they withdraw from trying. To overcome this negative attitude, the teacher begins with activities simple enough to ensure success. Any effort by the student, even when successful, must be generously praised and further attempts encouraged. When more complex movements are introduced, the mental retardate may fail to perform the total movement successfully but will likely perform some part of it satisfactorily. The teacher should point out his success and use the resulting feeling of accomplishment to stimulate further attempts to achieve the entire movement.

If mentally retarded students are brought together with normal peers for physical education, the benefits that can result from this association will be realized only if the mentally retarded youngster feels adequate and accepted by the class. If dual scheduling has been arranged, the teacher will be able to prepare the normal class in advance by promoting an understanding of the mentally retarded as an individual who has a specific weakness but also has certain strengths, as we all have. It is not a matter of developing tolerance for his weakness but of developing an attitude of acceptance of him as a person.

The mentally retarded student will feel more secure if he is introduced to the activity in a separate class before he joins the regular group. He may be taught something about the activity and given a chance to practice the skill

before entering the regular class. Hence, in the beginning, he will be sufficiently ahead of the class to feel confident about his performance and so will
enjoy participation.

The program for mentally retarded children must be carefully planned, taking into consideration their mental ability and any physical handicapping conditions. The instructional period must be relatively short since they perform
skills best during the first attempts. Practice should continue in brief sessions
over a long period of time.

Verbal instruction should be limited to short concise clear statements. It is
often desirable to repeat the instructions several times using the same word
patterns as in the original instruction. Demonstration is more effective in most
situations than verbal explanation in teaching a skill. The mentally retarded
usually comprehend more readily by watching than by listening. Furthermore,
they enjoy mimicking the teacher. Manual kinesthesis is also very effective as a
method of instruction, especially with a non-verbal child. Leading a child
through a desired movement, such as tossing a ball, often enables the student
to grasp the concept of the movement when all other methods have failed.

In determining the physical fitness level of the mentally retarded, the in-

Figure 17–4 Activities should be
chosen in accordance with the child's ability
to perform. (Challenge.)

ability of a child to comprehend the directions and to remember the pattern of movement the test requires makes it difficult to secure a true measurment of the fitness level with tests designed for normal youngsters. The scores are likely to be influenced by the failure to understand or remember. It is recommended, therefore, that for testing the physical fitness of trainable and educable mentally retarded students, a specially designed test battery be administered (see Appendix II).

EMOTIONALLY DISTURBED CHILDREN

Emotionally disturbed children vary so considerably in the behavior traits they display that it is nearly impossible to characterize them as a group. There is, however, a common denominator in their behavior and that is their inability to adapt to a changing environment. The lack of ability to adapt results in behavior that ranges from hyperactivity at one end of the scale to withdrawal at the other extreme. Children between the two extremes display less marked but still highly inappropriate responses in normal situations. Their emotional impairment manifests itself in the classroom and playground in disruptions, lack of cooperation, and inability to function adequately.

The cause of emotional disturbance in children is not yet fully understood. Many authorities believe the cause to be environmental in nature, i.e., some circumstance in the early life of the child, such as family disorganization, produces a block to normal emotional maturation. Other experts believe the source of the disturbance is a faulty physiological condition of the nervous system.

With respect to physical education, many emotionally disturbed children have difficulty performing activities in which motor control and perception are important elements. Those who lack motor control exhibit a lack of coordination in their movements. Deficiencies in perception show up in the inability to move the body through space effectively. In addition, some of the children may display psychosomatic reactions when they feel inadequate in movement and perform poorly.

Curriculum Objectives

Suggested objectives for the physical education for emotionally disturbed children are:

TO DEVELOP AND/OR MAINTAIN AN OPTIMUM LEVEL OF PHYSICAL FITNESS

The level of physical fitness will vary greatly among emotionally disturbed children. Those who are hyperactive may demonstrate a high level of development of some or all of the physical fitness components, while those who are withdrawn and, therefore, not physically active will exhibit generally low levels in all components of physical fitness. For those among the former group who lack development only in some of the physical fitness factors, it is necessary to redirect their interest to activities that foster the development of those components in which they are deficient. For the others, considerable ingenuity will be needed to interest and involve them in appropriate physically vigorous activities.

TO DEVELOP BASIC MOTOR AND SPORT SKILLS

Children who are emotionally disturbed need to improve their basic motor skills for the same reason as other children—to enable them to perform the everyday activities of life more effectively. Since these motor skills are also the basis for learning sport skills, they must be developed before the social learning and skill refinement opportunities afforded by participation in the various sports can be available to these children.

TO AID THE DEVELOPMENT OF SELF-CONFIDENCE IN PHYSICAL EDUCATION ACTIVITIES

Success is important in helping the emotionally disturbed child achieve satisfactory adjustment. Enabling him to achieve success in the activities of the physical education program bolsters the child's confidence in his ability to perform well in physical situations.

TO AID THE DEVELOPMENT OF SOCIALLY ACCEPTABLE RESPONSES

The emotionally disturbed child needs a great deal of help in developing responses that are acceptable to others. Since many physical education activities are social in nature, they are a good medium through which to provide experiences in which the emotionally disturbed child can make independent adjustments that are acceptable to those with whom he is playing.

Teaching Hints

In their reaction to the teaching of physical education activities, the emotionally disturbed represent an extremely heterogeneous group. Approaches that are effective with some will be disturbing to others. Hence, successful teaching of the emotionally disturbed child depends upon finding the method and procedures that evoke the most positive responses. The teacher must explore all the possibilities carefully, adapting, revising, or eliminating as appears to be indicated. The child may be included in the regular program when he can successfully participate; however, when he cannot, he should be placed in a separate or individual program.

A variety of activities should be presented since the shorter attention span so often present in emotionally disturbed children makes concentration on one activity for any length of time difficult. It is helpful to remove distracting objects before the teaching session begins for, as a general rule, the attention span can be increased if extraneous objects are removed from the immediate environment. The same holds true for other activities occurring at the same time.

It is desirable for the teacher to make available alternatives in the learning environment by providing various activities from which the child may make a selection. He should be encouraged to explore and try new experiences whenever it appears that he might be willing to do so. Activities or situations that encourage immediate success provide the best results. The activities provided should also involve as many of the senses as possible.

To help the child understand and interpret his behavioral response to the experiences he is having, the teacher should provide cues that demonstrate the relationship of a new experience to an old one. The child should be encouraged to reflect on the experiences he has and to arrive independently at judgments concerning behavior that will be acceptable to others. Authoritarian control in aiding a child to adjust to a situation should be avoided.

DISADVANTAGED CHILDREN

Increased awareness of the plight of poor families in the inner cities and depressed rural regions of our country has focused attention on the special educational needs of the children of these families. Numerous research studies and special programs have been undertaken to determine how the educational system can better serve these children who are virtually handicapped in educational achievement by the circumstances of their lives. The results of the studies and experimental programs give ample evidence of the adverse effects upon learning of poor nutrition, lack of medical and dental care, disruptive home life, and a general poor environment for the promotion of physical, mental, and emotional well-being. The obvious conclusion to be made from this evidence is that the root conditions must be eliminated as speedily as possible. Unfortunately, the school is limited by financial and legal authority in its ability to effect the remedies. Consequently, the school must rely on its teachers to implement ways of improving conditions for disadvantaged children through adapting methods and materials to serve their special needs.

To create more meaningful programs and present them in ways that will better serve the disadvantaged, teachers must understand their special needs, interests, and abilities. Achieving an understanding is not always easy for a teacher whose own circumstances and education reflect middle class standards, values, and goals. Children from disadvantaged homes, although handicapped by many deficiencies and limitations, do possess certain strengths that can be utilized in improving education programs for them. It is often difficult for the teacher to differentiate between the strengths and weaknesses of the disadvantaged child, for what may be viewed a weakness as judged by the teacher's standards may well be a strength that makes survival possible for the child in his environment.

The discussion which follows presents certain characteristics of strengths and weaknesses that have been observed by those who have worked extensively with disadvantaged youngsters both inside and outside the school. The presentation is limited to those characteristics that should receive consideration in planning the physical education program. More comprehensive discussions will be found in the references listed in the Supplementary Readings.

The reader must bear in mind that the characteristics described do not apply to every disadvantaged child. For various reasons, most children will exhibit different degrees of the characteristics while some will evidence no trait of the characteristic at all. They are discussed here to give the prospective teacher some basis for understanding these children and planning an effective program of physical education for them.

Traits of Negative Consequences

1. POOR PHYSICAL HEALTH. The disadvantaged child's environment is not conducive to the development of sound health. The poor health conditions that surround him as well as the lack of medical care throughout his life tend to increase his vulnerability to disease and illness, thereby depriving him of the vigor necessary for participation in physical education.

Malnutrition is prevalent among disadvantaged children; it is not uncommon for a child to arrive at school hungry and with a limited supply of reserved energy. In taking part in strenuous physical education activity, the child frequently uses up his meager supply of energy, leaving him weak and exhausted and unable to be effective in anything else he undertakes in school. The teacher of physical education must be aware of and make allowance for illness and poor health, fatigue, and a lack of interest that stems from lack of energy.

2. LOW ACHIEVEMENT ORIENTATION.   Research indicates that the disadvantaged child does lack drive and ambition as compared to the general population of school children. This lack is often interpreted as a negative or defeatist attitude on the part of the child. However, more frequently than not, this attitude stems from the child's firm grip on reality and his ability to view life pragmatically. The environment, as he knows it, is a hostile one. The life he leads is a difficult one and offers little hope for the future. The disadvantaged child is often criticized for not taking his work seriously or for playing around even in serious situations. This type of action is actually a necessary adaptive mechanism used by the child to make a difficult life bearable.

Understanding the influences that are at work, the teacher will better understand why the child does not strive for the goals accepted by most of the middle class society. If he is to be effective with the disadvantaged child, the teacher must not attempt to force upon him his own values that had been nurtured in a different class culture.

3. ANTI-INTELLECTUALISM.   It is common for those who have never had the opportunity to learn to reason and to think objectively to develop an anti-intellectual attitude. The disadvantaged seldom have this opportunity, for their learning experiences are founded upon a physical or motoric-visual orientation to learning, i.e., answers to problems are arrived at through physical manipulation.

When his learning is based entirely upon a motoric-visual orientation, the individual often comes to regard "book knowledge" and abstract concepts as impractical and holds them in small regard. This attitude often develops into an antagonism toward books, schools, and teachers that represent, as one disadvantaged child has stated it, "intellectual stuff that has no value in real life."

Physical education is uniquely structured to help the child bridge the gap between symbolic and motoric-visual learning. Although the research is limited and very little practical application has yet been made of the problem-solving method in physical education to making this bridge, it would appear that the method could be used most effectively to achieve this end, for the nature of the problem in physical education is such that both types of approach may be used in solving them. As children become engrossed in the physical manipulation required to solve a problem, they may actually begin to employ symbolic reasoning without being aware of it. When this occurs, the children may be helped by the teacher to recognize the practical value of its use. Having become aware in this small way of the merit of the reasoning process, they are likely to look with greater favor upon it.

4. FRUSTRATIONS OF ALIENATION.   All too frequently the disadvantaged child feels alienated from society. He feels left out, passed by. The frus-

tration of finding avenues to success and happiness closed to him most often expresses itself in a lack of respect for authority.

It is difficult for the disadvantaged child, especially as he grows older, to trust leaders and teachers and to cooperate with them to achieve a common goal. His reaction becomes one of antagonism to all individuals in positions of authority.

Because respect earns respect, the teacher's most successful efforts in reducing alienation will be achieved by developing a genuine respect for the efforts of the disadvantaged child in coping with the difficulties of his life. Only when mutual respect is achieved can the alienation of the student be broken down.

Respect should not be confused with authority. Rigid dictatorial control of the class may bring compliance and the appearance of respect from the students, but it will prove defeating. True respect grows from the knowledge that the teacher is fair, considerate, knowledgeable, and willing to admit error or lack of information, and that he respects his students as individuals.

Teachers of physical education tend to use commands, military formations, and other authoritarian techniques to teach and control the class. This is undesirable in any situation, but it is particularly damaging where one is dealing with youngsters who distrust authority.

Traits of Positive Consequences

1. PHYSICALLY STRONG AND WELL-COORDINATED. The disadvantaged child, if he escapes serious illness and malnutrition, is often physically strong and well-coordinated, because his environment forces him into physical activities which develop physical fitness and motor skills. Because physical powers are necessary to his survival, he generally has a keen interest in developing himself physically. For those who teach physical education, the significance of this is obvious. Capitalizing on the existing interest, the teacher can guide the students into a well-rounded program of motor skill and physical fitness development.

2. MOTORIC-VISUALLY ORIENTED. As pointed out above, the disadvantaged child learns by moving the body or manipulating objects. While this is to his disadvantage when confronted with symbols and abstract concepts, it is a distinct advantage in physical education. Here he is able to perform successfully and to take satisfaction in achievement.

3. EARLY DEVELOPMENT OF INDEPENDENCE AND RESPONSIBILITY. The disadvantaged child develops independence and responsibility at an early age. While still very young, he is involved with such serious adult problems as unemployment, drug addiction, and prostitution. He often has to be responsible for the care of younger brothers and sisters. His childhood contains no room for fantasy and fairy tales. He never needs to make a transition from the make-believe world to the real world. He is part of that real world and has been since birth.

Because of the responsibilities that fall upon him, he develops an independence far beyond his years. He has learned to do things for himself; as a consequence, he meets his problems head-on and does not depend on help from others.

Again, here is a strength that can be utilized in teaching physical education. When students are responsible and independent enough to accept and carry out individual assignments in motor movement, a much more exciting and productive class is possible. The teacher is freer to move about to give individual help and encouragement, and the students are able to work at their own rate in activities suited to their individual needs and interests.

4. SOCIALLY ORIENTED. The home life of the disadvantaged child provides abundant opportunities for social interaction. The home is generally crowded with people with whom he must learn to interact in order to survive. There is no place to which he can retreat or hide; he simply has to learn to cope with a variety of personalities and behavior patterns. Although this early and continuous involvement with people may make it difficult for the young child to concentrate in the classroom on inanimate objects such as numbers and words, it does prepare him for involvement in activity with others in the physical education program. The teacher does not have to spend time preparing these youngsters to accept each other as partners in play. The time thus gained can be put to good advantage in helping in the areas of greatest weakness.

Curriculum Objectives

The specific objectives and the kind of emphasis needed to accomplish them are listed below.

TO DEVELOP MOTOR SKILLS OF MOVEMENT. Although the disadvantaged child frequently has had a broad experience in motor movement in his daily "play" (even though he lacks the conventional play experiences of the middle class), the physical education program can contribute to the further development of the basic skills, i.e., improving running, dodging, and balancing. In a large number of cases, for some reason or other, the child has not developed the wide range of ability in the basic skills and needs special help.

A further development of sports skills is, of course, desirable to provide the child with additional recreation opportunities as well as providing him a means of gaining acceptance in a society that respects physical ability.

TO CONTRIBUTE TO THE DEVELOPMENT OF PHYSICAL FITNESS. The admiration among disadvantaged youths of such factors of fitness as strength and endurance contributes to their desire to develop and maintain a high level of physical fitness. Therefore, probably no special emphasis need be placed on physical fitness for many of the children, except to capture their interest in physical education. For those whose physical fitness level is low, special attention must be given to improvement. However, if malnutrition or illness, which as noted above is more common among these youngsters, is a contributing cause, alleviation of the condition must occur before physical fitness in physical education can be emphasized. If the low physical fitness level is due to withdrawal from activity, the approach to the problem is similar to that discussed in Chapter 7.

TO INCREASE SOCIAL AND EMOTIONAL DEVELOPMENT. Before the disadvantaged child can experience any positive social and emotional development, it is necessary for him to develop a feeling of individual worth. The total physical education experience like all educational experiences should provide the child with opportunities that help him to develop respect for himself. His respect may grow from pride in his achievements in physical education, but it should not be confined to this. His physical education experiences should contribute to his feeling of worth as an individual.

TO DEVELOP SELF-DIRECTION IN MOVEMENT AND UNDERSTANDING HOW HIS BODY MOVES IN ITS ENVIRONMENT. Although the disadvantaged child has an advanced development of some motor skills, a better understanding of how his body moves will increase his ability to explore and experiment with movement to find out how to use his body better.

TO DEVELOP THE CONCEPT OF THE PROPER PLACE OF MOTOR ABILITY IN THE TOTAL PICTURE OF EDUCATION. Physical prowess is generally highly respected by disadvantaged youths. It is, in fact, generally accorded a higher place in their hierarchy of values than academic abilities. Many youngsters in their exaggerated respect for physical powers have developed a stongly anti-intellectual attitude. Under proper guidance, physical education can help these children gain a better perspective of the total educational picture and the relative positions of physical and mental ability in it.

Teaching Hints

Programing is much more likely to be successful if it is built on play activities that the children regularly engage in outside of school. The games these children play on their own are simply structured with clear-cut goals. The elements of the game usually are free from abstract complications; they are concerned with direct action and tangible results. As such, they reflect the motoric-visual orientation of the children. By choosing games, dances, and activities that utilize the same basic patterns of their free-time play activities, the teacher can capitalize on the students' interest to introduce new activities that might otherwise be received with apprehension. For the same reason, games and dances related to the culture of the neighborhood are good selections.

The teachers must contantly be alert to the physical condition of the children. Those who fatigue easily and those who are malnourished must conserve their energy and should not take part in the more strenuous activities. It is important that in excusing them from participation, the attention of the other children not be directed to the deficiency of those who are not able to participate. An effective solution is to give these children obviously useful jobs such as keeping score, timing, and so forth, making these seem important rather than something to keep them occupied. (While it is recognized that this is not "physical education," the thoughtful teacher recognizes that these children will be incapable of taking the regular course of physical education until their nutrition has improved). If a dual class arrangement exists, weak and malnourished children may be placed in the adaptive class rather than accommodated in the regular class.

Rules and regulations for the conduct of the class should be simple and as few in number as possible. The children need to understand why the rules are necessary and this may best be accomplished by a discussion in which the teacher elicits from the children reasons why certain rules must be followed.

Children from disadvantaged homes want and need rules and order; they desire clearly defined limits; they want the teacher to be firm but consistent in meting out punishment for violation of the rules. Firmness and consistency are two universally important assets every teacher must develop. Consistency here refers to a pattern of response to children and to classroom situations that is essentially the same day after day. Firmness indicates a no-nonsense but unemotional response; it does not mean rigidity and a dictatorial attitude, nor does it mean harshness and severity.

SUPPLEMENTARY READINGS

American Association for Health, Physical Education and Recreation: *Best of Challenge.* Washington, D.C., American Association for Health, Physical Education and Recreation, 1973.

American Alliance for Health, Physical Education and Recreation: *Integrating Persons with Handicapping Conditions into Regular Physical Education and Recreation Programs.* Washington, D.C., A merican Alliance for Health, Physical Education and Recreation, 1975.

American Alliance for Health, Physical Education and Recreation: *Physical Education and Recreation for Individuals with Multiple Handicapping Conditions.* Washington, D.C., American Alliance for Health, Physical Education and Recreation, 1975.

American Association for Health, Physical Education and Recreation: *Physical Education and Recreation for the Visually Handicapped.* Washington, D.C., American Association for Health, Physical Education and Recreation, 1973.

Cheyney, Arnold B.: *Teaching Culturally Disadvantaged in the Elementary School.* Columbus, Ohio, Charles E. Merrill Publishing Co., 1967.

Clarke, Harrison H., and Clarke, David H.: *Developmental and Adapted Physical Education.* Englewood Cliffs, New Jersey, Prentice-Hall, Inc., 1963.

Cratty, Bryant J.: *Motor Activity and the Education of Retardates.* Ed. 2. Philadelphia, Lea and Febiger, 1974.

Drowatzky, John N.: *Physical Education for the Mentally Retarded.* Philadelphia, Lea and Febiger, 1971.

Fait, Hollis F.: *Special Physical Education: Adapted, Corrective, Developmental.* Ed. 3. Philadelphia, W. B. Saunders Co., 1972.

Lowman, Charles: *Postural Fitness.* Philadelphia, Lea and Febiger, 1960.

Shivers, Jay, and Fait, Hollis F.: *Therapeutic and Adapted Recreational Services.* Philadelphia, Lea and Febiger, 1975.

BIBLIOGRAPHY

[1]Fait, Hollis F.: *Special Physical Education: Adapted, Corrective, Developmental.* Ed. 3. Philadelphia, W. B. Saunders Co., 1972. pp. 208–210.

chapter eighteen

games for playground and self-directed play

PLAYGROUND SUPERVISION
PLAYGROUND AND SELF-DIRECTED
    ACTIVITIES

The classroom teacher can usually expect to serve at certain scheduled hours as supervisor of the playgrounds during recess and free play periods. Since children of all ages are on the playground together at such times, it is customary in the interest of safety to have certain areas of the playground designated for the specific use of the younger and older children. Primary grades are, preferably, assigned an area close to their classrooms and provided with equipment scaled to their size. Outlying areas and playing fields are set aside for the upper grades, and the equipment is of a size and nature to serve the needs and interests of older children.

PLAYGROUND SUPERVISION

The teacher has several important duties in supervising the playground. The good supervisor does not reduce these duties to policing the children's activities but performs them in a positive way so that both the safety and the enjoyment of the free play periods are created and preserved.

SAFETY. The teacher must be alert to keep children from careless practices which may result in injury such as, for example, standing too near swinging apparatus, throwing the bat after hitting the ball, and attempting skills which are too advanced for the maturity and ability of the child.

COURTEOUS CONDUCT. Unless reminded by the teacher that good manners and sportsmanlike conduct must prevail during these free play periods the same as elsewhere, some pupils may make of free play a "free-for-all."

PARTICIPATION OF CHILDREN. The teacher should make an effort to encourage participation in play by those who are not aggressive enough to make an effort to be included. If there is a group of several such children, the teacher may help by assisting them in starting a game of their own rather than trying to work them all into an already existing game.

RULE ENFORCEMENT. Children should have a clear understanding of the rules and regulations concerning use of equipment, areas in which they may and may not play, and general conduct on the playground. Hopefully, the rules needed will be small in number and simple in nature so that they can be readily understood and remembered. The teacher should be firm in dealing with violators; punishment should be consistent with school policy. Deprivation of privileges is very effective with most youngsters.

RESPECT FOR PROPERTY. Many adults have little respect for public property as evidenced by the huge sums of money spent by municipalities in restoring defaced buildings, repairing damaged lawns, and cleaning up after litterers. Schools could do a great deal more toward instilling respect for public property in young people than they do; and the free play period provides opportunities for such lessons. Children can and should be made to understand that equipment destroyed by carelessness and abuse must be replaced with money that might otherwise be spent for additional equipment for their benefit and enjoyment.

EQUIPMENT

We have noted in the discussion of facilities in a previous chapter that the outside play space should be a large fenced area of turf and hard surfacing adjacent to the classrooms. Playground apparatus should be the kind that provides opportunities to engage in a wide variety of movements and encourages safe motor exploration as well as providing enjoyment. Apparatus may be of the traditional variety, which has been described as "sit and ride" equipment, or the free form, generally referred to as creative play equipment. Although the latter provides more opportunities for skill development and creative play, some of the items of traditional equipment, e.g., swings, slides, and teeter-totters, still have a justifiable place on the playground. Swings and teeter-totters provide excellent experience in dynamic balance for very young children, while slides offer climbing experiences and the challenge to overcome fear. It is only when play on these pieces of equipment is allowed to substitute completely for other play experiences that their use becomes questionable. Children will tend

Figure 18–1 Developmental equipment provides opportunities for self-directed play. (Mexico Forge, Inc.)

to overemphasize the use of these pieces unless they are taught skills that can be used on other apparatus and are encouraged to use them.

Items of equipment recommended for the playground are described below.

Basketball Goals. It is suggested that basketball goals be set at two different heights: 10 feet (regulation height) for older children and 7 feet for younger children.

Balance Beams. Balance beams should be of different widths, 2 inches and 4 inches, to accommodate students with different balancing abilities. The beams should be permanently installed and may be arranged in various patterns. The height of the beams from the ground should not be over 24 inches. The wider beams may be placed as low as 8 to 12 inches from the ground for younger children.

Creative Play Equipment. This kind of equipment is available in a variety of imaginative forms that children can climb on, over, under, and through. It is also possible to use assorted scrap materials to construct equipment that offers similar opportunities.

Sandboxes. The boxes should be a minimum of 6 by 10 feet. They should be made so that it is possible to cover them when not in use.

Slides. It is recommended that slides be a maximum height of 8 feet and have a safety platform at the top.

Softball Backstops. Stops may be fixed, or they may be portable to allow their being moved from field to field.

Swings. No more than two swings should be in a row to avoid accidents that may occur if a child runs to a swing in the center of a row of three or more swings. Many safety experts recommend canvas seats to prevent possible head injuries if the seat should hit a fallen "swinger."

Figure 18–2 Opportunities for crawling activities are readily provided by improvised playground equipment. (Recreation Magazine.)

Tether Ball Stands. The stands should have a fastening device so that the ball may be removed from the stand for safekeeping.

Overall Standards. It is recommended that standards be adjustable so that a net may be either placed at regulation height or lowered for use by younger children.

Stationary Bars. There should be bars of several heights, ranging from 3 feet to 7 feet, in order to accommodate all sizes and degrees of ability among children.

Climbing Equipment. Vertical and parallel ladders can be combined for an arrangement that can be used for vertical and horizontal climbing and for hanging. Tires tied to a frame with ropes make an excellent improvised climbing device (Figure 18–3).

CARE. The vigorous use given any apparatus and equipment on the playground necessitates close observation of the amount of wear they evidence. Every teacher who supervises the playground should consider it a special responsibility to check for worn parts and to report these to the proper authorities so that they may be repaired before they become the cause of accidental injury to the children.

Other procedures which should be observed for the maintenance of a safe and pleasant outdoor play space include:

1. Painting the wood and metal apparatus, supports, standards, etc., to prevent rotting or rusting. Gay colors also help create more pleasant surroundings.

2. Sweeping the hard surfaced portion of the playground to keep it clean of dirt, sand, gravel, and trash.

3. Raking the turf to keep it free from debris which may cause players to trip and fall.

4. Raking and refilling sandboxes and jumping pits.

5. Repainting court markings.

6. Maintaining the fences which enclose the area.

IMPROVISED EQUIPMENT.   Except for large pieces of traditional equipment, no school need spend great sums of money to purchase playground apparatus, for these can be more readily improvised than any other type of playing equipment. Discarded railroad tracks or ties make excellent balance beams. Old culverts and large tree stumps provide crawling and climbing activity for younger children. Ladders no longer used by householders may be repaired for playground use. Packing boxes and planks used in combination with the ladders or separately promote climbing, hanging, balancing, and other developmental activities. Some schools have even found that an old fire engine or automobile with the hazardous parts removed inspires endless creative activity. All improvised materials should, of course, be sturdy, free of nails and splinters, and preferably painted.

PLAYGROUND AND SELF-DIRECTED ACTIVITIES

Play activities during recess and free play periods are for fun and relaxation; children play at whatever they wish and any organized activity is promoted by the children themselves. The teacher may give some assistance to the organizational efforts, but the children are given as much opportunity as possible to put into practice during these self-directed periods the teaching of the classroom and physical education period. There will be times when the teacher will be asked, "What can we play?" There will be times, too, when the teacher will feel it is necessary to redirect the children's play interest to some other game. Games suitable for either situation are described on the following pages.

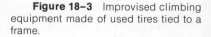
Figure 18–3 Improvised climbing equipment made of used tires tied to a frame.

Hopscotch (Grades 1–4)

GENERAL RULES.   The court is painted or drawn with chalk on the playing surface; any number of children may play. Any flat object such as a checker, a hockey puck, a stone, etc., may serve as the puck. When throwing the puck, the player must stand behind the base line and may not lean forward over this line; if the puck touches a line, the player is out. Players follow an established order of competing throughout the game and each begins his next turn at the point where he previously missed. Playing out of turn, making an incorrect play, or stepping over a line constitutes a miss. The winner is the player who has gone through the entire game with the fewest misses, all other players having had their turn.

AMERICAN HOPSCOTCH.   The general rules are applicable to American Hopscotch. The court is made as shown in Figure 18–4. Each player has a puck. The layer stands behind the base line and tosses his puck into the first box. He then hops into the two adjacent boxes with one foot in each box having skipped the first box. He then hops forward landing on one foot in the adjacent triangle. On the next move he hops into the two triangles which have a common apex, landing with one foot in each triangle. He then hops into the remaining triangle on one foot, followed by a hop forward to land with one foot in each of the two adjacent boxes. He hops into the last single box with one foot, turns around, and hops in reverse order back to the first box. Without stepping into the first box, he picks up his puck and hops into the first box and out. He then tosses his puck into the left box of the double boxes and begins to hop into the court areas in the same sequence as before. He must not jump into the space containing his puck until he returns and retrieves it from that space. Play continues in this way with the puck being advanced one space until the player has reached the final box and returned in reverse order to the starting box. The first player to do this is the winner.

COMMON HOPSCOTCH.   This variation of hopscotch is played like American Hopscotch with the player hopping on one foot in the single boxes and on both feet in the adjacent boxes. The court is shown in Figure 18–5. After landing in the last two adjacent boxes with one foot in each box, the player jumps up and turns around to land in the same two boxes and then proceeds to hop back to the first box in reverse order.

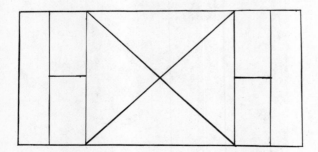

Figure 18–4 American hopscotch court.

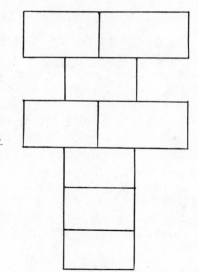

Figure 18–5 Common hopscotch court.

SQUARE HOPSCOTCH. This game is played on a court marked as shown in Figure 18–6. No puck is used. The player begins by hopping into the first square on his right and continues hopping into each square above the starting square, across to the top square of the next row, into each square below, across to the bottom square of the final row, and into each square above to end in the upper left square. He then proceeds to hop back through the squares in reverse order. If he makes it successfully back to the starting place, he places his initials in any of the squares he chooses. No other player may hop into that square as he plays the game. However, a player may hop with one or both feet into a square which has been initialed by him.

VARIATIONS IN COURTS. For additional variety in playing hopscotch the court may be drawn in the shape of a question mark or in the shape of a snail, using a double line to outline each and connecting the double lines with straight lines to divide the area into a series of boxes. Play follows the general rules with the player hopping from one box to the next without missing.

Figure 18–6 Square hopscotch court.

Marbles (Grades 1–3)

DESCRIPTION OF GAME. Two to eight players may participate in one game. Each player must have several marbles. One marble is placed by each player in the center of a ring drawn on the playing surface. The ring is from 4 to 6 feet in diameter. To determine in which order the players will shoot, they "lag" or roll their "taws" (the marble they will shoot) toward a line, the player whose marble is nearest the line being the first to play. Each player in turn shoots his taw from the edge of the ring in an attempt to knock marbles out of the ring. Any marbles which he succeeds in knocking out become his. The player with the most marbles at the end of the playing period is the winner.

Teaching Hints. Young children may roll their taws to knock marbles out of the ring. Older players may learn to shoot their taws by grasping the marble between the cushion of the finger tip of the pointer and the first knuckle of the thumb. The marble is flipped forward by extending the thumb forcefully.

Scully (Grades 1–4)

DESCRIPTION OF GAME. Scully, also called loadies or checkers, is a New York City street game played with bottle caps that are filled with wax, clay, or chewing gum. The court is drawn on the floor or sidewalk as shown in Figure 18–7. The dimensions are adapted to the space available. Generally the game is played with four or more players who are paired. Each player shoots the bottle cap at the numbers in order, beginning with number 1. If he is successful in landing his cap in the right number, he continues playing. If he misses, he loses his turn. A direct hit on another player's cap allows him to proceed to the next number. If a player's cap lands in the box surrounding the number 13, which is called "muds," the player cannot play again until his cap is knocked from the box by another player. After reaching the highest number, the player must go back to 1 in reverse order. When he reaches 13, he must then knock his cap into "muds" in succession from 1 to 4. The winner is the player who is finished first.

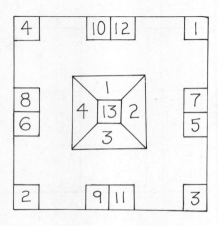

Figure 18–17 Scully court.

Jacks (Grades 2–4)

DESCRIPTION OF GAME.   A set of jacks and a small ball are needed. Two to four children may play with one set of jacks. The first player throws the jacks on the playing surface. The ball is tossed into the air with one hand, and with this same hand the player picks up one jack and catches the ball after one bounce. The jack is transferred to the other hand. Play continues in this way until all the jacks have been picked up or the player fails to pick up a jack or misses the ball, in which case the next player begins play. As soon as a player has picked up all the jacks singly, he attempts to pick them up two at a time, then three, and so on. After he has picked up all of the jacks at one time, he begins again by picking up one jack at a time during the bouncing of the ball; but this time the jack must be transferred to the other hand before the ball is caught—"Eggs in the Basket." After successfully progressing through the entire set using this technique, the player begins again with one jack. This time the jacks are swept through the arched fingers of the opposite hand which is placed against the playing surface. This is followed by "Pigs over the Fence" in which the jacks are thrown over the "fence" which is created by placing the edge of the opposite hand against the playing surface with the fingers out-stretched and the thumb up. In the final round, "No Bounce," the ball is not per-mitted to bounce before being caught. Whenever a player misses, the next player takes his turn. When the player who missed has a turn again, he must start at the beginning of the set in which his miss occurred.

Quoits (Grades 2–6)

DESCRIPTION OF GAME.   A playing court is established by driving a stake into the ground and marking a restraining line 15 to 20 feet from it. Two or four may play. Each player has four quoits and, standing behind the restraining line, tries in turn to ring the stake with his quoits. In scoring, a ringer counts 5 points. All quoits within the distance of the diameter of a quoit count 1 point. A game consists of 21 points.

Teaching Hints.   Quoits may be improvised from pieces of heavy rope at least 18 inches long. The ends are taped together to form a circle.

Rope Jumping (Grades 2–6)

DESCRIPTION OF ACTIVITY.   The rope is swung by wrist action rather than with elbow or shoulder action. The legs are kept relatively straight, and the hop is made on the balls of the feet utilizing ankle extension to lift the body just high enough to clear the rope. Good posture should be maintained while jump-ing as it increases the likelihood of success.

VARIATIONS.   While young children enjoy the success of merely jumping over the rope successively, older children are challenged by the many varia-tions which make rope jumping a complex and vigorous activity. The following are varieties of movement in rope jumping.

The Rope Is Turned from Behind the Body, Over the Head, and Then Under the Feet. The child hops on two feet, on the right foot only, on the left foot only, alternately on the right and then on the left, or on both feet with the rope crossed. (For the last, arms should begin to cross when the rope is over the head and finish with arms crossed at the wrists at waist height—wrist action is required.)

Or the child hops on both feet with the rope held in a crossed position on one hop and uncrossed on the succeeding hop. The jumper may also try hopping on the right or left foot with the opposite leg extended forward, on the right or left foot with the opposite leg swinging alternately forward and backward, or on both feet while in a full squat position. (The back should be vertical and the hopping must be done on the toes.)

Other possibilities are taking two hops to every turn of the rope, completing two revolutions of the rope on every second hop or every hop, turning the rope while running or skipping forward, turning the rope while running backward, and doing a Russian double kazotski on every turn of the rope. (While hopping in a full squat position both legs are extended forward and returned to the squat position on each turn of the rope. The back should be kept vertical and the hips low.)

The Rope Is Turned from in Front of the Body, Over the Head, and Then Under the Feet. The child hops on two feet, on the right foot only, on the left foot only, alternately on the right and then on the left foot, or walks or runs in place through the rope.

With a Partner and One Rope. Facing one another, the partners hop on both feet, on one foot, on alternate feet, or walk or run in place through the rope. All the above stunts may be performed with partners facing the same direction, with partners standing side by side, the one on the right turning the rope with his right hand while the one on the left turns it with his left hand, and with partners standing back to back. One partner may turn while the other hops and turns to face different directions.

Two Partners Each Turn a Rope Necessitating a Double Hop. The partners face the same direction, face one another, or hop back to back.

With One Long Rope, Two Turners, and One Jumper. The child runs in "the front door" and hops as the rope at the bottom of its swing is moving toward him; or he runs in "the back door" and hops as the rope at the bottom of its swing is moving away from him. The performer may take two jumps to each turn of the rope, two turns of the rope to each jump, or jump "hot pepper" (very fast hopping and turning).

The children may also turn 180 degrees on each hop, hop in a full squat position, on all fours facing the side, on the right foot, on the left foot, alternately on right and left feet, on the right or left foot with the opposite leg extended forward, or on the right or left foot while swinging the opposite leg alternately forward and backward.

The jumper may do the "double kazotski," hopping in a squat position and on each hop extending both legs forward and flexing them again to return to the squat position with the back vertical and the weight on the balls of the feet, or he may try the "bucking bronco": as the rope at the bottom of its swing approaches the jumper, he drives his hips upward to land on his hands in or near a handstand position and snaps down to his feet again by flexing his hips.

Ditties. Children enjoy singing ditties as they jump or skip rope. Following are several which children have sung for many years:

Mable, Mable
Set the table
And don't forget
The Red Hot Pepper
   (Here rope turned very fast.)

Ika, backa, ika backa
Ika backa boo
If your father chew tobacco
He's a dirty old shoe.

One, two, buckle my shoe
Three, four, shut the door
Five, six, do some tricks,
Seven, eight, don't be late
Nine, ten, big fat hen
Eleven, twelve, bake her well.

Bubble gum, bubble gum,
Chew and blow,
Bubble gum, bubble gum,
Scrape your toe,
Bubble gum, bubble gum,
Tastes so sweet,
Get that bubble gum off your feet.

Ice cream soda
Delaware punch
Tell me the name
Of your honey bunch
Alphabet a, b, c — (continued through the entire
   alphabet or until the jumper misses).

Teddie bear, Teddie bear,
Turn around
Teddie bear, Teddie bear
Touch the ground
Teddie bear, Teddie bear
Go upstairs (jumper moves toward
   one of the turners)
Teddie bear, Teddie bear
Say your prayers
Teddie bear, Teddie bear
Turn out the light
Teddie bear, Teddie bear
Say good night.

Down in the meadow
Where the green grass grows
There sat (name of jumper)
As sweet as a rose
She sang and she sang
And she sang so sweet
Along came (name of boy friend)
And kissed her on the cheek.
How many kisses did she get?
　　(Count the hops until jumper misses.)

Tether Ball (Grades 4–8)

DESCRIPTION OF GAME.   The equipment for tether ball consists of a tether ball attached by means of a long rope to the top of a pole which is set firmly in the ground. The pole is 8 to 10 feet in height, and the rope should come to about 3½ or 4 feet from the ground. Two or four players may participate; however, the game is more active if play is limited to two players. In a game of singles (two players), the players stand opposite each other with the pole in the center. In doubles (four players) partners stand together on opposite sides of the pole. The object of the game is to hit the ball with the hand so as to cause the rope to wind around the pole clockwise. The game begins with a serve of the ball similar to the volleyball serve. The server stands on his side of the pole, holds the ball in one hand, and strikes it with the other driving it clockwise around the pole. As the ball swings toward the opponent's side, the opponent attempts to knock the ball back in the opposite direction so that the rope will wind around the pole. The side which first winds the rope completely around the pole is the winner.

Deck Tennis (Grades 4–8)

DESCRIPTION OF GAME.   The official playing court is 14 by 40 feet for singles and 17 by 40 feet for doubles (Fig. 18–8); however, a smaller court will do for younger children. Two or four may play. In singles the two players face each other at opposite ends of the court; in doubles partners play on the same side. The game is played with a round rubber deck tennis ring. A net is stretched across the center of the court so that its top is 5 feet from the floor. For younger children, the height may be lowered to 4 feet from the floor. The game

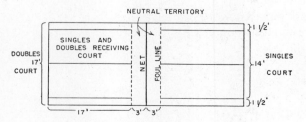

Figure 18–8 Deck tennis court. (From Fait et al.: *A Manual of Physical Education Activities,* Ed. 3. W. B. Saunders Company.)

Figure 18–9 Shuffleboard court. (From Fait et al.: *A Manual of Physical Education Activities*, Ed. 3. W. B. Saunders Company.)

is started with an underhand serve from the base line behind the right receiving court to the opposite right receiving court. Thereafter the server alternates from left to right. The serve must not "wobble" or waiver in flight. The receiver catches the ring with one hand only and without hesitation returns it over the net with an underhand throw. Scoring follows volleyball rules.

Shuffleboard (Grades 6–8)

DESCRIPTION OF GAME. Needed for play are a shuffleboard court (Fig. 18–9), two or four cues, and eight disks. Two players (singles) or four players (doubles) may participate on one court. The object of the game is to push one's own disks with the cue into the scoring spaces on the court and to prevent the opponent from doing likewise by knocking his disks out of the scoring section. In singles both players push their disks from the same end of the court and then move to the opposite end to count the score and play the disks back to the original end. In doubles play, the partners play at opposite ends of the court during the entire game. The disks are shot from the "Ten Off" zone each time. To push the disk, the player stands facing the opposite end of the court. The cue is grasped lightly but firmly and the head of it rests on the court behind the disk. The player takes one step forward with the left foot (if righthanded) and pushes the cue forward. The score is added after all the disks have been shot from one end. Only those *wholly* within a scoring area may be counted; a disk touching the line does not count. If there is a disk in the "Ten Off" zone, 10 points are subtracted from the total. The first person or team scoring 50 points wins the game.

Teaching Hints. Beginners will not be concerned with strategy to any great extent. However, as skill increases, the game will become dull for the player if he merely plays every disk to score or knock out the opponent's disks. At this point, the player should be introduced to blocks or "pilot shots" which are plays that are placed outside the scoring area prior to a placement of a disk in a scoring area to protect a score from the opponent (Fig. 18–10).

Horseshoes (Grades 6–8)

DESCRIPTION OF GAME. A regulation horseshoes court measures 40 feet between the stakes; however, for young children and inexperienced players, it is recommended that the distance be reduced to 20 or 30 feet. Two

Figure 18–10 Disk placement. (From Fait et al.: *A Manual of Physical Educational Activities*, Ed. 3. W. B. Saunders Company.)

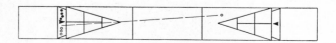

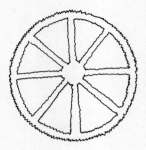

Figure 18–11   Fox and Geese court.

stakes are driven into the ground at each end of the court. The stakes extend 1 foot above the ground. Four metal horseshoes are needed although for beginners hard rubber shoes are preferred. Two or four children may participate at one time. When two are playing, they both pitch their shoes from the same end and move together to the other end to score and play back to the original end. When there are four players, partners remain together at one end of the court. One player starts the game by pitching at the opposite stake. The players alternate to pitch. The horseshoe nearest the stake scores one point. If both shoes of one player are closer than either of the opponent's shoes, they score two points. A ringer scores three points. To be a ringer, the horseshoe must encircle the stake far enough to allow a straight ruler to touch both sides of the horseshoes and clear the stake. The game in singles is 21 points and in doubles, 50 points.

Fox and Geese (Grades 6–8)

DESCRIPTION OF GAME.   Fox and Geese is generally played by children after the first snow of the year although it can be played without snow by marking the trail on the ground. The trail takes the form of a wheel with a hub and spokes as shown in Figure 18–11. The snow is trampled down to form the outline. One child is selected to be the "fox," and the other children are "geese." The fox attempts to catch the geese. If one is caught, he joins the fox to help catch others. Neither the fox nor the geese may leave the trail. The geese are safe only if they are in the center of the circle (hub).

Teaching Hints.   To increase the skill demand of the game, a second smaller circular path may be made inside the larger one.

SUPPLEMENTARY READINGS

Fait, Hollis F., et al.: *A Manual of Physical Education Activities.* Philadelphia, Ed. 3. W. B. Saunders Co., 1967.

Stone, J.: *Play and Playgrounds.* Washington, D.C., National Association for the Education of Young Children, 1970.

Vannier, Maryhelen, et al.: *Teaching Physical Education in Elementary Schools.* Ed. 5. Philadelphia, W. B. Saunders Co., 1973.

chapter nineteen

the extra-class program

GROUPING FOR PARTICIPATION
TOURNAMENTS
INTRAMURALS
INTERSCHOLASTIC SPORTS
PLAY DAYS AND SPORTS DAYS
DEMONSTRATIONS FOR PARENTS AND
    PUBLIC
COMMUNITY SCHOOL

The extra-class program consists of activities related to physical education which are conducted outside the physical education class during free periods in the school day schedule or in the after-school hours under the supervision of school personnel. The extra-class activities most often found in our elementary schools are: intramurals, interscholastic athletics, play or sport days, and demonstrations. They serve the very necessary function of extending physical education beyond the allotted class periods.

Except for physical education demonstrations, most of the activities offered in the extra-class program are based on competition. Most children enjoy the competitive element in play; they like to test their skills against others both as individual participants and as members of teams. The enthusiasm engendered by competitive play provides the teacher with one of the best of all motivational tools, but it must be used with discretion and wisdom. Winning must never be permitted to become the game's most important objective. It is not the competi-

491

tion in our physical education programs which is unsound, although this is where the criticism is usually directed, but the overemphasis on winning and the stigma attached to losing.

Nearly all games feature some degree of competition and could, therefore, be used as contests for intramural and interscholastic play and for play and sports days. Some are better suited to certain of these events than others because the number of players, the space requirements, seasonal restrictions, and other like considerations make them more easily administered. The selection of games for competitive play purposes must always be based upon needs, interests, and abilities of the age group involved.

GROUPING FOR PARTICIPATION

Grouping students for team participation in the extra-class program is far too often done without regard to their levels of readiness, maturation, and ability to perform. The program will be more successful and educationally sound if these factors are given proper consideration.

A common means of grouping is that of classrooms at the same grade level. Since the youngsters at a given grade level are of about the same chronological age, the uses of the already existing divisions of classes appears to be a sound and expedient way of grouping. While it is expedient—and its usefulness in this respect is granted—this method of grouping does not give consideration to the wide range of abilities and differences in maturation levels that usually exist in every classroom.

Another frequently used means of grouping is the choosing of team members by certain students designated as team captains. This method almost always results in unbalanced teams; moreover, it creates the undesirable situation of last choices being made of those children who perform poorly. It is so educationally unsound that it should never be used for grouping in any school program.

More effective and desirable are the methods of grouping that are based upon the factors of age and weight, which provide a rough indication of motor ability levels of elementary school-age children. One excellent means of grouping, based upon these factors, is the McCloy Classification Index.[1] The formula used is (10 $\times$ age) + weight. The scores can be used to determine groups of similar abilities and also to set equal competition between individual players.

TOURNAMENTS

Tournaments for competitive play in the extra-class program on the elementary school level take several forms: elimination, ladder, round robin, and pyramid.

SINGLE ELIMINATION. As its name implies, this type of tournament progresses to its conclusion through a series of contests in which the losers are

TABLE 19–1 Single Elimination Tournament

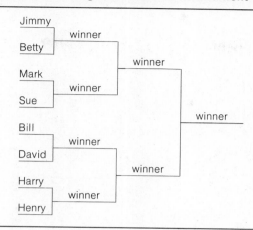

eliminated from further play. Winners of each round of play meet for subsequent rounds until the final round in which the winner of the tournament is determined. The elimination tournament is the shortest type in point of time required to play it off and, as such, has certain advantages where time is limited.

The tournament is easily set up if the number of individual contestants or teams is a power of 2 (Table 19–1). When the number is not, "byes" (no opponent) are used in the first round so that in the second round the number will be a power of 2. The number of "byes" is found by subtracting the number of entries from the next highest power of 2. In Table 19–2 this was 1.

DOUBLE ELIMINATION.   In the double elimination tournament, no loser is eliminated from play after his first contest. Instead losers move to the left (Table 19–3) for the second round of play while winners move to the right as in the single elimination. It should be noted that when the winner of the first elimi-

TABLE 19–2 Single Elimination Tournament with a Bye

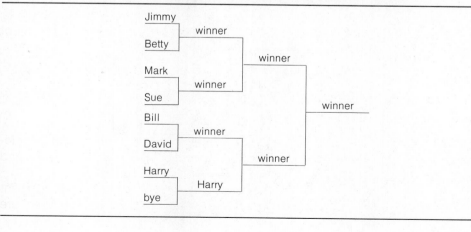

TABLE 19-3　Double Elimination Tournament

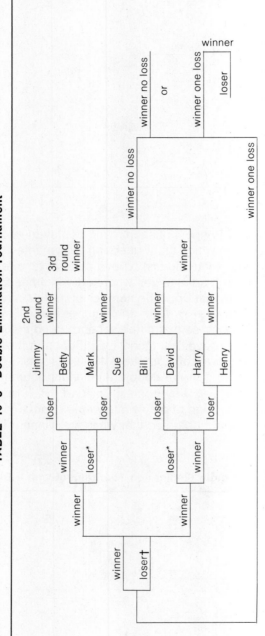

*Losers of second round on right side.
†Loser of third round on right side.

TABLE 19–4   Ladder Tournament

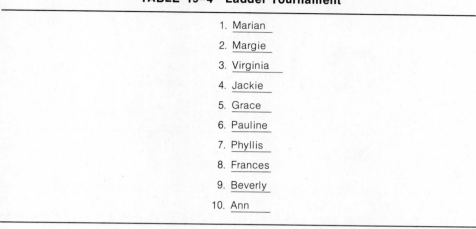

1. Marian
2. Margie
3. Virginia
4. Jackie
5. Grace
6. Pauline
7. Phyllis
8. Frances
9. Beverly
10. Ann

nation loses to the winner of the second elimination, this is his first loss and another game must be played by the two before a winner is declared. The advantage of this type of tournament is that affords more participation than the single elimination; however, it is much more time consuming.

LADDER.   For a ladder tournament, the names of the players or teams are entered upon movable cards arranged one above the other as on a ladder (Table 19–4). The objective is to climb to the top of the ladder, and any player or team on a lower rung of the ladder may challenge those above to a match. (Usually the challenge is limited to one or two names above.) If a player is successful, his name card is exchanged with that of the defeated opponent. If not successful, his name remains in its position and he must not challenge the victor again until he has met one other opponent. The winner of the ladder tournament is the one whose name is at the top of the ladder on the day which has been set for the end of the tournament. The ladder tournament is better suited to individual contests than to teams because it is more difficult for an entire team to be available to respond to a challenge on a given day.

PYRAMID.   The pyramid formation is similar in objective to the ladder tournament and has the same advantages while providing for more opportunities to play by making possible more challenges. In the pyramid tournament, players may challenge those in the row above or in their own row (Table 19–5).

TABLE 19–5   Pyramid Tournament

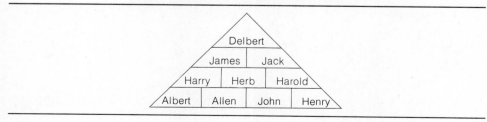

TABLE 19–6   Round Robin Tournament

1st round	2nd round	3rd round
1–2	1–3	1–5
3–4	5–2	6–3
5–6	6–4	4–2

	4th round	5th round	
	1–6	1–4	
	4–5	2–6	
	2–3	3–5	

The final winner is the one who attains the top of the pyramid on the date on which the tournament closes.

ROUND ROBIN.   To set up a round robin tournament, the participating players or teams are given numbers. The number of rounds to be played will be one less than the total number of entrants. In each round, games are scheduled for all those entered with the pairing different (Table 19–6). When the scheduling of the round has been completed, the names of the participants can be substituted for the appropriate numbers. In the case of an uneven number of entrants, a "bye" is added. The team with a "bye" does not play in that particular round. One of the best features of this type of tournament is that it provides for maximum participation because the winner is determined by the number of games won in the duration of the tournament.

INTRAMURALS

Intramurals are contests of sports and games conducted between students within the same school. The Youth Fitness Council[2] recommends that intramurals begin in the fourth grade for both boys and girls and continue throughout their school years. Intramural activities can be offered to children younger than this, but they must be selected with consideration of their interests, needs, and skills. Team sports will be, for the most part, beyond their skill abilities and their interest; moreover, their need to play with teammates doesn't manifest itself until fourth grade and later.

Activities which might appropriately be included in an intramural program for children below the fourth grade are:

Hop scotch	Kicking balls for distance
Rope jumping	Throwing at targets
Relays	Individual stunts and
Stunts	self-testing activities

Activities suggested by the Conference on Intramurals for Elementary

School Children[3] as suitable for intramural programs for youngsters in the upper grades are:

Lead-Up Skills and Games for Team Sports

TOUCH FOOTBALL TYPE
Punt for accuracy or
    distance
Pass for accuracy or
    distance
Place kick for accuracy
    or distance
Pass or punt-back game
Passing relays
Punting relays
Centering relays
Football Newcomb
Team football keep away
Modified touch football
SOCCER TYPE
Dribbling for time
Obstacle dribbling
Goal kicking
Heading for accuracy
Dribbling relays
Passing relays
Circle soccer
Circle soccer dodge ball
Soccer goal kick
Line soccer
Crab soccer
Seven or nine man
    soccer
Seven or nine man
    speedball
VOLLEYBALL TYPE
Ball keep-up
Serving for accuracy
Volleying for accuracy
Volleying relays
Catch and bat volleyball
One bounce volleyball

Volley-tennis
Beachball volleyball
Modified volleyball
SOFTBALL TYPE
Throw for accuracy and
    distance
Base running for time
Batting for distance
Long base
Bat ball
Kickball
Whiffle ball
Modified softball
BASKETBALL TYPE
Basket shooting contest
Obstacle dribbling
Dribbling for time
Passing for speed
Twenty-one
Follow the leader
Dribbling, shooting,
    passing
Relays
Sideline basketball
Nine court basketball
Two court basketball
MISCELLANEOUS
TEAM GAMES
Circle team dodgeball
End-zone dodgeball
Newbomb
Volley baseball
    basketball
Modified field hockey
Modified lacrosse

Individual Sports and Contests

TRACK AND FIELD
40 to 60 yd. dashes
220 to 440 yd. distance
　events
Hurdle dash
High jump
Standing broad jump
Running broad jump
Modified shot put
Standing hop-step-jump
Throw for distance
Shuttle relays
Circular relays
SWIMMING
Speed or distance
　swimming in single
　and combination
　strokes
Swimming relays

STUNTS, TUMBLING,
APPARATUS
Stationary stunts, e.g.,
　free hand, head
　stand, pyramids
Moving stunts, e.g.,
　forward roll, back
　roll, cartwheel
Apparatus, e.g.,
　trampoline, parallel
　bars, vaulting, rings,
　rope climbing

Miscellaneous Activities

Paddle tennis, table
　tennis, deck tennis
Badminton
Tennis
Shuffleboard
Horseshoes

Tetherball
Four square
Rope jumping
Bowling
Handball

INTERSCHOLASTIC SPORTS

Interscholastic athletics are those sports in which teams representing one school compete against those from other schools. Although, generally, all those who are interested in participating are urged to "come out," the number who can play on any one team is limited and a system of eliminating those with less ability must necessarily be employed. Those who become members of the team are usually those who have superior skills and so the interscholastic program is often thought of as a special opportunity for the athletically gifted. Few schools have such programs below the sixth grade; the most common practice is to include them at the seventh and eighth grades.

There has been much criticism of the interscholastic sports program. Opponents have been concerned chiefly about the detrimental effects on the health of immature youngsters resulting from the strenuous play, and the fact that winning becomes so important that the educational values are lost sight of.

Proponents argue that there are less dangers to the participants in school sponsored programs than they would experience in rough and tumble sandlot play.
Moreover, their argument goes, competitive play fosters the loftiest concepts of
fair play and sportsmanship.

Research into the effects of competitive athletics on elementary school
children indicates that most of the concern for health of the young participants is unfounded. In most cases, the vigorous activity is beneficial to the
competitor. However, there is much evidence to indicate that the concern for
the loss of positive education values is justified. The emphasis on winning all
too often negates the desirable learning that could occur. The educational
value of an interscholastic program is entirely dependent upon the leadership
and direction it is given, and its inclusion in the elementary school program can
be justified only if winning is never allowed to outweigh the educational considerations.

Because of the widespread criticism and concern about competitive athletics for children of elementary school age, a joint policy statement[4] has been
drawn up with the approval of several professional groups* to serve as a
guideline for creating good programs. The statement stresses that decisions
about implementing competitive athletic programs should give careful consideration to: proper physical conditioning of the participants; competent teaching
and supervision with regard for the relative hazards of each particular sport and
modification of rules, game equipment, and facilities to suit the maturity level of
the participants; qualified officials; careful grouping according to weight, size,
sex, skill, and physical maturation when indicated; good protective equipment,
properly fitted; well-maintained facilities suitable for the sport involved; proper
delineation of the spheres of authority and responsibility for school administrators, family, sponsor, physician, coach, and athlete; and adequate medical care
with periodic health appraisal, including a careful health history, and a physician present or readily available during games and practices.

The policy states further that, before an athletic program for elementary
schools is started, steps should be taken to ensure: (1) provision for daily physical education instruction for all children, under supervision of certified physical education teachers; (2) opportunities for every child in the upper elementary grades to participate in an organized and supervised intramural athletic
program; and (3) that the athletic program will not curtail the time or budget of
the normal school program (i.e., will not utilize school time, facilities, personnel,
or funds in any way which would jeopardize the total educational experience of
the participants or of other children).

PLAY DAYS AND SPORTS DAYS

Many elementary schools sponsor a special day on which individual contestants and teams engage in a variety of games and sport events throughout

---

*American Academy of Pediatrics, American Alliance for Health, Physical Education and Recre-
ation, American Medical Association Committee on Medical Aspects of Sports, and Society of State
Directors of Health, Physical Education and Recreation.

the day. The day is usually referred to as "Play Day" if all the grades are participating and as "Sports Day" if grades from the fourth or fifth grade and up are
involved. Usually, although not always, in the latter case the activities are
limited to track and field events, volleyball, or softball. Participation in both
kinds of "days" may be restricted to one school or may include one or more
schools from the same or neighboring towns.

Both are an extension of the physical education program and represent an
effort to give the students additional opportunities for vigorous play. Consequently, some schools hold a sport or play day several times a year as the
weather permits. Most schools, however, hold it only as an annual event near
the end of the school year. Activities for the play day are those which the children have liked particularly during the year. Parents may be invited to observe
the progress their children have made throughout the year. When they are to be
present, some activities may be selected to show new skills which have been
developed.

Sports Days devoted to track and field activities present events for both
boys and girls. Commonly included are the dash, relay race, football and softball
throw for distance, the running broad jump, and the high jump.

To realize the greatest value from these days, participation must be open to
all. Even in situations in which visiting schools are included in the program,
there should be no restriction of play to those who are most likely to win over
the visitors. If there is a wish to have some competition between teams (including mixed teams) or individuals of superior abilities, all the participants should
be classified according to ability and matched with opponents of like ability.
However, fun should be the key word for play and sports days, and too much
stress on competition may mar the fun for many students.

DEMONSTRATIONS FOR PARENTS AND PUBLIC

The physical education demonstration is, as its name implies, a showing of
the physical education program to the public. It is an opportunity for the teacher
to present and for parents to learn about the objectives of their children's physical education and how these are achieved. Demonstrations may show how a
class is conducted from beginning to end on a typical day; they may demonstrate skill progression; they may show special activities which have been
learned; or they may present a bird's eye view of all that has been learned
throughout the year. The number of students is the determining factor in selecting what is to be demonstrated for everyone should participate. Each student
need not participate in every activity presented by his class, but no one should
be omitted entirely.

It is best for the demonstration to run no longer than an hour and a half; the
amount of time allotted to each class must be reduced according to the number
of classes to be presented. To ensure that the events will move as smoothly as
possible within the time limit, one or two rehearsals may be necessary. The
teacher should strive for an orderly progression rather than a polished performance. Taking large blocks of time from the physical education periods to "prac-

tice" for the demonstration deprives the children of other physical education opportunities which they deserve to have during this allotted time.

COMMUNITY SCHOOL

Community School is the name given to a program of educational and recreational opportunities that extends beyond the traditional school day, beyond the school year, and both before and beyond the years of formal education. The philosophy of the Community School is that education is a life-long process and that the school facilities which are supported by the community should be open to everyone in the community to pursue his educational needs and recreational interests. The program may contain anything from enrichment courses to hobby groups, from vocational skills to athletic activities.

Community Schools are increasing at an ever-accelerating pace as their enormous values are recognized. One of their important advantages is that the total use of the school plant means that taxpayers are receiving far greater returns on their investment, for no longer does an expensive building stand empty and unused from late afternoon to early morning and on weekends and through the summer. Equally important, perhaps more so, is the improved community-school relationship that is engendered by the participation of parents and elderly residents in the activities of the program that bring them into the school. School age children, likewise, develop a more positive attitude toward the school, which has been demonstrated to have a very definite beneficial effect upon their educational progress. Still another dividend is realized in the closing of the generation gap as children and parents come to know and understand each other through involvement in a program that brings them together for common purposes.

Teachers for the Community School are recruited both from the citizens of the community and from the school faculty. Naturally, those with training in physical education are much in demand to teach various motor skills and to organize and supervise play activities. All the information and recommendations contained in this textbook to help the elementary school teacher better serve the needs, interests, and abilities of young children through physical education are applicable to physical education offerings for children below high school age in the Community School.

SUPPLEMENTARY READINGS

American Association for Health, Physical Education and Recreation: *Desirable Athletic Competition for Children of Elementary School Age.* Washington, D.C., American Association for Health, Physical Education and Recreation, 1968.

Kleindienst, Viola K., and Weston, Arthur: *Intramurals and Recreation Programs for Schools and Colleges.* New York, Appleton-Century-Crofts, Inc., 1964.

Mathews, David, Editor: *Intramurals for Elementary School Children.* Chicago, The Athletic Institute, 1964.

Totten, Fred W., and Manley, Frank J.: *The Community School: Basic Concepts, Function and Organization.* Galien, Michigan, Allied Education Council, 1969.

Vannier, Maryhelen, and Fait, Hollis F.: *Teaching Physical Education in Secondary Schools*. Ed. 4. Philadelphia, W. B. Saunders Co., 1975.

BIBLIOGRAPHY

[1]McCloy, Charles H., and Young, Norma: *Tests and Measurements in Physical Education.* Ed. 3. New York, Appleton-Century-Crofts, Inc., 1954.
[2]President's Council on Youth Fitness: *Youth Physical Fitness.* Washington, D.C., Superintendent of Documents. (No date.)
[3]The Athletic Institute: *Intramurals for Elementary School Children.* Chicago, The Athletic Institute, 1964.
[4]American Association for Health, Physical Education and Recreation: *Desirable Athletic Competition for Children of Elementary School Age.* Washington, D.C., American Association for Health, Physical Education and Recreation, 1968.

sources of motor skill tests for intermediate and junior high school grades

American Association for Health, Physical Education and Recreation: *Skills Test Manual.* (A series of booklets for a number of team and individual sports.)

Bontz, Jean: *An Experiment in the Construction of a Test for Measurement Ability in Some of the Fundamental Skills Used by Fifth and Sixth Grade Children in Soccer.* Unpublished Master Thesis, State University of Iowa, 1942.

Hanson, Margie: *Motor Performance Testing of Elementary School Age Children.* Unpublished Doctoral Dissertation, University of Washington, 1965.

Johnson, Robert: Measurement in fundamental skills of elementary school children. *Research Quarterly,* March 1962.

Kelson, R. C.: Baseball classification play for boys. *Research Quarterly,* October 1953.

Lamp, Nancy: Volleyball skills of junior high school students as a function of physical size and maturity. *Research Quarterly,* May 1954.

Russell, Naomi, and Lange, Elizabeth: Achievement tests in volleyball for junior high school girls. *Research Quarterly,* December 1940.

Shaufele, Evelyn: *The Establishment of Objective Tests for Girls of the Ninth and Tenth Grades to Determine Soccer Ability.* Unpublished Master Thesis, State University of Iowa, 1940.

Wilke, Lester: *Analysis and Standardization of a Progressive Testing Program in Physical Education for the Elementary Grades,* Unpublished Master Thesis, State University of Iowa, 1942.

physical fitness tests for the mentally retarded (trainable and educable)*

Administering the Tests

If the items are all to be given in one day, they should be placed in an order that will not require the subject to perform a test that may fatigue him in certain portions of the body to the detriment of his score on the following item. For example, running the 300 yard run-walk test item is likely to create enough fatigue to affect the score of the 25 yard dash if it is run immediately after the former, even though one is basically involved with the factor of speed and the other with endurance. The following order is recommended to eliminate fatigue as a factor: 25 yard dash, bent arm hang, leg lift, static balance test, thrust, and 300 yard run-walk.

Facilities and Equipment

The test items may be given indoors or outside with equal ease, with the exception of the 300 yard run-walk. The space required for this item is such that it can be performed inside only if the participants run in laps, and keeping track of the number of laps which have been run may create confusion. The administration of the 25 yard dash requires a 35 yard straight runway and something against which the foot can be placed for a brace to start the race. A cleared wall may be used for this purpose inside the building. When testing outdoors, a board 2 inches high by 4 inches wide and by 2 or 3 feet long may be secured to the ground for a starting block. The leg raise will require a mat at least 6 by 4 feet in size. If a mat is not available, a mattress with a clean cover or several layers of blankets may be substituted. For the bent arm hang a bar is needed. If a stationary bar is not available, a door bar may be used. Other items of equipment necessary for the testing are stop watches and scoring cards.

---

*Tests were developed at the University of Connecticut by Dr. Hollis F. Fait, financed by a grant from the Joseph P. Kennedy, Jr., Foundation.

Testing Stations

For maximum efficiency in giving the test items, five testing stations should be set up with a tester at each station. If the testing stations are placed in an ordered sequence, most mentally retarded subjects will be able to move from station to station without difficulty. It is helpful to have an assistant to keep the subjects moving in the right direction to the next station.

Recording Scores

For ease in recording the scores, a 4 by 6 inch card with his name on it may be carried by each student from station to station. Students incapable of carrying the card without losing or mutilating it may have their cards pinned to their shirts. The tester at each station records the score on the student's card as soon as he completes the test.

Personnel

Only one person is required to administer the 25 yard dash if he serves as both timer and starter. He will need to stand at the finish line and give the command to start from there. One person is able to administer the bent arm hang, static balance test, and thrust. An assistant will be needed for the leg lift. The 300 yard run-walk should be the last test item given. Two people, a timer and a scorer, will be required to administer the test.

Uniformity in Testing

In administering the test items, extreme care must be taken to ensure that each item is performed uniformly by all the subjects. Unless this is done, the comparison with norms will not be meaningful nor will the comparison of one student's scores with another's have any valid meaning. If a subject is unable to perform in the prescribed manner, his score, however, need not be discarded entirely as a measurement of the fitness factor being tested. The score may still be used as a basis for comparison of his future scores on that item to determine the extent of improvement achieved by the subject.

Description of Test Items

Twenty-five Yard Run (Measures the Speed of Running Short Distances)

The subject places either foot against the wall or block with the foot parallel to it. The other foot and trunk are turned in the direction he is to run. He then takes a semi-crouch position with the hands resting lightly on the knees. His head is held up so that he is looking toward the finish line. At the command of "Ready . . . Go!" the subject begins the run. The watch is started on the "Go" and is stopped as the subject passes the finish line. However, the subject is directed to run to a second line, which is about 5 feet beyond the finish line, to prevent his slowing down as he approaches the true finish line. The time of the run is recorded to the nearest one-tenth of a second.

Bent Arm Hang (Measures Static Muscular Endurance of the Arm and Shoulder Girdle)

A horizontal bar or doorway bar may be used for this test. A stool approximately 12 inches high is placed under the bar. The subject steps onto the stool and takes hold of the bar with both hands, using a reverse grip (palms toward the face). The hands are shoulders' width apart. The subject brings his head to the bar, presses the bridge of the nose to the bar and steps off the stool. He holds this position as long as possible. The timer starts the watch as the subject's nose presses to the bar and the body weight is taken on the arms. The watch is stopped when the subject drops away from the bar. The tester should be ready to catch the subject in the event that he falls. The number of seconds the subject held the position is recorded on the score card.

Leg Lift (Measures Dynamic Muscular Endurance of the Flexor Muscles of the Leg and of the Abdominal Muscles)

The subject lies flat on his back with his hands clasped behind the neck. A helper should hold the subject's elbows to the mat. The subject raises his legs, keeping the knees straight until they are at a 90 degree angle. Another helper, who stands to the side of the subject, extends one hand over the subject's abdomen at the height of the ankles when the legs are fully lifted. This serves as a guide to the subject in achieving the desired angle and encourages him to keep the legs straight. He should be instructed to touch the shins against the helper's arm. The subject is to do as many leg lifts as possible in the 20 second time limit. He begins on the command of "Go" and ceases on the command of "Stop." The score is the number of leg lifts performed during the 20 seconds.

Static Balance Test (Measures Ability to Maintain Balance in a Stationary Position)

The subject places his hands on his hips, lifts one leg and places the foot on the inside of the knee of the other leg. He then closes his eyes and maintains his balance in this position as long as he can. The watch is started the moment he closes his eyes. As soon as the subject loses his balance, the watch is stopped. The score is the number of seconds, to the nearest one-tenth of a second.

Thrust (Measures the Specific Type of Agility That Is Measured by the Squat Thrust or Burpee)

The subject takes a squatting position with the feet and hands flat on the floor. The knees should make contact with the arms. At the command "Go," the stop watch is started. The subject takes the weight upon his hands so that he may thrust his legs straight out behind him. The legs are returned to the original position. The score is the number of complete thrusts the subject is able to perform in 20 seconds.

300 Yard Run-Walk (Measures Cardiorespiratory Endurance)

In the starting position, the runner places one foot comfortably ahead of the other. A semicrouch position with the hands resting lightly on the knees is taken. At the command to go, the stop watch is started. The subject runs the prescribed course. He is allowed to walk part of the distance if he is unable to run the total distance. The time required to complete the run-walk is the score.

Achievement Scales of Physical Fitness Tests for Mentally Retarded Youths

(Score in seconds)

25 YARD RUN

Boys

Age	Trainable			Educable		
	Low	Av.	Good	Low	Av.	Good
9–12	7.0	6.0	5.2	6.2	5.2	4.4
13–16	6.5	5.5	4.7	5.4	4.7	4.2
17–20	6.0	5.0	4.2	5.1	4.4	3.9

Girls

Age	Low	Av.	Good	Low	Av.	Good
9–12	7.4	6.3	5.3	5.8	5.4	5.2
13–16	6.7	5.6	4.7	6.1	5.2	4.3
17–20	7.3	6.1	5.1	6.4	5.4	4.7

BENT ARM HANG

Boys

Age	Trainable			Educable		
	Low	Av.	Good	Low	Av.	Good
9–12	2.0	10.0	16.0	3.0	19.0	33.0
13–16	11.2	22.0	30.2	5.0	25.0	43.0
17–20	23.0	23.0	31.0	8.0	30.0	50.0

Girls

Age	Low	Av.	Good	Low	Av.	Good
9–12	2.0	8.0	12.0	3.0	9.0	13.0
13–16	4.0	14.0	22.0	5.0	15.0	23.0
17–20	3.0	9.0	13.0	4.0	12.0	18.0

LEG LIFT

Boys

Age	Trainable			Educable		
	Low	Av.	Good	Low	Av.	Good
9–12	6	9	12	7	10	13
13–16	6	9	12	8	11	14
17–20	7	10	13	8	11	14

Girls

Age	Low	Av.	Good	Low	Av.	Good
9–12	6	10	14	6	10	14
13–16	7	11	15	7	11	15
17–20	6	10	14	6	10	14

(Table continued on the following page.)

(Score in seconds)

STATIC BALANCE

Boys

	Trainable				Educable		
Age	Low	Av.	Good		Low	Av.	Good
9–12	3.0	4.4	5.8		4.0	5.0	6.0
13–16	3.1	4.5	5.9		5.0	6.0	7.0
17–20	3.2	4.6	6.0		5.0	10.0	15.0

Girls

9–12	2.2	3.2	4.2		2.5	3.5	4.5
13–16	5.1	6.1	7.1		8.6	9.6	10.6
17–20	4.9	5.9	6.9		5.2	6.2	7.2

THRUST

Boys

	Trainable				Educable		
Age	Low	Av.	Good		Low	Av.	Good
9–12	4	8	10		6	12	14
13–16	4	8	10		8	14	16
17–20	5	9	11		8	14	16

Girls

9–12	4	8	10		5	9	11
13–16	4	8	10		8	12	14
17–20	5	9	11		5	9	11

300 YARD RUN-WALK

Boys

	Trainable				Educable		
Age	Low	Av.	Good		Low	Av.	Good
9–12	145	115	95		105	80	60
13–16	111	86	66		95	75	55
17–20	104	79	59		74	59	39

Girls

9–12	198	148	108		143	113	83
13–16	158	108	65		125	91	61
17–20	159	107	66		142	102	71

improvised equipment

Instructions and illustrations for the construction of pieces of improvised equipment are given in the text where the discussion of their use occurs. Page numbers are given below:

1. Balance platform from lumber—pages 163 and 167
2. Scoop from bleach bottle—page 222
3. Target from muffin pan—page 235
4. Target from old umbrella—page 235
5. Target from egg carton—page 235
6. Ring toss stake from chair—pages 231–232
7. Stilts from lumber—pages 231–232
8. Stilts from cans—page 231
9. Building blocks from lumber—page 228
10. Rocking "raft" from rockers of an old rocking chair—page 227
11. Jouncing or bouncing board from lumber—page 228
12. Drum from large can—page 238
13. Drum from metal tray—page 238
14. Rhythm blocks from scrap lumber and sandpaper—page 238
15. Gym mat from used mattress—page 349
16. Mat cart from lumber—page 349
17. Kickboard from wooden plank—page 431
18. Supporting device from inner tube—page 431
19. Balance beam from railroad tie—page 481
20. Crawling and climbing devices from assorted materials—pages 229 and 481

index of dances, games and stunts

(directions for performing)

DANCES

GAMES

Active Table Games

Aquatic Games

511

Basic Skill Games

STUNTS

Trampolining

subject index

Boldface words also appear in the Index of
Dances, Games, and Stunts